Water Management

WATER MANAGEMENT
Technology and Institutions

Warren Viessman, Jr.
University of Florida

Claire Welty
Massachusetts Institute of Technology

1817

HARPER & ROW, PUBLISHERS, New York
Cambridge, Philadelphia, San Francisco,
London, Mexico City, São Paulo, Singapore, Sydney

Photo Credit: A Flaming Gorge Unit, Colorado River Storage Project—Utah. (*Courtesy of the Bureau of Reclamation, U.S. Department of the Interior.* Photo by Stan Rasmussen.)

Sponsoring Editor: Cliff Robichaud
Project Editor: Eleanor Castellano
Cover Design: Robert Sugar
Text Art: Fine Line Inc.
Production: Marion Palen/Delia Tedoff
Compositor: ComCom Division of Haddon Craftsmen, Inc.

WATER MANAGEMENT: Technology and Institutions

Library of Congress Cataloging in Publication Data

Viessman, Warren.
    Water management.

    Includes bibliographies and index.
    1. Water resources development—United States.
2. Water-supply—United States—Management. I. Welty,
Claire, 1954–   II. Title.
TC423.V54   1985   333.91′00973   84–10864
ISBN 0–06–046818–1

90 91 9 8 7 6 5 4 3

To our parents, without
whose guidance and help
this book would not have
been possible.

Contents

Chapter 6
Water and the Environment   164

Chapter 7
Natural Water Supply Processes   184

Chapter 13
Case Studies of Water Resources Systems   570

Chapter 14
Outlook for Tomorrow   580

Preface

The availability, use, development, and management of water resources are receiving increasing attention worldwide. Population increases have brought about growing demands for new or expanded supplies of good quality water for direct human consumption, as well as for agricultural and industrial use. In the process of satisfying these expansions, many water sources have been depleted or despoiled. Furthermore, studies conducted by the United Nations indicate that about two-thirds of the populations of developing countries do not have access to safe and adequate drinking water supplies. Even in technically advanced nations, drinking water sources are menaced by improper waste disposal practices or by a lack of understanding of the potential for harmful effects stemming from trace impurities of complex chemical substances.

Increased pressures to provide more water to feed the needy and to develop energy resources such as coal and oil shale are stressing local and regional water resources systems. In addition, many of our water institutions (laws, regulations, administrative actions, organizations) have become outmoded and impede rather than facilitate the changes needed to resolve critical water problems. A further complication is that increasing concern about maintaining or improving the quality of the environment has intensified conflicts in water allocation.

Avoiding water shortages in the future will require an approach that combines the best elements of technology with the practical realities of contemporary political and social systems. It is in such a context that this book has been written. Today's world is unlike that of even a few years ago. The pace of technological change, the rapid shifting in value structures of people, and the coming of age of the computer provide us with the ability to attain futures that until recently were only vague embryos in the minds of dreamers. Such a state requires a cooperative interface among engineers, scientists, planners, citizens, and policymakers, as well as an understanding of the totality of the world—an appreciation of how engineering designs and objectives relate to human and environmental factors and an appreciation of what should be "engineered" and what should not.

The engineers and scientists of tomorrow will require ethics of practice that permit them to range beyond the technicalities of design and into the realm of shaping policy that ultimately specifies what those designs should be. Imaginative and creative individuals are needed who can perceive and respect technical, nontechnical, and combination solutions to society's problems; who can set forth and assess viable alternatives; and who can understand environmental issues and design workable systems accordingly. Engineers and scientists, in particular, should be prepared to take leadership roles in guiding those in decision-making capacities to create the best possible programs and regulations for the management of water and other resources. The challenge is to produce technically qualified individuals who can relate their knowledge to the realities of the political, economic, and social settings in which all water problems must be solved.

Furthermore, environmentalists, managers, and planners concerned with the use and development of water resources have as great an obligation to understand something about technology as engineers do to understand related but nontechnical fields. Nontechnical policymakers should not have to rely solely on engineers and scientists to provide analyses of the technical data needed for them to formulate workable programs to manage water resources. A second goal of this book thus is to provide, for students of environmental management, planning, and related fields, an understanding of the engineering and scientific factors that must be considered in making decisions.

The book is designed to be used in undergraduate and introductory graduate courses in water resources management, engineering, and related physical sciences—as well as in nontechnical courses in planning and environmental and natural resources sciences. An attempt has been made to present the technical elements of water resources systems in the context of the political, social, and other environments in which they exist. This is done so that the engineering-oriented student will come to understand the tradeoffs that must be made between economically and technically efficient solutions to water resources problems and "realizable" solutions that can be implemented in the face of social and regulatory influences. Similarly, the nontechnical student will come to understand the technological considerations involved in planning, developing, and managing water resources systems.

For the technical reader, frequent citations are made to computer applications and statistical and numerical methods. By omitting Chapter 9 and the technical portions of Chapters 7, 10, 11, and 12, those who are not technically inclined should find the text informative and easy to understand. The book is also designed to serve as a reference for professionals involved in water resources decision-making processes.

Many sources of information have been drawn on for the subject matter of the book. The authors hope that suitable acknowledgment has been given to them. The helpful comments of colleagues and students are also acknowledged. Dr. Ronald M. North of the University of Georgia wrote the chapter on economics and financing, and we greatly appreciate this contribution. Dr. Daniel P. Loucks of Cornell University supplied most of the material for the chapter on case studies, and his kindness is hereby acknowledged. A debt of gratitude is also owed to Dr. Frederick Welty, who painstakingly reviewed and edited the manuscript. Finally, thanks are given to Pearl E. Summers and Sharon L. Nixon for typing the manuscript.

WARREN VIESSMAN, JR.
CLAIRE WELTY

Water Management

Chapter 1
Introduction

This is a book about water, but more than that, it is a book about politics, laws, organizations, economics, and environmental concerns and how all these diverse social elements affect the way we use and misuse water and make decisions about water management. A few years ago this book might have been titled "Engineering for Water Development"; not today. The engineering aspect is still prominent, but in a very different context. The authors maintain that engineering expertise, while an important and necessary component of the water resources problem-solving machinery, is not sufficient in itself to resolve the many politically and socially sensitive issues surrounding today's concerns about water. Thus, it is the intent here to present the technological role in a setting of the many constraining and/or influencing legal, social, political, and economic elements within which it is bound. The expectation is that the engineering student can, by means of the discussions and examples presented, learn to function as an effective participant in society's water resources decision-making processes. In like manner, it is the intent that the nontechnical student will be able to see more clearly the nature of the technical role and the potential and limitations it has for addressing far-ranging water-environment issues. The day of the "individual water project" solution to water resources problem solving is drawing to a close. With its demise, there is a need for engineers, environmental scientists, planners, resource managers, and others who can break the narrow confines of their disciplines and function as informed citizens and professionals in devising solutions to the many water problems being recognized worldwide. These solutions must not only be feasible in a technical sense but also must be socially and politically acceptable, and thus have a high probability of implementation. It is with this objective in mind that the book has been written.

1-1 WATER RESOURCES DEVELOPMENT: YESTERDAY AND TOMORROW

The history of water resources development in the United States can be traced to the early days of the country's settlement. The first need for water was to satisfy basic living requirements. Water was also an important element in transportation. Soon thereafter, agriculture and industry demonstrated their large water requirements. Initially, most water developments were on an individual or small-community basis. Later, as water issues became not only of local but of national concern, the federal government became actively engaged in a host of activities such as navigation improvements and flood control. For many years, in fact well into the twentieth century, the focus of most developmental efforts was on single-purpose water projects. Eventually, the philosophy of multiple-use facilities emerged, but even then the solution of water resources problems was usually carried out on an individual project level, not on the basis of a comprehensive plan. Concern for how water use and management affected other decisions regarding a region's goals and objectives was slow in coming and, in fact, is still often lacking. Politically strong local constituencies found they could influence congressional delegations to bring home water projects. This practice strengthened the chances of reelection of many public servants, and the concept of "pork barrel" politics emerged. It should be noted, though, that a sweeping generalization that most water projects are political gifts is to overlook the importance of hundreds of water resources developments in providing dependable water supplies, food and fiber, jobs, recreation, and safe areas in which to live.

But now, in the 1980s, a fresh approach to the solution of water problems seems in order. Many of the historical reasons for developing water projects are no longer valid. The objective of settling arid lands in the western U.S. through irrigation development is not a principal theme of national policy today. Thus the mandate to provide federally subsidized irrigation water is no longer rational. Large-scale flood control projects on most of the nation's major rivers have already been built, and so has much of the inland waterways navigation system. The population is increasing, however, and it is also shifting from some of the previously populous regions, such as the northeast, to the more favorable climate of the nation's sun belt. Furthermore, the energy crisis of the 1970s has stimulated plans for developing the coal and oil shale resources of the western U.S. at an accelerated pace. The water requirements for this are substantial, and to meet them some reallocation of water in the west will likely be necessary.

What this all means is that the nature of water problems is changing, and accompanying this change is the need to realize that today's and tomorrow's problems cannot be solved with yesterday's policies and/or philosophies.

The water problems faced by the United States and other industrialized nations are of both physical dimensions, that is, the availability of water, and of institutional dimensions, that is, the nature of laws, organizations, and customs that are in force. As used here, institution means any or all of a combination of laws, regulations, organizations, and customs. Unfortunately, at least in the United States, the prevailing institutional arrangements are often the crucial factors in a region's water supply problems. Many valid technical solutions cannot be implemented because of a variety of institutional constraints.

It is the intent of this book to convey the need for a broadened outlook on water resources problem solving, one that fits the context of the resource availability and the existing institutional structures. It is hoped that the nontechnical reader can gain an insight into the opportunities that exist for technological impact on contemporary water problems. It is also hoped that the technical reader will learn that his or her conception of an optimal technical solution to a problem might have little or no chance of implementation unless it is also politically and socially feasible.

The authors believe that some elements of existing physical and institutional systems are subject to change in the short run whereas others are not. Thus we must learn to produce functional systems that can operate within existing constraints, but at the same time develop the hard data needed to support revision of the presently immovable system elements. Both physical and institutional aspects of water issues must be dealt with. Their features are discussed in the chapters that follow. Several case studies are also presented to illustrate how the various features of a water resources system can be considered comprehensively.

1-2   WATER AVAILABILITY AND USE IN THE UNITED STATES

All water problems are tied to the various uses the resource is put to and/or the extent to which it is efficiently managed. In the earliest periods of settlement, drinking, cooking, and bathing were the main foci. With the passage of time, navigation, industrial processing, fire fighting, irrigation, cooling, and other uses assumed importance. Several of these, namely irrigation and power cooling, now dominate water use patterns in the United States and in many other industrialized nations. As agricultural production and industrial development became more widespread, there emerged a companion water quality problem of great proportions. Concern about this, combined with increasing fears of irreversible environmental degradation, has now kindled a strong interest in reserving some of the nation's waters for many purposes other than the more traditional ones. These include fish and wildlife maintenance, recreation, water quality protection, and the protection of aquatic plants. The types of water uses, their geographical distribution, and associated problems are summarized on a state-by-state basis in the table in Appendix D.

Given unlimited water resources, all the many competing uses could be accommodated. But in reality this condition is not met, and in fact it is not even approximated in many areas, especially in the more arid regions. The problem of allocating available water so as to satisfy a multiplicity of users is the fundamental water problem. It presents a challenge of great scale.

The first step in addressing this issue is to determine the availability of the water resource; the second is to estimate what the future has in store. One would think that the first part of this assessment would be straightforward. Unfortunately, this is not always the case. Given that this is so, it does not take much imagination to see that ascertaining the future demands on available water supplies is a hazardous business at best. Methods for estimating a baseline from which to make decisions about future allocations and for constructing reasonable trends are discussed in Chapter 4. A brief summary of trends in water use follows here to acquaint the reader with the major water-using sectors and the variances in estimates with which the water resources planner or manager must deal.

During the 25-year period ending in 1980, freshwater use in the United States increased about 175 percent. Forecasts made for the period from 1975 to 2000 range from a high of about a fourfold increase to a low of a slight decline from the 1975 figure. Although no one can accurately predict the future, it seems likely that more moderate trends in water use rates will be the norm. Increased costs, environmental concerns, and a growing conservation philosophy are key factors.

During 1980, the nation's water withdrawals (fresh and saline) for all purposes averaged 450 billion gallons per day (bgd) (1).* This included a substantial reuse of flows. Of the total amount used, approximately 100 bgd were consumed through evaporation or incorporation into products. The latter figure is important since water consumed is unavailable for further use in the locality of withdrawal.

Nationwide, there is ample water to meet projected needs well beyond 1985 (the average annual stream flow in the coterminous United States is about 1200 bgd alone). This optimistic view must be tempered, however, by the realization that national totals mask geographical and temporal variations, and that some severe local, state, and regional problems exist and others can be expected. According to the U.S. Water Re-

*Numbers in parentheses refer to references at the end of the chapter.

sources Council (WRC), the water supply outlook for the eastern third of the nation is generally good to the year 2000 (2). Exceptions are the Miami–Ft. Lauderdale and Chicago areas. In the west, the picture is less favorable. Major water supply problems exist or are expected in southern California, the Great Basin, the lower Colorado, the Rio Grande, the High Plains of Texas, and the south-central portion of the Missouri River Basin. Many of these areas are large agricultural water users, and expected water use for development and processing of coal and oil shale deposits in some of them will add to the difficulties. Unless there is some adjustment in water allocations, water may already be limiting growth in the more critical areas.

Table 1-1 shows the average annual stream flow, the estimated dependable water supply in 1980 (minimum monthly stream flow under existing conditions of development augmented in some cases by groundwater and imported water), and the annual flow that is exceeded 90 percent of the time for WRCs 21 water resources regions (Figure 1-1) (1). For the year 1975, the table also shows combined freshwater and saline water withdrawals from all sources (surface and underground) (col. 5), fresh water withdrawn (col. 6), and fresh water consumed (col. 7). Consumptive use is that portion of the water which is withdrawn from a source and not returned for further use; in general it is water that evaporates or is used by plants. By comparing columns 3 and 4 with columns 5, 6, and 7, areas of shortage and adequacy can be identified. For example, in the eastern regions (excluding the Great Lakes) and in the Pacific northwest region, the recorded annual flows exceeded 90 percent of all years are large compared with dependable water supplies and withdrawals. This indicates a natural dependability of supply. On the other hand, in 1975 both water withdrawals and consumptive use exceeded the supply originating in the lower Colorado region. This situation is possible only because water is imported, groundwater is mined, and there is repeated reuse of the same surface water. In the long run, however, such measures cannot be counted on to solve water supply problems.

Figure 1-2 shows historical and expected freshwater withdrawals in the United States as determined by the U.S. Geological Survey (USGS, for historical data) and WRC (projections from 1975 to 2000). The figure also shows the relative differences in water use by the principal water-using sectors. Note that irrigation and steam electric generation (cooling) are by far the largest water users. A study of the figure suggests that if significant reductions in quantities of water used are to be achieved through conservation, for example, then the largest water users are the ones that must be dealt with. Local water shortages might be alleviated by conserving drinking water or commercial water, but the problems of major river basins are not likely to be eased much unless irrigation and/or power plant cooling are dealt with.

Table 1-1 COMPARISON OF WATER SUPPLY WITH CUMULATIVE OFF-CHANNEL WITHDRAWALS FOR THE COTERMINOUS UNITED STATES IN 1975[a]

(1)	(2)	(3)	(4)	(5)	(6)	(7)
REGION	AVERAGE ANNUAL FLOW (BGD)	ANNUAL FLOW EXCEEDED IN 90 PERCENT OF YEARS (BGD)	ESTIMATED[b] DEPENDABLE WATER SUPPLY 1980 (BGD)	TOTAL WATER WITHDRAWALS 1975: FRESH WATER AND SALINE WATER (BGD)	FRESH SURFACE WATER WITHDRAWN 1975 (BGD)	FRESH WATER CONSUMED 1975 (BGD)
New England	67	49	22	14	4.4	0.44
Mid-Atlantic	84	68	36	52	22	1.6
South Atlantic–Gulf	197	129	75	43	24	3.7
Great Lakes	75	54	69	36	35	1.1
Ohio	125	75	48	36	34	1.2
Tennessee	41	28	14	11	10	0.28
Upper Mississippi	65	36	31	19	16	0.80
Lower Mississippi	79	38	25	16	11	5.5
Souris-Red-Rainy	6.2	2	3	0.4	0.3	0.09
Missouri Basin	54	29	30	35	25	15
Arkansas-White-Red	73	36	20	15	6.2	9.0
Texas-Gulf	32	11	17	22	9.7	8.0
Rio Grande	5.0	2	3	5.4	3.0	3.5
Upper Colorado	13	8	13	4.1	3.9	1.7
Lower Colorado	3.2	1	2	8.5	3.5	6.3
Great Basin	7.5	3	9	6.9	5.4	3.6
Pacific Northwest	210	148	70	33	26	11
California	62	30	28	51	22	23
United States (coterminous)	1200	747	515	409	261	95

SOURCE: Modified from Table 4, USGS Circular 765, 1977, p. 19.
[a]Partial figures may not add up to totals because of independent rounding.
[b]Minimum monthly streamflow under existing conditions of development augmented in some cases by groundwater and imported water.

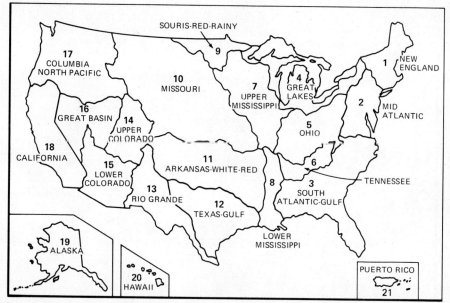

Figure 1-1   Principal water resources regions in the United States as designated by the Water Resources Council.

Tables 1-2 and 1-3 show historical (1975) and projected trends in total water withdrawals (fresh plus saline) and consumptive use to the year 2000. The wide range in estimates given illustrates the dilemma of the decision maker faced with interpreting and using them. Many factors shape water use trends, and projections of these are of doubtful validity. In general, the older the estimate, the more likely it is to be off target due to influences unrecognized at the time it was made or to understatement or overstatement of other conditions.

1-3 FEDERAL WATER AGENCIES

A number of federal agencies in the United States have responsibility for one or more aspects of water resources development and management. On the water quality side, the Environmental Protection Agency (EPA) is the principal actor. On the water supply side, the Army Corps of Engineers (CE), the Bureau of Reclamation (USBR), the Soil Conservation Service (SCS), and the Tennessee Valley Authority (TVA) are the most significant. The Water Resources Council (WRC) was, until its termination in 1982, the principal body for coordinating federal water programs and analyzing national water policy. Several other agencies, the Economic Development Administration (EDA), Small Business Administration (SBA), Farmers Home Administration (FmHA), and the Department of Housing and Urban Development (HUD), assist rural and economically

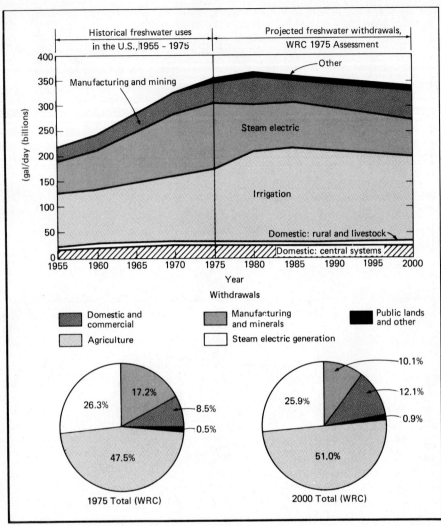

Figure 1-2   Historical and projected freshwater withdrawals in the United States, 1955 to 2000 (figure constructed from data reported by the USGS and WRC, references 1 and 2).

depressed areas to build and maintain adequate water supply and wastewater disposal facilities. A brief description of the role of each of these agencies is given in Table 1-4.

1-4 WATER RESOURCES ISSUES

Although the quantity of water available worldwide is fixed, local depletions and excesses occur and the quality of the water resource is continually subjected to change. Constructed facilities have served to increase the

Table 1-2 PROJECTED UNITED STATES WATER WITHDRAWALS[a]

	PROJECTED WITHDRAWAL (BGD)			
STUDY BY[b]	1975	1980	1985	2000
USGS (1975)	420[c]	—	—	—
USDC (1960)	450	494	—	—
SSC (1961)	—	559[d]	—	888[d]
WRC (1968)	—	443	—	805
RFF (1971)	—	335–509	—	391–848
NWC (1973)	—	382–556	—	590–1319
WRC (1975)	398[c]	—	422	425

SOURCE: Data for the table were reported in references 1 to 7.
[a]Withdrawal means water taken from a surface or groundwater source for offstream use.
[b]USGS: U.S. Geological Survey; USDC: U.S. Department of Commerce; SSC: Senate Select Committee; WRC: Water Resources Council; RFF: Resources for the Future, Inc.; NWC: National Water Commission.
[c]Historical data.
[d]Does not include saline water use, which was about 70 bgd in 1975 and was estimated by the WRC to be about 119 bgd in 2000.

Table 1-3 PROJECTED UNITED STATES CONSUMPTIVE USE[a]

	PROJECTED CONSUMPTIVE USE (BGD)			
STUDY BY	1975	1980	1985	2000
USGS (1975)	96[b]	—	—	—
USDC (1960)	170	183	—	—
SSC (1961)	—	119	—	156
WRC (1968)	—	104	—	128
RFF (1971)	—	116–133	—	125–172
NWC (1973)	—	116–143	—	133–180
WRC (1975)	107[b]	—	121	135

SOURCE: Data for the table were obtained from references 1 to 7.
[a]Consumptive use: portion of water withdrawn for offstream uses and not returned to a surface water or groundwater source.
[b]Historical data.

availability of water for some localities and conversely have depleted and despoiled other water sources. A shifting away from some traditional water uses to new ones and an intensified focus on environmental quality and public health add new dimensions to old water problems.

In reality, most water problems have both physical and institutional dimensions, but some classification is useful to enhance understanding. Thus the issues discussed in the following paragraphs have been categorized as institutional (for those topics dealing mainly with laws, regulations, and/or organizations), water quality (for those subjects in which the constituents of or substances in the water are of primary concern), and water quantity (for those issues in which water allocation is the main

Table 1-4 PRINCIPAL UNITED STATES WATER RESOURCES PLANNING AND DEVELOPMENT AGENCIES

AGENCY	MISSION
Army Corps of Engineers (CE)	Planning, constructing, operating, and maintaining a wide variety of water resources facilities including those for navigation, flood control, water supply, recreation, hydroelectric power generation, water quality control, and other purposes. Nationwide activities.
United States Bureau of Reclamation (USBR)	Planning, constructing, operating, and maintaining facilities for irrigation, power generation, recreation, fish and wildlife preservation, and municipal water supply. Most activities are confined to the 17 western states. Original efforts were concentrated on irrigation.
Soil Conservation Service (SCS)	Carries out a national soil and water conservation program. Provides technical and financial assistance for flood prevention, recreation, and water supply development in small watersheds (fewer than 250,000 acres). Also appraises the nation's soil, water, and related resources.
Tennessee Valley Authority (TVA)	Planning, constructing, operating, and maintaining facilities in the Tennessee River Basin for navigation, flood control, and the generation of electricity. The TVA is a unique regional organization that has worked well in the United States.
U.S. Environmental Protection Agency (EPA)	Abatement and control of pollution. Provision of financial and technical assistance to states and local governments for constructing wastewater treatment facilities and for water quality management planning. Coordination of national programs and policies relating to water quality. Its principal role is regulatory.
U.S. Water Resources Council (WRC)	Principal role was the coordination of regional and river basin plans, assessing the adequacy of the

Table 1-4(*Continued*)

AGENCY	MISSION
	nation's water and related land resources, suggesting changes in national policy related to water matters, and assisting the states in developing water planning capability. Although terminated in 1982, the WRC exemplified the long-sought mechanism for water program coordination and water policy analysis that was recommended by many study commissions since the early 1900s. A new organization with many of the WRCs roles is almost sure to come.
Economic Development Administration (EDA), Small Business Administration (SBA), Farmers Home Administration (FmHA), and the Department of Housing and Urban Development (HUD)	In the water resources field, the principal role of these agencies is to assist rural and economically depressed areas to develop and maintain water and wastewater conveyance, processing, and other related facilities. This is accomplished mainly through grant and loan programs.

focus). These topics are treated extensively in later sections of the text, but they are summarized here to acquaint the reader with the scope of the problems that must be dealt with. Although many of these have particular relevance to American systems or practices, most of the issues are important in all parts of the world.

Institutions

The use of water to satisfy competing users is affected by, and often constrained by, legal, social, political, organizational, environmental, and economic factors. As the nation's waters have been more and more dedicated to specific uses, the potential for escalation in conflicts among environmentalists, ranchers, irrigators, well users, energy firms, cities, and industries has grown. For example, agricultural development in the west has grown to the point where newly emerging demands on western waters for purposes such as energy production are making some farmers uneasy about the future. In some cases, water is hard to come by, but in others, it is available but is not used or is poorly used because of regulations, laws, and/or other institutional elements. A complicating factor is that many water allocation problems are tied to long-standing social customs and provincial biases that are not receptive to easy change.

ROLES OF FEDERAL, STATE, AND LOCAL GOVERNMENTS

There is a need to define more explicitly the roles to be played by federal, state, and local governments in developing and managing the nation's water resources. Federal water resources development appears to have little additional role in opening up new lands for irrigation, for stimulating regional economic growth, or for meeting some of the other traditional objectives that are now less important than before. Furthermore, many water problems are taking on localized dimensions. Thus, a restructuring of historical governmental responsibilities seems in order. Considerable legislative time, dispute, and political risk may be involved in resolving this issue, but it is arguable that unless it is addressed, less than optimal solutions to water problems will be the result. Uncertainty about who is to do what leads to delays, duplications, and other forms of inefficiency.

STATE AND FEDERAL WATER LAWS

Countless laws share in allocating the nation's waters. Many of these arose out of local needs and/or disputes and at the time were adequate for the task to which they were committed. Today, however, some of these laws have outlived their usefulness, and they themselves generate conflicts and impose barriers on good water resources management. The nonuniformity and occasional cross-purposes of state and federal water laws must be reckoned with.

WATER QUANTITY–WATER QUALITY COORDINATION

Although technical understanding of the inseparability of water quality and water quantity issues is complete, there has been a minimal carry-over of this knowledge into operational planning and management programs. This is true not only at the federal level but also at state and local levels of government. The Environmental Protection Agency is concerned with water quality planning and management, whereas other federal water agencies direct most of their attention to issues of water allocation and control. Counterparts at state and local levels function in a similar fashion and the result is that the nation appears to be getting less than its money's worth out of the large investments in water-related facilities. Rapid progress toward a "total water management" philosophy cannot be attained unless all aspects of water are considered simultaneously.

Water Quality

According to the twelfth annual report of the president's Council on Environmental Quality (CEQ), the nation's waters continue to be damaged by pollution and misuse (8). The report cites water problems throughout the country and notes that although improvements in water quality are substantial in some localities, nationally, water quality changed little from 1975 to 1980. Sewer overflows, urban and agricultural runoff, overloaded sewage treatment plants and toxic wastes were identified as principal offenders. The CEQ noted that nationwide measurements of six key pollutants showed little overall change in levels from 1975 to 1979. Limited funds combined with less than optimal approaches to water quality control have been major factors in slowing the effort to improve the quality of the nation's waters.

Although it is not always thought of in the context of water quality management, the issue of sewage and other sludge management and disposal is also of great importance. It is clear that the liquid fraction of wastewater has always received the most attention (9). This is unfortunate in many respects because the sludge produced in wastewater treatment processes is a far more intractable waste material than the liquid.

NON-POINT-SOURCE POLLUTION

Most of the water quality effort in the United States through the 1970s was related to point sources of pollution and to particular pollutants. The scale of the nonpoint problem is of such magnitude, however, that substantial further progress in cleaning up watercourses in the United States seems unlikely unless a major effort in controlling diffuse sources is mounted. For example, the CEQ reported in 1979 that sediment flows from nonpoint sources were about 360 times greater than those from municipal and industrial outlets. Another important factor is that large amounts of sediment and other pollutants are produced naturally and not just by human actions. Expected yields of from 200 to 300 tons of sediment per square mile per year from undisturbed southern pine forests of the Coastal Plain illustrates this point.

In 1976 it was estimated that nonpoint sources contributed about 65 to 75 percent of the phosphorous and nitrogen loadings to water bodies in the United States. Urban agricultural lands also contribute much of the biochemical oxygen demand (BOD) load to streams, sometimes greater than that of the point sources they surround (10). It has also been reported that both concentrations and volumes of zinc and lead in sediments from urban runoff may exceed those of many municipal wastes. Urban runoff also contributes about 80 to 90 percent of the petroleum products delivered to many of the nation's harbor areas.

Although the nature and in many cases the extent of the nonpoint pollution problem have been identified, the solution is complex. Conventional point source treatment methods are usually not applicable, costs for urban runoff control are high, and agricultural conservation techniques are often not considered cost-effective from the farmer's point of view. The benefits of non-point-source pollution control must be carefully evaluated in setting priorities for water quality management actions. Furthermore, the political, financial, legal, and social issues surrounding the use of regulatory processes for land use control as a means of reducing the nonpoint pollution problem are complex and have to be dealt with cautiously.

ACID PRECIPITATION

Acid precipitation has been reported to have damaged crops, forests, soil fertility, lakes, fish, and structures. It has killed fish in New York's Adirondack wilderness, pelted the Rocky Mountains, and affected Scandinavia, much of western Europe, and Japan. It is an increasingly harmful kind of pollution, invisible and operating inconspicuously. Acid precipitation is caused largely by sulfur dioxide emissions from coal-burning power plants, smelters, and factories. To a lesser extent, nitrogen oxides from car exhausts and industry contribute to the problem.

Environmental impacts of fossil-fuel burning associated with acid rain have serious implications for national energy policy. Questions surrounding this issue include: To what degree should pollution controls be required? and Is it necessary to impose stringent federally mandated emission standards on existing and converted coal-fired power plants?

GROUNDWATER POLLUTION

Groundwater is a major source of water supply in many parts of the world. In the United States, about 25 percent of all fresh water used, 95 percent of the total domestic and industrial needs of the rural population, and 50 percent of all water used in agriculture is withdrawn from the ground (2). Groundwater is also a major drinking water source for 32 states and is the only source in many localities.

Severe problems related to both the quantity and the quality of groundwater are arising throughout the world. Many groundwater resources are being contaminated by poor waste management practices and others are being rapidly depleted. There is inadequate information about the social and economic impacts resulting from contamination and closing of wells, and in many cases there is inadequate technical data for making good decisions about managing the groundwater resource. There is also an inadequate understanding of the physical and chemical processes involved in changes of water quality that occur in groundwater systems. Important influencing factors include the original water conditions, the chemistry of the soils and the aquifer formations, and the pollution loading of recharging waters.

WATER QUALITY CONTROL

The trend in water quality management in the United States has been toward centralization and the imposition of uniform rules. Although an effort was made in the Water Quality Act Amendments of 1965 to relate water quality to the functioning of the nation's river systems, this ap-

proach was abandoned and a technology-based standards program was
instituted in its place (P.L. 92–500). After about 10 years of observing how
well this has worked, many experts are convinced that the policy needs
revision.

Careful reexamination of the nation's approach to water quality management appears to be in order. Pertinent questions include: What should
our clean water goals be? How can the high costs of sewage treatment
works be reduced? What is the appropriate role of advanced waste treatment? How can innovative options, including land application of effluents
and wastewater reuse, be encouraged and more widely implemented?
What is the proper role of federal, state, and local governments and private industry?

SAFE DRINKING WATER
Since it was first discovered that disease could be transmitted by water,
people have sought means to provide safe drinking supplies. In this century, the scourges of cholera, typhoid, dysentery, and other communicable
waterborne diseases have all but vanished in the United States (9). In fact,
it appears that science and technology can provide reasonable guarantees
that concerns about questionable drinking water can be eliminated given
the time, funds, and incentives to do so. It is mostly a question of where
society places its priorities (9).

Today the standards for drinking water quality in this country are set
by the Safe Drinking Water Act (P.L. 93–523). But the mandates of the act
are thought by many to be overly restrictive in their requirements to
remove various constituents that have not been proved conclusively to be
harmful to humans. The costs of overtreatment must be carefully balanced
against less expensive approaches that may not adequately ensure the
safety of drinking water supplies. This is an area clearly in need of additional study. It is often almost impossible to accurately determine what
hazards are tolerable. Simon Ramo said, "The unwanted ills conceivably
present are too numerous and not always quantifiable. Even if for every
activity we could measure every possible menace, we would not learn
thereby what threshold level of impairment is acceptable" (11).

Water Quantity

Providing water in sufficient quantity for the various uses of humans has
long been an objective of water resources developers. In the early part of
this century an aggressive program to add to the stock of dependable
water supplies was set in motion and carried forward. Then in about the
mid-1970s the program slowed considerably, mainly due to the opposition
to water projects on environmental grounds. Following this came a period
of interest in exploring conservation techniques and other approaches to
solving water problems rather than depending on the traditional building

of new works to store, convey, treat, and otherwise modify existing natural water systems. Add to this the economic problems of the late 1970s and early 1980s and it is easy to understand why the approach to water quantity management is taking on new dimensions. Still there is a need to increase water supplies, and this issue is explored in the following paragraphs.

WATER ALLOCATION AMONG COMPETING USES

A basic problem is how to allocate water for environmental enhancement, food and energy production, recreation, municipal and industrial water supply, and other purposes. Ways to accommodate new and expanded uses include development of water storage and conveyance facilities, reduction of the quantities of water used, and better management. It is often difficult to implement these options, however, because of many hard to deal with constraints such as conflicting water laws, uncoordinated management of ground and surface waters, lack of coordination of water quality and water quantity programs, unwillingness of many to accept nontraditional growth patterns in water use, and the failure to price water commensurate with its value in use.

The southwest's water problems are strongly tied to pricing policies in that region, for example. It has been said that the southwest is "running low on cheap water" but not running out of water (12). Federal subsidies have kept water prices artificially low. Replacement costs for water are estimated to be 50 times what some farmers were paying in 1981. Water from new federal projects would cost about $160 an acre-foot if construction and operation and maintenance costs were included (12). But the reality is that very few agricultural users pay more than a fraction of this rate and some farmers in California's Central Valley pay as little as $3.50 an acre-foot. On this basis it is easy to see that there is little incentive to conserve or to explore policies for reallocation that would jeopardize this attractive situation.

There are many avenues that can be followed in shifting water from one use to another or for increasing the availability of water for various purposes. These may be classified roughly as structural (building various works) and nonstructural (using regulatory and other associated measures). Although the nonstructural approach has been much talked about during the past 15 years, it has not been extensively used. This is because structural solutions often involve "distributional policies" in which the public pays for something that benefits specific interests and there are generally clear winners and no specific losers (that is, the loss is diffuse and often nonspecific), whereas nonstructural solutions that involve regulatory or redistributive measures tend to be associated with clearly defined losers and no specific winners (13). Thus nonstructural solutions usually encounter heavy opposition in political processes even though they may often be the most efficient and sometimes the only real option for solving the allocation problem.

GROUNDWATER MANAGEMENT

Augmenting the nation's surface water resources are about 50 billion acre-feet of economically accessible groundwater. Only about 2 percent of this is available on a continuing basis, however, and most of it is located in humid regions (14). Much of the nonrenewable groundwater in the arid regions is being exhausted at a rate that will cause significant reductions in total groundwater availability by the year 2000. For example, the Ogallala aquifer, which supplies water to the semiarid agricultural states from Texas to South Dakota, is being depleted much faster than it is being replenished.

Relative to this issue there are many questions, including: How can incentives and/or penalties be used effectively to facilitate good groundwater management and encourage conjunctive use of surface and groundwater supplies? What are the major constraints on wise use of groundwater resources? How can these be modified? What are the principal threats to groundwater quality? Are special institutions needed to manage groundwater and if so, what form should they take?

FLOODPLAIN MANAGEMENT

Large areas of the United States and other nations are subject to periodic flooding. In the United States, average annual flood damages run into the billions of dollars, and unfortunately about 80 lives are lost each year (2).

Early efforts to mitigate flooding problems were mostly structural, in the form of dams, levees, and channel modifications. The approach is changing, however, and federal involvement is now aimed mainly at breaking the ever-enlarging cycle of flood destruction through floodplain management. There has been a shifting away from a narrow focus on flood modification through structural means to a more nonstructural approach that deals with how humans occupy the floodplain, how they manage it, and how they adjust to the dangers of occupancy.

The regulation of existing and future floodplain development is a critical element for limiting flood damages. Without increased floodplain regulation, WRC estimates that by the year 2000 urban flood damages could increase by 38 percent. Agricultural damages are forecast to increase less rapidly but to still be widespread. Thus the federal government is faced with the prospect of rising flood damages and associated disaster relief costs, which, in the absence of adequate floodplain management, could have a substantial adverse effect on the national budget.

INSTREAM FLOWS

Instream flows may be reserved for sustaining fish and wildlife populations, outdoor recreation, navigation, hydroelectric power generation, waste assimilation, conveyance to downstream points of withdrawal, and ecosystems. In particular, the determination of the quantities of water needed to protect the aquatic, biologic, and aesthetic values of a stream and preserve existing fisheries is very difficult. This is due to the wide variety of habitats and streamflow conditions encountered and the lack of hard data.

Present instream flow estimates are crude and should be used with caution in evaluating the prospects for future water allocations. Of importance, however, is the fact that these flows may be substantial, and if reservations are made to keep them instream, major conflicts with withdrawal users are likely. In the western United States, conflicts with irrigated agriculture and energy developers could be severe.

Questions about instream flows include: How can reasonable estimates of instream flow uses for fish and wildlife be obtained? and What are practical mechanisms for maximizing the compatibility of instream and offstream uses of water?

WATER FOR ENERGY RESOURCES DEVELOPMENT

Almost every energy system requires water for one or more of its elements. These include mining, processing, cooling, and waste treatment. Thus policy decisions regarding energy are of importance to water resources developers, planners, and managers. The WRCs 1975 assessment pointed out that increased energy demands are creating both water quality and quantity problems in water-short regions. Water demands for energy will have to be weighed against those for other purposes such as irrigated agriculture, and tradeoffs will have to be made.

There are many questions surrounding the energy-water issue. These include: What quantities of water are needed for various levels of energy resources development? How important is water quality for the associated uses? Are the limits of development of needed energy resources set by the actual availability of water or are the real barriers institutions? What changes in laws, institutions for water management, and technologies are needed to ensure adequate water supplies?

HYDROELECTRIC DEVELOPMENT

The "energy crisis" has kindled a new interest in hydroelectric facilities development and/or modification. In particular, the idea of installing small units on minor rivers and tributaries has become popular. Many previously developed sites, now abandoned, offer attractive possibilities for augmenting electrical energy needs. Hydroelectric facilities do not consume fuel and do not create air or water pollution problems.

In the United States in 1979, hydroelectric power was providing about 64,000 megawatts (MW) of electrical energy from 1251 facilities. This was approximately 13 percent of the nation's electrical generating capacity. The total hydroelectric potential from existing locations and undeveloped sites is estimated, however, to be more than 512,000 MW (15). In addition, preliminary estimates by the Corps of Engineers suggest that development of 4500 potentially feasible undeveloped sites could raise the nation's generating capacity by 354,000 MW. This would be in addition to new incremental power that could be generated at approximately 5400 existing locations. Although as much as 50 percent of the estimated potential might be difficult to realize, the remainder is great enough to warrant consideration for development. The constraints on this appear to be mainly economic and institutional.

RURAL WATER SUPPLY AND WASTEWATER DISPOSAL

According to a national demonstration water project (1977), as many as 30 million residents in rural communities experience some form of problem related to the quantity of drinking water supplies or the adequacy of wastewater disposal systems (16). For many of these communities designing and financing water supply and/or wastewater disposal systems are beyond their resources. An added problem has been the movement of former city dwellers to rural communities. Questions appropriate to this issue include: How valid are the EPA's drinking water requirements for small communities? Are special grant and/or loan programs needed to assist rural communities? and What is the potential for regional systems to accommodate several users, thereby providing economies of scale and consolidating needs for technical personnel?

URBAN WATER SYSTEMS

There are thousands of miles of water and sewer lines buried beneath American cities and towns. Many of these, and their associated treatment works, were built as long as 50 or 100 years ago. This is especially true in the northeastern and eastern United States. These systems, serving enormous populations, are frequently being stressed and some are disintegrating at an alarming rate. What is to be their fate and who should pay the costs of repairs or improvements that are both labor- and fuel-intensive? The scale of this problem is clear when one considers that the 1980 Intergovernmental Task Force on Water Policy found that the capital expenditure needs for urban water systems could reach $110 billion by the year 2000 (17). This would include $50 to $80 billion for replacement and rehabilitation of worn-out system elements.

While there is considerable debate as to the wisdom of the federal government entering the realm of direct funding for construction and rehabilitation of urban water systems, escalation of interest rates in combination with weakening tax bases in many cities gives this problem an urgent dimension. Historically, localities have paid for their own water supplies. Can they continue to do so? This issue is really institutional rather than technical, involving the means to repair and maintain existing municipal water supply system elements and to finance the construction, operation, and maintenance of system expansions.

WATER FOR AGRICULTURE

American agriculture depends heavily on irrigation water. Although irrigated cropland constitutes only about 13 percent of the total acreage farmed, it accounts for 27 percent of the value of all crops produced.

Worldwide, the figures are about 10 percent and 40 percent respectively. Declining groundwater reserves, escalating energy costs, overallocation of surface-water supplies, and increasing competition for western water from expanding urban areas, energy firms, and instream flow preservation advocates are issues creating concern over the future of growth of western agriculture and, in fact, over the stability to maintain present levels of productivity.

In addition to using large amounts of water, agriculture also influences the quality and quantity of water for other functions. Agricultural pollutants entering streams present significant water quality problems in the humid east as well as in the arid west. Erosion of topsoil, leaching of pesticides and fertilizers, drainage from animal feedlots, and irrigation-induced stream salinity are principal forms of agricultural water pollution. Application of more stringent regulations on the control of agricultural pollution could result in a reduction in cropland reserves; such a tradeoff would require careful examination. A balance must be struck to provide for meeting domestic and international food and fiber needs while at the same time safeguarding the environment and stimulating more efficient use of water in agricultural regions. The overwhelming importance of this issue deserves special attention.

NAVIGATION

Rivers and lakes have long served as avenues for public and commercial transportation and for recreational boating. The nation's inland and inter-coastal waterway system now comprises more than 25,000 miles of navigable channels and canals. In 1965, total domestic waterborne traffic was 829 million tons. By the year 2000, it is expected to almost double to 1.5 billion tons. While the WRC forecasts that the water supply should be adequate for navigation in most of its water resources regions, there are many problems of channel maintenance and rehabilitation, tie-ups in traffic at critical locks and dams, and issues of payment for facilities and operation of the waterways that bear continuing attention.

OTHER ISSUES

Other issues that relate directly or in part to water resources management and development include erosion and sedimentation; wetlands management; degradation of bay, estuary, and coastal waters; preservation of unique ecological areas; and land use planning and management.

1-5 OPTIONS FOR SOLVING WATER PROBLEMS

There are many options that might be exercised in solving the water problems reviewed in the preceding section. A summary of these is given here. The major options are treated in detail later.

Surface-Water Development

Development of water storage capacity can ease the effects of sporadic streamflows. According to the WRC, existing storage facilities can convert about 30 percent of nature's annual water supply to human use. By developing additional storage capacity, a higher percentage conversion can be realized. Although there is much opposition to dam building, these structures are often the most dependable means for increasing local water supplies.

Another aspect of water containment deserving attention is conjunctive use. This is based on the coordinated operation of surface-water and groundwater storages. Annual water requirements are generally met by surface storage whereas groundwater storage is used to meet cyclic requirements covering dry years. The operational procedure involves a lowering of groundwater levels during periods of below-average precipitation and a subsequent raising of levels during wet years. Transfer rates of surface waters to underground storage must be large enough to ensure that surface water reservoirs will be drawn down sufficiently to permit impounding significant volumes of water during periods of high runoff. To provide the required transfer capacity, methods of artificial recharge such as spreading, ponding, injecting, returning flows from irrigation, or other techniques can be used (14).

Opportunities for conjuctive use of water supplies are extensive in the midwest and western United States, but widespread implementation of these systems is constrained by state water laws and related institutions and the general anti-dam-building attitude of the public, which grew out of the environmental movement and has been supported by the widespread belief that many dams are more costly than beneficial. Are reforms needed to utilize this approach to water management? What role should the federal government play? These are principal questions surrounding the issue.

Groundwater Development

The nation's groundwater reserves are enormous, but they are not evenly distributed geographically. Groundwater supplies are widely used for drinking water and they are heavily depended on in the western states for irrigation. The most serious groundwater overdraft problems in the nation center on the High Plains region of western Texas and eastern New Mexico (18). In that locality, groundwater supplies are steadily being depleted (mined), since natural recharge of the aquifer is far below the rate of withdrawal. In other areas, varying opportunities exist for new groundwater developments or expanded use of already tapped resources. There is even potential in some of the driest areas, as exemplified by a news release on July 6, 1977, by the USGS noting that groundwater use could be greatly increased in the drought-plagued Great Basin region of Nevada.

In the long run, unless groundwater recharge balances groundwater withdrawals, the supplying aquifers will be mined out. The enduring nature of solutions to regional water supply problems through expansion of groundwater use will thus depend on how aquifers are managed and on local climatic conditions. Properly managed, the nation's groundwater resources can be operated to minimize water supply problems during low-flow periods, and in some cases they can serve as the sole source of supply for indefinite or extended periods of time if recharge by natural or artificial means is sufficient to balance, or at least minimize, the deficit between water supply and demand.

Weather Modification

Precipitation management technology has been developing rapidly, and some forms of precipitation augmentation are feasible for increasing water supplies. Studies supported by the U.S. Bureau of Reclamation in 1973 demonstrated that as much as 1.8 million acre-feet (maf) of new water could be provided in the upper Missouri River Basin by seeding winter orographic storms. The cost of providing this water was estimated to be relatively low compared to that of developing like amounts of water by other means.

The status of operational weather modification programs is such that meaningful economic and technical evaluation is limited to special, localized cases. There is a need for more information on the processes to be altered, the methods that can be used to achieve such alterations, and the extent to which resulting effects can be predicted in time, space, and degree.

It appears that a workable technology for augmenting rain and snow from certain types of clouds is scientifically feasible. Except for seeding of supercooled fogs and stratus, however, weather modification is largely in the experimental stage, and much additional study is needed. Furthermore, the legal and social aspects of "rainmaking" are potentially of enormous dimensions.

Water Conservation

Conservation as a means of stretching water supplies has long been recognized. It has been difficult, however, to obtain acceptance and employment of the known technology (19).

Large quantities of water are wasted, and opportunities abound for meeting many projected water needs through conservation rather than new development. For example, estimates of the water savings attainable through increasing efficiency in irrigation water management have been reported to range between 20 and 50 percent. The significance of this as a potential means of easing water supply problems in the western states is plain when one considers that irrigation is the largest single depletor of water in the United States. In the Missouri River Basin, for example, year 2000 estimates of depletions by irrigated agriculture range up to 23 million acre-feet per year, more than the mean annual flow in the water-short upper Colorado River Basin. On the municipal and industrial scene, large reductions in water use through conservation are also possible. Savings of 20 percent or more are feasible by changing patterns of water use and developing plumbing codes that require installation of water-saving devices in new construction of living and working quarters.

A word of caution is in order, however. Although conservation measures can theoretically provide substantial water savings, they should not be looked on as the sole means of addressing problems of water shortage. Once the maximum level of conservation is achieved in a locality, additional growth can only be supported by developing new water supplies.

Some important questions about conservation include: What impacts would specific conservation practices have on energy consumption? Under what conditions should conservation programs be implemented? What would be the costs of converting present irrigation systems to more efficient forms? How could this be accomplished and financed? What might be the negative impacts of implementing large-scale conservation programs?

Interbasin Transfers of Water

Interbasin transfers of water offer technical solutions to regional water problems. Popular attitudes toward such undertakings range from approval to strong condemnation, especially on environmental grounds. The northwestern United States has been very negative about plans for exporting water to the southwest, for example.

Many large-scale interbasin transfer schemes have been proposed. Several of the most well known are the Pacific Southwest Water Plan, the North American Water and Power Alliance (NAWAPA), and the Texas Water Plan. These projects would transport up to 10 million acre-feet of water annually (20). Many existing and/or anticipated water shortages could be resolved in this manner, but the tradeoffs that would have to be made deserve careful attention, and the environmental implications of some of them could be very severe.

Wastewater Reuse

Wastewater reuse is gaining recognition as an option for augmenting local supplies. Pressures of population concentration, limited availability of water supplies, and political-financial factors associated with water importation from other regions are all factors making use of reclaimed wastewater more attractive.

Direct reuse of treatment plant effluents is becoming increasingly popular for many purposes, drinking water supplies excepted. However, the barriers to this form of reuse are likely to fall as matters of public health are resolved.

Municipal wastewater reuse has been most pronounced in the semiarid southwest where water is in short supply. In 1971 irrigators used most of the 133 billion gallons of wastewater available to that region. Next in line were industry, recreation, and nonpotable domestic water users.

Industries use waste flows extensively in their processing water and cooling water stages of production. In 1965 each gallon of industrial water averaged recirculation two and a-quarter times before being discharged or consumed. In agriculture, the reuse of irrigation return flows has been practiced for centuries. Of the water diverted for irrigation in the United States, approximately 30 percent returns to streams and is then available for reuse by others.

Desalination

Desalination is technically feasible, but the economics of conversion from salt to fresh water limit its practical application. In 1952 desalted water cost upward of $7 per 1000 gallons. By 1971 this cost had been reduced to about $1 per 1000 gallons, but to be widely competitive, it would have had to be reduced even further at that time. Efforts to reduce desalination costs are continuing, but rapidly increasing energy costs have adversely affected these efforts.

Environmental problems involving the disposal of saline-water conversion wastes are also significant. For example, for each million gallons of fresh water produced, about 2000 tons of brine waste may be generated. For seawater conversion plants, ocean discharge of wastes is sometimes acceptable, but the waste disposal problems of inland plants are more complex. Inland disposal methods include evaporation ponds, transport by pipeline, deep well injection, and central stockpiling of dry salts. Each method has associated costs and environmental problems.

Today's price for desalted water rules out its use for irrigation, but there are opportunities for municipal water supply applications. At the Foss Reservoir in western Oklahoma, for example, a reverse osmosis desalination plant converts high chloride and sulfate water to potable water for municipal use.

Phasing Out Marginal Uses

Phasing out marginally efficient water uses could make additional water supplies available for other purposes, but hardships resulting from such actions would have to be considered. Methods to effect phaseouts include pricing water to eliminate subsidies, levying taxes, and implementing appropriate regulations.

Improved Management and Operation of Existing Facilities

No longer is the massive structural project looked on as the principal means for solving the nation's water problems. This is partly due to the fact that most good reservoir sites have already been developed and partly due to increased concerns about the environmental impacts of large-scale structural developments. This does not mean that structural action is no longer needed to address troublesome water allocation issues, but it does suggest that innovative approaches combined with the more traditional ones will be required in the future. One of these is the assessment of existing systems to determine whether or not they can be revised and/or operated more efficiently to meet current and projected water requirements and thereby eliminate or defer the need for new or expanded system elements. This approach offers some attractive prospects for the future. An example of the payoff of such an approach is given relative to the Potomac River Basin in Chapter 13.

Other Approaches

In addition to the methods already mentioned for saving or providing additional water, there are other avenues that hold promise for the future.

A solution to the water supply problems of southern California and the lower Colorado River Basin through the use of Antarctic icebergs has been suggested (13). In a National Science Foundation study, it was found that Antarctic icebergs might be economically and technically developable as a source of water for these regions. The icebergs would be harvested, cabled together to form "trains," and covered with plastic to inhibit evaporation. Nuclear-powered tugs would then push the trains into prevailing ocean currents and guide them to parking areas along the shore near Los Angeles. Waste heat from electric-generating plants would be used along with the heat exchanged from the ambient sea water to melt the ice. Once melted, the water would be transported inland where it is estimated that it could reduce the intake water to southern California from the Colorado River by about one million acre-feet each year (13).

Another promising avenue for reducing freshwater requirements in arid lands is the development of salt-tolerant crops. Many wild plants grow in saline environments, and scientists are enthusiastic about the prospects for genetic solutions to the problem of salinity (13). A key question is whether suitable salt-tolerant crops will be developed in time to maintain the current level of agricultural productivity in areas such as California's San Joaquin Valley and Central Valley. Raising of crops under saline conditions is not new, however; such practices are being carried out in Israel, for example, where fresh water is in short supply.

Vegetation modification and the use of native plant varieties are other approaches to conserving water, especially in arid and semiarid regions. Finally, the development of plant varieties that transpire less water is being pursued by agricultural scientists. such an approach could have a high payoff, especially in those areas that depend heavily on irrigation.

There are many possibilities for improving the water supply picture of all regions. Some of these will require considerable research to perfect whereas others will require only the funds for implementation or the willingness of people to adopt them.

1-6 WATER RESOURCES MANAGEMENT: THE DIRECTION OF THE FUTURE

For many years the water resources fraternity focused on development. The reason for this is clear. Not long ago settlers were moving westward, industry was rapidly developing, and energy producers looked to rapid expansion. Population was also on the increase, as was the standard of living. New water-using devices were coming on the market: washing machines, air conditioners, dishwashers, and others. In fact, the philosophy of the nation was one of growth in terms of both people and economic well-being. This outlook was embraced by those involved in guarding against the ravages of uncontrolled streams as well as by those concerned about increased food production and stepped-up industrial activity. One of the measures of water use is the per capita base. This too became caught up in a growth fixation: the widespread belief was, and unfortunately still is in the minds of many, that as population increased, not only was one faced with an increased water requirement due to this growth but also the per capita water use figure would have to rise to meet hoped-for improvements in the standard of living. Such a doctrine is not a threat where water is in surplus, but where supplies are short, or are expected to be in the future, decision making based on this philosophy can lead to undesirable increases in population as well as fostering waste in all water-using sectors.

The liberal use of water (for many it is considered to be a "free" commodity) has led to the intense development of water-short regions such as southern California. To ensure continued growth in these areas, major water development schemes have been proposed and implemented (the California Water Plan, for example). Today, however, the attitude of many people is moving away from the desirability of expanding a city's limits or fostering new agricultural and/or industrial development. This shift is partly due to a greater concern about environmental values, but it is also tied to the fact that the policies of the past, which for a variety of reasons encouraged excessive growth and waste, have now resulted in a level of development that, in many regions, is close to an upper limit.

Short of large-scale interbasin transfers of water or a shifting of water allocations away from some current uses, easing the water problems in these areas will be difficult.

In many river basins in the United States the level of development is high, and improved water management will be the key to adjusting to future growth and/or change. This may include development of new facilities, but more broadly the focus will be on operating existing systems in a manner permitting more conservative use of water, acceptable reallocation of water supplies among users, and more efficient scheduling of streamflows during dry periods. Aversion of local and/or regional water shortages will depend in large measure on the ability of water managers to innovate and to manipulate the physical and institutional elements of their systems within feasible bounds. The time for moving forward with well-designed management programs is at hand (1).

1-7 THE TECHNOLOGICAL ROLE

A technological solution to a water problem that is generated in isolation from institutional factors will probably not be implemented. It is unfortunate that with so much technical capability there is not a better understanding of how technology relates to society's needs and the extent to which it can produce feasible solutions within the context of prevailing institutional structures.

Good decision making requires good information to support it, and this is part of the technological role. For example, a well-conceived technological solution to a regional water problem might not be permitted by federal regulations. If the payoff from implementing the proposed scheme is well documented and the consequences of choosing other alternatives are displayed relative to it, then this exercise might lead to regulatory reform. On the other hand, if the option is merely presented and the decision makers realize only that it is constrained by current regulations, then their attitude might be one of rejection without considering the merits of pursuing that option further. If the technician is called on to address a water issue, then he or she must be able to deal with the institutional elements that will ultimately determine whether his or her proposal is worth the effort or not. The water manager of the future must be able to accept reality, bring about change where feasible, recognize and deal with prevailing system constraints, and explicitly state his or her case where significant legal, regulatory, economic, or social changes are needed to effectively deal with the problem at hand. The technical role is important, for without an understanding of the hydrologic and hydraulic systems involved, there will be no effective solutions to water problems. But technology is not enough; it is only part of the system, and if this is recognized and accepted, then the technologist will be able to contribute significantly to meeting the world's water supply needs.

PROBLEMS

1-1. For your state, identify what you believe to be the three most pressing water resources problems.

1-2. For the problems cataloged in Problem 1-1, suggest solutions you believe would be feasible. Indicate why you think the approaches selected would work.

1-3. What is the major water-using sector in your state? From reference 1 determine that sector's magnitude in 1980. Do the same for the second- and third-highest uses.

1-4. How much of a reduction in the major water-using sector do you think could be obtained by the implementation of conservation practices? Do you believe that the costs of achieving this reduction would be large, moderate, or small? Why?

1-5. Identify the principal state agencies in your state having jurisdiction over water-related issues. Briefly describe the function of each of these.

1-6. Identify the principal local agencies in your city or town having interest in water issues. Describe their functions.

1-7. Determine the degree to which the local agencies listed in Problem 1-6 coordinate their activities with those of the state agencies you identified in Problem 1-5.

1-8. What do you see as the major institutional problems related to water management in your state? Describe these and indicate what you think can be done about them.

References

1. U.S. Geological Survey, *Estimated Water Use in the United States in 1980,* Geological Survey Circular 1001, U.S. Gov't. Print. Off., Washington, D.C., 1983.
2. U.S. Water Resources Council, *The Nation's Water Resources 1975–2000,* U.S. Gov't. Print. Off., Washington, D.C., 1978.
3. U.S. Department of Commerce, Business and Defense Services Administration, *Water Use in the United States (1950–1980),* U.S. Gov't. Print. Off., Washington, D.C., March 1960.
4. U.S. Congress, Senate, *Report of the Select Committee on National Water Resources,* Rep. No. 29, 87th Cong., 1st Sess., U.S. Gov't. Print. Off., Washington, D.C., January 1961.
5. U.S. Water Resources Council, *The Nation's Water Resources,* U.S. Gov't. Print. Off., Washington, D.C., 1968.
6. N. Wollman and G. E. Bonem, *The Outlook for Water Quality, Quantity and National Growth,* Resources for the Future, Inc., Johns Hopkins Press, Baltimore, MD, 1971.
7. National Water Commission, *Water Policies for the Future,* U.S. Gov't. Print. Off., Washington, D.C., 1973.
8. Council on Environmental Quality, *Twelfth Annual Report,* U.S. Gov't. Print. Off., Washington, D.C., 1981.
9. Abel Wolman, "When the Well Is Dry," *Proc. of the National Water Conference,* Philadelphia Academy of Natural Sciences, Philadelphia, PA., January 1982.

10. M. G. Wolman and C. C. Chamberlin, "Non-Point Sources," *Proc. of the National Water Conference,* Philadelphia Academy of Natural Sciences, Philadelphia, PA., January 1982.
11. Simon Ramo, "Regulation of Technological Activities: A New Approach," *Science,* vol. 213, no. 4150, August 21, 1981.
12. Julia Vitullo-Martin, "Ending the Southwest's Water Binge," *Fortune,* February 23, 1981.
13. David Sheridan, "The Underwatered West," *Environment,* vol. 23, no. 2, March 1981.
14. J. W. Clark, W. Viessman, Jr., and M. J. Hammer, *Water Supply and Pollution Control,* 3d ed., Harper & Row, New York, 1977.
15. W. Viessman and Christine DeMoncada, *Hydroelectric Development of Existing Facilities,* Congressional Research Service, Issue Brief No. IB78035, Washington, D.C., February 1978.
16. National Demonstration Water Project, *Drinking Water Supplies in Rural America,* Washington, D.C., 1978.
17. The President's Intergovernmental Water Policy Task Force, Subcommittee on Urban Water Supply, *Urban Water Systems: Problems and Alternative Approaches to Solutions,* Washington, D.C., June 1980.
18. General Accounting Office, Comptroller General of the United States, *Ground Water: An Overview,* Pub. CED-77-69, Washington, D.C., June 1977.
19. W. Viessman, Jr., *Water and Energy Conservation in Irrigated Agriculture,* Congressional Research Service, Issue Brief No. IB77072, Washington, D.C., 1977.
20. C. W. Howe and K. W. Easter, *Interbasin Transfers of Water,* Johns Hopkins Press, Baltimore, MD, 1971.

Chapter 2
Water Resources
Development,
1900 to 1980

Many organizations are responsible for planning, designing, constructing, and managing facilities needed to develop and use water, and it is important to understand the roles these agencies play. Furthermore, a history of how these roles have developed and changed over the years and how water policy has evolved will make it easier for the reader to understand how technology and its application to water problems are influenced by, and sometimes constrained by, historical events and agency biases (1–7).

2-1   TRENDS IN WATER RESOURCES DEVELOPMENT

From the earliest historical times, the federal government has been concerned with the nation's waters. The first area receiving attention was navigation. The Gallatin report of 1808 proposed, in part, an extensive system of canals and river improvements (7). Economic development of the west, political unity, and national defense were given as the basis. As an outcome of the Gallatin report and subsequent congressional actions, the Corps of Engineers became the first major water construction agency in the United States. The responsibilities of the Corps for planning river and harbor improvements were established in about 1824, and in 1826 the Omnibus Rivers and Harbors Act, authorizing specific waterway improvements and surveys, was passed. For a number of years, authorizations (providing the authority to act) and appropriations (providing the funds for authorized actions) for river and harbor improvements were made in the same bill. Later, however, the Omnibus Rivers and Harbors Act, separately authorizing the planning stages of some projects and construction phases of others, became the type of legislation that enabled the Corps to carry on its navigation improvements and flood control programs.

Flood control was originally seen as a local responsibility, but as the flood-ravaged lower Mississippi River Basin was settled, the country's interest in this area intensified. In 1874 Congress appointed a commission to report on a permanent plan for reclaiming a part of the Mississippi that was subjected to heavy flooding. This led to the establishment in 1879 of the Mississippi River Commission. This commission was given the authority to survey the river and prepare plans that would improve navigation and prevent floods.

The federal government did not become active in the development of irrigation facilities until after its flood control and navigation programs were well established. In 1877 the Desert Land Act authorized the sale of 640-acre tracts of arid lands in four states and eight territories to persons who would agree to irrigate them within three years. Following this, in 1890, a statute reserved to the United States a right of way for ditches and canals that it might later construct on public lands west of the 100th meridian if such ditches and canals were patented under any of the land laws of the United States. This statute paved the way for the Reclamation Act of 1902, out of which flow most major irrigation developments today.

Another area in which the federal government took an early interest was water power. In about 1879, and thereafter, Congress enacted numerous statutes that provided for the leasing of water power or surplus water to private companies or authorized the construction of private power dams. In 1890 Congress prohibited the building of dams in navigable waters without permission of the Secretary of War.

The ways in which resources programs have evolved in the United States since 1900 are discussed in the following paragraphs. Most of the material referenced was obtained from the works of Holmes (6, 7). Her reports are among the most comprehensive treatments of the history of water-related activities in the United States. For quick reference, Table 2-1 summarizes the major attributes of each of the time periods that are described in more detail in the narrative.

1900 to 1921: The Progressive Period

This period had its real beginning when Theodore Roosevelt was in office (7). As related to water resources planning, its major elements were:

Conservation of natural resources

A desire to encourage small, independent enterprises, such as the family farm

Belief in a strong federal government having the ability to affect the nation's economic life

Table 2-1 A HISTORY OF WATER RESOURCES PROGRAMS IN THE UNITED STATES FROM 1900 TO 1980

TIME PERIOD	SIGNIFICANT FEATURES OF THE PERIOD
1900 to 1921 Progressive period[a]	Emphasis on conservation and family farm development. Corps of Engineers' functions were expanded to include construction of flood control facilities as well as navigation improvements. The Bureau of Reclamation was established and authorized to plan and build irrigation works. The concept of multiple-purpose water resources planning emerged but was not carried out to any significant degree.
1921 to 1933 Post–World War I years	Unified national planning of public works and multiple-purpose planning with drainage basins was advocated. Planning functions of the CE and USBR were greatly expanded and increased emphasis was placed on hydroelectric development. The Corps was authorized to study water resources development on navigable streams. A sweeping program for flood control was adopted by Congress. The principal motivation for water resources planning stemmed from the localities that would receive the benefits from the projects proposed.
1933 to 1943 New Deal era	The primary concern during this period was the need to stimulate the nation's economy through the provision of jobs. Large public works projects including those for water resources development were looked on as a way to do this. Consequently, this period was one of construction. The TVA was created and other water agencies were given expanded roles. Several efforts in multiple-purpose planning became established. These included an expansion of the CE's river basin studies and of the efforts of interagency and intergovernmental teams led by national resources planning organizations. Another feature of the period was the formalization of the economic evaluation of water projects. Cooperation with local governments and encouragement of local participation in water programs was well ingrained in the New Deal philosophy.
1943 to 1960 Period of tightening congressional control	The National Resources Planning Board was abolished, and with its demise water resources planning became fragmented and narrower in scope. New water resources programs were mostly the work of congressional committees responsible for individual agency programs. All the construction agencies expanded their

Table 2-1(*Continued*)

TIME PERIOD	SIGNIFICANT FEATURES OF THE PERIOD
	programs (CE, USBR, SCS, and TVA). In 1948 a program of pollution control planning was authorized by Congress. In addition, grants were provided for the construction by local governments of sewage treatment works. The Fish and Wildlife Coordination Act provided that more formal consideration be given the protection of various creatures affected by water resources construction activities. Increased emphasis was placed on the economic evaluation of water projects and on the methodology of these evaluations. A number of study commissions were formed, and these were very consistent in their recommendations that planning for river basins be carried out comprehensively as opposed to on an individual purpose or project basis.
1960 to 1980 Environmental era	The U.S. water program from 1961 to 1965 was one of development. Construction of facilities was widespread and the construction agencies received the spotlight. The 1961 report of the Senate Select Committee on Water Resources ushered in a new era in water resources planning. The construction agencies were given new roles relative to water quality, municipal and industrial water supply, recreation, fish and wildlife protection, and regulation of floodplains. In 1966 President Johnson began to sharply focus his attention on water quality. This, combined with the environmental movement of the 1960s, led to the enactment of the sweeping Water Pollution Control Act Amendments of 1972. The Environmental Protection Agency was formed, and this was seen by the administration as a way of ensuring that the environment would be looked on as a single, interrelated system. Pollution control rather than water supply became the target of interest and funding.
1980 and beyond Devolution era	This period appears to be characterized by a shifting of authority and responsibility for water projects and programs from the federal government to state and local governments. An important issue is the ability of these governments to take on this added burden. It is likely that the trend in the future will be toward better management of existing systems and less construction of new facilities.

[a]Period designations generally follow those of Holmes (7).

Protecting equal opportunity and promoting the well-being of the
  people
Guarding the public domain from giveaways to special interests

During the progressive period much innovative thinking stemmed
from several official study commissions: the 1908 report of the Inland
Waterways Commission, the 1909 report of the National Conservation
Commission, and the 1912 report of the National Waterways Commission.
The last of these reports urged specific navigation improvements, prevention of deforestation of land bordering mountain streams, and the promotion of water power development. It also advocated a federal reservoir
system for flood control, noting that the costs could be justified by multiple-purpose benefits.

In addition to the already established planning role of the Corps,
several new water resources planning agencies were created during the
period from 1901 to 1920. These included the Reclamation Service (now
the Bureau of Reclamation), the Forest Service, the Waterways Commission (1900–1920), and the Federal Power Commission (now the Federal
Energy Regulatory Commission). The Corps of Engineers' planning functions were expanded to include water power development and flood control.

In 1912 Congress gave discretionary authority to the Secretary of War
to include, in permanent facilities for navigation, works that may be desirable for future development of water power. Follow-up legislation in 1913
required that reports on examinations and surveys include information
related to the development and use of water power. The Flood Control
Act of 1917 provided that comprehensive studies of watersheds include
consideration of the possible economical development of water power.
The Flood Control Act also gave the Corps responsibility for planning and
building flood control works, such as levees, on the Mississippi and Sacramento rivers, but reservoirs were not included.

Some historians have noted that the Corps was somewhat resistant to
the idea of multiple-purpose planning during the progressive period (7).
Nevertheless, legislation affecting that agency showed great accommodation of this philosophy. For example, general legislation in 1910 provided
that each survey of a navigable stream should include various measurements and investigations necessary for planning and proper consideration
of all uses of the stream that would affect navigation.

The Reclamation Act of 1902 directed the Secretary of the Interior
to make examinations and surveys and to locate and build works needed
for irrigation. It also required that the Secretary estimate the costs of
proposed works and determine the quantity and location of lands to be
irrigated. All facts related to the practicability of each irrigation project
were to be assembled. This act ushered in a major federal involvement in
providing water for opening the west to settlement.

The 1920 Federal Water Power Act gave the Federal Power Commission (FPC) authority to conduct continuing surveys of water power development and potentials across the United States. It also permitted determination of whether power derived from federal dams could be used to advantage for public purposes.

Most activities resulting from the legislation during the progressive period occurred in the west, midwest, or south. The reclamation program was designed to provide irrigation benefits to 17 western states. Most waterway improvements were for the benefit of midwestern farmers and businesses on the Ohio, Missouri, and Mississippi rivers. The flood control programs carried out were directed mainly to Mississippi Valley cities, and water power development tended to focus on aiding industries and the public in the west, midwest, and south. Nevertheless, irrigation, development of waterways, power production, and flood control were all part of a clear national ideological program. Although multiple-purpose water resources planning was broadly discussed and encouraged during the progressive period, it was not accomplished to any significant degree (7).

1921 to 1933: Post–World War I Years

During 12 years of Republican power from 1921 to 1933, it became the norm to remove as much competition between the federal government and private enterprise as possible. But even so, the ideology of the progressive period continued to influence water resources policies and programs at the national level. A new type of conservative attitude toward water resources planning was seen under Herbert Hoover, first as Secretary of Commerce and later as president. While he was Secretary of Commerce, Hoover advocated unified national planning of public works and multiple-purpose planning by drainage basin commissions. He also promoted several planning efforts that later, when he became president, resulted in many waterway improvements. These included projects on the Great Lakes, Hoover Dam, the Grand Coulee and Central Valley projects, and eventually the St. Lawrence Seaway.

The so-called era of normalcy following World War I also saw greatly expanded planning functions of the Corps and the Bureau of Reclamation (7). In 1925 Congress directed the Corps and the FPC to jointly prepare a list and estimate the cost of determining where power development might be practicable on navigable streams. The idea behind this was to produce general plans for the improvement of those streams for navigation in combination with the development of power, flood control, and irrigation. A list of streams was submitted to Congress in 1927. Since it was printed as House Document 308, the surveys became known as the 308 reports. In 1928, following a series of ravaging floods on the Mississippi River, Congress adopted a sweeping program for the control of floods on that river. It was stated that the federal government would bear the entire cost of this program. Although the 1928 act provided only for levees and diversion floodways as the immediate approach to the problem, one section of the act called for reports on the effect on lower Mississippi flood control of a reservoir system on its tributaries. Studies made pursuant to this section of the act showed that the CE believed that reservoirs were needed to reduce flood heights and that the Corps recommend construction of such works. The CE believed that there should be local participation in the planning and financing of the construction. The general investigative authority of the 308 reports permitted the CE to make general plans for all river basins in the United States except the Colorado, which was assigned jurisdiction by the USBR. These 308 studies took over 20 years to complete. They formed the basis of much of the water resources development that took place during the New Deal and post–World War II periods.

The Bureau of Reclamation also acquired regional multiple-purpose planning functions during the 1920s, when the 1920 Kincaid Act directed the Secretary of the Interior to investigate the Imperial Valley of California and consider the potential for irrigating it by diverting water from the lower Colorado River. The report, which came out of this 1922 study, recommended construction of several facilities and suggested that all future developments along the Colorado River be undertaken by the federal government. In 1928 the Boulder Canyon Project Act provided authority for studies of the feasibility of multiple-purpose projects in six other Colorado Basin states. The objective of these studies was to formulate a comprehensive plan for development and control of the Colorado River and its tributaries.

During the 1920s the principal motivation for planning stemmed from the localities that would receive the benefits of the developmental works. At the same time, the ideological issues that were receiving national attention, such as multiple-purpose projects and power development, continued to influence water planning directions.

1933 to 1943: The New Deal Era

The New Deal period, insofar as water resources matters were concerned, dealt mostly with the desire to stimulate the nation's economy through the provision of jobs. Large water resources projects were an integral part of this program. At the same time, however, leaders of the administration were concerned that the public works activities might be looked on as "pork barrel" in nature, and so they specified that all water projects should be related to and coordinated with plans for comprehensive river basin development. Many of the ideals of the former progressive movement were carried forward by the New Deal planners. Furthermore, the New Deal planning agencies put forward the notion that they must deal with "national" resources, which were defined to include human resources and institutions in addition to the traditional elements of land, water, and minerals (7).

During the New Deal period, the Tennessee Valley Authority was created. This unique organization is the only one in the United States which is empowered to exercise all federal functions related to the development and management of land and water resources within a defined geographical region. The TVA was authorized to plan, construct, and operate dam and reservoir projects for the primary purposes of navigation and flood control and also for generating electric power. In addition to the TVA, four national resource planning organizations emerged during the New Deal period as well as several emergency planning agencies. All of these had some role to play relative to the development and/or management of the nation's waters. The National Planning Board was created in 1933. It was given several tasks, but its most important accomplishment relative to water was coordinating the work of the President's Committee on Water Flow (7). That committee's report included multiple-purpose plans for 10 river basins. Many of the projects suggested by the report were later authorized for development. In June 1934 the National Planning Board was reorganized as the National Resources Board. The NRB recommended that studies of water projects for consideration by Congress should be based on drainage basins as comprehensive units and that a wide variety of water uses and controls should be considered in the plans. The NRB passed out of existence after a brief life and was replaced by the National Resources Committee (NRC) in 1935. The new committee's most significant achievement was a nationwide study of drainage basin problems and programs. The study included recommendations for both federal and state action and it was undertaken in cooperation with newly formed state planning boards. In 1939 the Executive Office of the President was created, and with its creation the NRC was reconstituted as the National Resources Planning Board (NRPB). The NRPB was authorized to undertake research and analyze problems involving water and other resources and to report its plans and programs to the president and Congress. The NRPB was also assigned joint responsibility with the Bureau of the Budget (now the Office of Management and Budget, OMB) for executive review of studies and plans of the construction agencies and for all construction agency reports to Congress. In many respects this marked the beginning of intense economic analysis of water projects. Two emergency planning agencies of importance to the water field were also established during the New Deal period. These were the Public Works Administration and the Works Progress Administration. These two agencies were responsible for the financial support of state and local planning and of projects constructed by state, local, and federal agencies.

While a number of new agencies emerged during the 1930s, that period also witnessed an increase in functions of the old agencies, principally the CE, FPC, and the Department of Agriculture. In 1935 Congress authorized the CE to supplement its completed 308 surveys with additional studies where needed, "to take into account important changes in economic factors as they occur and additional streamflow records or other factual data." This amounted to a nationwide framework river basin planning program. The Department of Agriculture was involved in coordinating water resources planning sponsored by the national resources planning organizations. In addition, it became active in participating in investigating certain agricultural aspects of USBR projects.

Two parallel efforts in multiple-purpose planning became established during the New Deal period. One was the continued and expanded effort of the CE through its 308 studies program. The other effort was that of the interagency and intergovernmental teams led by the national resources planning organizations. Their studies included assembling data on stream pollution and pollution abatement, municipal water supplies, soil erosion, reforestation, land drainage, recreation, wildlife conservation, and institutional issues.

Another milestone in water resources planning and evaluation occurred during the 1930s. This was the formalization of the economic evaluation of water projects. The general use of benefit-cost analysis to test a project's worth is attributed mainly to the Flood Control Act of 1936. The act provided that "the Federal Government should improve or participate in the improvement of navigable waters or their tributaries, including watersheds thereof, for flood control purposes if the benefits to whomsoever they may accrue are in excess of the estimated costs. . . ." Although this provision applied only to flood control works of the CE and Department of Agriculture, it was soon adopted by other water planning agencies for all purposes (7). Unfortunately, the various agencies were not always consistent in the way they defined terms or went about their analyses, a fact that has led to much controversy relative to benefit-cost analysis over the years. Another area of concern that emerged during the New Deal period was that of who should pay the cost of water projects. The question of cost sharing came up at that time and is still being argued about by Congress and the various administrations. Fundamentally, the question is one of subsidy: how much of the cost of a certain project function, such as flood control, should be borne by the federal government and how much, if anything, should state and local participants be expected to contribute. The earliest notions were that major works for purposes such as flood control were in the national interest and the cost should be assumed by the federal government. As time passed, the attitudes of citizens and members of Congress shifted and today the general attitude is one of "user pays the costs."

Cooperation with local governments and encouragement of local participation in water programs were basic to the New Deal philosophy. Even so, the policies espoused by the resources planning organizations were usually based on national ideological concerns. These included the provision of low-cost electricity and water for 160-acre western farms. Finally, although the attempt was made to foster local cooperation, there were often examples of intense local opposition to water proposals. The broadening of outlook away from the single-purpose project with its attractiveness to local supporters and toward multiple-purpose projects with their potential for conflict among project purposes seems to have played an important role in building the opposition that did occur.

1943 to 1960: A Period of Tightening Congressional Control

Once the National Resources Planning Board was abolished, federal water resources planning became fragmented and of narrower scope. The executive branch of the government no longer had the capability to develop comprehensive water resources plans or to evaluate the plans prepared by the construction agencies. The new water resources programs that developed were mostly the work of the congressional committees responsible for individual agency programs. As a result, each of the construction agencies developed close ties with its congressional supporters and the programs that evolved were heavily oriented to agency missions and geographical areas of responsibility. The CE was motivated by desires of local communities seeking flood protection, the USBR was motivated to stimulate economic development in the west through irrigation development, and the SCS set out to conserve the nation's soil and water through its watershed conservation programs. During this period, congressional sponsorship was based more on serving local constituencies than on furthering national ideologies.

During the 1940s and 1950s, all the construction agencies expanded their programs significantly even though there was little national interest in water programs other than the continuing concern for the ravages of floods. But by the end of the 1950s, some water resources issues began to capture wider national concern. These were associated with an awakening concern about the nation's environment.

In the period following World War II, the CE continued to be the major construction agency in water resources, with more than 50 percent of federal authorizations and appropriations going to programs of the Corps. Flood control issues dominated the CE work, but navigation ran a close second. The Flood Control Act of 1944 was the CE's main governing policy statement during this period. The same act also authorized the USBR to participate in the Pick-Sloan plan (Missouri River Basin development plan), which was the largest project of its type the bureau had participated in so far.

In addition, the 1944 act gave Congress the responsibility for coordinating the work of the CE and USBR. In 1953 the role of the SCS was strengthened when it was given full administrative responsibility for watershed programs. In 1954 Public Law 566 was passed. The law provided that for watersheds not exceeding 250,000 acres, the Department of Agriculture was authorized to help local organizations conduct works of improvement for flood prevention and agricultural aspects of water use and conservation. This included studies, plans, and financial assistance for the conduct of appropriate programs. This small watershed program carried out by SCS could not support the construction of large dams such as permitted by the authorities of the CE, USBR, and TVA, but it permitted the SCS to engage in a multitude of nationwide projects related to the needs of rural areas. At the same time that the involvements of the other construction agencies were expanding, so were those of the TVA. After World War II, the TVA's dam and reservoir program was accelerated. It was found, however, that many communities in the TVA's region were still subject to damaging floods and that structural solutions (building dams and levees) to these problems were often not economically feasible. As a result, the TVA began a cooperative program with state and local governments that involved land use planning to help communities avoid or minimize flood damages where they could not prevent floods. This was one of the earliest efforts at nonstructural flood control, now a widely accepted and practiced approach.

During the period after World War II, there also emerged several new planning agencies with responsibilities for water resources. These included the Public Health Service, the Fish and Wildlife Service, and the National Park Service. The 1948 Water Pollution Control Act authorized the U.S. Surgeon General of the Public Health Service to work with federal, state, interstate, and local agencies in preparing comprehensive pollution control plans for interstate rivers. The legislation also had a pollution abatement procedure but did not provide for enforcement action without approval of the state involved. Another provision of the 1948 legislation was the authorization of grants and loans to local governments for construction of sewage treatment works. No funds were appropriated for this purpose, however. In 1956 a much stronger pollution control bill was passed. This 1956 act authorized a program of 30 percent incentive grants to subsidize municipal wastewater treatment plant construction. In addition, the federal abatement procedure was strengthened.

The 1946 Fish and Wildlife Coordination Act provided for cooperative efforts among water agencies to prevent harm to or loss of wildlife as a result of federal actions to impound, divert, or control water. The act also provided that the cost of planning, construction, and maintenance of facilities for protection of wildlife should be part of the cost of the project involved. In 1958 the act was amended to add wildlife enhancement to the planning purposes for which the federal agencies would have to consult the Fish and Wildlife Service.

The National Park Service started reporting to the USBR in the 1940s regarding the recreational potential of reservoir sites and river basins. Then in 1947 the service was given responsibility for recreation planning at reclamation projects. In 1945 it began recreation planning for CE projects also, but only when requested to do so. The National Park Service did not always share the views of the CE and USBR relative to their water development programs. As a result, it was not uncommon for the Park Service to oppose the projects of both construction agencies.

After the National Resources Planning Board died in 1943, the executive branch no longer had a mechanism for proposing overall priorities for federal water resources programs. The congressional committees assumed this role, but at the time they were often more responsive to the desires of local constituencies and agency biases than to national ideologies. As a result, both Congress and the Bureau of the Budget (BOB) required that all projects pass a test of economic feasibility. Thus, it became necessary for the water planner to prove that the benefits of the project exceeded the costs and that local interests had agreed to repay (and likely could repay) the costs that were not to be assumed by the federal government. Initially, the Bureau of the Budget's role in this process was very limited. But in December 1952, during the last days of the Truman administration, BOB developed what became known as Circular A-47. This circular, adopted by the Eisenhower administration, contained the provision that not only must total project benefits exceed the costs but the benefits of individual purposes of multiple-purpose projects must exceed the costs of including such purposes. It also included several cost-sharing provisions and set a maximum period of 50 years for repayment of federal investments in water resources projects.

After about 1943, there was a flurry of activity relative to the coordination of water resources plans and programs. A number of interagency coordinating committees and official study commissions were established. It seemed clear to both the executive and the legislative branches of the government that something was wrong with the methods with which federal water resources programs were being managed and focused. As a result, the recommendations of study commissions composed of respected experts were sought. The most prominent of these commissions were the U.S. Commission on the Organization of the Executive Branch of the Government, 1949; the President's Water Resources Policy Commission, 1950; the Subcommittee to Study Civil Works of the House Committee on Public Works, 82d Congress, 2d Session, 1952; and the Presidential Advisory Committee on Water Resources Policy, 1955 (7). The four study commissions produced work that was given careful consideration by the legislative and the executive branches of the government and, although there were differences in the recommendations of these commissions, they were generally in close agreement on their recommendations regarding the approach to water resources planning. All the commissions favored planning for river basins on a comprehensive rather than an individual purpose or project basis. They also favored integration of planning by federal, state, and local planners on a river basin level. All the commissions favored the establishment of fair policies for economic evaluation of projects and repayments of costs. The recommendations of these study commissions were later considered by other analysts and eventually led to many of the reforms in water resources organizational structure and management that emerged in the late 1960s.

1960 to 1980: The Environmental Era

During the years 1961 to 1965, the federal water resources program in the United States can be characterized as one of development. Construction of facilities was widespread, and construction was the focus of most thrusts in funding, staffing, and attention of the public. A second important function during that time was the continued operation and maintenance of facilities that had been constructed earlier. Because of this emphasis, the principal construction agencies dominated the river basin planning of the day and played principal roles in the planning organizations that were functional at the time.

On April 20, 1959, the Senate Select Committee on Water Resources was established. The committee made five broad recommendations (8). First, it called for the federal government, in cooperation with the states, to prepare comprehensive water development and management plans for all major river basins of the United States. Second, the committee recommended that the federal government encourage the states to more actively participate in planning and implementing water development and management activities. A third recommendation was that a periodic assessment of water supply and demand relations be made for each water resources region of the United States. Fourth, the committee recommended a federal program of coordinated scientific research on water, and finally, it recommended a specific program to encourage efficiency in water development and use.

Although the Senate Select Committee made no legislative proposals, the Water Resources Planning Act of 1965 was an outgrowth of its work. This act was designed to encourage conservation, development, and use of the nation's water and related land resources on a comprehensive and coordinated basis. The act established the Water Resources Council, provided for river basin commissions, and authorized financial assistance to the states for comprehensive water resources planning.

The recommendations of the Senate Select Committee in 1961 are often thought to be the starting point of a new era in water resources planning and development in the United States. The report gave the executive branch approval to initiate radically new policy directions (6). The role of existing construction agencies was expanded to include emphasis on topics such as water quality storage, municipal and industrial water supply, recreation, fish and wildlife protection, and the regulation of floodplains. It was also recognized that the traditional focus of water programs was in need of revision to ensure proper handling of the most urgent water problems identified in the 1960s.

When President Kennedy was inaugurated in 1961, a number of issues related to the nation's waters had emerged as matters of concern to the political and social systems of the United States. The federal programs functioning at that time were generally conceived by most observers to have been rooted in national ideologies, even though the direct benefits of some of them were actually quite local. It is also apparent that once a federal program had been established to address an important issue, the nation tended to lose interest in the issue (6). Momentum for the program was then provided by the agencies responsible for administering it and by local recipients of project or program benefits. This did not mean, however, that the prevailing ideology was abandoned or could not be called again into play if the situation warranted it.

The changes in water resources programs that emerged during the Kennedy years were mostly development oriented. Senate Document 97 changed the standards for making benefit-cost analyses in such a way that more projects were expected to meet the test of economic efficiency and thus be eligible for authorization. Many new projects were authorized and initiated. These included a wide array of projects that would have substantial impact on the environment. Projects such as the USBR's Fryingpan-Arkansas transmountain diversion and new canals that would greatly increase the length of the nation's inland waterways system emerged (6).

President Johnson endorsed most of Kennedy's ideas about water resources planning, research, and development, but when Johnson was elected president he also made the preservation of nature a keystone of his domestic policy. In 1966 Johnson began to sharply focus his attention on water quality. It was his position that the entire river basin, rather than a locality, should be the focus of pollution control efforts. He proposed a "clean rivers demonstration program" in which the federal government would provide funds to interstate and/or regional water pollution control authorities on a first-ready, first-served basis. Those participating in the program would be required to have permanent water quality planning organizations, water quality standards, and implementation plans in effect for all waters of the basin designated.

When the Clean Rivers Restoration Act was passed in 1966, it contained no provision for Johnson's demonstration program. It did, however, acknowledge his river basin planning concept. But the greatest effect of the 1966 act was its substantial increase in the level of funding that could be appropriated for the construction of wastewater treatment facilities. Unfortunately, due to the increasing costs of the Vietnam war, the construction grant program was not funded at the levels authorized in the 1966 act.

In 1969 the Nixon administration took office. At that time it had good conservation credentials, but it was also hampered in its efforts by budgetary restraints imposed by the Vietnam conflict. Nevertheless, Congress prodded the new administration to take action in the areas of water pollution control and environmental policy. This prodding was supported by a strong environmental movement, which had been swelling during the last part of the 1960s. By 1970 the Nixon administration became convinced that there was need for a massive federal investment in the sewage treatment plant construction program. In his February 1970 Message on Environmental Quality, President Nixon proposed a four-year, $10 billion program of state, federal, and local investment in wastewater treatment facilities. The federal share of this investment was to be $1 billion per year. Although this amount lagged behind actual authorized funding levels and was less than many environmental advocates desired to see spent, it was much more than any previous presidential request (6).

In 1970 the National Environmental Policy Act was passed (NEPA, 1969). The act was praised by President Nixon, who proclaimed that the three-member Council on Environmental Quality (CEQ) would be a great asset in informing the president on important environmental issues. The Nixon administration promptly put the provisions of NEPA into effect. On March 5, 1970, the president issued an executive order instructing all federal agencies to report on possible variances of their authorities, policies, and so on with NEPA's purposes. Then on April 30, 1970, CEQ issued interim guidelines for the preparation of environmental statements.

In December of 1970, as an outgrowth of the administration's environmental interests, a new independent body, the Environmental Protection Agency (EPA), was created. This organization assumed the functions of several existing agencies relative to matters of environmental management. It brought together under one roof all the pollution control programs related to water, air, solid wastes, pesticides, and radiation. The organization of the EPA was seen by the administration as the most effective way of recognizing that the environment must be looked on as a single, interrelated system. It is noteworthy, however, that the creation of the EPA made even more pronounced the separation of water quality from other water programs. It appears that the public sentiment at the time was that water resources development and water pollution control were "at best unrelated, and at worst antagonistic, concerns" (6).

Even with the enactment of NEPA, it was clear that a comprehensive response to water pollution issues was still lacking. Relative to the construction grants program, it became evident during congressional hearings in 1971 that the program was underfunded. To rectify the situation, Congress passed the Water Pollution Control Act Amendments of 1972 over President Nixon's veto. The 1972 amendments:

Increased federal funding for wastewater treatment facilities
Increased planning responsibilities at all levels of government

Established a regulatory mechanism requiring uniform technology-
based effluent standards along with a permit system for all point
source discharges

Provided the federal government with final authority over most aspects of the program (9)

The 1972 amendments recognized the importance of the water
quality management problem and the urgency to act on it quickly. It
was estimated by the National League of Cities and U.S. Conference of
Mayors, for example, that a financial commitment of $33 to $37 billion
would be needed for water pollution control programs during the remainder of the 1970s (9). The 1972 act committed the federal government to carrying 75 percent of the costs associated with the construction of wastewater treatment facilities and authorized $18 billion of
contract authority.

After the passage of P.L. 92-500, there was a transition from research-
ing the water pollution problem to implementation of solutions (9). For
example, Section 101 of the act states goals of fishable and swimmable
waters and the prohibition of toxic discharges. These goals required put-
ting programs into operation to reverse the threats that scientists had
identified. The 1972 Clean Water Act provided the framework for a concerted effort on water pollution control. Contract authority to construct
treatment facilities combined with meaningful enforcement procedures
set in motion a policy to reverse the water quality degrading practices of
the past.

Then in 1977, in response to the indicated need to address deficiencies in the 1972 act, the Clean Water Act was revised. The salient points
of the 1977 act include:

States were specifically mandated primacy over water quality and
water use issues

Municipalities were given evidence of a federal commitment in the
form of construction grants and training assistance

The public received assurances of the priority of water quality in the
form of effective enforcement and incentive provisions for governments and industries to achieve the goal of fishable and swimmable
waters

Industry received necessary extensions of compliance deadlines
under the effluent discharge limitations provision

Environmental groups witnessed the incorporation of a Resource Defense Council–EPA consent decree into the law that established
toxic effluent standards and set forth a comprehensible process to
implement effluent limitations (9)

As a result of water pollution control efforts from 1972 to 1980, the
tide of pollution was noted to have been turned in many localities. But in

1981 the Reagan administration, in its efforts to curtail federal expenditures, encouraged passage of the 1981 Municipal Wastewater Treatment Construction Grant Amendments. Among the key provisions of this act were reduced funding levels, shifting of construction costs to municipalities, and limiting eligible categories for funding. This reduced funding commitment at the federal level superficially appears to reflect a lessened priority for environmental uses, but whether or not this is actually the case remains to be seen.

Aside from work on pollution control, activity in most other water resources programs (particularly development oriented) slowed considerably after about 1970. Some changes in water policy occurred as a result of presidential initiatives, but studies and regulations were the principal products, not water. During the Carter years many issues were debated between the executive and legislative branches of the government, but the outcome was generally a stalemate. Every energy and water appropriations bill before Congress after 1976 was a major area of conflict. President Carter's 1977 "hit list" of what his administration felt to be unsound water projects typified the antagonism between the president and many pro-water-development members of Congress. The Reagan administration took a more receptive stand on water projects, but the worsening state of the nation's economy in the early 1980s limited funds for any significant revitalization of water resources development activities at that time.

Although the future is clouded, it appears that the trend will be toward improved management of existing water resources systems rather than the construction of new facilities (10). Interest in water quality management remains high as does interest in environmental protection. Programs in these areas will certainly continue, but they may take a different form and be financed to a greater extent with state and local, rather than federal, funds.

1980 and Beyond: The Devolution Era

Since the late 1970s there has been a decided move by the Carter and the Reagan administrations to shift both authority and responsibility for many water resources programs from the federal government to the states. Whether this trend will persist into the future is hard to say. But one thing seems clear: the days when most of the planning, designing, and development were carried out almost exclusively by the federal government are at an end. The states and local governments are assuming more important roles; the difficulty is that as of 1984 not all of them were adequately prepared to take on the new responsibilities. Changing attitudes on federal-state partnerships are emerging and with them a clearer definition of responsibilities at all levels of government may be expected.

2-2 LESSONS FROM HISTORY

Since the turn of the century, interest in water resources has shifted from emphasis on navigation and flood control to multiple-purpose water projects and then to concern about broad environmental issues. Although the focus of attention has changed over the years, many of the old ideologies and traditions carry on. It is difficult if not impossible to effectively take on today's water issues without having some knowledge of what has gone before. It is not only that popular perceptions are sometimes slow to change; they are also locked into laws and regulations of a bygone day. These exert a constraining influence on what we do.

A review of history reveals several interesting points:

United States water resources development has been heavily influenced by local political pressures

Strong national interests and/or crises have been the major motivators for legislative action

Recognition of regional differences and the need to appropriately address them in planning processes has persisted for years, but regional or river basin planning efforts have often been ineffectual or poorly done

As society's interests have changed, attitudes toward water resources development have also shifted

Planners and developers have often been slow to react to signals from the public

Although not written explicitly, a national water policy does exist and it can be traced through the eras discussed in this chapter

New legislation to react to shifting political and social pressures has not been accompanied by needed revisions and/or deletions of previous laws

The concept of planning ahead to meet and/or stave off future problems is well recognized but short-range concerns having more immediate political payoff have tended to dominate and preclude the mounting of effective efforts to adequately prepare for events that are expected to take place

Water resources development is largely an outcome of political processes and the need to provide better information on which to make decisions is clear

The level of funding provided for most major programs has usually fallen far short of projected needs

A careful review of past proposals for regional and river basin management, coordination of agencies and programs, planning of water resources facilities, and consolidation of managing agencies shows that the "wheel" has been invented and reinvented many times. The examples of starting from ground zero on water issues by new administrations are legion. Often these efforts ignored the lessons of the past. This is unfortunate, but it is typical of human nature.

PROBLEMS

2-1. Trace out a brief history of water resources development in your state. Does it follow the national pattern? If not, how does it differ and why?

2-2. List the principal state water resources agencies in your location. What are the similarities between these and the federal agencies discussed in Chapter 1?

2-3. How are the programs of the various agencies in your state coordinated? Is the approach effective? If not, what do you think could be done to improve it?

2-4. What improvements do you think are needed in the way that your state develops and manages its water resources?

2-5. What do you think should be the federal role in assisting your state to carry out its water programs?

References

1. Department of the Army, Office of the Chief of Engineers, *The Corps in Perspective Since 1775,* EP 360-1-9, Washington, D.C., December 1976.

2. Lewis H. Blakey, "The Corps of Engineers Water Resources Planning Program as an Information Resource for State Water Planners," *Interstate Conference on Water Problems,* Washington, D.C., rep., vol. 1, no. 5, Washington, D.C., August 12, 1982.

3. U.S. Department of the Interior, *Water and Power Resources Service—Its Mission, Its Programs,* Washington, D.C., 1980.

4. U.S. Department of Agriculture, Soil Conservation Service, *Assistance Available from the Soil Conservation Service,* Agriculture Information Bull. 345, December 1980.

5. Martha Derthick, *Between State and Nation—Regional Organizations of the United States,* The Brookings Institution, Washington, D.C., 1974.

6. Beatrice H. Holmes, *History of Federal Water Resources Programs and Policies, 1961–1970,* U.S. Department of Agriculture, Miscellaneous Pub. No. 1379, Washington, D.C., September 1979.

7. Beatrice H. Holmes, *A History of Federal Water Resources Programs 1800–1960,* U.S. Department of Agriculture, Miscellaneous Pub. No. 1233, Washington, D.C., June 1972.

8. U.S. Congress, Senate, Committee on Interior and Insular Affairs, *History of the Implementation of the Recommendations of the Senate Select Committee on National Water Resources,* 90th Cong., 2d Sess., U.S. Gov't. Print. Off., Washington, D.C., 1969.

9. Ron M. Linton, *The Politics of Clean Water,* Chemtech, July 1982.

10. Federal Reserve Bank of Kansas City, *Western Water Resources: Coming Problems and the Policy Alternatives,* Westview Press, Boulder, CO, 1980.

Chapter 3
Water Policy and
Institutions

The development and management of American water resources have been influenced by many social, political, organizational, and economic factors. Unfortunately, many of these conflict with one another and act more as obstacles to good water management than promoters. A complication is that many people do not recognize that institutions, rather than physical conditions, are often the cause of shortfalls in water supply. In fact, many physical problems cannot be overcome without accompanying changes in institutional elements. Water resources planners, developers, and managers must be aware of this; otherwise, their plans and designs may have little hope for realization.

3-1 NATIONAL WATER POLICY

United States water policy exists implicitly in numerous statutes, regulations, and administrative actions. It includes plans for flood control, navigation, fish and wildlife preservation, reclamation of arid lands, conservation, elimination of pollutants, recreation, municipal and industrial water supply, and other water-related features.

The Reclamation Act of 1902; the 1909 Rivers and Harbors Act; the Flood Control acts of 1917, 1936, and 1944; the Water Resources Planning Act of 1965; and the Federal Water Pollution Control Act amendments of 1972 and 1977 are a sampling of the pertinent federal laws.

Over the years, as national goals have changed, so has the nation's water policy. For the most part, redirections have been associated with

49

piecemeal efforts, however, and new provisions have been layered over the old, often with little thought given to the inconsistencies created in the process.

Modern attempts (since 1970) to reshape water policy can be associated heavily with the recommendations of the National Water Commission (NWC) in 1973, with those stemming from President Carter's Water Policy Initiatives in 1978, and with the deliberations of President Reagan's Cabinet Council on Natural Resources and Environment (established in 1981) (1, 2).

The NWC stressed the need for a more direct embodiment of environmental considerations in water resources planning processes and embraced the principle that users should pay the full costs of water projects. It also emphasized the need for an aggressive effort to improve the quality of the nation's waters but believed that the nationwide uniform treatment provisions of P.L. 92-500 would not lead to the most rapid or cost-effective solution to water quality improvement. The NWC's analysis was comprehensive, and although it included many recommendations for action by the federal government, few of them have been implemented.

President Carter's water policy reform proposals were designed to improve water resources planning and management, to permit construction of sound water projects, to emphasize water conservation, to enhance federal-state cooperation, and to increase the focus on environmental quality (2). Although some changes resulted from this effort, studies and regulations were the main products and few new facilities to meet emerging water needs materialized. By 1980 the entire United States federal water program appeared to be suffering from a negative image. This was created partly by the environmental movement of the 1960s and partly by an emerging general belief, sometimes poorly founded, that most water projects were overpriced and of greater detriment to society than benefit.

The Reagan administration, like its predecessor, established machinery to consider water policy reform. The Cabinet Council was established and the Assistant Secretaries Working Group on Water Resources was set up to assist it. The early focus of these organizations was on reviewing the principles and standards for water and related land resources planning (P&S, see Chapter 4) and on developing revised cost-sharing policies to move toward full cost recovery for water projects where beneficiaries could be clearly identified. Fundamentally, however, the Reagan administration espoused the principle that the states should assume greater responsibility for the planning, design, construction, management, and financing of water resources projects. A transition from mainly federal to state responsibility in water programs is slowly emerging. This significant institutional shift has many problems associated with it, but one thing is certain: the states will have to develop a level of competency in dealing with water matters that in many instances is not presently (1984) apparent.

3-2 POLICY FORMATION PROCESSES

The management of water and other resources is carried out in accordance with policies set at various levels of government. These broad policies are exemplified by the following statements: provide adequate quantities of water for human needs, ensure the maintenance of good quality water, guard against the ravages of floods, and protect the environment. Such policies are translated into action by statutes, regulations, and administrative actions. The design of these policies and their plans for implementation are fundamental determinants of how the world's water resources are used and managed. The institutions discussed in this chapter are at the same time derivatives of water policy and constraints on forming new or revised policies. It is important that they be understood in this context.

Policymaking is an outcome of political forces operating in different political arenas. Conflict is an inherent element of these political processes, and it serves to ensure that a multiplicity of values is represented. Compromise is a partner to all policymaking and the art of reaching this compromise can be greatly enhanced by appropriate technological input and the use of state-of-the-art analytical techniques.

Water managers at various levels face local institutional frameworks that define and limit their actions. Where constraints appear overly restrictive, suggested policy changes should follow. Policy analysts, using the feedback from current management stances, can begin to shape new policy choices. According to Stokey and Zeckhauser, these choices may be made after the following process: establishing the nature of the issue to be dealt with, presenting alternative methods for addressing the issue, predicting the consequences of the suggested alternative courses of action, and placing values on the outcomes produced, monetary or otherwise (3). This procedural framework is well suited to a variety of modeling approaches such as those discussed later in this text. Important to the successful use of such models is the inclusion in them of the institutional constraints that limit what can be done.

The goal of the process to guide policymaking should be the provision of the best information given that time, basic data, and manpower may be limiting. Choosing among competing options is not easy, as the future is unknown, but by doing a better job of assessing the outcomes of various alternatives and establishing a mechanism for evaluating their consequences, better decisions and consequently policies should be the result. The reader should keep this in mind as he or she moves through the discussions on analytical methods that follow.

3-3 INSTITUTIONAL ISSUES

Water supplies are thought to be inadequate in many locations, and it is commonly believed that the only way to solve this problem is to tap new sources. In some cases, water availability is limited and technical solutions are appropriate. In other cases, the water is physically available but locked out of use due to laws, regulations, or other institutional mechanisms. Unfortunately, these institutional elements are sometimes hard to change because they may involve political sensitivities and may also be tied to local traditions. They are the heart of many water problems, however, and deserve attention accordingly. Institutional issues of importance include:

The nonuniform, incomplete, and sometimes conflicting coverage of state and federal water laws. At the federal level, Indian and federal reserved water rights issues are compelling. Uncertainties created by unquantified water rights may constrain planning and inhibit investments in water management facilities.

The failure of laws, agencies, and water users to recognize the interrelations of surface waters and groundwaters. The use of water from one source often affects the availability from another. Efficient regional water management cannot be achieved unless surface waters and groundwaters are used in a coordinated fashion.

The separation by statutes and administrative processes of water quality and water quantity. Water quality decisions affect water quantity decisions and vice versa, and yet they are often made without regard for one another.

The failure to recognize that water is not a free commodity. Users often pay far less than the cost of providing the water they use. Furthermore, fees collected for water services are sometimes channeled to purposes other than defraying the capital costs of new water projects or for meeting operation and maintenance expenses.

The focus on projects as opposed to comprehensive plans for achieving water resources goals. Historically approaches to water resources development have often been piecemeal and narrow in perspective. This has resulted in less than optimal regional systems of development and questionable federal investments in facilities.

The lack of effective national, state, and regional mechanisms for setting priorities for water resources investments. Good investment decisions require mechanisms to set water development priorities in the context of all options for water resources expenditures and within the broader framework of other needs for federal outlays of funds. The principal yardstick used at present is the project-oriented benefit-cost analysis.

The lack of mechanisms for ensuring implementation of plans. A great deficiency in water resources planning systems has been the inability of planners to influence decisions through their plans. If plans are worth developing, they should be used in decision-making processes.

The diffusion of legislative jurisdictions at all levels of government. Split legislative committee jurisdictions, for example, foster inconsistencies in programs, duplication of efforts, and conflicts in management.

The inability of federal, state, and local agencies to coordinate their programs.

The proliferation of regulations, many of which constrain rather than promote the effective use of the nation's waters. The construction of wastewater treatment facilities has been impeded, for example, by confusing regulatory requirements. Some requirements have been imposed retroactively in the middle of design procedures, adding millions of dollars to project costs.

The nonuniformity in requirements for evaluating water resources projects. Sewage treatment plants, for example, are not judged in the same manner as water storage works. Dams are subjected to detailed benefit-cost analyses whereas sewage treatment plants must only be cost-effective.

The variety of and sometimes conflicting purposes of state and federal water laws, the proliferation of water agencies, and the ill-defined roles of federal, state, and local governments are prime aspects of institutional elements that must be reckoned with and overcome. The enormous body of environmental laws and regulations that has been produced in recent years is also troublesome. The sometimes inconsistent interpretation of these laws and regulations by federal agencies and the courts has, for example, hindered the construction of even beneficial water projects. Furthermore, various laws and regulations have sometimes been used inappropriately as tools to derail or delay water and other types of development.

3-4   ROLES OF FEDERAL, STATE, AND LOCAL GOVERNMENTS

Basic to the resolution of many water problems is clarification of the roles of federal, state, and local governments in addressing them. In its 1973 report, "Water Policies for the Future," the National Water Commission stated that "development, management, and protection of water resources should be controlled by that level of government nearest the problem and most capable of effectively representing the vital interest involved" (1). The commission envisioned a continuing federal role in planning and financing but believed it should gradually diminish. The report also proposed that "Regional and State entities, as well as local units of government, should assume increasing roles in the control of water resource use and preservation."

President Carter's water policy reforms of 1978 included emphasis on an increasing role for the states (2); the Reagan administration has taken a similar position. Unfortunately, there has been little evidence to indicate how some of the states might be able to take on added burdens such as this along with their own fiscal problems and sometimes limited technical cadres. If a successful transfer of authority is to be made, some federal guidance and technical support will probably be required and innovative financing options may be needed to permit some of the less well-to-do states to carry on a determined effort.

3-5 STATE AND FEDERAL WATER LAW

Many of the laws that share in allocating this nation's waters came about as a result of local disputes and/or circumstances. At the time of their design, they were usually appropriate, but today many of them have outlived their usefulness and some even constrain efficient water management.

State Water Law

Water law in the United States is mostly property law and almost entirely state law with the exception of Federal Reserved Water Rights and Indian Water Rights, which are covered later (4, 5, 6). There is also a distinction between groundwater law and surface-water law, and this imposes an added difficulty for water managers. The extent to which these two legal systems vary is dependent on the individual state. It has been common practice, however, for states to use separate laws for groundwater and surface water even where the two systems are physically interconnected. Different rules sometimes apply to waters moving downward through the ground than for those already stored and moving underground. A particularly troublesome point is that rechargeable and nonrechargeable aquifers are often treated the same in state laws. In this case, the argument can be strongly made that the renewable segment of the groundwater resource should be treated differently from the nonrenewable or "stock" resource.

The interface between the hydrologic system and the legal system is depicted in Figure 3-1 (6). Hopefully, the trend in the future will be to bring legal systems dealing with water into closer balance with hydrologic systems. In particular, interactive surface waters and groundwaters should be managed conjunctively and water stored in aquifers having insubstantial mechanisms for recharge should be treated independently as a stock resource. In the meantime, planners and managers will have to deal with the legal systems that are already established. A good summary of the various state water laws was published by the National Water Commission in 1973 (7).

SURFACE-WATER RIGHTS

There are two principal doctrines regarding surface water in the United States (4, 5, 6): the surface-water rights system that prevails in the eastern

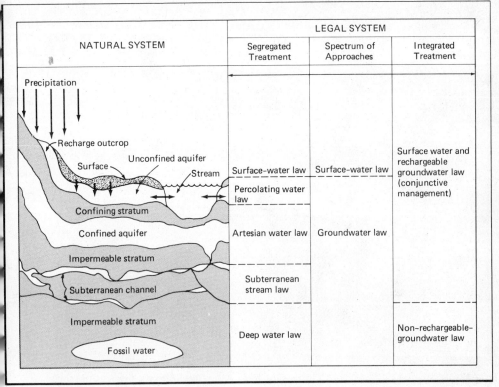

NATURAL SYSTEM	LEGAL SYSTEM		
	Segregated Treatment	Spectrum of Approaches	Integrated Treatment
Precipitation / Recharge outcrop / Surface / Unconfined aquifer / Stream	Surface-water law	Surface-water law	Surface water and rechargeable groundwater law (conjunctive management)
	Percolating water law		
Confining stratum / Confined aquifer	Artesian water law	Groundwater law	
Impermeable stratum			
Subterranean channel	Subterranean stream law		
Impermeable stratum / Fossil water	Deep water law		Non–rechargeable-groundwater law

Figure 3-1   Natural system–legal system interface. (After the John Muir Institute, Inc., reference 6.)

United States is that of riparian rights, whereas the system of appropriation rights is the one generally followed in the west (Figures 3-2 and 3-3).

• *Riparian Rights.* Water law in the eastern United States was modeled mostly after the system that evolved in England. In that scheme, lakes and streams were considered as "private" waters and the right to use them was given the owners of "riparian land" (land that borders on, or encompasses, a surface-water system). The water was expected to be used for beneficial purposes and was not to be impaired in quality or diminished in quantity when returned to the source. This provision was considered to be overly restrictive for American practices, and in the eastern United States a doctrine of "reasonable use" was generally established. This doctrine permitted a riparian landowner to modify the quantity and quality of water withdrawn within the bounds of reason so long as the water was used for the purpose for which the land was dedicated.

Riparian water rights are generally obtained along with the purchase of riparian land. It is possible, however, for riparian land to be sold with a provision in the deed stating that the water rights are to be retained by

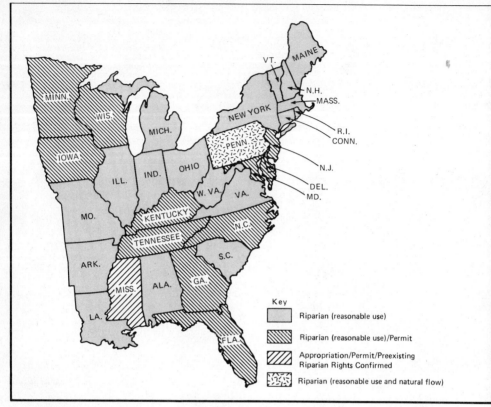

Figure 3-2   Surface water rights systems in the eastern United States. (After the John Muir Institute, Inc., reference 6.)

the seller. Although tradition has been that riparian landholders are entitled to withdraw reasonable quantities of water whenever they desire to do so, many states are now beginning to impose permit requirements. When this is done, the riparian owner must secure a permit from an appropriate state agency before withdrawals can be made. Such permits are often conditioned to ensure noninterference with existing water users served by the same source and to ensure that adequate flows for instream purposes are maintained and that water quality is not impaired.

Riparian rights are usually considered to be coequal, that is, there is no priority assigned the most senior user. In times of shortage, all users are expected to curtail their uses on a pro rata basis. It is generally expected that riparian waters must be used on the owner's land, but there is usually no restriction placed on the type of use.

As water uses have increased and the number of withdrawal locations has grown, the tendency of riparian states to move toward permit systems has accelerated. Concern about maintaining adequate instream levels for fish and wildlife has been an important factor in bringing this about.

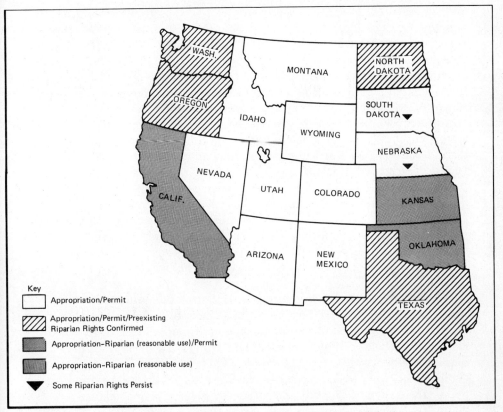

Figure 3-3 Surface water rights systems in the western United States. (After the John Muir Institute, Inc., reference 6.)

Where permits are required, they may impose restrictions on where withdrawals may be made, on the quantities of water that may be withdrawn, and on the period of time over which the withdrawals may be made. In some cases, some uses may also be assigned a higher priority than others so that during times of limited supply, the users having the highest priority may be able to continue their operations uncurtailed, while other users may be required to limit their uses. Permits may also specify that the nature of a water use cannot be altered without approval of the water rights agency. All these modifications of the early riparian system have come about as water supplies have become more heavily used and their quantity diminished. The intent of the permitting system is to ensure that essential water uses are maintained during critical periods, that the quality of the water is protected, and that waste is guarded against.

• *Appropriation Rights.* The surface-water rights that predominate in the western United States are for the most part appropriation rights. In the early days of western settlement, the commonest enterprises were mining and agriculture. Both of these endeavors required large amounts of water, and the location of the water use was often not suited to the eastern riparian system, that is, the land under development was not always adjacent to a surface-water source. The appropriation doctrine was thus devised, permitting water withdrawals to be made and applied to lands for beneficial purposes regardless of the ownership of the land. The principal means by which appropriation rights may be obtained are demonstrating an intent to withdraw water for a beneficial use, actually diverting the water, and applying the diverted water to a beneficial use (6). Another distinguishing feature about appropriation rights is their priority system. Unlike riparian water users, appropriators are assigned a level of priority based on their seniority of water use. Thus the concept of "first in time, first in right" emerged. Basically, the idea was that the most senior appropriator could, during times of shortage, use the full amount of water to which he or she was entitled before the next senior appropriator could exercise his or her right and so on. Under this system it is therefore possible for junior appropriators to be left without water during critical periods.

Appropriation rights are generally obtained by applying to a designated state agency, and if the application is accepted, its date becomes the mechanism by which the priority is established. Permits are usually granted if they are found not to create conflicts with existing users, if unappropriated water is available, and if the proposed project is not in conflict with the public interest. A key aspect of the appropriation doctrine is the designation of what is considered to be a "beneficial use." Many water rights statutes term this the "basis, measure, and limit" of the right to use water (6). Historically, beneficial uses have been described as those uses having clear economic value. Generally these include uses for domestic, agricultural, industrial, mining, and municipal purposes. More recently, some states have defined nontraditional uses as being beneficial. In particular, several western states now recognize instream flow uses as beneficial. Some states also give preference to certain uses over others so that during times of stress, these favored uses will be satisfied even though their priority might be lower than that of another use. In most cases, preference is given to domestic and municipal uses and often to agricultural uses.

Once a right to use water has been obtained by an appropriator, he or she must exercise this right or it may be lost through nonuse. Thus the concept of "use it or lose it" was established. This is declared by many to encourage waste rather than conservation. The problem is that there is no incentive for appropriators to conserve since they cannot usually benefit from the water saved and may even be penalized if they forfeit the right to water they may desire to use in the future.

Appropriation water rights can usually be sold, although the new owner may be required to file for a permit if he or she wishes to change the nature of the water use or the place of use or withdrawal. In some states there are restrictions on using water outside of the basin of origin or outside of the state. Furthermore, some applications for change in water use may be refused because the state recognizes a preference for the original type of water use.

• *Weather Modification Rights.* Although weather modification is still in its infancy, California Pacific Gas and Electric and Southern California Edison have sponsored cloud-seeding operations. Legal problems associated with such practices are also emerging. Basically, these relate to the right to seed, the rights to the water generated, and the adverse effects of seeding operations on others.

In 1978 the Department of Energy (DOE) reported that 33 states had laws relating to weather control (6). Only three states were known to have statutes allocating water rights from seeding operations; two of these followed the appropriations doctrine whereas the other one tied the rights to laws regulating natural precipitation (6). The legal aspects of weather modification will unfold as controllable systems appear and are put into practice. As this occurs, controversy and litigation are likely to be extensive.

GROUNDWATER RIGHTS

There are four doctrines applicable to groundwater rights in the United States (5, 6). These are the common law of unlimited withdrawals, the rule of reasonable use, the correlative rights rule, and appropriation rules (Figures 3-4 and 3-5).

Groundwater law is generally more local in dimension than is surface-water law and has been defined as having been heavily influenced by technological changes that have made possible an ever increasing facility in pumping and spreading water (5). One aspect of groundwater law, which makes it more complex to deal with than its surface-water counterpart, is that it is not consistently defined among the states. Various subdivisions are used, including channelized, artesian, percolating, tributary, rechargeable, and nonrechargeable (6). Another complication arises from the fact that under some circumstances, groundwater may be classified as "mineral" or "geothermal," subjecting it to a different set of laws entirely (6). The uncertainties created by these different designations make the groundwater management task all the more difficult. Furthermore, some localities have little or no mechanism for dealing with groundwater withdrawals and use, and this often leads to misuse and sometimes to conflict with surface-water withdrawals.

Where groundwater permitting systems exist, there may be provisions for perpetual use, subject to conditions on nonuse or wasteful use, or for use for limited periods of time. The latter arrangement is gaining in popularity and will likely be commoner in the future. Another feature of

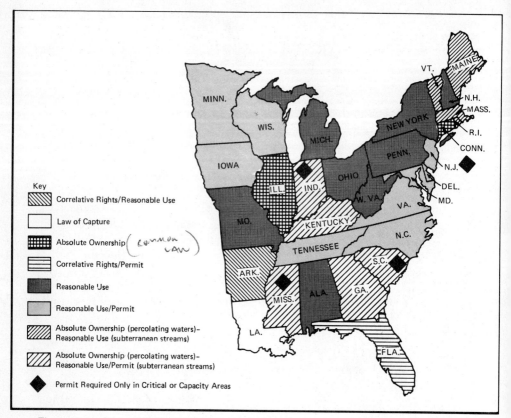

Figure 3-4   Groundwater legal systems in the eastern United States. (After the John Muir Institute, Inc., reference 6.)

groundwater regulatory systems is the designation of critical or closed areas. Usually these are locations where the annual recharge from all sources is less than the annual withdrawal. These are circumstances usually referred to as "mining." If a state declares a "critical area," then it may regulate the number of wells in the area, limit pumping, and restrict new development.

• *Common Law.* In the common law system, an overlying landowner can withdraw groundwater in any amount for any purpose. This sytem was borrowed from English common law, that is, law that grew out of court decisions. Under the common law system there is no liability for damage to any other user of the same groundwater system. This means that a user can lower the water level to the extent that wells of other users might become useless without any fear of recrimination. In days when groundwater withdrawals were small, this was not important to consider, but in modern times, the technical ability to withdraw large quantities of water

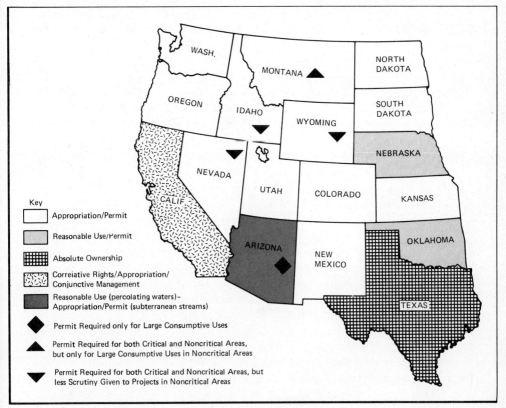

Figure 3-5 Groundwater legal systems in the western United States. (After the John Muir Institute, Inc., reference 6.)

from the ground emphasizes the need to properly evaluate the influences of these withdrawals on others and to provide reasonable safeguards.

• *Reasonable Use.* Under the doctrine of reasonable use, overlying landowners are considered to have coequal rights. This system, which also requires nonwasteful use, was established to counteract some of the more troublesome aspects of the common law doctrine.

• *Correlative Rights.* In this system, rights are allocated in proportion to the extent of ownership of the overlying land. The concept of reasonable use may also be incorporated. This doctrine has not found widespread use in the United States although it is used in California, Arkansas, and several other states (6).

• *Appropriation Rights.* The system of prior appropriation for groundwater is similar to its surface-water counterpart. In this case, a permit must be obtained from an appropriate state agency. This sets a priority based on time. Most states in the west follow the doctrine of prior appropriation, but there are exceptions. For example, Texas, a major groundwater user, follows the common law doctrine.

STATE WATER RIGHTS ISSUES

There are many inconsistencies in state water rights laws. Some of these constrain new water resource developments and inhibit or foreclose exercising the best available water management practices. In Nebraska, for example, water rights are specific to the type and place of use and this cannot be changed. In Colorado, on the other hand, water rights are separable from the land and may be freely sold or transferred. Third-party interests are another issue that is hard to deal with. What must be considered here are the possible consequences for harm to a third party by actions taken as a result of transfer of water rights from one user to another in which some change in use or point of withdrawal of use occurs.

In the east, common law water rights doctrines often forbid the transfer of groundwater from overlying land, and where surface-water use is regulated by permit systems, similar restrictions are also common. In theory, at least, many western states can accommodate water rights transfers. This does not mean the same thing in all states, however, and even transfers that are legal are sometimes difficult to implement (4).

Some common constraints that have bearing on the acquisition and use of water for various purposes are the following: restrictions on groundwater mining; restrictions on off-site use; prohibition of transwatershed export, restrictions on interstate transport of waters; provisions protecting other water rights; preferential treatment of some beneficial uses; restrictions on type of water use; antispeculation prohibitions; uncertain status of deep groundwater, saline groundwater, and geothermal waters; and uncertainty concerning the use of aquifers to store, transport, or comingle artificially recharged waters (6).

There are many approaches that might be taken to deal with constraints imposed by water laws. These include legislative change, court action (often not a preferred approach but sometimes the only option), providing reliable data to reduce uncertainty, agreeing to compensate injured parties, augmenting water supplies, improving water quality, mitigating impacts, substituting new water uses for old ones, regulating rates of withdrawal of groundwater, metering water use, and developing educational programs.

Many water laws are coming under scrutiny as legal constraints on water development and use arise. According to one recognized authority on water law, Frank J. Trelease, the ideal system of water rights should promote efficiency in water use by providing "both security and flexibility of water rights" (4). This means that holders of water rights should be given sufficient tenure in their rights so that they will not be hesitant to make needed investments in facilities. At the same time, there must be a mechanism for shifting from low production to high production uses when this is considered necessary.

The foregoing ideals could be achieved in several ways. One approach would be to develop a system of administrative allocation. In this case, the water to be allocated would be put in the hands of an administrator who would make decisions about how and where it should be used. Alternatively, changes could be made in the appropriation doctrine to permit needed transfers and reallocations of water during critical periods and to guard against waste. Trelease cautions that care would have to be exercised in using the administrative approach because it might unduly focus power in the hands of a single individual. Either system could be designed to incorporate the features considered important to a region's water management. In the future it is likely that modified water rights systems will incorporate some elements of each.

Federal Reserved Water Rights

National parks, national forests, and other federal lands withdrawn from the public domain have rights to sufficient water to serve the purposes for which the reservations were intended. This doctrine was enunciated in the 1955 *Pelton Dam* decision by the U.S. Supreme Court, *Federal Power Commission v. Oregon,* 349 U.S. 435 (1955), and reaffirmed by *Arizona v. California,* 373 U.S. 546 (1963).

If federal reserved rights are not quantified, planning for future water allocations becomes uncertain, and needed developments might be delayed or forgone because developers fear that the exercise of the federal right at some future time might restrict or destroy their proposed operations. A priority is assigned the federal right based on the date the reservation was created, and since this might predate a more recent application for a water right from the same source, the potential for conflict is easy to see. As of 1980, adjudication (explicit determination) of federal reserved rights had not been extensive.

Originally, the notion of federal reserved water rights applied only to Indian reservations. Later, the doctrine was extended to land reserved for national forests, parks, and recreational areas; for national monuments; and for wildlife refuges (6). Reserved water rights may involve both surface water and groundwater. Only waters unappropriated at the time of the reservation are affected, however, and the federal government must compensate for damages to those holding rights predating those of the reservation.

Key issues are the quantity of water to be reserved and the use to which it is to be put. A 1978 court decision (U.S. v. New Mexico) held that reserved water may be used only for the original purpose of the federal reservation. This finding narrowed the scope of the reservation doctrine, and in so doing removed some of the uncertainty associated with the doctrine. One other modifying influence on the doctrine is that the determination of federal reserved water rights may be made in state courts (6). The fact that recent legislation and court decisions tend to restrict the reservation doctrine is of great importance to the states. A broad interpretation of the reservation doctrine could lead to confrontation with state constitutional or statutory provisions and generally interfere with the operation of state water rights systems. By integrating federal reserved water rights into existing state water rights systems, the limit of the rights can be determined and planning uncertainties can be minimized.

Indian Water Rights

Indians have been settled on reservations that were set aside for the purpose of promoting agriculture and "civilization." In the arid west, the lands of most of the reservations were considered to be of little value unless water was provided. This basic concept of Indian water rights was established in law by the 1908 case of *Winters v. United States,* 207 U.S. 564.

Indian water rights under the Winters doctrine are separate and distinct from water rights established under the prior appropriation concept used in most western states. Indian water rights arise in federal law and generally are established at the time a reservation is created. When the reservation is on lands aboriginally owned by the Indian tribe, the water rights may be considered to exist from time immemorial (1). Ordinary appropriated waters have a priority in time dating to the time of first use or from the date of a permit whereas Indian rights have a priority in time dating at least to the date the reservation was established. Indian reservations considered to have aboriginal rights would have first priority on the body of water serving their supply.

On a historical basis, the amount of the water right would seem to be sufficient water to satisfy agricultural and related needs. Thus far, there has been only one major adjudication of the Winters doctrine rights. This was by the 1963 *Arizona v. California* decision, 373 U.S. 546, which paved the way for authorization of the Central Arizona Project. The decision in that case was that the five central tribes of Arizona had the right to sufficient water to irrigate all the "practicably irrigable acreage" on their reservations. Future adjudications may face a variety of issues such as the eligibility of municipal and industrial needs for water rights, the ability to use irrigation-based rights for other purposes, and whether the water rights should be permanently fixed or allowed to change with the times (8). The amount of water needed to irrigate acreage practicably appears to be the principal component of the Winters doctrine rights, however.

The competition between Indian and non-Indian water rights poses some significant problems, especially in the west. Most Indian reservations predate major water projects in that region, although heavy use of water by the Indians has generally developed in relatively recent times. An important factor to be dealt with is that the resource potentials of Indian reservations are often large. In the northern Great Plains, for example, most Indian lands are underlain with hugh reserves of coal and other valuable minerals, many have outstanding recreation features, and many contain large areas suitable for agriculture. The tribes are concerned that water used for non-Indian purposes will adversely affect their water rights and lead to depletions on their reservations. They seek assurances that their water requirements will be fairly considered by those outside the Indian community. Although many studies have addressed the issue of Indian water use, the fact remains that the quantities of water needed are generally unknown or are in dispute. Until this matter is resolved, uncertainty will surround plans for future water allocations, and even the maintenance of existing operations at current levels may be subject to question.

Interstate and International Water Law

There is no general federal policy regarding interstate and international waters, but there are devices available to resolve questions of water quality or water allocation among the states or between the United States and Canada or Mexico. For international issues, the usual approach is by the use of a treaty. Examples are the Mexican Water Treaty of 1944, which provides for Mexico's share of Colorado River water, and the Boundary Waters Treaty of 1909 with Canada, which allocates waters of the Milk River.

Means to allocate and manage interstate waters are interstate compacts, Supreme Court litigation, and congressional allocation (9). The most widely used of these instruments is the compact. Compacts can be used to allocate interstate waters, to regulate water quality, and for other purposes. As of 1977, there were 35 compacts in force dealing with various aspects of water management (9). These include the Colorado River Compact of 1922, the Rio Grande Compact of 1938, the Potomac River Basin Compact of 1940, and the Delaware River Basin Compact of 1961(10).

3-6 REGULATIONS

Once a new agency or program is established by law, regulations pertaining to its purpose are drawn up. In the early part of the twentieth century, this was not especially troublesome, but today the number of laws and their accompanying regulations sometimes pose formidable obstacles to those they are intended to guide (11).

A good many of the policy conflicts and added costs due to regulatory requirements can be traced to the rapid expansion of environmental law that took place after the environmental movement of the 1960s. Although recognition of the need to provide adequate and reasonable safeguards for the environment was probably long overdue, the zealous efforts that took place in the late 1960s and early 1970s were unfortunately often uncoordinated and in some cases poorly thought out. The result is that today there are thousands of legal and regulatory measures that affect all aspects of water resources development and management and, contrary to their original intent, they sometimes confuse, delay, and limit our ability to achieve the most efficient solutions to water and related problems. It has been said that the current laws are too complex, too inflexible, and constructed so as to foster procedural complexities (12, 13).

Some idea of the scope of this issue can be had by considering that the 185-page Clean Air Act has generated over 2500 pages of regulations to implement it. The Clean Water Act, which is about 125 pages in length, has an associated compilation of regulations that exceeds 1200 pages. It has been reported that "no one at EPA headquarters fully understands even a single program . . ." (13).

Regulatory reform is needed, as is a new approach to environmental law that recognizes regional differences, permits alternative solutions rather than requiring a uniform fix, assesses the likelihood of practical compliance, and accepts the premise that methods other than new laws may sometimes be more efficient for solving environmental problems. According to Orloff, what is needed is "a set of guiding principles, clarity, straightforwardness, consistency, knowledge of the intrinsic limits of legislation, and a solid informational base . . ." (13).

The point is that a balanced approach to environmental protection is needed, one that permits attainment of environmental objectives while at the same time permitting the use of the most efficient technologies and procedures for achieving them.

3-7 TRADITIONS AND SOCIAL CUSTOMS

While laws and regulations directly influence actions taken with respect to water resources, traditions and social customs play a more subtle but no less important role. In the United States there are a number of factors that give rise to local practices and traditions. These include the historical dominance of a water use (irrigation in the western states), farming practices, climate; federal subsidies, the nature of the water storage and distribution systems that are in place, the cost of water, the nature of industrial operations and plant designs, the desire to maintain local or individual control of water and/or other natural resources, and resistance to change. In a worldwide setting, especially in developing or undeveloped regions, endemic religious traditions may be very influential as well. Planners confronted with the task of providing water that is safe to use and of ample quantity to satisfy the expanded needs of present users and needs of new users must be careful to see that their proposals will gain local acceptance and fit the character of the region to be served. If this is not done, there may be little hope of securing the necessary funding for the works envisioned. Furthermore, even if financing is available, facilities having features considered objectionable on religious or other grounds may not be used.

3-8 ORGANIZATIONS

One would have to return to very primitive times to find a period in which some significant conflicts in water use were not apparent. The resolution of these combined with the need to provide water to a variety of users has led to the development of an extensive system of organizations at all levels of government. Many of these organizations arose from a single need and were not designed to consider closely related or inextricably linked aspects of the water resource. This narrow special-interest focus has resulted in literally thousands of agencies and governmental units with responsibility for some facet of water resources development, management, or control. Many of these entities were well conceived at the time of their formation but have long since outlived their usefulness or ability to perform their functions effectively. The situation is parallel to that of the manner in which federal, state, and local laws have evolved over the years. The unfortunate aspect of all this is that there are few examples where existing organizations or laws have been eliminated as a first step in introducing new ones more consistent with the times. As a result, great inconsistencies, inefficiencies, duplications, and conflicts have been the product. The fundamental question is: What are the organizational needs for optimum water resources planning, development, and management? Associated questions are: What are the options for consolidating and/or eliminating existing organizations? and How can the many activities of these organizations, operating at all levels of government, be coordinated so as to minimize conflict and facilitate good water management? Answers to these questions have been sought for years, but many proposed mechanisms for achieving an efficient level of management or control have been difficult to implement due to strong intergovernmental and interagency jealousies and mistrusts. Those who are responsible for planning, constructing, regulating, and operating water resources systems must be able to face the prevailing organizational systems and develop workable policies for functioning within them if changes in these structures cannot be made (14, 15, 16).

Regional

Since the early 1900s, many commissions have considered the merits of regional or river basin organizations to carry on water resources planning and other related functions. The notion is still strong that regional, in addition to state and local, perspectives are needed if wise decisions are to be made regarding federal investments in water resources projects and programs.

The first and perhaps best known of the regional organizations is the Tennessee Valley Authority, which was established in 1933. The TVA is a public corporation created to "improve the navagability and provide for the flood control of the Tennessee River; to provide for reforestation and the proper use of marginal lands in the Tennessee Valley; to provide for the agricultural and industrial developments of said valley; to provide for the national defense by the creation of a corporation for the operation of Government properties at and near Muscle Shoals in the State of Alabama." The TVA has had a long and successful history, but it is unique in form, and not likely to be duplicated (10). The strength of the TVA stems from the fact that the organization has broad operating, management, and regulatory functions.

After 1945 the federal Interagency River Basin Committee program was established, which encouraged the creation of informal, voluntary interagency committees. Three of these, the Arkansas-White-Red, the Southeast Basins, and the Pacific Southwest committees are still in operation. Three others became the Pacific Northwest, Missouri, and New England River Basin commissions. These three have now been abolished. The interagency committees have little power and their main accomplishment has been in providing a forum for communication among the several state and federal agencies and units of government involved.

In 1961, the states of New York, New Jersey, Pennsylvania, and Delaware joined with the federal government in creating the Delaware River Basin Commission. Like the TVA, the DRBC has broad powers, which include both planning functions and implementation and operation. In theory, the DRBC has the power to do much more than it has done, but it has been very successful in settling disputes over water allocation among the participating states. As pointed out by Derthick, "a coordinating organization will work only to the extent that the participants share an interest in making it work" (10). One other commission designed along the lines of the DRBC has been formed: the Susquehanna River Basin Commission, established in 1973. The DRBC and SRBC are state-federal compact commissions and their creation requires a consensus of the states who would be participants. Many such compact commissions have been proposed, but a lack of consensus has stifled all efforts other than those for the Delaware and Susquehanna.

The most recent type of river basin organization grew out of the Water Resources Planning Act of 1965. These were the Pacific Northwest, Missouri River, Upper Mississippi River, Great Lakes Basin, Ohio River, and New England river basins commissions. These RBCs were designed to be planning-coordinating entities and forums where representatives of states and federal agencies could coordinate activities and jointly develop

river basin or regional plans for water and related land resources. They
had no management or operating authority and did not replace functions
of the federal agencies.

An independent chairperson, appointed by the president, coordinated the activities of the commissions. Each federal agency with an
interest in the river basin was entitled to membership, as was each state
lying totally or partially within the basin. The act provided that every
reasonable effort be made to arrive at a consensus on all issues.

Creation of an independent chairperson and staff, divorced from federal and state agencies, was an important departure from the rotating
chairships of predecessor interagency committees. It provided a loyality
to the institution and an opportunity for focusing on regional goals rather
than on the narrower objectives of the member states and federal agencies. A lack of control over members limited this authority, however.

The performance of the RBCs was hampered by budgetary constraints, problems of coordination, lack of authority to enforce decisions,
and the necessity to act through consensus. Obligations of members to
their parent organizations, the voluntary nature of the coordination process, and the limited capacity of members to speak for their organizations
added to the difficulties. The result was that the RBCs fell short of expectations and on July 28, 1981, they were abolished.

The former RBCs have been reshaped into various forms of interstate
entities charged with coordination of interstate activities and water resources planning. How long these organizations will survive is hard to
predict, as is the role they will play in future decision-making processes
in their regions.

It seems clear that interest in regional efforts is still high but that
politically acceptable regional institutional arrangements are elusive. Furthermore, it seems that institutional arrangements will have to be tailored
to suit the region. Experience shows that what will work in one place will
not work in another, and that the imposition of uniform rules or systems
nationally is doomed to failure.

State, Federal, and Local

Federal agencies involved in water programs have played significant roles
in determining the types and locations of water developments that have
taken place. The principal construction agencies, the Corps of Engineers,
the Bureau of Reclamation, and the Soil Conservation Service, are still
very influential. The major regulatory agency, the EPA, has become a
dominant factor since the early 1970s in terms of both federal budget and
the influence of its regulations on all aspects of water use and development.

Most states have agencies that are, in some ways, counterparts of the
federal agencies. This has come about since the states have needed institu-

tions to manage the many diverse federal programs in which they desire to participate or are required by law to be a party to. The water agencies of some states such as Texas and California have large expert staffs, but others depend for assistance on technical matters from appropriate federal agencies. The western states in particular have agencies charged with administering their water rights systems. Where permits are required in the east, a similar situation exists. The details of the wide variety of state agencies cannot be treated here. The important point to remember, however, is that they must be dealt with by those engaged in the water resources profession and a knowledge of them is a prerequisite to performing most jobs successfully. Another feature to be kept in mind is that state, federal, and local agencies and organizations may have powers ranging from comprehensive (planning, constructing, and managing) to very narrow, encompassing only such functions as planning, or coordinating, or issuing of permits. Agencies with wide-ranging powers offer the attraction of minimizing the number of entities that must be dealt with but have the drawback of minimizing checks and balances.

At the local level there are also many organizations that manage or relate to water programs. These include municipal water and sewer departments, local planning units, special-purpose local districts, and local agencies for health and environmental control.

Other Organizational Arrangements

In recent years, the problems of fragmented interests in water problems in many states and the extension of problems beyond the jurisdictions of some governmental units has led to the consolidation of organizations and the emergence of new authorities having capabilities for managing some aspect or aspects of water over an intergovernmental region. Two such endeavors will be presented here. They are the formation of consolidated natural resource districts in Nebraska, and the Southwest Florida Water Management District designed for flood control and water management over a 10,000 square mile area of Florida.

NEBRASKA NATURAL RESOURCE DISTRICTS

In 1939 there were 172 special-purpose entities in Nebraska designed to deal with some aspects of the state's waters (17). As greater demands were placed on this resource, additional governmental units emerged to address special needs. By 1969 the number of such organizations had grown to about 500. The result was a host of narrowly focused organizations, overlapping responsibilities, duplication of services and taxation, and limited ability to cope with problems encompassing more than one jurisdiction. There were about 15 types of organizations that had been authorized by the state legislature. These included soil and water conservation districts, watershed conservancy districts, watershed districts, watershed planning boards, irrigation districts, reclamation districts, sanitary drainage districts, drainage districts, and groundwater conservation districts.

To provide a better focus on solving the state's water problems, the legislature determined that a consolidation of these many districts would be needed and that a new set of regional water management districts should be devised to blanket the state. Action was taken in 1969 when the state legislature established 24 natural resource districts (NRDs). It was the intent of the legislature to create governmental units with sufficient powers to address a broad range of natural resources issues and to implement programs or projects to resolve them. Although only about 300 of the previous districts were merged or abolished in the process of setting up the NRDs, the new organizations had much greater capacity for managing water and other natural resources than their predecessors (17). The original intent of the NRD movement was to bring about a total consolidation of existing entities. This was not politically feasible at the time and so a compromise was struck. Nevertheless, the remaining districts were encouraged to cooperate and if possible to merge with the NRDs. In addition, the legislature specified that no new districts of previous form could be established after the passage of the legislation.

The supervisory control of the NRDs is vested in the state's Natural Resources Commission. This semiautonomous agency has broad powers and is charged with the task of coordinating the activities of the NRDs, other state agencies responsible for some aspect of natural resources, and other substate entities including counties, municipalities, and those special-purpose districts that were not abolished or merged into the NRDs. The principal state agencies to be dealt with are the Department of Water Resources (responsible for administering the water rights of the state), the Department of Agriculture, and the Department of Environmental Control (the state's counterpart to the EPA). The Natural Resources Commission (NRC) must also interface with those federal agencies whose programs apply to various aspects of developing and managing the state's waters. Even with the consolidation brought about by the formation of the NRDs, there are still many federal, state, and local agencies or units of government that must be dealt with. The NRC is thus faced with an important role in coordinating these units and their activities.

In establishing the NRDs, the Nebraska legislature gave them broad responsibilities. These include soil conservation and erosion control; flood and sedimentation control; water supply; development and management of groundwaters and surface waters; solid waste disposal, sanitary drainage, and pollution control; drainage and channel improvements; and responsibilities relative to fish and wildlife habitats, recreation, forestry, and range management.

In keeping with the assignment of many areas of responsibility, the legislature did not overlook providing the needed authority to get the job done. The powers of the NRDs include taxation; eminent domain; construction and maintenance of facilities; acquisition and disposal of water rights; financial assistance for projects; regulation of groundwater use; development, storage, and distribution of water; regulation of land use in certain cases; rate setting for water furnished; development of facilities for solid waste disposal; provision of technical assistance; assignment of charges to beneficiaries for services; and initiation and conduct of studies.

While the NRDs may obtain rights, they have little real control over surface water or groundwater allocations. The rights to divert waters are administered by the Department of Water Resources. In addition, the quantity and quality of streamflows are largely determined by the Department of Environmental Control and the state's Game and Parks Commission.

One of the advantages the NRDs hold over their predecessors is that of dimension. On the average, the NRDs are about four times larger than the average Nebraska county. This scale gives the NRDs the financial capability to obtain qualified technical staffs. Furthermore, the NRDs have access to a state resource development fund that may be used to fund or partially fund meritorious state projects. The size of the districts also suggests that many localized problems can be resolved within the bounds of a single NRD (17).

On the negative side, it has been argued that the choice of watershed boundaries was not wise, since most NRDs cover only parts of a basin. More importantly, because most state data are reported on a county basis, many believe that aggregations of counties would provide better limits of operation (17). The fact that not all of the special-purpose districts existing before the NRD legislation were disbanded or merged with the NRDs is another weakness. This is important since some of these other districts, the irrigation districts, for example, are powerful in their own right and thus dilute the authority of the NRDs.

Regardless of some of the weak spots, the NRD movement in Nebraska has much to recommend it. The NRDs are acting to facilitate coordination and are becoming a recognized force in dealing with intrastate water problems. The essence of the NRD model is sound and could be transferred to other states having a highly fractured approach to water management such as was in evidence in Nebraska in the late 1960s.

SOUTHWEST FLORIDA WATER MANAGEMENT DISTRICT

It is almost a universal rule that decisive political action relative to water resources management follows some period of crisis. So it was with the formation of the Southwest Florida Water Management District (SWFWMD). The legislation that created the district followed widespread flooding in Florida, which resulted in deaths and injuries and damages of about $200 million (18).

The SWFWMD is a regional flood control and water management regulatory agency. It covers about 10,000 square miles centered around the Tampa–St. Petersburg metropolitan region. The district was created in 1961. Its responsibilities have progressed from sponsorship of flood control projects to groundwater regulation, issuance of consumptive use permits, and management and storage of surface water (18). The district, which is now one of five similar districts that blanket the state, is governed by an unsalaried board that has taxing authority.

The governing board consists of nine leading citizens appointed by the governor and confirmed by the state senate. This board sets district policy, carries out regulatory responsibilities, enters into contracts, and authorizes tax levies. The district is subdivided into nine watershed basins. These basins generally follow hydrologic boundaries and all have their own basin boards except one. That basin, because of its special importance, is controlled by the district's own governing board. The basin boards are action oriented and may initiate projects to solve water problems. They also levy the necessary ad valorem taxes to support their budgets. The basin boards do not have the authority to regulate, however; that is retained by the governing board.

The taxing authority of the SWFWMD is substantial. Based on 1980 figures, tax revenues could have totaled about $28 million, although this level of assessment was not considered necessary and the income was closer to $7 million (18).

In 1974, legislation was passed in the Florida legislature allowing the establishment of regional water supply authorities. These authorities may develop, store, and transport water for sale to cities and counties. Concurrently the same act authorized the water management districts to plan, design, construct, and operate regional water supply facilities, but only if requested to do so by a county, city, or regional water supply authority. The effect of this action by the legislature was to add the potential for additional substate entities rather than vesting this authority totally in the hands of the water management districts.

A recognized strength of the district is that by having a responsible unpaid board as the executive head, a high degree of insulation from political pressures is evident. Furthermore, the nature of the board is such that maximum familiarity with local problems is achieved. Other advantages of the water management districts are their taxing authority; transcendence of local political boundaries; and capability to conduct studies, develop solutions, prepare plans and to design, construct, and operate water management systems. Weaknesses of the district system include lack of authority to plan and implement water supply projects unless invited to do so; lack of authority to regulate water quality; and lack of authority to construct, operate, or maintain sewage treatment facilities.

The district has compiled a good record of dealing with water issues in the region for which it has authority. Like the NRDs, there are limits to responsibility that keep the SWFWMD from attaining the theoretical maximum level of coordination. Even so, the district exemplifies another

effective move at the substate level to reduce conflicts in water management, to minimize overlapping areas of responsibility, and to provide
institutions capable of seeing their plans through to completion.

3-9 POLITICS

The political aspects of water resources development and management
are probably the most difficult of all to deal with. They are very important,
however, since almost every major decision dealing with public facilities
is reached in the political arena. The political processes are complex, ever
changing, and subject to high levels of emotionalism. In the final analysis,
political feasibility determines the nature of actions that are taken.

The Decision-Making Arena

Politics may be considered the art of maneuvering to gain a particular
objective. In the field of water resources, political decisions at all levels of
government affect water availability and use. The city council makes
recommendations regarding expansion of the city's water treatment
plant, the governing board of an irrigation district considers regulating
groundwater withdrawals, the governor of one state joins with that of
another to seek an interstate agreement, and members of Congress respond to requests from their constituents for new water supplies. Whenever decisions related to the public interest and public investments must
be made, the political process is called into play.

While it is hardly possible to address more than a few aspects of the
political process here, it is instructive to give some examples of the complexity of the process, the many decision points, and the roles of various
actors. In the realm of federally funded water projects or projects that are
at least partially supported by the taxpayer at large, a system has evolved
of first obtaining authorization for the project and second of obtaining
appropriations to implement the project. This authorization and appropriations process involves individuals, groups, agencies, governmental
units, and others in making choices in a variety of settings (19). Local
interests envision the need for some type of water project or program and
then devise a scheme to generate enough political support to bring their
project to fruition. In the process, a given proposal may be considered and
reconsidered at many levels before it finally reaches Congress for consideration. If congressional action is favorable, the bill will be passed on to
the president for signature or veto. The time scale of this process may be
20 or more years for major projects, and during this period the project
proponents will likely face many obstacles and can expect frequent periods of frustration.

The Congress of the United States authorizes the construction of
water projects in response to political demands for them. Water projects
usually distribute benefits directly to congressional constituencies while

indirectly allocating costs. Thus the political rewards for bringing home a project are easily accounted for while the costs are diluted through funding mechanisms. The costs of a water project that has its major benefits in Colorado, for example, might be shared by taxpayers nationwide. Congressional selection has been strongly influenced by the desire to accommodate local constituencies. Unfortunately, this is not always compatible with building either the best or the most needed projects.

Proposals to construct water projects that are sent to Congress for consideration are referred to appropriate authorizing committees for review. Projects having social merit and obvious political support are usually received with favor. While economic and environmental selection criteria are important factors, strong political support at state and local levels is essential for positive action (19).

After a project has been authorized, funds for it must be appropriated if it is to be implemented. Congressional appropriations committees review project authorizations and determine which of these are to be funded and when. Thus obtaining project authorization is only the first part of the political process that must be successfully navigated if a project is ever to materialize. The political backing of project proponents must be powerful enough to pass both of these congressional hurdles.

The executive office of the president also plays a role in water project and program selection. In this case, the Office of Management and Budget (OMB), representing the president's position, reviews agency recommendations for new water projects and/or programs. Agency recommendations not conforming to OMB's interpretation of the administration's views are opposed. Based on OMB views, as well as on those of other policy officials of the executive office of the president and those of the agency heads themselves, the president decides which water projects he will recommend to Congress for funding. A project included in the president's budget is not assured of funding, however, as members of the appropriations committee might oppose it. In a like manner, a project not included in the president's budget might still be included in the budget bill by Congress if it is supportive. Obviously, project proponents must be prepared to convince both Congress and the administration if they are to be successful in their efforts.

Since the environmental movement of the 1960s, the traditional support for water projects has been eroding. It is becoming more and more difficult to assemble the coalitions needed to provide the political strength to implement any but the most socially and economically desirable projects. With this trend it is likely that some changes in project selection mechanisms by Congress will also take place. Even so, political rationale rather than technical judgment will still be the determining factor in the decisions that are made.

In an excellent study of political aspects of water resources development, Helen Ingram made a detailed analysis of New Mexico's role in the bill authorizing the Central Arizona Project (CAP) (20). Some of her findings are presented here as examples of the vagaries of the politics of water. The report deals mainly with two water projects in New Mexico that were included as part of the congressional package authorizing CAP.

The Ingram report noted that the inclusion of the two New Mexico water projects in the bill was "a curious event." It was said that the connection between the New Mexico projects and CAP was neither direct nor clear. Furthermore, it was pointed out that the effects of the two projects on CAP were detrimental. The report concluded that: "In terms of hydrology and engineering, economics and financing, the association of these projects in a single package appears irrational; its rationale appears only when the politics of the Colorado Basin Act are laid out." The role played by New Mexico in bringing this about was considered to underscore the overriding importance of political feasibility in setting water policy.

In the case of the CAP bill, local activists in New Mexico exerted considerable pressure to influence the political process at the most significant level. This was achieved by convincing Congressman Aspinall of Colorado that it was to his advantage to move quickly on one of the projects of interest to New Mexico (Animas-La Plata). Another political mechanism for consent-building, the practice of noninterference, also came into play.

In the case of CAP, its supporters were concerned mainly with whether the inclusion of New Mexico's demands would result in building added political support for the package that had CAP as its core. The Ingram study showed that where such political feasibility was found to exist there was no further questioning. This is the political technique of avoiding conflict by accommodating polar interests without confrontation. The idea is to "live and let live." Another finding of the analysis, and one of great importance today, was that activists who did not share the basic local concern about water were very hard to accommodate. The idea of mutual noninterference is not applicable to conservationists or environmentalist factions. It has become increasingly clear, however, that the views of these groups are having a much greater impact on the traditional game of water politics. This adds considerable time and difficulty to consent-building processes and may ultimately lead to changed perceptions and altered political patterns (20). The Ingram study also commented that even after CAP was taken up in earnest, it still took three Congresses and over five years to pass the bill. In view of today's concern about environmental and economic issues, it is not likely that another massive water project such as the CAP could make it through the political hurdles even that easily, if at all. Finally, it must be observed that while the rationality of water policy may be questioned on technical and other grounds, it is, in fact, politically rational. It represents the net effect of risks and rewards associated with the issues (20).

Political Constraints

The political process is one of consent-building to the level needed to gain support of Congress, a state legislature, or a local governing body. For each activist supporting a proposal and for each level of interaction there may be a counteractivist and an equal opportunity for interaction. What is meant here by interaction is the interface between the activist and those institutions in the political system where sufficient authority resides to make policy. The actions taken by those opposing a project or program thus may be considered as political constraints. These political constraints can be formidable and may in many cases be the determinant of the outcome of a given proposal. They may be defined as that class of institutional constraints stemming from the deliberate action of factions seeking to delay, inhibit, or prevent some proposal for water use or development (6).

Political constraints are born out of the interest of someone or some group to oppose an action being sponsored by others. These constraints may be imposed by the direct intervention of counteractivists in normal planning, approval, and implementation processes, or they may occur as a result of influencing elected officials who can then sway the outcome of a project. The goal of the counteractivists is to delay, change, or prevent some proposed action. In days gone by, the environmental embodiment of the counteractivist was the "little old lady in tennis shoes." This is no longer the case; the eccentric lone advocate has been replaced by a throng of Rotarian types. Environmentalists, conservationists, and preservationists, for example, have taken strong positions in recent years on various aspects of many water projects. These groups are no longer the weakly heard "voices in the wilderness." Today many of them are well organized, sophisticated, experienced in all aspects of lobbying, and knowledgeable in methods for gaining strong public support for their views. Where such groups elect to oppose an issue, the proponents can expect a time-consuming and difficult uphill fight.

Opposition to a particular project may be confined initially to a few individuals or small groups. As time goes on, however, many of these will seek support from other groups who, although they may have different interests, generally stand against the type of action being considered. This combination of opponents increases the strength of the opposition and gives it a more formidable political dimension. The strategies of those opposing water projects may range from mass appeals and protests to testimony before review and regulatory bodies, to lobbying of elected officials, and to court action (6). Generally several or all of these mechanisms will be used simultaneously. Political constraints have an air of unpredictability associated with them. This is because they are subject to frequent adjustment by their creators as conditions and/or levels of support change. They represent the interests of their designers, however, and they must be reckoned with by those proposing new water developments or changes in water use. It has been said that political opposition "can turn what are otherwise procedural matters into major obstacles" (6). Political deterrents reflect the points of view of important interest groups and as such may be the most difficult of all institutional constraints to deal with.

Those seeking to implement water projects or programs are well advised to assess carefully the political feasibility of their proposals. Unless political support appears to be a likelihood, efforts to modify proposed courses of action to achieve the needed backing will be more productive than attempts to overcome hard-to-deal-with political constraints. For a broader view of the political process, the reader is referred to references 1, 4, 6, 9, 19, 20, 21, 22, 23, 24, 25, and 26.

3-10 TECHNOLOGICAL PROBLEM SOLVING UNDER INSTITUTIONAL CONSTRAINTS

Only those technical solutions to problems that are politically feasible, socially acceptable, and legally permissible will have any chance of implementation, short of lifting some of the constraints. The scientist and engineer must be prepared to evaluate the array of institutional constraints and then proceed to develop alternatives that can function within these limits. To seek the "best" technical solution without regard for its acceptability is to invite delay, added cost, and even total failure. On the other hand, the technologist has an important role to play in providing explicit analyses of the impact of existing constraints on addressing the water issues of his or her region. If the benefits to society can be clearly shown to increase as the result of modifying laws, changing regulations, developing new organizations, and so on, then the prospects for eventual reform in these areas will be enhanced.

PROBLEMS

3-1. List the major water planning, development, and management organizations in your state. Briefly describe their roles.
3-2. Are the operations of the organizations listed in Problem 3-1 coordinated? If so, how is this done?
3-3. Do you believe your state agencies should be consolidated or partly consolidated to permit more efficient water management? Discuss.
3-4. Summarize your state's water rights laws. Do they permit easy transfer of water rights? Do they encourage waste?
3-5. What are the principal institutional problems in your state? Discuss.
3-6. Are there any regional organizations with water management authority in your state? Discuss the strong and weak points.
3-7. Describe the degree of coordination between water quality and water quantity management in your state.
3-8. What long-standing social customs in your state have the greatest impact on

water allocation and use? Do you think these customs can be altered? If so, how?

3-9. Discuss the nature of water "politics" in your state.

References

1. National Water Commission, *Water Policies for the Future,* U.S. Gov't. Print. Off., Washington, D.C., 1973.
2. U.S. Congress, Senate, Committee on Energy and Natural Resources, *An Analysis of the President's Water Policy Initiatives,* Committee Print, 95th Cong., 2d Sess., Pub. No. 95-129, U.S. Gov't. Print. Off., Washington, D.C., 1978.
3. E. Stokey and R. Zeckhauser, *A Primer for Policy Analysis,* Norton, New York, 1978.
4. Federal Reserve Bank of Kansas City, *Western Water Resources: Coming Problems and the Policy Alternatives,* Westview Press, Boulder, CO, 1980.
5. U.S. Department of Energy, *Ground Water and Energy,* CONF-800137, National Technical Information Service, U.S. Department of Commerce, Springfield, VA, November 1980.
6. U.S. Department of Energy, *Institutional Constraints on Alternative Water for Energy,* DOE/EV/10180-01, National Technical Information Service, U.S. Department of Commerce, Springfield, VA, November 1980.
7. National Water Commission, *A Summary-Digest of State Water Laws,* U.S. Gov't. Print. Off., Washington, D.C., 1973.
8. U.S. Department of the Interior, *Report on Phase I of Water Policy Implementation,* Office of the Secretary, Washington, D.C., June 6, 1980.
9. V. P. Nana (ed.), *Water Needs for the Future—Political, Economic, Legal, and Technological Issues in a National and International Framework,* Westview Press, Boulder, CO, 1977.
10. M. Derthick, *Between State and Nation—Regional Organizations of the United States,* The Brookings Institution, Washington, D.C., 1974.
11. E. J. Cleary, "Frustrated Aspirations for Watershed Quality Management," *Journal of the Water Pollution Control Federation,* vol. 53, no. 3, March 1981.
12. J. A. McClure, "Adverse Effects of Federal Regulation," *Mining Congress Journal,* vol. 66, no. 12, December 1980.
13. N. Orloff, "Environmental Law in the Eighties," *Engineering Cornell Quarterly,* vol. 15, no. 4, Ithaca, NY, Spring 1981.
14. Ernst Liebman, *The Water Resources Council,* National Technical Information Service, PB 211443, Springfield, VA, 1972.
15. Beatrice H. Holmes, *A History of Federal Water Resources Programs, 1800–1960,* U.S. Department of Agriculture, Miscellaneous Pub. No. 1233, Washington, D.C., June 1971.
16. *History of the Implementation of the Recommendations of the Senate Select Committee on Natural Resources,* Committee on Interior and Insular Affairs, U.S. Senate, 90th Cong., 2d Sess., 1969.
17. L. K. Fischer, "A Critique of Nebraska Natural Resource Districts," Department of Agricultural Economics, University of Nebraska, Lincoln, unpublished, 1981.
18. D. R. Feaster, "From Flood Control to Water Management—The Florida

Experience," paper presented at the annual meeting of the American Water Resources Association, Atlanta, GA, unpublished, 1981.

19. D. J. Allee and H. M. Ingram, *Authorization and Appropriation Processes in Water Resources Development,* National Technical Information Service, PB 212-140, Springfield, VA, 1972.

20. H. M. Ingram, *Patterns of Politics in Water Resource Development: A Case Study of New Mexico's Role in the Colorado River Basin Bill,* Div. of Government Research, University of New Mexico, Albuquerque, December 1969.

21. The John Muir Institute, Inc., *Western Water Institutions in a Changing Environment,* vol. 1, Napa, CA, 1980.

22. The John Muir Institute, Inc., *Western Water Institutions in a Changing Environment,* vol. 2, Napa, CA, 1980.

23. S. Alnes, "State-of-the-Art: The Geo-Political Perspective," *Futurics,* vol. 5, no. 1, 1981.

24. A. Maass, *Muddy Waters: The Army Engineers and the Nation's Rivers,* Da Capo Press, New York, 1974.

25. A. Hoffman, *Vision or Villainy—Origins of the Owens Valley–Los Angeles Water Controversy,* Texas A&M University Press, College Station, 1981.

26. J. A. Ferejohn, *Pork Barrel Politics,* Stanford University Press, 1974.

Chapter 4
Water Resources
Planning

Water is so essential to human life that planning for its future use and protection is a necessity. Planning is both a means for ensuring that the needs of future generations will be recognized and a mechanism for resolving conflicts of interest. It is a chart for "progress and social change" (1, 2). Unfortunately, planning is an inexact process involving a good deal of uncertainty. Closely allied to planning is forecasting. Forecasting is the methodology of looking into the future whereas planning is the strategy for coping with it.

The elements of a water resources plan include identification of human needs, assessment of water sources, and design of means for meeting the anticipated needs in the context of prevailing constraints. The philosophies of planning change with time as cities are built, people move, and attitudes about the environment and other subjects shift. Regional differences in climate, geography, social customs, and so on are also influential in planning processes. Although there can be no set formula for describing all the elements of any given plan, there are some underlying themes that most modern water planners keep in mind. The contemporary ones appear to be embodied in the findings of the National Water Commission in 1973 (1). They are:

1. The level of future demands for water is not inevitable but derives in large part from policy decisions within the control of society.
2. There has been a shift in national priorities from development of water resources to restoration and enhancement of water quality.

It is interesting to note that national opinion polls in 1982 sustained the strong commitment of the United States public to this concept even in the face of severe economic conditions.

3. Water resources planning must be tied more closely to land use planning. If environmental quality is to be optimized, then water uses and land uses must be considered concurrently.

4. Sound economic principles should be applied to decisions as to whether or not water projects are to be built. This holds true also for water programs.

5. Policies are needed that will lead to more conservative use of water.

6. Laws and legal institutions should be reexamined in the light of contemporary water issues.

7. Development, management, and protection of water resources should be controlled by that level of government nearest the problem and most capable of effectively representing the vital interests involved.

There is one more subject that should be introduced at this point: coordination of plans. Water planners and other planners often fail to realize, or overlook the fact, that their plans may have far-reaching significance for what is happening or will happen in other sectors. Extension of sewer mains in one direction will generate development in that area. This may be contrary, however, to the plans of recreationists desiring to maintain the locality in its undisturbed state. It does not take much imagination to envision a variety of conflicts that might emerge from uncoordinated plans. This problem has long been recognized, but in general it has not been resolved.

Formal mechanisms for planning coordination include consolidation of planning agencies, establishment of joint advisory boards, and requirement of joint review of proposals having consequences outside a planning agency's jurisdiction. Where such consolidations or formal linkages can be arranged, they can be very useful, but such changes may require legislative or other involved action and may not be easy to bring about. Sometimes an informal approach, based mostly on interpersonal relations, may be the only reasonable course to follow. If this proves workable, it may become the catalyst for a more formal institutional change.

4-1   SOCIETAL GOALS AND PUBLIC INVOLVEMENT

In all planning processes, the goals of society should be considered to be guiding principles. Such goals are usually not written explicitly but instead are embodied in legislative, administrative, regulatory, and other actions. Furthermore, goals are constantly changing. Once we sanctioned irrigation development in the west as a means to populate that region of the United States. Today there are many who oppose any further irrigation development on environmental or other grounds. Complicating the picture is the fact that there are often multiple goals, and some of these are not compatible. There is a very complex relation between social and political forces that feeds the goal-setting process. Often there will be far from unanimous agreement on any goal whether it be national, regional, or local. The planner is caught up in this controversy. While planners should not consider themselves to be society's goal setters, they can assist the public in this regard by providing the kinds of information needed to bring about informed choices.

The best way to gain public support for planning processes is to seek this support before the fact. Plans developed in secrecy have little chance for acceptance by the public. This is especially true if the appropriate goals are not kept in mind or if the plans developed are contrary to the interests of influential sectors of society. On the other hand, planning cannot be done efficiently by committee, and a strategy for public involvement must be set so that planners can take advantage of public input but still be able to function effectively.

Since the 1960s, the American public has become very concerned about water resources issues, especially those involving possible construction. As a result, federal water agencies have all developed detailed procedures for public involvement in their planning processes (3–5). Most planners believe that if the public's involvement is to be effective, it should be associated with all phases of the planning process. Usually citizen input is sought on identification of problems, ranking of problems, identification of water-related goals, determination of how these goals relate to other goals of society, types of water development and/or management activities that are acceptable for achievement of goals, identification of possible conflicts that might arise from various management or development options, the degree of public acceptance that might be expected for a particular course of action, and the nature of negative impacts possibly associated with a particular plan.

A number of mechanisms can be employed to foster communication between citizens and planners. These include citizens' advisory committees; planning and zoning boards; public hearings; the use of radio, TV, and newspapers; town meetings, conferences; referenda; seminars; and public opinion surveys. The important point to remember is that the public will ultimately, through their political representatives, determine the fate of any plan that is developed. If they are informed and involved, so that their input has been wisely used and the plans hold no surprises, the likelihood of implementation is good. If this is not the case, the converse can be expected. Figure 4-1 charts the points at which citizen input should be considered in water planning processes.

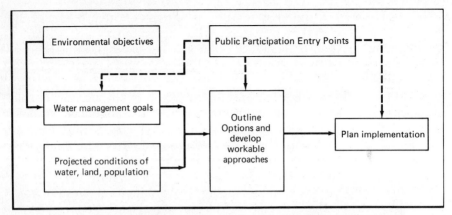

Figure 4-1 Public participation and the water resources planning process.

4-2 POLITICS AND WATER RESOURCES PLANNING

Water resources planning is often subjected to intense political pressure. As was pointed out in Chapter 3, planners and others who believe that they can devise strategies for the future based only on sound technical considerations are in for a rude awakening. Water, like other natural resources, is perceived in different ways by different people. Consider a proposed reservoir: a boating enthusiast might desire a full impoundment at all times, an irrigator would probably want to deplete it during the summer, and a white-water canoeist might oppose the project altogether. The decision on whether to build or not to build and on how to regulate the water level will be politically based. It will be strongly flavored by the relative political strengths of the competing interests. These viewpoints must be recognized by the planner if he or she is to be successful. The challenge is how to accommodate them, if this is possible.

The implications of water planning are necessarily different at various levels of government (national, regional, or local). For large projects, the world food supply, regional industrial growth, and the future development of major cities might be affected (6). Small projects might only influence whether the southern or the northern parts of a town will grow. In either case, people's lives are affected, and this occasions strong political interplays. Some will win and some will lose in the process; the planner's role is partly to minimize and compromise these losses.

To ensure that political decisions are made recognizing what is called the "common good," certain measures are used to assess the plans that are proposed. In the United States, these measures are largely economic and environmental. Generally, water resources plans are expected to be economically efficient (provide maximum return for the investment), equitable (not place an unfair burden on any sector), and environmentally sound (2).

4-3 LEVELS OF PLANNING

Most nations conduct water planning at several levels. These depend on the nature of the problems to be addressed. In the United States, water resources planning occurs at national, state, regional, and local levels. A general rule is that planning should be done at the lowest level that is competent to develop the plan and see it to completion.

National level planning is ordinarily directed toward identifying those problems that are pervasive in the country and thus worthy of consideration for technical and/or economic assistance by the highest level of government. The Water Resources Council and the principal federal water agencies in the United States have cooperated in such processes for years. Their findings and recommendations often result in action by Congress to authorize programs or projects and to appropriate funds to implement them.

Regional planning considers the fact that most nations are composed of subareas that have varying properties and thus require individual consideration. National level planning is often too coarse for regional work and state or lower level planning is sometimes too parochial to reflect or consider regional interactions or influences. River basin commissions and other regional authorities can be used to provide the needed regional focus and to coordinate water resources programs in their areas. The Delaware River Basin Commission is one example, the Southeast Basins Interagency Committee is another, and the TVA is a third.

All the states in this country and most of their counterparts around the world have some form of planning agency. In many cases water is a specific planning function. Often it is further divided into quality and quantity aspects, and sometimes even into groundwater and surface water or other categories. In those areas of the United States where a regional water planning agency exists, the states act as partners. The degree of cooperation and coordination achieved in such arrangements is not consistent from one area to another, however. It has already been pointed out that coordination of the various planning sectors is hard to accomplish. It must also be said that even where the focus is common, as in the case of water, the problems associated with coordinating the activities of the many actors are still complex.

Most plans include recommendations for action, and the proposed actions often apply to specific locations within a broader planning area. Local planners must thus be prepared to carefully consider these proposals by higher-level planning agencies so that final designs are compatible with their area's requirements and their constituency's interests. The success or failure of local planners rests on their understanding of the desires of the citizenry and their ability to see that these are adequately reflected in regional plans and are ultimately translated into action. Small watershed or other local planning units can be especially attractive vehicles for effectiveness because of the intense community interest they can generate.

4-4   STATIC V. DYNAMIC PLANNING

Not many years ago, the development of a "master plan" and then discontinuance of the planning process was the order of the day. Bookshelves are filled with such plans, and often the space they occupy is all that remains to show for the effort that went into them. Even now, in the 1980s, there are many who refer to "the plan" as if it were an instrument capable of guiding decisions over long periods of time with infallibility. While a plan for the construction of a specific water treatment plant might be considered a final product, plans for river basin management involving many projects and programs are subject to many rapidly changing influences, and these cannot be effectively dealt with on a one-time-only basis.

Planning must be considered a dynamic process if it is to be efficient and up to date. The process involves an initial assembly of data whose interpretation in the light of identified goals leads to the development of one or more alternatives for addressing the issues of concern. As time goes on, the data base expands as more current information becomes available about the region being planned for. Identified changes in the state of the system become the feedback by which planners continuously adjust their plans to reflect the most current trends and simultaneously improve their forecasts about the future. Such a feedback-looping system consisting of improved information, adjusted plans, revised recommendations, and so on allows the maximum level of flexibility in decision making. As the need for change becomes apparent, a dynamic process affords frequent opportunities to make revisions in programs and/or facilities proposed in earlier plans. Dynamic planning provides the best measure of the current pulse of the planning region and of emerging trends. Because of its flexibility, it is ideally suited to rapidly changing circumstances. For example, if there is some question about the ultimate amount of storage needed for a community, a small dam might be built and then raised at a later date. Staging such as this increases the likelihood of good investments and aids in maximizing opportunities for diverting available funds to as many needy areas as possible.

4-5   FORECASTING TECHNIQUES

Since plans are designed to anticipate future conditions and make provision for accommodating them, they must incorporate forecasts of many factors that have an impact on the elements being planned for. In the field of water resources, it is often necessary to look ahead as far as 50 to 100 years. This is especially true where large projects are involved. These often take as much as 25 years from time of conception to time of operation, and, if they are to be in place when needed, their plans must be completed many years in advance. The problems associated with such long-range planning and the forecasts it must rely on are many. In fact, it is sometimes difficult to plan even a few years ahead.

Some of the difficulties in dealing with the future can be overcome by developing plans for a set of alternative futures rather than by making a single projection and assuming that it will occur. Use of the dynamic planning process, already discussed, is another means of accommodating the time-varying nature of influencing factors. Changes in technology, societal attitudes, economic conditions, level of popular education, and many other factors must be taken into account. The degree to which these changes can be anticipated is a function of both the nature of the planning process and the ingenuity and creativity of the planners involved. At present there is no panacea.

Numerous forecasting techniques are available, and new ones are constantly emerging. All these approaches may be classified roughly into the following categories: methods using historical data, techniques based on models and simulations, and qualitative and holistic approaches. Several procedures will be discussed here: the Delphi technique, scenario writing, trend extrapolation, trend impact analysis, and simulation.

Forecasts are needed to support planning processes, but in themselves, forecasts are not plans. Forecasts may be designed to predict what will actually happen at some target date, or they may be designed to define plausible alternatives. In choosing a forecasting method, it is wise to estimate the payoff that will be associated with the accuracy of the forecast and to weigh this against the cost of achieving greater reliability. Finally, forecasts are only approximations of what might occur. They should never be looked on as accurate portrayals of the future.

Delphi

The Delphi technique is used to assemble and analyze information from a group of experts in a particular field (7–9). The Delphi approach has been used to address problems in economics, environmental control, water resources planning, regulatory decision making, and policy setting.

In a typical Delphi exercise, a group of respondents (experts) is selected and a questionnaire prepared. This questionnaire (often termed the round 1 questionnaire) poses both quantitative and qualitative questions about the subject under study. In the case of quantitative estimates, the respondents are usually expected to give their rationale and/or source of information. A second questionnaire (round 2) follows the first and normally contains some (or all) of the same questions asked in the first round plus a statistical summary of first-round findings. The idea is that the respondents will use the feedback from round 1 to adjust their answers to critical questions if it seems warranted. The second-round questionnaire may also contain some new questions. The second round is followed by a third, usually the final round. In the final round the respondents are asked to take one more look at most or all of the previous questions and then to make some judgments about policies that might be instituted to address the problem or problems being considered. It is assumed that by round 3 the views of the respondents will have converged, at least to a degree, or the reasons for nonconvergence will have been identified. If underlying assumptions considered by the respondents at the several stages are not reported for others to see at follow-up rounds, convergence is less likely to be achieved.

The Delphi approach differs from the common polling method in which people are asked to express their views about an issue. The Delphi panel is composed of experts only, and the objective is to get them, through a feedback process, to provide a basis for making some assumption or assumptions about the future. In water resources planning, for example, a Delphi panel might be assembled to estimate the likelihood of a shift in power cooling practices. Both the nature of the shift and its timing would be important considerations. The information obtained could then be used in forecasting future water use trends for power cooling. The Delphi method is an excellent vehicle for thorough assessment of the assumptions about an issue (10–13).

Scenario Writing

Most people think of a scenario as a manuscript or plot outline that describes some sequence of actions, characters, and scenes. Herman Kahn and other policy analysts have defined the scenario as a hypothetical series of events constructed for the purpose of focusing attention on causal processes and points at which decisions might be made (14). In this context, the scenario becomes a consistent, carefully thought out, detailed set of circumstances that is plausible and permits the user to understand and easily translate the circumstances into planning or other decisions.

To be of value to planners, scenarios should be developed early in the planning process. First-stage scenarios help to focus an analyst's attention on the future in concrete terms. They also provide a structural framework for continued analysis (14). Scenarios are an aid in exploring issues and can provide a basis for more rigorous phases of analysis. They can incorporate nonquantitative factors into decision-making processes that some of the more analytical techniques cannot accommodate. The target date for the scenario should be the planning horizon. Furthermore, close attention should be paid to the present set of circumstances and to the time path extending into the future.

The number of scenarios to be used in the planning process must be determined. Generally it is difficult to use more than a few, and most studies involve only three or four carefully selected ones. Sometimes one of the scenarios is labeled the baseline (alternatively called a surprise-free scenario), and two others are used to define the upper and lower limits on what the future might have in store. The range in these extremes is thus a guide to the amount of variation that might have to be accommodated in the planning process. It is considered best not to attempt to label one scenario as the "most likely" or "most probable." Such labels tend to lead analysts and others into believing that particular scenario is really the only one deserving of attention. In reality, all the scenarios generated may be considered to have a low probability of occurrence since they are all simply concepts of the trend of future events.

In judging the value of a scenario, the most important criterion is credibility. Since scenarios must relate to the world in which we live, they must be plausible (believable) at every time step and internally consistent (14). A scenario based on some incredible discovery might be of interest, but it would not likely be considered plausible. It should be made clear, however, that plausibility and predictive accuracy are not one and the same. Scenarios are designed to illustrate what might happen, not what will happen. Finally, a scenario should be easy to understand and it must have utility (include enough detail so that its implications can be readily translated into plans or decisions).

Scenario writing is subjective, and the value of any scenario is highly dependent on the abilities of the writer and on how it is interpreted in light of the issue or issues being analyzed (15, 16). On the other hand, a carefully prepared scenario can raise questions or pose conditions that might be overlooked by an analyst using more structured forecasting techniques.

Trend Extrapolation

Trends are directions a variable has taken over time. Projection of a trend into the future is called trend extrapolation. This process is probably one of the oldest of the forecasting technologies. It is also one of the easiest to use. The time scale employed in tracing a trend can be minutes, days, years, and so on, depending on the process being studied. The change in value of the variable with time constitutes the trend.

When extending historical trends into the future, a good rule to follow is that the extension should not exceed the length of the historical trace. In reality, even small extensions of a few years may be grossly in error if unforeseen circumstances that directly influence the trend occur. The methods used to extrapolate trends may be classified as sensory (judgmental, intuitive, and visual) and mathematical (7). Techniques falling in the first category involve extending a trend by subjective methods (graphical curve extension, for example), whereas the second category makes use of various curve-fitting procedures. Although there are many computerized approaches to trend extrapolation, their mathematical formality should not mislead one into believing that they will always give good results.

Some positive aspects of trend extrapolation are that the progressive history of the trend is clearly presented, the approach has wide applicability to problems associated with both scientific and social variables, the method is easy to use, and extrapolations may be accomplished rapidly by both hand and computerized methods (7). Limitations on trend extrapolation include the assumption that the conditions that generated the historical trend will continue unchanged into the future, and the adequacy of the extent and reliability of the data base.

Trend Impact Analysis

Trend extrapolation is based on the premise that the social, economic, political, and other forces that controlled the trend in the past will prevail in the future. The further ahead one attempts to project, the less accurate is this assumption. To compensate for the likelihood that historical influences alone are often not sufficient as a sole basis for making inferences about the future, a technique called trend impact analysis has been developed (7). This procedure is designed to add the effects of unexpected events to extrapolated historical trends. The procedure can be initiated by identifying all major events that might significantly affect the trend to be projected, estimating the probability of these events, calculating the impact of each event on the trend (impacts may be positive or negative and must be defined quantitatively over time, as shown in Figure 4-2), calculating the combined impacts of all events on the trend by letting each event happen at each time step according to its chances of happening, and modifying the extrapolated trend at each time step by the net change occasioned by the impacts.

Trend impact analysis produces information on the likelihood of a trend being modified by various influences over time and serves to quantify the magnitude of such changes. The method relies heavily on judgmental estimates of events, probabilities, and so on and thus is limited by the reliability of these evaluations. Often techniques such as the Delphi are used to explore potential trend-impacting influences and to arrive at their probabilities of occurrence.

Simulation

Simulation is the process of mimicking the dynamic behavior of some system over time. The simulation model is the surrogate (substitute) of its prototype (real world) system. The results of simulation runs can be used to describe (forecast) future states of a system of interest. The method facilitates generation of data that otherwise might take months or years to assemble. Simulation models can also be used to assess policy impacts on the performance of the system. Simulation models may incorporate statistical correlations, empirical formulas, probabilistic estimating methods, and equations based on scientific principles. Since the subject of

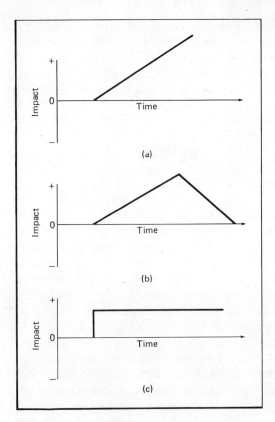

Figure 4-2 Some simple impact shapes: (a) increasing impact; (b) transitory impact; (c) sudden, stable impact.

simulation is covered extensively in Chapter 10, it will not be addressed further here. The potential of simulation models for use as forecasting tools should be easy to see, however (17, 18).

4-6 POPULATION

Generally, the greater the number of people residing in an area, the more will be the water use. Furthermore, it is not only the number of people that is important but also their ages, level of education, social background, religious beliefs, and other factors.

Population issues include the way in which the current population is, and the future population will be, distributed geographically; the trend in population growth rate and the likelihood that it will shift; the measures that might be taken to influence the growth rate; and how the population growth rate affects the economy, natural resources, labor force, energy requirements, urban facilities, world food supply, and so on.

Historical data are basic to estimating future levels of population, but unfortunately these data are not always handy. The problem is especially severe in some developing countries. And even in the United States, errors in current estimates are common. For example, it has been reported that about five million people were unaccounted for in the 1970 census. Due to data deficiencies or discrepancies and the many uncertain factors influencing population change (fertility, mortality, migration, and so on), most forecasters suggest the use of at least three possible trends in growth based on plausible mixes of influencing factors.

Impacts of Population on Water Resources Development

MUNICIPAL AND INDUSTRIAL WATER SUPPLIES

The water-using sector most directly sensitive to population size is the domestic or residential one. This is understandable because domestic water use is based on the way people use water in their households and the number of people served. The more the population of a city expands, the greater will be its demands for water. However, a doubling of population does not necessarily mean a doubling of the demand for water. If we were using the minimum amount of water needed to sustain life this would be true, but we are not and there are many opportunities to reduce per capita water use without creating hardship. Still, population shifts must be accommodated by local water suppliers and future trends must be recognized early enough so that the necessary facilities are in place to meet needs as they arise. The industrial picture is similar. Generally, expansion of a water-using industry will require added water. If the water-using processes are made more efficient, however, an actual reduction in water use could occur. Industrial expansion (contraction) is frequently tied to population trends because industries expand (contract) to meet increased (decreased) needs for their products and these needs are reflected by changes in population.

In addition to expansion, there is another population-related aspect of municipal water supply that must sometimes be dealt with. This is the case where a once-viable community finds that it is losing rather than gaining population. This condition is not uncommon today, especially in some of the older cities in the northeastern United States, where people have moved away to more favorable climates or increased employment opportunities. If the population loss is great, a city water department could be faced with operating and maintaining a system that has become oversized for its use. Consideration might then have to be given to eliminating some of the system's elements, revamping treatment facilities, operating storages in a different manner, and/or modifying unit water prices.

FOOD PRODUCTION

Food and fiber needs to support global population growth are increasing. In the early 1970s, 2.47 acres (one hectare) of land under agriculture supported approximately 2.6 persons (19). By the year 2000, it is estimated that four persons will have to be supported by the same amount of land. Increases in food production of this magnitude are within technical feasibility, but very large capital investments will be required to attain them. Furthermore, humans are not the only ones placing demands on the world's food supplies. It has been reported, for example, that livestock feeding might represent about five times, in population equivalents, the number of people being fed (20). Raising the food to support an expanding global population is of international concern. The quantities of water associated with it will be large, and some believe that water, rather than land, could become the limiting factor in food production.

There is reason to be concerned about more efficient water use practices in the agricultural sector. Beyond this there is an apparent need to explore new crop varieties that are less water demanding and other agricultural and land management practices that could cut the per-acre water requirements for the principal crops needed to support worldwide population increases.

PUBLIC WORKS

Most facilities for water supply and wastewater treatment are very costly. That the investment of funds in such facilities should be done with wisdom is not hard to see. The problem associated with these commitments is that they must be made well in advance of the need so that planning and construction lags can be accommodated in the intervening time. If the facilities are not large enough at the time they are completed, added outlays will be needed, with the usual result that costs will be greatly increased over those that would have resulted if the original facility had been correctly sized. On the other hand, if the growth forecasts are scaled down and the constructed facilities are much larger than needed, then some of the investment was made unnecessarily and could have been diverted to other purposes. Since project sizing usually involves some measure of future population, it is clear that erroneous projections of water requirements based on faulty population projections can have significant consequences for public works investments. Both the size of the facility and the timing of its construction are tied to estimates of population growth or decline.

MANAGEMENT OF EXISTING FACILITIES

The water management systems in place in the United States represent an investment of billions of dollars. Furthermore, the job is not finished once a project is completed. It still must be operated, maintained, and sometimes totally or partially replaced as its elements decay with time. The ability of cities, irrigation districts, and other water management institutions to carry out these functions depends mostly on the availability of users to pay the costs. If some of the users depart, system managers must still provide for the upkeep of facilities unless, of course, there is total abandonment. Local shifts in population can significantly affect the operation of an area's water management facilities.

DEVELOPMENT OF ENERGY RESOURCES

Energy resources are developed for heating, operation of machinery, transportation, raising of crops, running hospitals, and other purposes. This resource development is often accompanied by large water requirements for cooling, processing, and restoring mined lands. Although the area in which the resource development activity occurs may be far removed from the region in which the developed energy is used, the locality of the resource development is the one having to provide water and other resources to convert its coal, oil, oil shale, and so on into a useful form. Furthermore, the population-related stresses imposed by such developments may go far beyond those associated with mining, drilling, processing, and other operations. Development of resources on a large scale requires a large labor force and a good deal of backup support (commercial services, schools, etc.). In many localities where resource development is proposed, there are not enough people to support the operation. Thus labor must be imported, with the result that a once-small community might double or triple in size in a few months or years. These rapid population shifts are cause for concern. They may create a burden on local services and stress or exceed the limits of the local water facilities, waste treatment plants, schools, stores, police, and so on. In fact, it is possible that some situations may create a water demand, tied to the population influx that equals or exceeds that created by the resource development industry itself. Furthermore, if the proposed energy-associated development is expected to last only a few years or some other limited time, the host community will ultimately have to face a possible large-scale abandonment at some future time. A water system capable of serving 100,000 persons is not an asset to a community of 25,000.

Factors Affecting Population Trends

The rate of population change at any location and at any time is determined by many factors, some of which are interactive. They include birthrate, death rate, immigration, emigration, government policies, societal attitudes, religious beliefs, education, technological change, and war. The components of population change (births, deaths, net migration) can be linked together to form the fundamental population equation:

$$P_2 = P_1 + B - D \pm M \tag{4-1}$$

where P_2 is the size of the population at the end of the time interval
$\quad\quad\quad$ P_1 is the size of the population at the beginning of the interval

B is the number of births occurring in the population during the interval

D is the number of deaths occurring in the population during the interval

M is the net number of migrants moving to or away from the area during the interval

A very important population factor in the United States, especially in recent years, has been the internal migration from the northeast and other areas to the south and west. Another problem is that associated with the trend toward out-migration from central cities. Both of these aspects have strong implications for the water management field.

It has been reported that the number of people living in central cities declined about 4.6 percent from 1970 to 1977 (21). Most of the cities showing declines are in the northeast, but cities larger than one million in population are showing similar declines even in the south. With the decline in population of these cities has also come a shifting of composition. For example, the more affluent people are generally leaving, so that the remainder, the poorer people, are left to shoulder the tax burdens, maintain services, and so on. This trend is placing great stress on the traditional mechanisms of municipal finance. In the water supply area it is manifest in the problem of maintaining a large infrastructure already in place with fewer resources to do it.

Questions of concern to planners are: Can the city be revived? What are the mechanisms to accomplish this? How can the in-place facilities be operated and managed more efficiently with reduced use? and What system elements should be eliminated? The answers to these questions may be very difficult to obtain. Furthermore, any dismantling of facilities could present a problem if at some future time the trends were suddenly reversed.

A second problem area is rural migration. After about 1970, the rate of population growth of nonmetropolitan counties exceeded the growth rate of metropolitan areas (21, 22). This was due to the belief by many urban Americans that rural locations were more attractive, and in some cases less expensive, places for residence. This issue is companion to the loss of population from central cities. In some cases, the rapid shifting of the population to areas previously settled sparsely creates significant problems of providing needed services, water and wastewater among them. How long this trend continues cannot be easily predicted. Factors that could counter it include escalating energy costs, making transportation to jobs more costly, and urban renewal projects in downtown areas offering modern accommodations combined with convenience to city attractions.

Finally, a phenomenon known as the sun-belt trend has brought about major regional shifts in the United States population since the 1960s. The population in the northeast and north central states has been steadily declining; whereas, growth in the south and particularly the west has been accelerating. For example, between 1970 and 1977 the population of the west grew 31 times more rapidly than the population of the northeast (21).

The types of internal flows of people just discussed must be given serious consideration by planners and managers. The impacts of rapid increases or decreases in population have been pointed out. Beyond this, there is the question of how long some of these trends might prevail and whether they will ever reverse and, if so, to what degree.

Population Estimating

Both short- and long-term population projections are needed for many aspects of water resources planning. These estimates may be made by the Bureau of the Census, by a state agency, or by a local governmental agency. Water resources planners may also be called on to make population projections or, if not to make them, to interpret them. Most estimates incorporate the use of analytical techniques and judgment.

METHODS OF FORECASTING

There are many forecasting techniques. Some are designed simply to extend historical trends whereas others use historical data to define only an initial condition and then relate future trends to estimated changes in those variables that most significantly affect the trend.

Trend extrapolation may be accomplished by graphical means or by mathematical curve fitting. Historical data for such exercises may be obtained from the U.S. Bureau of the Census, local planning commissions, bureaus of vital statistics, local utilities, moving companies, and chambers of commerce.

Short-term estimates are usually those involving extensions of less than about 10 years. For large regions, these estimates, if based on simple extrapolations, are often fairly good. But for small subdivisions such as a town, curve extensions even for a few years might be very misleading. This is because the move of a major industry or a similar happening can significantly affect (create a sharp discontinuity) in what might have been perceived as a fairly uniform trend. For large regions local shifts are often dampened.

Projections can be made by plotting historical data on population versus time and simply extending the trend by graphical means. Alternatively, a mathematical curve-fitting process might be used. Such processes usually recognize that the generalized shape of a population trend will be of the S form shown in Figure 4-3. This typical growth curve recognizes an initial period of geometric increase (constant percentage) followed by a period of arithmetic growth (constant rate) and finally by a period of decreasing rate of growth.

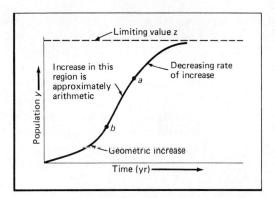

Figure 4-3 Population growth curve.

The arithmetic increase is represented by the following equation:

$$\frac{dY}{dt} = K_u \tag{4-2}$$

where Y = population
t = time
K_u = a uniform growth rate constant

If Y_2 is the last-recorded population and Y_1 is the population Δt years before Y_2, then the population Y at some time t_f (time in the future measured forward from the last recorded population) will be given by

$$Y = Y_2 + [(Y_2 - Y_1)/\Delta t](t_f - t) \tag{4-3}$$

If it is believed that the growth is following a geometric pattern, then we may write

$$\frac{dY}{dt} = K_p Y \tag{4-4}$$

where the variables are as defined before except that K_p represents a constant percentage increase. Thus if the population had grown 10 percent in some time period, it would be assumed to increase 10 percent in the next equal time period. The short-term geometric increase is thus

$$\ln Y = \ln Y_2 + K_p \Delta t \tag{4-5}$$

Base 10 logarithms may also be used.

Estimates made under the assumption that the rate of increase in population is decreasing assume that

$$\frac{dY}{dt} = K(Z - Y) \tag{4-6}$$

where Z is a limiting value that must be estimated and K_d is the rate constant (23).

The choice of the mathematical representation should be based on an examination of the historical data or other information. Often if the historical data are to be extended only a few years, a simple graphical extrapolation may be expected to give results as reliable as the more formal procedures given here. Long-term trend extrapolations (usually considered to exceed 10 years) may be accomplished by curve-fitting techniques, graphical methods, or comparisons of data for similar cities or areas that are larger but seem to be characterized by the same types of growth patterns as the locality in question. The latter approach amounts to transferring the trends of other localities to the area of concern (23).

One technique used to estimate long-term trends is logistic curve fitting (24). The equation used for this purpose is

$$Y_c = \frac{K}{1 + 10^{a+bX}} \tag{4-7}$$

where
Y_c = ordinate of the curve
X = time period in years (10-year intervals are frequently chosen)
K, a, b = constants

In order to fit the logistic curve, three points in time (years), each equidistant from the others, must be selected. These we shall designate as X_0, X_1, and X_2. The usual practice is to select one of these years near the beginning of the historical record, one near the middle and one near the end. The fitted curve will pass through the three populations associated with the years X_0, X_1, and X_2. The populations we shall designate as Y_0, Y_1, and Y_2. In the fitting process, the origin on the x axis will be the year X_0. The number of years between X_0 and X_1 or X_1 and X_2 is designated as n. The constants K, a, and b are estimated as follows:

$$K = \frac{2Y_0 Y_1 Y_2 - Y_1^2(Y_0 + Y_2)}{Y_0 Y_2 - Y_1^2} \tag{4-8}$$

$$a = \log \frac{K - Y_0}{Y_0} \tag{4-9}$$

$$b = \frac{1}{n}\left[\log\frac{Y_0(K - Y_1)}{Y_1(K - Y_0)}\right] \tag{4-10}$$

Once these values are substituted in Equation 4-7, any future or intermediate population Y_c may be determined for its associated value of X. The use of this technique is illustrated in the following example.

Example 4-1

Given the population data for the continental United States for the period 1810 to 1950 (Table 4-1), fit a logistic curve to the data and from this fitted curve, estimate the 1980 population of the United States.

SOLUTION

1. Plot the data as shown in Figure 4-4. If we exclude the years 1810 and 1950, the end points become 1820 and 1940. The year 1880 falls halfway between, and we shall choose it as our central value. Rather than use the populations recorded at each of these three years, we shall take an average of the populations 10 years greater and 10 years less than the central value plus the central value and use these averages for our values of Y_0, Y_1, and Y_2. Because the population data we are dealing with are more in the nature of a geometric progression than an arithmetic one, we shall choose the geometric mean values. These are obtained as the antilogs of $(\Sigma \log Y)/N$, where N is the number of observations (three in this case). For the data from the years 1810, 1820, and 1830, the geometric mean is found to be 9.6. The values to be centered at 1880 and 1940 are found to be 50.2 and 134.6 respectively. If, as shown in Table 4-1, we let X be measured in multiples of 10 years, then n in Equation 4-10 is 6 or $\dfrac{60}{10}$.

Table 4-1 CALCULATED POPULATION OF THE COTERMINOUS UNITED STATES FROM 1810 TO 1980 USING A LOGISTIC CURVE

(1)	(2)	(3)	(4)
		POPULATION, MILLIONS	COMPUTED POPULATION, MILLIONS
YEAR	X	(Y)	(Y_c)
1810	−1	7.2	7.1
1820	0	9.6	9.6
1830	1	12.9	13.0
1840	2	17.1	17.4
1850	3	23.2	23.1
1860	4	31.4	30.3
1870	5	39.8	39.3
1880	6	50.2	50.2
1890	7	62.9	62.8
1900	8	76.0	76.8
1910	9	92.0	91.7
1920	10	105.7	106.8
1930	11	122.8	121.3
1940	12	131.7	134.6
1950	13	150.7	146.3
1980	16	—	170.5

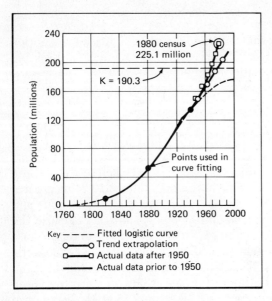

Figure 4-4   Historical population of the coterminous United States from 1810 to 1950 and fitted logistic curve extended to 2000.

2. Using the values of Y_0, Y_1, and Y_2 determined as the geometric means and Equations 4-8, 4-9, and 4-10, we find the values of the constants K, a, and b to be: K = 190.3, a = 1.275, and b = −0.138.

3. Equation 4-7, with substitution of these values, is then used to estimate the values of Y for the associated X values. These are shown in column 4 of Table 4-1. The origin is the year 1820 and the X units are multiples of 10 years.

4. The trend values obtained by using Equation 4-7 are shown in Figure 4-4. A look at this plot clearly illustrates how well the fitted curve matches the historical data.

5. Of particular concern to us, however, is that even though the historical record extended until 1950, the estimated value for 1960 (about 156 million, see Figure 4-4) is about 13 percent less than the actual recorded 1960 coterminous population of about 178 million. Going further, to 1980, the estimated population of 170.50 million is about 24 percent less than the 1980 census value of about 225.1 million. What this tells us is that although we may be able to fit a historical trace very closely with a mathematical fitting technique, the projection of the trend this provides may be far from reliable.

■

It is instructive to note that in our example, had we elected to use a linear extrapolation of the trend (see Figure 4-4), we would have projected the 1960 population to be about 170 million and the 1980 population to be about 200 million, about 5 percent and 11 percent too low, respectively. Obviously, these last two estimates were obtained in a few seconds compared with the several minutes required to calculate the values of the logistic curve and then use the logistic equation to estimate the populations at the years of interest. This should not be interpreted to imply that the more complex approach may not be better than a simpler counterpart, but it does strongly suggest that good judgment should be exercised in picking the approach to use and in making assumptions about the nature of the trend. A study of Figure 4-4 would convince many that the linear extrapolation approach might be more representative of the future than that represented by the logistic model. A simple plot of the historical data is all that is needed to make such a judgment in this case. ∎

The final comment related to trend fitting is that unless there is reason to believe that the historical trend will be preserved for some period into the future, then trend extrapolations, whether graphical or mathematical, may be very poor indicators of the future. In such cases an extrapolated trend might be adjusted using supplemental information on factory closings, immigration, birthrate or any other external influences that might reshape the previously recorded pattern of growth.

NATIONAL FORECASTS

Several agencies estimate national population trends (25–30). Most of these use historical Bureau of the Census records and assumptions about future birthrates, death rates, and immigration and emigration rates to establish both short- and long-term national trends.

In its second assessment, the Water Resources Council used two sets of projections for economic activity and population growth, the National Future (NF) and the State-Regional Future (SRF). The population projection used by the WRC was based on the assumption that there would be a birthrate modified by a labor force movement that would in time yield zero population growth, exclusive of immigration (25). The State-Regional Future estimates were based on information compiled by assessment teams in each of the WRC's 21 regions or from state population estimates.

According to the WRC, the national population is expected to increase about 24 percent from 1975 to 2000, an annual growth rate of about 0.9 percent. This growth rate will not be uniformly distributed across the nation. Large increases in the sun-belt regions are expected; whereas, some areas such as the Souris-Red-Rainy River Basin area in the north central United States are expected to show declines.

The standard in national population estimating is set in the U.S. Department of Commerce, Bureau of the Census (27–30). The Bureau of the Census estimates that the population of the United States will continue to grow throughout this century at rates that could fall below those in the late 1970s (29). Their Series II projection, which assumes a fertility rate of about the level in 1977, indicates that the total United States population will be about 260 million in the year 2000, an increase of about 21 percent from 1976 (29). It is estimated under Series II that the annual growth rate will increase to 0.9 percent during the 1980s and then decline to about 0.6 percent by the end of the century. Population projections to the year 2025 for Series II and two other series, I and III, are shown in Table 4-2. The fertility assumptions for Series I and III were chosen to give a range likely to bracket future fertility in the United States. The resulting range in population projections is from 246 million (Series III) to 283 million (Series I). For Series I, the growth rate from 1976 to 2000 would be in the 1.0 to 1.3 percent range, whereas for Series III, the growth rate for the same period would be only about 0.3 percent by 2000 (29).

National population estimates by the Bureau of the Census are updated periodically and/or as required. The bureau also provides population estimates on a state-by-state basis. The information about specific regions, towns, cities, and so on must usually be obtained from local plan-

Table 4-2   ESTIMATES AND PROJECTIONS OF TOTAL POPULATION, 1930 TO 2025, IN THOUSANDS AS OF JULY 1.[a]

YEAR	SERIES I	SERIES II	SERIES III
ESTIMATES			
1930[b]		123,188	
1935[b]		127,362	
1940[c]		132,594	
1945		140,468	
1950		152,271	
1955		165,931	
1960		180,671	
1965		194,303	
1970		204,878	
1975		213,540	
1976		215,118	
PROJECTIONS			
1980	224,066	222,159	220,732
1985	238,878	232,880	228,879
1990	254,715	243,513	236,264
1995	269,384	252,750	241,973
2000	282,837	260,378	245,876
2005	297,600	267,603	248,631
2010	315,248	275,335	250,892
2015	334,708	283,164	252,548
2020	354,108	290,115	253,011
2025	373,053	295,742	251,915

SOURCE: *Current Population Reports,* series P-25, no. 632, tables 1, 2, 5, and 6, Bureau of the Census.
[a]Includes armed forces overseas.
[b]Excludes Alaska and Hawaii.
[c]The figure excluding Alaska and Hawaii is 132,122.

ning agencies, utility companies, and other local public or private agencies or businesses.

POPULATION DENSITIES

In addition to determining overall population growth, it is important to know where these people will be located. For example, it makes a great deal of difference to the designer of a municipal water distribution network extension to know whether a pipeline must serve 16 persons per acre or 300.

According to the WRC, the density of population is an index reflecting pressures on the nation's water resources (25). From 1950 to 1975, the average population density in the United States increased from about 43 to 61 persons per square mile. If the estimated year 2000 population of about 260 million is reached, the density will average about 75 per square mile. There are, however, wide variations from one region to another. For example, the population density in the Caribbean is about 859 per square mile whereas that in the upper Colorado and Alaska regions is three and one per square mile respectively (1975 data, reference 25).

Generally, population densities are high in urban areas and industrialized states. They are lowest in agricultural areas and in much of the region west of the Mississippi River except for California and some large cities in southwestern states. Zoning ordinances, histories of settlement, topography, and other factors may be useful guides for estimating or projecting population densities.

4-7 WATER USE

Past histories of water use are valuable aids in making estimates of future water use. They indicate the principal influencing factors and how these factors might be manipulated to affect future water withdrawals or consumptive uses. Projected trends, on the other hand, serve as measures to guide planners as they propose new water resources facilities, modifications of existing systems, new or revised operating rules, regulatory changes, revised laws, organizational changes, and research.

As of 1980, the United States was withdrawing about 450 billion gallons of water each day (31). This represented an average of about 2000 gallons per capita per day (gpcd) for all purposes. From 1950 to 1980, United States water use more than doubled, but as shown in Figure 4-5, the rate of water use increase has slowed. In fact, it diminished from about a 12 percent increase during the period 1970 to 1975 to about an 8 percent increase from 1975 to 1980. The U.S. Geological Survey study also revealed some other interesting facts. The average per capita water use per day varied strikingly from state to state, with the highest rates being associated with sparsely populated states with large tracts of irrigated land. California withdrew more water than any other state, and 25 percent of the total United States withdrawals could be accounted for by the states of California, Florida, Texas, and Idaho. More water was used for industry than for any other offstream use, with about 83 percent of this use being associated with thermoelectric power production. Irrigation was the second largest offstream user (see Figure 4.5).

Analyses of water use projections made since 1970 show that an increasing rate of per capita water use is less likely than estimators of the

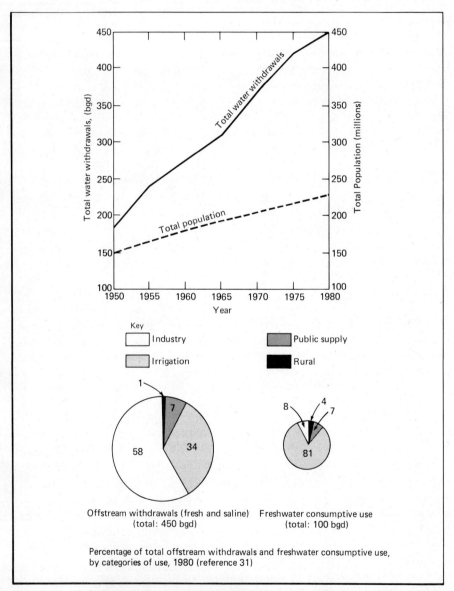

Figure 4-5   Trends in total water withdrawals in the United States, 1950 to 1980.

1950s and 1960s would have believed. Another lesson is that national or regional trends are not always indicative of state and local trends. Thus, planners must be equipped to deal with developments and management options at several geographical levels so that special local and regional influences can be accommodated. While the overall tendency in water use to the year 2000 appears to be more conservative than that of the past, striking local variances can be expected. Projected trends for several states with different types of economic activity, varying prospects for developing new water supplies, and a diversity of regional climatic and water use characteristics are illustrative.

Figures 4-6 to 4-9 show historical trends to 1975 and projected trends in water withdrawals and consumptive use to the year 2000 for the states of Alabama, Arizona, Pennsylvania, and Nebraska (32). These states represent (a) climates ranging from humid to semiarid and (b) economic bases ranging from heavily agricultural to intensely industrial. A careful evaluation of these by the reader will lead to a better understanding of the importance of regional differences in water use patterns and why generalized national trends can be misleading for any given locality.

Figure 4-6 for Alabama is representative of a well-watered region that has its major water withdrawals dedicated to the steam electric sector. Alabama's forecasts of significant increases in electric-generating capacity to be provided about equally by plants with once-through cooling and by plants with recirculating cooling are responsible for the large increases in withdrawals projected. A phasing-out of older coal-fired plants with new facilities using evaporative cooling resulting in part from stricter environmental controls on thermal discharges could alter the trends shown. In any event, for Alabama it is easy to see that any efforts to reduce water withdrawals significantly should focus on the power cooling sector.

Figure 4-7, in contrast to that for Alabama, is descriptive of one of the most water-short regions in the Untied States. The Arizona population growth rate is expected to exceed the national average through the turn of the century. Thus, residential and commercial water uses are also expected to be on the rise. This growth coupled with expected significant new requirements for steam electric generation and minerals production will add to the heavy stress of irrigation water use. The Arizona Water Commission has taken an alternative futures approach to making its projections to 2000. The highest and lowest forecasts are labeled Alternative I and Alternative III respectively, and they are displayed in the figure. Of considerable importance is the amount of water consumptively used. Note from Figure 4-7 that under Alternative I the consumptive use in 2000 would be about 50 percent of withdrawals, whereas in Alabama the consumptive use projected for 2000 would be only about 4 percent of the water withdrawn. The analyses made by the Arizona Water Commission were designed in part to determine what would be needed to bring the state's water supply and demand into balance by 2000. The most restric-

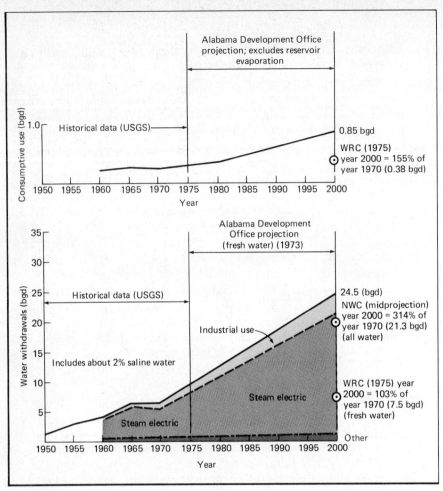

Figure 4-6 Alabama water withdrawals and consumptive use (actual, 1950 to 1975, projected, 1975 to 2000). Note that circled values labled WRC and NWC are year 2000 estimates based on average projected national water use increases from 1970 to 2000 as determined by the Water Resources Council and the National Water Commission, reference 32.

tive alternative, Alternative III, would come close to meeting this but would still result in an accumulated overdraft during the period from 1990 to 2000 of about four million acre-feet. It should be clear to the reader that measures to reduce water use in the agricultural sector are the only ones that will have any great significance in alleviating Arizona's water supply problems.

Pennsylvania's water withdrawals as projected to the year 2000 by the Pennsylvania Department of Environmental Resources reflect the generally more conservative attitude toward water resource development that has been emerging since the 1960s (see Figure 4-8). Note that the major water-using sectors are industry and steam electric generation. In this

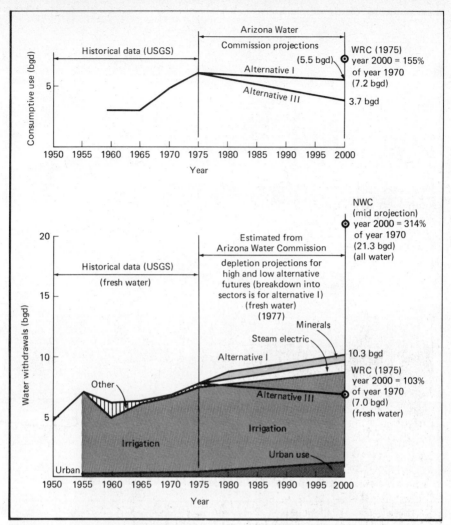

Figure 4-7 Arizona water withdrawals and consumptive use (actual, 1950 to 1975; projected, 1975 to 2000).

case, projected expansion of activity in these sectors is expected to involve greater levels of recycling and decreased once-through cooling. It is also anticipated that existing operations would be increasingly subjected to water-conserving management systems, the net effect being a slight decline in total water withdrawals from 1975 to 2000. The reader should observe, however, that the reduction of withdrawals is usually indicative of increased levels of consumptive use (see Figure 4-8) when the sector under consideration is steam electric generation or industry. On the other hand, reducing agricultural water withdrawals does reduce consumptive use as well. This is an important consideration in the western United States.

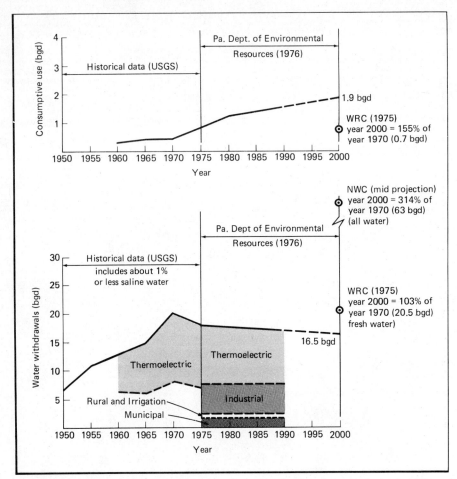

Figure 4-8 Pennsylvania water withdrawals and consumptive use (actual, 1950 to 1975; projected, 1975 to 2000).

The final state trend shown is for Nebraska (Figure 4-9). This important agricultural producer in the midwest is located in a region in which there are fairly large surface water supplies available combined with an extensive groundwater system. Nebraska represents one of the few localities in the United States where irrigated agriculture is expected to expand significantly up to the year 2000. The trend indicated on the figure shows that the dominant water use is by agriculture and that the rate of increase projected is fairly steep. No doubt the anticipated growth could be supported by more conservative water use, but the general availability of large quantities of good groundwater provides less incentive for conservation than the rapidly disappearing groundwater reserves in the southwest. The figure also shows the large amount of water consumed and clearly

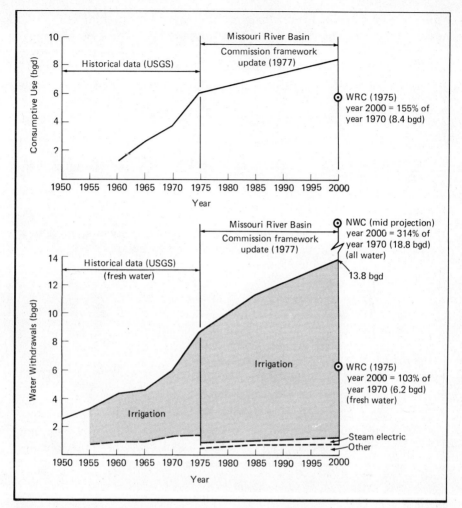

Figure 4-9 Nebraska water withdrawals and consumptive use (actual, 1950 to 1975; projected, 1975 to 2000)

demonstrates that any appreciable modification of withdrawals in Nebraska must be at the expense of the agricultural sector.

Example 4-2

A community having a population of 250,000 in 1980 estimates that its population will increase to 400,000 by the year 2000. The water treatment facilities in place can process up to 55 millions of gallons per day (mgd). The 1980 per capita water use rate was found to be 160 gpcd. Estimate the water requirements for the community in 2000 assuming that the per capita use rate remains unchanged. Will new treatment facilities be needed to accommodate this growth in population? If revised plumbing codes were adopted during the period of growth, and if these changes resulted in an overall reduction in the community's water use by 15 percent, what would the water requirement be in 2000? Could expansion of treatment facilities be deferred until after the year 2000 under these conditions?

SOLUTION

1. The water requirement in the year 2000 for a population of 400,000 and a per capita use rate of 160 gpcd would be

   $$400{,}000 \times 160 = 64 \text{ mgd}$$

2. Since 64 mgd exceeds the 1980 treatment capacity of 55 mgd, new facilities would be needed before the year 2000.

3. For a 15 percent reduction in water use, the per capita water requirements would be

   $$160 \times 0.85 = 136 \text{ gpcd}$$

   Water use in 2000 would be

   $$136 \times 400{,}000 = 54.4 \text{ mgd}$$

4. Under these conditions, expansion of water treatment facilities could be deferred until after the year 2000, since the demand of 54.4 mgd is less than the treatment plant capacity of 55 mgd.

   This example illustrates that an alternative to providing new facilities to meet expanding water needs could be more efficient use of the water already at hand. ■

Example 4-3

For the state of Nebraska (Figure 4-9), graphically determine how well population correlates with total water withdrawals and with total water withdrawals minus irrigation water use. The data are tabulated in Figure 4-10. Population figures were obtained from "Statistical Abstract of the United States—1980," U.S. Department of Commerce, Bureau of the Census. Water withdrawal data were scaled from Figure 4-9. Note that the 1950 value for water withdrawal exclusive of irrigation was obtained by projecting the historical trend back from 1955 to 1950 and the 1980 figure for that category was estimated by projecting the historical trend forward from 1975. The discontinuity shown in Figure 4-9 for water withdrawals other than for agriculture in 1975 reflects two estimates for that year by different organizations. In this example, the historical trend was used as the data base.

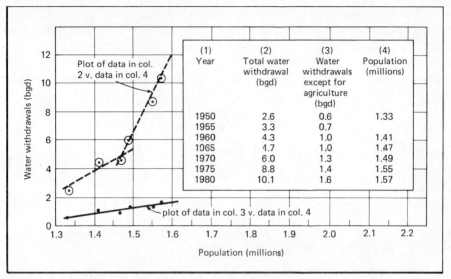

Figure 4-10   Plot of water withdrawals v. population for Example 4-3.

Discontinuities such as those mentioned are not uncommon when dealing with data derived by different organizations. This is unfortunate and serves as a further caution to accepting data without understanding underlying assumptions. In reality, if all water use terms were defined consistently among agencies involved in collecting and reporting data, there should be no disagreement on historical data. The water withdrawal figure for total water use was taken as the projected value given in Figure 4-9.

A plot of the data clearly shows the high degree of correlation of primarily municipal water use with population. The plot of total water use presents a different picture, however. In this case the correlation is, as would be expected, much weaker. For the Nebraska data a sharp break in trend appears in about 1965. This occurred as a result of an accelerated installation of center pivot irrigation systems (see Chapter 12) in the state.

This example shows that population may or may not be highly correlated with water use trends. In the absence of other data about the future, population data can be used to extend historical trends, but this should be done with caution. The validity of such projections would be greatest for municipal water uses and would be far less for other sectors, especially irrigated agriculture and steam electric generation. ■

Example 4-4

Consider that in 1980 a state had a total water withdrawal of eight billion gallons per day (bgd), distributed as follows: municipal water use, 1 bgd; steam electric generation, 5 bgd; and irrigated agriculture, 2 bgd. The

1980 population was 11.7 million and by the year 2000 it is expected that the population will increase to 13.2 million. Furthermore, it is estimated that 4000 megawatts (MW) of new electric-generating capacity will be installed by 2000 and that irrigated acreage will expand by 500,000 acres. Estimate the total water withdrawal in 2000 and the withdrawal for each of the three sectors.

SOLUTION

1. Estimated water use in the municipal sector can be obtained by using the projected change in population and an estimate of per capita water use in the year 2000. Assume the latter to be 140 gpcd.

   Change in population 1980 to 2000 = 13.2 − 11.7 = 1.5 million
   1.5 × 140 = 210 mgd = 0.21 bgd increase in municipal water use from 1980 to 2000

2. Assume that the water requirements for the crops to be raised average 3 acre-ft per acre.

   500,000 (acres) × 3 (acre-ft/per acre) = 1,500,000 acre-ft irrigation water needed annually in 2000. Since 1.12 million acre-ft/yr = 1 bgd, 1.5/1.12 = 1.34 bgd, the added irrigation water requirement in the year 2000.

3. Assume that the plant capacity factor for the steam electric facilities to be built is 60 percent (this measures the percentage of the nameplate, or installed capacity, of generating facilities that is actually realized in operation). At a 60 percent capacity factor, one kilowatt of installed capacity would produce 14.4 kilowatt-hours (kWh) of electrical energy each day. Note also that the WRC indicates that new steam electric facilities using once-through cooling (which we shall assume here) will require about 50 gallons of water per kilowatt-hour. Then

   4000 MW × 1000 (kW/MW) × 14.4 = 57,600,000 kWh per day
   57.6 × 10^6 × 50 (gal/kWh) = 2880 mgd or 2.88 bgd, the water requirement for steam electric cooling to be added during the interval 1980 to 2000

4. The added water requirements to the year 2000 are thus obtained by totaling the incremental increases for the three sectors:

   0.21 + 1.34 + 2.88 = 4.43 bgd increase; thus, the total water withdrawal in 2000 would be 4.43 + 8.00 = 12.43 bgd. The combined withdrawal use in 2000 would thus be about 1.6 times that of 1980.

   This example further supports the position that projections of future
water use are more likely to be in error in their totals if significant withdrawals for irrigation and steam electric cooling are expected. It also
illustrates that major reductions in water withdrawals are not likely to be
achieved in most regions unless more conservative measures are taken in
the agricultural and power cooling sectors. ■

Importance of Water Use Projections

There are two fundamental types of data with which the water resources
planner and manager must be familiar. These are the amount of water
available and the amount of water being used. Armed with this knowledge, determinations can be made of the likelihood of periodic water
shortages under the currently prevailing conditions and also the potential
for expanded use of the water resource.
   Evaluation of the supply that can be depended on with various
probabilities can be determined through the use of hydrologic-data-gath-
ering programs coupled with statistical analyses of these data. Various
analytical and modeling techniques that might be employed are discussed
in Chapter 7. It should be made clear, however, that adequate historical
data are not always available, even in highly developed nations such as the
United States. It is therefore necessary on occasion for approximations to
be made based on data from areas considered to be hydrologically similar,
or based on data generated from assumptions about local hydrologic conditions.
   The probabilistic nature of hydrologic variables must always be kept
in mind. Even where historical data are available, it must be recognized
that the period of record might represent a very wet or very dry time at
the locality in question. Thus estimates of future water supply availability
might be significantly in error on either the high or the low side. A classic
example is the estimate of average annual streamflow in the Colorado
River Basin. This region is one of the most critical in terms of water supply
in the United States. Water in the basin is allocated according to the
Colorado River Compact of 1922, which provides for the upper basin, the
lower basin, and Mexico. At the time the compact was drawn up, it was
estimated that the average annual flow of the Colorado River at Lee Ferry
Arizona was about 15 million acre-feet (maf). Since that time it has been
determined that the actual mean value might be closer to 12 maf, a very
considerable difference in a region where paper water rights already
exceed the apparently inflated compact flow.
   Although it is possible to measure the flow in a river at any point in
time, the calculation of what its value will be at some future time cannot
be made. At best, only the probability of some baseline flow being equaled
or exceeded can be estimated. An accurate prediction about the future is
elusive, and planners and managers must be satisfied to deal with the

liklihood of meeting a given target. They can never be sure, however, that conditions will not be worse than anticipated.

On the demand side, similar problems of estimation are encountered. Obtaining reliable figures on current water use is easier said than done, although at least in theory, water uses are all subject to measurement. When it comes to forecasting 10 or 20 years ahead, the planner is on shaky ground at best. There are many factors that affect water use and they must be understood by those seeking to make projections. Given the context of tight money and environmental concern, a knowledge of which factors can be most easily manipulated to bring about more conservative water use trends is important.

Planners are always faced with having to anticipate the future. It is necessary that this be done. Yet the validity of many forecasts is short-lived, and those making projections are faced with long odds. Estimates of future water use patterns are needed by decision makers in the United States and in all other parts of the world. Unfortunately, as pointed out by Wollman and Bonem, "the art of making comprehensive projections remains more primitive for water than for a number of other resource commodities . . ." (33). Their reasons for this finding include the local and regional rather than national dimensions of most water problems, the lack of a comprehensive market for water, the multiple use of water from the same source that affects the supply in different ways, and interdependence of water quantity and water quality, which makes quantity alone an inadequate measure of water supply.

All projections are associated with uncertainties such as the rate of technological advance, changing economic conditions, shifts in national and world politics, and the unpredictability of human nature. Still, projections are needed and it is encumbent on forecasters to use the data available to them as wisely as possible and to clearly state their assumptions so that those desiring to use the projections will not be misled. The inability to predict the future with confidence suggests that forecasting efforts should be accompanied by suitable feedback processes so that as events unfold, changes can be made to reflect unforeseen events or modified circumstances. Finally, projections should be looked on only as guidelines for decision making. They should be used cautiously and not accepted as accurate portrayals of what is to come.

Influencing Water Use Trends

The water use patterns that have emerged in the United States and other countries have been molded by many factors. There are, however, opportunities to purposely modify these trends if it is desired to do so. Mechanisms that can be used to this end include implementing conservation programs, regulating energy costs, restricting grant and loan programs to only those new facilities that are designed and operated to minimize water use, imposing environmental regulations such as limitations on thermal discharges, initiating educational programs to instill in citizens a more conservation-oriented approach to water use, encouraging reuse and recycling of water, limiting funding for construction of new water resources facilities, developing and marketing more efficient devices for using water in homes and industries, and employing pricing policies, taxes, and special incentives to encourage greater water use efficiency.

4-8 ELEMENTS OF A WATER RESOURCES PLAN

Water resources planning involves both a process and a scope. The process is the method by which the planning is carried out, and the scope is the measure of what is included in the plan. In general, water resources planning must deal with the following issues: the availability of water (all sources); the uses to which the water is to be put (amount and timing); the impacts of the various water uses on water quality and on the environment; deficits or surpluses in water supply; constraints on water development and/or management; prevailing legal, social, and population patterns; economic conditions; and the nature of local water politics. Figure 4-11 illustrates the elements of a typical planning process.

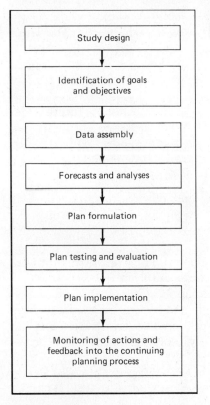

Figure 4-11 A water resources planning process.

Objectives

Water resources planning must address the goals and preferences of society if it is to result in action. In the United States, the principal water resources planning objectives have been to maximize national economic development and to maintain the integrity of environmental quality. Social well-being and regional development have also been objectives. Once the planning goals are established in an area, a plan or plans can be developed to achieve these goals. The planning process begins with the identification of problems that must be resolved in order to meet the specified goals. Once this has been done, alternative approaches to solving the problems are formulated. These alternatives must then be evaluated according to prescribed performance criteria, such as providing a positive benefit-cost ratio. Furthermore, the impact of any alternative on the environment must be evaluated in order to determine the extent and severity of any adverse consequences. Approval is then sought for implementation of various plan elements, and the process is subjected to periodic updating.

Data Assembly

Good planning requires an adequate data base. This includes both physical information about such things as water availability and information about such things as public preferences and shifts in social goals. The latter dimensions are often gained only through carefully designed programs for public participation in the planning process. The reasonableness of plans depends heavily on good information about the historical and present state of the system under consideration.

Because water planning is concerned about determining future water requirements, appraising various means to meet these requirements, and identification of alternatives for providing these means, many detailed studies and investigations are usually required. These include the following:

1. Population, economic, land use, and other associated planning studies that are needed for the prediction of water quality and quantity requirements for water uses anticipated during the planning period.
2. Hydrologic investigations to provide estimates of the quantities of fresh surface water and groundwater entering the region and of the temporal distribution of these supplies. It is often the case that sufficient data on the meteorologic and hydrologic characteristics of the region are not available. Additional field measurements and statistical analyses must frequently be relied on to yield the required information.
3. Comprehensive field investigations to evaluate the physical, chemical, radiological, and biological characteristics of the waters in the

region. This information will guide deliberations about treatment requirements, recreational values, and water quality control measures.

4. Studies of the storage capacities and uses of existing and proposed reservoirs. In some cases it will also be necessary to make detailed studies of the topography and geology of the region, with the objective of determining additional storage sites of an acceptable nature. Storage volume estimates for potential sites would also be required.

5. Investigations to determine the location and extent of groundwater storage, aquifer characteristics, and the quality of the underground water supplies.

6. Studies to provide information on anticipated and existing sources of wastes that might be introduced into surface water or groundwater. A knowledge of the characteristics and amounts of these wastes is essential.

7. Estimates of water requirements to be used to augment low flows of streams in the region. Low-flow augmentation can play an important role in fish and wildlife preservation and in combating pollution.

8. Evaluation of the costs and benefits of the various actions that might be proposed to solve the region's water problems.

9. Studies of environmental impacts of possible actions that might be proposed in the planning process. The data from these analyses will be necessary for developing a credible environmental impact statement.

Although the list presented above is not exhaustive, it gives an idea of the variety of data-generating studies that could be required in a typical water resources planning effort.

Planning Horizons

The planning horizon is the furthest point in time considered in an economic study of a region's water resources. While forecasting difficulties suggest that planning periods be kept as short as possible, the need to evaluate the longer-term consequences of short-term actions and to prepare for distant water shortages or other problems requires that planning cover many years into the future. In terms of facilities that might be built as the result of a plan, it has been suggested that there are actually four time periods that must be considered (4): the economic life, the physical life, the period of analysis, and the construction horizon.

Economic life extends until incremental benefits from operating a facility no longer exceed incremental costs of operating the facility. The physical life is said to end when the facility can no longer accomplish its function. The period of analysis is the time span over which the project consequences are considered in a study. For most large-scale water development undertakings, the period of analysis is in the range of from 50 to 100 years. The construction horizon is the point in time at which the constructed facilities can no longer be expected to satisfy all of the future demands. The fact that long time scales are used in water resources planning strongly recommends the dynamic planning process with its frequent adjustments.

Alternative Futures

Because of the great uncertainties surrounding forecasts, it is becoming common for planners to explore several plausible alternative futures rather than to make single projections. As was pointed out in our discussion on scenario writing, several futures that bracket the best and the worst situations and that represent some continuation of current trends can be very useful in suggesting and evaluating the consequences of courses of action to be followed in meeting long-range water requirements.

Historically, most estimates of future demands for water and associated activities were based on a single projection of the principal variables affecting water use (1). In the future the quantities of water used will depend, however, on many variables, including (1) population; (2) the rate of national income growth; (3) per capita energy consumption; (4) factors affecting demands for food and fiber for domestic use and for export, including the lifestyles and eating habits of people; (5) government programs dealing with resource development and distribution, such as environmental protection goals and crop price support programs; (6) the rate of technological change; (7) recreational water uses; and (8) the price of water to the users. Efforts to identify emerging water resources problems and to plan for solving them should consider these and other factors carefully.

Because it is difficult if not impossible to make single "best" estimates of the values of these variables over periods of 100, 50, 20, or even 10 years, planners should not be bound by any particular projection or forecast. Instead, an alternative-futures approach of assessing future water requirements by investigating a range of possible outcomes should be used. In this way, an array of policy choices, tradeoffs, and options for water use can be evaluated (1).

The alternative-futures approach permits the greatest possible latitude in assessing the implications of proposed actions and thus makes possible selecting that course of action which has the greatest flexibility to accommodate changes as they might occur (34, 35). Although in theory an infinite number of futures might be envisioned, the human mind can deal with but a few at any one time. Considering this, a review of alternative strategies bracketing best and worst cases (or some reasonable outer limits) and considering intermediate conditions has the attraction of informing decision makers of the range of possibilities that might be encountered and the implications of making decisions based on a specific target future if a different future actually occurs.

For each alternative future projected, it is common practice to formulate one or more approaches that will meet the requirements of that future. These plans may embody alternative physical works, structural v. nonstructural approaches to water management, alternative organizational arrangements for constructing and/or managing the facilities proposed, and alternatives in timing (scheduling) of developments. The alternatives might also include different projections for population growth, economic development, social programs, industrial activity, technological change, and other factors. Note that the alternative ways of meeting the water requirements of a particular future should not be confused with the term alternative futures. The latter represents the state of a region at some future date whereas the former is an alternative method of meeting some particular objective.

In past years, the tendency in planning not only was toward making a single projection regarding the future but also was heavily biased (at least in the United States) by an ingrained philosophy of growth: in each succeeding year there will be more people, they will drive bigger cars, they will each use more water, they will each generate more wastes, and so on. Since the Arab oil embargo in the 1970s and the environmental movement of the 1960s, this notion of growth as the norm has been somewhat altered. Nevertheless, there are still many water planners who are driven by the idea that their region must "grow" and that the services provided to support the new growth must somehow be more per capita than the old ones. This type of thinking leads to increasing rate-of-use projections, and in developing plans to meet them, the trap is that overbuilding may occur or the lure of excess capacity will generate a growth that might not have occurred naturally, and that might not be desirable. By exploring alternative futures, information will be generated that, at the least, may show that some declines are possible in population or services or both. Furthermore, consideration of various growth level futures results in creating an awareness of options that might be exercised to minimize the need for new facilities even though substantial increases in population, industrial activity, or agricultural development are anticipated.

Although it is easy for most planners to foresee patterns of growth, it is often less likely that they will think seriously about no-growth or declining-growth patterns. In constructing alternative futures, it is important that these possibilities be kept in mind. Demographic patterns in the United States have been undergoing rapid change, and while many regions may expect continued growth, there are others that are already mature and may decline in the future. This signals the need for some revised and imaginative thinking on the part of planners and engineers. Historical practice in designing a municipal water treatment plant was to provide a generous margin of excess capacity to compensate for expected population increases. Schuler notes, however, that in an area experiencing decline, "today's margin of safety may become tomorrow's albatross" (6). This is because in a declining situation, the amount of excess capacity increases with time, and the costs of operating the system must be spread over fewer users. Planners are well advised to anticipate the prospects of such occurrences, and it may be important for them to consider modifications of existing systems to function more efficiently at reduced loadings. In some cases, an option to be considered might be abandonment of some area whose future costs would be excessive relative to the benefits of maintaining it. Alternative-futures planning offers the vehicle to explore several possible time streams in an area, time streams that might reflect growth as well as no-growth or even decline.

4-9 PLAN EVALUATION

Once a plan or plans have been formulated, they must be evaluated according to some measures of worth. Such measures are usually economic, environmental, and social in character. They determine whether a proposed plan has a positive or negative effect on the economy; whether there are adverse environmental consequences; whether the social costs associated with relocating people, or minimizing their access to a water body, are reasonable in terms of possible benefits from the proposal; whether the region will benefit and in what way; whether people will accept the plan; and whether the available financial resources are such as to ensure implementation (36–42).

Evaluation Criteria

In the United States there are well-established criteria for evaluating water resources plans. For actions proposed for support totally by the private sector or by local governmental units, the comprehensive criteria may be departed from, but in almost every case there will be some standard of judgment. Generally, the following criteria are used:

ECONOMIC

Traditionally, the test of whether or not a plan would be implemented has been an economic one. This test usually takes the form of determining if the proposal has positive net benefits, or at least if the activity is cost-effective. The former measure has been the standard for most structural development of water resources in the United States whereas the latter has been used mostly for assessing waste treatment facilities. In this context, the EPA has defined cost-effectiveness analysis as a systematic comparison of alternatives that reliably meet given goals and objectives, in order to identify a solution that minimizes the long-range total cost to society.

A good economic analysis requires that alternatives be defined in enough detail so that associated costs and benefits can be reliably estimated. The methods used in estimating these must be such that the worth of the alternatives can be directly compared. The time value of money is represented by the use of an appropriate discount rate. Since a detailed accounting of methods used in economic analysis is given in Chapter 5, no more need be said here.

ENVIRONMENTAL

Since the 1960s, water planning in the United States has been greatly influenced by the desires of society to minimize the effects of water resources developments on the environment. Water projects are often opposed on environmental grounds and many proposed projects have been delayed, altered in concept, or scuttled as a result. And while some worthy water projects have been jeopardized by environmental actions, the net effect has been one of creating an awareness of environmental concerns and a formal process to give these the attention they deserve. Furthermore, a positive spin-off has been the general expansion of approaches considered in devising alternatives. For example, water supply needs might be met by developing new sources of water or they might be met, for a period of time, by reducing local demands. The latter approach is obviously one less likely to affect adversely the environment than the former. It is also the approach that would minimize the need for funds. The environmental movement has encouraged us to explore ways to reduce water requirements; more seriously consider nonstructural approaches to water management; think more intensively about reusing waste streams; evaluate more fully the linkages between water management activities and those related to air pollution control, solid waste disposal, transportation, and other areas; and intensify research efforts to quantify the ecological consequences of various courses of action.

Today most planning processes include an environmental impact assessment. The National Environmental Policy Act of 1969 formalized this process with its requirement that an environmental impact statement (EIS) be prepared with respect to the planning, constructing, and operating phases of any federally supported project (43). Minimal elements of such a statement include:

1. A description of what is proposed, including the data needed to make a reliable assessment
2. Comment on the probable environmental impact of the proposed action
3. Identification of adverse effects that cannot be avoided

4. A statement of alternatives considered, their environmental impacts, and the reasons they were not followed up
5. An accounting of both the short- and long-range implications of the proposed action
6. A statement of commitments of resources required to complete the proposed action, giving information on whether or not these commitments would be reversible.

Although the preparation of an EIS is a special legal requirement, evaluation of the environmental consequences of planning alternatives should be an integral part of every plan. If the EIS is thorough, it can be the basis for supporting plan implementation; if it is done poorly, it can spell delays at best and failure of the plan at worst.

REGIONAL

Decision makers are always concerned about the regional implications of plans. They desire to improve the lot of their constituents and to guard against losses to their regions. Measures used to evaluate the regional dimensions of plans include the value of increased goods and services that will result from implementation of the plan, impact on job opportunities, effects of the plan on population growth and/or distribution, regional environmental impacts, the effect of the plan on the region's economy, and the relation of the plan to other proposals for regional development.

SOCIAL

The well-being of people residing in a planning region must be considered in plan evaluation. Factors that are used to measure the effects of a plan on social welfare include income distribution; life, health, and safety implications; educational, cultural, and recreational opportunities; and the degree to which the plan provides for protection of water supplies and/or other services during times of emergency.

PUBLIC ACCEPTANCE

No planning effort can be successful if the plan is not acceptable to those whom it will affect. We have already noted that appropriate public involvement in the planning process is the key to gaining this acceptance.

IMPLEMENTATION OPPORTUNITY

Although a plan may meet the tests of economic efficiency, environmental acceptability, regional benefits, and enhancement of social well-being and be acceptable to the public, it still may not be translated into action. This last step cannot take place unless there are adequate legal authorities and feasible mechanisms for financing the proposed projects or programs. Unless funding sources can be identified and payback arrangements made, long delays in project implementation or even cancellation of projects can be anticipated.

WRC's Principles and Guidelines

In 1982 the governing procedures for evaluation of water resources plans requiring federal involvement were the "Principles and Guidelines for Planning Water and Related Land Resources." These evolved from the 1973 "Principles and Standards" (P&S) after a long transition in planning criteria development set in motion when the Flood Control Act of 1936 established that investments in public works for water resources development be made on the basis that "the benefits to whomsoever they may accrue" should be "in excess of the estimated costs." From this start, a systematic accounting system has evolved. Over the years, many refinements in it have taken place, and by 1982 the focus was on nonmonetary effects of water resources development, on the actual distribution of costs and benefits, and on simplification of procedures.

The modern accounting system took shape in the recommendations of a 1969 WRC task force proposing that benefits and costs should be summarized in four accounts: (1) national economic development, (2) environmental quality, (3) social well-being, and (4) regional development. In devising this system, the WRC hypothesized that the primary objectives of water and related land use policy were:

To enhance national economic development by increasing the value of the nation's output of goods and services and improving national economic efficiency

To enhance the quality of the environment by the management, conservation, preservation, creation, restoration, or improvement of the quality of certain natural and cultural resources and ecological systems

To enhance social well-being by the equitable distribution of real income, employment, and population, with special concern for the incidence of the consequences of a plan on affected persons or groups; by contributing to the security of life and health; by providing educational, cultural, and recreational opportunities; and by contributing to national security

To enhance regional development through increases in a region's income; increases in employment; and improvements of its economic base, environment, social well-being, and other specified components of the regional objective

Resulting from this effort was the first edition of the "Principles and Standards for Planning Water and Related Land Resources." It appeared in the *Federal Register* on September 10, 1973 (42). Of the four objectives originally considered by the WRC, only the first two, national economic development (NED) and enhancement of environmental quality (EQ), were retained. It was required, however, that beneficial and adverse effects relative to these objectives be displayed in four accounts, namely NED, EQ, regional development, and social well-being.

In an article titled "Principles and Standards," Warren Fairchild (a former WRC director) pointed out that the new "Principles and Standards" "place environmental concerns on a basis equal to economic development. This allows planners to truly recognize the environmental trade-offs in resource planning." In addition, the P&S "represent a real effort on the part of water resource officials and agencies to make the planning process relevant to today's situation." In addition, the P&S allow the public arena to "participate on the basis that there are alternatives to react to . . . ." Finally, the P&S "provide that measurements will be in quantitative or qualitative terms appropriate to the definition of the component being evaluated . . ." (44).

Since their emergence in 1973, the P&S have undergone refinements and have been subjected to a continuing critique by both proponents and opponents. A major change in emphasis was proposed by President Carter in his Water Policy Initiatives of June 6, 1978. In that statement he noted that conservation would be added as a specific component of the economic and environmental objectives of the P&S. He also called for greater consistency and uniformity among the federal agencies in conducting benefit-cost analyses. The result of all this was the publication in 1980 of revised P&S reflecting the conservation component and other changes. The 1980 revisions of the P&S established new procedures for evaluating benefits and costs for Level C or Implementation studies (program or project feasibility studies that are expected to result in project authorization, funding, and implementation) of federal water and related land resources projects. These procedures were considered to use the best techniques available and were believed to ensure consistency and accuracy among agencies in the economic evaluation of federal water resources projects.

A key revision made in 1980 was the requirement that water conservation be integrated fully into "project and program planning and review." The revised "Standards" section stated that this insertion was "a means of achieving both the national economic development and environmental quality objectives." Water conservation was defined as actions that would "(a) reduce the demand for water; (b) improve efficiency in use and reduce losses and waste; and (c) conserve water." It clearly excluded storage facilities for water supplies, however.

Another change in the P&S made in 1980 was requiring that "at least one primarily nonstructural plan" be included in plan preparation. It was theorized that since nonstructural plans are generally conceived to be demand-reducing measures, they may offer special benefits in terms of maximizing economic development at the least cost to the environment. The 1973 section on flood control, land stabilization, and related activities was also significantly changed. The 1973 version called for the "prevention or reduction of inundation" and the "prevention of damage from inadequate drainage," while the new approach stressed environmentally sound flood control or land stabilization measures. Finally, the 1980 version of the P&S recognized that plans and planning procedures could only "contribute" to meeting needs or achieving policy objectives but could not alone guarantee meeting these needs.

When the Reagan administration took office, it expressed the belief that various aspects of the P&S were an impediment to the expeditious development of the nation's waters and that they needed streamlining and a greater degree of state input. As a result, the Assistant Secretaries Work Group on Water Resources was assigned the mission of reviewing the P&S and making recommendations to the President's Cabinet Council on Natural Resources and the Environment. The principal features of these recommendations were a proposal to convert the P&S to guideline status and to consider NED as the single planning objective. The work group's recommendations were that:

The planning framework would be in the form of flexible guidelines, as opposed to inflexible rules. Explicit provisions would be made for abbreviation of steps where appropriate.

The guidelines would have a single national planning objective with flexibility provided to address other concerns relevant to the planning setting.

Provisions would be made to encourage planners to also formulate cost-effective alternatives that contribute to social, regional, and environmental goals and address state and local concerns not fully accommodated by the NED objective.

Emphasis would be placed on avoiding or mitigating adverse effects of alternative plans and on protecting the nation's environment pursuant to national environmental statutes and executive branch policies.

State participation would be encouraged in all aspects of planning.

While emphasis would be placed on ensuring that all reasonable alternatives were considered, the only required plan would be the one that reasonably maximizes net economic benefits and other alternative plans required to satisfy the intent of the National Environmental Policy Act.

The plan with the greatest net economic benefits would be recommended. However, there would be a provision for the secretary of a department or the chairman of the TVA to recommend an exception, if and only if the exception was approved by the Cabinet Council on Natural Resources and Environment.

Estimates of the economic impacts of plans would be made in accord with existing detailed procedures that would be incorporated into the guidelines. Abbreviation of the procedures would be permitted, and when an alternative procedure provided a more accurate estimate of the benefit, it also could be shown.

Existing detailed procedures for evaluating environmental quality impacts would be included as one suggested procedure for evaluating environmental effects.

A formal, detailed accounting of the economic benefits and costs of alternative plans presented to decision makers would be required. Other impacts of plans would be shown as required by law and to the extent they would have a material bearing on the decision-making process.

The new "Principles and Guidelines" (P&G) were printed in draft form in the *Federal Register* on March 22, 1982. Final action was taken in November 1982. The P&G include:

A single federal objective (NED)

An emphasis on addressing state, local, and international concerns

A requirement for a secretarial exemption if a plan other than the NED is required

Elimination of the grandfather clause that limited applicability of previous P&S

A role for the Cabinet Council in reviewing water policy changes

4-10 PLAN IMPLEMENTATION

The purpose of planning is to determine some strategy or strategies for overcoming problems and meeting anticipated needs. If a plan is not put to use, then the resources invested in its development are lost, and no value is gained from the effort. All too often, this is what happens. The reasons why many plans are not executed include failure of planners to present economically and politically acceptable alternatives, lack of public support, inability of planners to present their plans in a timely fashion, lack of coordination between planning and developmental agencies, and ineffective linkages between planning agencies and decision-making bodies.

River basin planning is a case in point. For years plans have been developed for these areas, but many of them have been given little consideration by Congress or other legislative bodies. On the other hand, strong local constituencies have often been very influential in determining what projects are built or programs are implemented in their regions. These decisions have not always been in the best interests of the nation or of the region. Nevertheless, they were made because the proponents could marshal the needed political support. An additional problem stems from the fact that what is considered best in a regional or national sense is not always considered best when viewed from the eyes of a local community.

For implementation it is necessary that a plan be highly visible, competent, backed by factual data, and specific and clear in its establishment of priorities and the implications of not observing them. Good information and strong arguments supporting the options presented by the plan can go a long way toward convincing those making the decisions that the plan is worth paying attention to. Public support is part of this, and thus the electorate's participation must be given more than lip service. When the planning process is carried out by a governmental unit, the best mechanism for ensuring that it will be seriously considered is to establish a statutory requirement that it be the basis or at least part of the basis for legislative action. If plans are to be given this prominence, they must be good, however, and must be in a form that provides explicit guidance for decision making. Too many plans are simply "wish lists" with little or no attention paid to the relative importance of planning elements or their timing. For plans such as these, it is little wonder that politicians turn for help to constituencies that can make a convincing case, even though it might not be the best one.

PROBLEMS

4-1. Are the water quality and water quantity planning programs in your state coordinated? If so, how is this accomplished? Can you suggest improvements? Discuss three ways in which you believe public participation in planning processes can be accommodated.

4-2. For a region of your choice, identify the most pressing water problems and suggest a strategy for developing options for addressing them. What baseline data would be needed? Are they available? If not, what would you do to compensate for the deficiency?

4-3. Discuss the pros and cons of using a mathematical model as an aid in water resources planning.

4-4. For your state, what level of coordination exists among planning programs for water, transportation, land use, etc.? Is it sufficient? How could it be improved?

4-5. Review an already developed water plan for your state, region, or some other area and discuss how the planners dealt with problems of uncertainty. Could their approach be improved on? How?

4-6. Use the following data to estimate the 1985 and 1990 populations by assuming arithmetic and geometric rates of increase.

YEAR	POPULATION (THOUSANDS)
1910	6
1920	12
1930	22
1940	27
1950	31
1960	38
1970	42
1980	44

4-7. If the minimum flow of a stream having a 100 mi^2 watershed is 0.10 ft^3/s/m^2, what population might be supplied continuously from the stream? Assume that only distribution storage is provided. Consider a maximum daily water use of 160 gpcd.

4-8. Estimate the 1985, 1990, and 2000 population of a community for the data of Problem 4-6 by plotting the data for 1910 onward on arithmetic coordinate paper and extending the curve by eye. Compare these results with those obtained in Problem 4-6 for 1985 and 1990.

4-9. Given the following population data, fit a logistic curve to the data and determine an estimate of the 1995 population. How much confidence do you place in this estimate?

YEAR	POPULATION (THOUSANDS)	YEAR	POPULATION (THOUSANDS)
1850	25	1910	98
1860	33	1920	113
1870	42	1930	130
1880	53	1940	139
1890	67	1950	153
1900	79	1960	161
		1970	172

4-10. Obtain population data for your state from 1900 to 1980. Fit a logistic curve and estimate the population in 1990 and 2000.

4-11. Use the data for Problem 4-9 and find the 1990 and 2000 populations by a simple trend extrapolation. Compare the results with those obtained in Problem 4-9. Discuss the differences, pointing out whether you believe them to be important.

4-12. By considering all the factors you think might influence population trends in your state to the year 2000, develop three alternative future population levels for that year. Discuss the significance and plausibility of each.

4-13. Given that the population of a state was 7.2 million people in 1970, and that the population is projected to increase to 9.8 million in the year 2020, and further that the amount of water withdrawn in the state in 1970 was 6.3 bgd, make a rough projection of the level of water withdrawal in 2020. How reliable do you think this projection is? Would the projection likely be more accurate if the major growth in the state's economic activity was in the manufacturing sector or if it was related to irrigated agriculture? Explain your reasoning.

4-14. A community has a population of 200,000 in 1980 and it is expected that this will increase to 260,000 by 2000. The water treatment capacity at 1980 was 43 mgd. A survey in 1977 showed that the average per capita water use rate was 143 gpcd. Estimate the community's water requirements in 2000 assuming (a) no change in use rate and (b) a reduced rate of 135 gpcd. Will expanded treatment facilities be needed by 2000 for condition (a)? For condition (b)?

4-15. Obtain historical water use data for your state, or use the data provided in one of the figures on state water use given in the chapter, and correlate total water withdrawals and withdrawals for each of the water-using sectors with population data for the state you choose. Which sector correlates most highly? Explain. For sectors showing poor correlation see if you can determine the factor or factors most responsible for the deviation.

4-16. Refer to Figure 1-1 and determine in which of the WRC's designated regions you reside. For that region, make a determination of which water-using sectors are most dominant. How did you arrive at this determination? Do you think the past trends will continue into the future? If so, why? If not, why not? Are there water supply problems in the region? If so, could these be alleviated by modifying water use rates in one or more of the water-using sectors? How much of a reduction below current rates of use do you think could be achieved? What revision in facilities or systems operation would be required to bring about this reduction?

4-17. Consider that a state had a total water withdrawal of 7.5 bgd in 1980. This was distributed as follows: municipal use, 1.5 bgd; industrial water use, 2 bgd; and steam electric cooling, 4 bgd. Assume that the 1980 population was 10 million and that it is expected to increase by 10 percent in 2000. It is estimated that an additional 3000 MW of electric generating capacity will be added by the year 2000 and that cooling water requirements for this will be 55 gallons per kWh. Furthermore, an industrial expansion of 10 percent is also projected by 2000. Estimate the total water withdrawal in each sector and the grand total as well. State your assumptions and indicate any reservations you have about the projections you make.

References

1. National Water Commission, *Water Policies for the Future,* U.S. Gov.'t. Print. Off., Washington, D.C., 1973.
2. D. J. Parker and E. C. Penning-Roswell, *Water Planning in Britain,* George Allen and Unwin, London, 1980.
3. V. Novotny and G. Chesters, *Handbook of Nonpoint Pollution,* Van Nostrand, New York, 1981.
4. L. D. James and R. R. Lee, *Economics of Water Resources Planning,* McGraw-Hill, New York, 1971.
5. R. K. Linsley and J. B. Franzini, *Water Resources Engineering,* McGraw-Hill, New York, 1979.
6. R. E. Schuler, "Engineering for Decline—A Challenge in the Eighties," *Engineering: Cornell Quarterly,* vol. 16, no. 1, Summer 1981.
7. Susan R. Abbasi et al., *Long Range Planning,* Committee Print, U.S. House of Representatives, Committee on Science and Technology, 94th Cong., Washington, D.C., May 1976.
8. U.S. Army Corps of Engineers, *Handbook of Forecasting Techniques,* Fort Belvoir, VA, December 1975.
9. Roy Amara, *Some Methods of Futures Research,* WP–23, Menlo Park, CA, Institute for the Future, December 1975.
10. Joseph F. Coates, "In Defense of Delphi," *Technological Forecasting and Social Change,* vol. 7, no. 2, 1975.

11. Harold A. Linstone and Turoff Murray (eds.), *The Delphi Method: Techniques and Application,* foreword by Olaf Helmer, Addison-Wesley, Reading, MA, 1975.
12. University of Minnesota, "Report of Delphi Inquiry into the Future of American Water Resource Utilization and Development," Office for Applied Social Science and the Future, Minneapolis, January 15, 1973.
13. John Stover, *Probabilistic System Dynamics,* The Futures Group, Glastonbury, CT, March 1975.
14. Herman Kahn and Anthony Wiener, *The Year 2000,* Macmillan, New York, 1967.
15. Rene D. Zentner, "Scenarios in Forecasting," *Chemical and Engineering News,* vol. 53, October 1975.
16. Theodore J. Gordon, "The Current Methods of Futures Research," in *The Futuristics,* Alvin Toffler (ed.), Random House, New York, 1972.
17. U.S. Environmental Protection Agency, *A Guide to Models in Governmental Planning and Operations* (prepared for the Office of Research and Development), U.S. Environmental Protection Agency, Washington, D.C., August 1974.
18. U.S. Congress, House, Committee on Merchant Marine and Fisheries, Subcommittee on Fisheries and Wildlife Conservation and the Environment, *Computer Simulation Methods to Aid National Growth Policy,* U.S. Gov't. Print. Off., Washington, D.C., 1975.
19. D. M. Roth and D. L. Little, *Rapid Population Growth in Third World Countries: An Overview of Social and Economic Effects and Their Relationships to U.S. Multinations Corporations,* Congressional Research Service, Library of Congress, Washington, D.C., 1981.
20. G. T. T. Molitor, *Food and Population: Future Crises?* Industrial Management Center, Castine, ME, June 8, 1977.
21. D. L. Little, *Population Trends and Energy Consumption,* Congressional Research Service, Library of Congress, Washington, D.C., October 1980.
22. *The Revival of Population Growth in Nonmetropolitan America,* Economic Research Service, U.S. Department of Agriculture, ERS-605, Washington, D.C., June 1975.
23. J. W. Clark et al., *Water Supply and Pollution Control,* 3d ed., Harper & Row, New York, 1977.
24. W. Isard et al., *Methods of Regional Analysis: An Introduction to Regional Science,* Technology Press of M.I.T. and Wiley, New York, 1960.
25. U.S. Water Resources Council, *The Nation's Water Resources 1975–2000,* vol. 2, *Water Quantity, Quality and Related Land Considerations,* Washington, D.C., 1978.
26. U.S. Department of Commerce and U.S. Department of Agriculture, *1972 OBERS Projections—Economic Activity in the United States,* Washington, D.C., September 1972.
27. U.S. Department of Commerce, Bureau of the Census, *1980 Census of Population and Housing,* PHC80-V-1, United States Summary, Washington, D.C., April 1981.
28. U.S. Department of Commerce, Bureau of the Census, *Statistical Abstract of the United States 1980,* 101st ed., *National Data Book and Guide to Sources,* Washington, D.C., 1980.

29. U.S. Department of Commerce, Bureau of the Census, *Population Estimates and Projections,* series P-25, no. 704, Washington, D.C., July 1977.
30. U.S. Department of Commerce, Bureau of the Census, *Comparison of Current Trends with the 1977 Population Projections,* series P-25, no. 889, Washington, D.C., August 1980.
31. U.S. Geological Survey, *Estimated Water Use in the United States in 1980,* Geological Survey Circular 1001, U.S. Gov't. Print. Off., Washington, D.C., 1982.
32. U.S. Congress, Senate, *State and National Water Use Trends to the Year 2000,* serial no. 96-12, 96th Cong., 2d Sess., U.S. Gov't. Print. Off., Washington, D.C., 1980.
33. N. Wollman and G. W. Bonem, *The Outlook for Water Quality, Quantity and National Growth,* Resources for the Future, Inc., Johns Hopkins Press, Baltimore, MD, 1971.
34. Duane S. Elgin, David C. MacMichael, and Peter Schwartz, *Alternative Futures for Environmental Policy Planning: 1975–2000,* Center for Study of Social Policy, Standford Research Institute, Menlo Park, CA, 1975.
35. U.S. Congress, Senate, Committee on Agriculture and Forestry, *Alternative Futures for U.S. Agriculture, Part I,* 94th Cong., 1st Sess., U.S. Gov't. Print. Off., Washington, D.C., 1975.
36. General Accounting Office, *An Overview of Benefit-Cost Analysis for Water Resources Projects—Improvements Still Needed,* Rep. CED-78-127, Washington, D.C., August 7, 1978.
37. Joseph Carroll et. al., *Benefits or Costs II—An Analysis of the Water Resources Council's Manual of Procedures for Evaluation of Benefits and Costs,* National Wildlife Federation, Washington, D.C., August 1979.
38. S. H. Hanke, "On the Feasibility of Benefit-Cost Analysis," *Public Policy,* vol. 29, no. 2, Spring 1981.
39. *Policies, Standards, and Procedures in the Formulation, Evaluation, and Review of Plans for Use and Development of Water and Related Land Resources,* 87th Cong., 2d Sess., Senate Document no. 97, U.S. Gov't. Print. Off., Washington, D.C., May 29, 1952.
40. *Federal Register,* notices, Water Resources Council, "Proposed Principles and Standards for Planning Water and Related Land Resources," Notice of Public Review and Hearing, vol. 36, no. 245, December 21, 1971.
41. U.S. Water Resources Council, *Summary and Analysis of Public Response to the Proposed Principles and Standards for Planning Water and Related Land Resources and Draft Environmental Statement,* Washington, D.C., July 1972.
42. *Federal Register,* Water Resources Council, "Establishment of Principles and Standards for Planning Water and Related Land Resources," vol. 38, no. 174, part III, Washington, D.C., September 10, 1973.
43. Anon., *National Environmental Policy Act,* P.L. 91–190, U.S. Cong., Washington, D.C., 1969.
44. W. D. Fairchild, "Principles and Standards—The President's Announcement," *Water Spectrum,* vol. 5, no. 4, Washington, D.C., 1973.

Chapter 5
Economics and Financing

Ronald M. North*

This chapter is designed to acquaint the reader with the application of economic theory to the planning, design, and management of water resources systems. Several principles of economic analysis are discussed. They include theories of supply and demand (price theory), the theory of welfare economics, and investment theory. Price theory emanates from positive economics where market conditions are accepted as given. The theory of welfare economics considers the ability of an economic system to attain goals that are presumed to maximize human welfare. The theory of welfare economics grew out of the work of Pigou (1), with the realization that certain desirable social gains and undesirable social costs were not fully accounted for in a private, profit-maximizing, market economy. Welfare economic theory supports the evaluation of public policies as well as private market decisions when the objective is the improvement of net social welfare. Price theory and welfare economic theory embrace static analyses that involve no significant time horizon whereas investment theory (financial analysis) involves a study of values through time. This theory seeks to evaluate the impacts of changing conditions over time with respect to supply, demand, and prices. In the final analysis, it is the welfare theory that drives economic analyses of most water resources projects and programs.

Price theory, welfare economic theory, and investment theory are important elements in benefit-cost analyses for water resources projects.

*Professor of Agricultural Economics, University of Georgia.

These analyses, appropriately made, reveal the full extent of all private and social costs and benefits with respect to their impact on national income (real wealth) and on the distribution of that income among the various sectors of the population in the present and future.

The reader desiring more background than can be given here will profit from reviewing several of the classics in the literature of water resource economics. The authors suggest as basics the book by Pigou (1), the Flood Control Act of 1936 (2), and the "Green Book" of 1950 (3). Several other classics include books by Hirshleifer, DeHaven, and Milliman (4); Krutilla and Eckstein (5); Eckstein (6); and McKean (7). The reader will also enhance his or her background by reading *Economic Philosophy* by Joan Robinson (8) and *The Impact of the Social Sciences* by Kenneth Boulding (9). Additional background on the theory of welfare economics can be obtained from Little (10) and Baumol (11).

Since these contributions to the literature, the use of economic analysis has expanded substantially and has become more sophisticated. The central theme during the three decades preceding the 1960s was focused on developing and refining the benefit-cost analysis of water resources projects and their component functions such as flood control, water supply, irrigation, navigation, and hydroelectric power generation. Since that time, much of the focus has been on broader issues (often described as environmental economics) and the emphasis has shifted to studies of social costs and methods of dealing with social costs. These include such subjects as regulation, subsidies and penalties, methods and institutions for managing water resources, and cost sharing (allocating benefits and costs). Emphasis has also shifted, from a focus on the economic functions produced by the water resources processes described above, to focuses of maintaining, enhancing, conserving, and preserving the quality of water and other natural resources.

5-1 OBJECTIVES OF ECONOMIC ANALYSIS

Water resources have usually been managed and allocated in the public sector. As governments have perceived specific needs for water-related services they have not hesitated to exercise their authority to provide water services. When the nation needed a better transportation system, both federal and state or local governments were active in developing navigable waterways and ports. When the nation needed more electricity, the federal government was active in developing water resources for the production of power. When many of the nation's waters became contaminated and polluted, federal and state governments began regulating effluent disposal and providing capital to improve the water quality. Such responses are indicative of the ability of political systems to respond to market-type signals to provide goods and services from water resources.

The goal of economic analysis is the understanding and prediction of human behavior in the face of scarcity. The question to be answered is that of how one manages the relative scarcities of resources and products. Economists are concerned with managing these relative scarcities for maximum long-run human advantages.

The water resources problem is basically that of the allocation of water among competing users as a resource input, and among consumers as a product, to obtain an optimum value in terms of market or welfare measures or both. There are two important effects of any activity in the economy that allocates or reallocates scarce items. These are referred to as (1) *the efficiency effect* and (2) *the equity or distribution effect.* The two effects can be identified but their precise measurement is difficult. The two effects are not necessarily complementary. Increased efficiency may not always result in the desired distribution. Involuntary redistribution often results in gross inefficiencies.

The efficiency effect refers to the size of the economic pie available (net national product or welfare) whereas the distribution effect refers to the number and size of the slices (income or wealth) accruing to each party or segment of society. Optimum economic efficiency may be defined as the allocation of resources (land, labor, capital) among competing users such that desired results (profits or sales) are maximized. Optimum economic distribution may be defined as the allocation of payments for resources such that the needed resources are retained in the desired productive activities. However, society is not always satisfied with the distribution of benefits and costs that results from an unrestrained market. Institutions are devised by society to effect redistributions through systems of transfers. These redistributions are defined in subjective terms such as "social benefits" or "social costs." The objective of economic activity is to maximize net social welfare, which includes consideration of both individual and societal benefits as well as all private and social costs.

For example, if an additional acre-foot of water used in irrigation produces a product valued at $100, and if the same marginal acre-foot of water produces a product worth $150 when used in textile finishing, then economic efficiency is increased by transfer of all or part of the marginal acre-foot of water to use in textile finishing. This is an efficiency effect. Why? In the unrestrained market the textile finisher could pay the irrigator something more than $100 but no more than $150 for the acre-foot of water. Both parties would have their positions improved through such a willing transaction, the total value of economic activity would be increased, and economic efficiency would be improved.

The final allocation of water and products produced by water between the irrigator and the textile finisher is an equity issue. If, as is sometimes the case with water resources, there is no market mechanism for the transfer of the water and some arbitrary and uncompensated assignment of the water is made to the manufacturer from the irrigator, then the reduction of income to the irrigator and the increase of income to the textile finisher is clearly an adverse distribution effect. In this case one party gains at the expense of the other. An arbitrary assignment of the water to maximize social welfare is difficult to make without knowledge of the values attached to the marginal acre-foot of water by each competitor. The economist is not usually able to make interpersonal comparisons as to the value of water or other resources. The *equimarginal principle of allocation* will indicate how an optimum allocation of resources to achieve efficiency and equity is attained in the unrestrained, competitive market. A less than competitive market in the allocation of resources and products can achieve high levels of efficiency and equity in the society at large, but components of the economy will not achieve maximum efficiency as measured by a competitive market standard.

5-2 ECONOMIC MODELS

An economic model may be defined as a device relating the desires of the consumer to the resources that can be used to satisfy these desires. Such models include demand functions for goods, services, and productive resources; production functions for goods and services; and supply functions for resources. The marketplace provides a means of transformation of various resources into goods and services and permits the delivery of products to the consumer. Desires of the consumer are transmitted through the system, and these in turn influence the outcome. All these features constitute components of economic models for water use.

Product Demand Functions

In the most elementary form, the demand function for goods and services may be represented graphically by a price-quantity relation that slopes downward to the right. This is illustrated in Figure 5-1. A study of the figure shows that in general, the lower the cost the larger will be the quantity taken by the consumer. To qualify this statement, however, it should be understood that the consumers have specified incomes, tastes, and preferences and that other competing goods and services are available. Shifts in the demand function for any particular product may result from variations in any or all of these factors.

Water is in demand for many purposes, as has already been discussed. Some of these are (1) domestic uses, (2) recreational uses, and (3) uses in the production of other products. It is expected that consumers will be willing to pay a fairly high price for water rather than go without it. In addition, to meet basic domestic needs, the demand will be relatively constant regardless of price. In other words, we are going to use a certain amount of water for cooking, washing, and maintaining health standards even if water is expensive. At the same time, we are not going to use much more water than we really need no matter how cheap the water is. Thus

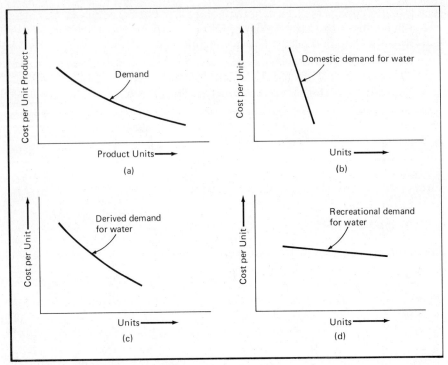

Figure 5-1   Examples of supply and demand curves.

the price-quantity relation for domestic use is very steep and approaches the vertical (Figure 5-1b). The demand for products derived from water may not be so steep, particularly if the products are luxury items or if the products can be substituted for (Figure 5-1c). Evidence indicates that the price-quantity relation for recreational water use may have a relatively flat slope. This can be explained in part by the fact that if water recreation costs become too high, other forms of recreation will be substituted.

It is likely that the demand functions engineers and planners will encounter are more complex than the simple cases outlined here. This is because of variations in such factors as income, personal preferences, and the relations of other products and their prices. In a more complex sense, the demand function for water is represented by an n-dimensional demand surface that takes into consideration many variables.

Production Functions

In general, the development of useful products depends on the combination of various resources through the utilization of certain production techniques. For example, the development of a specified head for power production may require the construction of a dam and other engineering works, all of which represent a resource input to obtain a product output. Agricultural production functions include water, technology, land, labor, capital, and other items among the factors of production.

Water is an independent and productive resource that has economic utility in both industry and agriculture. Thus it can be employed at a greater than zero price. It is also well established that production techniques are subject to change, which implies that additional products can be obtained using the same inputs. The difficulty is that it is usually not possible to predict accurately what the future will bring in the field of technological improvement. Nevertheless, it can be stated that products of the past can be employed in developing new techniques through research. Thus the proper management of resources can lead to capital creation, which in turn will produce useful products and new techniques.

A study of the production processes that include water as an input will serve as the basis for allocating the water resource among alternative uses. To illustrate this, consider that a specific allocation of irrigation water can be used to produce a variety of crops. On a given land area and with a defined growing season, the farmer cannot hope to raise every type of crop that could possibly be raised on his land. He must make a decision based on the net payment he can expect to receive from the final product. In other words, he should choose some combination of crops so that he will obtain the maximum return from his available resources. Product prices may be obtained from demand functions.

The farmer establishes demand functions for the resources (including water) he must use to produce his crops. These demand functions are based on the alternatives of production he can choose among and the consumer's alternative demand functions. The demand function for water or any other resource is also a price-quantity relation. For agricultural water use this is generally a curve that slopes downward to the right. Figure 5-1c is somewhat representative. In general, the farmer will take larger quantities of water as the price is lowered, but the amount he can use may be limited by the number of acres he can farm or other restrictions.

If the farmer desires to maximize his profits, he will commit water to his production process until the cost of the final unit of water added is equal to the value of the product that is produced by this last unit of water. Mathematically this may be stated as

$$\frac{\partial (PF)}{\partial R}(P_P) = P_R \tag{5-1}$$

where PF = production function
   R = resource
   P_P = price of the product
   P_R = price of the resource

By equating these values for all the products he produces, the farmer can make allocation of water among the several alternatives indicated as profitable by consumer-demand information. Thus, production methods and consumer demands play an important role in influencing the allocation or use of resources such as water.

It will take but little imagination for the reader to see that the relative value of water resources for use in various ways is strikingly affected by consumer desires.

Resource-Supply Functions

The resource-supply function may be defined as the quantity of resource made available per unit time as a function of the price per unit of resource. Figure 5-2 illustrates a typical price-quantity relation for resource supply. In general, this relation indicates that if the price for a given resource is high, the resource supplier will be willing to deliver a large quantity.

In the case of water resources, additional quantities can be made available through storage, development of well fields, diversions, and so on if the price is right. Of course, other factors (political, social, health) may also influence the resource supply. Whenever money must be spent to develop water resources, the development costs must be carefully considered in the economic decision-making process regarding the degree, mode of development, and allocation of the water resource.

For the rational allocation of water resources among numerous alternatives, information on demand, production, and resource supply must be had. Unfortunately, information of this type is often not available and in many instances it cannot be accurately determined. If water supplies are plentiful in relation to demands, the cost of water may be low. On the other hand, in regions of short supply, high prices might be paid to satisfy various water requirements. For a given supply, as demands increase, water users such as industries, which can afford to pay more per unit volume of water than agriculture, for example, may transfer additional increments of the available supply to themselves while agricultural pro-

Figure 5-2   Resource-supply function.

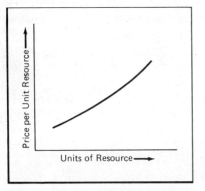

duction declines. Theoretically, under the ordinary market-price system, water can be readily transferred from low-value uses to high-value uses. Again, political pressures or legal restrictions may significantly influence the process.

5-3 INVESTMENT CONCEPTS

A subpart of economic analyses is investment analysis. In this special case, the analyst's main objective is the allocation of resources over time. This temporal allocation also affects the distribution of benefits and costs over time. In the simplest case, investment analysis allocates resources between present consumption and future consumption. In the most primitive society one can imagine that all allocation is in the present, when consumption is direct and there is no deferral of present consumption to the future. When the concept of storage for future consumption evolves, the storage facility then requires capital investment or abstention from current consumption in order to construct the storage facility. As society becomes more complex and the parties who consume are different from the parties who save and/or invest, the issue of compensation to those who defer present consumption becomes relevant. At what rate should savers (that is, those who abstain from present consumption) and investors (those who use such savings to create future products for consumption) be compensated by those who will be consuming in the future?

These concepts are also related to the economic differentiation between a fixed investment cost and a variable or operating cost. The appropriate rate of compensation for savers or investors can be most accurately described as the discount rate.

Discount Rate Theories and Interest Rates

The appropriate *discount rate* is defined as that rate at the margin that is just sufficient to equate the demand for investment capital with the supply of savings or abstention from current consumption. The use of resources for current consumption (a reduction of savings) is described as the demand for liquidity. The function of the discount rate is to allocate resources among sectors of the economy over the long term and to allocate rationed capital to the most efficient projects in the short term.

There is no single discount rate that prevails in a market economy, just as there is no single predetermined correct price for wheat. The issue of an appropriate discount rate is sufficiently complex and controversial with respect to water resources projects that we must consider in concept three levels of discount rates, any one of which may be preferred by various groups for different reasons. These concepts also describe our view of *time preference* with respect to both the private sector and the public sector as well as the relations between the two sectors.

Time preference is the choice people make with respect to current consumption v. future consumption. The discount rate measures these preferences along with other considerations. There are three concepts of discount rates that affect the selection of the appropriate discount rate level. These include (1) the social time preference, (2) the market rates of interest (costs of funds), and (3) the opportunity cost of capital. Each of these concepts involves several distinctions depending on the sources of funds and the uses intended as well as the special conditions that affect the net values of either.

It is necessary to differentiate between discount rate theories as they apply to the discount rate levels and the actual capital market allocating mechanisms. The latter we refer to as the interest rate and define this specifically as the price of money or capital. The distinction serves mostly as an expository device. The prices of money, or interest rates, are the prevailing rates on the specific instruments or transactions that allocate the savings of consumers to the investors, normally through financial intermediaries in the capital markets. There is always the tendency toward equilibrium between savings (the supply of money) and investments (the demand for money) as registered through prevailing interest rates.

All investment decisions in the private sector are based on anticipated demands for products or services for future consumption, and it is this expected rate of return that influences or limits the prevailing interest rate. No investor would pay more for investment capital than the expected rate of return from the investment, adjusted for prevailing risks and uncertainty estimates.

SOCIAL TIME PREFERENCE

The *social discount rate* is not likely to be an interest rate, although it may be very near in some cases. The social time preference rate can be specifically defined as that rate of discount that is completely free of all risk and uncertainty considerations. It is the pure rate of discount that equates the preference of consumers for present consumption to that of future consumption. By the strictest definition, the social time preference would prevail only in an economy of stable prices and economic conditions in which there is no expectation of changes in the value of goods and services to be purchased for a given sum in the future and in which the cost of capital transactions (that is, the matching of savers with investors) is zero. One can argue successfully that in modern society there does exist a social rate of discount or a social time preference composed of the aggregate willingness of consumers to defer some consumption to the future. This social discount rate is the lowest real discount rate that might exist.

In the mind's eye of those who argue the appropriate levels of discount rates, the social discount rate would be in the range of 2 to 4 percent per annum. The interest rate that most nearly approximates the social discount rate would be the rate on long-term government bonds of small denominations sold directly to savers when there is no expectation of either inflation or deflation and the public has a very high level of confidence in the stability of the government's economic policies.

In the business of planning water resources projects, the social time preference rate of discount has been the prevailing concept applied. This social rate of discount for planning has been justified as the appropriate rate over a half-century. It equated the interest rate of long-term government savings instruments with the concept of the social discount rate in an environment of price stability and a prevailing public attitude that assigned heavy emphasis to improving social welfare through the public sector. In this case it has been alleged that the government should invest in water resources development projects at the social discount rate, partly out of concern for the welfare of future generations. Occasionally, the discount rate was represented as risk-free to the government on the basis that all government funds for the nation were pooled and thus individual projects were not subject to the same risk and uncertainty of unexpected outcomes as they might be in the private sector.

COST OF FUNDS THEORY

The cost of funds theory supports the concept that the appropriate discount rate is the "market rate" of interest, defined as the cost of borrowing to finance the investment. The market rate of interest always reflects expectations for price instability (inflation and deflation) as well as the risk and uncertainty of estimated benefits and costs. Market rates are affected by the prevailing incentives and penalties related to taxing policies and regulations on capital. Such constraints create many different market rates of interest as found in the different instruments used. There are short-term and long-term bonds or bonds v. equity instruments. The rates of each depend on whether the instruments are issued by the private sector or the public sector and whether special tax treatments are given the various credit instruments.

There are two general categories of market rates of interest that are advocated for use as the planning discount rate for water resources projects. One is the cost of government borrowing and the other is the cost of private sector borrowing. The correct discount rate to use would be the government long-term bond rate for government projects and either long-term corporate bond yields or the prime rate (short term) for privately financed projects. These rates would reflect, respectively, the risks to each sector. Even the government borrowing rate will vary between federal government v. state and local governments, and for all three, the terms and conditions will affect the rates.

The short-term cost of federal government borrowing is reflected by current treasury bill rates whereas the long-term cost is reflected by long-term government bonds (maturities in excess of 15 years). Some would argue that since most government revenue comes from general taxes the use of bond rates is not appropriate as a discount rate. However, when government depends on borrowed funds for its operations and investments, one must advocate a discount rate at least equal to the long-term government borrowing cost to reflect some of the forgone opportunities for the use of capital.

The private cost of funds rate may be adopted as the appropriate discount rate. The private cost of borrowing is approximated by the current yields on corporate bonds. For water resources projects this yield is for long-term bonds because of the long-term nature of water resources projects. If the private sector cost of funds is used for public projects, then private projects would be in a more competitive situation with respect to capital markets since there would be no financial advantage to users from government construction. Private sector cost of funds is more appropriate for the discount rate in planning privately financed projects whereas the government cost of funds rate is more appropriate for public water resources projects when one assumes that the projects are in a different risk category.

If we are trying to establish an acceptable discount rate, tax considerations that affect yields of investors should not be considered. This means that either the government or the private sector cost of funds before tax adjustments should be used. The cost of funds discount rate, for either public or private projects, greatly improves efficiency in the allocation of capital resources both within project selection processes and between water projects and other investments.

OPPORTUNITY COST OF CAPITAL

The opportunity cost of capital is defined as the return that funds would yield if invested in those projects with the highest available yields. Under conditions of limited capital, *the opportunity cost of capital discount rate* will always be higher than the social discount rate or the cost of funds discount rate. When this discount rate is used, the implication is that both public and private water resources projects will compete equally with all other available investment for capital resources. This approach would ensure that water resources projects would only be built when their economic efficiency and/or financial efficiency were highest among all projects or at least equal to alternative investment opportunities. Theoretically, one could use the opportunity cost of government capital in public projects and the opportunity cost of capital in private sector alternatives for privately financed projects.

In practice, there is no acceptable measure of the opportunity cost of capital for alternative government projects or programs. This leaves the calculation of the opportunity cost of capital as an estimate derived from the private sector, which does know reasonably well its opportunity costs. Possibly the lowest readily available estimate of the cost of capital is the after-tax profits on stockholder equity. Substantial premiums for inflation and risk have been included in this rate. However, in the private sector the opportunity cost of capital is considerably higher than the return on stockholder equity, before or after taxes. Under conditions of rationed capital most private sector firms have substantial alternative investment opportunities at rates several percentage points above the market rates of interest. This level of discount rate would be the most economically effi-cient discount rate to use and it would ensure that only the most produc-tive water resources projects would be constructed by either the public or the private sector. It would mean also that fewer water resource proj-ects would be built since project construction decisions would be based on much higher discount rates.

Many privately owned power companies, irrigation districts, and municipalities invest in water resources projects and compete for private capital. They do consider the opportunity cost of alternative water re-sources projects as well as alternative investment opportunities. In most cases, public utilities are concerned only with alternative methods of achieving their needs, such as power generation or water supply, at the lowest capital cost because their responsibilities for these services are part of their franchise, that is, they are not free to choose to invest only for maximum returns.

APPLICATIONS TO WATER RESOURCE PROJECTS

Application of a discount rate that is too low results in overbuilding or overinvestment in those projects vis-à-vis other, more efficient, projects in which appropriate discount rates are applied. It is important to use a discount rate that is competitive in the industry for all project design work in which different sizes of projects and different lengths of project life exist. Comparisons of project design, the mix of purposes, and project scale cannot be made in the absence of an appropriate discount rate. The discount rate is the mechanism that equates these differences to a com-mon denominator of present value.

At the policy level, the choice of the appropriate discount rate will depend heavily on the prevailing views of the social value of water re-sources projects or the prevailing perceived value of investing current resources for future goods and services. The question now is, How much and in what types of projects should we invest for posterity?

Historically, water resources projects have been evaluated and com-pared in the planning process on the basis of discount rates approximating the social time preference rates. It should be noted that these discount rates are for planning purposes only and are useful only for comparing similar types of projects, that is, the federal government investment port-folio, which will be constructed from funds budgeted for this purpose on a political basis. All projects that are being considered for construction out of the same capital pool should be evaluated at the same discount rate. Some economists include premiums or discounts to account for variations in risk and uncertainty. This adjustment is not inappropriate although other, more explicit risk adjustment methods are available.

There have been continuous pressures since the 1950s for upward adjustments in water resources project discount rates toward at least the market rate of interest, obstensibly to achieve greater efficiency in the use of government funds. Some adjustments have been made by the adoption of various formulas that tie the water resources discount rate for planning to yields on government securities. The current method specified in the U.S. Water Resources Council's operating procedure (P.L. 93-254) requires the secretary of the treasury to calculate the current discount rate annually on the basis of the average yield during the preceding fiscal year on interest-bearing marketable securities of the United States that have terms of maturity remaining in excess of 15 years. However, there is a limit of one-fourth of one percent per year on the change in the discount rate, regardless of the calculated rate. The official water resources planning discount rate in 1982 was 7.625 percent.

Financial Analyses

In this chapter we shall consider financial analyses to include a simplified cash flow analysis based on the use of discounting techniques. The methods of cash flow analysis and discounting are then used in benefit-cost analyses. Most investment decisions involve multiple time periods that are not a part of a standard economic analysis based on supply and demand theory. Financial analyses are more closely related to the long-run considerations discussed in economic theory rather than to the short-run maximum profit model. We consider that capital is the limiting factor and that the goal is to maximize the rate of return to capital, not necessarily to maximize net profits, a short-term concept. However, profits are important to the extent that they provide the funds necessary to amortize investments.

In the public sector this amortization normally takes the form of cost recovery. A basic assumption in financing is that an investment will be made in a current period with the expectation that revenues in the future will be sufficient to recover the cost at a positive rate of interest at least equal to the cost of borrowing funds or to the alternative opportunities. The revenues flowing from this investment will occur in the future and are at best expectations based on the best information available to the analyst. These expectations of future returns involve elements of risk and uncertainty. Also, most investment projects, including water resources projects, have a specific life history in which they are constructed, operated at various levels of intensity, and eventually decline in usefulness either through wearing out of the assets or obsolescence or both. Also, during the operating life of the investment, costs will be incurred to operate and maintain the project. In investment analyses we are concerned with the issue of measuring the performance of a project over time when investment capital is to be committed to a long-life project.

MEASURING PERFORMANCE OF CAPITAL INVESTMENTS

There are four types of criteria for measuring performance of capital investments in either the private or the public sector. These are stated in terms of objectives: (1) maximize average return on average investment, (2) minimize payback period, (3) maximize present value, and (4) maximize internal rate of return.

The first two criteria are unsuitable for multiple-period analysis of water resources projects, and thus we turn our attention to the two acceptable methods that have the advantage of considering, on an equivalent basis, all differences of time that result from uneven flows of either costs or revenues. Furthermore, the use of a discount rate in the net present value and internal rate of return criteria enables the analyst to use the discount rate to adjust for differences in risk. We shall consider both the present value and the internal rate of return together.

The *net present value method* discounts each annual payoff (net profit) by the selected discount rate and accumulates the discounted present value for a net present value estimate. There are three possible methods of calculation, depending on whether the annual payoff value is different from year to year, whether it is equal in all years, or whether the equal periodic payoff extends to infinity. The net present value methods provide a result equivalent to subtracting all discounted costs from the discounted stream of income. The present value calculation can be converted directly into a benefit-cost ratio.

The internal rate of return is the rate of discount that makes the present value of a stream of income less its cost equal to zero. It is a statement of expected yield over the life of a project. It is a single valued estimate in which investments can be compared with each other and selected on the basis of the maximum internal rate of return or on the basis of investing in those projects that yield an internal rate of return above some minimum cutoff point.

The net present value method provides net dollar amounts expected from the investment at the selected discount rate. The present value (V_0) of a stream of payoffs (income, profits) $P_1, \ldots, P_r$ is defined as

$$V_0 = \frac{P_1}{(1 + r)} + \frac{P_2}{(1 + r)^2} + \cdots + \frac{P_r}{(1 + r)^n} \qquad (5\text{-}2)$$

For example, if P_1 and P_2 are $100 each and the discount rate r is 5 percent:

$$\begin{aligned} V_0 &= \frac{\$100}{(1.05)} + \frac{\$100}{(1.05)^2} \\ &= \$95.24 + \$90.70 \\ &= \$185.94 \end{aligned}$$

When the payoffs are equal in each period or recalculated as an annual average, the net present value calculation may be simplified to

$$V_0 = P_a \left[\frac{1}{(1 + r)} + \frac{1}{(1 + r)^2} + \dots + \frac{1}{(1 + r)^n} \right] \qquad (5\text{-}3)$$
$$= \$100(0.9524 + 0.9070)$$
$$= \$100(1.8594)$$
$$= \$185.94$$

Note that the value 1.8594 is a discount factor commonly found in prepared financial or discount tables to include both time and discount rate considerations for an annuity of two years at 5 percent. For perspective, the present value of this payoff at 5 percent for 50 years is $1825.59.

5-4   BENEFIT-COST ANALYSIS

The objective of a water-resources system design is to select that combination of variables which will maximize the net benefits resulting from the system in accordance with imposed design criterion. For a single-purpose project that is not dependent economically or physically on any other project, this can be accomplished in a relatively simple and straightforward manner. In this case, calculations of benefits minus costs can be used to indicate the degree of project development that will produce the largest net benefit. For independent multiple-purpose projects a net benefit surface must be defined. If two uses are dominant, the response surface will be of the form indicated in Figure 5-3. For n uses, an $(n + 1)$-dimensional space results, and detailed operations studies for each proposed system must be conducted.

Unfortunately, it is often difficult to estimate the benefits and costs (especially the benefits) expected from either private or public investments in water resources projects and programs. A part of this difficulty stems from the fact that much of the effort and methodology has been

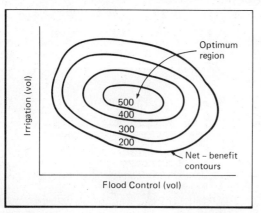

Figure 5-3   Net response surface for an independent multiple-purpose project.

developed with some bias toward the justification of project expenditures. The technical issues of benefit estimation are often clouded by agency requirements and rules that mandate specific procedures for expediency or consistency or some other reason not related to economic theory or practice.

Externalities

In many production and policy situations involving water resources there are certain social costs and benefits that occur outside the market mechanisms previously described, both competitive and monopolistic. These are defined as nonmarket benefits and costs when such values are not reflected in market prices. Some nonmarket benefits (positive externalities) from investments in water resources, such as recreation or enhanced water quality or flood control, accrue to society at large or to those who will not pay voluntarily. Normally, they cannot be excluded because of the public-good nature of the benefit. Policies are often developed by governments to internalize the external benefit through systems of user charges or tax assessments that are not necessarily scaled proportionately to those who benefit in the same sense as they would be for market goods.

There are also *external* or *nonmarket costs* such as pollution from waste disposal that are not included in the prices of goods and services marketed from the polluting production. In the case of external costs (negative externalities) the most pervasive is pollution. There are many schemes available to internalize these costs in a way so as to achieve a higher level of economic efficiency and to reduce distributional inequities. Some of these methods include direct regulation through either stream standards or effluent standards, effluent charges, and abatement subsidies. As one might expect, it is difficult but not impossible to estimate the approximate private values of social costs and benefits and to identify the parties who incur the costs or reap the benefits. However, this exercise is a major element of the economic analyses of water resources projects and programs, so much so that the fate of both private and public sector projects is determined by the credibility of the benefit-cost estimates.

Methods of Measuring Benefits and Costs

MARKET OBSERVATIONS

Benefits and costs may be measured as the *net market value* of changes in the quantities of outputs and inputs. Observed or adjusted market prices of goods and services are multiplied by the changes in outputs to obtain gross benefits. The cost of additional inputs associated with the change in outputs that results from the project provides an estimate of total benefits which permits estimation of net benefits.

Market prices are assumed to be competitive when the increases or decreases with the project are very small relative to the total market. Production relations must be known so that costs of factors and best-output combinations can be estimated. The use of market observations is the preferred method of measuring benefits and costs when such data are available.

COST OF THE LEAST-COST ALTERNATIVE

Benefits may also be measured in terms of the cost of the least-cost alternative. Since a proposed project would result in a loss of some goods and services presently enjoyed, this technique uses market data to estimate the cost of providing the same goods and services by the least-cost alternative means. The necessary assumptions are that (1) sufficient economic and technological information exists to identify a least-cost alternative, (2) market prices and production relations pertinent to a least-cost alternative are observed and competitive, and (3) if goods and services are made available by a least-cost alternative, demand must be sufficient to cover real cost.

MARKET SURROGATES

Where observed market prices are nonexistent or inadequate to provide a reliable guide to economic value, other valuation methods that are based on signals from potential consumers may be used as market surrogates. These are inferential methods with which economists attempt to use market-generated data about the demand for related goods and services to infer the value of nonmarket goods and services. For many kinds of nonmarket goods, no suitable market data have been identified, and in many cases where a data base has been identified, the necessary analytical assumptions are violated. These techniques use a market-generated data base rather than a hypothetical data base. For example, benefits may be measured as *gross willingness to spend.* This is known also as the *travel cost method.* Expenditures on access and travel to recreation sites provide evidence of the revealed demand for recreation opportunities. Travel cost is a function of distance from a residence to a site. An increase in travel cost or access is assumed to have the same effect on use as an increase in price or cost of a market service.

Techniques of Benefit-Cost Analysis

The technical aspects of benefit-cost analysis are generally specified in the operating handbooks of the agencies charged with the responsibility for project evaluation. These agencies are guided in principle by a series of historical documents that have contributed to or modified their handbook procedures. These began with the Flood Control Act of 1936, P.L. 74-738 (2). Significant benchmarks have included "Proposed Practices for Economic Analysis for River Basin Projects," popularly known as the "Green

Book" (3); "Policies, Standards, and Procedures in the Formulation, Evaluation, and Review of Plans for Use and Development of Water and Related Land Resources," popularly known as "Senate Document 97" (12); and "Water and Related Land Resources: Establishment of Principles and Standards for Planning," usually referred to as "the Principles and Standards" (13).

Traditionally, project costs have followed accounting procedures in which only the resources used were included in the cost estimates. Such cost estimates are based on project design and associated engineering costs to include lands, easements, and rights-of-way, construction of all facilities, general expenses, and contingencies. Economists generally recommend that interest during construction be added either to the total estimated project cost during the construction period or progressively as construction is completed. Costs should also be adjusted for changes in the general price levels of resources that are expected to occur during the construction period. In addition to these construction or implementation costs, estimates must be made of the annual operating maintenance and replacement costs (OM&R) that will be required to operate the project at its design capacity.

A typical cost tabulation for a multiple-purpose small watershed-type project is given in Table 5-1. The reader should note that there are two major categories of costs. The first category, capital costs (also referred to as implementation, construction, or sometimes as initial costs), is approximately the same as "fixed" costs in financial and economic analyses. The second category, operating costs, is the OM&R. These costs are approximately equivalent to the "variable" costs in economics. There is a category of annual fixed costs, that is, those OM&R costs that do not vary with the level of output.

Conventional presentations organize implementation costs on the basis of present values of costs expected at the time of project completion. OM&R costs are usually presented on an average annual basis, as estimated from previous project experiences or rules of thumb. The reader can easily convert implementation costs to an annual basis or annual costs to a capitalized basis using standard discount factors. In all cases, the benefit-cost analysis must be completed on the basis of comparable costs, either capitalized or annualized, for a complete presentation.

Benefits in a multiple-purpose project are estimated one by one, using one of the methodologies previously described or some variation thereof. Most benefit measurements are based on some measure of consumer willingness to pay. The first priority for the economist is to estimate the primary or direct benefits, that is, the outputs produced by an investment in the water resources project. The primary benefits attributable to a project are equal to the total primary benefits less any costs associated with the production of project goods and services but not included in the direct cost of resources used in the project itself.

Table 5-1 COSTS ASSOCIATED WITH A TYPICAL MULTIPLE-PURPOSE
PROJECT (DISCOUNT RATE, 3⅛ PERCENT; PROJECT LIFE, 50 YEARS)

RESOURCE USED OR OPERATING ACTIVITY	PRESENT VALUE (MIL. $)	ANNUAL VALUE (1000 $)
IMPLEMENTATION		
Land and easements	4.517	
Reservoir construction	7.364	
Dam and spillway	4.723	
Channel clearing	1.787	
Total direct costs	18.391	
Overhead and contingency	5.609	
Interest during construction	0.900	
Total implementation costs	24.900	816.4
OPERATION AND MAINTENANCE		
Upkeep of dams and reservoir		20.0
Channel maintenance		17.0
Silt removal (5-year intervals)		13.0
Administrative expense		10.0
Total OM&R costs	1.830	60.0
PROJECT COMPOSITE COSTS	26.730	876.4

Historically, secondary benefits and costs have been included in economic analyses. These secondary benefits and costs are values of goods and services over and above the values of immediate inputs or outputs associated with the project. Because these are second-round benefits or costs that would not be particularly different for other kinds of investment, such as that from the private sector, they should not be considered in project economic analysis. The correct economic analysis would include only direct project costs and direct project benefits as well as associated costs and benefits. No secondary benefits should be considered in a project evaluation unless it can be shown that the secondary benefits would not accrue in the absence of the specific water resources project. In most cases, efforts to include secondary benefits in project analyses result in substantial double counting such that the credibility of the economic analysis is reduced by their inclusion. In most economic analyses, including those made for the public sector, the primary benefits and costs plus the due consideration of externalities are sufficient to judge the viability of a project, especially in the prevailing conditions of scarcity of capital.

The benefits by functional purposes for a typical small, multiple-purpose watershed project are shown in Table 5-2. The benefits are presented

Table 5-2 BENEFIT ESTIMATES FOR A TYPICAL SMALL WATERSHED
PROJECT (DISCOUNT RATE, 3⅛ PERCENT; PROJECT LIFE, 50 YEARS)

BENEFIT DESCRIPTION	PRESENT VALUE (MIL. $)	ANNUAL VALUE (1000 $)
Flood reduction		
Agriculture	11.219	368.0
System	2.460	80.6
Roads and bridges	0.305	10.0
Subtotal	13.984	458.6
General recreation	6.151	102.75
Hydropower generation	NA	NA
Fish and wildlife enhancement	3.278	107.6
Navigation	NA	NA
Redevelopment	3.800	114.0
Water Supply		
Irrigation	NA	NA
M&I	2.200	66.0
Water quality control	0.467	15.3
Shoreline development	4.795	143.85
Total direct benefits	$34.675 = B_0$	$1107.1 = B_a$
Less OM&R costs	$1.830 = OMR_0$	$60.0 = OMR_a$
Operating benefits	$32.845 = OB_0$	$1047.1 = OB_a$
Less amortized capital	$24.900 = C_0$	$816.4 = C_a$
Net project benefits	$7.945 = NB_0$	$230.7 = NB_a$

in official documents as average annual values. It is not difficult to capital-
ize the annual values to compare benefits with costs in either annualized
or capitalized values. In the given example, total direct benefits are
summed for each project output and the operating maintenance and
repair costs are subtracted to provide an estimate of operating benefits.
When the amortized capital costs are subtracted, the net project benefits
are generated. The net project benefits are the most effective measure of
an efficient use of economic resources. In this case, the benefits minus costs
(the net benefit criterion) should be maximized to determine the proper
scale of the project and to rank each project with all others in the selection
process. This maximum net benefit criterion is superior to all other methods of benefit-cost comparison such as the benefit-cost ratio or the internal
rate of return.

An example will serve to illustrate the application of benefit-cost data
in analyzing a water resources project.

Example 5-1

A flood control district can construct several alternative control works to
alleviate flooding. These alternatives include the construction of dam

A, dam B, and a system of levees C. Each of these works can be built to function alone or together with any other or all other projects. Thus we have a possibility of the following combinations: ABC, A, B, C, AB, AC, and BC. The life of each dam is considered to be 80 years and the life of the levee system is expected to be 60 years. The cost of capital is 4 percent. Information on total investment, operating and maintenance costs, and average annual flood damages is given in Table 5-3. Which flood control undertaking would be the most economical?

SOLUTION

1. Compute the average annual investment charges for each project by using the capital recovery factors of Table 5-4 with the appropriate structure life and interest rate. Note that the appropriate factor to convert an investment into an equivalent annual cost is designated as the capital recovery factor (CRF). It may be computed from the expression $i(1 + i)^N/[(1 + i)^N - 1]$, where i is the interest rate per year (expressed as a decimal fraction) and N represents the years of estimated life. When a present sum of money is multiplied by the capital recovery factor for N years and interest rate i, the product is an annual figure sufficient to repay exactly the present sum in N years with interest rate i. The CRF is often given as the ratio of an annual payment to the present worth.

   For dam A = 6,000,000 × 0.04181 = \$251,000/yr
   For dam B = 5,000,000 × 0.04181 = \$209,000/yr
   For levees C = 6,000,000 × 0.04420 = \$265,000/yr
   For AB = \$460,000/yr
   For AC = \$516,000/yr
   For BC = \$474,000/yr
   For ABC = \$725,000/yr

2. To these values, add annual operating and maintenance costs to yield total annual costs.

Table 5-3 FLOOD CONTROL PROJECT DATA

PROJECT	TOTAL INVESTMENT (\$)	ANNUAL OPERATION AND MAINTENANCE (\$)	AVERAGE ANNUAL FLOOD DAMAGES (\$)
Reservoir A	\$ 6,000,000	\$ 90,000	\$1,100,000
Reservoir B	5,000,000	80,000	1,300,000
Levees C	6,000,000	100,000	700,000
Combination AB	11,000,000	170,000	900,000
Combination AC	10,000,000	190,000	400,000
Combination BC	9,000,000	180,000	500,000
Combination ABC	15,000,000	270,000	250,000
No control at all	0	0	2,000,000

Table 5-4 CAPITAL RECOVERY FACTORS (CRF) FOR VARIOUS PROJECT LIVES AND INTEREST RATES

YEARS OF LIFE	INTEREST RATE (%)							
	0	2	3	4	5	6	8	10
5	0.20000	0.21216	0.21835	0.22463	0.23097	0.23740	0.25046	0.26380
10	0.10000	0.11133	0.11723	0.12329	0.12950	0.13587	0.14903	0.16275
15	0.06667	0.07783	0.08377	0.08994	0.09634	0.10296	0.11683	0.13147
20	0.05000	0.06116	0.06722	0.07354	0.08024	0.08718	0.10185	0.11746
25	0.04000	0.05122	0.05743	0.06401	0.07095	0.07823	0.09368	0.11017
30	0.03333	0.04465	0.05102	0.05783	0.06505	0.07265	0.08883	0.10608
35	0.02857	0.04000	0.04654	0.05358	0.06107	0.06897	0.08580	0.10369
40	0.02500	0.03656	0.04326	0.05052	0.05828	0.06646	0.08386	0.10226
50	0.02000	0.03182	0.03887	0.04655	0.05478	0.06344	0.08174	0.10086
60	0.01667	0.02877	0.03613	0.04420	0.05283	0.06188	0.08080	0.10033
80	0.01250	0.02516	0.03311	0.04181	0.05103	0.06057	0.08017	0.10005
100	0.01000	0.02320	0.03165	0.04081	0.05038	0.06018	0.08004	0.10001

$$A = \$341,000/\text{yr}$$
$$B = \$289,000/\text{yr}$$
$$C = \$365,000/\text{yr}$$
$$AB = \$630,000/\text{yr}$$
$$AC = \$706,000/\text{yr}$$
$$BC = \$654,000/\text{yr}$$
$$ABC = \$995,000/\text{yr}$$

3. Find the annual benefits for each type of project by subtracting average annual flood damages (Table 5-3) from $2,000,000.
4. Tabulate the information in (2) and (3) in the form shown in Table 5-5 and compute benefit-cost ratios and benefits minus costs for each type of project.

The most economical design is selected from Table 5-5 as the one in which the greatest excess of benefits over costs is displayed. In this case, the system of levees alone would be selected for construction. Note that if the cost of capital were increased to 8 percent, the benefits minus costs would be as shown in column 6. Project C would still be selected, but observe that project AB now shows little positive net benefits and a further increase in discount rate would completely rule out some projects. At 10 percent, for example, project AB would have costs exceeding benefits by $170,000. ■

5-5 FINANCING WATER PROJECTS AND PROGRAMS

Every water project and program must be paid for, and often it is the ability or inability of the sponsoring government, industry, or other agency to secure the needed funds that spells the difference between realization of the proposed action and failure. Thus it is important that some aspects of financing be considered here.

Table 5-5 BENEFIT-COST ANALYSIS FOR EXAMPLE 5-1

(1) PROJECT	(2) ANNUAL BENEFITS ($)	(3) ANNUAL COSTS ($) FOR COST OF CAPITAL = 4%	(4) BENEFIT-COST RATIO FOR COST OF CAPITAL = 4%	(5) BENEFITS MINUS COSTS FOR COST OF CAPITAL = 4%	(6) BENEFITS MINUS COSTS FOR COST OF CAPITAL = 8%
A	$ 900,000	$ 341,000	2.64	$ 559,000	$ 328,980
B	700,000	289,000	2.42	411,000	219,150
C	1,300,000	365,000	3.56	935,000[a]	715,200[a]
AB	1,100,000	630,000	1.75	470,000	48,130
AC	1,600,000	706,000	2.27	894,000	444,180
BC	1,500,000	654,000	2.29	846,000	434,350
ABC	1,750,000	995,000	1.76	755,000	113,330

[a]Optimum design.

Federal Financing

In the past, most major water resources projects were financed heavily by the federal government. Many water projects were considered to be in the national interest and it was believed that taxpayers at large should share in the costs associated with their development. This practice often favored specific localities in terms of their receipt of federal dollars and was responsible for the assignment of the "pork barrel" label to many construction activities of the federal water agencies. The justification for federal involvement in water resources programs and projects can be summarized as follows (14):

1. Meeting national priorities, either constitutionally specified or jointly agreed on by federal and nonfederal interests
2. Providing and allocating public goods or services associated with water development
3. Providing reservations for the future
4. Providing a response to emergency and critical needs

The federal government's participation in water project financing has mostly been motivated by national priorities that shift continuously with time. Over the years, the focus has included navigation, irrigation, flood control, water quality improvement, and other areas. The extent of the federal involvement has also varied from almost total to slight, although historically the federal government has picked up most of the tab. Very significant differences exist among repayment arrangements for federal water projects. On a national average, the estimated effective composite nonfederal cost share is about 30 percent of the total cost of the federal and federally assisted water and related land programs. Recent trends are to increase the nonfederal share of project costs with the general philosophy tending toward the principle of "user pays the costs."

State and Local Government Financing

Most water resources financing lies within the jurisdictions of state and local governments and of special districts. Exclusive of federal aid in the form of grants and revenue sharing, the major mechanisms of state and local financing are current revenues and proceeds derived from assuming a debt obligation. At the state level, current revenues consist mostly of taxes generated through sales, licensing, and individual and corporate income and property assessments.

Private Sector Financing

Private sector financing in the water field is handled in generally the same manner as that in the public sector except that taxing is not included. The common instruments are selling stock, issuing bonds, drawing from retained earnings, and incurring long-term debt.

In the section that follows, on financing urban and rural water supply systems, additional details on the foregoing and other financing approaches are discussed.

Financing Urban and Rural Water Supply Systems

The financial solvency of urban and rural water supply systems has become a particularly important issue since the early 1970s. The problem is one of (1) accumulating sufficient capital to retire debts and pay for system rehabilitation, and (2) revising revenue-generating capabilities so that water supply systems can be financially self-sufficient. The challenges are to make up for past shortfalls and to establish revenue-generating measures that will ensure financial self-sufficiency. Options for generating capital for rehabilitation and retiring debts from past revenue shortfalls include selling bonds, creating special districts, establishing water banks and seeking funding from state and/or federal governments.

Many water utilities have a systemic problem of insufficient revenue-generating capabilities. They must establish means to generate sufficient income for operation and maintenance costs and for future capital needs. Water supply systems are administered by different types of authorities, including private water companies, quasi-government boards, and components of municipal services. Historically, water has been delivered at less than cost because it was considered a public good and a necessary prerequisite for economic development. The increasing cost of meeting and maintaining water quality standards required by federal regulations has added to water utilities' problems in generating sufficient revenues. Governments' costs and obligations to provide public services such as water are being reevaluated in light of fiscal restraints and greater recognition that private beneficiaries should pay a greater share of the service's cost than has historically been the case. An inevitable result is that beneficiaries of public services such as water will be expected to carry a larger share of the cost.

Various financing options may be used to deal with the infrastructure problem. Increasingly, states are favoring capital financing options other than traditional general obligation bonds, which typically require voter approval and are retired with receipts from property or other taxes. Many are examining revenue bonds or similar alternatives: mechanisms in which user charges collected over the operating life of a facility or enterprise go to pay off front-end financing. Such mechanisms are generally believed to promote sound financial management and citizen support, as does direct privatization of public works (private sector construction, ownership, and operation of a system).

States are exploring options such as tax increases with revenues dedicated to infrastructure needs (such as motor vehicle registration fees for highway work) or more comprehensive proposals. State banks to loan funds for infrastructure projects have also been considered. Monies in such banks might consist of federal aid, state appropriations, proceeds from state bonds, and possibly private capital. The National Water Symposium assembled the following recommendations relative to the urban-rural financing issue (15):

State laws should be revised to allow the use of a range of innovative financing mechanisms, including, for example, the dedication of state revenues to water infrastructure through taxes, fees, or other sources, and consideration of a state sales tax on water, with the revenues to be placed in a dedicated fund.

State laws regarding bonds should be revised to permit:

Reciprocity between states in recognizing the state income tax exempt status of funds issued by another state.

State guarantees to support municipal bond issues.

Price indexing of state bond issues.

Issuance of tax exempt bonds in smaller denominations.

Creation of state or regional authorities with bonding capacity.

Accumulation of budget surpluses from year to year to finance future costs.

Prohibition of transfer of funds from a dedicated revenue account.

Federal laws should be revised to allow for:

Elimination of the registration requirement for tax exempt bonds.

Reduction or elimination of tax exemption for bonds issued for nonpublic uses.

A National Water Bank, analogous to the National Land Bank, should be established by federal law.

Federal and state laws, where necessary, should be revised to provide for the creation of profit or nonprofit organizations or corporations for the purpose of pooling public and private funds to finance water infrastructure.

Cost Allocation, Cost Sharing, Cost Recovery

In order to enlist financial (or political) support for long-term investments in which the initial costs are the major part of the total cost, some justification is required for at least partial recovery of the cost of a project. In these cases, some method must be adopted to spread the investment costs to the various classes of beneficiaries. This issue of spreading joint costs is discussed in terms of cost allocation, cost sharing, and cost recovery, all of which are special aspects of financing water resources projects having multiple outputs. The previous economic models serve adequately for the comparison of costs, revenues, and the establishment of prices for investments that produce a single output.

The issue of cost allocation in water resources projects first arose with the Reclamation Act of 1902, but it was not until the Tennessee Valley Authority encountered similar problems with regard to the public power v. private power controversy that allocation of joint costs were taken seriously by the federal government. Although there were informal agreements among the four construction agencies to adopt a standard method of cost allocation, it was not until publication of the "Green Book" (3) in 1950 that a specific cost allocation policy was proposed. This method, known as the "separable cost–remaining benefits method" addressed only the issue of allocating joint cost, leaving open the issues of how much cost should be shared and the methods of cost recovery.

The next major development in cost allocation and cost sharing was the unpublished study by the U.S. Water Resources Council in 1975 and 1976. This study provided a basis for several congressional and presidential proposals beginning in 1976, all of which accepted the existing formulas for cost allocation but mandated specific divisions of cost between the federal government and nonfederal interests. These proposals were based on the sharing of costs on project outputs rather than on project measures or construction methods. Furthermore, these proposals would have provided for a method of joint federal and nonfederal (state) sharing of initial investment costs (financing) along with the sharing of cash flows or cash revenues generated from the vendible outputs produced by multiple-purpose projects. The extensive procedures for water and related land resources planning ("the Principles and Standards") promulgated by the WRC in 1973 adopted the basic cost allocation proposal from the Green Book without substantive change (13). In a multiple-purpose water project, for example, a reservoir, the raw material may produce several outputs (power, navigation, irrigation, and so on) among which the cost of the reservoir must be allocated for good practical reasons even if no contribution is made to economic efficiency by the allocation. Because of this dilemma, most of the cost allocation and the resultant cost-sharing practices in multiple-purpose water projects is determined politically in either an arbitrary manner or as a result of some consensus reached in a bargaining environment. It should be noted that the problem of cost allocation is an individual matter for each multiple-product manufacturing plant or for each multiple-output water resources project because of the different scales of plant and mix of outputs. General formulas would not be useful.

The decisions on allocation of costs are independent of the decisions on building or not building a project. The build decisions are based on the benefit-cost ratio, the net present value, the internal rate of return, or some other criterion. Nevertheless, the U.S. Congress has required that costs be allocated to the project purposes in order to provide some semblance of order in the recovery of cost from certain project outputs, especially those that compete with private enterprise. These outputs include electric power, irrigation water, and municipal and industrial water supplies. Costs for these outputs have been categorized as *reimbursable,* which means the full costs allocated to the particular purpose should be recovered from the beneficiaries. Other costs such as flood control, recreation, and navigation (before 1978) are often considered, at least partially, *nonreimbursable* because of their "public goods" nature. Such nonreimbursable costs are absorbed by the federal government (taxpayer) and thus do not become a part of the cost recovery process, even though the benefits are included in the economic justification. For those purposes in which full costs are recovered, one must set average revenue equal to average cost. The average total cost (fixed plus variable) cannot be determined except by some process of allocating the joint costs that may include both fixed and variable types of costs. There are three categories of cost allocation methods: (1) the proportionate use of capacity, (2) priority of use, and (3) various benefit methods. Each of these methods involves many variants depending on the type of project or program.

In addition to the issue of cost allocation, there are the companion issues of the sharing of costs and cost recovery. Traditionally, cost sharing between the federal government and nonfederal governments for flood control purposes included in federal projects would average about 20 percent in urban areas and 11 percent in rural areas for the nonfederal sponsors (13). Current policies attempt to recover about 20 percent of the federal cost of flood control for both structural and nonstructural methods from local beneficiaries. With regard to hydroelectric power, the prevailing policy is to recover the full cost—both allocated and separable cost—from the beneficiaries. This is done by charging the major power distributors a wholesale rate that is then passed on to their individual consumers. Preferences are given to municipalities, rural electric cooperatives, and other special interests such as national defense installations and irrigation projects.

Under the provisions of the Reclamation Act of 1902 and subsequent amendments, the full cost of irrigation water should be recovered from project beneficiaries. However, this allocated cost is limited to the ability of farmers to pay for these water services from customary production in the project area less allowances for minimum levels of living. The result has been an unexpected net cost recovery on a composite project basis (implementation plus OM&R costs) of about 19 percent of total allocated costs for all active project proposals in the federal inventory. Also, before 1978 local sponsors of certain navigation projects were required, by provisions in the various River and Harbors acts, to contribute the lands, easements, and rights-of-way necessary for the dredge and spoil disposal in maintaining waterways. These costs and other contributions will average about 7 percent of the total allocated costs (16). After 1978 navigation user charges were imposed on users of the inland waterways system in the form of a tax on fuel sufficient to recover the full allocated costs for inland waterways (shallow draft) navigation. It can be seen that policy decisions to declare certain costs nonreimbursable to the federal government, such as navigation and some kinds of irrigation costs, violate the concept of full cost recovery as well as the efficient and equitable allocation of resources.

The Reagan administration supported the following nonfederal levels for cost sharing on water resources projects as of 1983:

Flood control: 35 percent
Hydroelectric power: 100 percent
Municipal and industrial water: 100 percent
Recreation: 50 percent
Agricultural water: 35 percent
Beach erosion control, initial construction and periodic nourishment: 50 percent

PROBLEMS

5-1. Take the following set of data and complete a schedule for (1) physical production functions (total, average, marginal); (2) cost functions (total, average, marginal for both factor and product); (3) revenue functions (total, average, marginal for both a competitive market price of 15 cents per head of lettuce and for the industry demand schedule shown in column (3); (4) firm equilibrium positions for both the competitive and monopolistic price structures, demonstrating total revenues, total costs, and net revenues. What are the optimum levels of production and resource use under both pricing structures when water costs $40/acre-in and fixed costs are $160?

PRODUCTION FUNCTIONS, COST, AND
REVENUE RELATIONS FOR LETTUCE
PRODUCTION PER ACRE, ONE
VARIABLE INPUT

(1) ACRE-IN WATER	(2) PRODUCTION OF LETTUCE	(3) PRICE OF LETTUCE/HEAD
0	186	50¢
1	698	25
2	1185	20
3	1648	18
4	2085	17
5	2496	16
6	2883	15
7	3245	14
8	3582	13
9	3895	12
10	4181	10
11	4442	8
12	4679	6
13	4891	4

5-2. Given the following project evaluation data for a project that has an economic life ending with the fifth year:

END OF YEAR	BENEFITS	COSTS
1	$ 0	$ 10,000
2	2000	300
3	3000	400
4	4000	600
5	5000	700
6	0	0

a. Is the project economically feasible at a social discount? Why?
b. Is the project economically feasible at today's government short-term cost of borrowing? Why?
c. Is the project economically feasible at a zero discount rate? Why?
d. What is the approximate internal rate of return?
e. Would the project be economically feasible at a social discount rate if half of the benefits were from flood control and half from power generation? Why? Would it be financially feasible under these conditions?
f. Would a private power company build the project if all the benefits were from power generation? Why?
g. Is the project *financially* feasible for the government if all the costs are reimbursed at 6 percent interest on the basis of user charges collected in years 2 through 5?
h. What, in your opinion, is the appropriate discount rate for federal projects under today's economic conditions? Explain and justify.

5-3. Describe briefly the differences between a competitive market pricing system and a public utility pricing system. Be sure to note the conditions and limitations that affect each system as well as the efficiency and distribution consequences.

5-4. How would you explain the "demand for water" to a congressman based on both economic theory and empirical analyses? Should forecasts of water needs be based on this economic concept of "demand"?

5-5. Demonstrate the process of scaling the Nancy Creek watershed flood control project to optimum size to maximize net benefits. What will be the present value of net benefits. What will be the present value of net benefits at six percent discount rate and 50-year project life for the alternative selected? What will an approximate internal rate of return be for a 50-year project life for each alternative?

NANCY CREEK ALTERNATIVE MEASURES	DAMAGES	ANNUAL BENEFITS	COSTS	B/C RATIO
		--------(1000$)--------		
No improvement	1174.4	0.0	0.0	0.0
Floodproofing	579.3	594.7	369.8	1.61
Evacuation	40.0	1,134.4	929.6	1.22
Clearing and snagging	1,064.1	110.3	25.5	4.33
Modify bridges and cul.	1,022.7	151.7	57.2	2.65
Channel improvement	239.7	934.7	717.9	1.30
Floodproof and evac.	10.4	1164.0	1298.4	0.90

5-6. Economics is concerned with choices, that is, how do we make rational choices regarding the use of resources? Explain the differences and similarities between private sector decision making and public sector decision making regarding investments in natural resources projects with regard to (a) desirable (or conventional) objective(s), (b) criteria for measuring attainment of objective(s), (c) appropriate discount rates, (d) economic efficiency, (e) economic distribution, (f) environmental values, (g) pricing outputs, (h) cost allocation and cost recovery.

5-7. The town of Watkinsville has considered a series of alternative water supply systems with a 10-year expected life as follows:

TOTAL COST	ANNUAL AVERAGE REVENUES
1000	$ 150
1500	220
2000	320
2500	420
3000	505
3500	575
4000	625

If the acceptable discount rate is 8 percent, how large should the investment be based on (a) maximizing the net returns and/or (b) maximizing the benefit-cost ratio?

5-8. A flood control district can construct a number of alternative control works to alleviate the flood problem in that area. These alternatives include dam A, dam B, and a levee system C. The levee system can be built alone or in combination with dam A or B. Both dams cannot be built together but either one can function alone. The life of each dam is 80 years and the life of the levee system is 60 years. The cost of capital is 6 percent. Information on total investment, operating and maintenance costs, and average annual flood damages is given below. What form of flood control would be most economical?

PROJECT	TOTAL INVESTMENT ($)	ANNUAL OPERATION AND MAINTENANCE ($)	AVERAGE ANNUAL FLOOD DAMAGES ($)
No control at all	0	0	$2,150,000
Dam A	$6,200,000	$ 93,000	1,100,000
Dam B	5,300,000	89,000	1,400,000
Levees C	6,700,000	110,000	800,000

5-9. Solve Problem 5-8 if the cost of capital is 8 percent.

References

1. A. C. Pigou, *The Economics of Welfare*, 4th ed., Macmillan, London, 1932 (St. Martin's Press, New York, 1962).
2. *Flood Control Act of 1936*, Statutes at Large, 74th Cong., chap. 688, P.L. 74–738 and 33 USC 701, 49 Stat. 1570, Washington, D.C.

3. *Proposed Practices for Economic Analysis of River Basin Projects,* Report to Federal Interagency River Basin Committee, prepared by Subcommittee on Benefits and Costs, Washington, D.C., May 1950 (rev. May 1958).
4. J. Hirshleifer, J. C. DeHaven, and J. W. Milliman, *Water Supply Economics, Technology, and Policy,* University of Chicago Press, Chicago, 1960.
5. J. V. Krutilla and O. Eckstein, *Multiple Purpose River Development,* Johns Hopkins Press, Baltimore, 1958.
6. O. Eckstein, *Water Resource Development: The Economics of Project Evaluation,* Harvard University Press, Cambridge, 1961.
7. R. N. McKean, *Efficiency in Government Through Systems Analysis,* Wiley, New York, 1958.
8. J. Robinson, *Economic Philosophy,* Aldine, Chicago, 1962.
9. K. E. Boulding, *The Impact of the Social Sciences,* Rutgers University Press, New Brunswick, 1966.
10. I. M. D. Little, *A Critique of Welfare Economics,* Oxford University Press, London, 1960.
11. W. J. Baumol, *Welfare Economics and the Theory of the State,* 2d ed., Harvard University Press, Cambridge, 1965.
12. *Policies, Standards and Procedures in the Formulation, Evaluation, and Review of Plans for Use and Development of Water and Related Land Resources,* Senate Document 97, the President's Water Resources Council, 87th Cong., 2d sess., Washington, D.C., May 1962.
13. U.S. Water Resources Council, "Water and Related Land Resources: Establishment of Principles and Standards for Planning," *Federal Register,* pt. III, vol. 38, no. 174, pp. 24,778–824,874, Washington, D.C., September 10, 1973.
14. Federal Reserve Bank of Kansas City, *Western Water Resources: Coming Problems and the Policy Alternatives,* Westview Press, Boulder, CO, 1980.
15. "Changing Directions in Water Management," *Proc. of the National Water Symposium,* American Public Works Association, Washington, D.C., 1982.
16. Ronald M. North and Walter P. Neely, "A Model for Achieving Consistency for Cost Sharing in Water Resources Programs, *Water Resources Bull.,* vol. 13, no. 5, October 1977, pp. 995–1005.

Chapter 6
Water and the
Environment

Chapters 3, 4, 5, and 7 discuss some significant factors influencing the way our society shapes its decisions on how to develop and manage its water resources. These factors include the physical availability of water, water needs and use patterns, institutions (laws, regulations, organizations) controlling water, and the economics and financing of water management projects. This chapter examines a fifth factor that has come to be a viable force in shaping water policy and management practices in the United States over the past 20 years: the public concern over protecting its natural environment from deterioration caused by industrial, municipal, and agricultural development. Discussed briefly in this chapter are the impact of the environmental movement on water resources development, surface water and groundwater quality issues, water quantity issues, and the importance of coordinating water quality and quantity management.

6-1 IMPACT OF THE ENVIRONMENTAL MOVEMENT ON WATER RESOURCES DEVELOPMENT

National Interest in Preservation and Conservation

By the end of the 1960s, environmental causes had become a dominant force in national politics in the United States as a result of a growing, broad-based national interest in preserving natural resources and aesthetics of the environment, coupled with increased public awareness of the existence and health effects of pollution. As recounted by B. Holmes (1) the most significant events that contributed to the strong national movement to preserve the environment included:

Evidence that certain persistent insecticides (such as DDT) in soil and water tend to concentrate as they rise through the food chain, and that they have harmful effects on animals and possibly humans. Public interest in this issue was stimulated by several large fish kills culminating with a five-million fish kill on the Mississippi River in November 1963. Upon investigation, the incident was attributed to pollution of the river by the pesticide endrin.

The discovery in 1970 of dangerous concentrations of methyl mercury in United States waters from industrial waste discharges. Consumption of mercury-contaminated fish in Japan in the 1950s had demonstrated that methyl mercury was a water-soluble poison that rises in the food chain and causes brain damage in humans. As a result citizens clamored for government intervention to control industrial sources of pollution.

A growing public interest in preserving coastal beaches, estuaries, and Great Lakes bays and shorelines from further development. A steady, growing concern for the adverse effects on fish, wildlife, and water quality caused by human encroachment on these areas had begun to emerge. This was exemplified by the "Save the Bay" movement for the San Francisco Bay in the early 1960s, where citizens opposed further development of the marshland bay area for ecological reasons. From 1850 to 1957, 250 out of 300 square miles of marshland had been drained and filled for development.

The 1969 blowout of an offshore oil drilling site near Santa Barbara, California. The resulting oil spill spread over hundreds of square miles of coastal waters, covering 13 miles of beaches with oil, killing fish and wildlife, ruining beaches, and damaging the tourist industry of Santa Barbara. There had been strong local opposition to the offshore facility prior to its operation; the accident served to intensify public demands for conservation and environmental protection and caused fundamental changes in United States environmental policy in 1969 and 1970 (1).

Enactment of Environmental Laws

Events of the 1960s led to Congress passing the National Environmental Policy Act of 1969 (NEPA). The main thrust of NEPA was the requirement of environmental impact statements for all federally funded projects recommending major actions significantly affecting the quality of the human environment; for example, projects that would be expected to cause changes in aesthetics, air quality, water quality, noise levels, or fish and wildlife populations. This action was a triumph for preservationists who had tirelessly opposed water projects on environmental grounds.

Because of the significance that environmental protection and pollution control had achieved in the eyes of the public by 1970, President Nixon brought all the pollution control activities of various federal agencies together under the newly established Environmental Protection Agency (EPA) that year (see Chapter 2 for a history of the components of the agency). The 1970s witnessed a myriad of environmental laws issued by Congress giving the EPA the authority to regulate a broad spectrum of pollutants affecting all media: air, land, and water.

The principal statutes that enable the EPA to carry out its duties in protecting water quality today are the *Clean Water Act of 1977;* the *Marine Protection, Research and Sanctuaries Act of 1972;* the *Safe Drinking Water Act of 1974;* and the *Resource Conservation and Recovery Act of 1976.*

THE CLEAN WATER ACT

Under the Clean Water Act, the EPA is required to issue effluent guidelines, which are used in setting discharge limitations on wastewater pollutants produced by industrial and municipal sources. The act established two pollution control goals for the nation: (1) "fishable" and "swimmable" waters by 1983, and (2) elimination of discharge of all pollutants into navigable waterways by 1985 (2). Under the EPA's program, every industrial or municipal wastewater discharger must have a permit limiting its discharge. The permits are issued either by the federal government under the National Pollutant Discharge Elimination System (NPDES) or by states that have assumed responsibility for issuing the permits. The permits, based on effluent guidelines where available, specify the amount of pollution that can be legally discharged by a plant or other facility.

The EPA has now developed effluent guidelines for most industries. The states have set water quality standards, based on water quality criteria, that streams and lakes receiving discharges must meet, which in some cases result in more stringent industrial discharge requirements than those specified by the EPA effluent guidelines.

To limit pollution from municipal sources, the EPA administers a program of federal grants to cities and states for construction of municipal sewage treatment systems that are publicly owned. Under the Municipal Wastewater Treatment Construction Grant Amendments of 1981, all municipal wastewater treatment plants must comply with EPA requirements for secondary treatment by 1988 (see Chapter 12 for a discussion of secondary treatment requirements).

The authority for the EPA to administer grants to any state or municipality for this kind of construction is found in Section 201 of the Clean

Water Act. Congress originally had in mind, however, that any state or municipality should be required to evaluate waste management practices to demonstrate the need for construction before it would receive funds from the EPA. Therefore in Section 208 of the Clean Water Act Congress required localities with substantial water quality problems to develop management plans for area waste treatment. Each plan was to contain alternatives for treatment of all wastes generated in the designated geographical area. Each plan was to include (1) identification of treatment works necessary to meet the anticipated municipal and industrial waste treatment needs over a 20-year period, and (2) the establishment of construction priorities for such treatment works. Unfortunately, this "208 planning" failed to perform as Congress intended. By executive choice, the EPA decided to proceed with the construction of "201 projects" before much of the 208 planning was completed; consequently, much of the planning came after the fact.

THE MARINE PROTECTION, RESEARCH, AND SANCTUARIES ACT

Also known as the Ocean Dumping Act, this act prohibits ocean disposal of wastewater discharges, except that allowed by permits, in any waters under United States jurisdiction, by any vessel registered by the United States, or by any vessel sailing from United States ports. The act bans any dumping of radiological, chemical, or biological warfare agents or any high-level radioactive waste. The EPA issues permits for ocean disposal only after it determines that such disposal "will not unreasonably degrade or endanger human health, welfare, or amenities, or the marine environment, ecological systems, or economic potentialities" (3). The Corps of Engineers issues permits for ocean disposal of dredge spoils.

THE SAFE DRINKING WATER ACT

The Safe Drinking Water Act of 1974, as amended in 1977 and 1980, directs the administrator of the EPA to prescribe national drinking water standards to protect the public health, permits states to enforce the requirements, provides for the protection of underground sources of drinking water, and establishes a system for emergency allocation of chemicals necessary for water purification (4). The National Interim Primary Drinking Water Regulations and Secondary Drinking Water Regulations issued by the EPA under this act are discussed in Chapter 12 as they relate to water treatment technology.

THE RESOURCE CONSERVATION AND RECOVERY ACT OF 1976

The Resource Conservation and Recovery Act of 1976 (RCRA) indirectly gives the EPA the authority to protect water resources by requiring the regulatory control of land-disposed hazardous wastes. Under this act, the EPA is required to issue regulations to protect groundwater and surface water from any possible contamination by hazardous wastes disposed on the land in piles, landfills, surface impoundments, and underground injection wells (5).

Effects of Environmental Regulations

The intended result of Congress's passage of pollution control laws was for the EPA and the states to issue enforceable regulations to improve the quality of the nation's water resources and to prevent further deterioration. This had the effect of generating pollution control programs at every level of government to cope with implementing the regulations, through the necessary steps of issuing permits, inspecting regulated facilities, and enforcing the rules. In response, industries and municipalities found it necessary to organize internal pollution control programs to stay abreast of regulatory requirements, to work with plant personnel to attain compliance with regulations, to learn about environmental monitoring and sampling techniques, and to work with the regulatory agencies to obtain permits. In a sense, the 1970s was the period of the institutionalization of the ideals of the environmental movement prevalent in the 1960s.

Some 10 years later, the question is: Just how successful have pollution control efforts been in the United States? To provide an annual assessment of progress in combating environmental pollution, every year the president's Council on Environmental Quality (CEQ) issues an annual report (see, for example, reference 6). Some of the CEQ's findings are discussed later in this chapter.

6-2 SURFACE WATER QUALITY ISSUES

Sources of Pollution and Effects on Surface Water Quality

POINT SOURCES

Water pollution sources can be classified as *point* or *nonpoint* sources. Municipal and industrial wastewater discharge pipes emptying pollutants into a water body comprise point sources. Industrial point sources may be further classified as *direct* or *indirect* discharges. A direct discharger disposes of effluent straight to a receiving water body. An indirect discharger disposes of plant effluent to the municipal sewer, where it flows to the municipal wastewater treatment plant for treatment along with sanitary sewage before discharge to a receiving water body.

Point sources are by far the easier of the two types of pollution sources to control, because the quantity of flow and its physical, chemical, and biological properties can be accurately measured, providing baseline data to determine the extent of pollution. Once controls have been put in place, such monitoring data also provide information on the extent to which the pollutants are being removed from the effluent. Some pollutants of concern are heavy metals, organic matter that causes oxygen depletion in receiving waters, pathogenic microorganisms, toxic organic chemicals, temperature, and strong acids and bases. The significance and quantification of wastewater pollution from point sources is discussed in Section 12-6.

NONPOINT SOURCES

Runoff from rural areas (agricultural and silvicultural operations) and urban runoff are examples of *nonpoint sources* of pollution. These are diffuse sources that are not attributable to one particular discharge location but rather to a large area that imparts pollutants to storm water running over it. The commonest nonpoint pollutants are solids from soil erosion, pesticides, and fertilizers. Due to their nature, nonpoint sources are quite difficult to control, and they remain one of the most vexing problems facing the EPA and the states in attaining the goals of the Clean Water Act. Where the EPA can determine the parties responsible for a nonpoint pollution problem, the polluters may be required to employ "best management practices" to reduce the amount and impact of runoff. Urban runoff is discussed in more detail in Section 12-7.

ACID RAIN

The phenomenon of acid rain and its damaging effects on the nation's natural resources have received increased national and international attention in recent years. *Acid rain* refers to the wet and dry deposition of sulfuric, nitric, and in some locations hydrochloric acids from the atmosphere onto the land. Such deposition has had the effect of causing widespread damage to aquatic ecological systems, including loss of bicarbonate, increased acidity, and higher concentrations of heavy metals in those systems. The result has been the elimination of several species of fish and invertebrates over parts of their natural ranges (7).

Whereas the pH of pure precipitation is usually slightly acidic (pH = 5.6) due to reaction with atmospheric carbon dioxide, the pH of acid rain is well below this, on the order of an average of 4 to 5. The occurrence of acid rain is centered in the northeastern United States, as shown by the map in Figure 6-1. Remembering that a one-unit drop in pH means a 10-fold increase in acidity, the seriousness of this phenomenon can be inferred.

Natural sources contribute to acid rain, but the largest source by far is from human activities. The gaseous precursors to acid rain, sulfur and nitrogen oxides, are generated by the combustion of fossil fuels and the smelting of sulfide minerals. These react with atmospheric water and are deposited from the air, often entrained by precipitation.

Many questions concerning acid rain remain to be answered before a program for solving the problem can be formulated. An intense intera-

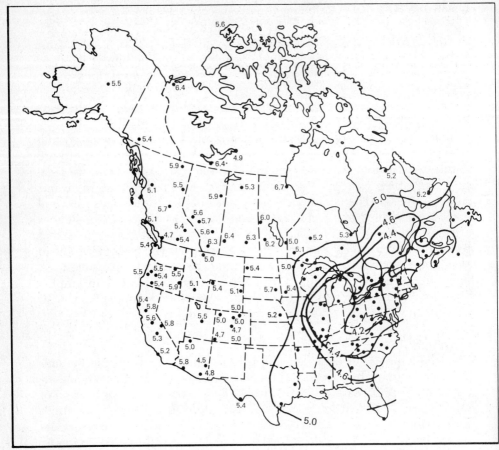

Figure 6-1 Acidity of North American precipitation (pH). (After the Interagency Task Force on Acid Precipitation.)

gency research program is now under way to determine more about the origin of acid rain and its chemistry, deposition, and ecological effects. For example, it is not clear how much damage is produced by a given degree of acid loading on a lake. Although many data gaps exist, some scientists believe that current information is compelling enough to warrant a major regulatory program aimed at reducing the gaseous precursors of acid rain in an effort to slow the rate of environmental degradation that it causes. Future amendments to the Clean Air Act indeed may reflect these concerns.

EFFECTS OF POLLUTION

The justification for water pollution control efforts should be obvious. Many pollutants entering water bodies are acutely poisonous to aquatic life; others may not be lethal but are concentrated in aquatic organisms and later cause adverse health effects in species further up the food chain.

Moreover, many surface-water bodies are sources of drinking water for human populations. The long-term effects of some water pollutants; for example, synthetic organic chemicals, have not yet been completely documented. In some instances it has been shown that these substances can cause cancer or other effects in humans, and the question of what is an acceptable level allowable in water has yet to be determined for many water pollutants. A summary of the environmental and health effects of 25 toxic chemical water pollutants appears in Table 6-1.

Cleanup Efforts and Results

In its 12th Annual Report, the Council on Environmental Quality stated that water pollution controls are having positive results in the United States (6). Every year the EPA reports success stories of rivers and lakes slowly returning to their natural state. Data collected by the U.S. Geographical Survey show that despite an increase in population and gross national product, water quality did not change significantly over the period of 1975 through 1980 (see Table 6-2). Table 6-2 also shows, however, that even though there has been no significant increase in deterioration of the nation's waters, pollution is still evident, and there is still much work to be done in cleaning up our water resources.

Future of Pollution Control Efforts in the United States

In 1980 the Reagan administration assessed the progress of pollution control programs to date and concluded that fundamental changes of the Clean Water Act and the Safe Drinking Water Act were in order if significant progress was to be realized in abating water pollution. Key to the Reagan philosophy is a reduction in the federal role, with more responsibility given to the states in implementing and enforcing water pollution control regulations. A basic question is whether the country should continue with its present programs or cut back due to the costs involved.

A major effort was started at the EPA under administrator Anne Burford to review all its regulations to determine whether the costs of pollution control could be lowered by modifying its regulatory approach. One outcome was the support of water quality standards in lieu of the technology-based standards that have been the fundamental basis of the Clean Water Act since 1972. (Water quality standards establish a designated use for a specified section of a water body, which is then balanced with the maximum amount of waste the water body can assimilate; technology-based standards are effluent limitations based on the levels of pollutant removal that can be achieved by modern wastewater treatment technology.)

The reasons Congress initiated the technology-based approach in the amendments to the Clean Water Act of 1972 were that the water-quality-based approach of the 1960s had failed to work due to difficulties of

Table 6-1 SELECTED HUMAN HEALTH AND ENVIRONMENTAL EFFECTS OF 25 TOXIC CHEMICALS[a]

| CHEMICAL | HUMAN HEALTH EFFECTS | | | ENVIRONMENTAL EFFECTS |
	CARCIN-OGEN	TERATO-GEN	OTHER EFFECTS	
Aldrin/dieldrin	●		Tremors, convulsions, kidney damage	Toxic to aquatic organisms, reproductive failure in birds and fish, bio-accumulates in aquatic organisms
Arsenic	●	●	Vomiting, poisoning, liver and kidney damage	Toxic to legume crops
Benzene	●		Anemia, bone marrow damage	Toxic to some fish and aquatic invertebrates
Bis(2-ethylhexyl) phthalate	●	●	Central nervous system damage	Eggshell thinning in birds, toxic to fish
Cadmium	●	●	Suspected causal factor in many human pathologies: tumors, renal dysfunction, hypertension, arterio-sclerosis; Itai-itai disease (weakened bones)	Toxic to fish, bio-accumulates in aquatic organisms
Carbon tetrachloride	●		Kidney and liver damage, heart failure	
Chloroform	●		Kidney and liver damage	
Chromium	●		Kidney and gastro-intestinal damage, respiratory complications	Toxic to some aquatic invertebrates
Copper			Gastrointestinal irritant, liver damage	Toxic to juvenile fish
Cyanide			Acutely toxic	Kills fish, reduces growth and development of fish

Table 6-1 *(Continued)*

CHEMICAL	HUMAN HEALTH EFFECTS			ENVIRONMENTAL EFFECTS
	CARCIN-OGEN	TERATO-GEN	OTHER EFFECTS	
DDT	●	●	Tremors, convulsions, kidney damage	Reproductive failure of birds and fish, bioaccumulates in aquatic organisms, biomagnifies in food chain
Di-*n*-butyl phthalate			Central nervous system damage	Eggshell thinning in birds, toxic to fish
Dioxin	●	●	Acute skin rashes	Bioaccumulates
Ethylbenzene				
Lead	●	●	Convulsions, anemia, kidney and brain damage	Toxic to domestic plants and animals, biomagnifies in food chain
Mercury		●	Irritability, depression, kidney and liver damage, Minamata disease	Reproductive failure in fish species, inhibits growth and kills fish, methyl-mercury biomagnifies
Methylene chloride (dichloromethane)				
Nickel	●		Gastrointestinal and central nervous system effects	Impairs reproduction of aquatic species
PCBs	●	●	Vomiting, abdominal pain, temporary blindness	Liver damage in mammals, kidney damage and eggshell thinning in birds, suspected reproductive failure in fish
Phenol				Reproductive effects in aquatic organisms, toxic to fish

Table 6-1 *(Continued)*

CHEMICAL	HUMAN HEALTH EFFECTS			ENVIRONMENTAL EFFECTS
	CARCIN-OGEN	TERATO-GEN	OTHER EFFECTS	
Silver				Toxic to aquatic organisms
Tetrachloro-ethylene	●		Central nervous system effects	
Toluene	●			Toxic to aquatic organisms at high concentrations
Toxaphene	●	●		Decreased productivity of phytoplankton communities, birth defects in fish and birds

Note: If a substance is identified as a carcinogen, there is evidence that it has the potential for causing cancer in humans. If a substance is identified as a teratogen, it has the potential for causing birth defects in humans.
[a]Courtesy of The Conservation Foundation.

enforcement and the limited availability of data for use in water quality models. The arguments in favor of a technology-based approach are as follows:

1. Technology-based standards are easy to enforce. This is important from an institutional perspective.
2. These standards are the first step toward the ultimate goal of zero discharge of pollutants to natural waters, as opposed to merely cleaning up waters to suit human objectives (the basis for water quality standards).

Table 6-2 NATIONAL AMBIENT VIOLATION RATES[a] FOR WATER POLLUTION INDICATORS, 1975–1980

POLLUTION INDICATOR	VIOLATION LEVEL[b]
Fecal coliform bacteria	Above 200 cells/100 ml
Dissolved oxygen	Below 5.0 mg/L
Total phosphorus	Above 0.1 mg/L
Total cadmium	Above 4.0 μg/L for soft water / Above 10.0 μg/L for hard water
Total lead	Above exp [1.51 ln (hardness)—3.37] μg/L
Total mercury	Above 0.05 μg/L

SOURCE: After the Council on Environmental Quality.
[a]The violation rate is the percentage of all measurements that exceeds the violation level specified.
[b]Based on U.S. EPA water quality definitions.

3. There are insufficient resources and knowledge to set water quality standards for all pollutants and locations. Technology-based standards are an interim approach to avoid pollution.
4. Nationwide uniformity in treatment standards minimizes economic dislocations.
5. This approach promotes equity among dischargers. No one should have the right to discharge more into the environment just because of geographical location.

The Reagan administration, however, contended that while technology-based standards were important in the past in providing impetus for local governments and industry to clean up pollution from their treatment facilities, the EPA now has the ability and sophistication to regulate discharge pollutants under water quality standards, and that the Clean Water Act should be amended accordingly. The Reagan administration believes that some of the advantages of water quality standards are as follows (8):

1. Water quality standards and the process by which they are adopted inherently encourage an assessment of costs and benefits, which is absent in the adoption and application of technology-based standards
2. They foster scientific debate that accelerates the advancement of the state of the art in predicting the fate and effects of pollutants
3. The debate takes place in a local/state arena and heightens awareness of local government, policymakers, and the public of the importance of water pollution control in their communities
4. The assertion of the primary right and responsibility of states to regulate pollutants is essential to establishing the appropriate balance of power between the federal establishment and state governments

1975	1976	1977	1978	1979	1980
39	32	34	35	34	31
5	6	11	5	4	5
47	47	48	48	47	48
7–17	4–12	4–13	4–6	7	2
18–42	18–38	20–41	23–27	27	15
50–61	40–63	32–45	25–60	34–81	67–81

5. Water-quality-based decisions can avoid requirements of treatment for treatment's sake, which can result from application of technology-based standards (8).

6-3   GROUNDWATER QUALITY ISSUES

Approximately 25 percent of all water used in the United States is withdrawn from groundwater supplies (9), which provide a major drinking water source in 32 states and the only drinking water sources in many localities. A map depicting the groundwater areas in the United States is given in Figure 7-23. Traditionally, groundwater has not been monitored for pollutants, because it was considered a pristine resource. It has only been in recent years that a number of incidents have documented the existence of groundwater contamination having human health implications at least as serious as those of surface-water pollution. The finding of synthetic organic chemicals and other substances in groundwater indicates that the pollution sources can be traced to human activities.

Sources of Groundwater Pollution and Effects on Water Quality

Groundwater contamination is caused primarily by seepage of toxic organic and inorganic chemicals into underground aquifers (water-bearing strata). Figure 6-2 illustrates that a variety of industrial, municipal, and private operations are responsible for groundwater pollution. These include seepage from agricultural activities, leakage from underground injection wells, leakage from sewer lines and septic systems, percolation from municipal and industrial landfills, and leakage from pits, ponds, and lagoons containing various wastes. Other sources of groundwater contamination include saltwater intrusion in coastal areas, leakage from buried storage tanks (for example, those storing gasoline), accidental spills of toxic materials, abandoned and leaking wells, artificial recharge operations, and highway deicing salts (10, 11).

AGRICULTURAL ACTIVITIES
Agricultural operations are a major source of pollution in many areas. Overapplication of water, pesticides, and fertilizers and improper management of animal wastes can give rise to a number of problems. Irrigation practices can raise the concentrations of salts and minerals in groundwater by leaching them out of the soil. Improper management of fertilizers can lead to excess levels of nitrates in the groundwater, sometimes to the point where the water is rendered unsuitable for consumption. Leachate from animal feedlot operations can infiltrate and contaminate usable aquifers if not managed properly. Pesticides may also contaminate groundwater under certain conditions.

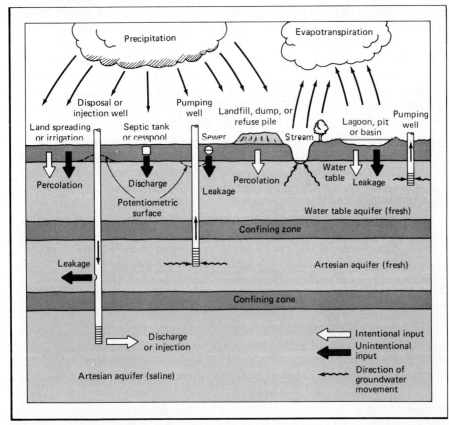

Figure 6-2 Sources of groundwater contamination. (After the U.S. EPA.)

UNDERGROUND INJECTION WELLS

Underground injection wells are used to dispose of industrial, municipal, radioactive, and hazardous wastes and brine from oil and gas production deep into subsurface aquifers that are unsuitable for bearing usable water (for example, saline aquifers). These wells often pass through aquifers used as drinking water sources and may cause contamination by leakage of pollutants through the wellhead, the well casing, or fractures in the rock layers confining the aquifers. Since many of the materials being disposed of are highly dangerous, potable groundwater contamination caused by leaking underground injection wells is a serious health concern.

SEPTIC TANKS AND ON-SITE WASTEWATER SYSTEMS

Septic tanks, soil adsorption systems, cesspools, pit privies, and other on-site wastewater disposal systems are the commonest alternatives to municipal sewerage and wastewater treatment systems in the United States. Over two trillion gallons of wastewater per year are discharged into groundwater as a result of their widespread use. The EPA has cited failing septic tanks and cesspools as one of the most serious sources of groundwater contamination (11).

On-site systems such as septic systems rely on three natural processes to cleanse the wastewater. Suspended solids are removed by *filtration* as the wastewater percolates through the soil, *biological degradation* of organic matter occurs in the settling tank and/or soil adsorption field, and undissolved solids are *adsorbed* onto soil particles and may later be used by plants. A system may fail due to either poor design or maintenance, causing discharge of bacteria, viruses, degradable organic compounds, synthetic detergents, chlorides, and nitrates into groundwater, with the potential for ultimately causing pollution of drinking water sources.

LAND DISPOSAL OF WASTES

One hundred fifty million tons of municipal refuse and 240 million tons (dry weight) of industrial wastes are placed in land disposal sites every year (11). Another 10 trillion gallons of liquid wastes are placed in surface impoundments (pits, ponds, lagoons). About 10 percent of all solid and liquid wastes are hazardous (toxic, explosive, flammable, or corrosive) to human health and the environment. If land-disposed solid and liquid wastes are not managed properly, precipitation and high water tables can leach dangerous contaminants from the wastes and eventually carry them to groundwater. Unlined or improperly lined surface impoundments can leak toxic waste constituents directly into groundwater supplies. The discovery in the late 1970s of many sites across the country where chemical wastes had been illegally dumped for years and were leaking into groundwater has led the EPA to brand the cleanup of this problem "the Challenge of the Eighties."

ACCIDENTAL SPILLS AND LEAKS

Accidental spills of toxic materials, liquid wastes, gasoline, and oil can occur at industrial sites, on highways and railways, on city streets, and at airports. The danger of large spills on permeable soils is that the materials may percolate easily to the water table and then move with the groundwater. Leaks from gas station and home fuel-storage tanks, industrial plants, and petroleum pipelines are also potential sources of groundwater contamination. In the case of contamination with petroleum products, the taste and odor of water are affected.

ABANDONED AND LEAKY WELLS

It is estimated that there are several million abandoned industrial and domestic wells in the United States. They can serve as sources of pollution in a number of ways. Demolition operations may inadvertently raze wells, thereby breaking surface casings and seals and providing a direct route for surface pollutants to enter groundwater aquifers. Abandoned oil and gas wells may continue to discharge brine to shallow freshwater aquifers in cases where salt water has migrated to an abandoned well. In addition, these wells are often convenient sites for illegal disposal of hazardous wastes. In some southern states, improperly constructed and abandoned wells are considered by health officials to be the most significant source of groundwater contamination.

ARTIFICIAL RECHARGE OPERATIONS
Artificial recharge is the replenishment of an aquifer by other than natural means. There are numerous techniques for performing artificial recharge, including irrigation, seepage ponds, injection wells, and land spreading. Municipal and industrial wastewater, urban storm water runoff, and irrigation return flows are some water sources that are used for these operations. These waters may contain pollutants that cannot be filtered out by the soils at a particular location, however, thereby posing a potential threat of groundwater pollution when such waters are used for aquifer recharge.

SALTWATER INTRUSION
Excess pumping of a freshwater aquifer located near an underground saline-water aquifer or the sea can result in the saline water being drawn into it. This may result in the entire freshwater aquifer becoming contaminated with saline water and rendered unfit for drinking or irrigation.

HIGHWAY DEICING SALTS
The United States uses about 4.5 million tons of sodium and calcium chloride every year to melt snow and ice on roads in northern climates. This practice is a source of both groundwater and surface water pollution. Runoff from salted roads can seep through the soil along the sides of the road and eventually reach groundwater.

GROUNDWATER POLLUTION EFFECTS
The effects on groundwater quality of the practices discussed above did not receive a great deal of public attention until the late 1970s (12). It was not until then that groundwater pollution was first documented and correlated with adverse health effects experienced by humans and animals consuming contaminated groundwater. Even today, the extent of groundwater contamination is not clear, because of its slow movement and the possibility of yet undiscovered sources of contamination. The Conservation Foundation, in its *State of the Environment 1982,* documented actual and anticipated groundwater quality problems in every region of the country (see Figure 6-3) (13). In 1981 the EPA conducted a survey of

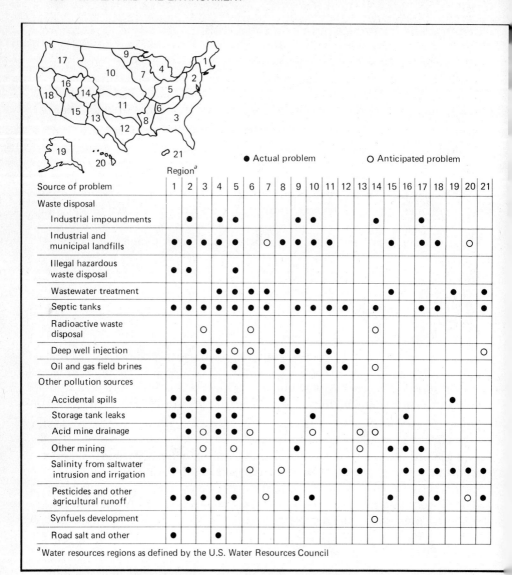

Source of problem	1	2	3	4	5	6	7	8	9	10	11	12	13	14	15	16	17	18	19	20	21
Waste disposal																					
Industrial impoundments		●		●	●				●	●				●			●				
Industrial and municipal landfills	●	●	●	●	●		○	●	●	●	●				●		●	●		○	
Illegal hazardous waste disposal	●	●			●																
Wastewater treatment				●	●	●	●								●			●			●
Septic tanks	●	●	●	●	●	●	●		●	●	●	●		●			●	●			●
Radioactive waste disposal			○			○								○							
Deep well injection				●	●	○	○		●	●		●									○
Oil and gas field brines			●		●				●			●	●	○							
Other pollution sources																					
Accidental spills	●	●	●	●	●				●										●		
Storage tank leaks	●	●		●	●					●						●					
Acid mine drainage		●	○	●	●	○				○			○	○							
Other mining			○		○				●					○		●	●	●			
Salinity from saltwater intrusion and irrigation	●	●	●			○		○				●	●		●	●	●	●	●	●	●
Pesticides and other agricultural runoff	●	●	●	●	●		○		●	●					●		●	●		○	●
Synfuels development														○							
Road salt and other	●			●																	

● Actual problem   ○ Anticipated problem

[a] Water resources regions as defined by the U.S. Water Resources Council

Figure 6-3   Actual and anticipated groundwater problems by region, 1980. (Courtesy of The Conservation Foundation.)

public water supply systems using groundwater and found that volatile organic chemicals (see Table 6-3) could be detected in approximately 45 percent of the systems serving over 10,000 people, and in approximately 12 percent of the systems serving fewer than 10,000 people. Most of the systems had one or more of these chemicals at very low levels, but a few systems had high levels of contamination (6). The health effects of some of these chemicals are documented in Table 6-1.

Table 6-3   SYNTHETIC ORGANIC CHEMICALS
MOST COMMONLY DETECTED IN GROUNDWATER

Trichloroethylene	Benzene
Tetrachloroethylene	Chlorobenzene
Carbon tetrachloride	Dichlorobenzene(s)
1,1,1-Trichloroethane	Trichlorobenzene(s)
1,2-Dichloroethane	1,1-Dichloroethylene
Vinyl chloride	*cis*-1,2,-Dichloroethylene
Methylene chloride	*trans*-1,2-Dichloroethylene

SOURCE: After U.S. EPA, Office of Drinking Water.

Difficulties of Protecting Groundwater

Groundwater moves at an exceedingly slow rate: on the order of five feet per day to a few feet per year. At this rate, it may take 100 or even 1000 years for contamination to be detected. Moreover, it is difficult to monitor for groundwater contamination, because once contaminants enter the groundwater system, they are dispersed in a plume. The shape of the plume and its velocity depend on local geological conditions. A further difficulty is that groundwater does not have the same self-cleansing properties as surface water; contaminants are likely to persist for years. Once groundwater contamination is detected, it is nearly impossible to remove, and it is quite expensive to treat if it can be extracted.

Future of Pollution Control Efforts in the United States

The EPA clearly feels that groundwater protection is one of the highest priority pollution control projects of the future. The agency believes that a unified strategy for national groundwater protection is needed. In 1980 the agency proposed several alternatives that might possibly be used to achieve this goal, including a scheme of classifying all groundwater aquifers based on primary use and regulating activities adversely affecting the designated use (14). A final announcement of a groundwater protection policy will most likely be forthcoming from the EPA within the next few years.

6-4   WATER QUANTITY ISSUES

Groundwater Depletion

Although the United States has more than enough water to provide for its requirements on a national scale, there are parts of the country experiencing severe water shortages at the local level (see Chapter 4). Most notable in this regard are the arid western states, where excessive water withdrawals are dangerously depleting some water sources. In some areas this practice has caused sinkholes or massive land subsidence, which has led to damage of structures, sewers, and drainage systems. Another effect of lowering the water table by excessive withdrawal is to raise pumping costs, which has a significant impact on the costs of irrigated farming in areas dependent on groundwater supplies. Groundwater overdrafts may also reduce base flows to surface streams, posing a potential danger to aquatic life during low precipitation periods. As discussed previously in this chapter and in Chapter 7, groundwater overdrafts in coastal areas often cause saltwater intrusion into freshwater aquifers. Rapid pumping also serves to spread any contamination present in an aquifer more quickly.

Instream Flow Use

In the west, development has been so rapid that surface-water supplies have been severely depleted in a number of areas, including the Rio Grande Basin, the lower Colorado Basin, and California. Water has been withdrawn to such an extent that too little or none is left for desirable instream uses such as navigation, recreation, hydroelectric power generation, and fish and wildlife. This has led to the passage of laws in some states requiring that a specified flow be maintained for instream use at all times, and withdrawals of water are regulated accordingly.

6-5 COORDINATION OF WATER QUALITY AND QUANTITY MANAGEMENT

In the federal government, agencies traditionally responsible for water quantity and water quality have been separate. As discussed in Chapter 2, the principal water resources planning and development agencies in the United States are the Corps of Engineers, the U.S. Bureau of Reclamation, the Soil Conservation Service, the Tennessee Valley Authority, and the U.S. Water Resources Council (now terminated). On the water quality side, the Environmental Protection Agency is the sole body responsible for a comprehensive program. With some of the issues outlined in this chapter, it is clear that there is a need for coordinated management of both quantity and quality aspects of groundwater and surface-water flow.

This attitude was reflected by the 97th Congress in its attempt to establish an independent National Ground Water Commission, responsible for comprehensive assessment of groundwater quality and quantity in the United States (15). Although the bill was not enacted by that Congress, it is likely that a similar measure will be considered in the future.

PROBLEMS

6-1. Describe some of the events that led to public demand for water pollution control.

6-2. What are the main statutes under which the EPA controls water pollution? Which aspects of water pollution may be regulated under each act?

6-3. Define point and nonpoint water pollution sources. Give five examples of each.

6-4. What is meant by "acid rain"? What are the chief causes of it and some of the environmental concerns?

6-5. List 10 adverse health effects that can be caused by toxic chemical pollutants.

6-6. In your opinion, what is the most significant source of groundwater pollution in this country? Explain.

6-7. What is the most significant source of groundwater pollution in your state? Describe the sources and effects of contamination to the extent they are known.

6-8. Why is groundwater contamination so difficult to detect and clean up? Research and briefly describe some of the techniques that are used in aquifer restoration.

6-9. Describe some of the hazards caused by groundwater depletion.

6-10. Why do you think it is important to plan water quality and quantity management together? Give examples.

6-11. Identify the agencies in your state responsible for managing (a) water quality and (b) water quantity.

References

1. Beatrice H. Holmes, *History of Federal Water Resources Programs and Policies, 1961–1970,* U.S. Department of Agriculture, Miscellaneous Pub. No. 1379, Washington, D.C., September 1979.
2. *Clean Water Act of 1977,* 33 U.S.C. §1251 et seq.
3. *Safe Drinking Water Act,* 42 U.S.C. §300 et seq.
4. *Marine Protection, Research, and Sanctuaries Act,* 33 U.S.C. §1401 et seq.
5. *Resource Conservation and Recovery Act of 1976,* 42 U.S.C. §§6901–6987.
6. *Twelfth Annual Report of the Council on Environmental Quality, 1981,* U.S. Gov't. Print. Off., Washington, D.C., December 1981.
7. National Research Council, *Atmosphere-Biosphere Interactions: Toward a Better Understanding of the Ecological Consequences of Fossil Fuel Combustion,* National Academy Press, Washington, D.C., 1981.
8. "Monitor: New Approaches and New Concerns," *J. Water Pollution Control Federation,* vol. 54, no. 12, December 1982.
9. U.S. Water Resources Council, *The Nation's Water Resources 1975–2000,* U.S. Gov't. Print. Off., Washington, D.C., 1978.
10. *Eleventh Annual Report of the Council on Environmental Quality, 1980,* U.S. Gov't. Print. Off., Washington, D.C., December 1980.
11. U.S. EPA, Office of Solid Waste, *Ground Water Protection,* SW-886, Washington, D.C., 1980.
12. U.S. EPA, *The Report to Congress: Waste Disposal Practices and Their Effects on Ground Water: Executive Summary,* Washington, D.C., 1977.
13. The Conservation Foundation, *State of the Environment 1982,* Washington, D.C., 1982.
14. U.S. EPA, Office of Drinking Water, *Proposed Ground Water Protection Strategy,* Washington, D.C., 1980.
15. *H.R. 6307,* 97th Cong., 2d Sess., September 13, 1982.

Chapter 7
Natural Water Supply Processes

In a global sense, the total quantity of water available is fixed. Natural forces continuously transfer water from one terrestrial or atmospheric reservoir to another. Although water is neither created nor destroyed in this overall cycling process, the amount available at any given time or location may vary widely. Once the physical system of water distribution —that is, its *hydrology*—is understood, its management can be attempted in the context of prevailing legal, social, and political factors.

The basic principles of surface-water and groundwater hydrology are presented in this chapter. A brief introduction to probability analysis of historical water flow data is included.

7-1 INTRODUCTION TO HYDROLOGY

Hydrology is the science that deals with the forces that distribute water on and beneath the earth's surface and in the atmosphere. The hydrologic cycle is the constant transfer of water from the land and the sea to the atmosphere and back again. The hydrologic (or water) budget is a mass balancing of water over time at a locality.

The Hydrologic Cycle

The ocean is the earth's principal reservoir; as shown by Table 7-1, it stores over 97 percent of the terrestrial water. The sun-driven hydrologic cycle transfers this water to land in usable form. The hydrologic cycle can be defined as the continuous process whereby water is evaporated by the sun,

Table 7-1 DISTRIBUTION OF THE WORLD'S ESTIMATED SUPPLY OF WATER

LOCATION	SURFACE AREA (1000 MI^2)	VOLUME OF WATER (1000 MI^3)	TOTAL WATER (PERCENT)
World area, total	197,000		
Land area	57,500		
Surface water, continental			
Polar ice and glaciers	6900	7300	2.24
Freshwater lakes	330	30	0.009
Saline lakes, inland seas	270	25	0.008
Stream channels, average		0.280	0.0001
Total surface water	7500	~7350	2.26
Subsurface water, continental			
Soil root zone	50,000	6	0.0018
Groundwater above 2640-ft depth		1000	0.306
Groundwater, 2640 to 13,200 ft depth		1000	0.306
Total subsurface water	50,000	2000	0.61
Total water on land		~9350	2.87
Oceans	139,000	317,000	97.13
Atmospheric moisture		3.1	0.0001
Total world supply of water		326,000	100

SOURCE: R. D. Hockensmith (ed.), *Water and Agriculture*, AAAS Pub. No. 62, Washington, D.C., 1960, p. 45. Copyright 1960 by AAAS.

is incorporated into clouds as water vapor, falls to land and sea as precipitation and, on land, ultimately travels into streams and back to the ocean. The hydrologic cycle can be considered a closed system for the earth, because the total amount of water in the cycle is constant even though its distribution in time and space varies. There are many subcycles within this worldwide system, however, and they are generally open-ended. It is these subsystems that give rise to the many problems of water supply and demand that confront hydrologists.

The hydrologic cycle is generally described in terms of six components: precipitation (P), infiltration (I), evaporation (E), transpiration (T), surface runoff (R), and groundwater flow (G). Figure 7-1 defines these components and illustrates their interrelation; it also indicates the cycling process. For example, some precipitation evaporates before reaching the earth and remains in the air as water vapor. Water also evaporates after precipitation reaches the earth. Plants take up infiltrated water and groundwater (in cases of some deep-rooted plants) and return part of this water to the atmosphere through their leaves by a process called *transpiration*. Some infiltrated water may emerge to surface-water bodies as

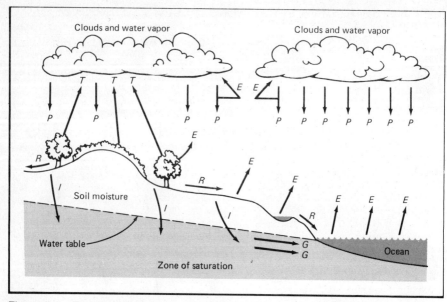

Figure 7-1   The hydrologic cycle: *T*, transpiration; *E*, evaporation; *P*, precipitation; *R*, surface runoff; *G*, groundwater flow; *I*, infiltration.

interflow, while other portions may become groundwater flow. Ground-water may ultimately be discharged into streams or may emerge as springs. After some initial filling of interception and depression storage, and providing that the precipitation rate exceeds the infiltration rate, overland flow (surface runoff) begins.

Also of importance is the fact that as water is transferred through the hydrologic cycle, its quality changes. Seawater is naturally desalted and purified by solar evaporation, but rainwater that falls from clouds may pick up new contaminants as it descends through the atmosphere, as it is used and discarded by humans, or as it flows over land. Soil acts as a natural filter and can adsorb pollutants from water that is seeping through it toward groundwater reserves. It is well known that the soil's capacity for purification has been exceeded in some areas where liquid wastes with high concentrations of chemical contaminants have been buried. In these cases the groundwater has been rendered unfit for certain, if not all, uses because the soil's capability for adsorption of contaminants has been exhausted. These and other water quality topics are discussed further in Chapters 6, 10, and 12.

The Hydrologic Budget

A water budget comprised of the components of the hydrologic cycle system can be formulated. It is an accounting of the inflow, outflow, and storage of water in a specified hydrologic system. Figure 7-2 illustrates a

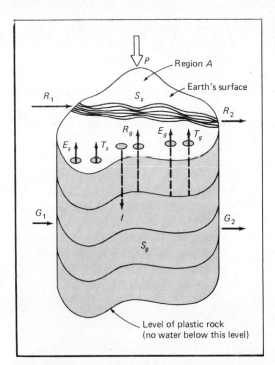

Figure 7-2 Schematic diagram of a hydrologic cycle for a region.

regional hydrologic system conceptualizing the components of the hydrologic cycle. With T, E, P, R, G, and I standing for the hydrologic components as shown in Figure 7-1 and ΔS standing for the change in storage, a hydrologic budget can be derived with the inflows to the region denoted as positive quantities and outflows as negative ones. The subscripts s and g indicate surface and underground components, respectively.

For surface flow, the hydrologic budget can be written as:

$$P + R_1 - R_2 + R_g - E_s - T_s - I = \Delta S_s \tag{7-1}$$

where precipitation, surface-water inflow, and groundwater appearing as surface water (R_g) are inflows; surface-water outflow, evaporation, and infiltration are outflows; and all variables are volumes per unit of time.

For underground flow, the hydrologic budget can be written as:

$$I + G_1 - G_2 - R_g - E_g - T_g = \Delta S_g \tag{7-2}$$

where infiltration and groundwater inflow are inflows; groundwater outflow, groundwater appearing as surface water, evaporation, and transpiration are outflows. The hydrologic budget for the region is derived by summing Equations 7-1 and 7-2:

$$P - (R_2 - R_1) - (E_s + E_g) - (T_s + T_g) - (G_2 - G_1)$$
$$= \Delta (S_s + S_g) \tag{7-3}$$

If the subscripts are dropped and the quantities in parentheses are taken as net changes, the equation reduces to

$$P - R - E - T - G = \Delta S \tag{7-4}$$

Equation 7-4 is the fundamental equation of hydrology. In practice, it is often used to estimate combined evaporation and transpiration, "evapotranspiration" (ET), for an area, if estimates of the other variables can reasonably be made. For example, in large river basins (measured in thousands of square miles), groundwater system boundaries often follow surface-water divides. In cases where this appears to be true, the ground-water flux into and out of the region can be assumed to be zero $(G = 0)$. In addition, over a long period of time (usually greater than five years), seasonal excesses and deficits in storage often tend to balance out in large systems, and in such cases the average condition for ΔS may sometimes be assumed to be equal to zero. Under these two particular assumptions, the hydrologic equation becomes

$$P - R - ET = 0 \tag{7-5}$$

and by knowing P and R, a rough estimate of ET can be obtained.

Example 7-1

The area of the drainage basin of the James River at Scottsville, Virginia, is 4571 mi^2. If the average annual runoff is determined to be 5102 ft^3/s and the average annual rainfall is 42.5 in, estimate the evapotranspiration losses for the area. How does this compare to the lake evaporation of 39 in/yr measured at Richmond, Virginia?

SOLUTION
1. Assuming that $G = 0$ and $\Delta S = 0$, Equation 7-5 can be used to estimate ET.
2. The runoff is converted from units of ft^3/s into units of in/yr as follows:

$$R = 5102 \text{ ft}^3/\text{s} \times \frac{1}{4571 \text{ mi}^2} \times \frac{1 \text{ mi}^2}{(5280 \text{ ft})^2} \times \frac{12 \text{ in}}{1 \text{ ft}}$$
$$\times \frac{(86,400)\,(365) \text{ s}}{\text{yr}} = 15.6 \text{ in/yr}$$

3. $ET = P - R = 42.5 \text{ in/yr} - 15.6 \text{ in/yr} = 26.9 \text{ in/yr}$

4. The estimated ET losses over the drainage basin are less than the measured lake ET losses at Richmond. (All ET losses over a lake are due to E only.) This shows that the ET rate is less for the vegetated drainage basin than for the open, available body of water. ∎

Hydrologic Components

If the hydrologic equation is to have practical application, numerical data must be available or derivable in order to evaluate its terms. Methods are discussed here for measuring or otherwise determining precipitation, surface runoff, evaporation, transpiration, and infiltration for use in hydrologic analyses.

PRECIPITATION

Precipitation occurs as rain, sleet, snow and hail. It is commonly expressed in the United States in units of inches per unit time or acre-feet per unit time.* The National Weather Service regularly measures and records precipitation at rain gauges located at numerous points throughout the United States. This recorded information is used in determining the nature of local storm events that must be considered in flood analyses and in estimating the long-term availability of water for cities, industries, and farms.

Precipitation varies in time and in space. Time variations on the order of minutes, hours, days, weeks, months, and years must sometimes be dealt with. The geographical variability of precipitation is an important factor in regional water planning. The variability for the United States is illustrated in Figure 7-3, which is an isohyetal map of the mean annual precipitation (*isohyets* are lines of equal rainfall depth). Note the extreme variability among the regions, for example, four inches per year in some parts of Arizona as opposed to 150 inches per year in some parts of Washington. On the average, the coterminous United States receives about 30 inches (4200 bgd) of precipitation per year.

The distribution of precipitation as it reaches the earth is depicted in Figure 7-4. *Interception storage* is the amount of precipitation that adheres to vegetation before the excess falls to the ground. Water contained in interception storage is eventually evaporated and returned to the atmosphere. A fraction of the water that falls to earth is stored in depressions on the surface and subsequently evaporates (*depression storage*), a fraction seeps into the soil (*infiltration*), and the remainder flows over land into stream channels. The time distribution of the components of a rainfall input is shown in Figure 7-5.

Precipitation losses due to evaporation during storm events, interception storage, depression storage, and infiltration account for the fact that only a fraction of the total precipitation reaches stream channels as surface runoff. This fraction is called *effective precipitation.*

Water that infiltrates the earth may take several courses. *Inter-*

*In this book, use will be made of the units of measure most commonly employed in the United States in the field of water resources management. Frequent reference will be made to the SI system of metrics to acquaint the student with these units. A complete conversion table is found in Appendix A.

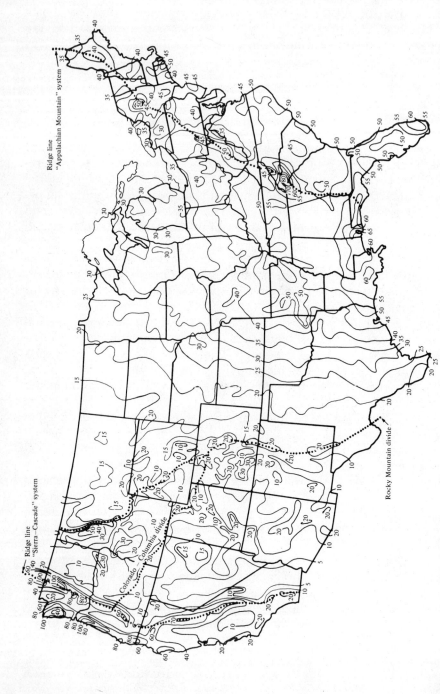

Figure 7-3 Average annual precipitation (in inches) in the United States. (After U.S. Department of Agriculture, Soil Conservation Service.)

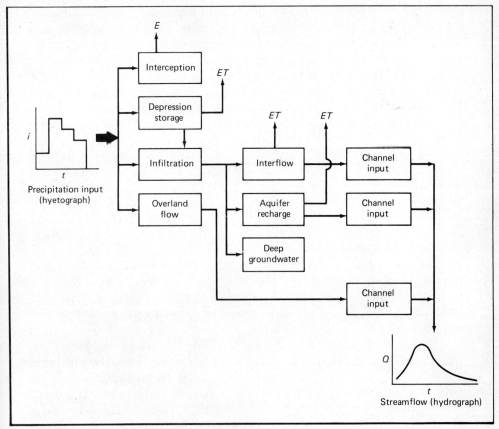

Figure 7-4 Distribution of precipitation input.

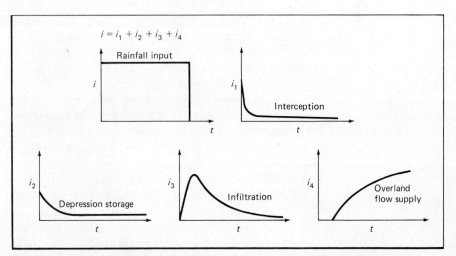

Figure 7-5 Disposition of rainfall input in terms of interception, depression storage, infiltration, and overland flow.

flow is that portion of subsurface flow which moves at shallow depths and flows laterally to surface channels. Other infiltrated water may seep into underground water storage areas called aquifers (water-bearing strata) before emerging to stream channels or to very deep underground areas from which the water cannot be withdrawn.

Precipitation data are recorded at specific locations, but the data obtained at a given station may not be representative of a very large area. For example, considerable rainfall variability is common even between points as close as 50 or 100 feet. In hydrologic analyses, a representative average areal rainfall is obtained by evaluating the data from several gauging sites in the area under study. Three methods that are widely used for determining such areal precipitation averages are (1) a simple arithmetic mean of existing precipitation data, (2) the Theissen method, and (3) the isohyetal method. The isohyetal method is considered to be the most accurate of the three, but accounting for variability in factors such as topography requires the skills of an experienced analyst. The Theissen method is discussed in references 1 and 2. The isohyetal method consists of plotting gauge locations and precipitation data, interpolating between gauges, and then connecting the points of equal precipitation. The average areal precipitation is calculated as the weighted average of the precipitation depths between isohyets.

When precipitation data are not available for a point of interest but data exist at surrounding points, precipitation estimates of the unknown point can be made by determining a weighted average of existing data from adjacent areas if the topography and local climatic conditions are reasonably similar. The U.S. National Weather Service has established a procedure for determining such missing data (3). References 1 and 2 can also be consulted for explanation.

EVAPORATION

Of the precipitation that reaches the United States, well over half is returned to the atmosphere by evaporation (4). Evaporation is particularly significant over large bodies of water such as lakes and reservoirs during dry periods.

Measured evaporation data are available for some areas of the United States. One source is the National Weather Service, which maintains records of evaporation data, commonly expressed in the same units as precipitation. A Weather Service map of the United States showing lines of equal lake evaporation is shown in Figure 7-6.

The Weather Service collects evaporation data by measuring the loss of water from large evaporation pans placed in the field. These data are converted to lake evaporation data by multiplying by an appropriate pan coefficient. For example, a "Class A" pan is four feet in diameter, 10 inches deep, and situated 12 inches above the ground on a wood frame. Lake evaporation data are derived from Class A pan data by multiplying the

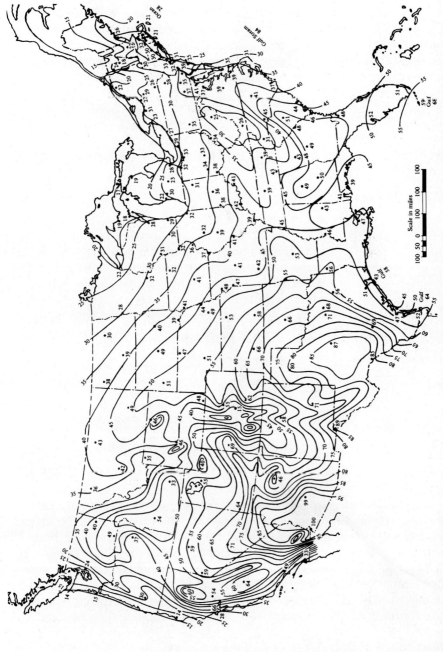

Figure 7-6 Average annual lake evaporation (in inches) in the United States. (After U.S. Department of Agriculture, Soil Conservation Service.)

193

latter by 0.7, which takes into account the effect of the differences observed between pan data and natural water bodies; this is known as the "pan coefficient."

Evaporation can be estimated from the hydrologic budget equation (Equation 7-4) if the precipitation, runoff, transpiration, and storage components are known. Another approach, which has been used for lake evaporation, is the energy budget method, where the budget equation is written in terms of energy and estimates are made of incoming, outgoing, and storage of energy in the system.

A third basis for estimating evaporation is a mass transfer approach that was first recognized by Dalton (5). This approach is based on the relation between evaporation and the difference between the vapor pressure of the water surface and the partial pressure of water vapor in the ambient air, that is,

$$E = K (e_0 - e_a) \tag{7-6}$$

where E = evaporation
K = a coefficient that depends on wind velocity, atmospheric pressure, and other factors
e_0 and e_a = water saturation vapor pressure of water at the water surface temperature and the actual vapor pressure in the air, respectively

One commonly used empirical formula based on this relation has been developed by Meyer (6). The equation is of the form

$$E = C(e_0 - e_a) (1 + W/10) \tag{7-7}$$

where E = daily evaporation in inches
e_0 and e_a = as previously defined but in units of inches of Hg
W = wind velocity in mph measured approximately 25 feet above the water surface
C = an empirical coefficient; equals approximately 0.36 for lakes and 0.50 for wet soil surfaces and small puddles

Accurate evaporation estimates are important for use in storage calculations for reservoirs. Some of the areas of the country that are the driest also have the highest average annual temperatures. In the cool, humid northeast, evaporation amounts to about 20 inches per year, whereas in the hot, dry southwest evaporation is on the order of 80 inches per year. If additional surface-water storage is planned for a western reservoir by adding to the height of a dam, a calculation of evaporation effects is crucial for determining whether any net increase in storage will be realized.

TRANSPIRATION AND EVAPOTRANSPIRATION
Transpiration, which is a difficult quantity to measure because of its dependence on phytological variables, is an important component in the water

budget of heavily vegetated areas. It is a function of the number and types of plants, soil moisture and soil type, season, temperature, and average annual precipitation. Because of the complexities of estimating evaporation and transpiration, they are often dealt with in a combined form known as *evapotranspiration* (ET). If precipitation over an area and net runoff are known, and estimates of groundwater flow and storage can be made, an estimate of ET can be derived from the basic hydrologic equation (see discussion of Equation 7-5).

In agricultural areas the estimated evapotranspiration or consumptive use of water by crops is of great importance in determining irrigation water requirements. One method for making such estimates is the Blaney-Criddle method (7), which states that consumptive use is given by

$$U = k_s B \tag{7-8}$$

where U = consumptive use of water during the growing season (in)
k_s = a seasonal consumptive use coefficient applicable to a particular crop, empirically derived (see reference 7)
B = summation of monthly consumptive use factors for a given season

The term B can be expressed as

$$B = \Sigma \left(\frac{tp}{100} \right) \tag{7-9}$$

where t = mean monthly temperature (°F)
p = monthly daytime hours given as percent of the year

Several values of consumptive use that are based on empirically derived values of k_s for various crops are given in Table 7-2. Example 12-1 demonstrates application of the Blaney-Criddle method.

Table 7-2   CONSUMPTIVE USE FOR CROPS IN THE MONTROSE, COLORADO, AREA DURING THE IRRIGATION OR GROWING SEASON

CROP	CONSUMPTIVE USE (IN)
Alfalfa	26.5
Corn	19.7
Small grain	14.9
Grass hay	23.3
Natural vegetation	37.3

SOURCE: H. F. Blaney, "Water and Our Crops," *Water, The Yearbook of Agriculture,* U.S. Department of Agriculture, Washington, D.C., 1955.

INFILTRATION

Infiltration is a function of soil type, ground slope, temperature, precipitation type and intensity, vegetation, and soil moisture. It is a key variable in the rainfall-runoff process (discussed in Section 7-3). Field measurement techniques, such as the use of ring infiltrometers, can be employed to obtain rates of infiltration. These devices consist of concentric metal rings inserted into the soil. Water is poured into them and the rate of infiltration is measured. These rate data can then be substituted into an equation relating infiltration to time to determine infiltration capacity.

In the early 1930s, Horton set forth the following relation for determining infiltration capacity (8):

$$f = f_c + (f_0 - f_c)e^{-kt} \tag{7-10}$$

where f = infiltration rate at time t (depth per unit time)
f_0 = infiltration rate at time $t = 0$
f_c = ultimate infiltration rate
k = a coefficient representing the rate of decrease in f capacity

The application of Horton's equation is limited by difficulties in determining f_0 and k. The equation has been used, however, in several watershed models. Its use in the EPA storm water management model is described in Chapter 10.

Two other methods commonly used to determine infiltration rate are those set forth by Holtan and Philip. Holtan's formula relates the infiltration rate to the exhaustion of available soil moisture storage (9). It is stated as

$$f = (a \times S_a^{1.4}) + f_c \tag{7-11}$$

where f = infiltration capacity (in/h)
a = infiltration capacity in in-h/(in)$^{1.4}$ of the available storage (index of surface-connected porosity)
S_a = available storage in approximately the first six inches of soil in inches of equivalent water
f_c = constant rate of infiltration after long wetting (in/h)

Holtan's equation has been used in the Stanford Watershed Model and the USDAHL Watershed Model. For the latter model, Equation 7-11 has been modified as follows (10):

$$f = GI \times a \times S_a^{1.4} + f_c \tag{7-12}$$

where a = a vegetation parameter
GI = growth index of crop in percent maturity

Examples of the growth index for various crops at a particular location are shown in Figure 7-7. Further information for estimates of GI and the

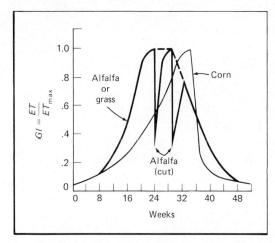

Figure 7-7 Growth index $GI = ET/ET_{max}$ from lysimeter records, irrigated corn and hay for 1955, Coshocton, Ohio. (After H. N. Holtan and N. C. Lopez, *USDAHL-74 Revised Watershed Hydrology,* U.S. Department of Agriculture, ARS Tech. Bull. No. 1518, Washington, D.C., 1975.)

vegetative parameter a can be obtained from the referenced USDA publication (11).

Philip's mathematical model of infiltration is incorporated in newer versions of the Hydrocomp simulation model (see Chapter 10). It also relates infiltration to soil moisture (12). Finally, infiltration indexes are sometimes used as rough approximations for distributing infiltration losses. Such indexes generally assume that infiltration occurs at some constant or average rate throughout a storm. Consequently, initial rates are underestimated and final rates are overstated if an entire storm sequence with little antecedent moisture is considered. The best application is to large storms on wet soils or storms where infiltration rates may be assumed to be relatively uniform (13).

Since the 1930s, when Horton introduced his now classic infiltration equation, the trend in hydrologic analysis has been toward the use of simulation models. Because most such models are actually accounting procedures in which the disposition of water in various stages and/or flow systems is being determined for sequential time steps, infiltration equations based on estimating soil moisture over time are better suited to the process than equations of the type developed by Horton. Equations such as that proposed by Holtan are now the most commonly used, and variations of these are widely encountered in most modern hydrologic modeling approaches.

STREAMFLOW

Streamflow is derived from overland flow, interflow, and groundwater flow, and it is commonly expressed in units of cubic feet per second or acre-feet per unit of time. The U.S. Geological Survey measures streamflow at about 9000 gauging stations across the United States. These measurements provide a good estimate of the total runoff at the gauged location. A plot of streamflow or stream stage (depth) v. time is called a *hydrograph*.

Unfortunately there are many ungauged streams in the United States. For these areas, synthetic streamflow data can sometimes be generated based on a knowledge of precipitation and drainage basin characteristics. Determining the appropriate precipitation input is of fundamental importance to hydrologists. Section 7-3 presents detailed methods for determining relations between precipitation and runoff.

Figure 7-8 shows the annual runoff in the United States in inches per year, which is but a fraction of the measured precipitation. The amount of precipitation that becomes runoff is not uniform from basin to basin, being dependent on many geological and climatological factors.

Hydrologic Budget of the United States

The Water Resources Council has estimated the hydrologic budget for the coterminous United States (4). Approximately 40,000 bgd of water passes over the United States as vapor. Of this amount, about 4200 bgd (equal to 30 inches per year) falls to earth as precipitation. About two-thirds of this (2750 bgd) is returned to the atmosphere by immediate evaporation or by transpiration. The remaining 1450 bgd is accounted for by storage; flows to Canada, Mexico, and the oceans; evaporation from surface-water storage; and consumptive use. Of the 1450 bgd that could potentially be used, the WRC considers only 675 bgd to be available in 95 out of 100 years. The components of the United States water budget are illustrated in Figure 7-9.

Concluding Remarks

In this section we have described the components of the hydrologic system and how these quantities can be measured. We showed that in order to evaluate the hydrologic budget for an area, there is a need for representative data for these components. Precipitation, streamflow, and pan evaporation data are available for many areas of the United States. Based on accurate characterization of vegetation, soil type, topography, and geology, other components of the system can be estimated. In Sections 7-3 and 7-4 we will show how time distributions of hydrologic variables can be used in operational studies of water resources systems.

In simulating hydrologic systems, the ability to quantify the components of the system is essential for verifying and calibrating the models used. An example of a flow process was given in Figure 7-4. In this system both precipitation and streamflow data are needed to determine whether the processes of interception, surface detention, and so on have been adequately calibrated to predict streamflow based on precipitation data. The use of hydrologic data in the simulation and optimization of water quantity and quality systems is the subject of Chapter 10.

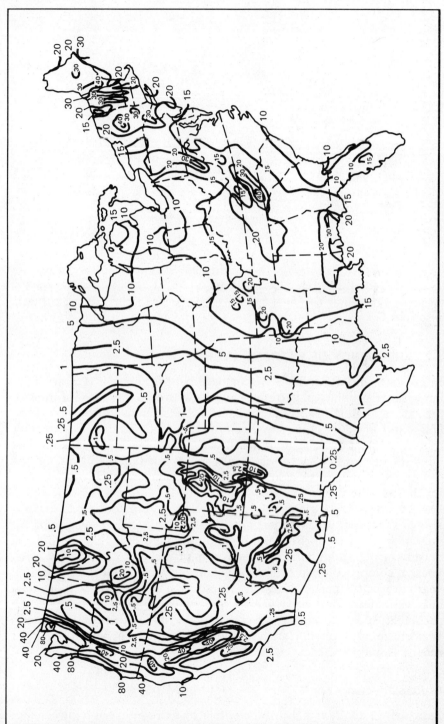

Figure 7-8 Normal annual runoff (in inches) in the United States. (After the U.S. Geological Survey.)

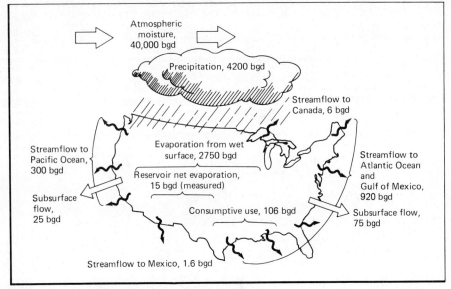

Figure 7-9 Hydrologic budget of the coterminous United States. (After the Water Resources Council.)

7-2 FREQUENCY OF EXTREME EVENTS

In planning and designing water management facilities, it is desirable to know the probability of extreme hydrologic events. Typically of interest are extreme rainfall depths and intensities, peak annual discharges, flood flows, and low-flow durations. For example, in designing a wastewater treatment plant discharging into a stream, a low flow with a small probability of occurrence (seven-day, 10-year) is used in determining the stream's minimum waste assimilative capacity, and thus the design criteria for the treatment plant.

Extreme hydrologic events are commonly estimated using what are known as *annual series* or *partial duration series* of historical data. An *annual series* is comprised of one extreme event (this may be either a maximum or a minimum) for each year of record. A *partial duration series* is comprised of all events exceeding a selected base value for each year of record. A partial duration series is used in cases where more than one event of significance occurs per year; for example, in determining the probability of low flow in an area characterized by two distinct dry seasons. In performing frequency analyses on historical data, at least 10 years of record should be used.

Probability Concepts

Basic to the definition of the probability of an extreme event is the concept of *recurrence interval* (synonymous with *return period*). *Recurrence in-*

terval is defined as the average interval in years between the occurrence of an event of stated magnitude and one of an equal or larger magnitude (see Example 7-3). If a hydrologic event has a recurrence interval of T_R years, the probability P that the magnitude of the event will occur or be exceeded in any particular year can be expressed as

$$P = \frac{1}{T_R} \tag{7-13}$$

and the additional following mathematical relations can be stated:

1. The probability that the magnitude of the event will *not* be exceeded in any one year is

$$1 - P = 1 - \frac{1}{T_R} \tag{7-14}$$

2. The probability that the magnitude of the event will not be exceeded for N successive years is

$$(1 - P)^N = \left(1 - \frac{1}{T_R}\right)^N \tag{7-15}$$

3. The probability that the magnitude of the event will occur once or more within N successive years is

$$1 - (1 - P)^N = 1 - \left(1 - \frac{1}{T_R}\right)^N \tag{7-16}$$

Practicing planners and engineers often express the recurrence interval as the "N-year" event, for example, a "50-year flood." A 50-year flood is a flood that can be expected to occur on the average of once in 50 years. It is important to note that the probability of a 50-year flood occurring within a fixed interval of 50 years is less than 1. In other words, within the next 50 years, a 50-year flood has a probability of occurrence of 64 percent, not 100 percent. Such statistics are helpful to an evaluator in assessing the adequacy of a design.

Figure 7-10 shows the probability of floods at several recurrence intervals occurring in any year up to 50 years in the future. The curves were derived by substituting various values of T_R and N into Equation 7-16. Such information is useful in estimating the chances of an extreme event occurring during a prescribed time span. For example, the graph shows that there is about a 40 percent chance of a 100-year flood happening in the next 50 years. This information would indicate that a structure having a design life of only 50 years might well be subjected to an extreme event having a much longer return period (see also Example 7-2).

Example 7-2

Using Figure 7-10, show in tabular form the percent probability of a 40-year flood occurring within 5, 10, 20, 30, 40, and 50 years in the future.

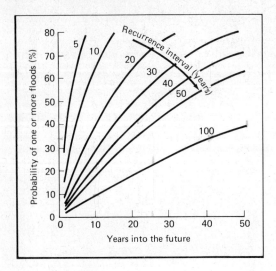

Figure 7-10   Flooding
probability chart.

Explain why this information is more useful than the simple statement
that a particular design is based on a 40-year flood.

SOLUTION
1. Using the 40-year recurrence interval curve in Figure 7-10, read
   off the ordinate (percent probability) for each abscissa (years into
   the future) specified in the problem.
2. Summarize the data in tabular form (see Table 7-3).
3. Often in proposing a plan or design for a water management facility, a planner or engineer is writing for a nontechnical audience.
   In describing that a particular water management project is based
   on a "40-year flood," information such as that presented in Table
   7-3 helps the audience to understand the true probabilities associated with the occurrence of a flood of that magnitude within
   a number of successive years into the future.   ■

Table 7-3   WHEN TO EXPECT A
40-YEAR FLOOD

YEARS INTO THE FUTURE	PROBABILITY OF OCCURRENCE (%)
5	12
10	22
20	40
30	53
40	64
50	72

Frequency Concepts

Graphical methods can be used to determine the recurrence interval and probability of extreme events. One such method has been set forth by Gumbel (14). This method makes use of logarithmic extremal probability paper where the probability (or recurrence interval, $1/P$) of the extreme events of the series are plotted against the magnitude of the events. The occurrence of the selected event is then read from the line best fitted through the plotted points.

Gumbel's method is most often applied to annual series of high flows or low flows. A *low flow* is defined as the lowest discharge occurring for the duration of a short period, on the average of once in a longer time period. In the United States, the most commonly used low flow in designing wastewater treatment facilities is the seven-day, 10-year low flow: the average low flow for seven consecutive days occurring on the average of once in 10 years. Determination of a seven-day, 10-year low flow from an annual series by the Gumbel method is illustrated in Example 7-3.

Example 7-3

Determine the seven-day, 10-year low flow from the data given below using the Gumbel method. Use logarithmic extreme value probability paper and solve the problem graphically.

SOLUTION

1. The data are arranged in Table 7-4 as follows:
   a. The 14 flow data points are arranged in order from the lowest to the highest value.
   b. Each flow value is assigned a rank from $m = 1$ to $m = 14$.

YEAR	LOWEST MEAN DISCHARGE FOR 7 CONSECUTIVE DAYS
1968	52.4
1969	57.5
1970	59.0
1971	45.4
1972	68.3
1973	43.6
1974	65.8
1975	61.2
1976	50.1
1977	48.7
1978	60.9
1979	49.8
1980	55.3
1981	51.0

Table 7-4 COMPUTATIONS FOR EXAMPLE
7-3

RANK	FLOW	RECURRENCE INTERVAL (YR) $T_R = (N + 1)/m;\ N = 14$
1	43.6	15
2	45.4	7.5
3	48.7	5.0
4	49.8	3.8
5	50.1	3.0
6	51.0	2.5
7	52.4	2.1
8	55.3	1.9
9	57.5	1.7
10	59.0	1.5
11	60.9	1.4
12	61.2	1.25
13	65.8	1.15
14	68.3	1.1

c. The recurrence interval is calculated for each year as

$$T_R = \frac{N + 1}{m}\ \text{yr}$$

where N is the number of years of data (14) and m is the rank of
the flow. Note that there are a number of formulas for estimating
T_R, the simplest being N/m. The one given above is perhaps the
most widely used, however (see reference 4).

2. The data are plotted on the logarithmic extreme value probability
paper with the recurrence intervals assigned to the x axis and the
corresponding flows to the y axis, and a line of best fit is drawn
through the points, as shown in Figure 7-11.

3. The flow of the 10-year recurrence interval is determined from the
graph to be 43 ft^3/s. ■

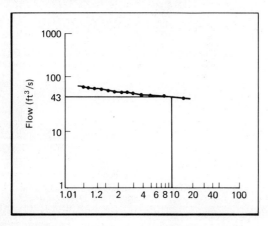

Figure 7-11 Low-flow
frequency curve for data given
in Example 7-3.

For reservoir design, the low flow of interest is usually a longer period of time, for example a number of consecutive months or even years, occurring on the average of once in 20, 50, or 100 years.

This section has dealt with simple frequency concepts applicable only to events observed at a single point. Chapter 10 extends this by covering frequency distributions and time series.

7-3   SURFACE-WATER HYDROLOGY

This section deals with methods to describe mathematically the behavior of water as it flows over the surface of the earth, and its response to natural or manmade changes in its path. The concept of a *hydrograph*—a time distribution of streamflow—is introduced. Once a river reach (section) is characterized by a hydrograph, the response of the reach to a change in input or output can be assessed. Armed with hydrograph concepts, an analyst can make estimates of reservoir storage capacity and reaction to flood waves of various magnitudes.

Hydrograph Analysis

The hydrologic budget (Equation 7-4) accounts for the inflows, outflows, and storage associated with the represented system. Most hydrologic process models are designed to accept precipitation as input, distribute this input to components such as infiltration, and finally produce an outflow hydrograph. The precipitation input is usually specified as a time distribution. Graphically it may be represented by a *hyetograph*, a plot of precipitation over time (see Figure 7-12). A *hydrograph* represents a time distribution of streamflow or discharge (see Figure 7-13). The peak areas of a hydrograph result from *direct surface runoff*, that is, the effective precipitation (total precipitation less losses due to interception, depression storage, infiltration, and evaporation) that finds its way to a watercourse.

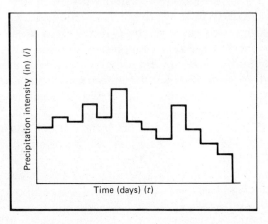

Figure 7-12   A hyetograph.

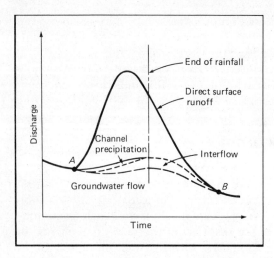

Figure 7-13 A hydrograph.

During dry periods, when streamflow exists, groundwater flow to the stream channel is the source of surface-water flow. This is called the *base flow*—the flow sustained by groundwater input into the system.

A hydrograph has four component elements: (1) direct surface runoff, (2) interflow, (3) groundwater or base flow, and (4) channel precipitation. The rising portion of the hydrograph is known as the *concentration curve*, the region in the vicinity of the peak is called the *crest segment*, and the falling portion is the *recession* (13). The shape of a hydrograph depends on precipitation pattern characteristics and basin properties. The time base of a hydrograph is considered to be the time at which the concentration curve begins until the direct-runoff component essentially reaches zero. Figure 7-13 illustrates these definitions.

In most hydrograph analyses, interflow and channel precipitation are grouped with surface runoff rather than treated independently. Channel precipitation begins with the inception of rainfall and ends with the storm. Its distribution with respect to time is highly correlated with the storm pattern. The relative volume contribution tends to increase somewhat as the storm proceeds, since stream levels rise and the water surface area tends to increase. The fraction of watershed area occupied by streams and lakes is generally small, usually on the order of 5 percent or less, so that the percentage of runoff related to channel precipitation is usually minor.

Interflow is that part of the subsurface flow that moves at shallow depths and reaches the surface channels in a relatively short period of time and is therefore commonly considered part of the direct surface runoff. Its distribution is commonly characterized by a slowly increasing rate up to the end of the storm period, followed by a gradual recession that terminates at the intersection of the surface flow hydrograph and base flow hydrograph. Figure 7-13 illustrates the approximate nature of the components of channel precipitation and interflow.

The base flow component is composed of water that percolates downward until it reaches the groundwater reservoir and then flows to surface streams as groundwater discharge. The groundwater hydrograph may or may not show an increase during the storm period. Groundwater accretion resulting from a particular storm is normally released over an extended period measured in days for small watersheds and often in months or years for large drainage areas.

The surface runoff component consists of water that flows overland until a stream channel is reached. During large storms it is the most significant hydrograph component. Figure 7-13 illustrates the surface runoff and groundwater components of a hydrograph. The relative magnitude of each component for a given storm is determined by a combination of many factors. Hydrographs are analyzed to provide knowledge of the way precipitation and watershed characteristics interact to form them. The degree of hydrograph separation required depends on the objective of the study. For most practical work, surface runoff and groundwater components only are required. Research projects or more sophisticated analyses may dictate consideration of all components. When multiple storms occur within short periods, it is sometimes necessary to separate the overlapping parts of consecutive surface runoff hydrographs.

Discharge from precipitation excess—that is, after abstractions are deducted from rainfall—constitutes the direct runoff hydrograph (DRH). Arrival of direct runoff at the outlet of a watershed causes an initial rise in the DRH. As precipitation excess continues, enough time elapses for progressively distant areas to add to the outlet flow. Consequently, the duration of rainfall dictates the proportionate area of the watershed amplifying the peak, and the intensity of rainfall during this period of time determines the resulting highest discharge.

A normal single-peak DRH generally possesses the shape shown in Figure 7-13. The time to peak magnitude of this hydrograph depends on the intensity and the duration of the rainfall and the size, slope, shape, and storage capacity of the watershed. Once peak flow has been reached for a given rainstorm, the DRH begins to descend, its source of supply coming largely from water accumulated within the watershed such as detention and channel storage.

Processes involved in forming the DRH can be better understood by visualizing precipitation excess as being partially disposed of as surface runoff while a portion remains held within the watershed boundaries. This water is released later from storage. Thus the shape and timing of the DRH are integrated effects of the duration and intensity of hydrometeorological factors as well as the effect of the physiographic factors of the watershed on the storage capacity.

The relative timing of hydrologic events must be known if drainage areas having subbasins are to be modeled or if continuous simulation is desired. A basic measure of timing is lag time or basin lag, which locates the hydrograph's position relative to the causative storm pattern. It is the property of a drainage area that is defined as the difference in time between the center of mass of effective rainfall and the center of mass of runoff produced. Other definitions are also used, mainly for ease of determination. Two of these are (1) the time interval from the maximum rainfall rate to the peak rate of runoff, and (2) the time from the center of mass of effective rainfall to the peak rate of flow. Time lag is characterized by the ratio of flow length to a mean velocity of flow and is a property that is influenced by the shape of the drainage area, the slope of the main channel, channel geometry, and the storm pattern. Another frequently used measure of timing in hydrologic studies is the time of concentration. It is defined as the flow time from the most remote point in the drainage area to the outlet of interest. It can be estimated for channels by the Chézy or Manning formulas (see Chapter 9).

THE UNIT HYDROGRAPH

A principal task of the hydrologist is to estimate streamflow hydrographs for prescribed conditions of precipitation and drainage basin characteristics. In the case of flood studies, the task is to determine the nature of the flood flow that would be produced by some extreme storm event. For drought emergency planning, estimates of low stream flows that might be expected during prolonged dry spells would be sought. Sometimes the objective is to produce only an event hydrograph (one associated with a particular rainfall, for example). In other cases, continuous hydrographs are needed such as in studies associated with reservoir filling or water supply. Regardless of the objective, there are a number of approaches that can be used to estimate hydrographs that would result from assumed conditions of precipitation. Several of these will be discussed in this chapter. We shall begin with the unit hydrograph, a procedure widely used in its original context and now used in many variations especially suited to computer modeling.

In 1932 Leroy Sherman proposed the concept of a *unit hydrograph* as a basis for analyzing surface-water systems (15). The unit hydrograph is defined as the hydrograph resulting from a storm delivering one inch of effective precipitation, during a specified time period (unit time), to a particular drainage area. The shape of the hydrograph is determined by the physical features of the drainage area. Although not theoretically accurate, it is assumed that the time base of the unit hydrograph is fixed for a given unit storm. Furthermore, for every unit storm a specific unit hydrograph can be derived for the area. A basic assumption of unit hydrograph theory is linearity. That is, the ordinates of the unit hydrograph are proportional to those of another hydrograph having the same time base but derived from a different effective precipitation volume (a hydrograph resulting from two inches of rainfall in the same unit time would have ordinates twice those of the unit hydrograph, and so on).

Unit hydrographs may be generated from any of three sources: field data, drainage basin characteristics, or conceptual models. To generate unit hydrographs from field data, rainfall and runoff records are needed. Synthetic unit hydrographs are derived from empirical equations based on various drainage basin characteristics. In conceptual models, theoretical equations are used as a model of the hydrograph shape.

To develop a unit hydrograph from field data, the data selected from historical records should have certain characteristics. The hydrographs should be single-peaked and they should be associated with storm patterns that are fairly uniform (see Figure 7-14). From these data a unit hydrograph can be determined in the following manner (see Figure 7-15):

1. Separate the base or groundwater flow so that the total direct runoff hydrograph may be obtained. A number of procedures can be used for this, but the most important point is to be consistent (1). A common method is to draw a straight line beginning at the point where the hydrograph begins to rise and ending where the hydrograph recession curve intersects this extension. Often a horizontal line is used (see Figure 7-15).
2. Determine the duration of effective rainfall. The effective rainfall volume is equivalent to the volume of direct surface runoff. The volume of direct surface runoff is obtained by calculating the area under the hydrograph that is above the base flow separation line. This volume is then used to adjust the rainfall pattern so that the duration of effective rainfall can be estimated. Note that the difference between the total volume of rainfall determined from the hyetograph and the volume of direct surface runoff is the amount

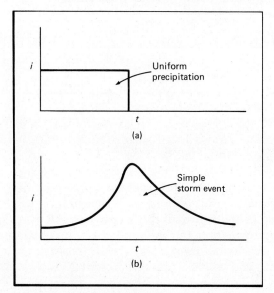

Figure 7-14　Field data needed for a unit hydrograph derivation: (a) uniform rainfall patterns; (b) single-peak storms.

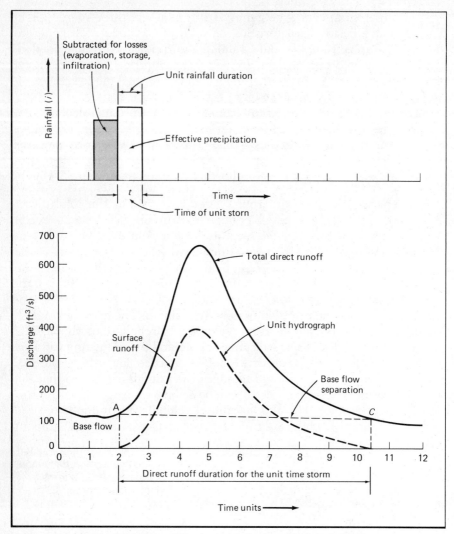

Figure 7-15 Derivation of a unit hydrograph from an isolated storm.

of rainfall that satisfies the various losses such as infiltration. By using mathematical representations of these loss functions or other estimating procedures, the volume of the loss can be deducted from the gross rainfall pattern to yield the effective precipitation pattern. Note that in Figure 7-15 it has simply been assumed that during the initial period of the storm all the losses were satisfied. This is a very rough approximation, but for large storms on extensive drainage areas, the procedure used in distributing losses is not critical. For small areas and storms, more representative tech-

niques should be used (1). The time base of the effective rainfall pattern is the time duration of the unit storm.
3. Tabulate the ordinates of direct runoff at sufficient points to determine the hydrograph shape. Note that the direct runoff ordinate is the vertical difference between the upper portion of the hydrograph and the base flow separation line.
4. Compute the ordinates of the unit hydrograph. The direct surface runoff hydrograph represents some volume of effective precipitation. This can be converted into a hydrograph representing one inch of effective precipitation (the unit hydrograph) using the hydrograph equation:

$$\frac{Q_s}{V_s} = \frac{Q_u}{V_u} \tag{7-17}$$

where Q_s = flow of direct surface runoff (ft^3/s)
V_s = volume of direct surface runoff (in)
Q_u = flow of unit hydrograph (ft^3/s)
V_u = volume of unit hydrograph = 1 in

Since Q_s and V_s are known from the input data, and $V_u = 1$ in, Q_u can be determined by dividing the direct surface runoff hydrograph into time steps and converting the ordinates of the time steps into unit hydrograph ordinates. This is done by dividing by effective precipitation volume, that is:

$$Q_u = \frac{Q_s}{V_s} \quad (ft^3/s)$$

The resultant hydrograph is the unit hydrograph for the area under study, and its points of intersection with the abscissa define the time base of the unit hydrograph. Application of the method is demonstrated in Example 7-4.

Example 7-4

Given an effective precipitation of 1.5 inches in one unit time and the runoff data given in Table 7-5, derive the unit hydrograph.

SOLUTION
1. The data are plotted as shown in Figure 7-16. The base flow is separated from the storm event by drawing a straight line from A to B on the hydrograph. Base flow values (column 2 of Table 7-5) are subtracted from the runoff values to obtain direct surface runoff (column 3).

Table 7-5   DERIVATION OF THE UNIT HYDROGRAPH FOR FIGURE 7-16

(1)	(2)	(3)	(4) TOTAL DIRECT RUNOFF	(5) UNIT HYDROGRAPH
TIME UNIT	TOTAL RUNOFF (FT³/S)	BASE FLOW (FT³/S)	(2) − (3) (FT³/S)	ORDINATE, (4)/1.5 (FT³/S)
1	105	105	0	0
1.5	105	103	2	1.3
2	125	102	23	15.3
2.5	200	100	100	66.7
3	350	99	251	167
3.5	500	98	402	268
4	575	96	479	319
4.5	500	94	406	271
5	400	92	308	205
5.5	325	90	235	157
6	250	89	161	107
6.5	200	88	112	74.7
7	175	86	89	59.3
8	125	83	42	28.0
9	100	80	20	13.3
10	75	75	0	0
11	75	75	0	0

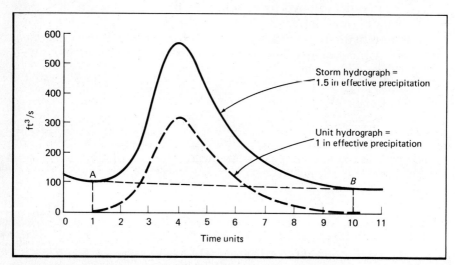

Figure 7-16   Derivation of a unit hydrograph for Example 7-4.

2. The direct surface runoff hydrograph represents 1.5 inches of effective precipitation. The unit hydrograph ordinates (Q_u) are derived by applying Equation 7-17, that is, by dividing the direct surface runoff ordinates (Q_s) by 1.5 in (V_s):

$$Q_u = Q_s/1.5$$

These values are entered in column 5 of Table 7-5. A plot of these values represents the unit hydrograph with a time base of nine time units and a peak flow of 319 cubic feet per second. ∎

Once a unit storm and a unit hydrograph are derived for a drainage area, a hydrograph can be calculated for any storm provided that the time base of effective precipitation is the same. Because of the linearity assumed by unit hydrograph theory, the ordinates of the unit hydrograph are simply multiplied by the volume of effective precipitation to derive a hydrograph for the storm of interest.

If the time base of the storm is not the same as that of the unit storm, a storm hydrograph may be derived from manipulations of the unit hydrograph as follows. The storm hyetograph is divided into blocks having the same time base as the unit storm. Hydrographs can then be determined for each storm block by multiplying the ordinates of the unit hydrograph by the effective precipitation of each block. The ordinates of the hydrographs are added to determine the composite storm hydrograph. Where it is expected that this approach will be used, the original unit hydrograph should be derived, if possible, from a short enough unit time storm so that other storm periods of interest will be approximate multiples of the original duration of effective precipitation.

Often it is desirable to use a unit hydrograph of a time duration different from that derived by using historical data. Methods for converting a unit hydrograph of one duration into another include the *lagging procedure* and the *S-hydrograph method*.

The lagging procedure is appropriate for deriving a unit hydrograph of a time duration that is an integral multiple of the original time duration. For example, suppose that, given a one-hour unit hydrograph, a three-hour unit hydrograph is desired. By the lagging method, three one-hour unit hydrographs are lagged by one hour and the ordinates are summed and divided by 3. The resultant ordinates represent one inch of precipitation spread over three hours (0.33 in/h) instead of one hour—a three-hour unit hydrograph (see Figure 7-17).

Alternatively, the S-hydrograph method can be used to derive the same result, and moreover it can be used to derive unit hydrographs having durations that are fractional multiples (either smaller or larger) of the original hydrograph. If many D-hour (for example, here one hour) unit hydrographs are lagged by D hours and their ordinates summed, an S hydrograph is formed that represents a storm with an intensity of one inch per hour continuing for an indefinite period. By lagging two S-hydrographs by the number of time units (t) of the duration of the desired unit hydrograph (for example, three hours), subtracting the S-curve ordinates and dividing the difference by the number of time units t, a hydrograph of the desired time duration can be derived (see Figure 7-18).

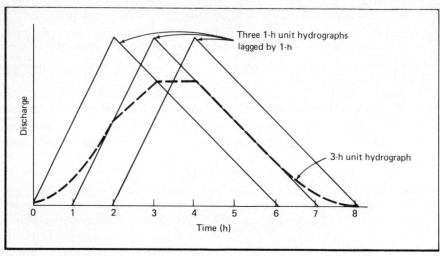

Figure 7-17   Lagging procedure.

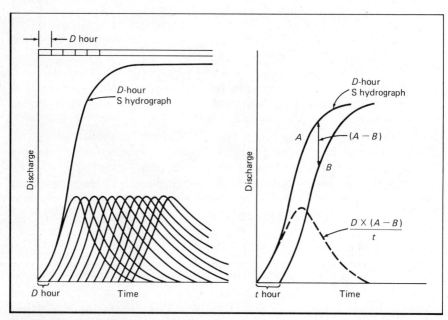

Figure 7-18   S-hydrograph method.

SYNTHETIC UNIT HYDROGRAPHS

The derivation of the unit hydrograph is impeded when historical rainfall and runoff data are not available for the watershed of interest. To deal with these cases, methods have been developed to correlate drainage basin properties with hydrograph characteristics to enable generation of artificial or *synthetic* unit hydrographs. These methods involve deriving empirical equations from field data to define the shape of a unit hydrograph for a particular drainage basin. Examples of such techniques are those that have been developed by Snyder, the Corps of Engineers, the Soil Conservation Service, Taylor and Schwarz, and Gray (16–20).

CONCEPTUAL HYDROGRAPH MODELS

Another method of generating unit hydrographs makes use of theoretical equations to define the shape of a hydrograph. A simple example is a model of a linear storage system where the storage equation and continuity equation are used to mathematically describe the shape of the system inflow and outflow hydrographs. The storage equation is:

$$S = KO \tag{7-18}$$

where S = volume of water stored
O = outflow per unit time
K = storage constant

and the continuity equation is:

$$I - O = \Delta S / \Delta T \tag{7-19}$$

where I = inflow per unit time
ΔS = change in volume of water stored
ΔT = change in time

By evaluating the storage constant K (using observed data or hydraulic principles) of the storage equation, a mathematical hydrograph of the system outflow can be generated.

An example of a more complex hydrograph model is the USGS rainfall-runoff model, which makes use of mathematical equations to describe moisture accounting, infiltration, and surface runoff to generate an outflow hydrograph. This model is presented in detail in Section 10-4.

SYNTHETIC STREAMFLOW GENERATION

Often the streamflow record for a drainage basin is of limited duration. But if it is long enough to permit valid statistical interpretation, synthetic streamflow traces can be generated based on the assumption that they are partially dependent on past occurrences and are partially random in nature. These statistical methods enable generation of long streamflow traces (histories) that are particularly useful for performing frequency analyses (Section 7-2). Additionally, streamflow data can be derived from rainfall data where no record of streamflow exists. Artificial rainfall records can be developed in the manner described above for streamflows and these records can then be converted into streamflows using rainfall-runoff models. The Markov process for generating synthetic streamflow is discussed in detail in Section 10-3.

Flow Routing

The use of a unit hydrograph to characterize the outflow of a river reach is limited to areas of about 2000 square miles due to the localized nature of rainfall events and the effects of time and changes in basin characteristics on the hydrograph as it moves downstream (13). To circumvent this problem, large watersheds can be divided into subwatersheds and each subwatershed characterized by its own hydrograph (see Figure 7-19). The problem is to determine how the subarea inflow hydrographs are combined to give an outflow hydrograph at some point downstream. Complicating factors are that tributaries contribute peak flows at different points in time, due to different travel distances and times to the downstream point of interest. Additionally, as flows are translated (move) downstream, they experience attenuation due to the storage characteristics of the system; the delay in flow arrival at the outlet due to storage dampens the hydrograph's peak and spreads its flow out over a longer time base (see Figure 7-20). Reservoirs also create a damping effect on hydrograph shape.

Flow-routing techniques are designed to account for the effects of the storage characteristics of a watershed or reservoir on flows in a stream channel. These techniques can be applied to flood forecasting, calculating hydrographs at various locations in a watershed, and deriving synthetic unit hydrographs. Routing methods are classified as being either *hydrologic* or *hydraulic.* Hydrologic routing employs the continuity equation and the storage equation, whereas hydraulic routing uses the basic equations of fluid flow and those of continuity and momentum (1, 2, 13). Hydraulic routing better models the dynamics of unsteady flow conditions that prevail in a moving flood wave, but it requires the use of a computer to solve the appropriate finite difference equations. Either method can be

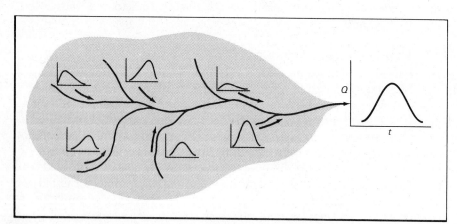

Figure 7-19   Characterization of subbasins by unit hydrographs.

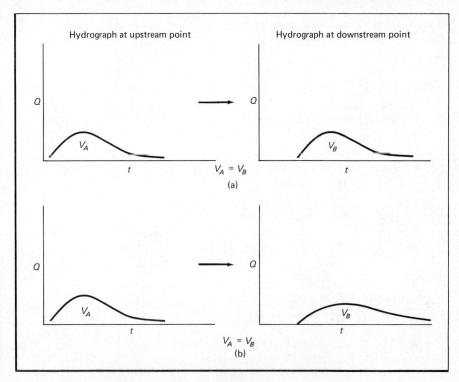

Figure 7-20 Attenuation and translation effects on a hydrograph as the peak flow moves downstream: (a) pure translation (change in timing only but no change in shape); (b) translation plus attenuation.

applied to streamflow routing, reservoir routing, or watershed routing; references 1, 2, and 13 give comprehensive treatment of these applications.

Simulation of Surface-Water Systems

Suppose that for a particular watershed it is desirable to determine the effects of a flood of a certain magnitude at the basin outlet. Given that the rainfall input is usually unevenly distributed over the basin and that the basin could be comprised of many tributaries, several reservoirs, and widely varying soil types, vegetation, topography, and degrees of urbanization, it is not hard to realize that calculating the system response to the input variables can become a complex task.

Because surface-water systems of interest are often extensive and intricate, and because it is often desirable to determine a system's response to varying inputs, *models* of the system that simulate the interrelations of the physical variables of concern at successive time steps are widely employed. These simulation models simply account for the allocation of water in a watershed. Their outputs are valuable to those making planning, design, and management decisions.

There are three types of models that find use in hydrologic analyses: physical, analog, and digital computer models. Physical models are built to mimic the real watershed on a small scale. Analog models are systems of circuits and resistors designed to imitate the hydrologic system electronically. Digital computer models are based on mathematical relations involving the variables that characterize the watershed's hydrology. By calibrating a computer model with known input and output data, such a model can be used to simulate a watershed's response to prescribed inputs. High-speed computers facilitate such calculations, especially when continuous output over many years is to be obtained.

Several hydrologic simulation models are discussed in Section 10-4. Included in the discussion are methods for estimating the physical parameters of the models and for calibrating the models for predictive use.

7-4 GROUNDWATER HYDROLOGY

The volume of groundwater in the United States greatly exceeds that stored in all of the nation's streams, rivers, reservoirs, and lakes, including the Great Lakes. This vast reservoir sustains streamflow during precipitation-free periods and constitutes the principal source of fresh water for many dry areas. Of particular interest is the total quantity of groundwater available for use; that is, that which can be withdrawn by wells and related manmade devices, or which forms the base flow of surface streams.

Groundwater flow is governed by a different set of physical principles than is surface-water flow. In evaluating the behavior of water underground, we must keep in mind that, for the most part, water is flowing at an exceedingly slow rate through a porous medium, namely through soil or through crevices in rocks.

In this section we shall look at the occurrence of groundwater supplies and the governing mathematical equations that describe the movement of groundwater under various conditions. Using these principles, we shall also look at methods for collecting groundwater for surface use. Finally, methods for artificially recharging depleted groundwater systems are discussed.

Aquifer Systems

Underground water is derived from infiltration of precipitation and surface water into subterranean zones. The unobservable flow of water beneath the surface of the earth makes it difficult to conceptualize, however. Except for a few isolated cases, groundwater does not flow in underground streams or lie in pools but rather is within the interstices of porous and permeable subsurface geological formations. The flow is exceedingly slow—on the order of five feet per day to a few feet per year.

VERTICAL DISTRIBUTION OF SUBSURFACE WATER

Figure 7-21 depicts various zones of water that occur beneath the earth's surface. In the zone of aeration, the rock or soil pores are filled partly with water and partly with air. In the zone of saturation, or the groundwater zone, the rock or soil pores are completely filled with water under hydrostatic pressure. The surface of the zone of saturation (for confined conditions explained later) is designated as the *water table,* and it is defined as the water surface under atmospheric pressure. The water table level is not static; rather, its elevation rises and falls depending on the net recharge of the groundwater system. In times when the discharge exceeds the recharge, the water table level will fall; in a similar manner, during times when the recharge exceeds the discharge, the level of the water table will rise.

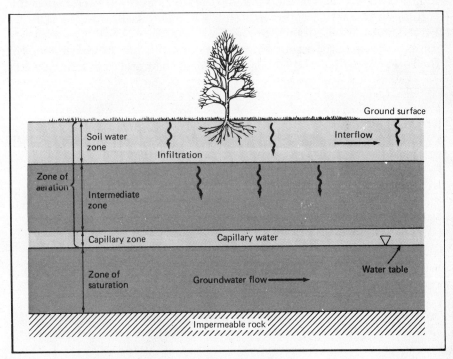

Figure 7-21   Vertical distribution of subsurface water.

TYPES OF AQUIFERS

A geological formation that will yield quantities of water that can be economically used and developed is defined as an aquifer. Figure 7-22 is an idealized depiction of two basic types of aquifers: confined and unconfined. In an unconfined aquifer the top of the zone of saturation is not restricted by an impermeable layer and is at atmospheric pressure. Note that if a well is drilled to an unconfined aquifer, the level of the water in the well rises to the level of the water table. In a confined or artesian aquifer the saturated zone is bound above by an impervious layer, which causes the water in a confined aquifer to be at a pressure greater than atmospheric. The free water surface occurs near the recharge area where the impervious layer no longer confines the water. When a well is drilled into a confined aquifer, the water in it will rise above the confining layer to the level of the artesian aquifer's piezometric surface, which is to say to a height above the pressurized aquifer corresponding to its hydrostatic head. In cases where the piezometric surface occurs above the ground surface, water will naturally flow up out of the ground.

OCCURRENCE OF AQUIFERS IN THE UNITED STATES

Figure 7-23 is a map of the groundwater areas in the United States. According to the WRC, approximately 25 percent of all water used in the United States is withdrawn from groundwater supplies (4). Groundwater sources provide 95 percent of the total domestic and industrial needs of the rural population and 50 percent of all agricultural needs. In 32 states

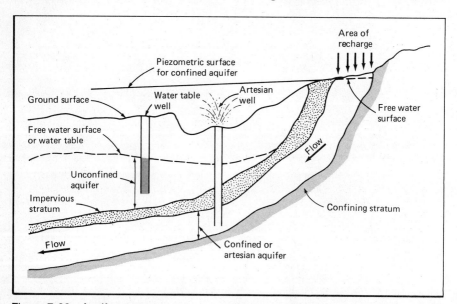

Figure 7-22   Aquifer systems.

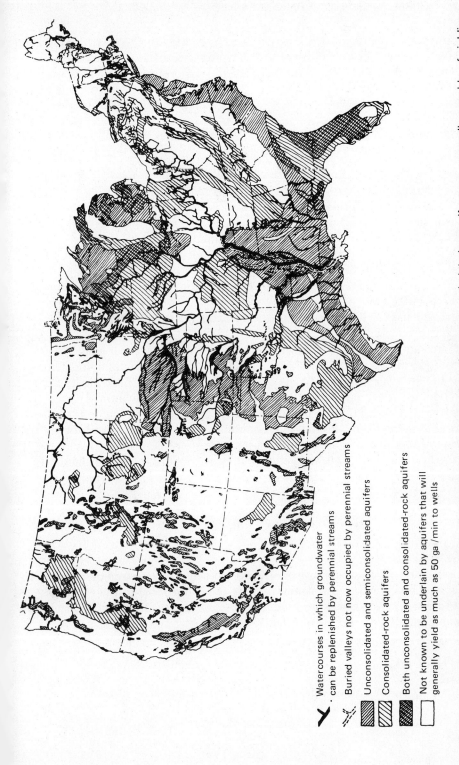

Figure 7-23   Groundwater areas of the United States. Patterns show that areas underlain by aquifers are generally capable of yielding to individual wells 50 gal/min or more of water containing not more than 2000 ppm of dissolved solids (includes some areas where more highly mineralized water is actually used). (After H. E. Thomas, "Underground Sources of Water," *The Yearbook of Agriculture,* U.S. Department of Agriculture, Washington, D.C., 1955.)

Watercourses in which groundwater can be replenished by perennial streams

Buried valleys not now occupied by perennial streams

Unconsolidated and semiconsolidated aquifers

Consolidated-rock aquifers

Both unconsolidated and consolidated-rock aquifers

Not known to be underlain by aquifers that will generally yield as much as 50 ga/min to wells groundwater is a major drinking water source, and it is the only source in many localities. The usability of groundwater depends very much on its quality. Factors affecting the quality of the groundwater in the United States are discussed in Chapter 6.

Safe Yield

In the past, *safe yield* has been defined as the quantity of water that can be withdrawn annually without ultimate depletion of the aquifer. This term has been viewed with disfavor in recent years because it is felt that the concept implies that it is desirable to avoid aquifer depletion. This is not necessarily the case, because sometimes it is not practical to operate in the safe yield mode. For example, where aquifer recharge amounts to virtually zero, a decision to mine the water may be made based on the lack of availability or on the quality of alternative water supplies. Mining an aquifer should therefore not be viewed as a practice to be avoided per se, but rather as a management option that should be exercised with full awareness of the impacts on the aquifer and its expected useful life.

For aquifers that are readily recharged, the safe yield management technique may be used for balancing aquifer recharge and depletion. One method for calculating safe yield has been developed by Hill. In this method, the mean annual draft is plotted against the mean annual change in groundwater level for a number of years approximating the long-term average water supply. For a basin receiving a fairly uniform water supply, the plotted points can be fitted by a straight line. The safe yield is taken as the draft that results in zero change in groundwater level. This method is illustrated in Figure 7-24.

Darcy's Law and Governing Equations

DARCY'S LAW

The basic equation used for groundwater flow analysis is based on Darcy's law, which states that the water velocity is proportional to the head loss in the system. A basic assumption is that groundwater flow velocities are exceedingly low—on the order of five feet per day to a few feet per year. Darcy's law can be stated as:

$$Q = -KA\, dh/dx \tag{7-20}$$

where Q = total discharge across a cross-sectional area of the
              permeable bed (vol/time)
       K = hydraulic conductivity of the material

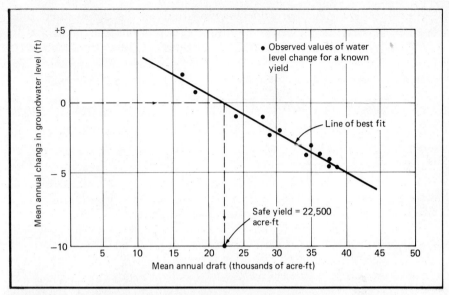

Figure 7-24 Example of the determination of safe yield with the Hill method.

A = cross-sectional area of the permeable bed
x = length of the bed under consideration

and

h, the total head or piezometric head at a selected elevation, can be expressed as (see Figure 7-25):

$$h = z_A + h_A \tag{7-21}$$

where z_A = elevation above a selected datum
h_A = head measured from selected elevation to water table

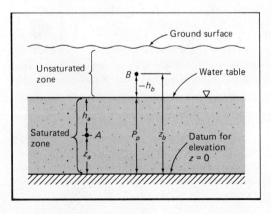

Figure 7-25 Definition sketch showing hydrostatic pressures in a porous medium.

Note that h is a negative value for elevations in the unsaturated zone, because z_B exceeds P_p under unsaturated conditions.

Equation 7-20 may be rewritten in terms of velocity, which is the form of Darcy's law used in solving most groundwater problems. The *Darcian velocity* is thus:

$$q = Q/A = - K \, dh/dx \qquad (7\text{-}22)$$

where q is also called the *specific discharge*, that is, the discharge per unit area, in units of velocity.

Another expression for q is:

$$q = nV_p \qquad (7\text{-}23)$$

where n = porosity of the permeable material
V_p = pore velocity

The hydraulic conductivity K (also called the coefficient of permeability) may be expressed in a number of ways. The USGS defines K_s, the standard coefficient of permeability, as the number of gallons per day of water that will pass through one square foot of a porous medium under a unit hydraulic gradient at 60°F. A *field coefficient of permeability*, K_f, may be derived from K_s by adjusting for the dynamic viscosity of water under field conditions based on the relation:

$$K_f = K_s \, (u_{60}/u_f) \qquad (7\text{-}24)$$

where u_{60} = dynamic viscosity of water at 60°F
u_f = dynamic viscosity at field temperature

Another useful coefficient in analyzing groundwater flow is the coefficient of transmissivity. It may be expressed as:

$$T = K_f b \qquad (7\text{-}25)$$

where K_f = field hydraulic conductivity or coefficient of permeability
b = the saturated depth of the aquifer

It is important to note that Darcy's law applies only to flow that can be characterized by a low Reynolds number (on the order of 1)—that is, in flow regimes where viscous forces predominate. The Reynolds number is an expression of the ratio of inertial forces to viscous forces acting on a fluid. The Reynolds number is designated as:

$$N_R = Vd/v \qquad (7\text{-}26)$$

where V = flow velocity
d = mean grain diameter
v = kinematic viscosity

Groundwater Collection Systems

Groundwater is collected primarily by means of wells and infiltration galleries. A water well is a hole or shaft, usually vertical, excavated in the earth for the purpose of bringing groundwater to the surface (6). An infiltration gallery is a horizontal conduit for intercepting and collecting groundwater by gravity flow. Because the latter systems depend on infiltrated water to derive most of their supply, they are commonly located near and parallel to riverbeds.

Darcy's law can be applied to wells and infiltration galleries to solve problems of groundwater flow. The appropriate equations for determining Q will be presented for steady, radial flow in an unconfined aquifer.

Before this discussion, attention should be given to some general characteristics of flows to wells. Figure 7-26 shows that after pumping begins, a head loss is encountered in the well. This is due to the frictional resistance of the soil to the flow through it that is generated by pumping. The piezometric surface surrounding the well becomes depressed as a result; this area is called the *cone of depression*. The cone of depression spreads until equilibrium conditions are reached. The height of the water in the well no longer rises to the level of the water table, but instead to some lower elevation h_w. The difference between the water table elevation and h_w is called the *drawdown*.

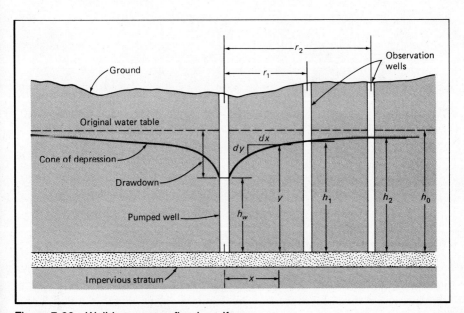

Figure 7-26   Well in an unconfined aquifer.

STEADY RADIAL FLOW TOWARD A WELL IN AN UNCONFINED AQUIFER

Referring to Figure 7-26, it is assumed that the original water table is horizontal, the flow to the well is radial, the well fully penetrates an aquifer of infinite areal extent, and steady-state conditions prevail. Given these conditions, the flow toward the well at any point x can be calculated as the product of the flow velocity and the cylindrical cross-sectional area at that point. Darcy's law allows us to state that

$$Q = 2\pi xy K_f(dy/dx) \tag{7-27}$$

where $2\pi xy$ = area of any cylindrical cross section with the well as
               its axis (ft^2)
       K_f = hydraulic conductivity (ft/s)
    dy/dx = the water table gradient at any distance x
        Q = the well discharge (ft^3/s)

Separating the variables and integrating x from the limits r_1 to r_2 and y from the limits h_1 to h_2:

$$\int_{r_1}^{r_2} Q \frac{dx}{x} = 2\pi K_f \int_{h_1}^{h_2} y \, dy \tag{7-28}$$

yields

$$Q \ln \frac{r_2}{r_1} = \frac{2\pi K_f(h_2^2 - h_1^2)}{2} \tag{7-29}$$

which can be simplified to

$$Q = \frac{\pi K_f(h_2^2 - h_1^2)}{\ln (r_2/r_1)} \tag{7-30}$$

If K_f is converted to units of gal/day/ft^2 and ln to log, Equation 7-30 can be rewritten as

$$K_f = \frac{1055Q \log (r_2/r_1)}{h_2^2 - h_1^2} \tag{7-31}$$

Simulation of Regional Groundwater Systems

The methods discussed above for analysis of groundwater flow are appropriate for solving local groundwater problems. For problems of regional scale, such as those for determining changes in water table level over a large area due to existing water use practices, the simulation methods presented in Chapter 10 are more appropriate. Such large systems lend themselves better to systems analysis due to the number of variables involved in formulating the problem, and due to the fact that the variables often change over time and space. Groundwater modeling techniques include porous media models, electrical analog models, and digital computer models for the solution of equations of groundwater flow. Computer simulation models are discussed in Chapter 10.

7-5   JOINT SURFACE-WATER–GROUNDWATER SYSTEMS

From the above discussions of surface-water hydrology and groundwater hydrology, it should be obvious that in many cases the two systems are physically inseparable—groundwater provides the base flow to streams and rivers and is in turn recharged by infiltration from water flowing over the earth's surface. Unfortunately, however, the two subsystems are often thought of as separate entities and are managed independently. Chapter 3 illustrates how the passage of water laws and regulations that do not recognize this physical relationship have contributed to this practice. Ideally, for the most efficient use of water resources, surface-water systems and groundwater systems should be operated together to take advantage of the best characteristics of each system. Such joint operation is called "conjunctive use."

In practice, this concept has been applied to the joint operation of surface reservoirs and nearby groundwater aquifers. It takes advantage of the fact that surface waters are available seasonally but at an uncertain time and in an uncertain amount. Surface waters can be collected and stored for future use in surface reservoirs, but a large amount of water may be lost by evaporation and infiltration. Groundwater storage, on the other hand, varies little over time and can be depended on for a predictable available quantity. By operating the two systems together, greater and more economical yields can be realized. This involves impoundment of surface water and using it to the greatest extent possible during periods of abundant precipitation and at the same time increasing groundwater supplies by artificial recharge. During dry periods, stored groundwater can be used since it is known that the water table can be replenished during the next wet period. In this manner the groundwater table can be allowed to fluctuate without cause for concern about permanent depletion of the aquifer.

Conjunctive use of surface water and groundwater requires careful planning and full understanding of the hydrogeological properties of the area under consideration. There must be sufficient storage space available in the aquifer for storing the amount of water needed to withstand a drought period. In addition, reservoir, pumping, and artificial recharge facilities must be available to control the surface-water system. An exam-

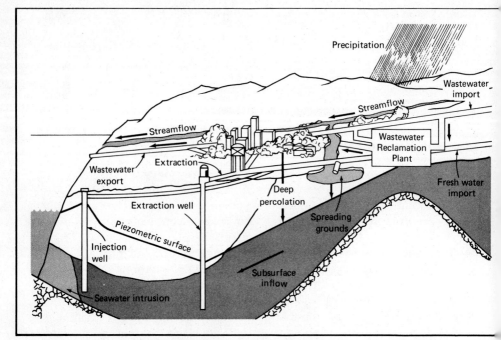

Figure 7-27   Pictorial representaion of conjunctive use of surface-water and groundwater resources, Los Angeles Coastal Plain, California. (After California Department of Water Resources, "Planned Utilization of Ground Water Basin: Coastal Plain of Los Angeles County," Bull. 104, Sacramento, 1968.)

ple of a conjunctive system in use in the United States is the extensive system in the Los Angeles Coastal Plain in California (21). A pictorial representation of this system is shown in Figure 7-27.

PROBLEMS

7-1. Derive a hydrologic budget for the atmospheric hydrologic system using the equation of continuity. Define the parameters and state your assumptions.

7-2. An impounding reservoir is to provide for constant withdrawal of 430 million gallons per square mile per year. The following record of monthly inflow values was selected from a critical period and was chosen as a basis for design. Find the amount of storage required in Mg/mi^2.

Month	J	F	M	A	M	J	J	A	S	O	N	D
Gauged inflow ($Mg/mi^2/mo$)	23	48	53	87	12	9	7	1	22	34	98	28

7-3. A particular river reach has an inflow of 250 ft^3/s and an outflow of 375 ft^3/s. Two hours later the inflow is 400 ft^3/s and the outflow is 450 ft^3/s. What is the change in storage in the reach after two hours? If, after two hours, the storage is 10.2 acre-ft, what was the initial storage, in acre-feet?

7-4. A 2500 mi^2 drainage basin receives 25 in/yr rainfall. The discharge of the river at the basin outlet is measured at an average of 650 ft^3/s. Assuming that the change in storage for the system is essentially zero, estimate the evapotranspiration losses for the area in inches, for the year. Be sure to state any assumptions that you make about the system.

7-5. Determine the daily evaporation from a lake for a day during which the following mean values were obtained: air temperature, 78°F; water temperature, 62°F; wind speed, 8 mph; and relative humidity, 45 percent.

7-6. Define recurrence interval. Explain what the "100-year flood" means. Show in tabular form the probability of a 100-year flood occurring within 10, 25, 40, and 50 years into the future.

7-7. Given the following storm pattern, unit storm, and unit hydrograph, determine the composite hydrograph.

UNIT STORM = 1 IN EFFECTIVE RAINFALL IN 1 H		
ACTUAL STORM PATTERN	TIME	VOLUME OF EFFECTIVE RAINFALL (IN)
	1:00	2
	2:00	2.5
	3:00	7
	4:00	3

Unit hydrograph (triangular) with base length = 5 h, time to peak flow = 1.5 h, and maximum ordinate = 0.4 in per h.

7-8. Using the derived unit hydrograph from Example 7-4, calculate the storm hydrograph for the following rainstorm pattern: time unit 1, rainfall = 1 in; time unit 2, rainfall = 3 in; time unit 3, rainfall = 2 in. Assume the storm data are effective rainfall.

7-9. The following hydrograph was measured on a creek for a storm that produced a total of 1.9 inches of rainfall in two hours. Losses due to depression storage, infiltration, and interception amounted to 0.4 inches.

	TIME FROM BEGINNING OF STORM (H)	DISCHARGE (FT^3/S)
	0	73
Storm begins	6	75
	12	900
	18	3400
	24	4350
	30	2900
	36	1450
	42	600
	48	450
	54	375
	60	250
	66	180
	72	135

A spillway design storm is 10 inches of effective rainfall in eight hours. Estimate the inflow hydrograph for the design storm.

7-10. The ordinates of a two-hour unit hydrograph are given in the following table. Derive a four-hour unit hydrograph from the two-hour unit hydrograph by (a) the lagging method and (b) the S-hydrograph method.

TIME UNIT	2-H UNIT HYDROGRAPH ORDINATES
0	0
1	200
2	400
3	300
4	200
5	100
6	0

7-11. Given the following data for mean annual draft and annual change in groundwater elevation, determine the safe yield.

MEAN ANNUAL DRAFT (1000s ACRE-FT)	MEAN ANNUAL CHANGE IN GROUNDWATER LEVEL (FT)
26	− 2
14	+ 2.5
36	− 4
21.5	+ 0.5
32	− 3
13	+ 2
32.5	− 2.5
26	− 0.5
19	+ 0.5
28	− 2

7-12. A well fully penetrates an unconfined aquifer. The coefficient of permeability is 750 gal/day/ft^2. The drawdown in an observation well located 50 ft away is 155 ft above datum and the drawdown at a second observation well 150 ft away is 165.5 ft above datum. Find the rate of flow to the well.

7-13. An industrial plant is restricted from discharging its wastewater to a stream when the average seven-day low flow is less than or equal to 75 ft^3/s. A cost analysis of proposed wastewater treatment and storage facilities requires knowledge of how frequently flow in the stream will fall below the critical level. Data over 32 years for seven-day low flows are given below. From these data determine (a) the probability that the seven-day low flow will be less than 75 ft^3/s in any given year; (b) the return period associated with 75 ft^3/s; (c) the probability that the seven-day low flow will be less than or equal to 75 ft^3/s for two years in a row; and (d) for at least one year in a three-year span.

YEAR	7-DAY LOW FLOW (FT³/S)	YEAR	7-DAY LOW FLOW (FT³/S)
1950	86.1	1966	102.0
1951	96.3	1967	117.0
1952	64.2	1968	70.0
1953	81.9	1969	63.6
1954	104.2	1970	61.4
1955	62.0	1971	89.0
1956	67.8	1972	95.0
1957	93.5	1973	51.4
1958	137.0	1974	124.0
1959	103.0	1975	60.2
1960	87.1	1976	55.1
1961	99.3	1977	83.9
1962	54.9	1978	92.6
1963	62.8	1979	110.0
1964	76.2	1980	73.5
1965	84.8	1981	98.4

7-14. Using the Gumbel method, plot the above data on extreme value probability paper and determine the seven-day, 10-year low flow.

References

1. W. Viessman, Jr., J. W. Knapp, G. L. Lewis, and T. E. Harbaugh, *Introduction to Hydrology,* 2d ed., Intext Educational Publishers, New York, 1977.
2. R. K. Linsley, M. A. Kohler, and J. L. H. Paulhus, *Hydrology for Engineers,* 2d ed., McGraw-Hill, New York, 1975.
3. Hydrologic Research Laboratory, *National Weather Service River Forecast Procedures,* NOAA Tech. Mem. NWS HYDRO 14, National Weather Service, Silver Spring, MD, December 1972.
4. Water Resources Council, *The Nation's Water Resources: 1975–2000,* U.S. Gov't. Print. Off., Washington, D.C., 1978.
5. E. R. Anderson, L. J. Anderson, and J. J. Marciano, "A Review of Evaporation Theory and Development of Instrumentation," Lake Mead Water Loss Investigation, Interim Report, Navy Electronics Lab. Rep. No. 159, February 1950.
6. A. F. Meyer, *Evaporation from Lakes and Reservoirs,* Minnesota Resources Commission, St. Paul, MN, June 1944.
7. W. D. Criddle, "Methods for Computing Consumptive Use of Water," *Proc. ASCE, J. Irrig. Drainage Div.,* 84 no. IRI, January 1958.
8. R. E. Horton, *Surface Runoff Phenomena: Part I, Analysis of the Hydrograph.* Horton Hydrol. Lab. Pub. 101, Edward Bros., Inc., Ann Arbor, MI, 1935.
9. H. N. Holtan, *A Concept for Infiltration Estimates in Watershed Engineering,* USDA, Agricultural Research Service, ARS 41–51, 1961.
10. Donn G. DeCoursey, *A Runoff Hydrograph Equation,* USDA, Agricultural Research Service, February 1966.

11. H. N. Holtan and N. C. Lopez, *USDAHL-74 Revised Watershed Hydrology*, USDA, ARS Tech. Bull. No. 1518, Washington, D.C., 1975.
12. J. R. Philip, "An Infiltration Equation with Physical Significance," *Soil Science*, vol. 77, 1954.
13. V. T. Chow (ed.), *Handbook of Applied Hydrology*, McGraw-Hill, New York, 1964.
14. E. J. Gumbel, "Statistical Theory of Droughts," *Proc. Am. Soc. Civil Engrs.*, vol. 80, separate no. 439, May 1954.
15. L. K. Sherman, "Streamflow from Rainfall by the Unit-Graph Method, *Engineering News-Record*, vol. 108, April 7, 1932.
16. F. F. Snyder, "Synthetic Unit Graphs," *Trans. Amer. Geophys. Union*, vol. 19, 1938, pp. 447–454.
17. U.S. Army Corps of Engineers, *Flood-Hydrograph Analysis and Computations*, Engineering Design Manuals, Em 1110-2-1405, U.S. Gov't. Print. Off., Washington, D.C., August 1959.
18. V. Mockus, *Use of Storm and Watershed Characteristics in Synthetic Hydrograph Analysis and Application*, USDA, Soil Conservation Service, 1957.
19. A. B. Taylor and H. E. Schwarz, "Unit Hydrograph Lag and Peak Flow Related to Basin Characteristics," *Trans. Amer. Geophys. Union*, vol. 33, 1952, pp. 235–246.
20. D. M. Gray, "Synthetic Unit Hydrographs for Small Drainage Areas," *Proc. ASCE, J. Hydraulics Div.*, vol. 87, no. HY4, July 1961.
21. California Dept. of Water Resources, *Planned Utilization of Ground Water Basin: Coastal Plain of Los Angeles County*, Bull. 104, Sacramento, 1968.

Chapter 8
Augmentation of Water Supplies

In Chapter 7 we considered nature's system for providing water supplies: the hydrologic cycle. In this chapter, we shall explore ways in which man can augment or modify this natural system to better suit his needs. A number of methods have been tested for augmenting water supplies that have met with varying degrees of success, as all are somewhat limited by geographical, economic, public health, and institutional factors. Water supply augmentation technologies discussed in this chapter include water conservation, wastewater reuse, storm water reuse, desalination of seawater and brackish water, interbasin water transfers, and precipitation enhancement via weather modification techniques.

8-1 CONSERVATION

Webster's *New Collegiate Dictionary* defines conservation as a careful preservation and protection of something; *particularly,* planned management of a natural resource to prevent exploitation, destruction, or neglect. In the United States, water conservation historically has *not* been planned but instead initiated in the face of emergency in response to forecasts of critical water shortages. In these situations, government officials imposing restrictions on water usage have often been surprised to find that when "backs are to the wall" a substantial amount of water can be conserved to survive the crisis. Learning from these experiences, many state and local governments have adopted permanent water conservation policies and even regulations to provide additional water for future use.

Impact of Conservation on the Various Water Use Sectors

When one thinks of water conservation, images of reduced lawn waterings and shorter showers are likely to come to mind. This is due to the effort and publicity that is directed toward *residential* water conservation, as opposed to conservation in other water use sectors. The information presented in Chapter 4 shows that domestic water use amounts to only a fraction of the national water use budget (see Figure 1-2). One may question the wisdom of placing such an emphasis on residential water conservation when much greater amounts could be conserved by large water use sectors, often with less effort. As an illustration, if a substantial effort was undertaken to reduce residential water use by 30 percent, the savings in 1985 would be $0.3 \times 26,000$ mgd, or 7800 mgd. The same amount of water conserved by irrigated agriculture would amount to less than 5 percent of total irrigation water use. Regional and other considerations dictate, however, the water use sector most promising for conservation.

Methods of Conserving Water

RESIDENTIAL WATER CONSERVATION

The average person in the United States uses water indoors at the rate of 90 gpcd for indoor use (based on a family of four, 1975) (1). Domestic water use outdoors is variable, but may exceed 70 gpcd in dry areas (1). For the average home, by far the greatest amount of water is used in the bathroom and outdoors. On a national basis, approximately 50 and 33 percent of total residential water are used for each of these two purposes, respectively (2, 3). Residential conservation efforts are frequently aimed at these two largest water consumers for maximum effectiveness. Several methods can be used to encourage, if not force, residential water conservation. The methods discussed in this chapter include installation of water-saving devices, changes in water use patterns, and adjustment of water metering rates.

• *Water-Saving Devices.* There are numerous devices that can be installed in the home to save water; some are available commercially. Certain of these items can be attached to existing water fixtures; others that could replace existing units are better suited to construction of new residential units. Several of these items and their potential water savings are presented in Table 8-1.

Other methods that can be considered for installation in new housing units are hot water pipe insulation, drip irrigation systems for shrubs and trees, automatic time-controlled sprinkler irrigation systems, and selection of drought-resistant landscaping.

• *Changes in Water Use Patterns.* Individuals may conserve water by cutting back on usage if they are convinced that there is a community need to do

Table 8-1 WATER SAVING DEVICES[a]

FIXTURE	TRADITIONAL WATER USE		WATER USE WITH CONSERVATION		
	QUANTITY		DEVICE	QUANTITY	
Toilet	5–7	gal/flush	Toilet modified w/plastic bottles	3.5+	gal/flush
			Reduced flow toilet	3.5	gal/flush
Shower head	4–15	gal/min	Flow restrictor in shower line	3	gal/min
			Modified shower head	2–3.5	gal/min
Faucet	4+	gal/min	Flow restrictor in faucet line	0.5–1	gal/min
Automatic washer	50+	gal/cycle	Water-saving model	30+	gal/cycle
Automatic dishwasher	13+	gal/cycle	Water-saving model	10+	gal/cycle

[a]References 1, 3, and 4

so, or if water prices are increased substantially. During drought conditions, massive public education programs can alert people about the need to save water and suggest ways to do so. Suggestions range from shorter shower times to fewer toilet flushings. In water-short areas, it is common for a municipality to restrict the use of water for residential irrigation and car washing. This may be enforced by the municipality or the community. Installation of water meters is an effective means of monitoring water use; penalties and prizes may be offered for over- and underaverage water usage rates.

Residential wastewater *recycling* is a means of reducing water consumption without reducing the frequency of established water use patterns. Reuse may be effected by segregating blackwater (wastewater from the toilet) and graywater (all other wastewater), and using the graywater one or more times before discharging to the sanitary sewer system. This practice can reduce water consumption significantly, but it involves some construction and special plumbing expenses (4). Examples of features of partial and total reuse systems are shown in Table 8-2.

• *Changes in Water Rate Structures.* Another method of encouraging changes in water use patterns is to adjust the water rate structure. Traditionally, declining block rates have been used in charging consumers for water in metered areas. This means that above a specified water use rate a customer is charged less per gallon of water used. In numerous areas across the country, reverse water rates (increasing block rates) have been enforced during drought conditions. In other words, if a customer uses more than a certain amount of water, the customer is charged a higher price per gallon. Success with reverse water rates has been limited. Experience has shown that the increase in price must be sufficiently high to have an influence on water use patterns.

CASE STUDY

In Sanibel, Florida, residential units were charged $5.25 per month to use up to 3000 gallons of water. They were charged an additional $1 per 1000 gallons for an additional use of 2000 gallons, and $1.45 per 1000 gallons for usage over

Table 8-2 RESIDENTIAL WASTEWATER REUSE SYSTEMS[a]

PARTIAL REUSE SYSTEM (REDUCES WATER CONSUMPTION BY 25%)
Toilet flushed partly with bathwater that has been filtered and stored in a holding tank Laundry water is used for landscape irrigation
TOTAL REUSE SYSTEM (REDUCES WATER CONSUMPTION BY 50%)
Bath/laundry water filtered into a holding tank and used for toilet flushing Overflow from holding tank plus kitchen sink wastes and blackwater discharged into on-site septic tank Leach field irrigation of rooted plants

[a]Reference 4.

5000 gallons. This pricing structure did not change water use patterns. On the other hand, a more stringent pricing system was implemented by the Washington Suburban Sanitary Commission. Water use at the rate of 100 gal/day was priced at $1.35 per 1000 gallons, while water use over 100 gal/day up to 500 gal/day was priced at $2.45 per 1000 gallons. This rating system reduced water demand by 20 gal/day per dwelling unit and had the effect of making 3 gal/day of sewage treatment capacity available (5).

INDUSTRIAL WATER CONSERVATION

Increased water prices have an influence on industrial water consumption, although not as much of an influence as on residential water consumption, due to the lower elasticity of demand that industrial water users exhibit in response to price increases (6, 7). Other factors that contribute to industrial water conservation are energy costs (for example, costs of pumping and heating) and costs of wastewater treatment and disposal (8). As the United States moves toward the Clean Water Act goal of zero discharge by 1985, environmental constraints will be even more of an impetus for conservation and reuse. In response to these factors, the industrial water use sector has been reducing water use by process modifications and recycling process wastewaters.

CASE STUDY

An example of water conservation practices resulting from environmental factors is illustrated by a process modification of a hot-rolling steel mill in Ohio (9). The plant formerly removed iron oxide scale from hot bars of steel with acid baths, followed by a water washing to remove the acid; the untreated acidic wastewater was discharged to a receiving water body. Under orders from the U.S. EPA to stop this practice, the company changed its descaling process by replacing the acid baths with a grinder wheel to remove the scale by mechanical means, thereby eliminating the generation of the acid wastewater.

In chemical processing industries, the greatest strides in water conservation have been made through increases in recycling capabilities of cooling tower recirculation systems. In 1972 the average recycle rate for cooling tower water was 4:1. By 1978 this was up to 7:1, with some companies reporting rates as high as 27:1 (10).

WATER CONSERVATION IN IRRIGATED AGRICULTURE

Because irrigation uses more water consumptively than any other sector in the United States and because irrigation practices are frequently inefficient, conservation in irrigation can result in substantial water savings. Billions of gallons of water are lost every year by inefficient distribution systems alone. Less than half the water delivered to farms is used by the crops, due to seepage through canal walls (11). This seepage could be reduced greatly by lining distribution canals with packed earth, concrete, or asphalt to prevent seepage, although this practice is very costly. Other methods of water conservation include:

Avoid overwatering

Improve scheduling of water application with the aid of soil detection devices to determine the optimum timing for irrigation

Reduce precipitation runoff from sloping fields by improving tillage and land management practices to provide additional water for irrigation

Use small surface impoundments to catch runoff and pump back to fields for reuse

Employ water-conserving irrigation methods such as drip irrigation or subsurface irrigation (these are described in Section 12-1)

The water saved by using these irrigation practices could increase the water supply for irrigated agriculture, energy development, environmental improvement, and recreation (11). Use of drip irrigation methods as opposed to others (see Chapter 12) is a proved method of water conservation.

Impact of Conservation on Wastewater Treatment Systems

Water conservation practices can have a significant influence on sewers and wastewater treatment plants. Under drought conditions, a reduced flow of wastewater to the sewer results in an increased pollutant loading, since the same mass of pollutants is discharged to the sewer in a more concentrated form. Table 8-3 illustrates the effect of conservation on the wastewater flow in a California community during the drought conditions of 1976–77. BOD levels increased by 33 percent and suspended solids concentrations increased by 21 percent (12). These low-flow conditions can result in accumulation of sediments in sewers, hydrogen sulfide gas formation, and clogging of sewer lines, because the sewers have been designed and installed at a certain slope (for example, 2 percent) to transport an average flow (12, 13).

Table 8-3 EFFECTS OF DROUGHT CONDITIONS IN CALIFORNIA IN 1976–77 ON THE MUNICIPAL WASTEWATER TREATMENT SYSTEM (POPULATION = 2,389,100)[a]

	1976	1977	PERCENT CHANGE
Wastewater flow, gpcd	113	92	−18
Biochemical oxygen demand			
mg/L	261	338	+33
lb/cap. day	0.23	0.23	0
Suspended solids			
mg/L	310	350	+21
lb/cap. day	0.27	0.24	0

[a]Reference 14.

Problems also arise at the wastewater treatment plant, where the increased loading is not compatible with the design parameters of the plant. If detention times of wastewater treatment processes are increased in an attempt to treat the more concentrated waste, septic conditions may result. One solution is to dilute the waste by recycling treated effluent to the plant influent. Another problem is that disinfection costs will rise as a result of the increased pollutant load. One beneficial impact of water conservation on wastewater treatment is that the total plant effluent loading to the receiving water body decreases, even though the concentration of the pollutants is greater (12, 13).

Detrimental effects on sewerage systems of strict water conservation practices can be avoided by implementing water conservation policies or regulations at the same time an existing wastewater system is expanded to serve a larger population. For areas where newly constructed systems are being planned and where conservation practices are in effect, consideration should be given to design changes, including slope of sewer pipes and perhaps increased design for peak grit removal if a system is subject to heavy rains (14, 15).

Is Conservation Worthwhile?

Water conservation policies have been recognized as a viable alternative in augmenting the nation's water supplies. When pressed by severe drought, communities have been able to conserve 20 to 50 percent of their normal water usage. Learning from these experiences, some jurisdictions have implemented permanent water conservation policies as a means of providing water supplies for the future, in lieu of searching for other water supplies or planning new water management facilities.

There is another school of thought on the subject, which says that conservation above and beyond flagrant waste elimination is not a beneficial practice for several reasons. First, strict conservation practice eliminates the "cushion" on which a community can fall back in case of drought or utility failure. Second, stringent conservation measures really only postpone the construction of new facilities for a number of years, rather than eliminate the need for them. It is argued that a more sensible approach is to stress programs to reduce wasteful usage, continue to plan water management facilities to serve communities as needed, and to use conservation only in emergencies (16).

8-2 WASTEWATER REUSE

As water resources become more scarce in arid and semiarid regions of the United States, as environmental regulations become more stringent, and while institutional constraints continue to preclude other water supply augmentation options, the practice of reusing wastewater is becoming more widespread. It is increasingly recognized that wastewater is a valuable resource and provides a steady source of water. In many cases energy savings are accrued by reusing wastewater before disposal. Although in the past, economic considerations have been a deterrent in implementing reuse systems, this is changing as alternatives are becoming more costly.

Wastewater generated by residential, commercial, industrial, and agricultural activities can be treated and utilized again for the same purpose or for another activity, depending on the quality of the wastewater generated and the quality of water desired for the new use. Treatment of wastewater for such reuse is called water reclamation. Wastewater may be reused without treatment in cases where lower water quality is acceptable.

In the past, the traditional impetus for wastewater reuse has been the necessity of resolving water quality problems caused by discharge to surface waters, the desire to reduce the high cost of effluent treatment, the existence of a large demand for water of a particular quality, or the existence of inadequate freshwater supplies. In recent years other factors have been recognized as being as important as the traditional ones in justifying wastewater reuse. Increasingly, in areas where water supplies are becoming alarmingly scarce, wastewater is being recognized as a potentially valuable resource in and of itself. In certain areas of the United States where the population is growing, particularly in the arid southwest, reuse of wastewater is seen as a means of easing the strains on a fixed amount of water. Even given that cost of treatment plays a large role in assessing the attractiveness of wastewater reuse, in those areas of the United States where water supplies are becoming scarce and alternative sources of water are becoming more expensive, wastewater reuse is becoming economically attractive as a means of supplementing the available water sources.

Some indirect benefits of reuse that may not be so obvious include improved quality of surface waters that no longer receive the reused wastewater (a benefit for downstream users and for aquatic life) and preservation of higher quality water for potable consumption. In addition, it has been recognized that reuse can reduce an area's total energy requirements, as well as conserve open space (where desirable) by the designation of land for disposal of reclaimed water (12).

Definitions

Several terms used to describe wastewater reuse are generally taken to mean the following:

Reuse means use by someone other than the original user, especially in an uncoordinated and random way.

Direct reuse means that wastewater is thoroughly treated and piped directly into a water supply system, without intervening travel dilution in natural surface or groundwater (13). For example, direct connection of a municipal wastewater plant to an irrigation site provides a direct water supply to that site.

Indirect reuse involves a middle step between generation of reclaimed water and reuse. This commonly includes discharge, retention, and mixing with another water supply before reuse.

Recycling means use by the same business, plant, or person two or more times in a coordinated, planned manner, sometimes with partial treatment between uses.

Sources and Characteristics of Reusable Wastewater

SOURCES

The most widely available and least variable source of wastewater for reuse purposes is municipal wastewater. Municipal wastewater can be relied on to provide a dependable continuous flow having consistent physical, chemical, and biological characteristics; reuse can be designed around these characteristics to achieve the degree of treatment desirable for end use. Reuse of municipal wastewater may be accomplished in a number of ways, with treatment ranging from none to that with the most advanced systems available, depending on the end use of the water. As an example of the diversity of reuses, the types of municipal wastewater reuses currently employed in California include fodder, fiber, and seed crop irrigation; landscape irrigation; orchard and vineyard irrigation; processed food crop irrigation; groundwater recharge; food crop irrigation (not processed); restricted recreational impoundments; landscape irrigation; pasture for dairy animals; and unrestricted recreational impoundments (17).

In industrialized sections of the United States, manufacturing operations can contribute heavily to the total wastewater generated in an area. The constituents of the wastewater are highly industry-specific and may limit the reuse options available for that wastewater. On-site wastewater reuse by manufacturing plants has become more important as environmental standards have been tightened by regulatory agencies.

In agriculture, wastewater from irrigation operations is a potential source of reusable water. The water is often highly contaminated with salts leached from the soil, however, and treatment is required in many cases if the water is to be reused on the fields. Desalination is technically feasible but often prohibitively expensive for the farmer.

CHARACTERISTICS

Wastewater reclamation processes must ensure removal of residual pollutants to such a degree as to make the water acceptable for the designated reuse. The pollutants that must be removed depend on the desired use of the water and its previous use. If municipal wastewater has undergone

secondary treatment (see Section 12-6), the remaining pollutants that
typically must be removed to make the wastewater suitable for reuse are
nitrates, phosphates, total dissolved solids, microorganisms, and refractory
organics such as trace levels of pesticides (13, 18). All these constituents
need not be removed should their presence be advantageous in the product water. For example, phosphates and nitrates are desirable in reclaimed water for use in irrigation because the constituents act as nutrients for plant life. The State of California has established water quality
requirements for different levels of reuse; these are shown in Figure 8-1
(19).

TREATMENT PROCESSES FOR WATER RECLAMATION
For high-quality effluent, *tertiary* or advanced treatment processes are
required to achieve the degree of contaminant removal beyond conventional treatment processes necessary to make wastewater acceptable for
reuse. A list of several common advanced treatment processes is given in

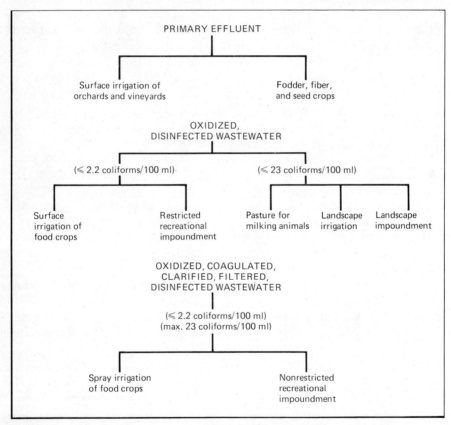

Figure 8-1   Water quality requirements for wastewater reuse in California.

Table 12-8, and several are discussed in Section 12-6. These processes are proved technologies for wastewater reclamation and some are readily available as "off-the-shelf" package units; economics is the driving factor in limiting the attractiveness of certain processes for widespread use in wastewater reclamation.

Municipal Reuse

Wastewater can be reused for municipal purposes either directly or indirectly. Direct municipal reuse requires advanced treatment of wastewater to meet stringent water quality requirements if the water is to be consumed for drinking water purposes. If a dual distribution system is available, water of lesser quality may be directly used for nonpotable purposes, such as landscape irrigation.

Indirect reuse is defined as the reuse of treated municipal wastewater as a raw water supply after the wastewater has entered, comingled, and essentially become a part of a natural surface- or groundwater resource. Anyone located in an area where the water supply system uses surface water for intake at a point downstream from a discharging municipal wastewater treatment plant is indirectly reusing the wastewater. The natural assimilative capacity of the river acts to purify and dilute the discharged water, to a degree, so as to make it more acceptable as intake water for municipal water supplies. This practice has been accepted for years with little questioning of its public health significance.

Indirect municipal reuse of wastewater is also accomplished by discharging reclaimed water into groundwater aquifers (artificial recharge) and later withdrawing the water for potable or other municipal reuse. Discharge into aquifers can be carried out by either deep well injection or shallow surface spreading with subsequent percolation into groundwater. The latter practice benefits from the extra purification provided by percolation through the soil. Both practices benefit from dilution of reclaimed water with existing groundwater. The natural aquifer provides a convenient storage area that is beneficial in case of uneven demand.

There are still many unanswered questions regarding the health effects of indirect (via groundwater) and direct wastewater reuses for drinking water purposes. There is a general fear on the part of the public that microorganisms and refractory organic chemicals in the wastewater designated for reuse may escape treatment, enter the water supply, and pose a threat to human health. Central unresolved issues are: What chemical constituents are acceptable in potable water and at what concentrations? Water Factory 21 in California is injecting reclaimed water of high quality into selected aquifers with the goal of someday reusing it for potable purposes, once health officials can agree on water quality standards that are also acceptable to the public.

CASE STUDY

Thus far, nowhere in the United States has wastewater been directly reused for drinking water purposes. Within the next decade, however, attainment of the goal of direct reuse is planned for the city of Denver. In 1970, when the Denver Water Board predicted future water shortages, a series of pilot studies were initiated to determine the feasibility of wastewater reclamation for direct potable consumption. With current usage of 100,000 acre-ft/yr from surface supplies and 250,000 acre-ft/yr from interbasin water transfers, the citizens of Denver perceived that an additional source of water was needed to allow for future growth. Pilot studies were completed in 1979. Although the water reclamation technology has proved effective on a pilot-scale basis, there is still the question of water quality. To provide data for a complete assessment of health-related issues, Denver is now in the process of building a 1-mgd demonstration plant consisting of lime clarification, recarbonation, filtration, selective ion exchange, first-stage carbon adsorption, ozonation, second-stage carbon adsorption, reverse osmosis, air stripping, and chlorine dioxide disinfection (see Figure 8-2). After start-up, planned for mid-1983, the plant will provide the water needed for complete analytical quality testing and health effects research, as well as the design criteria for scale-up to an operating facility. The testing program is scheduled for completion by mid-1987. This program, coupled with an extensive public education campaign, may pave the way for direct potable reuse in Denver by the turn of the century (20, 21).

Industrial Reuse

Scarcity of resources, environmental constraints, and economics are major factors that have caused industry to turn increasingly to recycling and reuse of its wastewater and to take in less raw water (22). These practices include (1) treating some or all process wastewaters to make them suitable for plant process makeup water, for example, cooling tower water; (2) recirculating the same water within a unit process or group of processes before discharge; and (3) sequential use of effluent from one process as input into another with optional treatment between processes (23–25). These practices also provide a significant savings in energy (for pumping, heating, and treating wastewater), as well as in water costs.

Reclaimed municipal wastewater is also a suitable source for certain industrial processes, depending on the economics of treatment and distribution and the quality of the water. The prime applications have been for use as cooling water and boiler feed water. Other uses will become feasible as the water quality of the reclaimed water increases (22).

Irrigation Reuse

Direct irrigation with wastewater has become a more widespread practice since land treatment of municipal wastewater has been encouraged by the

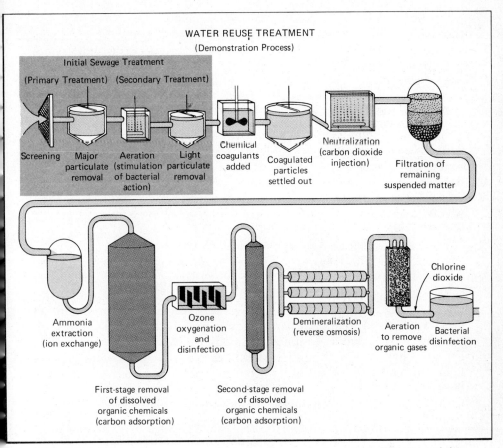

WATER REUSE TREATMENT
(Demonstration Process)

Initial Sewage Treatment

(Primary Treatment)   (Secondary Treatment)

Screening Major   Aeration   Light   Chemical   Neutralization
           particulate (stimulation particulate   coagulants   Coagulated   (carbon dioxide
           removal   of bacterial removal   added   particles   injection)   Filtration of
                      action)   settled out   remaining
                                                                                                  suspended matter

Ammonia   Ozone   Demineralization   Chlorine
extraction   oxygenation   (reverse osmosis)   Aeration dioxide
(ion exchange)   and   to remove Bacterial
                     disinfection   organic gases disinfection

First-stage removal   Second-stage removal
of dissolved   of dissolved
organic chemicals   organic chemicals
(carbon adsorption)   (carbon adsorption)

Figure 8-2   Denver wastewater reclamation demonstration plant. (Courtesy of the Denver Water Department.)

EPA as an "innovative and alternative" wastewater treatment technology. Both can be accomplished at the same time, yielding a savings in energy as well as in cost of treatment. Additional benefits include augmenting groundwater supplies, utilization of the nutrients in the wastewater as fertilizer, and preservation of the quality of surface waters.

The technology of land treatment of wastewater is discussed in Chapter 12. Land treatment involves spreading of wastewater on land and making use of natural filtration and adsorption properties of the soil to remove contaminants as wastewater percolates downward to the groundwater zone. Low-rate land application systems are suitable for irrigation. The detention times allow plants to take up nutrients from the wastewater. There are public health concerns, however, regarding the levels of nitrates, pathogens, and refractory organics that may be present in the wastewater.

Indirect reuse for irrigation is quite common, either from aquifers that have been recharged with reclaimed water, or from rivers downstream of a wastewater discharge where the river water is withdrawn for irrigation purposes.

Artificial Recharge

Groundwater aquifers are depleted by pumping, by natural discharge to surface-water systems, and to a minor extent by evaporation and transpiration. The balance between the depletion and recharge of the aquifer determines the average annual water table level. Aquifer recharge can be effected by natural recharge mechanisms, that is, by infiltration from precipitation and from surface-water bodies, or by man-induced means, which is called *artificial recharge.*

Artificial recharge is practiced for additional reasons beyond replenishment, including (1) storage of excess surface water, for example floodwaters, for future use; (2) amelioration of damage caused by excessive pumping, for example damage caused by lake level drawdown, saltwater intrusion (see Figure 8-3), or land subsidence; and (3) treatment of wastewater (land treatment) concurrently with recharge.

There are several common methods for performing artificial recharge. Those that will be discussed here are surface spreading, direct injection, and induced recharge from a stream. The method of choice depends on the availability and quality of water for recharge, the availability and cost of land overlying the aquifer, the aquifer type, the potential infiltration rate of the water, the storage capacity of the groundwater zone, and any effects of a nearby flowing surface-water body on the groundwater flow.

Surface spreading is a candidate recharge method where a recharge

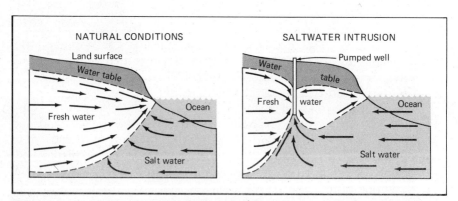

Figure 8-3 How intensive groundwater pumping can cause saltwater intrusion in coastal areas. (From *Ground Water,* U.S. Department of Interior/Geological Survey, Washington, D.C., 1980.)

area overlies an unconfined aquifer and water can percolate directly into the groundwater zone. The method involves periodic flooding of shallow basins where the rate of flooding is a function of the infiltration rate of the water. The recharged water may then be withdrawn from the aquifer by extraction wells located some distance from the spreading basins, with the distance of the wells being dependent on the desired degree of mixing with existing groundwater. Characteristic of surface-spreading operations is the formation of *groundwater mounds* directly beneath the recharge area (see Figure 8-4). The groundwater mounds grow in proportion to recharge rates. To avoid saturation of the upper portion of the soil moisture zone (the region depended on by most plants for water), often a series of recharge basins are flooded on an alternating basis to permit gradual seepage and to prevent the groundwater mound from becoming too large.

The feasibility of surface-water spreading is very much dependent on the availability and cost of the land overlying the aquifer. Operating costs of surface-water spreading are lower than direct injection, due to lower energy costs for delivering the water from the recharge area to the aquifer. One problem commonly encountered in recharge operations that must be controlled is the clogging of soil pores. In surface spreading this may be controlled by scraping off the clogged surface.

Direct injection is appropriate for areas overlying unconfined aquifers where lack of suitable land or high costs of land preclude recharge by surface spreading, and for areas overlying confined aquifers where an impervious layer would prevent infiltration of water from the vadose to the groundwater zone. The method involves the pumping of treated water under pressure directly into the groundwater zone (see Figure 8-5). The water may be withdrawn from the aquifer at the desired distance from the recharge area, allowing for mixing and dilution with existing groundwater. Direct injection is also used in coastal areas as a barrier to saltwater intrusion caused by previous excess pumping (see Figure 8-6).

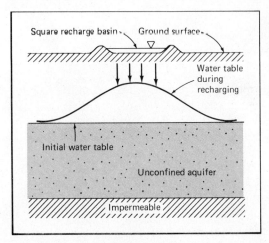

Figure 8-4 Recharge mound formed beneath a square spreading basin.

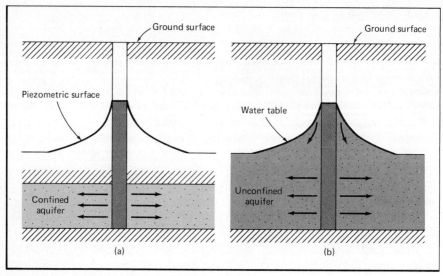

Figure 8-5 Radial flow from recharge wells penetrating (a) confined and (b) unconfined aquifers.

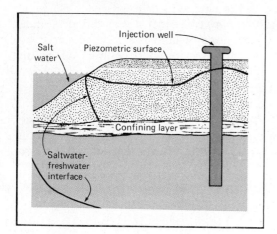

Figure 8-6 Injection as a barrier to saltwater intrusion.

Water recharged by direct injection does not benefit from the natural filtration and adsorption that water recharged by surface spreading receives from percolating through the vadose zone. Any soil pore clogging caused by particulates or organics is difficult to repair underground. Because of this potential problem, and because of other health issues associated with recharge operations, several states have adopted regulations requiring that stringent water quality standards be met before water is recharged by direct injection, to provide assurance that the groundwater will not become degraded by recharge activities.

Induced recharge from a stream is based on the principle that recharge from a stream to an aquifer can be increased by siting a well near a stream having a hydraulic connection to an aquifer (see Figure 8-7). Pumping the well forms a cone of depression that intersects the streambed, causing water to flow toward the well. The soil between the well and the river must have sufficient filtration capacity to provide the quality of water desired from the well. Care must be taken to determine that stream levels will not be drawn down so as to cause damage to river life or encroach on designated instream water uses.

As mentioned previously, at issue with all recharge operations where water may be withdrawn for future reuse is how stringent the water quality standards should be before recharged water is deemed fit for use in the potable water supply, although the reclaimed water may be of no worse quality than water withdrawn from a river for potable use downstream from a wastewater discharge point. When the day comes that the controversy over acceptable water quality for recharge to potable aquifers is resolved, artificial recharge may become a reality for augmenting the drinking water supply. Meanwhile, it has been proved viable to increase groundwater reserves for nonpotable reuse and as a means of checking saltwater intrusion.

CASE STUDY

As a result of rapid population growth in the 1950s, the coastal area of Orange County, California, experienced severe groundwater overdraft, resulting in a threat of saltwater intrusion of the water supply. To amelioriate the situation, the Orange County Water District undertook a program of groundwater injection to provide a water barrier to the intruding sea (see Figure 8-8). The water for injection is generated by Water Factory 21, an advanced wastewater treatment plant that includes a reverse osmosis (RO) system for removing dissolved minerals.

The advanced waste treatment processes consist of lime clarification with sludge recalcining, ammonia stripping, recarbonation, breakpoint chlorination, mixed media filtration, activated carbon adsorption with carbon regeneration, postchlorination, and reverse osmosis demineralization. The process configuration

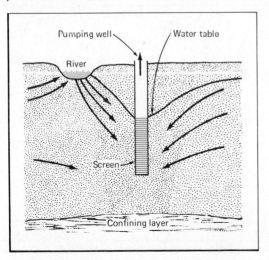

Figure 8-7 Induced recharge from a stream.

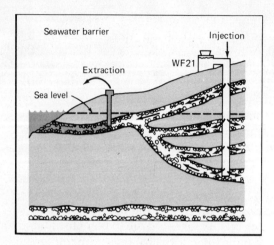

Figure 8-8 Orange County Water District injection well process. (From *Reverse Osmosis,* U.S. Department of the Interior, Office of Water Research and Technology, Washington, D.C., 1979.)

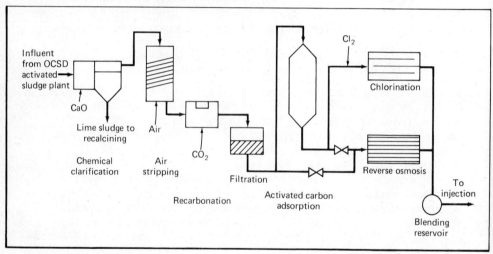

Figure 8-9 Process configuration of Water Factory 21. (Courtesy of Orange County Water District.)

of Water Factory 21 is depicted in Figure 8-9. The 5 mgd reverse osmosis system is designed to remove a maximum of 90 percent of all salts and to achieve at least 85 percent water recovery. The 5-mgd demineralized water is blended with 10 mgd of effluent from advance treatment before injection into the groundwater system (26). The water quality standards that the reclaimed water must meet are extremely stringent, since withdrawal for potable reuse is a possibility for the future.

8-3 REUSE OF URBAN STORM WATER

In urban areas where storm water is collected by a system separate from that which collects the municipal wastewater, a source of reusable water is provided to the city that, with a certain amount of treatment, is acceptable for a number of uses (27). Stormwater is typically low in BOD (comparable to the BOD level of effluent from a secondary municipal wastewater treatment plant), but high in suspended solids (often at a level comparable to that of raw municipal wastewater). Since the water is characteristically high in solids and has a highly variable flow rate, physical treatment processes are the most suitable for treating it. By employing various combinations of physical unit processes, effluents of various qualities can be produced. This flexibility is desirable because the end use of the water dictates the minimum degree of treatment needed to make it suitable for reuse. The characteristics and treatability of storm water are discussed in detail in Section 12-7.

Figure 8-10 shows the combinations of unit processes for treating storm water to render it suitable for four classes of end use: Class AA, high-quality application (for example, steam generation boiler feed); Class A, routine industrial supply; Class B, industrial cooling and recreational water for fishing; and Class C, lawn irrigation, fire protection, and land-

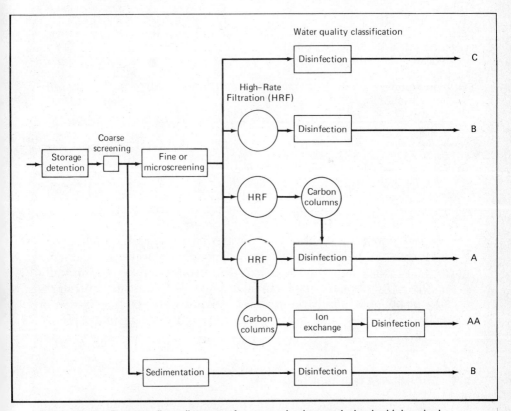

Figure 8-10 Process flow diagrams for several advanced physical/chemical storm water treatment systems. (After R. Field and C. Fan, "Recycling Urban Stormwater for Profit," *Water/Engineering and Management,* vol. 128, no. 4, 1981.)

Table 8-4 MAXIMUM CONCENTRATION OF SELECTED POLLUTANT BY REUSE CATEGORY[a]

CONSTITUENT (MG/L UNLESS INDICATED) WATER QUALITY CLASSIFICATION	REQUIRED WATER QUALITY[b] MAXIMUM CONCENTRATION			
	AA	A	B	C
Ammonia (NH_3)	0.5	0.5	0.5	0.5
Arsenic	0.01	0.05	0.05	0.05
Calcium	0.5	75.0	75.0	75.0
Chloride	50.0	250.0	250.0	250.0
Chromium (hexavalent)	0.05	0.05	0.05	0.05
Copper	1.0	1.0	1.5	1.5
Cyanide	0.01	0.2	0.2	0.2
Fluoride	1.5	3.0	3.0	3.0
Iron	0.1	0.3	0.3	0.3
Lead	0.05	0.1	0.1	0.1
Magnesium	0.5	150.0	150.0	150.0
Manganese	0.05	0.1	0.5	0.5
Nitrate (as NO_3)	45.0	50.0	50.0	50.0
Oxygen, dissolved (minimum)	5.0	5.0	4.0	4.0
Sulfate	50.0	200.0	400.0	400.0
Total solids	150.0	500.0	500.0	1500.0
Zinc	5.0	15.0	15.0	15.0
Coliform (Most Probable No. per 100 ml)	1	70	240	240
pH (units)	7.0	6.0	6.0	6.0
Color (units)	15	20	30	30
Turbidity (units)	0–3	3–8	8–15	15–20
Suspended solids	—	—	10.0[c]	30.0[c]
Phosphates	1.0	1.0	1.0	1.0

[a]Reference 33.
[b]Based on maximum concentrations allowed by the USPHS, the World Health Organization, and the Water Quality Standards of the State of Maryland.
[c]Higher suspended solids are permitted by various water quality standards. Limit based on sediment control and water contact recreation.

scape ponds. Table 8-4 lists the water quality standards for these end uses (28).

The advantages of treating storm water for these uses are numerous. When compared with the costs of using potable city water for the same purposes, physical treatment of urban storm water can be economically competitive. Additional benefits include improved drainage control, reduction of pollutant discharge to the receiving water body, creation of recreational and aesthetic ponds, and opportunity for groundwater recharge (27).

8-4 SALINE-WATER CONVERSION

As usable water supplies have become dangerously depleted or contaminated in recent years, the conversion of saline water to usable water has become more attractive as an alternative for augmentation of water supplies. Saline water is defined as containing more than 1000 ppm of total dissolved solids (TDS). Seawater contains an average of 35,000 ppm TDS, brackish water is characterized by 1000 to 35,000 ppm TDS, and brine is considered to be water containing over 35,000 ppm TDS (29).

With the oceans providing more than 97 percent of the world's water budget, it seems only logical to look to this vast reservoir as a source of water for augmenting freshwater supplies. Natural weather processes act to purify seawater by evaporating water from the oceans and leaving the salts behind; the purified water is subsequently returned to earth as fresh water. If seawater can be readily converted into fresh water by manmade processes that reproduce these natural processes, the oceans could indeed provide a limitless supply of fresh water.

The technology for doing this, in fact, exists. The problem with implementing the technology on a widespread basis is that it is limited by energy requirements, costs, and environmental constraints. To what degree these constraints act to impede desalination as a viable alternative for augmenting water supplies depends on how desalination measures up to the alternatives. For example, on ships it is cheaper to distill seawater than to carry a freshwater supply on board. For this reason conversion of saline water into drinking water by means of distillation has been used for years on oceangoing vessels.

In the face of shrinking land-based freshwater supplies in recent years, conversion of seawater into potable water has been investigated in coastal areas as an economically attractive alternative to other methods of augmenting water supplies such as long-distance water transportation. Even more recently, brackish water conversion has been looked to for desalination possibilities for inland populations where the only fresh- (ground) water supplies have been severely depleted or contaminated.

The primary saline-water conversion processes used commercially to augment water supplies are distillation and reverse osmosis. Several of these processes will be considered in detail in this section.

A typical desalination system consists of three subsystems: feedwater collection and conveyance, desalting processes with pretreatment and posttreatment, and brine conveyance and disposal. The desalting process consists of repeated units or modules; the volume of water to be treated dictates the number of modules needed.

Distillation Processes

Distillation is based on the simple principle of vaporizing pure water from salt water while leaving the salts behind as a concentrated brine, and condensing the product water vapor for subsequent use. Multistage flash distillation and vertical tube distillation are the two processes most commonly employed for large-scale desalination. As of 1978, multistage flash distillation (used primarily for seawater desalting) accounted for about 78 percent of the world's desalting capacity (30).

Both processes are based on the principle that water vaporizes at progressively lower temperatures when subjected to progressively lower pressures. A diagram of a typical multistage flash distillation system is depicted in Figure 8-11. In this system, the feedwater is heated under pressure to a temperature slightly below the boiling point and then injected into a chamber having a reduced pressure. The water then boils, producing a vapor that condenses on tubes cooled by feedwater, exchanging its energy with that of the incoming feedwater. The remaining feedwater in the first chamber, which is at a lower temperature, passes to the second chamber, which is at a lower pressure, and flashes, and again water condenses, forming product water. This process is repeated 30 to 40 times until the brine is relatively cool. Then the brine is mixed with more feedwater, reheated, and the process is repeated (29).

The vertical tube distillation process operates on the same principle, except that the steam generated in one chamber is condensed in the next chamber in order to aid vapor formation in that subsequent chamber. Each stage is called an "effect." Combination of vertical tube effects with alternating multistage flash distillation stages has been shown to be more cost-effective and thermodynamically efficient than vertical tube effects alone (31).

Several problems encountered with distillation processes are corrosion of the stills due to high salt concentrations and elevated temperatures, and scale formation on the heat-exchanger surfaces. The feedwater can be treated with acid or a polyphosphate compound to control scale, but such chemical additions can cause other problems. Distillation is higher in energy consumption than other desalination processes. Dual-purpose power plants generating electricity can provide an economical source of energy to the distillation process in the waste steam from the turbines (29).

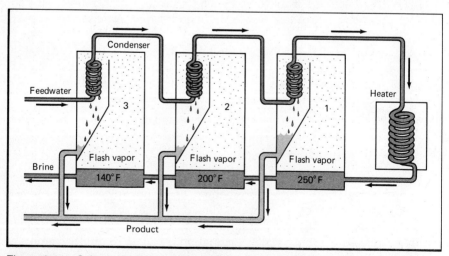

Figure 8-11 Schematic diagram of a typical multistage flash distillation system. (After the U.S. Department of Interior.)

Membrane Techniques

ELECTRODIALYSIS
As shown in Figure 8-12, an electrodialysis cell is comprised of two ion-selective membranes. An electric current applied to an electrodialysis cell provides the driving force of the process, and energy is used at a rate proportional to the quantity of salts to be removed. For this reason, primary application is to brackish waters with a total dissolved solids content of 1000 to 5000 ppm. Of the two ion-selective membranes, a cation-permeable membrane allows the sodium ions to pass through, while an anion-permeable membrane allows the negatively charged chloride ions to pass through; the process leaves fresh water between the membranes. Corrosion and scale formation are problems in electrodialysis; for this reason chemicals are added to the feedwater for control (29).

REVERSE OSMOSIS
When pure water and a salt solution are placed on opposite sides of a semipermeable membrane, the pure water diffuses through the membrane and dilutes the salt solution. This is known as osmosis. The effective force driving the flow is called osmotic pressure. By exerting pressure on the salt solution greater than its osmotic pressure, the process

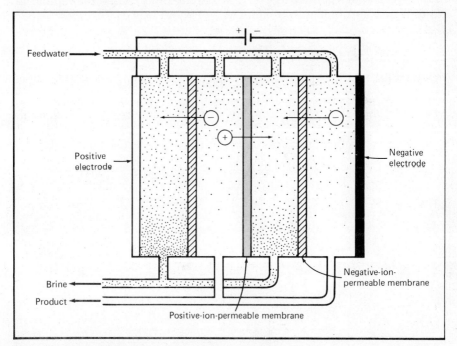

Figure 8-12   Generalized view of an electrodialysis desalting process. (After the U.S. Department of Interior.)

can be reversed. This is the principle behind desalting by reverse osmosis. Rather than an electric current driving the membrane process as in electrodialysis, here a hydraulic force is applied to separate the salts from the water. Energy consumption is proportional to the quantity of salts to be removed. For this reason, reverse osmosis is most economically applied to waters with a total dissolved content of 1000 to 10,000 ppm (31).

The basic components of a reverse osmosis system are the synthetic semipermeable membrane, a support structure for the membrane, a vessel in which the membrane can be exposed to water under very high pressures, and a high-pressure pump. A schematic of a typical reverse osmosis desalting system is depicted in Figure 8-13. The 5 mgd reverse osmosis plant at Water Factory 21 described previously is shown in Figure 8-14. Any number of reverse osmosis cells may constitute the system, depending on the quantity of water to be treated. Figure 8-15 shows one type of configuration of a reverse osmosis cell. This is called a tubular configuration. The membrane (typically made of cellulose acetate or polyamide) is placed within a porous tube and sealed into place. Multiple tubes are connected in series or parallel, the feedwater is forced through, and the purified water passes through the membrane and porous tube and is collected. For brackish water treatment, reverse osmosis membranes must be replaced about once every two to three years, due to membrane compression and biological fouling (32).

Economic Considerations

Capital costs of a desalination plant depend on the quality and quantity of water to be treated, the quality of product water desired, the price of land and construction materials, and the desalination process selected. Operating costs include energy costs, labor, supplies such as chemicals and process replacement parts, and administrative costs. Distillation is typi-

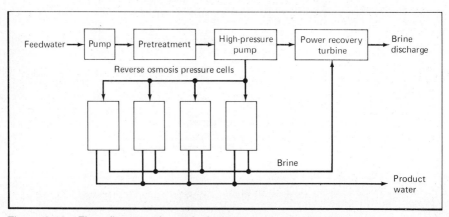

Figure 8-13   Flow diagram of a typical reverse osmosis desalting system.

Figure 8-14   5 mgd reverse osmosis wastewater desalting plant at Water Factory 21 in Orange County, California. (Courtesy of the Orange County Water District.)

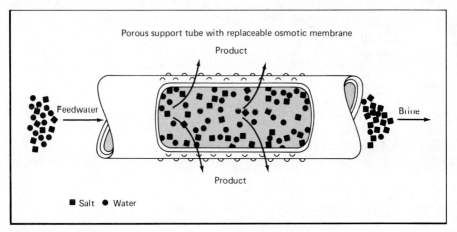

Figure 8-15   Illustration of basic reverse osmosis process.

cally the most expensive desalination process because of rising fuel costs and the excessive amounts of downtime that have been encountered historically in plant operation. As rapid advances are being made in membrane technology, reverse osmosis is being applied to more desalination operations as well as becoming a competitive low-energy alternative for desalting seawater (33).

8-5 INTERBASIN WATER TRANSFERS

Historically, man has made attempts to solve water-shortage problems by physically diverting water from areas of water surplus to areas of water deficit. What could be more illustrative of this practice than the construc-tion of the famous Roman aqueducts in ancient times? *Interbasin water transfers,* or *water importation,* refers to water withdrawal and removal by ditch, canal, or pipeline from a source containing excess water (the "exporting" drainage basin) to an adjacent area where water demands exceed existing water supplies (the "importing" drainage basin). On the surface, interbasin water transfers appear to offer an uncomplicated tech-nical solution to problems of regional water supply. Experiences with such projects have shown, however, that a multitude of social, economic, envi-ronmental, and political considerations often act to impede implementa-tion of these seemingly simple schemes.

Interbasin Transfers in the United States

Interbasin transfers of water have been used in the United States for irrigated agriculture as well as domestic and industrial uses. During the first half of the twentieth century, numerous interbasin water transfer projects were designed and implemented in the United States. As of 1965, 146 such existing projects were identified (34). Some of the more signifi-cant projects include the New York City water supply system, the Los Angeles Aqueduct, the Colorado River Aqueduct, the Central Valley Pro-ject in California, the California State Water Project, and the Colorado–Big Thompson project. The aqueduct length, safe yield, point of origin, and end use of the transferred water of these projects are summarized in Table 8-5 (35).

   During the 1960s numerous proposals for interbasin water transfers were made by scientists as correctives for shrinking water supplies and forecasted water shortages in many areas of the country. For example, the Texas Water Plan proposed to transfer water from areas of surplus in eastern Texas to the water-short areas of El Paso, the Trans-Pecos area, and the High Plains (36). The G.R.A.N.D. (Great Replenishment and Northern Development) Canal proposed to transfer 400,000 ft^3/s of fresh-water runoff from the James Bay Basin to the Great Lakes for storage for subsequent distribution to mid-North America (37). The North America Water and Power Alliance Plan called for transfer of about 90 million acre-feet of water annually from northwest Canada and Alaska to drier parts of Canada, the United States, and Mexico (38).

   These proposals gave rise to many feasibility studies and debates, but

Table 8-5 EXAMPLES OF INTERBASIN WATER TRANSFERS IN THE UNITED STATES

SYSTEM	YEAR BUILT	EXPORTING AREA	IMPORTING AREA	DISTANCE	SAFE YIELD	END USE
New York City	1842–1901	Croton River	New York City	250 km		
	1915–1924	Catskill system	New York City	400 km	1.3×10^9 m³/yr	Municipal and industrial
	1936	Delaware River	New York City	300 km		
Los Angeles	1913	Owens Valley (eastern side of Sierra Nevadas)	Mono Lake	500 km	580×10^6 m³/yr	Municipal
Colorado River Aqueduct	1928	Colorado River	California south coastal area	400 km	1.5×10^9 m³/yr	Recharge
Central Valley Project	1935	Northern California	San Joaquin Valley	600 km	3.4×10^9 m³/yr	Irrigation
California State Water Project		Feather River (northern California)	Los Angeles	800 km	2.5×10^9 m³/yr	Municipal
Colorado–Big Thompson Project		Colorado River	San Joaquin Valley	600 km 80 km (across Rockies)	2.7×10^9 m³/yr 370×10^6 m³/yr	Irrigation Irrigation and municipal

by the end of the decade interest in these solutions to water supply problems decreased due to rising construction costs and strong protests on environmental and political grounds. Indeed, such factors have remained as deterrents in implementing these widely publicized water transfer schemes.

A shift in water use allocation may serve to change this picture in the near future. As areas in the west become more involved in energy resources development (oil shale extraction, synthetic fuels production), which is highly water-intensive, and water use shifts away from irrigated agriculture to these more profitable uses, wealthy enterprising companies may be well able to afford the high price of water transfers.

Factors Affecting the Choice of Interbasin Transfers as a Viable Alternate Water Supply

ECONOMIC FACTORS

Certainly much has been learned from past experiences in proposing water transfer schemes. A large contribution to public opposition of these plans lies in a fundamental miscalculation of the true economic costs of the plan, especially in calculating costs to the water exporter. Too often construction and operation (that is, pumping) costs are considered as the only costs of the system. Surplus water is unfortunately regarded as a free commodity, rather than as a marketable resource for which the donor should be adequately reimbursed. If the donor is reimbursed, often administrative procedures involved with transfer of funds from the importer to the exporter may make such payment less than obvious to the water-donating locality (39). In addition, the economic advantages forgone by the exporter are usually neglected—for example, the costs of irrigation uses and power generation and the deterioration of water quality may be ignored (40).

ENVIRONMENTAL FACTORS

Altering the flow of a watercourse may result in severe environmental effects in the donating water basin downstream from the point of water withdrawal. Specifically, flow reduction can reduce the waste assimilative capacity of a river. The biological aquatic life may also be affected in downstream reaches of the altered waterway due to reduced flow and changes in sediment transport causing changes in life-supporting bed conditions of the stream (39).

SOCIAL AND POLITICAL FACTORS

In the western arid states where water rights have always been cause for emotional coloring of any water project, these sensitivities can be expected to affect strongly any proposal for water transfer if the reward or reimbursement to the donor is not sufficient or highly visible. A strong objection on the part of the donating party has been based on uncertainty of future demand for what may at the present time be considered surplus water. For example, future economic development in an area could cause a need for the surplus water. Since most water transfers involve treaties for a very long period of time (for example, 100 years), exporting communities are hesitant to get into such contracts if there is a chance that the water could benefit them in the future (39).

8-6 WEATHER MODIFICATION

Weather modification refers to man intervention in natural weather processes designed to induce a change to benefit man. This is usually accomplished by the purposeful dispersal of materials into clouds or fog to effect a change in meteorological conditions. Weather modification is not always planned, however. Inadvertent weather modification can occur as an unintended result of man's activities. For example, increased rainfall and severe storms, snow, and fog have been shown to occur as a result of the influence of industrial population centers (41).

Meteorological and Geographical Considerations

METEOROLOGICAL CONSIDERATIONS
Rain falls from clouds when moisture droplets become large enough in size and have sufficient velocity to overcome upward air motion (see Figure 8-16a). The principle behind weather modification is to induce these characteristics to initiate precipitation.

Both convective (cumulus) clouds and orographic (stationary) clouds are amenable to modification by seeding. Convective clouds are formed when unstable moist air is forced to rise by heating from below or by cooling from above and are characterized by short life cycles. Orographic clouds are stationary clouds (sometimes containing bands of convective activity) that are formed as a result of a layer of moist air moving horizontally and being forced to rise over a mountain. The clouds form as moist air cools, and subsequently precipitation falls on the windward side of the mountain.

There are two approaches to cloud modification, which can be used separately or together as a means of increasing precipitation. The first approach is to alter the colloidal stability of a cloud that possesses all the right characteristics for precipitation but where precipitation has not been initiated due to the low number of ice nuclei in the cloud. By adding ice nuclei to a cloud that contains sufficient supercooled moisture, the moisture is changed to ice, and the precipitation process is initiated early on in the life of the cloud, thereby improving the overall efficiency of the cloud. This type of modification is commonly used for winter orographic clouds and subfreezing convective clouds (see Figures 8-16a and 8-16b).

The second approach to cloud modification is to alter the cloud dynamics by adding an excess amount of seeding material. This action has the effect of converting a large amount of water into ice with the release of huge amounts of latent heat. This release produces additional uplift and hence growth of the cloud. The larger, modified cloud lasts longer than it would have lasted unmodified; thus more water is processed and converted into precipitation (see Figure 8-16c).

GEOGRAPHICAL CONSIDERATIONS

Successful weather modification has important implications for areas of the United States that experience long dry spells and hence water shortages, such as the west and midwest. To the west of the Rocky Mountains, most of the precipitation falls in the winter as snow, and rivers derive water from snowmelt in the spring. In these areas weather modification may be used to enhance winter snowpack so as to increase the water supply for the spring and summer.

To the east of the Rockies in the western and central states, convective clouds provide the summer precipitation, which comprises the bulk of the yearly rainfall for these areas. Because these areas include much of the vast agricultural section of our country, and because they produce most of the rain during the growing season, successful seeding of summer convective clouds is desirable. Results of summertime convective cloud seeding have met with only limited success, however (42).

Legal Considerations

Some interesting legal issues have surfaced as a result of planned weather modification activities. These issues center around the fact that weather modification that is to the advantage of one person may be to the disadvantage of a neighbor. For example, the extraction of precipitation from a cloud by seeding by one party could be said to be the cause of drought or flooding to another party close by. Is a weather modifier liable for such damages to a neighbor? Questions of "private rights" in the clouds have been raised (Does a weather modifier or landowner have private rights to atmospheric water over his or her property?) Problems of interstate and international significance could arise from pursuit of these issues as legal matters.

Figure 8-16 Weather modification: (a) natural cloud formation; (b) precipitation initiated by altering cloud stability; (c) precipitation initiated by altering cloud dynamics. (After D. F. Kostecki, "Weather Modification," *Water Spectrum*, Summer 1978, p. 32.)

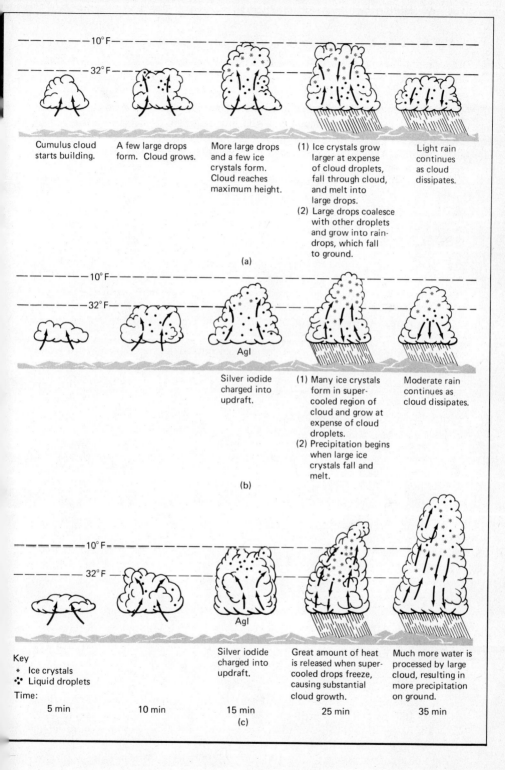

Cumulus cloud starts building.

A few large drops form. Cloud grows.

More large drops and a few ice crystals form. Cloud reaches maximum height.

(1) Ice crystals grow larger at expense of cloud droplets, fall through cloud, and melt into large drops.
(2) Large drops coalesce with other droplets and grow into rain-drops, which fall to ground.

Light rain continues as cloud dissipates.

(a)

Agl

Silver iodide charged into updraft.

(1) Many ice crystals form in super-cooled region of cloud and grow at expense of cloud droplets.
(2) Precipitation begins when large ice crystals fall and melt.

Moderate rain continues as cloud dissipates.

(b)

Agl

Key
*   Ice crystals
⁂   Liquid droplets

Time:

| 5 min | 10 min | 15 min | 25 min | 35 min |

Silver iodide charged into updraft.

Great amount of heat is released when super-cooled drops freeze, causing substantial cloud growth.

Much more water is processed by large cloud, resulting in more precipitation on ground.

(c)

263

CASE STUDY *The Colorado River Basin Pilot Project*

The Colorado River Basin suffers from some of the most severe water shortages in the United States. From 1967 to 1977 the Department of the Interior planned and conducted a study in the headwaters area of the Colorado River to determine the feasibility of seeding winter orographic clouds to increase snowpack in the San Juan Mountains and thus augment streamflow in the Colorado River Basin. The study area covered 1300 square miles in southwestern Colorado near Durango, at elevations from 9000 to 14,600 feet. Preliminary results showed that the cloud seeding was successful in increasing the average snowfall by 10 percent, which resulted in a potential increase in streamflow of 19 percent (42).

PROBLEMS

8-1. Look up the building codes for new construction in your area. Check state laws as well as local ordinances. Are water-saving devices required by law? If so, what year did these requirements become effective? Name the required devices and list the maximum flow restrictions. How do these restrictions compare with those (if any) previously required by law in terms of maximum allowable flow?

8-2. A household uses 130 gallons of water per person per day. The water uses and existing water control devices are as follows:

WATER USE	
Indoor water use	(gal)
Toilets	30
Bathing and personal use	
Shower	25
Toothbrushing	2
Other	6
Laundry	10
Dishwashing	5
Drinking and cooking	2
Outdoor water use	
Lawn watering	40
Car washing	10
Total	130

EXISTING WATER CONTROLS		
Faucet flow rate	4	gal/min
Shower flow rate	5.5	gal/min
Toilet	5	gal/flush

The area in which the house is located is hit by a severe drought. Residents are told by local authorities to reduce water demand by 30 percent. Devise a scheme to meet this standard by recommending a combination of water-saving devices and changes in water use patterns.

8-3. A city with a population of 100,000 uses 90 gallons of water per capita per day. Seventy percent of this water appears as wastewater in the sewerage system. The wastewater has a BOD content of 210 mg/L and a suspended solids content of 240 mg/L. What is the effect on the total flow, the BOD loading, and the suspended solids loading of the wastewater of implementing a water conservation policy that reduces water *use* by (a) 10 percent, (b) 25 percent, (c) 40 percent? What effect, in descriptive terms, will these new loadings have on the sewerage system and on the municipal wastewater treatment plant?

8-4. Determine the total quantity of water used for domestic purposes in your state in 1975. How does this amount compare with other water uses in your state for that year? If domestic water users were told to conserve 25 percent of their water under drought conditions, what percentage is this equivalent to in the largest water use sector in your state? Does this lead you to conclude that residential water conservation would be the most effective way to conserve water in your state? If not, what practices would you suggest for optimal water conservation?

8-5. What types of treatment processes (physical, chemical, biological) are the most suitable for storm water treatment? Why?

8-6. You have been given the job of designing a treatment system for a city's storm water. The product water is to be used for industrial cooling and recreation water for fishing. What are the maximum allowable concentrations of pollutants allowed for that reuse? What series of unit operations would you choose for treating the storm water to make it acceptable for this reuse?

8-7. Determine and describe the extent of wastewater reuse practices in your community. What quantity of water is reused on a daily (or yearly) basis for each purpose? Are you an indirect reuser of wastewater via your potable water supply? If so, how far away is the source of wastewater from your water supply intake?

8-8. What are the two primary purposes of recharging groundwater aquifers with reclaimed water? Why aren't aquifers that are recharged with reclaimed water used as a source of drinking water?

8-9. What is brackish water? Which desalination methods are the most suitable for water with this concentration of salt? Why are these methods unsuitable for waters containing higher concentrations of salt?

8-10. Define interbasin transfer. Is the water supply in your area augmented by interbasin transfer? If so, determine (a) where the water originates, (b) how far it is carried, (c) what compensation is given to the donating basin by the receiving basin, (d) the total quantity per year contributed to the water supply, and (e) the percentage of the total water demand that consists of the imported water.

8-11. Discuss the constraints of implementing interbasin transfers on a large-scale basis. What do you see as a possible solution to these constraints?

8-12. What are the two major types of cloud systems that are amenable to modification to increase precipitation? How is modification of each of these systems important in increasing the water supply?

References

1. U.S. Department of the Interior, *Water Conservation Devices: Residential Water Conservation*, U.S. Gov't. Print. Off., Washington, D.C., 1977.

2. W. D. Maddaus and D. L. Feuerstein, "Effect of Water Conservation on Water Demands," *J. Water Res. Div.*, ASCE, vol. 105, no. WR2, 1979, pp. 343–351.
3. M. Milne, *Residential Water Conservation*, California Water Resources Center Rep. No. 35, University of California/Davis, 1976.
4. M. Milne, *Residential Water Reuse*, California Water Resources Center Rep. No. 46, University of California/Davis, 1979.
5. W. S. Foster, "Reverse Water Rates Can Be a Useful Conservation Tool," *Am. City and County*, vol. 95, no. 2, 1980, p. 37.
6. C. W. Howe and F. P. Linaweaver, "The Impacts of Price on Residential Water Demand and Its Relation to System Design and Price Structure," *Water Resources Res.*, 1st quar., 1967.
7. S. H. Hanke and R. K. Davis, "Demand Management Through Responsive Pricing," *J. Am. Water Works Assn.*, vol. 63, no. 9, 1971, p. 555.
8. P. A. Rennison, "Water Conservation in Textile Finishing," *Am. Dyestuff Rep.*, vol. 66, no. 11, 1977, pp. 48–50.
9. "Republic Steel Recycling 80% of Steel-Mill Wastewater," *Civil. Eng.*, vol. 50, no. 6, 1980, pp. 102ff.
10. "Water Reuse: A Trickle Becomes a Torrent," *Chem. Eng.*, vol. 85, April 24, 1978, pp. 44ff.
11. Report to Congress by the Comptroller General of the United States, *More and Better Uses Could Be Made of Billions of Gallons of Water by Improving Irrigation Systems*, CED-77-117, September 2, 1977.
12. R. Von Dohren, "Consider the Many Reasons for Reuse," *Water and Wastes Eng.*, vol. 17, no. 9, 1980, pp. 74–78.
13. SCS Engineers Inc., *Contaminants Associated with Direct and Indirect Reuse of Municipal Wastewater*, U.S. EPA Rep. No. EPA-600/1-78-019, NTIS No. PB 280 482, March 1978.
14. W. J. Maier, J. DeZellar, and R. M. Miller, "Benefits from Water Conservation Depend on Comprehensive Planning," *Water Res. Bul.*, vol. 17, no. 4, 1981, pp. 672–677.
15. W. J. Maier and J. T. DeZellar, "Effects of Water Conservation on Sanitary Sewers and Wastewater Treatment Plants," *J. Water Pollut. Contr. Fed.*, vol. 52, no. 1, 1980, pp. 76–88.
16. S. Baxter, "Conservation Not the Answer to Water Problems," *Am. City and County*, vol. 94, no. 8, 1979, p. 29.
17. J. Crook, *Reliability of Wastewater Reclamation Facilities*, California Department of Health, Water Sanitation Section, Berkeley, CA, 1976.
18. W. E. Garrison and R. P. Miele, "Current Trends in Water Reclamation Technology," *J. Am. Water Works Assoc.*, vol. 69, no. 7, 1977, pp. 364–369.
19. California Department of Health, *Wastewater Reclamation Criteria*, California Administrative Code, Title 22, Div. 4, Water Sanitation Section, Berkeley, CA, 1975.
20. S. W. Work, M. R. Rothberg, and K. J. Miller, "Denver's Potable Reuse Project: Pathway to Public Acceptance," *J. Am. Water Works Assn.*, vol. 72, no. 8, 1980, pp. 435–440.
21. U.S. Congress, "Water Reuse Project Underway in Denver," *Congressional Record*, October 22, 1979, pp. E5191–E5192.
22. J. E. Matthews, *Industrial Reuse and Recycle of Wastewaters: Literature Review*, EPA Rep. No. EPA/600/2-80-183, U.S. EPA, Ada, OK, 1980.

23. B. A. Carnes, J. M. Eller, and J. C. Martin, "Reuse of Refinery and Petrochemical Wastewaters," *Indus. Water Eng.,* vol. 9, no. 4, 1979, p. 25.

24. L. E. Streebin, L. W. Canter, and J. R. Palafox, "Water Conservation and Reuse in the Canning Industry," *Proc. of the 26th Industrial Waste Conference,* pt. II, Purdue University, Lafayette, IN, 1971, p. 766.

25. C. A. Caswell, "Water Reuse in the Steel Industry," Am. Inst. of Chem. Eng., *Complete Water Reuse: Industry's Opportunity,* New York, 1973, p. 384.

26. U.S. Department of the Interior, *Water Factory 21,* Water Research Capsule Report, Office of Water Research and Technology, U.S. Gov't. Print. Off., Washington, D.C., 1978.

27. R. Field and C. Fan, "Recycling Urban Stormwater for Profit," *Water/Eng. and Management,* vol. 128, no. 4, 1981.

28. C. W. Mallory, *The Beneficial Uses of Stormwater,* U.S. EPA Rep. No. EPA-R2-73-139, NTIS No. PB 217506, January 1973.

29. U.S. Department of the Interior, Office of Saline Water, *The A-B-Seas of Desalting,* U.S. Gov't. Print. Off., Washington, D.C., 1968.

30. V. Cavaseno, "Desalting Takes Off," *Chem. Eng.,* vol. 85, March 13, 1978, pp. 41–44.

31. W. R. Walker, *Integrating Desalination and Salinity Control Alternatives,* U.S. EPA Rep. No. EPA-600/2-78-074, NTIS No. PB 281 381, Ada, OK, April 1978.

32. U.S. Department of the Interior, Office of Water Research and Technology, *Reverse Osmosis,* Water Research Capsule Report, U.S. Gov't. Print. Off., Washington, D.C., 1979.

33. "Water Desalination Gets Another Look," *Chem. and Eng. News,* vol. 58, February 4, 1980, pp. 26–30.

34. F. Quinn, "Water Transfers," *Geographical Review,* vol. 58, no. 1, 1968, pp. 108–132.

35. A. K. Biswas, "North American Water Transfers, An Overview," *Water Supply and Management,* vol. 2. no. 2, 1978, pp. 79–90.

36. Texas Water Development Board, *The Texas Water Plan,* Austin, Texas, 1968.

37. T. W. Kierns, "Thinking Big in North America: The Grand Canal Concept," *The Futurist,* December 1980.

38. A. H. Laycock, "Interbasin Transfer—The International Dimension," *Water Resources Bulletin,* vol. 7, no. 5, 1971.

39. G. Aron, E. L. White, and S. P. Coelen, "Feasibility of Interbasin Water Transfer," *Water Resources Bulletin,* vol. 13, no. 5, 1977.

40. C. W. Howe, "Economic Issues Related to Large-Scale Water Transfers in the U.S.A.," *Water Supply and Management,* vol. 2, no. 2, 1978, pp. 127–136.

41. "Weather Modification Could Solve Some Water Resource Problems," *Civil Eng.,* vol. 48, no. 9, 1978, pp. 107–109.

42. Congressional Research Service, Library of Congress, *Weather Modification: Programs, Problems, Policy and Potential,* committee print, 95th Cong., 2d Sess., U.S. Gov't. Print. Off., Washington, D.C., 1978.

Chapter 9
Flow of Water in Open Channels and Pipes

This chapter, which serves as background for the material presented in Chapters 10, 11, and 12, presents the principles governing the flow of water in open channels and in full-flowing pipes (pressure conduits). Also included is a discussion of methods of analysis for flow in pipe networks. A final section deals with pumping equipment used in water delivery systems.

9-1 OPEN CHANNEL FLOW SYSTEMS

Definitions

OPEN CHANNEL
An open channel is a natural or manmade waterway that carries water by the force of gravity due to the slope of the channel bottom. Because channel flow is bounded only on the sides and bottom by solid surfaces, the flow is characterized by a free water surface at atmospheric pressure. The hydraulics of open channel flow apply to natural rivers and streams and to manmade water conveyance structures such as canals and flumes, as well as to closed systems such as pipes, tunnels, and sewers that are flowing partly full. Their cross-sectional geometry varies from regular shapes such as rectangular, trapezoidal, or circular to irregular shapes that are characteristic of natural rivers and streams.

LAMINAR AND TURBULENT FLOW

An open channel flow regime can be classified in a number of ways. Flow is classified as being laminar or turbulent according to its *Reynolds number:* the ratio of inertial forces to viscous forces acting on fluid particles. The Reynolds number is expressed as:

$$Re = \rho R V / \mu = R V / \nu \tag{9-1}$$

where $\rho =$ fluid density (lb mass/ft^3)
$\mu =$ dynamic viscosity (lb mass/ft-s)
$R =$ hydraulic radius of channel (cross-sectional area divided by the wetted perimeter) (ft)
$V =$ mean stream velocity (ft/s)
$\mu/\rho = \nu =$ the kinematic viscosity (ft^2/s)

Laminar flow is defined as flow where viscous forces are strong relative to inertial forces, and where fluid particles travel in smooth, distinct paths. Laminar open channel flow is rarely encountered. For situations met within engineering designs, the flow in open channels is nearly always *turbulent;* that is, viscous forces are weak relative to inertial forces, and the fluid particles move in instantaneously irregular paths. Turbulent flow in open channels is usually associated with Reynolds numbers greater than 500.

STEADY AND UNSTEADY FLOW

Another way to classify flow is by its change in characteristics with respect to time. Given that the magnitude and direction of fluid velocity usually vary from point to point in a stream, if these conditions nonetheless remain constant at each point over *time,* the flow is called *steady flow.* True steady flow occurs only in laminar flow; however, steady flow is commonly defined for conditions that are really those of *mean steady flow,* that is, flow where velocity values at a point in a stream fluctuate about a constant mean velocity value for that point (1). Steady flow as used in this chapter is thus defined as mean steady flow.

If the mean velocity values at a given point continually vary over time, the flow is called *unsteady.* Examples of unsteady flow include flood wave propagation, the behavior of ocean waves, and the effects of tides on rivers and estuaries. Another important type of unsteady flow, discussed in Section 9-2, is *water hammer* or hydraulic surge.

UNIFORM FLOW

Whereas in steady flow the velocity conditions may vary from point to point in a stream (but remain constant over time), *uniform flow* is defined as flow in which the velocity is the same in magnitude and direction at every point in the stream. In practice, a modified definition is usually used for this characteristic: flow is considered to be uniform where discharge, cross section, and depth remain constant over a length (*reach*) of the channel. Uniform flow occurs at a depth called the *normal depth* (d_n) for a channel of constant slope, roughness, and cross-sectional area. We shall see that problems of uniform flow are more easily solved but are not usually encountered in open channel flow, and that problems of nonuniform flow may be converted to cases of uniform flow by dividing a channel into segments and performing calculations based on the assumption of average uniform flow in each segment.

SPECIFIC ENERGY AND CRITICAL FLOW

Channel flow may also be described in terms of its *specific energy* at a particular cross section with respect to the channel bottom. Specific energy, energy per pound of water, is defined as

$$E_s = d + V^2/2g \qquad (9\text{-}2)$$

where
$$d = \text{depth of water in the channel}$$
$$V^2/2g = \text{velocity head}$$
$$V = \text{mean velocity of flow}$$
$$g = \text{acceleration due to gravity (32 ft/s}^2)$$

Thus specific energy is expressed as the sum of depth and velocity head for a particular cross section. The relation between specific energy and depth of flow is shown in Figure 9-1.

Critical depth (d_c) is the depth of flow that occurs when specific energy is at a minimum. Discharge at critical depth is the maximum for

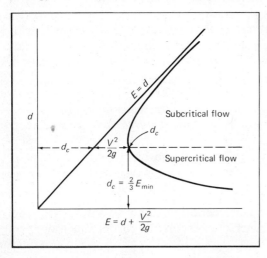

Figure 9-1 Relation between specific energy and depth of flow for a constant discharge Q. Note that d_c is two-thirds of the minimum specific energy ($\frac{2}{3} E_{min}$) and that the velocity head at E_{min} is thus equal to $\frac{1}{2} d_c$.

a given specific energy. Flow at critical depth is highly unstable and should therefore be avoided in design of open channel flow systems. Critical depth occurs at

$$d_c = \sqrt[3]{Q^2/gB^2}$$ (9-3)

where B is the width of the channel, or

$$d_c = \sqrt[3]{q^2/g}$$ (9-4)

where q is the discharge per unit width.

When the specific energy of the flow at a cross section is greater than the minimum, and therefore the depth of flow is greater *or* less than the critical depth, two possibilities for a flow regime exist. If the depth of flow is greater than the critical depth, the flow is classified as *subcritical.* Subcritical flow is characteristically deep, slow flow that would be expected to occur in channels having mild slopes. If the depth of flow is less than the critical flow, the flow is said to be *supercritical.* Supercritical flow is rapid, shallow flow that is typical of steep-sloping channels.

When there is a transition in flow from supercritical to subcritical or vice versa, the actual depth must pass through the critical value. Critical depth would also be expected to occur at a point of free outfall in a channel where the flow regime in the channel is subcritical, because the specific energy would be expected to be a minimum at this point.

The velocity associated with critical depth is the *critical velocity* and for any cross section is given by

$$V_c = (gd_c)^{1/2}$$ (9-5)

or

$$V_c = (gA/B)^{1/2}$$ (9-6)

where A = cross-sectional area of channel
B = width of channel at water surface
d_c = critical depth
g = acceleration due to gravity (32 ft/s^2) (9.8 m/s^2)

Uniform Flow in Open Channels

From Figure 9-2, the energy equation for uniform flow in a segment L between cross sections 1 and 2 of an open channel can be written as

$$Z_1 + d_1 + V_1^2/2g = Z_2 + d_2 + V_2^2/2g + H_L$$ (9-7)

where Z = elevation above an arbitrary datum (ft)
d = flow depth (ft)

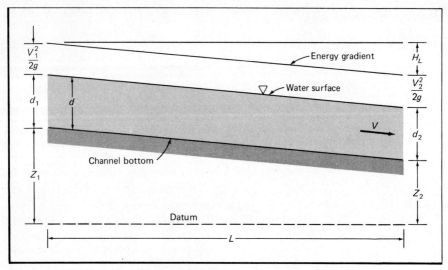

Figure 9-2   Uniform flow in an open channel.

$$V = \text{average velocity (ft/s)}$$
$$H_L = \text{total head loss (energy loss) between the two cross}$$
$$\text{sections}$$

The terms of the energy equation are all in units of energy per unit weight (ft-lb/lb), which is commonly expressed as units of length (ft) and called *head*. By definition, in uniform flow $d_1 = d_2$ and $V_1 = V_2$. Equation 9-7 thus becomes

$$Z_1 - Z_2 = H_L$$

or

$$\Delta Z = SL$$

where S is the slope of the energy gradient and L is the distance between two cross sections. In uniform flow, the slope of the energy gradient, the slope of the free water surface, and the slope of the channel bottom are all equal.

VELOCITY
There are several equations that can be used to calculate the velocity of flow in open channels. One equation is that proposed by Chézy in 1775, which states that

$$V = C(RS)^{1/2} \tag{9-8}$$

where V = velocity of flow (l/t)
R = hydraulic radius (cross-sectional area divided by the wetted perimeter) (l)
S = slope of the energy gradient
C = a coefficient with dimensions of $l^{1/2}t^{-1}$

Manning and others empirically determined that the Chézy coefficient is related to the hydraulic radius in the following manner:

(FPS units) $C = (1.49/n)(R^{1/6})$ (9-9a)
(SI units) $C = (1/n)(R^{1/6})$ (9-9b)

where n is a coefficient representing the roughness of the channel bottom. Combining these expressions for C with the Chézy equation (Equation 9-8) yields the widely used Manning equation:

(FPS units) $V = (1.49/n)(R^{2/3}S^{1/2})$ (9-10a)
(SI units) $V = (1/n)(R^{2/3}S^{1/2})$ (9-10b)

which can be rewritten to determine discharge in the form

(FPS units) $Q = (1.49/n)(AR^{2/3}S^{1/2})$ (9-11a)
(SI units) $Q = (1/n)(AR^{2/3}S^{1/2})$ (9-11b)

Various values for the roughness coefficient are given in Table 9-1. Manning's equation holds as long as S does not exceed 0.10. For channels with distinct changes in roughness across the width of a cross section, such as a paved channel with grassy sides, it is common to subdivide the cross section according to roughness, compute flow velocity for each subsection, and then sum the flows.

Example 9-1

Determine the discharge of a channel having a brick bottom and grassy sides, with dimensions as designated in Figure 9-3. Assume $S = 0.002$.

SOLUTION

1. Using Equation 9-11a, calculate the discharge for the portion of flow in the rectangular subsection. From Table 9-1, choose $n = 0.017$.

$R = (6)(12)/(12) = 6.0$ ft
$Q = (1.49/0.017)(72)(6.0)^{2/3}(0.002)^{1/2} = 931$ ft^3/s

Table 9-1 VALUES OF MANNING'S ROUGHNESS
COEFFICIENT n

NATURE OF SURFACE	MANNING'S n RANGE
Concrete pipe	0.011–0.013
Corrugated metal pipe	0.019–0.030
Vitrified clay pipe	0.012–0.014
Steel pipe	0.009–0.011
Monolithic concrete	0.012–0.017
Cement rubble	0.017–0.025
Brick	0.014–0.017
Laminated treated wood	0.015–0.017
Open channels	
Lined with concrete	0.013–0.022
Earth, clean, after weathering	0.018–0.020
Earth, with grass and some weeds	0.025–0.030
Excavated in rock, smooth	0.035–0.040
Excavated in rock, jagged and irregular	0.040–0.045
Natural stream channels:	
No boulders or brush	0.028–0.033
Dense growth of weeds	0.035–0.050
Bottom of cobbles with large boulders	0.050–0.070

SOURCE: *Design Charts for Open-Channel Flow,* U.S. Department of Transportation, Federal Highway Administration, Hydraulic Design Series No. 3, U.S. Gov.'t Print. Off., Washington, D.C., 1961.

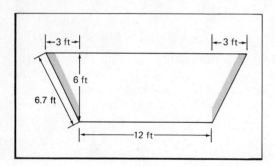

Figure 9-3   Figure for Example 9-1.

2. Calculate the discharge for the portion of flow in the grassy subsections of the channel. From Table 9-1, choose $n = 0.025$. For each side

$$A = (0.5)(3)(6) = 9 \text{ ft}^2$$
$$R = 9/4 = 2.25 \text{ ft}$$

For both sides

$$Q = 2[(1.49/0.025)(9)(2.25)^{2/3}(0.002)^{1/2}] = 83 \text{ ft}^3/\text{s}$$

3. The total discharge for the channel is thus

$$Q = 931 + 83 = 1014 \text{ ft}^3/\text{s} \quad \blacksquare$$

Many tables, charts, and nomographs are available to facilitate calculations using Manning's equation. Figure 9-4 is a nomograph based on Manning's formula that shows the relation between discharge, diameter of the conduit, slope, and velocity for a channel with $n = 0.013$. Values obtained from the nomograph can be adjusted to other values of n by making appropriate corrections, since V and Q are proportional to $1/n$ and S is proportional to n^2.

For open channels consisting of circular pipes or tunnels flowing partly full, calculation of hydraulic radius and cross-sectional area of flow can be cumbersome. Figure 9-5 facilitates these calculations by showing the relation between the hydraulic elements of a circular pipe, which allows the conditions of a pipe flowing partly full to be calculated from the conditions of a full-flowing pipe.

Example 9-2

If a pipe flowing full has a discharge of 12 m^3/s and a velocity of 2 m/s, find the velocity and depth of flow in the pipe when $Q = 8$ m^3/s.

SOLUTION
1. The problem is to determine the velocity and depth for a pipe flowing $8/12 = 67$ percent full.
2. From Figure 9-5, discharge at 67 percent full gives depth of flow $= 61$ percent full flow, and velocity $= 110$ percent full-flowing velocity:

$$(1.10)\ (2\ \text{m/s}) = 2.2\ \text{m/s} \quad \blacksquare$$

It should be noted that the maximum discharge in a pipe flowing partly full occurs when $AR^{2/3}$ is a maximum. This corresponds to a depth of $y = 0.94D$, where D is the diameter of the pipe (2).

From Manning's equation (Equation 9-10) it can be seen that for a cross section of any geometric shape, discharge is a maximum when the wetted perimeter is a minimum, given that the slope and channel roughness remain the same. Of all geometric shapes, the semicircular cross section is the most efficient for conveying water. However, the use of a semicircular contour for a channel is not always feasible, for example when using earthen materials or wood. The shape of the most efficient trapezoidal cross section is one where the hydraulic radius is equal to half the depth, so that, for example, the most hydraulically efficient rectangle is one in which the depth is half the width, and the most efficient trapezoid is the half-hexagon.

As mentioned previously, the normal depth d_n is the depth at which

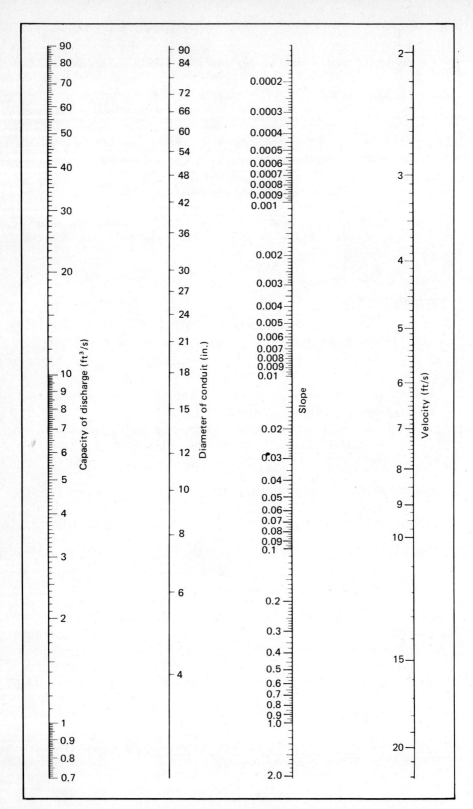

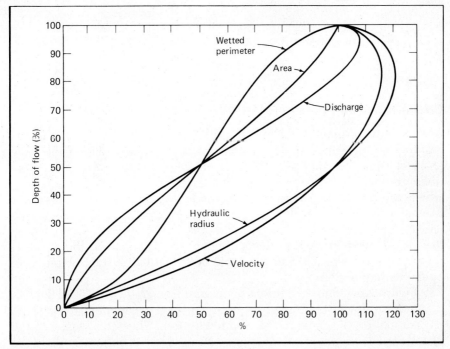

Figure 9-5   Hydraulic elements of a circular section.

uniform flow occurs. This depth may be calculated by using Manning's equation for discharge (Equation 9-11), expressing A and R in terms of depth, and then solving for depth by trial and error. The relation between critical depth and normal depth determines the flow regime. If $d_c > d_n$ (steep slopes), then the flow is supercritical. If $d_c < d_n$ (mild slopes), the flow is classified as subcritical.

Example 9-3

Discharge in a 30-ft-wide earthen canal is 600 ft^3/s. Assuming $S = 0.007$, $n = 0.017$, and conditions of uniform flow, determine (a) the normal depth and critical depth of flow, and (b) whether the flow is supercritical or subcritical.

SOLUTION

1. From Equation 9-11a, d_n is determined by trial and error:

$$600 = (1.49/0.017)(30d_n)(30d_n/(30 + 2d_n))^{2/3}(0.007)^{1/2}$$
$$d_n = 1.9$$

Figure 9-4   Nomograph based on Manning's formula for circular pipes flowing full in which $n = 0.013$. (Please see opposite page.)

2. From Equation 9-3, critical depth is determined:

$$d_c = [(600^2)/(32.2)(30)^2]^{1/3} = 2.3$$

3. Since $d_c > d_n$, flow is supercritical. ■

Gradually Varied Nonuniform Flow

Because flow, cross section, and depth frequently change over channel length, uniform flow is seldom encountered in the field. These changing channel conditions give rise instead to one of two *nonuniform flow* situations: gradually varied flow or rapidly varied flow. Gradually varied flow, which will be considered in this section, is nonuniform flow that results from gradual changes in flow regime over a long distance. Rapidly varied flow results from abrupt changes in flow regime that occur within a short distance. Determining the effects of channel conditions on the shape of the water surface profile and the depth of flow are important elements of open channel design.

Figure 9-6 defines conditions of nonuniform, gradually varied flow. In nonuniform flow, the slope of the water surface profile deviates from (is not parallel to) the slope of the channel bottom. The actual shape of the water surface depends on the slope of the channel bottom and on the relation of the actual depth of flow to the critical depth and to the normal depth for the channel reach under consideration. There are 12 possible shapes for water surface profiles in gradually varied flow; illustrations and detailed descriptions are given in references 1 and 3 to 5.

Problems of gradually varied nonuniform flow are solved by dividing

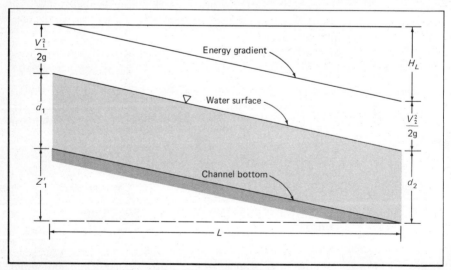

Figure 9-6 Nonuniform flow in an open channel.

a channel into reaches and treating each reach as being equivalent to conditions of uniform flow, using average hydraulic properties of the reach based on conditions at each of its ends. A common stepwise procedure that is used to determine water surface profiles (backwater curves) for gradually varied nonuniform flow is the *direct-step method.*

From Figure 9-6, the energy equation for gradually varied flow between cross sections 1 and 2 is given by

$$Z'_1 + d_1 + V_1^2/2g = d_2 + V_2^2/2g + H_L \tag{9-12}$$

Rearranging this equation in terms of specific energy E_s ($E_s = d + V^2/2g$) yields the form

$$(d_1 + V_1^2/2g) - (d_2 + V_2^2/2g) = H_L - Z'_1$$

or

$$E_1 - E_2 = H_L - Z'_1$$

Since $Z_1 = S_c L$, $H_L = \bar{S}_e L$, where S_c is the slope of the channel bottom and $\bar{S}_e$ is the slope of the energy gradient, Equation 9-12 can be rewritten as

$$E_1 - E_2 = \bar{S}_e L - S_c L$$

which in terms of L is

$$L = (E_1 - E_2)/(\bar{S}_e - S_c) \tag{9-13}$$

The slope of the energy gradient can be found by rearranging Manning's equation to the form

(FPS units) $S_e = n^2 V_{\text{av}}^2 / 2.22 R_{\text{av}}^{4/3}$ (9-14a)

(SI units) $S_e = n^2 V_{\text{av}}^2 / R_{\text{av}}^{4/3}$ (9-14b)

Equation 9-14 can be used to determine $\bar{S}_e$ for Equation 9-13 based on the assumptions that (1) the slope of the energy gradient for the reach is equivalent to the slope of the energy gradient for uniform flow with velocity and hydraulic radius equal to the average velocity and average hydraulic radius of the two cross sections, and (2) the slope of the energy gradient for uniform flow is equivalent to the average of the slopes at the two cross sections.

The direct-step method for computing backwater curves is carried out by dividing the channel into subreaches of specified depths at cross sections, and determining the distance between cross sections using Equation 9-13. This is done in an incremental fashion starting with a cross section of known depth at one end of the channel and computing the distance to each next cross section. By computing the critical depth and normal depth and comparing these values to the actual depth of flow, the shape of the water surface profile for each subreach can be determined.

HYDRAULIC JUMP

When the flow regime changes from supercritical to subcritical the result is a *hydraulic jump,* which is characterized by a discernible upward-sloping water surface profile and very turbulent flow. An example of one set of conditions that gives rise to a hydraulic jump is shown in Figure 9-7. The depths of flow before and after the hydraulic jump (the *conjugate depths*), as well as the length of the hydraulic jump, are of interest to engineers. The conjugate depths for a stationary hydraulic jump in a rectangular channel are given by the following equation:

$$d_2 = \frac{d_1}{2}\left(-1 + \sqrt{1 + \frac{8q^2}{gd_1^3}}\right) \tag{9-15}$$

where d_1 = smaller depth before hydraulic jump
d_2 = larger depth after hydraulic jump
q = specific discharge

Obviously, one depth must be known in order to calculate the other. This equation gives accurate results for determination of conjugate depths for channel slopes up to 0.10. Once the conjugate depths are found, the location of the hydraulic jump can be calculated using Equation 9-13.

Special Considerations in Design of Channels

CHANNEL TRANSITIONS

A channel transition is defined as a change in the direction, slope, or cross section of the channel that produces a change in the state of flow (3). Channel transitions may be constructed to connect channels of different sizes, to minimize head loss, or to change flow regime purposely. There are several shapes of channel transitions that are commonly used. These are illustrated in Figure 9-8. The same shape can be employed equally well for an expansion or a contraction; head loss is greater for expansions, however, so that providing smooth channel curvature in the expansion-

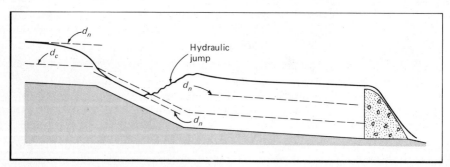

Figure 9-7   Example of a hydraulic jump.

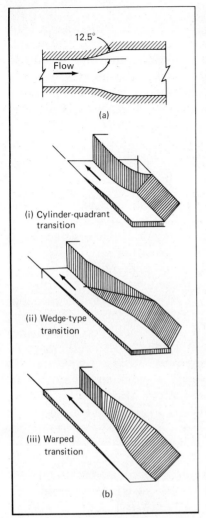

Figure 9-8   Transitions for subcritical flow: (a) simple straight-line expansion for two rectangular channels; (b) three types of contractions for connecting trapezoidal and rectangular channels.

transition region is particularly important in order to minimize head losses.

Figure 9-8a is a simple transition that is suitable for connecting two rectangular channels. An angle of 12.5° between channels minimizes head loss (4,5). Figure 9-8b shows the three commonest types of transitions used between trapezoidal and rectangular channels: the cylinder-quadrant transition, the wedge-type transition, and the warped transition. Note that these transition types are suitable only for transitions involving subcritical flow; the situation for supercritical flow is somewhat more complex and is outside the scope of this discussion. References 1 and 5 may be consulted for thorough treatment of the design of channel transitions for all flow regimes.

FLOW IN CURVED CHANNELS

Flow in curved channels must be given special consideration because of the effects of centrifugal force on the water surface. The depth of flow will be greater on the outside of the curve and therefore the outside walls of the channel must be high enough to accommodate this depth. The slope of the water at the channel bend may be determined from considerations of net pressure force and centrifugal force acting on the flow in the channel. Detailed discussions on the effects of these forces on open channel flow may be found in references 1 and 6.

SEDIMENT TRANSPORT

Of particular concern to the engineer is the interaction of channel flow with natural bottom sediment found in rivers and streams, and with sediment washed into both natural and lined channels from storm runoff. Depending on the velocity of channel flow and other factors, sediment transported by a channel may lead to channel scour or sediment deposition, either of which may present a problem to the intended operation of the channel. For example, when runoff from a severe storm contributes increased velocity of flow and quantity of coarse sediment to an open channel, the coarse particles carried by the fast-flowing water often cause channel scour. In the case of a storm sewer, this could very well mean accelerated erosion of the concrete conduit, leading to increased maintenance costs. Conversely, when channel flow velocity is greatly reduced, it can be expected that a portion of the suspended sediment will settle out of the flow and accumulate in the channel bottom. This situation is common where a stream intersects a reservoir (reservoir sedimentation) and at the mouth of a river (formation of a delta). Sedimentation can also be a problem in sanitary sewers, resulting in septic conditions, if the flow velocity is not sufficient to promote self-cleansing.

Channel sediment consists of two fractions, which can be designated as the *bed load* and the *suspended load.* The bed load is usually considered to consist of mostly sand-size and coarser sediment particles (> 0.06 mm in diameter) that roll along the bottom of the channel as a result of the drag force exerted by the fluid flow on the sediment grains. The suspended load consists of fine sediments—primarily silt and clay (< 0.06 mm in diameter)—that are eroded from the land and washed into the channel, and are usually carried in suspension by the channel flow because of their fine size. Some bed-load particles may jump into suspension when the flow velocity is increased, just as some suspended particles will settle out as the flow velocity is reduced.

Of importance to the engineer in designing a channel is the ability to determine the minimum velocity of flow that is necessary to prevent sediment buildup on the channel bottom. A number of relations for determining minimum velocity have been developed, all of which are based on the relation between the drag force of the fluid particles moving through the sediment layer and the resistive force exerted by the sediment particles in the layer that acts to prevent motion of the particles. One equation that has been presented by Fair and Geyer for determining minimum velocity of streamflow is (7)

$$V_m = C\sqrt{K\frac{\gamma_s - \gamma}{\gamma}d} \tag{9-16}$$

where V_m = minimum velocity necessary to prevent sediment deposition

   d = mean sediment particle diameter

   K = a measure of particle shape and cohesiveness and the effectiveness of scour, which must be determined experimentally

   γ_s = specific weight of the sediment particles

   γ = specific weight of water

   C = Chézy coefficient (see Equation 9-9)

The coefficient C is selected with consideration of the amount of solids present in the flow. Fair and Geyer have reported experimental values for K ranging from 0.04 for the initiation of scour to greater than 0.8 for effective cleansing (7).

9-2   FUNDAMENTALS OF FLOW IN PIPES

As stated in the previous section, a pipeline can act as an open channel if it is flowing only partly full, where water is conveyed under conditions of atmospheric pressure. Consideration is given in this section to the hydraulics of *full-flowing pipes* (*pressure conduits*) where water is conveyed at pressure greater than atmospheric. For most practical purposes, and in this section, pipe flow can be considered to be turbulent, that is, with Reynolds number greater than 2000. Pipelines are built to transport water where the topography is not favorable for construction of canals. Pipelines may be constructed either above or below ground and are usually made of concrete, steel, cast iron, asbestos cement, or plastics.

Calculation of Flow Velocity and Head Loss

Figure 9-9 defines the hydraulic and head elements of flow in a straight pipe of uniform diameter. The energy equation for flow in segment L between points 1 and 2 can be written as

$$Z_1 + p_1/\gamma + V_1^2/2g = Z_2 + p_2/\gamma + V_2^2/2g + H_L \tag{9-17}$$

where Z = elevation above an arbitrary datum (ft)

   p/γ = pressure head (ft)

   V = average velocity of flow (ft/s)

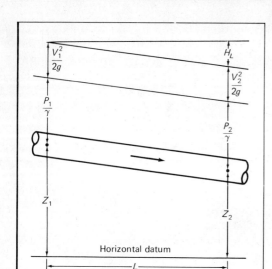

Figure 9-9 Definition sketch for pipe flow.

H_L = total head loss (energy loss) between the two cross sections

Note that the terms of the energy equation are all in units of energy per unit weight (ft-lb/lb), which reduce to units of length (ft). If a pump were inserted into the pipeline, the quantity H_p would be added to the left-hand side of the equation to account for the additional energy head resulting from the action of the pump. If a turbine were inserted in the pipeline in place of the pump, the positive quantity H_p would be replaced by a negative quantity H_t since a turbine converts the energy of flow into mechanical work, thereby consuming energy from the pipeflow instead of imparting energy to the flow as in the case of a pump.

Whereas the Chézy-Manning formula (Equation 9-10) is commonly used to calculate the velocity of flow in open channels, the Hazen-Williams equation is widely applied to determine velocity in pressure conduits. The Hazen-Williams equation is stated in the following form:

(FPS units) $V = 1.318CR^{0.63}S^{0.54}$ (9-18a)

(SI units) $V = 0.85CR^{0.63}S^{0.54}$ (9-18b)

where V = velocity of flow (ft/s or m/s)
   C = a coefficient that is a function of the construction material and age of the pipe
   R = hydraulic radius (cross-sectional area divided by the wetted perimeter) (ft or m)
   S = slope of energy gradient in feet per foot of length or meters per meter of length

For circular conduits flowing full, Equation 9-18 may be rewritten for determining discharge as follows:

(FPS units) $Q = 0.432CD^{2.63}S^{0.54}$ (9-19a)

(SI units) $Q = 0.278CD^{2.63}S^{0.54}$ (9-19b)

where Q = discharge (ft^3/s or m^3/s)
        D = pipe diameter (ft or m)

Some values of the coefficient C are given in Table 9-2. A nomograph for the Hazen-Williams formula for $C = 100$ is given in Figure 9-10. Other charts and nomographs for facilitating the solution of the Hazen-Williams formula can be found in most textbooks on hydraulics.

ESTIMATION OF HEAD LOSS
Total head loss in pipelines is due to pipe friction loss and to minor losses due to friction in piping auxiliaries. Minor losses include those resulting from valves, fittings, bends, changes in cross section, and changes in flow characteristics at inlets and outlets. Over long lengths of pipeline, minor losses can usually be ignored in calculations of head loss because they contribute a relatively small proportion to the total losses. On the other hand, minor losses in short water transportation systems, such as those in water and wastewater treatment plants, should not be ignored because their proportion of the total head loss is significantly larger. Minor losses are usually expressed as a function of the velocity head in performing calculations, that is, $H_L = KV^2/2g$.

The head loss resulting from pipe friction can be calculated by solving either the Chézy Manning equation (Equation 9-10) or the Hazen-Williams equation (Equation 9-18) for S and multiplying by the length of the pipe. Alternatively, the Darcy-Weisbach equation may be used to determine head loss, which is stated as

$$H_L = fLV^2/D2g \qquad\qquad (9\text{-}20)$$

where H_L = head loss
        L = pipe length
        D = pipe diameter

Table 9-2 SOME VALUES OF THE HAZEN-WILLIAMS COEFFICIENT

PIPE MATERIAL	C
New cast iron	130
5-year-old cast iron	120
20-year-old cast iron	100
Average concrete	130
New welded steel	120
Asbestos cement	140
Vitrified clay	110
Plastic	150

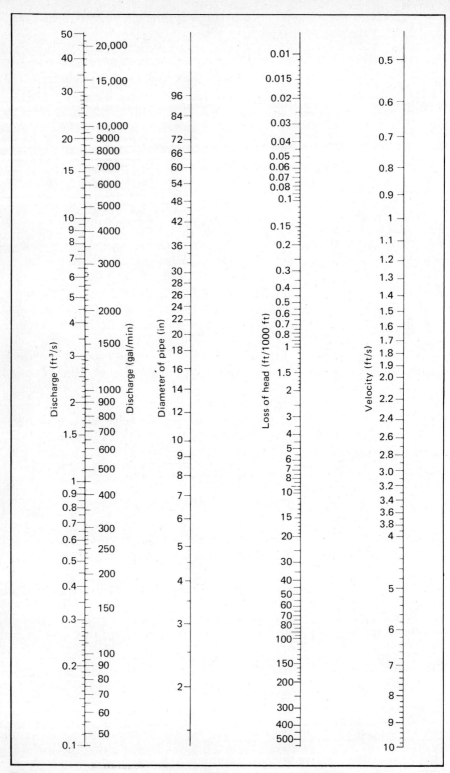

Figure 9-10   Nomograph for Hazen-Williams formula in which $C = 100$.

f = friction factor
V = flow velocity

The friction factor is a function of the Reynolds number and the relative roughness of the pipe. Friction factors for several pipe materials are given in Figure 9-11. Head losses in pipe fittings and transitions can be estimated using widely available tables and charts (1, 3, 6).

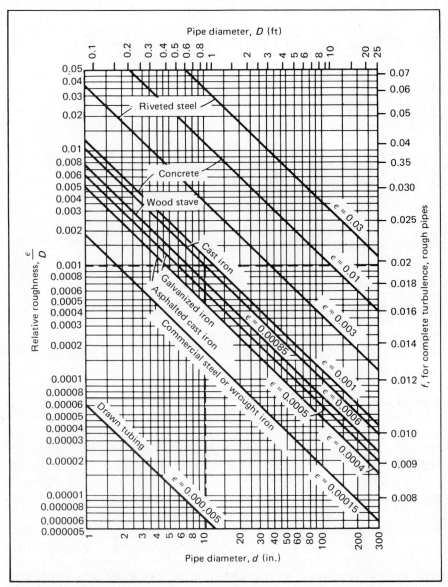

Figure 9-11 Relative roughness of pipe materials for complete turbulence. (Courtesy of Crane Co., Chicago.)

Example 9-4

Given flow in a 21-in concrete pipe 50 ft long with an average flow velocity of 9.5 ft/s, determine the head loss using the Manning equation, the Hazen-Williams equation, and the Darcy-Weisbach equation. Assume $n = 0.013$.

SOLUTION
1. The hydraulic radius is determined to be

$$D = \frac{21}{12} = 1.75 \text{ ft}$$

$$r = \frac{1.75}{2} = 0.875 \text{ ft}$$

$$R = \frac{\pi r^2}{2\pi r} = \frac{r}{2} = 0.4375 \text{ ft}$$

2. From Equation 9-10, solution by the Manning formula is:

$$S = n^2 V^2 / [(2.22)\ (R^{4/3})]$$
$$= (0.013)^2 (9.5)^2 / [(2.22)\ (0.4375)^{4/3}] = 0.021$$
$$H_L = SL = 0.021(50) = 1.03 \text{ ft}$$

3. Solution by the Hazen-Williams formula is:

$$S = [(V/1.318CR^{0.63})]^{1.85}$$
From Table 9-2 choose $C = 130$.

$$S = [(9.5/(1.318)\ (130)\ (0.4375)^{0.63}]^{1.85} = 0.012$$
$$H_L = SL = 0.012(50) = 0.62 \text{ ft}$$

4. Solution by the Darcy-Weisbach formula is

$$H_L = \frac{(0.016)\ (50)\ (9.5)^2}{(1.75)\ (2)\ (32.2)} = 0.64 \text{ ft}$$

where a friction factor of 0.016 is chosen from Figure 9-11. ∎

Flow in Complex Pipe Systems

FLOW IN BRANCHING PIPES
When several water management facilities are connected by a system of pipes, it is important to determine the direction and magnitude of flow in each pipe. This distribution will depend on the total head loss in each pipe, the diameter and length of the pipelines, and the number of connected facilities. A simple illustration is the classic *three-reservoir problem*, shown in Figure 9-12. Three reservoirs A, B, and C are connected by a system of pipelines that intersect at a single junction J. Given the lengths and diameters of the pipes and the elevations of the three reservoirs, the problem is to determine the magnitude and direction of flow in each pipe.

It should be obvious that the flow will be out of reservoir A and into

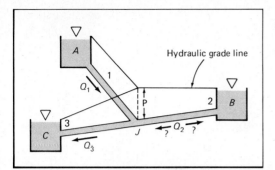

Figure 9-12   Branching pipe system with single junction.

reservoir C, but it is not immediately evident whether the flow will be into or out of reservoir B, because it is not known whether the pressure head at J is higher or lower than the water surface elevation at reservoir B. This problem can be solved by making use of the continuity equation and the energy equation, which indicate that the flow into J equals the flow out of J, and the pressure head for all three pipes is the same at the point of intersection. Thus, by continuity

$$Q_1 = Q_2 + Q_3 \qquad \text{if the flow is into reservoir } B \qquad (9\text{-}21a)$$

or

$$Q_1 + Q_2 = Q_3 \qquad \text{if the flow is out of reservoir } B \qquad (9\text{-}21b)$$

and, by energy equivalence

$$p_1/\gamma = p_2/\gamma = p_3/\gamma = P \qquad (9\text{-}22)$$

at J, where Q = flow in each pipe (vol/time)
p/γ = pressure head in each pipe (height in units of length)

The solution is derived by choosing a trial height for P and solving for Q_1, Q_2, and Q_3 using the Manning equation (Equation 9-10), the Hazen-Williams equation (Equation 9-18), or the Darcy-Weisbach equation (Equation 9-20). The trial-and-error process is repeated until the continuity equation is satisfied.

An alternate but more directly solved branching-pipe problem is to find the elevation of one reservoir given all pipe lengths and diameters, the surface elevations of the other two reservoirs, and the flow either to or from one reservoir. (See problems at the end of the chapter.)

FLOW IN PIPES IN SERIES
When a number of pipes of different diameters and lengths are connected in series, as depicted in Figure 9-13, the problem is either to determine the head loss given the flow, or to determine the flow given the head loss. The continuity equation allows us to state that the flow into and out of each

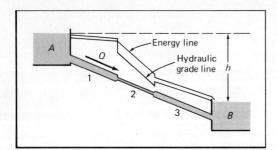

Figure 9-13   Flow in pipes in series.

section must be the same, and the energy equation allows us to state that the head loss for the system is the sum of the head losses for each section of pipe. In other words, for the example shown in Figure 9-13,

$$Q = Q_1 = Q_2 = Q_3 \qquad (9\text{-}23)$$

and

$$H_L = H_{L1} + H_{L2} + H_{L3} \qquad (9\text{-}24)$$

For cases where the total head loss is given and the problem is to find the flow, the total head loss is written in terms of the dimensions of the head loss of each section, which for Figure 9-13 would be

$$
\begin{aligned}
H_L = \ &[f_1(L_1/D_1)\,(V_1^2/2g) + \Sigma K(V_1^2/2g)] \\
&+ [f_2(L_2/D_2)\,(V_2^2/2g) + \Sigma K(V_2^2/2g)] \\
&+ [f_3(L_3/D_3)\,(V_3^2/2g) + \Sigma K(V_3^2/2g)]
\end{aligned}
\qquad (9\text{-}25)
$$

Minor losses are designated for each section as a function of velocity head, that is, $\Sigma K(V^2/2g)$. Since the flow is equivalent for each section, by continuity the velocity head for each section can be expressed as a function of the velocity head of any one section. For example, referring to Figure 9-13:

$$V_1^2/2g = V_2^2/2g(D_2/D_1)^4 \qquad (9\text{-}26)$$

and

$$V_1^2/2g = V_3^2/2g(D_3/D_1)^4 \qquad (9\text{-}27)$$

If a friction factor is assumed, the velocity of one section can be found and used in turn to calculate the flow, which would be the same for all sections.

Example 9-5

Find the discharge from reservoir A into reservoir B in Figure 9-13 if three cast iron pipes in series have diameters $D_1 = 15$ in, $D_2 = 10$ in, and $D_3 = 12$ in, and lengths $L_1 = 1500$ ft, $L_2 = 1350$ ft, and $L_3 = 2500$ ft, and the total head loss is 100 ft.

SOLUTION

1. Assuming $f = 0.01$ for all three pipes, and substituting the given values into the head loss equation given by Equation 9-25, the objective is to determine V_1, V_2, and V_3.

$$100 = 0.01 \, [1500/(15/12)] \, (V_1^2/2g)$$
$$+ \, 0.01 \, [1350/(10/12)](V_2^2/2g)$$
$$+ \, 0.01[2500/(12/12)](V_3^2/2g)$$

2. From Equations 9-26 and 9-27

$$V_1^2/2g \; = \; V_2^2/2g(10/15)^4 \; = \; 0.198(V_2^2/2g)$$
$$V_3^2/2g \; = \; V_2^2/2g(10/12)^4 \; = \; 0.482(V_2^2/2g)$$

3. Substituting back into the head loss equation:

$$100 = V_2^2/2g[12(0.198) + 16.2 + 25(0.482)]$$
$$V_2 = 14.5 \text{ ft/s}$$

4. Substituting V_2 back into the equations given in step 2,

$$V_1^2/2g = 0.198(14.5)^2/2g \qquad V_1 = 6.45 \text{ ft/s}$$
$$V_3^2/2g = 0.482(14.5)^2/2g \qquad V_3 = 10 \text{ ft/s}$$

5. Since $Q = Q_1 = Q_2 = Q_3$,

$$Q = Q_1 = V_1 A_1 = 6.45(\pi)(7.5/12)^2 = 7.9 \text{ ft/s}$$

As a check

$$Q = Q_2 = V_2 A_2 = 14.5(\pi)(5/12)^2 = 7.9 \text{ ft/s}$$
$$Q = Q_3 = V_3 A_3 = 10(\pi)(6/12)^2 = 7.9 \text{ ft/s} \quad \blacksquare$$

FLOW IN PARALLEL PIPES

In the case of pipes connected in parallel, the problem is again either to determine the head loss and distribution of flow for the system given the total flow, or to determine the total flow in the system given the head loss. For Figure 9-14, the continuity equation shows that the flow at the two junctions A and B is equivalent. In other words

$$Q_A = Q_1 + Q_2 + Q_3 = Q_B \tag{9-28}$$

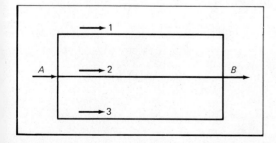

Figure 9-14   Flow in parallel pipes.

The head loss for the system can be shown by the energy equation to be equivalent to the head loss in each parallel pipe:

$$H_L = H_1 = H_2 = H_3 \qquad\qquad (9\text{-}29)$$

Given the total flow, the head loss distribution may be determined by solving the Darcy-Weisbach head loss equation (Equation 9-20) for V for each pipe,

$$V = [2gH_L/f(L/D)]^{1/2}$$

then substituting V into $Q = VA$, that is,

$$Q = A[2gH_L/f(L/D)]^{1/2} \qquad\qquad (9\text{-}30)$$

and writing Q as a function of the head loss and C where C is constant for a given pipe ($C = A[2g/f(L/D)]^{1/2}$):

$$Q = C(H_L)^{1/2} \qquad\qquad (9\text{-}31)$$

The flows for each pipe can then be summed and expressed as a function of the system head loss; for Figure 9-14, which has three pipes, this would be

$$Q = C_1(H_L)^{1/2} + C_2(H_L)^{1/2} + C_3(H_L)^{1/2}$$

From Equation 9-28 this becomes

$$Q = (H_L)^{1/2}(C_1 + C_2 + C_3)$$

An alternate method of analysis for simple systems of pipes in parallel or series is the *equivalent-pipe method.* In this method either a series of pipes or a system of parallel pipes is replaced with a pipe of equivalent head loss, for the purpose of simplifying calculations. This method can also be used to simplify portions of larger complex pipe systems.

FLOW IN PIPE NETWORKS

A pipe network is a system of parallel pipes that is interconnected by crossover pipes (pipes that operate in more than one circuit of flow), where flow may follow more than one path at a pipe junction, and where there are a number of withdrawal points throughout the system. Many municipal water distribution systems are complex pipe networks (see Section 11-2). A schematic of a simple pipe network is shown in Figure 9-15. Because pipe networks are more complex than the simple pipe systems just discussed, the methods of hydraulic analysis are accordingly somewhat more complicated. The most frequently used method of analysis is the Hardy-Cross method (8). Other methods include the circle method, the method of sections, and the linear theory method.

The Hardy-Cross method involves a series of successive approximations and corrections of pipe flow distribution until the system is hydrauli-

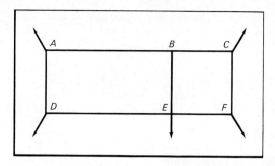

Figure 9-15 Example of a pipe network.

cally balanced (with an acceptable amount of error). The method is based on the following two principles:

1. The flow into a pipe junction equals the flow out of a junction (continuity is preserved)
2. The sum of the head losses (pressure drops) around a closed pipe circuit must equal zero

The Hardy-Cross method is used to determine the flow in pipe networks by the following steps:

1. At each junction, a first estimate of the division of flow must be made, so that each pipe section is assigned a quantity of flow such that the conditions of continuity are satisfied. This estimated assignment of flow allows us to state that for any section of pipe in the circuit

$$Q = Q_1 + \Delta Q \tag{9-32}$$

where Q is the actual flow, Q_1 is the assumed flow, and ΔQ is the flow correction. The objective is to determine ΔQ.

2. The head loss in each pipe section must next be determined. The Manning, Hazen-Williams, and Darcy-Weisbach equations used to determine head loss can be expressed in the general form

$$H_L = KQ^n \tag{9-33}$$

where H_L is the head loss, Q is the discharge, and K is a constant that accounts for the length, diameter, and roughness of the pipe and the units of measurement used. For the Hazen-Williams formula, for example, Equation 9-33 becomes

$$\text{(FPS units)} \quad H_L = KQ^{1.85} \tag{9-34}$$

which can then be directly used to determine head loss for each section of pipe. To satisfy the second principle on which this method is based, the sum of the head losses around the circuit should equal zero, that is,

$$\Sigma H_L = \Sigma KQ^n = 0 \tag{9-35}$$

where a sign convention of flow is assumed, for example, considering clockwise flows positive and counterclockwise flows negative. Note that satisfaction of Equation 9-35 depends on Q being accurate, which in turn depends on the determination of ΔQ.

4. ΔQ is derived in the following manner. First, substituting Equation 9-32 into Equation 9-33, for each pipe the head loss can be expressed as the binomial

$$H_L = KQ^n = K(Q_1 + \Delta Q)^n$$

which can be expanded to

$$H_L = K(Q_1{}^n + \Sigma n Q_1{}^{n-1}\Delta Q + \cdots)$$

If ΔQ is small, the terms in the expansion involving ΔQ to powers greater than 1 can be neglected. Because in a circuit ΔQ is the same for all pipes, the sum of the head losses for the circuit can be written as

$$\Sigma H_L = \Sigma KQ^n = \Sigma KQ_1{}^n + \Delta Q \Sigma K n Q_1{}^{n-1} = 0$$

Solving for ΔQ, this becomes

$$\Delta Q = -\Sigma KQ_1^n / \Sigma |KnQ_1{}^{n-1}|$$

and knowing from Equation 9-33 that $H_L/Q = KQ^{n-1}$:

$$\Delta Q = -\Sigma H_L / n \Sigma |H_L/Q_1| \tag{9-36}$$

keeping in mind that the numerator is an algebraic sum of the head losses following a sign convention indicating direction of flow, whereas the denominator is an arithmetic sum. If clockwise flows are indicated by a positive sign and counterclockwise flows by a negative sign, an excess of head in the clockwise direction is corrected by subtracting the ΔQ from the clockwise Q_1's and adding ΔQ to the counterclockwise Q_1's. If there is a deficiency of head in the clockwise direction, the opposite operations are performed.

5. Steps 1 through 4 are repeated until the head losses are balanced. The number of times that the process will have to be repeated depends on how good the initial estimates of flows were.

The iterative nature of the Hardy-Cross method makes the procedure well suited to solution by the use of a digital computer. An example of a computer solution to a pipe flow problem (written in Fortran IV) is given in reference 9.

As stated previously, although the Hardy-Cross method for network analysis is most commonly used, there are other suitable methods for analyzing pipe networks. Clark and Viessman discuss the method of sections in reference 6; Clark, Viessman, and Hammer present the linear theory method in reference 9, and Steel and McGhee summarize the circle method in reference 10.

Hydraulic Surge

Hydraulic surge or water hammer is generated when a valve in a pipeline flowing full is suddenly closed, creating a pressure increase that may be so intense as to cause rupture of the pipe. In cases where hydraulic surge cannot be avoided, such as in a hydroelectric plant where a sudden drop in load necessitates a rapid decrease in the flow of water to a turbine, relief measures must be provided for the pressure buildup, such as the use of a surge tank.

SURGE TANKS

One means to protect pipelines from hydraulic surge is to build surge tanks to relieve the excess pressure. These structures also serve to minimize the danger of negative pressure if a valve is suddenly opened. A simple surge tank may consist of a vertical standpipe open at the top and of sufficient height so that it will not overflow when the valve is closed. Figure 9-16 is a photograph of a simple surge tank constructed on the South Bay Aqueduct in California. Where very high heads are encountered, such a design may not be practical. In those cases some modification

Figure 9-16   Surge tanks at South Bay Pumping Plant. (Courtesy of the State of California Department of Water Resources.)

such as a restricted entrance or a closed top with an air cushion to absorb part of the pressure is often used.

9-3 PUMPING EQUIPMENT FOR WATER CONVEYANCE AND DISTRIBUTION SYSTEMS

Unless a source of water is at such an elevation that the water can flow to a desired location by gravity, some type of pump is needed to impart kinetic energy to the water so that it can overcome the hydraulic resistance of flow channels. This section discusses the types of pumps that are used in water conveyance systems, their power requirements, and some considerations in the design of pumping stations.

Types of Pumps and Source of Power

The two principal types of pumps used in water conveyance systems are termed *positive-displacement* and *centrifugal.* Other types of pumps that are sometimes used are air-lift pumps, jets, and hydraulic rams.

In positive-displacement pumps, a well-defined volume of water under pressure is displaced by a solid component moving through a close-fitting housing. The reciprocating type of positive-displacement pump operates by the action of a piston drawing water into a closed chamber on the intake stroke and then expelling it under pressure on the discharge stroke. The rotary type incorporates two rotating components moving in opposite directions, which trap water between them and the housing and sweep it from inlet to outlet chamber; as contrasted to the reciprocating type, the flow is steady rather than pulsating, and valves are not required.

Centrifugal pumps draw water in axially, impart centrifugal force by the action of rotating radial blades, and discharge under pressure at the periphery of the housings. The discharge is relatively free of pulsations, and the performance is efficient over a wide range of capacities and pressures at constant-speed operation.

Electric motors are usually employed to drive water pumps. Other types of drives that may be used include diesel engines, gasoline engines, direct-acting (reciprocating) steam engines, and steam turbines. It may be desirable to have one of these alternatively powered machines available at a pumping station in the event of electric power failure.

Considerations for the Design of Pumping Stations

In order to determine the appropriate size and type of equipment needed for a pumping station, certain characteristics of the water conveyance system must be determined. In addition, for a planner or engineer to be able to make a logical choice of pumping equipment, the characteristics of various pumping units available must be adequately described by the manufacturer.

SYSTEM REQUIREMENTS

It is important to characterize the water transportation or distribution system in terms of the total head against which the pump(s) must operate, the relation between total head and discharge, and the theoretical power requirements of the system.

The total head against which the pumps must operate is called the total dynamic head (TDH). It depends on the elevation of the surface of the source of water, the elevation of the water surface at the discharge point, and the elevation of the pump. The TDH is defined as

$$TDH = H_L + H_F + H_V \qquad (9\text{-}37)$$

where H_L = total static head or elevation difference between the pumping source and the point of delivery (see Figure 9-17)

H_F = the total friction head loss

H_V = the velocity head = $V^2/2g$

The relation between total dynamic head and discharge is defined by a curve designated the *system head*. Because the velocity head and the friction head, both components of the TDH, change with increasing discharge, the relation between TDH and discharge is not linear. In addition, if the static head level fluctuates, the system head curve will be displaced

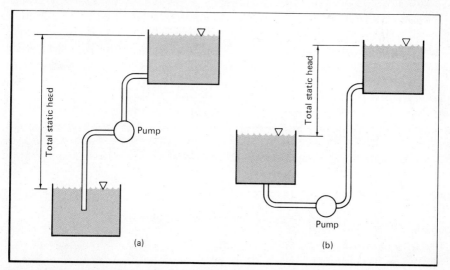

Figure 9-17 Total static head: (a) intake below pump centerline; (b) intake above pump centerline.

by a constant increment of TDH. An example of a set of system head curves for a fluctuating static head is illustrated in Figure 9-18.

The total dynamic head is also used in calculating the theoretical horsepower requirement for a particular system, for a known discharge, by

$$\text{hp} = Q\gamma H/550 \tag{9-38}$$

where
Q = discharge (ft^3/s)
γ = specific weight of water
H = total dynamic head
550 = conversion from foot-pounds per second to horsepower

The actual horsepower requirement is determined by dividing the theoretical horsepower requirement by the efficiency of the pump and driving unit. The latter two characteristics are provided by the equipment manufacturer.

PUMP CHARACTERISTICS

Whereas the water system characteristics must be determined by the engineer, the pump characteristics are provided by the manufacturer. These characteristics include the total head capacity, the efficiency, and the horsepower requirements for a range of discharge, and they are often illustrated by a set of *pump characteristic curves* as shown in Figure 9-19.

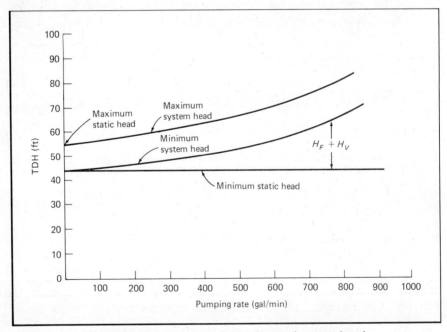

Figure 9-18   System-head curves for a fluctuating static pump head.

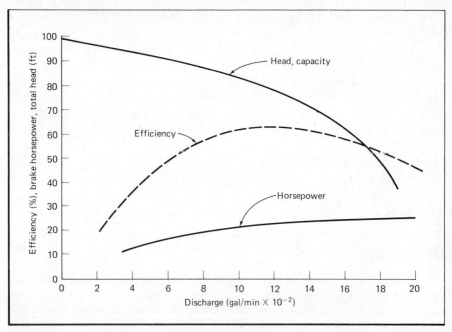

Figure 9-19 Typical pump characteristic curves.

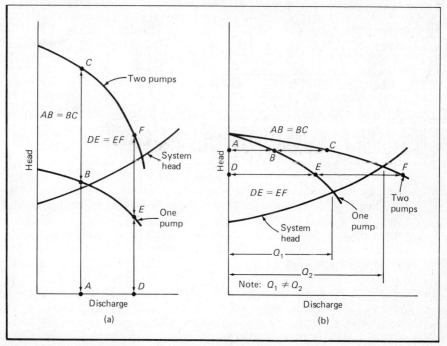

Figure 9-20 Characteristic curves for series and parallel pump operations of equal pumps: (a) series; (b) parallel.

The discharge at maximum efficiency is called the *normal* or *rated discharge* of the pump.

Pumps may be operated in series or in parallel. Series and parallel operation for two pumps is illustrated in Figure 9-20. Note that for pumps connected in series, the total head of the pumping system for a given discharge is the sum of the heads of the two pumps. For pumps connected in parallel, the total discharge of the pumping system for a given head is the sum of the discharges for the two pumps.

SELECTION OF PUMPING UNITS

When the system-head curve is plotted on the same sheet as the pump characteristic curves, the point(s) of intersection define the head and discharge at which the pump will operate to deliver the required flow.

PROBLEMS

9-1. Determine the Reynolds number for flow in a rectangular channel having a cross-sectional area of 160 ft^2, a depth of 8 ft, and flow with an average velocity of 4 ft/s. Is the flow regime supercritical or subcritical? Explain.

9-2. Given the following data on depth and velocity of flow for a cross section of a stream, determine the specific energy at each depth and plot a specific energy diagram for the data. At what depth does critical depth occur? If depth of flow were to suddenly change from 4 ft to 8 ft because of a downstream obstruction, what would be the result? Explain in terms of specific energy.

DEPTH (FT)	VELOCITY (FT/S)	DEPTH (FT)	VELOCITY (FT/S)
0.5	38.0	9.0	8.4
1.0	35.0	12.5	6.7
2.0	29.5	15.0	5.7
4.0	20.4		
6.0	13.9		

9-3. Given a V-shaped channel with a bottom slope of 0.001, a top width of 10 ft, and a depth of 5 ft, determine the velocity of flow. What is the discharge in ft^3/s?

9-4. A trapezoidal-shaped channel measures 3 m across the top and 1 m across the bottom. The depth of flow is 1.5 m. For $S = 0.005$ and $n = 0.012$, determine the velocity and discharge.

9-5. Given an 18 in concrete conduit with a roughness coefficient of $n = 0.013$, $S = 0.02$, and a discharge capacity of 15 ft^3/s. What diameter pipe would be required to quadruple the capacity?

9-6. Determine the dimensions of a rectangular concrete channel that is to carry a flow of 150 m^3/s, with a bottom slope of 0.015 and a mean velocity of 10.2 m/s.

9-7. A 21-in pipe flowing full has a discharge of 19 ft^3/s and a velocity of 6 ft/s. Determine (a) the velocity and depth of flow when $Q = 15$ ft^3/s and (b) the depth at which maximum discharge occurs.

9-8. Discharge in a 45-ft-wide rectangular canal of smooth rock cuts is 850 ft^3/s. Assuming $S = 0.005$ and conditions of uniform flow, determine (a) the normal depth and critical depth of flow and (b) whether the flow is supercritical or subcritical.

9-9. If flow in a rectangular concrete channel 15 ft wide is 750 ft^3/s and the slope of the channel bottom abruptly changes from 0.020 to 0.0015, (a) determine whether a hydraulic jump will occur and, (b) if so, the location of the jump and the depths of flows before and after the jump.

9-10. Determine the head loss in a 46-cm concrete pipe with an average velocity of flow $= 3.2$ m/s and $L = 30$ m.

9-11. Determine the discharge from a full-flowing cast iron pipe 24 in in diameter having a slope of 0.004.

9-12. Referring to Figure 9-12, assume reservoirs A, B, and C have water surface elevations of 150 ft, 90 ft, and 40 ft respectively and are connected by a system of concrete pipes. The pipe lengths are $L_1 = 2400$ ft, $L_2 = 1500$ ft, and $L_3 = 5500$ ft, and the pipe diameters are $D_1 = 8$ in, $D_2 = 12$ in, and $D_3 = 21$ in. Determine Q_1, Q_2, and Q_3 and the elevation of the hydraulic grade line at P.

9-13. Three reservoirs A, B, and C are connected by a branching cast iron pipe system. If the pipe lengths are $L_1 = 3000$ ft, $L_2 = 2200$ ft, and $L_3 = 1600$ ft; the pipe diameters are $D_1 = 15$ in, $D_2 = 10$ in, and $D_3 = 18$ in, respectively; and the surface elevations of two of the three reservoirs are $A = 125$ ft and $B = 55$ ft, find the elevation of the third reservoir C. Assume that the flow to reservoir C is 15 ft^3/s.

9-14. Solve Problem 9-13 assuming that the flow in pipe 3 is *from* reservoir C rather than *to* reservoir C.

9-15. Three riveted steel pipes are connected in series, with the flow through the system being 10 m^3/s. Determine the total head loss if the pipe diameters and lengths are $D_1 = 60$ cm, $D_2 = 40$ cm, $D_3 = 54$ cm; $L_1 = 400$ m, $L_2 = 450$ m, $L_3 = 750$ m.

9-16. Given the same lengths and diameters of pipes in series as in Problem 9-15, determine the total flow if the system head loss is 50 m and $C = 100$.

9-17. Consider the pipe system shown in the figure below. If the flow in BCD is 6 ft^3/s, find (a) the flow in BED, (b) the total flow, and (c) a length of 16-in pipe equivalent to the two parallel pipes.

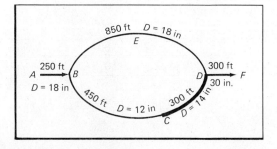

9-18. If a flow of 15 m^3/s is divided into three parallel pipes of diameters 30 cm, 20 cm, and 45 cm and lengths 30 m, 40 m, and 25 m respectively, determine the head loss and distribution of flow. Assume $f = 0.015$.

9-19. If a system of parallel pipes has diameters of 18 in, 8 in, and 21 in and lengths of 50 ft, 95 ft, and 60 ft respectively, determine the total flow in the system. Assume $f = 0.024$ and total head loss is 100 ft.

9-20. From the layout shown, determine the length of an equivalent 8-cm pipe.

600 m	1200 m	550 m
10 cm	5 cm	6 cm
A	B	C	D

9-21. Given the pipe layout shown, determine the diameter of an equivalent 1000-m pipe.

9-22. Given the pipe network shown below, determine the direction and magnitude of flow in each pipe by the Hardy-Cross method. Assume $C = 100$.

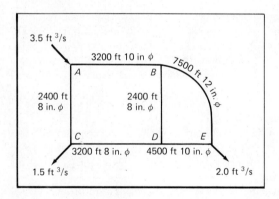

9-23. Determine the total dynamic head of a pumping system where the total static head is 50 ft, the total friction head loss is 5 ft, and the velocity head is 10 ft.

9-24. Calculate the horsepower requirements for the system described in Problem 9-23 if the flow is 25 ft^3/s.

9-25. Plot the system head from the following data:

Total dynamic head (ft)	55	60	65	70	75	80	85	90
Flow (gal/min)		200	500	700	850	975	1075	1200	1300

Plot the following pump characteristic data on the same curve. At what point should the pump operate?

EFFICIENCY (%)	HORSEPOWER (HP)	TOTAL HEAD (FT)	FLOW (GAL/MIN)
22	8	95	225
37	12	93	400
49	17	90	600
57	20	87	800
63	22	84	1000
64	23	78	1200
62	24	72	1400
59	25	64	1600
54	26	49	1800

References

1. R. L. Daugherty and J. B. Franzini, *Fluid Mechanics with Engineering Applications*, 7th ed., McGraw-Hill, New York, 1977.
2. "Design and Construction of Sanitary and Storm Sewers," *ASCE Manual of Practice 37*, rev. ed., 1976.
3. F. M. Henderson, *Open Channel Flow*, Macmillan, New York, 1966.
4. R. L. Linsley and J. B. Franzini, *Water Resources Engineering*, 3d ed., McGraw-Hill, New York, 1979.
5. H. Rouse (ed.), *Engineering Hydraulics*, Wiley, New York, 1950.
6. J. W. Clark and W. Viessman, Jr., *Water Supply and Pollution Control*, International Textbook Co., Scranton, PA, 1965.
7. G. M. Fair and J. C. Geyer, *Water Supply and Wastewater Disposal*, Wiley, New York, 1954.
8. H. Cross, "Analysis of Flow in Networks of Conduits or Conductors," *Univ. Ill. Engr. Experimental Station Bulletin*, no. 286, 1936.
9. J. W. Clark, W. Viessman, Jr., and M. J. Hammer, *Water Supply and Pollution Control*, 3d ed., Harper & Row, New York, 1977.
10. E. W. Steel and T. J. McGhee, *Water Supply and Sewerage*, 5th ed., McGraw-Hill, New York, 1979.

Chapter 10
Analyzing Water Resources Systems

In previous chapters various components of water resources systems have been discussed. These have been treated mainly in the context of their individual use and associated design and operational aspects. In this chapter, attention is turned toward the totality of water resources systems. The concern is with how all the many components interact, and with how they can be combined into efficient systems for meeting prescribed objectives. The approach is that of systems analysis. It relies extensively on two broad classifications of quantitative models: simulation and optimization.

10-1 CHARACTERISTICS OF WATER RESOURCES SYSTEMS

Simply put, a system is nothing more than a collection of components. In terms of water resources, systems of concern may range from individual water treatment processes to combinations of reservoirs, treatment works, distribution networks, and other elements occupying an entire river basin. The ease with which these widely varying systems may be analyzed is closely tied to the scale of the system and the nature of the findings required. Generally, it is necessary for the system to be described in mathematical terms.

Perhaps the most distinguishing feature of a systems analysis is its focus on the joint function of elements (components) of the system under various conditions that the system may be subjected to. These circumstances may be associated with wet or dry periods and they may be representative of short or long periods of time. In addition, the institutional aspects of the systems being dealt with must be considered. For example, laws and/or regulations may act as either constraints on, or facilitators of, technical approaches to solving problems of water allocation. Such factors must be dealt with directly by the analyst; otherwise, his or her proposed solutions may be grossly misrepresentative of the attainable.

According to Loucks et al., a systems approach is most fitting when objectives are reasonably well defined, there is good potential for implementing analytical findings, many alternatives for meeting the objectives are possible and the best of these is not apparent, mathematical representations of system elements can be constructed, and data are available to estimate the parameters of the models employed (1). In reality, all of these specifications may not be met, but even then, the use of systems techniques can often provide useful insights into system performance and aid in identifying those elements of data essential to reliable operation and interpretation of system models.

10-2 MODELING WATER RESOURCES SYSTEMS: AN OVERVIEW

Water resources systems are generally analyzed by using mathematical models. These models may be empirical, statistical, or founded on known physical laws. They may be used for such simple purposes as determining the depth of flow in a pipe for a specified discharge, or they may be used to guide decisions about the least costly way to develop a river basin for some overall basin objective. The choice of the model should be tailored to the purpose for which it is to be used. In general, the simplest model capable of producing results of desired reliability should be selected. Large computer models can be very expensive to operate. And while one of these may be counted on to do a given job, if the results sought can be obtained more inexpensively from another less sophisticated model, then it should be used.

Unfortunately, most water resources systems of practical concern are complex, involving both physical and human dimensions, and they cannot be described exactly by mathematical means. Furthermore, reliable historical data on a system to be modeled are often lacking. When one adds to this situation the fact that hydrologic systems are probabilistic in nature, it is clear that the modeler's task is not an easy one. In fact, it is often the case that the best that can be hoped for from a model is an enhanced general understanding of the system of interest. Even this may have great value, however, since it can lead to the establishment of needed data collection programs and ultimately to the ability to represent the system being studied well enough in quantitative terms to provide model solutions of practical value.

For the most part, mathematical models are designed to describe the way a system's elements interact to some type of stimulus. For example, a model of a groundwater system might be developed to show the effects on the water table of various schemes for pumping. The degree to which the model's components relate to actual system performance determines the fidelity of the model. Models that incorporate a high level of detail are sometimes more reliable than coarser ones, but coarse models are all that is needed for some purposes. Furthermore, crude models usually produce quick results, sometimes without the need for anything more than a desk calculator or paper and pencil. And the level of detail in a model does not always serve as an adequate measure of model performance. If field data to estimate the parameters of a sophisticated model are not available, or are of questionable worth, then the model's performance will be affected accordingly and the use of a crude estimating technique might produce results just as reliable. All of these factors must be kept in mind by both the designers and users of models.

Before a model is selected for a given job, its appropriateness should be thoroughly evaluated. In particular, its underlying assumptions must be understood. Where existing models can be used, they may prove to be the best option. Where they cannot, then suitable adjustments to them might be in order, or where even this would not work, a new model, tailored for the job, might have to be designed. In any event, the availability of a working model does not guarantee its worth unless it can be proved that it incorporates the controlling processes of the system to which it is to be applied. And the need to approximate real-world processes always raises questions about the validity of analyses based on these approximations.

As of today, many working models have been devised to address a wide spectrum of water resources problems. Some of these are transferrable from one locale to another; whereas, others are tied empirically to a given region or type of problem. Models can play a very useful role in planning and decision-making processes. They do not constitute a panacea, however, and their limitations must be recognized. The reader should keep in mind that models are only representations of real systems, to be used with that understanding and interpreted in that light.

Several of the current simulation and optimization models that have been proved in use will be discussed in this chapter. In the following section, some general comments about optimization and simulation are given in order to introduce the subject and to provide a background for the more technical treatment that follows.

Simulation

Simulation is the process whereby one attempts to represent the performance of some real-world system. The principal reason for doing this is to learn as much as possible about how the existing or proposed system will react to conditions that may be imposed on it or that might be expected to occur in the future. An example would be the determination of how

well a particular flood control configuration would perform when subjected to some design flood.

Simulation models may be physical (a scale model spillway operated
in a hydraulics laboratory), analog (a system of electrical components,
resistors and capacitors, arranged to act as analogs of pipe resistances and
storage elements), or mathematical (a compilation of equations that represent the actions of a system's elements). The vehicle used to operate
models of this type is normally the digital computer.

Simulation models may be used to evaluate single events (event simulation models) or they may be dynamic, designed to accommodate
changes with time and with time-varying interactions. Lumped parameter models ignore spatial variations in parameters; whereas, distributed
parameter models account for behavior variations at different points in a
system. Finally, stochastic models include elements of probability whereas
deterministic models do not. The type of model chosen depends on the
nature of the system being studied and the type of results desired from the
simulation.

Simulation models may be operated over short-term or long-term
time frames. Normally, short-term models can embody greater detail than
long-term models. This is because of limitations in computational ability,
even with today's large high-speed computers. The greater detail embodied in an event simulation model could balance the computational requirements of a coarser model operated for a much longer period of
projected time, for example.

If a simulation model can be developed and proved to represent a
prototype system, then it can provide, in seconds or less, answers about
how the real system might perform over years and under many conditions
of stress. Thus, costly proposed projects may be evaluated to judge
whether their performance would be adequate before investments are
made. In like manner, operating policies for facilities can be tested before
they are implemented in actual control situations. Where proposed designs and/or operating procedures do not meet the test, usually it is a
straightforward matter to revise the model to reflect changed policies
and/or structural configurations. Figure 10-1 depicts how a simulation
model might be used to estimate the behavior of a given variable under
continuation of current conditions and with the imposition of a new stimulus.

DEVELOPING A SIMULATION MODEL
The development of a simulation model begins with the identification of
a problem of concern. This might be the evaluation of flood control operating policies at a reservoir site to determine how they would affect downstream water depths; it could be the determination of how streamflows are
generated by a given sequence of storms, or it could be the evaluation of
downstream effects on water quality of some particular arrangement of

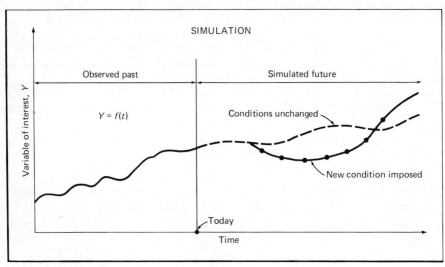

Figure 10-1 Hypothetical simulated traces.

wastewater treatment plants. Once the objective of the modeling procedure is prescribed, the next step is to conceptualize and develop an appropriate model. The model itself will be a set of equations describing the system to be simulated and an accompanying set of algorithms (procedures for effecting the solution of the equations).

In the model conceptualization stage it is necessary to conduct a detailed analysis of the system being modeled so that the appropriate governing equations can be developed and the data needs for determining parameter values and testing the model can be ascertained. No matter how well founded in theory the model may appear to be, unless data are available to set coefficients and evaluate the model's fidelity, little of practical value is likely to be achieved. In the conceptualization stage, additional data requirements often become apparent, and this sets in motion a feedback process in which improvements in model design and understanding continue to evolve. Once a determination is made that sufficient data are at hand and that the system's processes can be adequately represented, a computer program can be designed to permit the model's operation and interpretation.

Following problem identification and model formulation, the next procedures are model calibration and verification. The process of calibration requires observed data sets of both inputs to the model (rainfall, for example) and outputs from the model (streamflows, for example). During calibration, the objective is to adjust the model parameters and/or the model so that the computed output resembles the observed output as closely as desired. The evaluation of model parameters is very important to the production of a good working model. Usually this involves a subjec-tive trial-and-error procedure, although various analytical techniques are available to aid in this process (1). Model verification follows calibration and requires another independent set of input and output data. Care must be taken to ensure that these data are not the same as those used in calibrating the model; otherwise, there will be no true test of the model's validity. The model is considered to be verified when its output compares favorably with the observed data sets for some range of conditions other than those used in the calibration The degree of correspondence of mod-eled and observed outputs that constitutes verification is dependent on the objectives of the modeling process. In some cases models that indicate rough trends might be all that is required. In other cases, accurate portray-als of water levels might be the goal. Again, the model should suit the job. Oversophistication is as inefficient in some circumstances as oversimplifi-cation is in others. A good rule is to keep the model as simple as possible for the objective to be met.

After an acceptable model has been developed, it should be docu-mented so that its use can be facilitated. Basically, the documentation process is one of describing the data requirements for the model, indicat-ing how to set parameters, setting forth the model's underlying assump-tions, listing model limitations, and describing how to use the computer program and interpret its output.

Finally, the model is put to use in aiding design processes, guiding policy decisions, exploring impacts of various actions, or for other pur-poses. Several simulation models will be described later in this chapter, but the reader will benefit in understanding the modeling process by examining Figures 10-2 and 10-3. Figure 10-2 is a flow diagram for a groundwater management model developed by Huntoon and Viessman for use in Nebraska. The diagram indicates the nature of the system and the modeling process. Normally an early activity in the conceptualization process is the development of such a flowchart indicating the computa-tional sequences that must be incorporated in the computer program. The model depicted in the figure accepts historical data on precipitation and temperature and may use these data directly or use them to generate stochastic traces of precipitation to be used in computations. The objective of the model is to evaluate water level changes in an aquifer subjected to natural and artificial recharge and irrigation water withdrawals.

Figure 10-3 shows the model's output for a given location in the area studied. The curves shown on the figure illustrate predicted de-clines in water level to the year 2052 for several options related to regu-lation of the number of wells being pumped and/or supplementing natu-ral recharge by artificial means. In the latter case, the numerical values of groundwater level predicted for a given course of action were consid-ered to be representative only of what might happen. The model was

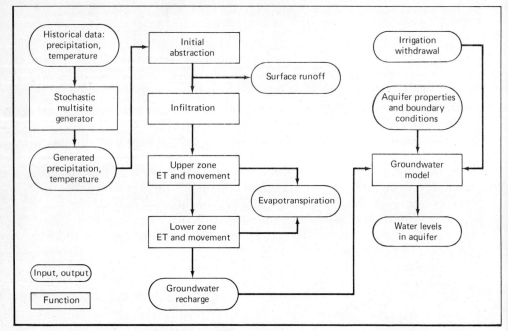

Figure 10-2   Flow diagram for the Big Blue River groundwater simulation model.

used to indicate trends in water level change associated with various management schemes. The information derived permitted evaluating the implications of instituting specific plans for aquifer recharge and/or well regulation.

PROS AND CONS OF SIMULATION MODELS

Simulation and other types of models can be valuable aids in decision making but their advantages and disadvantages must be weighed for the circumstances of concern. Some advantages of the use of simulation models include: they impose a logic and structure to analyses, they provide insights into systems behavior, their structure is ideally suited to experimental work, they may be designed to accommodate many options, projections into the future are facilitated with their use, and they can aid in communications between analysts and policymakers. On the negative side, simulation models sometimes have drawbacks such as oversimplifying real systems, data requirements that cannot be met, difficulty in handling of intangibles, high costs of development and/or use, problems of interpreting output, and problems of user acceptance. Furthermore, the use of models is sometimes inhibited because potential users fail to see their relevance, there are doubts about a model's validity, documentation may be poor, prospective users may lack understanding of a model or lack

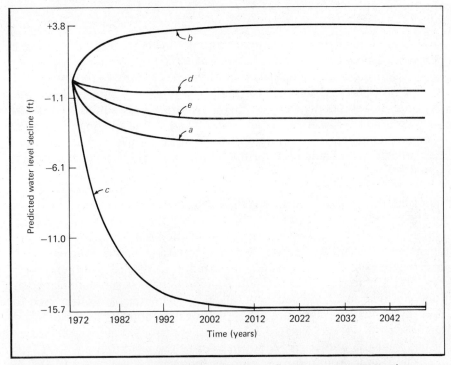

Figure 10-3 Groundwater declines resulting from five management practices as simulated for York County, Nebraska: (a) 1972 development; (b) half of 1972 development; (c) double 1972 development to six wells per section; (d) 1972 development plus double natural recharge; (e) 1972 development plus one recharge well per township.

the resources to be able to use it, and there is often a mistrust of mathematical representations.

Finally, those seeking models for use or exploring the worth of models for some application might ask the following questions as they make their judgments. Why was the model developed and does it meet its objectives? Is the model too detailed for its purpose? Are all significant variables and/or processes represented? Are the functional relations soundly based? What are the model's underlying assumptions and are they reasonable? Was the verification and calibration of the model adequate? Is the model easy to use and understand? Is the output subject to ready interpretation and application? There are many models that have been developed for a variety of circumstances. Some of these are good and others are of questionable worth. The prospective user must make the effort to ensure that if he or she chooses a model, its operation will produce reliable and not misleading results. A sophisticated computer output is no assurance that the results will come close to representing the system for which the model was designed.

Optimization

Optimization models are used to determine the "best" way to meet some objective. They might be used, for example, to select a group of treatment processes, from many candidates, to produce a required effluent quality at least cost. The final design of the system might be determined, however, by the use of simulation models that are more ideally suited to detailed analyses of specific alternatives and/or policies. In practice, many complex systems are analyzed by the coordinated use of simulation and optimization models, each being used for that part of the study for which it is best suited.

Optimization models are concerned with making choices where many alternative means may be employed to meet a particular objective. In theory, they can choose the "best" among hundreds of options. This capability could be achieved through simulation only by modeling every possible option and comparing them, an impossible undertaking except in trivial cases. On the other hand, optimization models cannot be used for the kind of fine tuning and design development that simulation models can be called on to do. Thus, optimization techniques are often used to determine the general nature of a system configuration while the detailed analysis of the system is carried out by simulation methods. Some examples of this joint use of models are given later in the chapter.

The use of an optimization model requires the definition of an objective that can be quantified. Often the objective is specified in economic terms, common ones being the maximization of benefits or profits, or the minimization of costs. Other objectives might be the minimization of a pollutant level or the maximization of water availability for fisheries preservation. An added feature of optimization models is their inclusion of constraints. In the classical sense, optimization is the mathematical notion of the calculus in which some function is minimized or maximized. The difference here is that the mathematical statement representing the optimization model may only have validity over some range of values. For example, quantities of water pumped can be zero or positive but cannot take on negative values. The constraints are introduced to ensure that the optimal solution obtained is actually feasible. The variables in the optimization model are called decision variables, as their values are "decided on" in meeting the stated objective in an "optimal" sense.

A pictorial representation of an optimization model is given in Figure 10-4. In this case, the objective is to design a treatment process so that the imposed effluent criteria are met at least cost. Given are the influent characteristics and the effluent characteristics to be met. The decision variables are the tank dimensions, the sludge storage volume, the hydraulic loading rates, and the amount of chemicals to be added. The solution will indicate those values of the decision variables that provide the least-

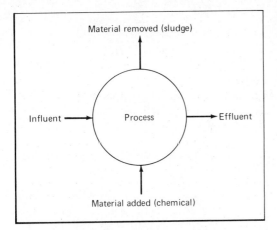

Figure 10-4 A simple process system. Decision variables: (1) tank dimensions; (2) sludge storage volume; (3) hydraulic loading rate; (4) required chemical supply.

cost configuration of the process within the bounds of the applicable constraints on the system.

Optimization problems are also classified as mathematical programming problems, which does not convey the same meaning as computer programming. A mathematical programming problem is one in which it is desired to determine the quantities assigned to variables of the problem in such a way that they satisfy the constraints imposed and optimize (maximize or minimize) some objective. There are a number of mathematical programming techniques that have been developed. Included among these are linear programming, dynamic programming, quadratic programming, and the use of Lagrangian undetermined multipliers. Some of these will be covered in more detail later. Many good textbooks are available on this subject, and the interested reader is encouraged to consult them (1–10).

Just as in the case of simulation, the validity of optimization models depends heavily on the reliability of the data used in their development and the adequacy of the model's formulation. In some cases, true optimal solutions can be obtained, but in others, the nature of the problem or the selected solution technique may lead only to a "local" rather than a "global" optimum. A mathematical function may have several peaks and valleys. If the greatest of the maxima is found, then the solution will be global. If a lesser peak is selected, the solution will be local. In any event, the use of mathematical programming techniques can shed much light on a system's performance. By conducting appropriate sensitivity analyses, a great deal can be learned about the importance of parameters and the influences of constraints. Such analyses can lead to policy modifications and can discourage unneeded refinements in data when such efforts would have little influence on the solution obtained.

A systems analysis approach can be very helpful to decision makers. The solutions sought may be design oriented, operations oriented, policy oriented, or some combination thereof. The systems analyst must recognize the circumstances of data availability and level of knowledge existing about the system with which he or she is concerned. Then, understanding these limitations, he or she can determine the feasibility of applying a model to meet the objectives. Where the situation precludes the reliable use of available models, a crude analytical effort might still provide insights about data needs and/or aid in devising models that will produce useful preliminary findings.

10-3 PROBABILITY CONCEPTS

A complicating factor in the analysis of water resources systems is the random nature of many of the variables that must be dealt with. This probabilistic dimension requires that most analyses be designed to deal with risk in one way or another. Some understanding of probability theory and statistical methods is thus necessary if one is to interpret the real significance of forecasted events. While it is impossible to treat this subject in any great depth here, it is important to present some concepts to permit better understanding of the models discussed later. A brief introduction to this topic has already been given in Chapter 7.

Probability theory deals with random variables. These are variables whose values depend on the outcome of some chance event. Random variables may be discrete, such as the positive integers, or continuous, wherein the variables take on all values within the range of their existence. In the case of a discrete variable we shall be dealing with the probability of a particular value. For a continuous random variable we shall be concerned with the probability of the variable falling within a given interval. The meaning of this will be made clear shortly. In some cases, continuous variables can be treated as discrete in order to facilitate analyses.

In analyzing or designing water resources systems it must be recognized that the availability of water at any given time is subject to the vagaries of streamflow created by prevailing weather conditions. Of particular concern are the extreme events, maximum and minimum flows, for example. Planners and engineers attempt to alleviate the influences of these events through regulation. The degree to which this can be accomplished depends mainly on the magnitude of the event, and thus it is important to know the frequency with which such an event might be expected to occur. Analyses of this type can be facilitated by probability methods.

Frequently Used Statistical Measures

Analysts desiring to model water resources systems are generally faced with having to obtain adequate and reliable data so that they can estimate model parameters, validate models, and/or estimate the probability of occurrences. In particular, it is common to be concerned about the frequency of low flows and floods of various severities. The numerical data of interest may be precipitation, streamflows, temperature, dissolved oxygen levels, water use, and so on. Useful information can be obtained by analyzing historical data to determine the range of observations, the manner in which these observations are clustered, and the average values of the data. Statisticians usually refer to these indicators as measures of central tendency and dispersion. Another measure, skewness, is also of interest and will be defined later.

MEASURES OF CENTRAL TENDENCY
The measures of central tendency that are used in analyzing data are the mean, median, and mode. For a given set of observations, these measures indicate that particular observation about which most of the data apper to cluster. The most stable of these measures, and hence the most frequently used, is the mean, which is defined by:

$$\bar{x} = \frac{1}{n} \sum_{i=1}^{n} x_i \tag{10-1}$$

where $\bar{x}$ is the sample mean, n is the number of observations, and the x_i are individual observations.

MEASURES OF DISPERSION
While knowledge of the mean value of a data set can be very useful, it tells nothing about the spread of the data. In most instances it is also important to know how much variation there is in values in the data set. Measures of dispersion that are used to do this include the range, standard deviation, and coefficient of variation.

The range is simply the interval between the smallest and the largest values in the data set. It indicates the scale of the variation in data but not the way the data are dispersed.

The standard deviation is the most useful statistical measures of dispersion. For sample data, it is calculated using the following equation:

$$s = \left[\frac{1}{n-1} \sum_{i=1}^{n} (x_i - \bar{x})^2 \right]^{1/2} \tag{10-2}$$

The coefficient of variation indicates how tightly the observations are grouped about the mean. It is given by:

$$C_v = s/\bar{x} \tag{10-3}$$

The smaller the ratio, the closer the grouping about the mean.

SKEWNESS

If sample data on some variable such as rainfall were grouped into intervals such as 30 to 35 inches, and if these grouped data were plotted v. the number of observations within an interval, a frequency plot would be the result. The ordinate of the graph would be the frequency and the abscissa would be rainfall in inches. Such a plot would graphically display the range in observations, give an indication of the central value, and also suggest whether or not the data were distributed symmetrically about the central value or whether they were skewed to the right or left. Hydrologic data generally tend to have a right (or positive) skew since they are constrained at zero on the left but are not constrained on the right. The degree to which the data are skewed is important in determining analytical methods to be used in their analyses. More will be said about this later, but the term used to evaluate skewness will be given here. It is known as the coefficient of skewness, and it may be calculated using the following expression:

$$C_s = \left[\frac{n}{(n-1)(n-2)} \sum_{i=1}^{n} (x_i - \bar{x})^3 \right] / s^3 \tag{10-4}$$

The reliability of estimates of skewness from less than 50 sample data points is subject to question. In such cases special procedures can be used, but they will not be described here (11).

Probability Distributions

Random variables are characterized by the distribution of probabilities associated with the values that the variables may take on. In the discussions that follow, random variables will be designated by capital letters whereas particular values they may assume will be designated by lower-case letters. Thus the probability that a random variable X takes on a particular value x_1 may be written as $P(X = x_1)$ or $P(x_1)$.

The cumulative distribution function, CDF, is convenient for describing probabilities. The CDF is the probability of any particular random event being less than or equal to a given limiting value. The CDF is denoted as $F(x)$ and it is equal to $P(X \leq x)$. This function, shown in Figure 10-5, increases monotonically from a lower limit of zero to an upper limit of 1. Another function of interest in dealing with probabilities is the probability density function, PDF. This function, $f(x)$, is the probability density at any point. It is depicted above the CDF in Figure 10-5. Note that the PDF is actually the derivative of $F(x)$ with respect to x.

For continuous variables, $f(x) \geq 0$, because negative probabilities are ruled out. It should be clear from the foregoing definitions that probability ranges from zero to 1, and thus,

$$\int_{-\infty}^{\infty} f(x)\, dx = 1 \tag{10-5}$$

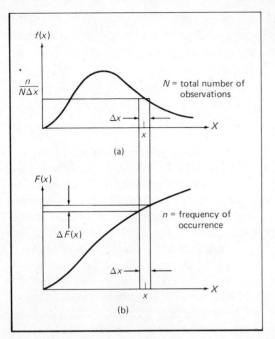

Figure 10-5 Continuous probability distributions: (a) probability density function; (b) cumulative distribution function.

The probability of a particular value of x falling between the limits a and b is given as:

$$P(a \leq X \leq b) = \int_a^b f(x) \, dx \tag{10-6}$$

But note that the probability that x takes on any specific value is zero. That is, probabilities are defined by the PDF only as areas under the curve between two limiting values. Finally, the CDF can be defined in terms of the PDF as follows:

$$F(x) - \int_{-\infty}^x f(x) \, dx \tag{10-7}$$

In the case of discrete distributions, there are mathematical expressions equivalent to those for the continuous variables that have been defined by equations 10-5, 10-6, and 10-7. These related forms are:

$$\sum_i f(x_i) = 1 \tag{10-8}$$

$$P(a \leq X \leq b) = \sum_{x_i \geq a}^{x_i \leq b} f(x_i) \tag{10-9}$$

$$P(X \leq x_k) = \sum_{i=1}^k f(x_i) \tag{10-10}$$

For a sample having a specified number of observations N, $f(x_i)$ is the probability for each outcome in the sample. This gives the probability of each observation as $1/N$ and thus $f(x_i)$ in Equations 10-8 to 10-10 can be replaced by $P(x_i) = 1/N$, providing the x_i are uniformly distributed over the range zero to N.

Continuous Frequency Distributions

A number of statistical distributions are used to represent historical sequences of hydrologic and other data of concern to water resources planners and managers. The premise is that the data are defined by continuous random processes and therefore can be represented by distributions. If a particular distribution can be determined to represent the variable of interest, then by estimating the distribution's parameters, one can make inferences about the recurrence of various events considered important by the analyst. The most commonly used distributions are the normal, log normal, log Pearson type III, Pearson type III, Gamma, and Gumbel's extremal distribution (discussed in Chapter 7). The normal and Pearson type distributions will be discussed here. For further information on other distributions the reader should consult references 1 and 2.

NORMAL DISTRIBUTION

The normal distribution is perhaps the best known and most widely used distribution since it describes many processes that are subject to random and independent variations. The normal distribution is symmetrical and bell shaped. Although it does not always fit sequences of hydrologic data very well, it finds widespread use in dealing with transformed data that do fit the distribution. For example, the logarithms of hydrologic variables often fit the normal distribution quite well, and the log-normal distribution is extensively used in analyzing such data.

The normal distribution is defined by two parameters, the mean and the standard deviation. Once estimates of these parameters are made, the entire shape of the distribution can be determined. The PDF for the normal distribution is given by:

$$f(x) = \frac{1}{s\sqrt{2\pi}} e^{-\frac{1}{2}[(x-\bar{x})/s]^2} \tag{10-11}$$

where the distribution's parameters are estimated using sample data. In this case s is the estimated value of the standard deviation, $\bar{x}$ is the mean obtained from the data, x is the value of an individual observation, and e is the base of naperian logarithms. The normal distribution can be easily transformed into a single parameter function by substituting $z = (x - \bar{x})/s$ and noting that $dx = s\,dz$. Then Equation 10-11 becomes:

$$f(z) = \frac{1}{\sqrt{2\pi}} e^{-z^2/2} \qquad (10\text{-}12)$$

The variable z is called the standard unit; it is normally distributed with zero mean and unit standard deviation. Tables of areas of the normal curve have been compiled for use with this standardization. An abbreviated table (Table 10-1) is given here, and its use will be demonstrated in Example 10-1.

The normal distribution ranges from $-\infty$ to $+\infty$ and the total area under the curve is equal to 1. Put another way, the probability of an observation being less than or equal to $+\infty$ is 1. The area under the curve for any value of x can be determined by using the probability integral,

$$A = \int_{-\infty}^{x} f(x)\,dx \qquad (10\text{-}13)$$

The meaning of this is of great practical value and is demonstrated in Example 10-1. Solution of the integral is facilitated by the use of tables such as Table 10-1. Note, for example, that the value of 0.341 shown in the second row and first column of the table indicates that at a deviation from the mean equal to one standard deviation, the area contained under the normal curve to that deviation is 34.1 percent.

LOG-NORMAL DISTRIBUTION

The distribution of many hydrologic variables is skewed to the right (positively skewed) due to the lower physical limit of zero and the theoretically unconstrained upper limit. In such cases the normal distribution may not be appropriate as a representation of the manner in which the data are actually distributed. This is especially true where the sample data are markedly skewed. Fortunately, these hydrologic data are often found to have the property that their logarithms follow the normal distribution. The PDF for this log-normal distribution is easily obtained by substituting the logarithm (ln) of x for the value of x in Equation 10-11. Both the normal and the log-normal distributions are two parameter and thus it is only necessary to compute the mean and standard deviation of the logarithms of the variables to define the distribution.

Table 10-1 ABBREVIATED TABLE OF AREAS UNDER THE NORMAL DISTRIBUTION IN TERMS OF MULTIPLES OF THE STANDARD DEVIATION MEASURED FROM THE MEAN

$(x-\bar{x})/s$	0.0	0.1	0.2	0.3	0.4	0.5	0.6	0.7	0.8	0.9
± 0	0.000	0.040	0.079	0.118	0.155	0.192	0.226	0.258	0.288	0.316
± 1	0.341	0.364	0.385	0.403	0.419	0.433	0.445	0.455	0.464	0.471
± 2	0.477	0.482	0.486	0.489	0.492	0.494	0.495	0.496	0.497	0.498

Example 10-1

If the mean annual rainfall in a region is 30 inches and the coefficient of variation is found to be 0.15, find (a) how often you might expect the rainfall to be greater than 42 inches, (b) the 10-year rainfall, and (c) the percent of the time the rainfall would be between 30 and 40 inches. Assume that the normal distribution is an adequate representation of the way the data are distributed.

SOLUTION

1. Use will be made of Table 10-1 and Figure 10-6. The table allows determination of probabilities whereas the figure shows pictorially how the table is used.
$C_v = s/\bar{x}$ (Equation 10-3), and thus $s = C_v\bar{x} = 0.15 \times 30$, or 4.5 inches. Now for part (a), $(x - \bar{x}) = 42 - 30 = 12$. Then $(x - \bar{x})/s = 12/4.5 = 2.7$. Looking at Figure 10-6a, we are seeking the area to the right of 42 inches and this lies at a distance of 2.7 standard deviations to the right of the mean. Now entering Table 10-1 at a value of $(x - \bar{x})/s = 2.7$, the area to the right of the mean up to $x = 42$ inches is found to be 0.496. Thus, the area to the right of 42 inches is gotten by subtracting 0.496 from 0.500, the total area

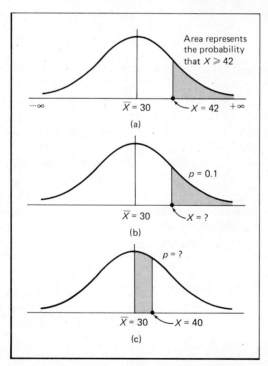

Figure 10-6   Diagram for Example 10-1.

under the curve to the right of the mean. Note that the values in the table are measured from the mean. For the problem at hand, the desired area, and hence probability, is $0.500 - 0.496 = 0.004$. Thus there is a 0.4 percent chance that the annual rainfall will equal or exceed 42 inches.

2. The 10-year rainfall has a frequency of 1/10 or 10 percent. This rainfall will be exceeded only 10 percent of the time. The area under the curve between the mean and the 10-year rainfall will thus be $0.500 - 0.100$, or 0.400. A glance at Table 10-1 for an area of 0.400 shows the closest value to be 0.403 at an $(x - \bar{x})/s$ value of 1.3. We shall accept this as close enough for our purposes. Now solving for $(x - \bar{x})$, $(x - \bar{x}) = 1.3 \times s$, or $1.3 \times 4.5 = 5.9$. Since the difference between the mean and the 10-year rainfall is 5.9 inches, the 10-year rainfall $= 30 + 5.9 = 35.9$ inches.

3. Part (c) of the problem requires a determination of the shaded area of Figure 10-6c. In this case, $(x - \bar{x})/s = (40 - 30)/4.5 = 2.22$. From Table 10-1 an area of approximately 0.487 is gotten by interpolation. Since the mean value in the example is 30 inches, the value of the area obtained from the table is the value being sought. Thus one could expect the annual rainfall to lie between 30 and 40 inches about 48.7 percent of the time.

This example illustrates the type of analyses that can be made using continuous probability distributions. It should be evident that if a particular distribution can be determined to fit the data of interest, many avenues for quantitative frequency estimates are opened. ■

PEARSON TYPE III DISTRIBUTIONS

The Pearson type III and log Pearson type III distributions have found widespread use in analyses of hydrologic variables. These distributions have three parameters, the mean, standard deviation, and coefficient of skewness. When skewness is zero, the Pearson type III distribution reduces to the normal distribution and the log Pearson type III reduces to the log normal. The Water Resources Council has specified that the log Pearson type III distribution should be the standard for analyzing annual series flood data. Flood magnitudes are estimated from

$$\log Q = \bar{x} + Ks \qquad\qquad (10\text{-}14)$$

where $\bar{x}$ is the mean of the logarithms of the flows and s is the standard deviation of the logarithms. K is a frequency factor that is a function of both skew and recurrence interval (Appendix C). The mean, standard deviation, and skew coefficient of observed data may be computed using Equation 10-1 for the mean, 10-2 for s, and 10-4 for C_s. In all of the above equations the variable x is the logarithm of the variable of interest.

In using the log Pearson type III distribution, it should be noted that C_s is sensitive to extreme events. The WRC states that for small samples, C_s is difficult to estimate and that a generalized estimate should be made (Figure 10-7) (11). Specifically, if records of 100 years or more are available, Equation 10-4 should be used. For records of 25 to 100 years, a weighted skew should be calculated in which the station skew is given a weight of $(n - 25)/75$, where n is the length of the record. This value is used with a generalized skew value to arrive at an adjusted value for use in computations. The generalized skew determined from special studies or from Figure 10-7 is given a weight of $1.0 - (n - 25)/75$ (11). Values of K to be used in Equation 10-14 are given in Appendix C. The use of the Pearson distributions is illustrated in the following section.

Frequency Analyses

Water resources systems analysts are confronted with many probabilistic phenomena such as rainfall, evaporation, streamflows, and temperature. It is often necessary to fit a probability distribution to the observations to permit required frequency analyses. The objective of these frequency analyses may be the estimation of the 25, 50, 100, or some other period

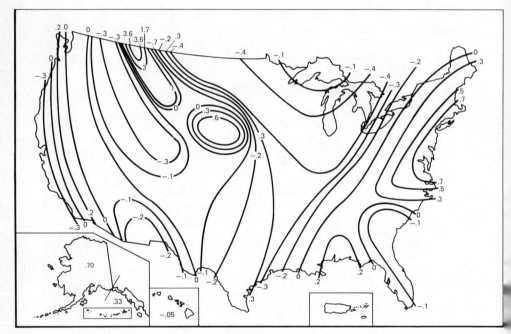

Figure 10-7   Generalized skew coefficients of logarithms of annual maximum streamflows (WRC, reference 11).

flood for a given drainage basin, the estimation of the seven- or 14-day low flow for use in water quality management studies, or the determination of the likelihood of achieving some target water storage. In general, frequency analyses should be avoided, or regarded cautiously, when records of fewer than 10 years are available. Furthermore, estimates of frequencies of occurrence that greatly exceed the length of the historical record from which they are derived are likely to have large errors associated with them. Frequency estimates exceeding twice the length of the record would be of questionable value, for example. For those seeking more detailed information, references 1, 2, and 11 to 15 will be helpful.

Example 10-2

Use the 40-year record of low flows for the Llano River at Junction, Texas, to estimate the 75-year low flow for that location. Fit a Pearson type III curve to the data and use the fitted curve to make the estimates. Does the fitted curve appear to be an acceptable representation of the distribution of the sample data?

SOLUTION
1. The data are tabulated in rank order from the lowest to the highest values in Table 10-2. The plotting position (percent) for each data point is tabulated in column 3.
2. Figure 10-8 shows the plotted data. The fitting of the Pearson type III curve requires calculation of the distribution's three parameters, $\bar{x}$, s, and C_s. These estimates are made using Equations 10-1, 10-2, and 10-4.

   The mean is obtained by summing the values in column 2 of Table 10-2 and dividing by the number of observations:

   $$\bar{x} = 1689/40 = 42.23 \text{ ft}^3/\text{s}$$

   The standard deviation is gotten by using

   $$s = [\Sigma (x - \bar{x})^2/(n-1)]^{1/2}$$

   The deviations from the mean are calculated in column 4, their squares in column 5, and their cubes in column 6. Using the calculated sum of the squares of the deviations,

   $$s = (16,205.1/39)^{1/2} = 20.4 \text{ ft}^3/\text{s}$$

   The coefficient of skewness is obtained by substituting the appropriate values in:

Table 10-2 DATA FOR EXAMPLE 10-2

(1)	(2)	(3)	(4)	(5)	(6)
RANK	LOW FLOW (ft^3/s)	PLOTTING POSITION $[m/(n+1)]$	DEVIATION FROM THE MEAN $(x-\bar{x})$	$(x-\bar{x})^2$	$(x-\bar{x})^3$
1	8	2.43	− 34.23	1171.7	− 40,118
2	8	4.87	− 34.23	1171.7	− 40,118
3	12	7.31	− 30.23	913.9	− 27,630
4	13	9.75	− 29.23	854.4	− 24,962
5	13	12.19	− 29.23	854.4	− 24,962
6	17	14.63	− 25.23	636.6	− 16,072
7	18	17.07	− 24.23	587.1	− 14,223
8	23	19.51	− 19.23	369.8	− 7115
9	27	21.95	− 15.23	232.0	− 3533
10	28	24.39	− 14.23	202.5	− 2889
11	31	26.82	− 11.23	126.1	− 1415
12	31	29.26	− 11.23	126.1	− 1415
13	33	31.70	− 9.23	85.2	− 785
14	33	34.14	− 9.23	85.2	− 785
15	37	36.58	− 5.23	27.4	− 143
16	39	39.02	− 3.23	10.4	− 34
17	41	41.46	− 1.23	1.5	− 2
18	42	43.90	− 0.23	0.0	− 0
19	42	46.34	− 0.23	0.0	− 0
20	43	48.78	+ 0.77	0.6	+ 0.5
21	44	51.21	+ 1.77	3.1	+ 5
22	46	53.65	+ 3.77	14.2	+ 54
23	46	56.09	+ 3.77	14.2	+ 54
24	48	58.53	+ 5.77	33.3	+ 190
25	48	60.97	+ 5.77	33.3	+ 190
26	48	63.41	+ 5.77	33.3	+ 190
27	50	65.85	+ 7.77	60.4	+ 466
28	50	68.29	+ 7.77	60.4	+ 466
29	50	70.73	+ 7.77	60.4	+ 466
30	52	73.17	+ 9.77	95.5	+ 938
31	53	75.60	+ 10.77	116.0	+ 1249
32	55	78.04	+ 12.77	163.1	+ 2082
33	55	80.48	+ 15.77	248.7	+ 3927
34	61	82.92	+ 18.77	352.3	+ 6607
35	63	85.36	+ 20.77	431.4	+ 8952
36	64	87.80	+ 21.77	473.9	+ 10,319
37	64	90.24	+ 21.77	473.9	+ 10,319
38	67	92.68	+ 24.77	613.6	+ 15,209
39	74	95.12	+ 31.77	1009.3	+ 32,056
40	109	97.56	+ 66.77	4458.2	+ 297,661
	1689			16,205.1	+ 185,200

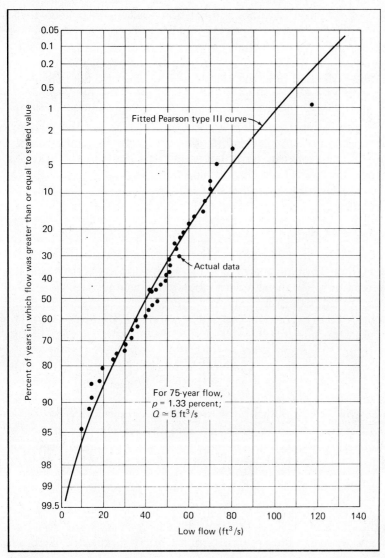

Figure 10-8 Graphical fitting of Pearson type III curve-to-streamflow data for the Llano River at Junction, Texas.

$$C_s = \left[\frac{n}{(n-1)(n-2)} \sum_{i=1}^{n} (x_i - \bar{x})^3 \right] / s^3$$

Thus

$$C_s = \left[\frac{40}{(39)(38)} (185,200) \right] / (20.4)^3$$

$$C_s = 0.59$$

Let us assume that other information leads us to believe that a value of 0.6 is slightly better. We shall use this revised value in our determination of the fitted curve.

3. Now using Appendix C, we can find the values of the frequency factor K needed to fit the curve. These values are taken from the appendix for a $C_s = 0.6$ for various values of the percent chance of occurrence. The selected values are tabulated in Table 10-3.

Now using the estimated values of the mean and standard deviation and employing Equation 10-14, the calculated values of the distribution can be obtained for the probabilities (percent chance) chosen. Note that Equation 10-14 was given for the log Pearson distribution. For the Pearson type III, the equation becomes:

$$Q = \bar{x} + Ks$$

where $\bar{x}$ is the mean of the observed data and s is the standard deviation. Thus, estimates of Q can be readily made for fitting the distribution. These values are tabulated in column 4 of Table 10-3.

4. Finally, the values in column 4 are plotted on Figure 10-8 and connected to represent the fitted Pearson type III distribution. The data fit this curve quite well. The 75-year low flow is obtained by entering the graph at a percentage point of $(1/75) \times 100 = 1.33$ percent chance that the flow will be less than or equal to that value (98.7 percent chance it will be $\geq$ that value). The estimated flow is seen to be about 5 ft^3/s.

This example illustrates the fitting technique for the three-parameter Pearson distribution and further clarifies the use of probability distributions for analyzing water resources problems.

∎

Time Series

Many of the random variables that must be dealt with in water resources planning and management are time dependent. The sequence of stream-

Table 10-3 FREQUENCY FACTORS FOR EXAMPLE 10-2

(1) P	(2) $K_{0.6,P}$	(3) Ks	(4) $Q=\bar{x} + Ks$
0.95	− 1.458	− 29.74	12.49
0.90	− 1.200	− 24.48	17.75
0.50	− 1.099	− 2.02	40.21
0.10	1.328	27.09	69.32
0.04	1.939	39.56	81.79
0.02	2.359	48.12	90.35
0.01	2.755	56.20	98.43

flows at a given point is an example. This sequence is referred to as a time series, and the value of any observation in such a series is often influenced by antecedent occurrences. In such cases, the observations are not independent, and their modeling requires the use of special techniques. Time series are often conceptualized as being single observations of a stochastic process (1). A stochastic process is one in which a random variable changes in value over time. Furthermore, the process is considered to be stationary if its probability distribution does not change with time.

A time series orders observations in their sequence of occurrence. Analyses of such series may reveal cycles, trends, or fluctuations. They also permit derivation of special processes for generating synthetic records of streamflows, rainfall, or other hydrologic variables. Figure 10-9 generalizes the nature of time series. Once a cycle or trend has been identified, there are many methods to fit a curve to the data so that the series can be represented by a mathematical model (2, 13).

STOCHASTIC TIME SERIES

When the events in a random process are not independent, then the nature of the correlation of these events must be determined if the process is to be modeled. The Markov process is one characterization used in such modeling (2, 14, 16).

When the dependence between sequential events in a random process is such that an event occurring at some point in time is dependent only on the immediately preceding event and not on any other past events, the process may be described as markovian. First-order Markov processes are ones exhibiting a step-by-step dependence. They are also described as having a lag-one serial correlation. This means that the event at one point in time is correlated only with the preceding event. The Markov theory can be extended theoretically, however, to include multiple-lag correlations. These processes are known as higher-order Markov processes. Regardless of the order, the process is defined in terms of discrete probabilities (2). Markov processes are widely used in simulating water resources systems (11). In particular, they are used to develop synthetic records of streamflows, rainfalls, or other hydrologic variables.

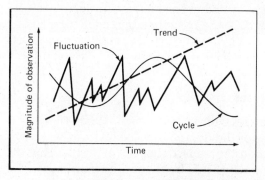

Figure 10-9 Time series representations.

SYNTHETIC STREAMFLOW GENERATION

It has already been pointed out that the use of frequency analyses based on historical records is limited in reliability when it comes to making estimates of occurrences with return periods very much outside the limits of the length of the record. This problem can be circumvented by generating synthetic histories of streamflows or other random variables that have longer periods of record. These records can then be analyzed by the methods already presented to identify extreme high or low flows, which may be more severe than those actually observed. The generating process, to be of value, must be selected so that the histories it creates are considered representative of actual ones that might have been recorded. The processes are chosen so that they preserve all the statistical features of the original data and thus yield other samples that the statistician could verify as having come from the same population (statistical set). The Markov process appears to do this and is therefore a useful tool to extend records and provide additional alternative futures that can be analyzed.

The assumption is made that streamflow is a random variable and that synthetic flow records can be generated by statistical methods. The Markov process can be used for this purpose. In this case, streamflows are considered to be chains of serially dependent values. Each value has a deterministic part (not subject to probability) and a random error part. For example, the lag-one single-period Markov chain assumes that the next flow in a series of flows is obtained by summing the mean flow, a dependent fractional part of the deviation of the preceding flow from its mean, and a random component (14).

It is the usual practice to generate synthetic sequences that are at least as long as the life of the project being studied. Ordinarily many such sequences would be derived. In fact, Linsley and Franzini recommended that about 1000 traces be generated and analyzed (16). Each generated trace might be used to determine the storage level of a proposed reservoir, for example. These storages then form a sample of storages from which the likelihood of requiring a specified storage level can be estimated.

The generating process described here is not valid if trends or cycles are known to exist. Usually, for the design periods encountered, this is not a problem. If records of actual streamflows are not available, or are very brief, then a Markov model might be used to generate rainfalls (if sufficient historical data are available). The generated rainfalls could then be used with an appropriate hydrologic model to simulate the desired streamflows.

Reliability of Statistical Analyses

The reliability of statistical analyses is directly tied to the size of the sample of data considered. A measure of the degree of reliability can be had by calculating confidence limits for estimated frequencies of events. Thus the estimate of the 10-year storm from a fitted frequency distribution can, for example, be subjected to a determination of the range of its likely error.

Unfortunately, most analyses of hydrologic systems suffer from limited data on the variables of concern. These data limitations, combined with the uncertainty associated with selecting appropriate distributions to represent the data, introduce errors into the frequency determinations that are made. The differences between population properties and estimates of these properties (mean, standard deviation, and so on) derived from sample data can be reduced only by obtaining additional data, improving the quality of the data, and/or making better determinations of the appropriate statistical methods to be used in their analyses. This is not always easy to do. In any case, it is usually important to obtain some indication of the reliability of the conclusions drawn from analyzing the data.

Those using frequency curves must accept the fact that the curve is only an approximation of the theoretical curve it is intended to model. Streamflows, rainfalls, temperatures, and other recorded observations are only samples and their use in making projections is greatly affected by the length of record, the reliability of the measurements, and whether the underlying statistical distribution is known. Confidence limits play an important role in measuring the uncertainty created by all of these conditions. Both the uncertainty of the estimated exceedance probability of a particular value and the uncertainty of the value at a selected exceedance probability can be determined. Various procedures for constructing confidence limits are reported in the literature (2, 11).

10-4 SURFACE-WATER SYSTEMS SIMULATION

Many cities, regions, and nations are in the process of reevaluating their water resources to determine the adequacy of these to sustain present uses and to ascertain the potential for new uses. Sometimes these determinations must be made with little or no data on either the hydrology or levels of water use being exercised in the region of concern. In such cases, simulation models can be called on to fill in missing records, to extend the length of records, to estimate data for ungauged sites, and to aid in determining the types of data and the frequency with which these data must be collected to provide adequate histories for further analyses. Where sufficient data are available, simulation models can be designed and/or used to test potential developments or operating procedures to guide decisions about water management.

Hydrocomp Simulation Model

One of the earliest digital simulation models to find wide use was the Stanford Watershed Model reported by Crawford and Linsley in 1966 (17). Since that time the model has undergone many revisions by its authors and others (18–25). The version discussed here is the Hydrocomp Simulation Program (18). This and other versions of the model have been used extensively for synthesizing continuous hydrographs of hourly or daily streamflows for watersheds of varying sizes and character.

The Hydrocomp Simulation Program (HSP) is actually a sequence of computational routines representing the major hydrologic processes. Figure 10-10, a flow diagram of the model, indicates the nature of the calculations that are made. Inputs to the model include precipitation, potential evapotranspiration, temperature, radiation, dew point, and wind. The last four of these are needed only if snowmelt is involved.

What the model does is to account for the initial moisture stored in the watershed and then determine the fate of a precipitation input. The hydrologic budget equation (Equation 7-5) is balanced for selected time

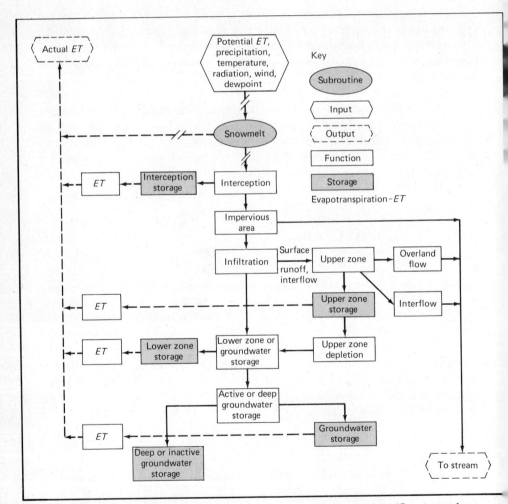

Figure 10-10 Flowchart for Hydrocomp simulation programming. (Courtesy of Hydrocomp International, Inc., Mountain View, California.)

steps so that the precipitation input can be converted into streamflow after the appropriate allocations to interception, evapotranspiration, and upper, lower, and deep groundwater storages have been made. Simply put, an equation of the following type is solved at each time step for streamflow:

$$R = P - ET - \Delta S \tag{10-15}$$

where
$P =$ precipitation
$R =$ streamflow
$ET =$ evapotranspiration
$\Delta S =$ total change in storage

The equation is balanced for each time step and the calculations proceed from interval to interval until there is no additional input of data.

SNOW ACCUMULATION AND MELT
In many parts of the United States and the world, snowmelt is the principal source of water supply. The HSP model has special subroutines to handle the snow accumulation and melt processes. Snowmelt hydrographs are generated and routed through the channel network in a similar manner to other channel inputs. Distribution from snowmelt to infiltration and ET is also made. For details on this aspect of HSP and on the modeling of snowmelt processes, the reader is referred to references 2, 16, 18, 26, and 27.

APPLICATIONS OF THE HSP MODEL
Use of the HSP model, or other versions of the original Stanford Watershed Model of which the HSP is an outgrowth, normally requires from three to six years of data so that the model can be calibrated for the watershed to which it is to be applied. During the process, parameters must be estimated and adjusted until the simulated and observed hydrographs are within acceptable limits of agreement. Once the model has been calibrated and verified, it is ready for use in analyzing a broad range of situations.

Typical simulation periods in HSP applications range from 20 to 50 years. The hydrologic traces generated are often used as data for probability studies of various aspects of water resources management.

USGS Rainfall-Runoff Model

The HSP model is a continuous-simulation model. Such models have great value when long histories must be generated. In many cases, however, it is only the simulation of some particular event that is needed. Models used for this purpose are classified as event simulation models.

Event simulation models are often used to imitate rainfall-runoff processes. Although lumped parameter models are widely used for such purposes, more sophisticated models are also common since the long-term computational sequences of continuous models are not required, and the analogous computer time can be used to incorporate greater detail in the event model. Normally, event simulation models are operated so that they calculate flows in a downstream manner from the uppermost reaches of a watershed. Unit hydrograph methods are commonly incorporated to estimate the outflows at designated points in a channel network.

Figure 10-11 illustrates the normal configuration of an event simulation model. The precipitation input is first applied uniformly over a subbasin, and losses to interception, infiltration, and evapotranspiration are calculated and deducted. This leaves an excess precipitation pattern,

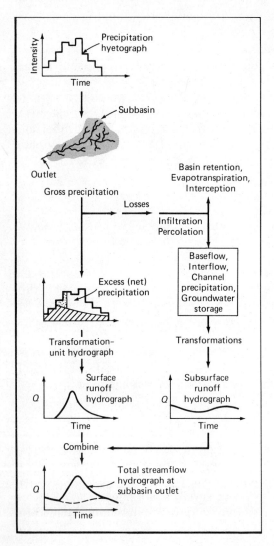

Figure 10-11 Flowchart for lumped parameter event simulation model.

which is then used to develop the surface runoff hydrograph using the chosen unit hydrograph model. One event simulation model will be discussed here. Viessman et al. describe the features of many other models (2, 28–33).

The USGS Rainfall-Runoff Model had its beginning in a 1972 study by Dawdy, Lichty, and Bergmann (2, 34–36). The model is used to evaluate short streamflow records and to calculate peak flow rates for natural drainage basins. Since the time the model was originally developed, it has undergone several modifications, namely the inclusion of internal optimization procedures for setting parameters, changes in routing procedures, and the inclusion of methods for considering uniformly distributed impervious areas.

The USGS model separates into three components of the hydrologic process: moisture accounting, infiltration, and surface runoff. The antecedent moisture accounting system is used to index soil moisture at the beginning of a time interval so that the infiltration rate for that time step can be determined. It also handles ET from the soil. The infiltration rate is estimated on the basis of Philip's equation and, similar to HSP, uses soil moisture determinations to set its rate (37). The final phase is routing of the rainfall excess pattern generated from the losses imposed on the original storm sequence by the antecedent moisture accounting process and infiltration. Rainfall excess is routed using a triangular-shaped translation hydrograph and a linear storage model. The manner in which the model functions is depicted in Figure 10-12.

The peak discharge for each storm within a year, as synthesized, can be ranked by the computer program. These ranked annual values can then be analyzed using the Pearson type III procedures discussed previously.

Conclusions

The foregoing discussion of continuous- and event simulation models should demonstrate the feasibility of using such models for a variety of purposes in planning and managing water resources systems. It should also be clear that there are many assumptions that must be made in developing and using models. Furthermore, there are often limited data, sometimes no data, available to evaluate model parameters and verify the model selected. Irrespective of these drawbacks, there are many opportunities to obtain valuable information from the use of models and to use model analyses as guides to technical, managerial, and political decisions. The key is understanding the limitations of models and knowing where they can be applied with the expectation of meaningful results. The technically trained person has an obligation to make such specifications clearly and to provide the needed guidance to those who seek to use model output but do not have the ability to understand a model's technical structure.

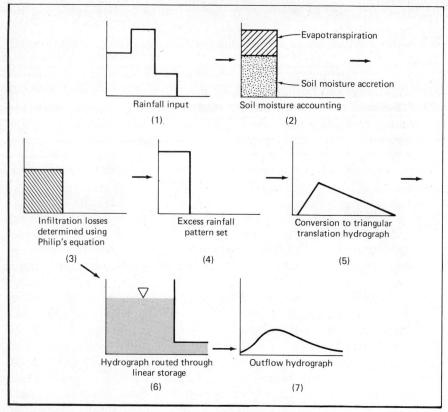

Figure 10-12 USGS Rainfall-Runoff Model flowchart.

10-5 GROUNDWATER SYSTEMS SIMULATION

In a general sense, groundwater may be considered as water in storage. These underground storages are often accessible to development; they lose little water to evaporation, they require no manmade works to contain the water, and the waters stored are often of good quality and low temperature. For these reasons, groundwater is an especially attractive source of water supply, and its natural storage reservoirs have the potential to supplement costly surface-water storage works.

Groundwater Modeling

Simulation models can be used to analyze the interdependencies of river-aquifer systems and to evaluate the impacts of systems for groundwater development and use. Variables that should be considered in studies of groundwater systems operation include the quantities and timing of diversions of water from interconnected streams; the timing, amount, and location of groundwater withdrawals; and the timing, location, and amounts of natural and artificial recharge. The model should be designed so that its output can be used to evaluate the net social impact associated with an array of options. The hydrological calculations made by the model should be translatable into an economic response mechanism representing the reactions of water users to changes in water supply and/or price.

A variety of groundwater modeling techniques have been developed (2, 37–49). These include porous media models, electrical analog models based on the comparability of Ohm's law and Darcy's law, and digital computer models for the numerical solution of the equations of groundwater flow. The latter type of model is the one that will be treated here. For details of other types of models, the reader is referred especially to Todd (40).

Finite Difference Methods

Digital simulation requires an adequate mathematical description of the physical processes to be modeled. For groundwater flow this description consists of a partial differential equation and accompanying boundary and initial conditions. The governing equation is integrated to produce a solution that gives the water levels or heads associated with the aquifer being studied at selected points in space and time. The model can simulate years of physical activity in a span of seconds, so that the consequences of proposed actions can be evaluated before decisions involving construction or social change are implemented. The expectation is that the model runs will lead to wiser and more cost-effective decisions (38–40).

The finite difference method is based on the subdivision of an aquifer into a grid and the analysis of flows associated with zones of the aquifer. The equation that must be solved is derived from continuity considerations and Darcy's law for groundwater motion. This yields the following partial differential equation describing flow through an areally extensive aquifer. Note that the equation presented here describes the two-dimensional case

$$\frac{\partial(T\frac{\partial h}{\partial x})}{\partial x} + \frac{\partial(T\frac{\partial h}{\partial y})}{\partial y} = S\frac{\partial h}{\partial t} + W \tag{10-16}$$

where h = total hydraulic head (L)
x = x direction in a cartesian coordinate system (L)
y = y direction in a cartesian coordinate system (L)
S = specific yield of the aquifer (dimensionless)
T = transmissivity of the aquifer (L^2/T)
W = source and sink term (L/T)

In the above equation, vertical flow velocities are considered to be negligible everywhere in the aquifer. The following assumptions are implicit in the derivation: the flow is two dimensional, fluid density is constant in time and space, hydraulic conductivity is uniform within the aquifer, flow obeys Darcy's law, and the specific yield of the aquifer is constant in space and time. Equation 10-16 is nonlinear for unconfined aquifers because transmissivity is a function of head and thus the dependent variable.

In order to integrate Equation 10-16, initial values of head, transmissivity, saturated thickness of the aquifer, and the amounts of water produced by sources and sinks must be identified for every point in the region of integration. The specific yield and location of geometric boundaries must also be defined. Unfortunately, analytic solutions to Equation 10-16 are impossible to obtain except for the most trivial cases. It is thus necessary to resort to numerical integration techniques to obtain the desired answers (39, 41–45).

Application of finite-difference techniques to groundwater flow problems requires that the region of concern be divided into many small subregions or elements (Figure 10-13). For each of these elements, characteristic values of all the variables in Equation 10-16 are specified. These values are assigned to the centers of the elements, which are called nodes. The heads in adjacent nodes are related through a finite difference equation that is derived from Equation 10-16. These difference equations can be derived by an appropriate Taylor's series expansion or by mass balance considerations (39). The resulting algebraic equations can then be solved simultaneously to yield the heads at each node for each time step considered.

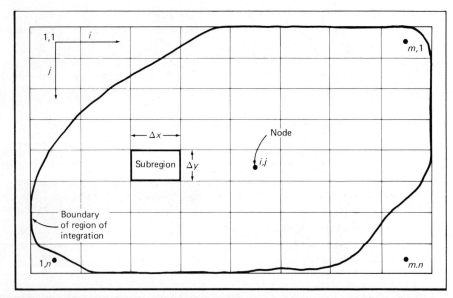

Figure 10-13   Subdivision of a region of intergration into computational elements for a finite difference problem formulation.

It should be understood that the simulation methods presented in this chapter are pointed toward the analysis of regional rather than localized groundwater problems such as the prediction of the drawdown at a particular well. In such cases, the methods discussed in Chapter 7 will usually be the most appropriate. Here we are mainly concerned with water level or head changes that might occur over a large area due to prescribed water use practices.

BOUNDARY CONDITIONS

In order to integrate Equation 10-16, the governing boundary conditions must be specified. Two types of boundary conditions will be discussed here. Where the region of integration is limited by a political or arbitrarily chosen boundary, it is often the policy to employ a constant gradient boundary condition (41). In this case, the assumption is made that the gradient of the water table will not change along the boundary even though the water level may rise or fall. Where streams with interconnections to the groundwater system are encountered, stream boundary conditions are employed. Constant gradient boundaries are expressed mathematically as

$$\frac{\partial h}{\partial s} = g(x, y) \tag{10-17}$$

where $g(x, y) =$ a constant specified at the location x, y throughout the period of simulation (dimensionless)
$h =$ hydraulic head (L)
$s =$ direction perpendicular to the boundary (L)

Stream boundaries are expressed as follows

$$h = f(x, y, t) \tag{10-18}$$

where $f(x, y, t) =$ a known function of time at the location x, y (dimensionless)
$h =$ hydraulic head (L)

The volumetric rate of flow across the constant gradient boundaries described by Equation 10-17 can be modeled at each time step using the Darcy equation (41):

$$Q = T\frac{\partial h}{\partial s}\Delta l \tag{10-19}$$

where $h =$ head (L)
$\Delta l =$ dummy variable denoting length of the side of the subregion perpendicular to s (L)

s = dummy variable denoting the direction of flow
perpendicular to the boundary (L)
Q = volumetric discharge (L^3/T)
T = transmissivity at the boundary (L^2/T)

The use of this equation at a boundary is illustrated by the notation
of Figure 10-14. Consider the flow from left to right in the x direction
across the left-hand side of the elemental region depicted. The node $i-1,j$ lies outside the region of integration and thus it may be assumed that
no information about it is available. An assumption may be made to cir-
cumvent this problem. It is that the transmissivity across the boundary is
uniform and equal to $T_{i,j}$.

In finite difference form the head-change term in Equation 10-19 can
be stated as

$$\frac{\partial h}{\partial x} = \frac{h_{i,j} - h_{i-1,j}}{\Delta x} \tag{10-20}$$

But the head $h_{i-1,j}$ does not exist, and another approximation is required:

$$h_{i,j} - h_{i-1,j} \simeq h_{i+1,j} - h_{i,j} \tag{10-21}$$

These two expressions are then substituted in Equation 10-19 to yield:

$$Q_{i-\frac{1}{2},j} \simeq T_{i,j}\frac{h_{i+1,j} - h_{i,j}}{\Delta x}\Delta y \tag{10-22}$$

At the beginning of each time step, a new volumetric flux is calculated
along each constant gradient boundary. This is accomplished by using the
heads and transmissivities computed in the previous time interval.

Surface streams are sometimes treated as constant head boundaries in
groundwater problems. This assumption is adequate where the water
level in the surface body is expected to remain unchanged during the time

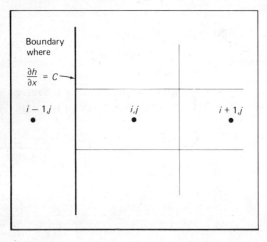

Boundary
where

$\frac{\partial h}{\partial x}$ = C

$i-1,j$

i,j

$i+1,j$

Figure 10-14 Subregions
adjacent to a constant gradient
boundary.

period of the modeling process. In many instances, however, surface flows and hence heads are significantly affected by withdrawals or recharges to the interconnected groundwater system. They may then be a limited source of water supply for the groundwater system. To accommodate the surface-water–groundwater linkage, a leakage term may be applied (41). After each time step the leakage from the stream to the aquifer is calculated and streamflows are depleted accordingly. If the streamflow at a particular node becomes zero, the model can be made to note that the stream is dry and break the hydraulic connection at that point (41)

TIME STEPS AND ELEMENT DIMENSIONS

The success of any finite difference scheme depends on the incremental values assigned the element dimensions and the time steps. In general, the smaller the dimensions of elements and time increments, the closer the finite difference approximation to the differential equation. However, as these partitions are made smaller, a price in computational costs and data needs must be paid. Furthermore, oversubdivision may even bring about computational intractability. Thus the object is to select the degree of definition that results in an adequate representation of the system while keeping data and computational costs at a minimum. There are many procedures for making such selections, but they will not be presented here (41–45).

Model Applications

To illustrate how simulation models can be used to provide insights into water management schemes, a model analysis of the upper Big Blue River Basin aquifer in Nebraska is presented (41).

The use of groundwater for irrigation in the upper Big Blue Basin was observed to be rapidly increasing and by 1972 about 3.3 wells per square mile were in operation. At that time farmers were becoming concerned about the progressive decline of the water level and were seeking guidance about the efficiency of implementing some form of basin-wide water management program. The University of Nebraska designed a model to evaluate the situation and to explore various proposals for recharging the aquifer and for estimating the long-term consequences of several scenarios of water use in the basin.

As might be suspected, the information of most concern to the local landowners and water planners was the rate of decline of the water table. In particular, they wanted to know how rapidly the groundwater resource would be depleted, where and when water level declines would pose an economic constraint on water use, and what impacts future development and/or management would have on the rate of decline.

The model developed to explore these features was a two-dimensional representation of flow through an areally extensive aquifer (41). Equation

10-16 along with the appropriate boundary conditions constituted the model. The region was divided into a finite difference grid, and after substitution of the nodal values T and S, the model was operated to predict water level changes to the year 2020 for various policies of recharge and for several levels of development. Calibration of the model was accomplished using historical data. The model was operated over the period 1953 to 1972 using the known distribution of wells and the average net pumpage per well to establish a match between observed and estimated water level changes. Once this was accomplished, the simulation of future trends proceeded. Figure 10-15 shows the correspondence achieved in the matching process.

On the basis of the model studies it was determined that water levels in the study area would continue to decline even if development was limited to the 1972 level. It was further predicted that some parts of the area would experience severe groundwater shortages by the year 2000. It was found, however, that by employing artificial recharge methods, permanent groundwater supplies could be ensured. To assess the effects of artificial recharge, two water delivery systems were modeled. Both of these delivered water from Platte River valley sources to recharge wells in the project area. Using these two water delivery systems, three recharge schemes were simulated. The gross effect of introducing the recharge wells was the cancellation of the effects of a proportionate number of pumping wells. Figure 10-16 shows the computed water level changes at one location under a graduated development plan (projected on the basis of the 1972 rate of development) with no recharge and then with graduated development for each of the three recharge schemes. The continual downward trend in water level with no recharge (curve 1) clearly shows the nature of the problem in the upper Big Blue Basin. The

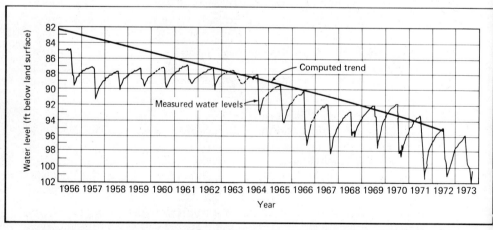

Figure 10-15   Measured and computed water level trends. (After Huntoon, reference 41.)

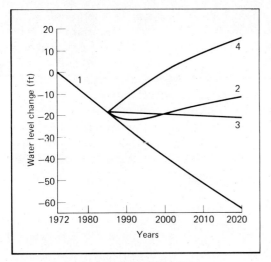

Figure 10-16   Computed water level changes under a plan of graduated development for conditions of (1) no recharge, (2) recharge under scheme 1, (3) recharge under scheme 2, and (4) recharge under scheme 3. (After Huntoon, reference 41.)

other curves, depicting the three artificial recharge options, show that stability can be achieved if such an approach is taken.

While the costs of implementing artificial recharge might be excessive, it is apparent that any long-term solution to the declining water table problem, short of reducing use, would require a supplemental source of water.

Operation of the model provided useful insights into the nature of the water table problem and suggested that the future for groundwater supplies is bleak and that the irrigators should be making water management decisions accordingly.

The modeling of groundwater systems is complex, and in the structuring of models such as that just discussed, many simplifying assumptions must usually be made. These have to do with aquifer parameters such as transmissivity, specific yield (for unconfined aquifers), and storage coefficient (for confined systems). Furthermore, the boundary conditions are normally approximations of what occurs in the physical system, and assumptions about the uniformity of materials in various subsurface strata are sometimes crude. This does not mean that groundwater models cannot be expected to yield useful results. It does imply that the users of the models must be cautious about how they interpret the output. For example, an areally extensive aquifer model such as that developed by Huntoon for analyzing the Blue River problem can be expected to give reliable information about water level trends for various configurations of development. It should not, on the other hand, be considered an accurate predictive tool for monitoring the water level change at some specific point in the region of concern. This type of information could be derived only from a more detailed modeling of the locality surrounding the point. The information provided by the Blue River model was targeted to show local landowners what the future might hold for several development levels and for several management options. The actual water levels predicted by the model were not of central concern; what was of interest was the determination that unless future development was restricted and supplemental water provided, or unless current uses could be significantly reduced, the outlook in the next 50 years was not good for irrigated farming.

The model thus provided the basis for making some quantitative observations about the future. It also provided insights into the relief that might be expected from artificial recharge. Beyond that it could be used to model other possible management options. A model such as this, carefully used and properly interpreted, can add a powerful dimension to decision-making processes.

10-6 WATER QUALITY SIMULATION MODELS

Water quality models may take the forms previously discussed for surface- and groundwater flow models, namely physical, analog, and digital, although our attention here will focus mainly on digital simulation. This form of modeling requires that there be mathematical expressions that equate water quality at a location of interest with factors that determine it. These models may be of varying degrees of complexity. Their nature depends on the application to be made of the model, the availability of data, and the level of understanding of the hydrochemical and hydrobiological processes involved. Unfortunately, the complexities of these processes, which are great, make the difficulties associated with hydrologic modeling seem inconsequential in comparison.

Water quality models usually accept inputs of pollutant (constituent) concentration (milligrams per liter, mg/L) v. time at points of entry to the system, description of the mixing and reaction kinetics in the stream element or groundwater element of concern, and synthesis of a time-distributed output indicating pollutant concentration at the outlet of the element (segment) being modeled. An analogy may be drawn to the discussion in Chapter 7 in which streamflow routing was described as being performed in a downstream sequence from one stream channel segment to another. In the case of water quality modeling, the common representation is the calculation of change in constituent concentration as it passes through successive elements of the water body being modeled.

As in the case of other water resources modeling processes, the approach may be deterministic or stochastic. In the case of water quality models, the stochastic approach is often ruled out because actual records of water quality parameters are unavailable for long enough periods to permit frequency methods to be used. Of course, generated sequences can be used for this purpose if adequate mathematical statements representing the kinetics of the system can be developed and their parameters determined.

The deterministic approach to water quality modeling requires that relations between water quality loading and the flow or hydraulic features of the system be established and that the appropriate chemical and/or biological reactions be tractable for solutions. Where theory-based relations cannot be employed, empirical relations are often used. The optimum model to use would naturally be the one best defining the actual water quality response of the system. Many models have been developed; some of them are described in references 50 to 65.

Pollutants may be classified as conservative or nonconservative (constituents having time-dependent decays); somewhat more specifically as organic, inorganic, radiological, thermal, or biological; and finally they may be categorized by specific forms such as biological oxygen demand (BOD), phosphorus, nitrogen, bacteria, viruses, specific toxic substances, and others. These pollutants may be loaded into a watercourse or groundwater system from either point or nonpoint sources.

The time rate of delivery of a pollutant must be determined if its characteristics are to be modified by management practices or its impact on some element of the system evaluated. For example, the consequences of some total quantity of silt delivered to a lake would not be the same if it were introduced over a period of five days as opposed to two hours. Thus monitoring of water quality must generally be on a continuous basis if the data are to be of value for planning and/or evaluating the performance of continuous-modeling processes.

Unstable pollutants such as radioactive materials, heat, biochemical oxygen demand, and living organisms all have time-dependent decays and are thus nonconservative in nature. For dealing with such constituents it is necessary that both the mixing properties and the reaction kinetics of the system be known or approximated. On the other hand, many inorganic pollutants are conservative in nature and their handling depends mainly on the ability to model the mixing mechanics of the receiving body of water.

The problems associated with modeling chemical and biological changes in a water body are many and complex. The field conditions encountered in natural water systems are highly varied and often negate the validity of reaction rate and other mechanisms determined under laboratory conditions. Furthermore, pollutants derived from nonpoint sources are subjected to many alterations in their travels over and/or through the ground before they reach a watercourse. The highly varied chemical, biological, and hydraulic characteristics of the land must be dealt with in estimating pollutant loadings from these sources. Although qualitative descriptions of hydrochemical and hydrobiological processes are easy to come by, their quantification is something else again. Fortunately, in some cases, empirical relations between pollutant concentration and streamflow or other hydrologic variables can be used to describe water quality loading mechanisms that cannot be obtained on a more theoretical basis. Again it should be stressed that a model is only as good as the data and scientific relations that it is based on.

Types of Water Quality Models

Most water quality models in use today are designed to trace the movement of pollutants through streams, rivers, lakes, estuaries, and other open bodies of water. Groundwater quality models have also been developed, but these generally lag the surface-water models in their state-of-the-art status. Water quality models may be equipped to accept pollutant loadings at specific locations (points) and to accept pollutant inflows along a watercourse (nonpoint inputs) as well.

Point source water quality models generally deal only with confined bodies (channels, groundwater systems) of water whereas nonpoint models must also take into consideration most other phases of the hydrologic cycle (Figure 10-17). Since nonpoint pollutants are moved to streams, estuaries, and so on in overland flow, interflow, and groundwater flow processes, the representative models must include these phases of the hydrologic cycle in addition to the channel phase. As a result, nonpoint models are often thought of as "loading models," which act to trace the movement of pollutants from their originating locations to watercourses. Once a watercourse is reached, these loads (pollutant inputs) can be handled by stream quality models or groundwater quality models as the case may be. Since nonpoint models represent the introduction of pollutants

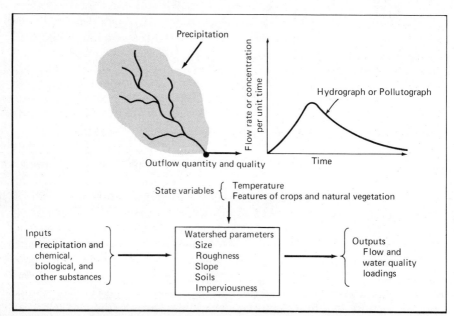

Figure 10-17 Black box concept of watershed modeling.

to watercourses from land surfaces, they are strongly associated with the occurrence of precipitation events. Point source models, on the other hand, usually represent continuous inputs of pollutants, primarily from the discharge of waste treatment works.

Many water quality models are extensions of equations developed in 1925 by Streeter and Phelps for predicting BOD and dissolved oxygen (DO) in flowing streams (1). These equations are often supplemented by various simple first-order reaction equations and mixing and sedimentation models. The trend, however, is toward more complex multiconstituent water quality models that can handle interactions involving numerous chemical constituents and biological organisms. Although such models require considerable data and are often demanding of computer time, they offer the promise of better understanding of water quality mechanics and have the potential for bringing about more efficient policies for water quality management.

Water quality models may be steady state or time varying in design. The former classification can be used where the principal variables are not time dependent or can be assumed to be so within a given stream reach or segment. These models are simpler and less expensive to operate than time-varying models, but they cannot handle rapidly changing situations such as the introduction of nonpoint pollutants during a storm. In general, steady-state models are more suited to long-range planning whereas time-varying models fit the need for setting policies for event management such as that associated with an intense storm.

It has already been pointed out that models may be deterministic or stochastic. Deterministic models deal mainly with projections of mean values of pollutant concentrations whereas stochastic models incorporate the randomness of the physical, chemical, and biological processes being studied. While all real systems are three dimensional, the models employed to represent these systems may be one-, two-, or three-dimensional in character. The choice depends on the use to be put to the model's results and on the nature of the system being modeled. Where one-dimensional models are used, complete mixing is assumed in the vertical and lateral directions. For two-dimensional models, either vertical or lateral mixing may be assumed, the choice depending on the nature of the system.

As in the case of water quantity modeling, both simulation and optimization models may be employed. Each has its own place. Simulation models calculate the values of water quality variables for given hydrologic, waste treatment, boundary, and initial conditions. Optimization models are used to identify management options that best fit preset management conditions.

Finally, as in the case of water quantity simulation, both lumped and distributed parameter approaches may be taken. Lumped parameter models are especially suited to large-scale systems analysis, whereas distributed parameter models can provide a greater level of detail where localized decisions must be made. In either case, the models may be operated continuously or tailored to the simulation of specific events. Continuous simulation can produce water quality histories that can be further analyzed by frequency methods so that inferences can be drawn about the risk associated with possible happenings. Event simulation models can be used to gather rather detailed information about the policies needed to cope with extreme occurrences.

An Elementary Water Quality Model

Water quality modeling efforts have been on the increase since the early 1960s. In the beginning, the commonest parameters included in such models were temperature, BOD, and DO. The list has steadily increased until today many models incorporate salinity; carbonaceous, nitrogenous, and benthic BOD; temperature; total organic carbon; refractory organic carbon; sedimentary, soluble, and organic phosphorus; ammonia, nitrite, nitrate, and organic nitrogen; dissolved oxygen; toxic compounds; phytoplankton; and zooplankton (57). The precision with which all of these constituents can be modeled is not uniform, however, and in some cases more research is clearly needed. It has already been pointed out that modeling natural systems is very difficult due to the many interactions and influences involved.

To provide some understanding of the way in which a water quality model might be formulated we shall consider a simple problem involving the discharge of waste into a receiving stream and the impact of this on the DO level at a downstream location. The nature of the problem is illustrated in Figure 10-18. The waste flow from a city q is found to have a DO level of zero and an ultimate BOD of BODUW. This waste flow is discharged to a receiving stream having a flow of Q, a DO level of DOS, and an ultimate BOD of BODUS. Let us assume that the BOD rate constant K_1 and the stream reaeration coefficient K_2 are known. The problem is to formulate a model that can predict the DO level at point C in the sketch, given the information above. Since the concern here is with the model formulation, it will not be necessary to assign numerical values to the variables and parameters specified above.

The principal components of the model will be the streamflow Q, the waste flow q, the average flow velocity u, the DO upstream of the waste discharge DOS, the DO of the waste $DOW = 0$, the ultimate BOD of the waste flow and the stream BODUW and BODUS, the coefficients K_1 and K_2, and any sources or sinks of oxygen in the region from B to C. The sources of oxygen supply could include photosynthesis, reaeration, and the supply available in the stream. Oxygen sinks would be the BOD in the flows and could also include sludge deposits on the stream bottom and algal respiration.

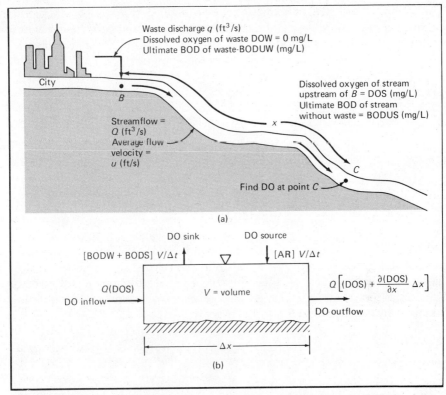

Figure 10-18   Definition sketch for DO model: (a) problem setting; (b) DO accounting in the stream segment.

For illustrative purposes we shall make the following assumptions: (1) steady flow (no variation with time), (2) the wastes are distributed uniformly across the stream cross section, (3) there is no dispersion along the stream path (no mixing in the downstream direction, (4) the decay rate for the waste may be represented by a first-order reaction, (5) there is only one point of waste entry in the stream segment of concern, and (6) the effects of algae and bottom sludge deposits may be neglected. It should be recognized that the foregoing assumptions may not be valid under many actual conditions encountered in the field. They are made here to simplify the model development and to emphasize again that all models include assumptions of varying severity and that these must be understood by model users before they decide on its suitability for their purposes.

Now that we have described the problem, made some simplifying assumptions, and made some statements about what is known (DOS and so on), we can begin to formulate the model. Refer again to Figure 10-18 and note that the stream segment of interest is of length Δx, that its cross-sectional area will be defined as A, and that the volume of water contained in the stream from B to C will be designated V. With this additional definition, we can begin the model formulation by considering that between sections B and C of the stream a continuity equation involving DO can be written. This takes the following form:

DO inflow + sources of DO − (DO outflow + DO sinks)
= change in DO storage in segment

or

$$Q(\text{DOS}) + g(\text{AR})V - \left\{ Q[(\text{DOS}) + \frac{\partial(\text{DOS})}{\partial x}\Delta x] + f(\text{BODW} \right.$$

$$\left. + \text{BODS})V \right\} = \frac{V\Delta(\text{DOS})}{\Delta t} \tag{10-23}$$

where $g(\text{AR})$ is a function of reaeration and $f(\text{BODW} + \text{BODS})$ is a function of the BOD exerted by the waste in the stream segment per unit of time. After insertion for Q of its equivalent $u \times (A)$ (the product of velocity and cross-sectional area), collecting terms, rearranging, and dividing through by V, Equation 10-23 becomes:

$$\frac{\Delta(\text{DOS})}{\Delta t} = -u\frac{\partial(\text{DOS})}{\partial x} - f(\text{BODW} + \text{BODS}) + g(\text{AR}) \tag{10-24}$$

Since we have assumed that the flow in the stream segment is steady (streamflow and waste flow are constant so that eventually the DO concentration in the stream will also be unchanging), the left-hand term in Equation 10-24 becomes zero and we can write:

$$u\frac{\partial(\text{DOS})}{\partial x} = -f(\text{BODW} + \text{BODS}) + g(\text{AR}) \tag{10-25}$$

This equation may be written in terms of the dissolved oxygen deficit at a given location (57). Thus we may deal with the difference between DO under saturated conditions and the level of DO that actually exists at the location. If the equation is written in this form and integrated, the result is the classical Streeter-Phelps equation for dissolved oxygen deficit (1, 57, 63):

$$D = \frac{K_1 L_0}{K_2 - K_1}\left(\exp\left(-K_1 x/u\right) - \exp\left(-K_2 x/u\right) \right)$$

$$+ D_0 \exp\left(-K_2 x/u\right) \tag{10-26}$$

where L_0 is the initial BOD load exerted on the stream by the waste (BODW) and organic material in the stream itself (BODS), D_0 is the initial level of DO in the stream, and D is the dissolved oxygen deficit at the downstream location at a distance of x units from the initial point (point C in Figure 10-18).

This equation and variations of it find wide use in water quality modeling of DO. It is the standard deterministic form and can be used successfully for its purpose if the assumptions made are valid for the situation and satisfactory values of the constants K_1 and K_2 can be obtained. Note that these two parameters are actually functions of pollution loading and rate of streamflow. Thus the assignment of fixed values is only an approximation that must be evaluated for its reasonableness at the conditions under which the model is to be used.

The foregoing discussion should convey to the reader that the formulation of water quality models follows the same general pattern as that for hydrologic models. Both include continuity considerations combined with appropriate equations of motion and reaction (BOD decay, for example). The beginning of the modeling process is thus an understanding of the mechanics of the system of concern and an ability to represent its mechanics in adequate mathematical terms. The following descriptions of several types of water quality models currently being used will bring these ideas into sharper focus.

EPA Storm Water Management Model

A widely used storm water runoff model with the capability for modeling the movement of certain water quality constituents in urban areas is the EPA Storm Water Management Model (SWMM) (2, 51, 52, 56). The model can simulate the runoff from an area of concern for any prescribed rainfall pattern. In using the model, the drainage area is broken up into a number of subareas having approximately uniform properties. The flow diagram for the runoff portion of the model is given in Figure 10-19.

The model has the capability of determining storm water flows and water quality at locations in a storm water system and receiving body of water. It is really a nonpoint pollution model since it deals with the movement of pollutants from the land surface of the area to combined sewers or storm drainage outfalls. The model is of the event simulation type and is not designed to develop long continuous histories.

Simulation is facilitated by the use of five special subroutine blocks. These are the executive, runoff, transport, storage, and receiving blocks. The executive block is the first and last to be called and it provides the interfacing needed between the other blocks. In the runoff block, Manning's equation is used to route the applied rainfall over the land surfaces, through the sewer system, and into the receiving stream. The runoff block also produces pollutographs (time-dependent plots of constituent concentration v. time). The transport block calculates infiltration (leakage into the sewer system), the amount and quality of dry weather flows, water quality

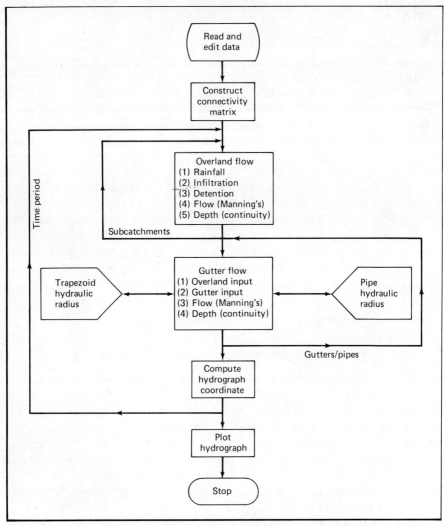

Figure 10-19 Flowchart for hydrographic computation. (After Metcalf and Eddy, Inc., University of Florida, Water Resources Engineers, Inc., reference 51.)

in the system, and costs associated with providing internal storages for dry weather and infiltrated flows if this is desired (51).

The storage block permits the model user to select or have the model select sizes of several treatment processes in a wastewater treatment facility that can accommodate a desired percentage of the peak flow from the area being modeled. When this option is selected, the program calculates the changes in nature of the hydrographs and pollutographs passing through the various treatment elements. The receiving block is used to determine the effects of the effluent from the sewer system on the quantity and quality of the receiving body of water. A detailed discussion of the hydrologic part of the model is given in references 2, 51, 52, and 56.

The input to the water quality portion of the Storm Water Management Model consists of hydrographs developed in the hydrologic phase of the model. The output takes the form of pollutographs for each of the pollutants modeled. The hydrographs and pollutographs that are calculated are then introduced into the transport block, which combines them with the dry weather and infiltrated flow components to produce the actual outfall graphs for water quality and quantity. The SWMM is capable of predicting the concentrations of suspended solids, BOD, total coliform, COD, settleable solids, nitrates, phosphates, and grease in storm water runoff (56).

The SWMM makes use of the assumption that the amount of a pollutant that can be removed from a drainage area during a storm event is a function of the storm duration and initial quantity of the pollutant. This can be represented by a first-order differential equation of the form

$$-\frac{dP}{dt} = kP \tag{10-27}$$

which integrates to

$$P_0 - P = P_0 \, (1 - e^{-kt}) \tag{10-28}$$

where $P_0 =$ initial amount of pollutant per unit area
        $P =$ remaining amount of pollutant per unit area at time t
        $k =$ decay rate

The value of k is assumed to be directly proportional to the rate of runoff. In the model this is represented as $k = br$, where b is a constant and r is the runoff rate. A value of 4.6 has been used for k based on analyses of storm event data from urban areas. This implies identical rainfall intensities and wash-off rates for all storms, a condition not met with in reality.

For the prediction of suspended solids and BOD, it has been determined that a modification of Equation 10-28 is needed. This change incorporates an availability factor A_0, which represents the percentage of the pollutant P_0 that is available for capture by a storm (56). Thus Equation 10-28 becomes

$$P_0 - P = A_0 P_0 (1 - e^{-kt}) \tag{10-29}$$

Coliform densities are predicted as the product of the suspended solids concentration and an appropriate conversion factor. The EPA provides complete information on methods used to establish the required model parameters (51).

For each time step in the modeling process, the rate of runoff is calculated using the hydrologic model. A value of P is also determined (Equation 10-28 or 10-29) and then becomes the value of P_0 for the next time step. Then, during the time interval, the change in value of P can be related to the quantity of flow from the area to produce the pollutograph of the constituent of interest. Calculations proceed from one time step to the next until the storm event has ended.

Calibration of the model centers around a trial-and-error procedure to determine the ideal combination of loading rate and removal coefficient that would result in a satisfactory match of the observed and computed pollutographs. The parameters derived in this manner are valid only for the particular storm used in the calibration and should not be used for other storms unless their features are considered to be quite similar. The SWMM has the flexibility to determine pollutant loading from a variety of urban land use characterizations. It can also be used to generate input data for use in stream quality models such as the one discussed in the preceding section. Reference 56 summarizes the model's application to a number of urban areas and storm events.

EPA Qual-II Model

Qual II is a comprehensive stream water quality model that can simulate up to 13 water quality constituents in any desired combination. The model can accommodate DO, BOD, temperature, algae as chlorophyll a, ammonia, nitrite, nitrate nitrogen, dissolved orthophosphate as P, coliforms, an arbitrary nonconservative constituent, and three conservative constituents (54). The model may be applied to branching stream systems that are well mixed. An assumption is made that advection and dispersion are only significant in the principal direction of flow. Multiple waste discharges, withdrawals, tributary flows, and incremental (lateral) inflows can be incorporated in the model.

The model is limited to the simulation of time periods during which streamflows are approximately constant and waste inputs are constant as well. It is possible, however, to operate the model in both steady-state and dynamic modes. In the latter case, diurnal variations in water quality can be studied. The model is an outgrowth of an earlier version, Qual I, which was developed in 1970 (62). It has seen wide use in water quality planning and management programs, and Qual II permits input and/or output of data in metric units (2, 54, 55).

THE QUAL-II CONCEPTUAL FORM

Figure 10-20 illustrates a stream reach that has been separated into several subreaches or computational elements. For each computational element of length Δx, a hydrologic balance can be written in terms of flow into the upstream face of the element, external sources or withdrawals, and the outflow across the downstream face of the element. The nomenclature for these flow components is given in Figure 10-20. Note that this accounting follows that for the elementary DO model discussed earlier and for several of the hydrologic models presented as well. In a similar fashion, a materials

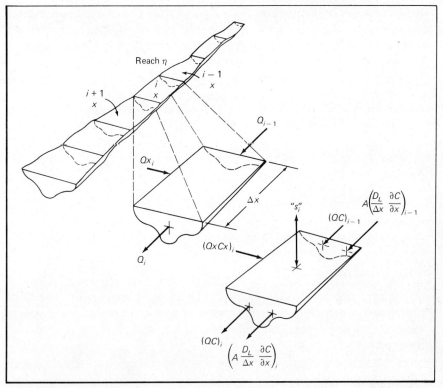

Figure 10-20   Discretized stream system. (After Water Resources Engineers, Inc., reference 65.)

balance for any water quality constituent of interest can also be struck. In the material balance we consider both advection (transport) and dispersion as mechanisms for moving the constituent mass along the stream axis. Mass can be added by waste streams and internal sources such as bottom deposits (benthic sources). It can also be removed by internal sinks of the same nature. The model assumes that there is complete mixing within each computational element.

Referring to Figure 10-20 again, one will see that the stream can be likened to a series of completely mixed reactors (computational elements) that are connected by the mechanisms of advection and dispersion. Groups of such elements in sequence constitute reaches that are assumed to have the same properties relative to hydraulic character, biological and chemical rate constants, and other factors. The groupings of reaches ultimately define the entire stream system.

FUNCTIONAL REPRESENTATION
The basic equation of the Qual-II model is the advection-dispersion mass transport equation, which was conceptualized in Figure 10-20 (54). This equation is numerically integrated over time for each water quality con-

stituent of concern. Embodied in the equation are the effects of advection, dispersion, dilution, reactions and interactions of constituents, and any identified sources or sinks. For a particular constituent C, the equation may be written as

$$\frac{\partial C}{\partial t} = \frac{\partial (A_x D_L \frac{\partial C}{\partial x})}{A_x \partial x} - \frac{\partial (A_x \bar{u} C)}{A_x \partial x} + \frac{dC}{dt} + \frac{s}{V} \tag{10-30}$$

where
x = distance (L)
t = time (T)
C = concentration (M/L^3)
A_x = cross-sectional area (L^2)
D_L = dispersion coefficient (L^2/T)
u = mean velocity (L/T)
s = external source or sinks (M/T)

The right-hand-side terms represent dispersion, advection, constituent changes and external sources, and/or sinks, in that order. The term dC/dt reflects constituent changes such as decay or growth. Examples of such changes are reaeration, coliform die-off, and algal respiration and photosynthesis.

Groundwater Quality Models

Groundwater quality has become a major source of concern in recent years. This has come about from the realization that many groundwater sources that were at one time considered almost pristine have now been degraded in quality by seepages from dumps, by leakage from industrial waste holding ponds, and by other waste disposal and/or industrial and agricultural practices. To deal with such problems, there has been an expanding movement to develop quantitative techniques to understand the mechanics of groundwater quality. These models, although not as advanced as their surface-water counterparts, are now beginning to play a useful role in water quality management.

In 1974, Gelhar and Wilson developed a lumped parameter model for dealing with water quality in a stream-aquifer system. The nomenclature and conceptualization of their model are shown in Figure 10-21 (64). The rationale for using a lumped parameter approach was that when dealing with changes in groundwater quality over long periods of time, temporal rather than spatial variations are the most important.

Changes in water table in the Gelhar-Wilson (GW) model are represented by the following equation:

$$p\frac{dh}{dt} = -q + \epsilon + q_r - q_p \tag{10-31}$$

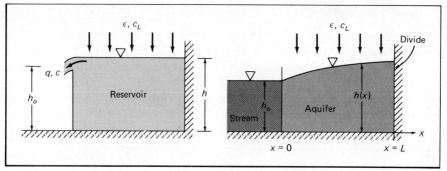

Figure 10-21   Schematic of the Gelhar-Wilson model. (After Novotny and Chesters, reference 52.)

where h = average thickness of the saturated zone
   p = average effective porosity
   ϵ = natural recharge rate
   q = natural outflow from aquifer
   q_r = artificial recharge/unit area
   q_p = pumping rate/unit area
   t = time

This is just another form of the continuity equation relating inflow, outflow, and the change in storage (left-hand term in Equation 10-31). The change in concentration of a constituent is given by:

$$ph\frac{dc}{dt} + (\epsilon + q_r + \alpha ph)c = \epsilon c_L + q_r c_r \qquad (10\text{-}32)$$

where c = concentration
   c_L = concentration of the natural recharge
   c_r = concentration of the artificial recharge
   α = a first-order rate constant for degradation of the contaminant

The GW model assumes that dispersion is negligible. This assumption may be made on the basis that the objective of the model is to estimate regional-average concentrations (52). The model also provides for the determination of hydraulic and solute response times for the system. These are measures of the lag that occurs in the movement of both water and constituent inputs to the system. Gelhar and Wilson assume that the response of an aquifer to a specific input can be likened to that of a well-mixed linear reservoir. Their studies showed that the model's determination of the concentration of constituents leaving an aquifer is representative of the average concentration of the constituent in the aquifer. On this basis it appears that the model is well suited to estimating the quality of groundwater discharging into a surface stream, provided the aquifer is narrow relative to the length along which discharge occurs.

Reliability of Water Quality Models

Although water quality models have become recognized tools to aid planners and managers, it must be understood that their usefulness, reliability, and acceptance are quite variable. Even when the theory underlying a given situation to be modeled is well understood, the complexity of most issues requires that simplifying assumptions be made. The introduction of such assumptions creates an element of uncertainty in model output. The degree of uncertainty depends on the nature of the model and the conditions specified.

The blind acceptance by planners and managers of the sophisticated-looking outputs of many models is cause for concern. Most models are only rough approximations and their use must incorporate this understanding. On the other hand, the wise application of modeling techniques to planning and management issues adds a dimension of power that should be made the most of. If one understands the model and its limitations, one's interpretation of its results can be enlightening. Models are often most useful for comparing impacts of alternative courses of action rather than for being depended on to produce single outcomes.

10-7 OPTIMIZATION MODELS

Optimization models are especially suited to the selection of a so-called "best" alternative from among many. They are often known as screening models because they are used to filter out economically or otherwise inefficient alternatives and to identify options deserving of evaluation in greater detail by simulation or other methods. Used jointly to take advantage of the special features of each, simulation and optimization models can provide a powerful added dimension to the traditional technologies (66–93).

The development of an optimization model may be roughly divided into several phases. These are problem formulation, model construction, data assembly, model testing, model application, and finally implementation of model findings. Although a lot of time is often spent on the model construction phase, it is often the case that the other elements in the process are more important. It is not unusual for the theoretician to discover that the data needed for model calibration are not available, are not of good quality, or are too costly to obtain. Furthermore, since the objective of model building should be to produce planning and management guidance through application of the model, the implementation of a model's results is really the proof of the pudding. All too often this final process is the weak one, either because the model did not really address the right questions or because its development and application were clouded in jargon incomprehensible to the potential user.

If implementation of model results is to be expected, then problem formulation must be considered a very important part of the model development process. Modelers not only must formulate models within their ability to secure the needed data but also must be mindful of so orienting them that their results will have a high probability of being accepted and used. A properly designed output stream is essential. In addition, this output stream must be translated into a form easily understood by less technically based individuals.

Some Common Terminology

Every field of endeavor has its own special vocabulary and this is also true for optimization modeling (also known as systems analysis and operations research). The terminology presented here circumscribes the principal notions embodied in optimization modeling. Basic to model development are various types of "functions." Some common labels are objective, cost, benefit, and performance.

In simple terms, an optimization model is devised to maximize or minimize some "objective function" subject to certain conditions called constraints. It is common for the objective function to reflect the costs of doing something or the benefits that might be obtained in the process. In the former situation, the intent would be to minimize the costs whereas in the latter case the objective would be to maximize the benefits. An objective function might also be constructed to maximize benefits minus costs, to maximize price, to maximize or minimize the amount of a water quality constituent, or for other purposes. In every case, however, the terms in the objective function must be commensurate in their units. That is to say, all terms must be dollars, milligrams per liter, and so on. Because economy is so important in such engineering works as dams and hydroelectric plants, it is usually the case that the objective functions used in water systems analysis are cast in economic terms.

A cost function is used to represent the cost of constructing, operating, or maintaining a water resources system or any combination of the three. The development of appropriate cost functions is an essential element of an optimization modeling process. Figure 10-22 illustrates what a cost function might look like for a dam. In this example, cost is shown as a function of elevation, but it could also be related to dam height or reservoir capacity. As with most cost functions, the relation used in the model is often a composite of cost curves developed for several variables. For example, in the figure it is assumed that the cost shown for any elevation is the actual cost associated with the sum of the costs of land acquisition, damages and relocations, construction, and appurtenances. The composite cost function (shown) is thus the sum of several elevation v. cost curves. Such functions are usually continuous nonlinear functions, but in some cases there may be discontinuities. This might result from the need to relocate an industry if a certain elevation is selected and an abrupt

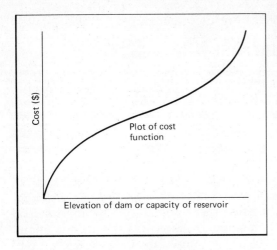

Figure 10-22   Illustration of a cost function. For any elevation, the cost consists of (1) reservoir land aquisition, *L;* (2) damages and relocations, *R;* (3) dam construction, *D;* (4) spillway construction, *S;* (5) appurtenances, *A.* Cost = *f(L, R, D, S, A)* = *f*(elev).

increase in costs at that elevation would be the result. Although the ingredients of a cost function are easy to identify, the development of the function is not always straightforward. This is because data are sometimes hard to come by. They must then be derived, and this can be both time consuming and costly.

Benefit functions describe the payoff associated with some activity such as providing water for irrigation, cities, or recreation. Figure 10-23 illustrates two types of benefit functions. The upper illustration depicts a recreation benefit function associated with a reservoir. Benefits in this example are assumed to exist only during the months of May to September, inclusive. For these months, benefits are a function of pool elevation. If the pool falls below elevation *A,* boat docks might be left high and dry, and benefits would cease. At some pool level *B,* recreation opportunity would be at its maximum. At level *C,* the depth of water would be so great as to make the lake inaccessible, and benefits would drop to zero. The benefit function shown in Figure 10-23b is typical of the type of function

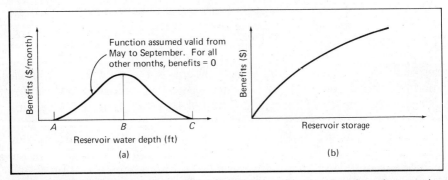

Figure 10-23   Benefit functions. (a) recreation benefits as a function of reservoir water depth; (b) benefit function for irrigation water use.

that might relate reservoir capacity to irrigation income potential. The problems encountered in developing cost functions, described above, also abound in the development of benefit functions.

The objective function, that is, the function to be optimized in the analysis, is commonly a cost function, a benefit function, or some combination of the two (benefits minus costs, for example).

The final function we shall describe here is called a performance function. Such a function is depicted in Figure 10-24. Performance functions indicate how elements of a system perform in meeting objectives or how system elements operate. In the example shown in Figure 10-24, the water supply of the town can be augmented by constructing a reservoir at the upstream location shown. For specific values of flow augmentation, the performance function shows the reservoir capacity required to meet this need.

What is important to remember about all of these functions is that they are descriptive of some part of a system's behavior. The systems analyst must identify and compile all such functions that are needed for an adequate description of the system he or she is working with. To do this, it is usually necessary to form composite representations of total behavior for various system elements from isolated component functions, which are the ones most easily obtained from parties with narrower interests. Agencies dealing with lands might have information on the costs of obtaining land for potential reservoir sites, whereas engineering offices would very likely have construction cost data for dams, channels, and so on.

It is also necessary to identify constraints that might act to limit the range of any particular decision variable (a variable whose value is to be determined in the optimization process). Such constraints might be physical, legal, economic, political, organizational, or regulatory in nature. Whatever the nature, these constraints must be quantified and presented in mathematical form for use in the modeling process. More will be said about this later in the section on linear programming.

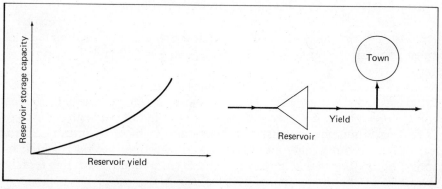

Figure 10-24 Performance function.

Optimization Methodology

The term optimization as used in this book implies the definition of a set of feasible alternatives and some objective to be optimized. In the optimization process the alternatives may be identified explicitly or they may be bracketed by giving ranges over which governing variables can operate. Simply put, the optimization process is one of searching the alternatives to find the alternative that results in the optimal (maximum or minimum) value of the objective function. For very small problems, the search may be conducted by enumeration, comparison of the few options possible. In most instances of practical importance, however, it is necessary to employ some mathematical procedure to perform the screening.

The value of the results obtained in an optimization process depends on the degree to which the problem is properly specified and its constraints dealt with. Problems associated with formulating an appropriate objective function include the intangible nature of some social goals and the fact that objectives often have multiple dimensions, such as providing irrigation water from a reservoir that must also serve to minimize downstream flood damages. Unless the intangible elements can be quantified in some way (use of indices, for example) and the various objectives related functionally, there is no way in which an optimal solution can be obtained by the methods to be presented.

Except in trivial situations, optimization models, like simulation models, are only approximate representations of the systems they are intended to simulate. In a very general sense, errors may stem from both the constraint set and the objective function. These errors are not mistakes in the classical sense but rather deficiencies due to our limited ability to formulate properly the model or to specify all the operative constraints.

Constraint errors tend to permit solutions that in reality may not be feasible (the law says you can't do this but the model didn't recognize it) or to exclude solutions that are really feasible (a model constraint is overrestrictive, perhaps due to limited data). Errors resulting from deficiencies in the objective function take on a different nature (70). If the coefficients used in the objective function (OBJ) are all incorrect by a constant percentage, such as might occur if the effects of inflation had not been properly accounted for, then the solution will still be optimal in terms of the policy it specifies, although the actual value obtained will be wrong. On the other hand, if some elements of the OBJ are correct and others are in error by varying amounts, then the solution will not be optimal even though it may still be feasible. What this all comes down to is that care must be exercised in using the results of optimization processes. The optimal values obtained may be questionable, but the policies indicated may be highly valuable to the decision maker. It is this type of guidance by the model that is really of the most value.

Some of the uses to which optimization models can be put include enhancement of understanding of the modeled system, exploration of cost differences under varying assumptions, screening large numbers of alternatives, and evaluating the impacts of various policies.

Problems to be solved using optimization techniques may be broadly classified as linear or nonlinear in character. Some nonlinear problems can be approximated by linear systems. In other cases, nonlinear functions may be approximated using a series of linear segments. Where these simplifications cannot be made, nonlinear methods of analysis must be used. Optimization methods include linear programming, nonlinear programming, integer programming, dynamic programming, and simulation. Of these methods, linear programming and dynamic programming will be discussed in the sections that follow. For information on other techniques the reader should consult references 1 and 66 through 74.

Before going on to a particular methodology, let us look briefly at the conceptualization of an optimization problem. Consider the problem of supplying water from a reservoir to irrigate land. For the system shown in Figure 10-25 there are a number of elements that could be dealt with by optimization techniques. A benefit function for irrigation water use (written in terms of dollar benefits for various reservoir capacities) might be used as the OBJ to be maximized. Additionally, objectives of minimizing canal costs and the costs of distributing water to the land could be formulated. Furthermore, the selection of the crop or crops to be grown that will maximize returns under the limitations of water availability is another aspect of the problem to be considered. Note that the elements of the system could be optimized individually or collectively. The decisions associated with the individual optimizations might not be the same as those determined for the combined system, however. This is because what is optimal at one system level may not be optimal when that subsystem is considered in the context of the more expansive system. When it is time for a raise in pay, you would consider the maximum level you could

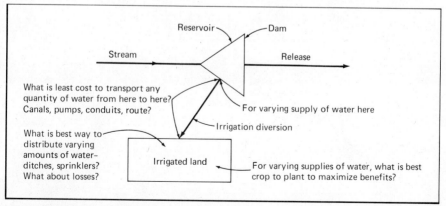

Figure 10-25 Elements of an irrigation system.

receive under company policy as optimal from your point of view. Your employer, who must deal with other employees as well, might consider this decision far from optimal from his or her decision-making point of view.

Linear Programming

Linear programming is a mathematical method that can be used to determine the optimum allocation of a resource such as water when there are alternative uses for the resource. It is the most widely used optimization method and it is available as a "package" for all major computing systems. Users of linear programming systems do not have to understand the details of the algorithm but must be acquainted with its nature and the limitations of the method. Although the method is one that requires the system being analyzed to be linear, some nonlinearities can be dealt with using special techniques.

THE LINEAR PROGRAMMING MODEL

In the linear programming model the objective function and constraints must all be expressed as simple linear algebraic equations. These equations may take the form of equalities or inequalities. Furthermore, the objective function must be convex, and the constraints must form a convex solution space (see Figures 10-26 through 10-28 for definition). The importance of this condition will be made clear when we discuss linearization of nonlinear functions. A final requirement is that the decision variables be allowed to take on only nonnegative values.

The solution to a linear programming problem is achieved by use of the Simplex method. The procedure evaluates the objective function at corner points of the policy space until it locates that corner at which no further improvement in value of the OBJ can be obtained. In maximizing, the solution will occur at the farthest corner point from the origin that still includes at least one feasible policy (point A in Figure 10-27).

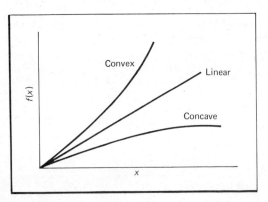

Figure 10-26 Functions of a single variable.

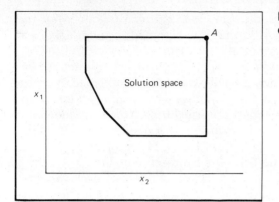

Figure 10-27 Convex constraint set.

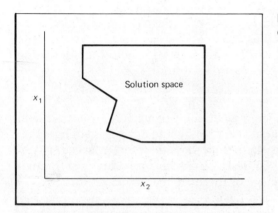

Figure 10-28 Concave constraint set.

The general statement of the linear programming problem is

Find the values of
$X_1, X_2, \ldots, X_n$
which minimize (maximize)
$Z = c_1 X_1 + c_2 X_2 + \cdots + c_n X_n$
subject to:
$X_j \geq 0, \quad j = 1, 2, \ldots, n$
and
$$a_{11} X_1 + a_{12} X_2 + \cdots + a_{1n} X_n = b_1$$
$$a_{21} X_1 + a_{22} X_2 + \cdots + a_{2n} X_n = b_2$$
$$\vdots \qquad \vdots \qquad \qquad \vdots \qquad \vdots$$
$$a_{m1} X_1 + a_{m2} X_2 + \cdots + a_{mn} X_n = b_m$$
where a_{ij}, b_i, c_j are given constants
$\qquad i = 1, 2, \ldots, m$
$\qquad j = 1, 2, \ldots, n$

Once the problem is formulated in this fashion it can be coded for the computer and run. If the algorithm used is designed to minimize, then maximization may be achieved simply by changing the signs in the OBJ, that is, minimizing a function $f(X_1, X_2, \ldots, X_n)$ subject to a set of constraints is equivalent to maximizing $-f(X_1, X_2, \ldots, X_n)$ subject to the same considerations. Note also that the constraint set written above as equalities is formed by converting inequalities into equalities by the introduction of special slack variables. This transformation is made automatically by the commercial linear programming (LP) packages. Thus a statement of the form $aX_1 + bX_2 \leq R$ can be converted into an equality of the form $aX_1 + bX_2 + S_1 = R$, where S_1 is a slack variable. These slack variables represent the distance to a constraint. For detailed information on the intricacies of the LP model see references 1, 73, and 74.

Linear programming is a powerful tool, and where it can be applied, many insights into water management strategies can be obtained. The large commercial systems such as IBM's MPSX can handle thousands of constraints and many variables. They are thus well suited to addressing problems related to large water resources systems (74).

LINEAR SYSTEMS ANALYSIS

Since about 1960, there has been a great flurry of activity associated with the use of optimization techniques (especially linear programming) (1, 2, 71–87). The analyses recorded range from those targeted to large regional systems to the study of so-called best designs for individual water treatment processes. A good summary of these is given by Greenberg (73).

Linear programming models have been designed to maximize the energy output from a series of reservoirs, develop reservoir operating rules, determine reservoir capacities that minimize dam size while providing anticipated water requirements, determine the cost-effectiveness of taking water from alternative sources, select least-cost water transmission systems, site and size new or expanded facilities for various water management purposes, estimate optimal values of hydrologic parameters, allocate the assimilative capacity of streams for handling oxygen-demanding wastes, determine optimal waste load allocations for streams, and select the most efficient systems for irrigation. It must be recognized, however, that even though LP has wide potential for use by water managers, it is still limited in many cases by the availability of good data for determining parameters, the occasional inability of investigators to identify appropriate cost and/or benefit functions properly, and the difficulty in all efforts to estimate future levels of water use and other variables that serve as model inputs. Still, if wisely used, LP can provide great insights into a system's performance and can be an effective tool for identifying those features of a model that need strengthening and for spotlighting coefficients that must be accurately quantified if the model is to produce meaningful results.

Some specific applications of LP to water resources problems follow. They are intended to acquaint the reader with the technique and to illustrate the general approach to problem structuring for this optimization method.

Example 10-3

A city has the ability to draw water from two streams and one well field (Figure 10-29). It is proposed to determine what mix of sources of supply would provide for the city's demands (water requirements) at minimum cost.

Numerical values for flows and coefficients are not given in this example. The problem is to formulate the LP model. Consider that all flows and the city's demand are in units of mgd and that all cost coefficients are given as $/MG. The following data are assumed to be given.

The period of operation of the model is one year divided into four seasons (I), season 1-spring, season 2-summer, season 3-fall, and season 4-winter. The seasonal cost coefficients for the two water treatment plants, TP1 and TP2, are CT1 (I) and CT2(I) respectively. The cost coefficient for delivering water from the well field is CP(I), and since we shall consider

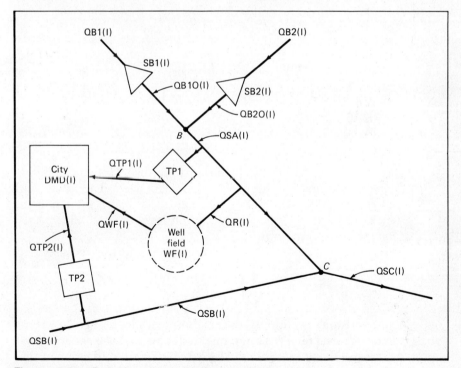

Figure 10-29 Definition sketch for Example 10-3.

that the well field requires recharge, the added cost of this will be reflected by the coefficient CR(I). It is assumed that both reservoirs must be full at the beginning of season 2 and that the groundwater reservoir will also be full at this time. The groundwater reservoir must also be recharged by the end of season 1. The amount of artificial recharge required for this purpose is designated as QR(I). The city's water requirements are DMD(I) and the number of days in each season is TDAS(I). Assume also that stream flow QSA(I) cannot exceed QSAMAX and that QSC(I) cannot fall below QSCMIN. Further conditions are maximum treatment plant capacities— TP1MAX and TP2MAX, maximum groundwater storage WFMAX, and maximum reservoir capacities QB1MAX and QB2MAX. The following seasonal flows are given: QB1(I), QB2(I), and QSB(I). To simplify the problem we shall assume that the water processed by the two treatment plants QTP1(I) and QTP2(I) finds its way back into the streams undiminished in quantity and that the consumptive use by the city is represented by the amount of water drawn from the well field.

SOLUTION

1. The first step is to develop the OBJ. In this case we have been asked to minimize the cost of providing the city's water requirement in each of four seasons. The OBJ will thus be the sum of products of costs/MG and water deliveries from the various sources in MG. Since the seasons range from 1 to 4, we can write the following:

$$
\begin{aligned}
\text{OBJ} = \text{minimum of} \sum_{I=1}^{I=4} &[\text{CT1(I)}*\text{QTP1(I)}*(\text{TDAS(I)} \\
&+ \text{CT2(I)}*\text{QTP2(I)}*\text{TDAS(I)} + \text{CP(I)}*\text{QWF(I)}*\text{TDAS(I)} \\
&+ \text{CR(I)}*\text{QR(I)}*\text{TDAS(I)}]
\end{aligned}
$$

   where the flows in mgd must be multiplied by the number of days in the season to convert to MG.

2. Having developed our OBJ, the next step is to set forth the required constraints. In this problem the data needed are given and they reflect physical limitations of facilities and sources and policies such as requiring a specified minimum level of streamflow.

3. *Constraints at Stream Junctions*
   The continuity of flows must be preserved and this requirement necessitates the following constraints:

$$\text{QSA(I)} - \text{QR(I)} + \text{QSB(I)} - \text{QSC(I)} = 0 \qquad I = 1\text{-}4$$

   This constraint represents an accounting at junction *C*. Note that the withdrawal for TP1 is not included since we have assumed that it is returned undiminished to the stream. The second junction that must be dealt with is *B*. The appropriate equation is

$$QB1O(I) + QB2O(I) - QSA(I) = 0 \qquad I = 1\text{--}4$$

Note that the above equations must actually be written for each season $I = 1\text{--}4$ and thus they represent a total of 8 constraint equations that would be included in the model.

4. *Constraints on Treatment Plant Capacities*
   Since the treatment facilities have limitations on the quantities of water they can treat, we must reflect this in the constraint set:

$QTP1(I) \leq TP1MAX$	$I = 1\text{--}4$
$QTP2(I) \leq TP2MAX$	$I = 1\text{--}4$
$QTP2(I) \leq QSB(I)$	$I = 1\text{--}4$
$QR(I) \leq QSA(I)$	$I = 1\text{--}4$

5. *Constraints on Meeting the City's Water Requirements*
   Since the objective is to see that the city is adequately supplied with water we must recognize this in the model:

   $$QTP2(I) + QTP1(I) + QWF(I) \geq DMD(I) \qquad I = 1\text{--}4$$

6. *Constraints Reflecting Flow Policies*

$QSA(I) \leq QSAMAX$	$I = 1\text{--}4$
$QSC(I) \geq QSCMIN$	$I = 1\text{--}4$

   These conditions were given in the problem statement. The second equation might reflect an instream flow policy for protecting fisheries, for example.

7. *Constraints on Reservoir Storage*
   Just as we did earlier for the junctions, we must consider the operation of the reservoirs such that continuity is preserved. This is done as follows using the data given in the problem and writing the continuity equation for each season:

$SB1(I) = QB1MAX$	$I = 1$
$SB2(I) = QB2MAX$	$I = 1$
$SB1(I) \leq QB1MAX$	$I = 2\text{--}4$
$SB2(I) \leq QB2MAX$	$I = 2\text{--}4$
$SB1(I) - SB1(I-1) - QB1(I)*TDAS(I)$ $+ QB1O(I)*TDAS(I) = 0$	$I = 2\text{--}4$
$SB1(1) - SB1(4) - QB1(I)*TDAS(I)$ $+ QB1O(I)*TDAS(I) = 0$	$I = 1$
$SB2(I) - SB2(I-1) - QB2(I)*TDAS(I)$ $+ QB2O(I)*TDAS(I) = 0$	$I = 2\text{--}4$
$SB2(1) - SB2(4) - QB2(I)*TDAS(I)$ $+ QB2O(I)*TDAS(I) = 0$	$I = 1$

   The first two equations simply specify that the reservoir storages must be full in season 1 as specified in the problem statement. The next two equations state that the storages cannot be permitted to exceed the maximum capacity of the reservoirs. Equations 5 through 8 are the continuity equations written in subscripted form. In all there are 16 equations.

8. *Constraints on the Groundwater System*

Finally, we must also consider limitations on the use of the well field. These conditions are reflected in the following constraint set:

$$WF(I) = WFMAX \qquad\qquad I = 1$$
$$WF(I) \le WFMAX \qquad\qquad I = 2\text{--}4$$
$$WF(I) - WF(I-1) - QR(I)*TDAS(I)$$
$$+ QWF(I)*TDAS(I) = 0 \qquad I = 2\text{--}4$$
$$WF(1) - WF(4) - QR(I)*TDAS(I)$$
$$+ QWF(I)*TDAS(I) = 0 \qquad I = 1$$

If we had been given numerical values for the various coefficients and streamflows, we could then code the data for solution by LP. The model development here should serve, however, to acquaint the reader with the nature of problem formulation for solution by LP techniques. In the final analysis, it is the ability to properly formulate a problem and quantify the needed parameters that determines the value of the model. Since the solution technique is standard, model formulation and output interpretation are really the key elements in using LP where it can be applied. ∎

Example 10-4

A large farming operation in the western United States has three tracts that can be used for two-season crop production. The total output of the farming operation is limited by the amount of water and land available. Three crops may be grown in any combination on the land available for farming. Crop x may be grown in season 1 only, and federal regulations require that the acreage not exceed 1500. Using the land, water, and pricing data given below, find the two-season crop-acreage allocation that maximizes profit for the farm.

Tracts 1, 2, and 3 include 480, 960, and 780 acres respectively. The water available in each season for irrigation use is 7 acre-ft/acre, 8 acre-ft/acre, and unlimited for tracts 1, 2, and 3 respectively. The three crop types are x, y, and z. The crop water requirements for these are 4.5, 3.0, and 3.5 acre-ft/acre respectively. Finally, the profit per acre that can be expected from crops x, y, and z is \$430, \$340, and \$380 in that order.

SOLUTION

1. The first requirement is to formulate the OBJ. It has been specified that we are to maximize profit. The OBJ will therefore be written

in terms of the profit to be obtained from each crop planted on the three tracts over the two seasons. Thus we can write

$$
\begin{aligned}
\text{OBJ} = \text{maximize} \; [& (\text{A1X1} + \text{A2X1} + \text{A3X1})*430 \\
& + (\text{A1Y1} + \text{A1Y2} + \text{A2Y1} + \text{A2Y2} + \text{A3Y1} \\
& + \text{A3Y2})*340 + (\text{A1Z1} + \text{A1Z2} + \text{A2Z1} + \text{A2Z2} \\
& + \text{A3Z1} + \text{A3Z2})*380]
\end{aligned}
$$

where A1X1 = acres of land for crop x at tract 1, season 1

A1Y1 = " " " " crop y at tract 1, season 1
A2Y1 = " " " " crop y at tract 2, season 1
A2Y2 = " " " " crop y at tract 2, season 2

etc.

2. The constraints reflect limitations relative to land, water, and regulation. The constraints on water are

WATR1: 4.5(A1X1) + 3.0(A1Y1 + A1Y2) + 3.5(A1Z1 + A1Z2) $\leq$ 3360
WATR2: 4.5(A2X1) + 3.0(A2Y1 + A2Y2) + 3.5(A2Z1 + A2Z2) $\leq$ 7680
WATR3: 4.5(A3X1) + 3.0(A3Y1 + A3Y2) + 3.5(A3Z1 + A3Z2) $\geq$ 0

Note that since crop x can only be grown in season 1, it appears only once in the first term of the above equations. Furthermore, since the algorithm we shall use ensures nonnegativity, we do not really need the third equation. These equations ensure that the amount of water available is not exceeded in the solution. The right-hand sides of the equations are gotten by multiplying the number of acres in a tract by the amount of water available. For example, equation WATR1 refers to tract 1 and the product of seven acre-ft/acre, and the tract size of 480 acres gives 3360 acre-ft as the maximum amount of water that can be allocated to that tract in each season. The fact that there is no limit to water supply for tract 3 is unreal in the physical sense, but in terms of the quantities that could be used on the tract, it indicates that no problem would be anticipated at this level of supply. The above constraints represent the amount of water used for each crop on each tract for the two seasons and they ensure that water availability is not violated.

3. Next we must develop the constraints on land. These will ensure that we are not attempting to irrigate more land than is available. They take the following form:

LND1A: A1X1 + A1Y1 + A1Z1 $\leq$ 480
LND1B: A1Y2 + A1Z2 $\leq$ 480
LND2A: A2X1 + A2Y1 + A2Z1 $\leq$ 960
LND2B: A2Y2 + A2Z2 $\leq$ 960

LND3A: $A3X1 + A3Y1 + A3Z1 \leq 780$
LND2B: $A3Y2 + A3Z2 \leq 780$

The first equation states, for example, that the acreages allotted to crops x, y, and z in season 1 on tract 1 must not exceed the size of the tract.

4. Our final constraint reflects the federal regulatory policy regarding crop x. It states that the acreage allocated to crop x on all three tracts must not exceed 1500 acres.

REG1: $A1X1 + A2X1 + A3X1 \leq 1500$

Note that we have named all the equations written in the model (REG1, for example). This is done because to use any of the packaged programs it is necessary to name (identify) the equations constituting the model to be operated on. In this example we shall use a system called LP1 to solve for the optimal value of the OBJ (identified by the term PROFIT in the computer input). LP1 is a proprietary system developed by Cyberware Computer Systems Limited. Many other LP solution systems are also available, however.

For the problem formulated, the input to LP1 appears as follows:

MAXIMIZE
PROFIT: 430A1X1 + 430A2X1 + 430A3X1 + 340A1Y1 + 340A1Y2 + 340A2Y1 + 340A2Y2 + 340A3Y1 + 340A3Y2 + 380A1Z1 + 380A1Z2 + 380A2Z1 + 380A2Z2 + 380A3Z1 + 380A3Z2;
SUBJECT TO
WATR1: 4.5A1X1 + 3.0A1Y1 + 3.0A1Y2 + 3.5A1Z1 + 3.5A1Z2 <3360,
WATR2: 4.5A2X1 + 3.0A2Y1 + 3.0A2Y2 + 3.5A2Z1 + 3.5A2Z2 <7680,
LND1A: A1X1 + A1Y1 + A1Z1 < 480,
LND1B: A1Y2 + A1Z2 < 480,
LND2A: A2X1 + A2Y1 + A2Z1 < 960,
LND2B: A2Y2 + A2Z2 < 960,
LND3A: A3X1 + A3Y1 + A3Z1 < 780,
LND3B: A3Y2 + A3Z2 < 780,
REG1: A1X1 + A2X1 + A3X1 < 1500,
COMPUTE CROPX: A1X1 + A2X1 + A3X1,
CROPY: A1Y1 + A1Y2 + A2Y1 + A2Y2 + A3Y1 + A3Y2,
CROPZ: A1Z1 + A1Z2 + A2Z1 + A2Z2 + A3Z1 + A3Z2;

The solution to the problem as obtained by the computer is:

A2X1 = 720 acres, A1Z1 = 480 acres, A2Z2 = 960 acres, A3X1 = 780 acres, A1Z2 = 480 acres, A3Z2 = 780 acres, and A2Z1 = 240 acres. Over the two seasons it can be determined that crop x uses its full possible allocation of 1500 acres (all restricted to season 1) and crop z is planted on 2940 acres. There is no allocation of land to crop y, which is obviously less profitable than crops x or z.

Certainly we are interested in the result, but it should be pointed out here that additional analyses could be made relative to the example with very little effort using some special features of LP1. We could, for example, look at possible changes in crop prices, water availability, and other factors to see how such changes might affect the optimal solution. A more complete discussion of this topic will be given later. ■

NONLINEAR SYSTEMS ANALYSIS

Most students of water resources realize that it is hard to find natural systems or constructed systems for storing, conveying, and processing water that are truly linear. The question arises as to the utility of a tool such as LP for addressing such problems. Fortunately, it has been found that assumptions of linearity often serve as good approximations to nonlinear systems. The unit hydrograph, a linear model, has been widely used to good purpose for hydrologic calculations, for example. The difficulty is in determining under what conditions linear approximations may be safely made. There is no simple answer to this question, but where the problem is very complex and known to be highly nonlinear, then a nonlinear model may be the only hope for a solution. On the other hand, if certain conditions that we shall describe later can be met, the system may be converted to a form that allows the use of linear analytical techniques such as LP even though its elements are totally or partially nonlinear. Furthermore, if it can be established that the optimal solution to a nonlinear problem occurs within a narrowly defined range, then any linear approximation need be accurate only in the region of the solution. Because of the ease of use of LP and because many nonlinear problems can be formulated to take advantage of this powerful tool, it has found wide use in tackling certain types of nonlinear problems. Where linear approximations would clearly lead to erroneous conclusions, approaches such as dynamic programming (discussed later) may produce the desired results.

The LP model can be generalized to include nonlinear objective functions and/or constraints. The model takes the form:

Maximize (minimize) $f(X_1, X_2, \ldots, X_n)$ subject to the conditions

$$g_i(X_1, X_2, \ldots, X_n) \leq b_i \quad \text{for } i = 1, 2, \ldots, m \quad \text{and} \quad X_j \geq 0$$
$$\text{for } j = 1, 2, \ldots, n \tag{10-34}$$

where $f(X_1, X_2,. . ., X_n)$ and $g(X_1, X_2,. . ., X_n)$ may be both nonlinear or one or the other may be nonlinear (71). Note that the form given above (Equation 10-34) is identical to that described by the general LP model (Equation 10-33).

There are a number of underlying assumptions that must be met in complying with an LP model (71). One of these is that the variables be additive. That is to say, the cost of producing some nth unit of a variable X_j would be the same as the cost of producing any other unit of X_j. It is in this additivity that the fundamental difference between linear and nonlinear programming lies. In a nonlinear programming model it is recognized that the cost of producing the nth unit might be more or less than the cost of producing some other unit.

The properties of convexity and concavity have already been referred to, but because they are so important in the nonlinear situation, further amplification is needed. These properties are very influential in determining whether an optimal solution is global or local in nature.

In general, if the constraint set is convex and the OBJ is also convex and if the objective is to minimize, then a global optimum can be expected. Conversely, if the OBJ is concave and the objective is to minimize, then a nonlinear programming model might lead to a local optimum (71). If, however, the objective is to maximize, then the reverse is true. In this case a concave OBJ maximized over a convex constraint set would likely lead to global optimum, whereas a convex OBJ could yield only a local optimum. Regardless of the nature of the OBJ, concavity in the constraint set will probably produce problems. In formulating a nonlinear programming problem, it is thus important to determine the properties of convexity or concavity of the OBJ and the constraints. In some cases, this might not be possible, and caution should be exercised.

A particularly useful technique for addressing nonlinear programming problems is separable programming (1, 71). It arises from the requirement that all nonlinear functions in a problem that are not already functions of single variables be separated into sums and differences of nonlinear functions of single variables. Thus if the OBJ can be written in the form

$$f_1(X_1) + f_2(X_2) + \cdots + f_n(X_n) \tag{10-35}$$

where each $f_j(X_j)$ is a specific function of that X_j only, then the function is separable. Application of separable programming requires that a nonlinear function of a single variable be approximated by some composite linear function. The manner in which this piecewise linear approximation can be accomplished is illustrated in Figure 10-30.

The approximation method described here is sometimes called the bounded variable method (71). The first step is to redefine the variable (x in this case) by using a series of approximations to the nonlinear function. As shown in the figure, we can replace x by the following relation:

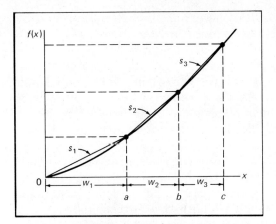

Figure 10-30 Piecewise approximation of a convex function.

$$x = w_1 + w_2 + w_3 \tag{10-36}$$

After this approximation has been made, the value of x in each constraint in which it is included must be replaced by the right-hand side of Equation 10-36. In like fashion the function $f(x)$ must be redefined as

$$f(x) = s_1 w_1 + s_2 w_2 + s_3 w_3 \tag{10-37}$$

where the s_j are the slopes of the linear segments. A further requirement of the method is that we bind each w_i within its applicable range. This may be done by adding a new constraint for each of the w_i terms. For the situation illustrated in the figure, three constraints would be required. They would take the form

$$
\begin{aligned}
w_1 &\leq a \\
w_2 &\leq (b-a) \\
w_3 &\leq (c-b)
\end{aligned} \tag{10-38}
$$

where a, b, and c are as indicated on the figure.

The value of separable programming lies in the fact that (a) it permits the Simplex procedure to be used and (b) it permits fairly easy conversion of nonlinear functions into linearized forms. Most proprietary LP packages include a separable programming function. It should be obvious from the foregoing discussion that in linearizing a problem, dimensionality may be increased significantly. Because of this it is sometimes useful to start with a rather coarse approximation to get some notion of the optimal region. Then a new linearization, having finer detail in what is believed to be the optimal region, can be made. The model is then rerun and further refinements can be made if it is found to be necessary.

Some of the concepts of applying LP to nonlinear problems can be illustrated by the following example of a water quality model designed to deal with the assimilative capacity of a river system. The problem discussed follows the reasoning of ReVelle et al., although it incorporates a nonlinear component that was not included in their original analysis (75).

One approach to water quality management is to develop stream standards that specify the quality of water that will be permitted in a stream or a segment of a stream. This was the original approach taken in the United States, although it has been replaced by technology-based standards (standards generally requiring the same level of treatment everywhere). Experience with the latter approach has indicated many inefficiencies and high costs.

As a result, there is a rethinking of the approach, and the notion of stream standards is again being considered. The analysis suggested here would be appropriate in guiding decisions about developing waste treatment facilities for compliance with established stream standards.

The linear programming formulation presented is based on the oxygen-sag equation. The problem is to determine the degree of treatment that would be required at a series of wastewater treatment plants discharging into a stream in order to minimize the cost of treatment and at the same time ensure that a specified dissolved oxygen (DO) level is maintained in the stream. The treatment requirement will be measured in terms of percent biological oxygen demand (BOD) removal. We shall explore a method for determining the combination of treatment plant efficiencies that will meet our standard.

Refer to Figure 10-31 for the configuration of the system we shall be dealing with. Note that there are two communities discharging wastes from their treatment works into the stream. We shall assume we are given a minimum level of DO that is acceptable in the stream. The question is the degree of treatment required to do this at least cost. Note that the approach outlined would work just as well for more than two communities, but to minimize the repetitiveness of the formulations, we shall deal only with two. Since we shall be concerned with costs, it will be necessary to know how many dollars must be spent to achieve a certain level of plant efficiency. This type of data would be derived from engineering firms that have studied waste treatment plant designs and the costs of constructing them. Figure 10-32 shows a typical cost function. Note that the function

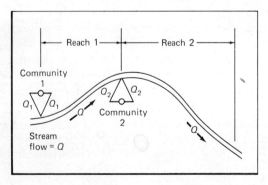

Figure 10-31 Hypothetical river system.

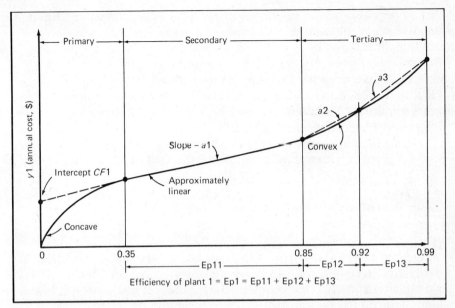

Figure 10-32 Typical cost function.

is quite nonlinear and in fact has both concave and convex portions. Since the objective function in this case will consist of the cost functions of the various treatment plants, and since that portion of the cost curve to the right of an efficiency of 35 percent is convex, our previous discussions of convexity and concavity lead us to believe that if the constraint set is convex and if we are minimizing, and if we deal only with this convex portion, we shall likely achieve a global optimum. Armed with this knowledge, and on the basis of some given conditions, we are ready to tackle the OBJ.

Let us assume that primary treatment is required at all locations by law. Even if this were not the case, we would probably want to provide it anyway. On the strength of this assumption we can rule out, by constraint, that portion of the cost curve which is concave (efficiency less than 35 percent). The remaining portion of the cost curve can be dealt with even though the portion to the right of an efficiency of 85 percent is nonlinear. Before we write that portion of the OBJ contributed by plant 1, some definitions are in order:

$Ep1$ = the efficiency of treatment plant 1; it is the percent removal of BOD divided by 100. Note also since we must linearize the cost curve, $Ep1$ is the sum of $Ep11$, $Ep12$, and $Ep13$, where the designations 11, 12, and 13 refer to plant 1, segment 1, and so on.

$y1$ = the annual cost of treatment for plant 1, in dollars.

$a1$ = the slope of segment 1, $a2$, and $a3$ are defined in similar fashion. The slopes are given in dollars/degree efficiency.

$CF1$ = the intercept of the cost curve. Since this is a fixed cost that will be required due to our commitment to at least primary treatment, it will not affect the solution and can be added to the optimal value of the solution after it has been obtained. It should be pointed out that even if the slope $(a1)$ projected back actually represented the cost function, we could not have dealt with the curve directly using the LP techniques we have reviewed. Such "setup" costs (involving an intercept greater than zero) require special treatment, which we shall not discuss here. For more information see references 1, 66, and 73.

Using the above definitions we can formulate the cost-efficiency function for plant 1. This will also be part of the OBJ.

$$y1 = (a1)(\text{Ep}11) + (a2)(\text{Ep}12) + (a3)(\text{Ep}13) + CF1 \qquad (10\text{-}39)$$

In similar fashion we can write for plant 2,

$$y2 = (b1)(\text{Ep}21) + (b2)(\text{Ep}22) + (b3)(\text{Ep}23) + CF2 \qquad (10\text{-}40)$$

where the bi are the slopes of the cost curve for plant 2. Note that for illustrative purposes, only three segments were used for each plant. Had we been setting up a real problem, the number of segments would have been determined by the shape of the curve and our concern about the desired closeness of the linear approximation.

The OBJ for our problem will be the sum of the two cost functions

$$\begin{aligned} \text{OBJ} &= \text{minimize } (y1 + y2) \quad \text{or} \qquad (10\text{-}41)\\ \text{OBJ} &= (a1)(\text{Ep}11) + (a2)(\text{Ep}12) + (a3)(\text{Ep}13)\\ &\quad + (b1)(\text{Ep}21) + (b2)(\text{Ep}22) + (b3)(\text{Ep}23)\\ &\quad + CF1 + CF2 \end{aligned}$$

Since the last two terms are not active in the solution they may be dropped in the model and their sum added to the least cost obtained from the OBJ without their inclusion. If the cost functions had been strictly linear, the OBJ would have consisted of only two terms (exclusive of $CF1$ and $CF2$) rather than six. If we had felt inclined to use more segments, the number of terms would have been even greater. Furthermore, we shall have to introduce some extra constraints due to our linearization.

Now that we have the OBJ, we must next formulate the appropriate constraints. First let us deal with the efficiency constraints. Since we require at least primary treatment, we must write for each plant:

$$\text{Ep}11 \geq 0.35 \qquad (10\text{-}42)$$
$$\text{Ep}21 \geq 0.35 \qquad (10\text{-}43)$$

Furthermore, because we have linearized the cost functions, we shall have to write bounds for each of the linear segments. These will take the form:

$$\text{Ep}11 \leq 0.85$$
$$\text{Ep}12 \leq 0.07$$
$$\text{Ep}13 \leq 0.07$$

$$Ep21 \leq 0.85 \qquad\qquad (10\text{-}44)$$
$$Ep22 \leq 0.07$$
$$Ep23 \leq 0.07$$

Except for the requirement that efficiency must exceed 35 percent, we do not need lower bounds on the other segments. This is because the increasing slope of the successive terms ensures that the next term will not enter the solution until the previous one has been extended to its limit. Obviously it is less expensive to remove BOD at $a1$ per unit than at $a2$. This illustrates another useful property of convexity. Note that the values 0.07 shown above are the intervals over which $Ep12$, $Ep13$, etc., are operative. For illustrative purposes, we have assumed that the break points in the linearization process for both plants are the same, but it should be recognized that this does not have to be the case.

In addition to the efficiency requirements, there are several other specifications that must be made. These additional requirements relate to the linkage between plant efficiency and BOD discharged, budgeting equations to account for wastes and oxygen at points of mixture in the stream, and water quality standards (75). The definition of efficiency serves to set the first type of additional constraint. The second type is basically a mass balancing of the form we have discussed many times. The third type of added constraint sets the allowable deficit in DO at any point in the stream (Figure 10-33).

• *Plant Efficiency–BOD Constraints.* Treatment plant efficiency is determined by the quantity of BOD removed divided by the amount originally introduced. For plant 1, it is given by

$$Ep1 = Ep11 + Ep12 + Ep13 = (P1 - M1)/P1 \qquad (10\text{-}45)$$

where $P1$ is the concentration of BOD entering the plant (mg/L) and $M1$ is the concentration of BOD leaving the plant (mg/L). The right-hand-

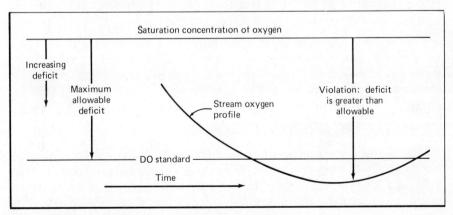

Figure 10-33   Definition of allowable deficit in DO.

side term can be written as $1 - (M1/P1)$. Making this transformation, inserting in 10-45 and moving all terms to the left-hand side except the numerical value of 1, we get

$$\text{Ep}11 + \text{Ep}12 + \text{Ep}13 + (M1/P1) = 1 \qquad (10\text{-}46)$$

For treatment plant 2 the constraint linking efficiency and BOD removal would be

$$\text{Ep}21 + \text{Ep}22 + \text{Ep}23 + (M2/P2) = 1 \qquad (10\text{-}47)$$

In these equations $P1$ or $P2$ is the concentration of BOD entering the plant (mg/L) and $M1$ or $M2$ is the concentration of BOD leaving the plant. Equations 10-46 and 10-47 are linear equations in the unknown plant efficiencies and effluent BOD.

• *Constraint on Deficit Inventory in Reach 1.* Before the deficit inventory constraints can be written, some additional definition is required:

$EO =$ the known oxygen deficit in the stream just above community 1 (mg/L).

$M1 =$ BOD concentration in the effluent of plant 1 (mg/L). This term was also defined previously for Equations 10-46 and 10-47.

$Q1 =$ the flow discharged by treatment plant 1 (mgd).

$T1 =$ the known deficit of the waste flow (mg/L).

$Q =$ the streamflow into reach 1 (mgd). This might be the seven-day, 10-year low flow for example.

$FO =$ known BOD concentration in the stream just upstream of community 1 (mg/L).

$L1 =$ BOD concentration in the stream just downstream of community 1 after mixing with the wastewater effluent (mg/L).

$D1 =$ the DO deficit in the stream at the beginning of reach 1 after mixing with the waste flow (mg/L).

By writing a mass balance at the beginning of reach 1, equations for $L1$ and $D1$ can be obtained. It is assumed that perfect mixing of the wastewater and streamflows occurs at the point of waste introduction. This assumption is not unrealistic for rapidly moving turbulent streams. By striking a mass balance on DO deficit at the beginning of reach 1 we get

$$EO(Q - Q1) + (T1)(Q1) = (D1)(Q) \qquad (10\text{-}48)$$

where the first term expresses the deficit in the stream just after the community withdraws $Q1$ and the second term expresses the deficit of the incoming waste stream. Note that we have assumed that the quantity of water withdrawn by the city is the same as the amount discharged. It would be easy to add a refinement to reflect consumptive use if this was desired. The right-hand-side term is the combined streamflow and waste flow deficit. Since we have stated that EO and $T1$ are known, we can solve Equation 10-48 for $D1$. It does not have to be written as a constraint in this case. Nevertheless, because the same type of relation will be needed at other waste discharge points and at these locations the terms will not all be known, we shall write it in the form in which it would generally appear in the constraint set:

$$(Q)(D1) - (Q - Q1)EO = (T1)(Q1) \tag{10-49}$$

where the right-hand side is known. This equation represents the inventory of deficit mixing at the beginning of reach 1.

• *BOD Inventory in Reach 1.* The BOD inventory is obtained in similar fashion to that for the DO deficit. It can be written as

$$(Q)(L1) - (Q1)(M1) - (Q - Q1)FO = 0 \tag{10-50}$$

where the equation simply states that the BOD in the stream before the introduction of the waste stream combined with the amount added by the waste flow must equal the BOD load just after the two flows mix.

• *Water Quality Constraints for Reach 1.* The final constraints needed relate to our water quality requirement. To construct these constraints we shall make use of the Streeter-Phelps model for DO sag (Equation 10-26). In this case we will change some of the variable names and write

$$D = \frac{k1}{(k2 - k1)} [(\exp - (k1)(t)) - (\exp - (k2)(t))]L1 \\ + [\exp - (k2)(t)]D1 \tag{10-51}$$

where exp represents the base of naperian logarithms (e) raised to some power. The term $\exp - (k1)(t)$ is thus equivalent to $e^{-(k1)(t)}$. The other terms are defined as follows:

$D =$ DO deficit at time t (mg/L)
$D1 =$ DO deficit at $t = 0$, just after mixing occurs at the beginning of the reach (mg/L)
$k2 =$ reaeration coefficient in the reach (days^{-1})
$k1 =$ bio-oxidation constant in the reach due to the waste stream from the plant (days^{-1})
$L1 =$ BOD at $t=0$, just after mixing occurs at the beginning of the reach (mg/L)
$t =$ time of flow in the reach

The DO deficit is constrained within the river reach so that it is not allowed to fall below a base level. To ensure that this requirement is met, it is necessary to evaluate the deficit at various locations along the stream so that the calculated values can be compared with the maximum allowable deficit. For more details on ways to select appropriate locations for testing, the reader should consult references 1 and 75. At the top of the reach we know that the deficit must be less than the maximum allowable:

$$D1 \leq DA \tag{10-52}$$

where DA is the maximum allowable deficit. For illustrative purposes we shall arbitrarily choose two points in the first reach. The first point will lie downstream of community 1 a time distance of $t1$; the second point will be at a time distance of $t2$. This second point will also be the beginning point of reach 2.

At point 1 in reach 1, we shall designate the deficit $D(t1)$. As before, this deficit must not exceed the maximum allowable, DA. Thus

$$D(t1) \leq DA \tag{10-53}$$

At the flow time $t1$, we shall define the coefficient of $L1$ in Equation 10-51 as

$$A1 = \frac{k1}{k2 - k1} \left[(\exp - (k1)(t1)) - (\exp - (k2)(t1)) \right] \tag{10-54}$$

Having done this, we may write an expression for the deficit at point 1. It will take the form

$$D(t1) = (A1)(L1) + [\exp - (k2)(t1)]D1 \tag{10-55}$$

Now if we substitute this expression in Equation 10-53, we obtain for the deficit constraint at point 1 the following:

$$D(t1) = (A1)(L1) + [\exp - (k2)(t1)]D1 \leq DA \tag{10-56}$$

Using the same line of reasoning and noting that at point 2 the time will be $t2$, we can define the coefficient of $L1$ at point 2 as $A2$. The deficit at point 2 must also be less than the maximum allowable (or equal to it) and thus we can write:

$$D(t2) = (A2)(L1) + [\exp - (k2)(t2)]D1 \leq DA \tag{10-57}$$

Now if we collect the terms in Equations 10-56 and 10-57 and rewrite the equations so that the right-hand sides include only the knowns, we get

$$(A1)(L1) + [\exp - (k2)(t1)]D1 \leq DA \tag{10-58}$$

and

$$(A2)(L1) + [\exp - (k2)(t2)]D1 \leq DA \tag{10-59}$$

Equations 10-58 and 10-59 are the constraints we are seeking. They are the oxygen-sag equations constrained to be less than or equal to the stream standard for the DO deficit we have set.

The constraint set for reach 1 is now complete. Next we shall proceed to develop similar equations for reach 2.

• *Deficit Inventory for Reach 2.* Terms similar to those used for reach 1 will be used to define the appropriate processes for reach 2. The following definitions will be used:

$E1 =$ the DO deficit at the end of reach 1
$T2 =$ the deficit from plant 2
$M2 =$ the BOD load from plant 2
$Q2 =$ the outflow from plant 2
$F1 =$ the BOD at the end of reach 1
$L2 =$ the BOD at the beginning of reach 2 after mixing with the plant effluent
$D2 =$ the DO deficit at the beginning of reach 2 after mixing

The units of these variables are all as given for reach 1.

It should be clear that the deficit $E1$ at the end of reach 1 is given by Equation 10-57. Thus $E1 = D(t2)$ for reach 1. We can therefore write:

$$E1 = (A2)(L1) + [\exp - (k2)(t2)]D1$$

or

$$E1 - (A2)(L1) - [\exp - (k2)(t2)]D1 = 0 \qquad (10\text{-}60)$$

Again using a mass balance to represent the deficit inventory in reach 2, we can write:

$$E1(Q - Q2) + (T2)(Q2) = (D2)Q$$

or

$$Q(D2) - (Q - Q2)E1 = (T2)(Q2) \qquad (10\text{-}61)$$

• *BOD Accounting in Reach 2.* Just as was done in reach 1, we must inventory the BOD in reach 2. The BOD decay that takes place in reach 1 can be expressed as

$$L = L1[\exp - (k1)(t)] \qquad (10\text{-}62)$$

where L is the BOD at time of flow t (mg/L). At the end of reach 1 we may calculate the remaining BOD loading in the following manner:

$$F1 = L1[\exp - (k1)(t2)]$$

or

$$F1 - [\exp - (k1)(t2)]L1 = 0 \qquad (10\text{-}63)$$

Note that the flow time is for reach 1 and so is the value of $k1$. Having determined $F1$, we can proceed to determine the mass balance as

$$(M2)(Q2) + F1(Q - Q2) = (L2)Q$$

or

$$Q(L2) - (Q2)(M2) - (Q - Q2)F1 = 0 \qquad \text{(10-64)}$$

The final step is to write the water quality constraints for reach 2.

• *Water Quality Constraints for Reach 2.* It will be assumed that the waste from plant 2 and the waste in the stream at the discharge point of plant 2 will be completely mixed. Furthermore, it will be assumed that the bio-oxidation rate in reach 2 can be approximated as the average of the rates of the two wastes. This assumption appears to be reasonable in many cases according to ReVelle et al. (75). The oxygen-sag equation for reach 2 is the same as that given for reach 1 (Equation 10-51) except that $L2$ and $D2$ are substituted for $L1$ and $D1$. Furthermore, although the reaeration coefficient and bio-oxidation rate constant are not subscripted by reach in our development, it should be noted that in an actual situation, these parameters would be expected to vary by reach. Flow times used in the sag equation are for the reach being studied also.

Following the same approach as before for reach 1, it is clear that $D2$, the deficit at the beginning of reach 2, must not violate the standard. Thus

$$D2 \leq DA \qquad \text{(10-65)}$$

As in the case of reach 1 we shall also consider two other points for evaluating the deficit. One of these will be along the reach and the other at its end. The appropriate deficit constraints are

$$(B1)(L2) + [\exp - (k2)(t1)]D2 \leq DA \qquad \text{(10-66)}$$

and

$$(B2)(L2) + [\exp - (k2)(t2)] D2 \leq DA \qquad \text{(10-67)}$$

where the coefficients $B1$ and $B2$ are derived in the same manner as $A1$ and $A2$ for reach 1. This completes the constraint set. Note that all of the equations are linear.

If we had wanted to consider further reaches of the stream, we could have done so in the same manner demonstrated. Summarizing the constraints that have been developed, we see that there are equations representing the piecewise linear approximations used for the cost functions, equations defining plant efficiency in terms of BOD loading in the plant effluent, inventory (mass balance) equations relating inputs and outputs at load points, and constraints on water quality imposed by the restriction that the DO deficit could not exceed a maximum prescribed value. The OBJ was designed to meet the water quality standard in the least-cost manner.

The OBJ and the constraints are summarized below.

OBJECTIVE FUNCTION

Minimize: $(a1)(\text{Ep}11) + (a2)(\text{Ep}12) + (a3)(\text{EP}13) + (b1)(\text{Ep}21) + (b2)(\text{Ep}22) + (b3)(\text{Ep}23)$ subject to the following constraints:

CONSTRAINTS ON LINEAR SEGMENTS

$\text{Ep}11 \geq 0.35$	$\text{Ep}13 \leq 0.07$
$\text{Ep}21 \geq 0.35$	$\text{Ep}21 \leq 0.85$
$\text{Ep}11 \leq 0.85$	$\text{Ep}22 \leq 0.07$
$\text{Ep}12 \leq 0.07$	$\text{Ep}23 \leq 0.07$

CONSTRAINTS DEFINING EFFICIENCIES

$$\text{Ep}11 + \text{Ep}12 + \text{Ep}13 + (M1/P1) = 1$$
$$\text{Ep}21 + \text{Ep}22 + \text{Ep}23 + (M2/P2) = 1$$

INVENTORY AT THE START OF REACH 1

$$Q(D1) - (Q - Q1)EO = (T1)(Q1)$$
$$Q(L1) - (Q1)(M1) - (Q - Q1)FO = 0$$

WATER QUALITY CONSTRAINTS FOR REACH 1

$$D1 \leq DA$$
$$(A1)(L1) + [\exp -(k2)(t1)]\,D1 \leq DA$$
$$(A2)(L1) + [\exp -(k2)(t2)]D1 \leq DA$$

INVENTORY AT START OF REACH 2

$$E1 - (A2)(L1) - [\exp -(k2)(t2)]DI = 0$$
$$Q(D2) - (Q - Q2)E1 = (T2)(Q2)$$
$$F1 - [\exp -(k1)(t2)]L1 = 0$$
$$Q(L2) - (Q2)(M2) - (Q - Q2)F1 = 0$$

WATER QUALITY CONSTRAINTS FOR REACH 2

$$D2 \leq DA$$
$$(B1)(L2) + [\exp -(k2)(t1)]D2 \leq DA$$
$$(B2)(L2) + [\exp -(k2)(t2)]D2 \leq DA$$

The foregoing problem formulation should serve to acquaint the reader with the way a problem can be organized for separable programming. It should also serve to further illustrate how models might be used to facilitate decisions about facilities requirements and water management in general.

SENSITIVITY ANALYSIS

Before leaving the subject of LP, some discussion of sensitivity analysis seems in order. Often it is the opportunity to explore sensitivities of problem solutions to changes in parameters that is of the greatest value to decision makers. Rarely are the parameters of a programming model known with certainty. Furthermore, even though values might be assigned to them that are considered appropriate today, they may change significantly with time (interest rates, rate of inflation, and so on). Thus the analyst is often concerned with exploring how the coefficients in the OBJ, the right-hand-side values of the constraint set, and/or the coefficients in the constraints themselves influence the policies generated by a model.

The approach taken is known as sensitivity analysis. This can be accomplished by varying the magnitude of various model parameters to see how they affect the system's performance. The procedure provides insights into targeting those parameters to which the system is the most sensitive. When this has been done, it can be determined whether better definition is needed and how it should be obtained. All major LP computing systems have provisions for conducting a variety of sensitivity analyses.

Example 10-5

Given the data in Table 10-4 and the schematic diagram and cost data of Figure 10-34, find the minimum cost of treatment to comply with a DO deficit maximum allowable figure of 4.5 mg/L. Also plot a curve of DO v. time as determined by the model.

SOLUTION

1. With the exception of the third treatment plant, this problem follows the discussion just presented. First, the OBJ must be formulated. This will be done using the cost curves given in Figure 10-34. For the sake of simplicity, we shall assume that the cost functions can be divided into three segments each. The segments and their limits are shown on the figure. Once the segments have been decided on, their slopes must be estimated. These values are recorded on the figure also. We are going to make the assumption that primary treatment will be required (efficiency $= 0.35$). This eliminates the concave portion of the cost functions and allows us to proceed with a separable programming approach dealing only with convex functions. Using the notation previously described, we may write the cost function as: Minimize $(s11)(Ep11) + (s12)(Ep12) + (s13)(Ep13) + (s21)(Ep21) + (s22)(Ep22) + (s23)(Ep23) + (s31)(Ep31) + (s32)(Ep32) + (s33)(Ep33) + (CF1 + CF2 + CF3)$ where $Ep11$ is the efficiency associated with segment 1 of the

Table 10-4 DATA FOR EXAMPLE 10-5

PARAMETER	VALUE		
	Reach 1	*Reach 2*	*Reach 3*
Bio-oxidation constant (days^{-1})	$k11 = 0.31$	$k12 = 0.27$	$k13 = 0.28$
Reaeration constant (days^{-1})	$k21 = 0.39$	$k22 = 0.44$	$k23 = 0.63$
Flow time for half reach (days)	$t11 = 0.50$	$t12 = 1.10$	$t13 = 0.70$
Flow time for reach (days)	$t21 = 1.00$	$t22 = 2.20$	$t23 = 1.40$
Treatment plant discharge (mgd)	$Q1 = 40$	$Q2 = 35$	$Q3 = 16$
BOD concentration entering the plant (mg/L)	$P1 = 275$	$P2 = 390$	$P3 = 160$
Deficit of plant discharge (mg/L)	$T1 = 7$	$T2 = 7$	$T3 = 7$
Streamflow	420 mgd $= QS$		
Deficit above reach 1	0.50 mg/L $= EO$		
BOD above reach 1	1.00 mg/L $= FO$		
Allowable DO deficit	4.5 mg/L $= DA$		
Saturation concentration of oxygen	8.2 mg/L $= CS$		

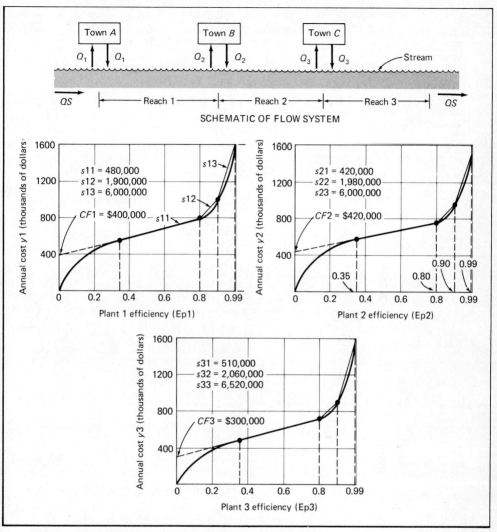

Figure 10-34 Diagram and cost data for example 10-5.

cost function for plant 1. The slope of this segment is denoted as $s11$ (Figure 10-34). Since the summation of the three intercepts does not affect the solution to the problem, we shall remove these terms from our OBJ and simply add them to the least cost found in the linear programming run:

$$(CF1 + CF2 + CF3) = 400,000 + 420,000 + 300,000 = \$1,120,000$$

Inserting the appropriate coefficients (sii terms) in the OBJ we get

$$4.8 \times 10^5 \ (\text{Ep11}) + 19 \times 10^5 \ (\text{Ep12}) + 60 \times 10^5 \ (\text{Ep13}) +$$
$$4.2 \times 10^5 \ (\text{Ep21}) + 19.8 \times 10^5 \ (\text{Ep22}) + 60 \times 10^5 \ (\text{Ep23}) +$$
$$5.1 \times 10^5 \ (\text{Ep31}) + 20.6 \times 10^5 \ (\text{Ep32}) + 65.2 \times 10^5 \ (\text{Ep33})$$

where the numerical values are the cost coefficients. The OBJ is thus ready to be entered into our computer program.

2. The next step is to use the given data and formulate the constraint set. This is done in a manner similar to that just described for the OBJ. The result is the LP1 formulation for the computer shown below.

1	MINIMIZE COST:	480000EP11 + 1900000EP12 + 6000000EP13 +
2		420000EP21 + 1980000EP22 + 6000000EP23 +
3		510000EP31 + 2060000EP32 + 6520000EP33;
4	SUBJECT TO C1:	EP11 GE 0.35,
5	C2:	EP21 GE 0.35,
6	C3:	EP31 GE 0.35,
7	C4:	EP11 LE 0.80,
8	C5:	EP21 LE 0.80,
9	C6:	EP31 LE 0.80,
10	C7:	EP12 LE 0.10,
11	C8:	EP13 LE 0.09,
12	C9:	EP22 LE 0.10,
13	C10:	EP23 LE 0.09,
14	C11:	EP32 LE 0.10,
15	C12:	EP33 LE 0.09,
16	C13:	0.0036M1 + EP11 + EP12 + EP13 = 1.0,
17	C14:	0.0025M2 + EP21 + EP22 + EP23 = 1.0,
18	C15:	0.0062M3 + EP31 + EP32 + EP33 = 1.0,
19	C16:	420L1 − 40 M1 = 380,
20	C17:	D2 LE 4.5,
21	C18:	D3 LE 4.5,
22	C19:	0.124L1 LE 3.58,
23	C20:	0.217L1 LE 3.74,
24	C21:	0.202L2 + 0.615D2 LE 4.5,
25	C22:	0.280L2 + 0.380D2 LE 4.5,
26	C23:	0.142L3 + 0.644D3 LE 4.5,
27	C24:	0.208L3 + 0.414D3 LE 4.5,
28	C25:	E1 − 0.217L1 = .758,
29	C26:	420D2 − 385E1 = 245,

30	C27: $F1 - 0.733L1 = 0,$
31	C28: $420L2 - 35M2 - 385F1 = 0,$
32	C29: $E2 - 0.280L2 - 0.380D2 = 0,$
33	C30: $420D3 - 404E2 = 112,$
34	C31: $F2 - 0.556L2 = 0,$
35	C32: $420L3 - 16M3 - 404F2 = 0;$

The problem was run for an allowable deficit of 4.5 mg/L, as stated in the problem. Subsequently, it was also run for $DA = 4.0$, 3.5, 3.0, 2.5, 2.0, and 1.5. The results of these runs are tabulated in Table 10-5. A plot of the oxygen-sag curve for $DA = 4.5$ is shown in Figure 10-35.

Table 10-5 shows that as the water quality standard gets more stringent (DA decreases), the cost of treatment rises accordingly as does the degree of treatment. It can be seen that for DA values greater than about 3.5, primary and secondary treatment combinations suffice (assuming that tertiary treatment begins when efficiency is equal to or greater than 90 percent). Once the DA standard drops below 3.0, it becomes necessary to implement tertiary treatment at one or more of the plants.

Obviously the range of data presented in the table for several values of the water quality standard is of much greater value for decision making than the single set for $DA = 4.5$ would be alone. It is such use of programming models to evaluate solutions for varying circumstances that makes them so useful.

The oxygen-sag curve for $DA = 4.5$ is plotted to demonstrate what happens between the points of computation used in the model. If the time points had been too widely spaced, it would have been possible for the maximum deficit to be violated between check points even though the model constrained it at its maximum allowable at any determining location. In such a case, the time spacing would have had to be shortened and the model rerun.

This example demonstrated the formulation of a separable programming problem. It also demonstrated the way in which optimization models might be used to guide decisions about the capacities of treatment plants or other facilities. Other parameters could also be selected for analysis to determine how their variance might affect the solution obtained with the model. ■

A further example of how LP can be used to aid in decision making may be had by referring to Figure 10-36. Using the model just discussed, Welty showed that correlations among the cost of providing waste treatment, low-flow period and its frequency of occurrence, and a water quality standard such as DA could be developed and displayed in a manner easy to interpret by those concerned about regulation and its costs but not technically qualified to make such analyses. For example, it can be seen

Table 10-5 OPTIMAL VALUES OF TREATMENT PLANT EFFICIENCIES FOR VARIOUS MAXIMUM ALLOWABLE DISSOLVED OXYGEN STANDARDS (EXAMPLE 10-5)

Measure	DISSOLVED OXYGEN DEFICIT, DA (mg/L)						
	$DA = 4.5$	$DA = 4.0$	$DA = 3.5$	$DA = 3.0$	$DA = 2.5$	$DA = 2.0$[a]
Efficiency of plant 1 (%)	0.74	0.80	0.80	0.84	0.90	0.90
Efficiency of plant 2 (%)	0.80	0.81	0.87	0.90	0.90	0.96
Efficiency of plant 3 (%)	0.35	0.35	0.35	0.35	0.47	0.51
Cost of treatment[b]	8.699×10^5	9.208×10^5	1.031×10^6	1.163×10^6	1.367×10^6	1.723×10^6

[a] $DA = 2.0$ was the last increment of 0.5 mg/L for which a feasible solution could be obtained. At $DA = 1.5$ the problem was infeasible.
[b] To all costs, an additional 1.120×10^6 (the intercept value determined at the outset of the problem) would have to be added.

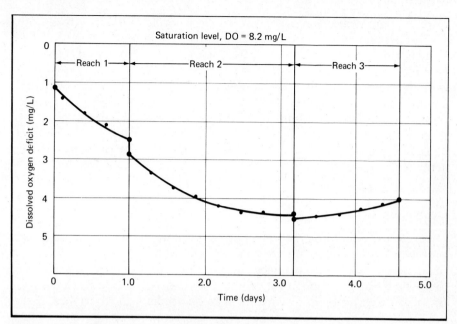

Figure 10-35   DO sag curve for DA less than or equal to 4.5 mg/L.

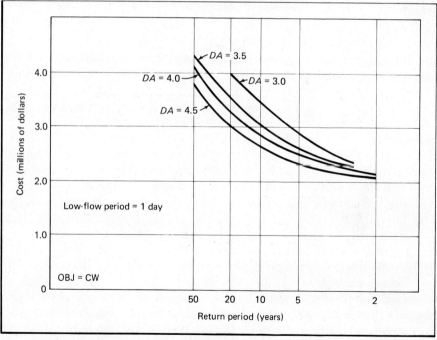

Figure 10-36   Cost v. DA v. return period curves for a prescribed low-flow period. (After Welty.)

from the figure that for a particular low-flow period of interest (three day, seven day, and so on) the costs of providing treatment needed to meet some standard such as $DA = 4.5$ decrease as the return period decreases. In addition it can be seen that for a given return period, the costs of providing treatment increase as the standard becomes more stringent (going from $DA = 4.5$ to $DA = 3.5$, for example). A little thought will make it clear that plots such as the one shown could be useful guides to those charged with setting standards, since they display the variation of costs and indicate the risks (return periods) associated with each course of action (87).

Dynamic Programming

Dynamic programming is a multistage or sequential process for analyzing problems. It is a systematic method for determining that combination of decisions made at various stages of a problem that produces a maximum (66). The method, although conceptually simple, requires individual structuring of each problem to which it is to be applied. Furthermore, there is no universal algorithm such as is the case for LP. Thus a program must be written to fit the exercise at hand. It has the advantage over LP of being able to handle any type of function, linear or nonlinear, and it can even accommodate discontinuities if they are present.

FEATURES OF DYNAMIC PROGRAMMING

In dynamic programming applications, the problem is transformed into a series of single-stage problems that are easy to solve. Problems with N decision variables are changed into N subproblems that have only one decision variable. This type of transformation can result in very significant savings in computational effort and can mean the difference between being able to solve a problem at all, or at great expense, and being able to solve it with little computer time (88). Since a standard mathematical formulation does not exist for dynamic programming (DP) the types of problems for which the method can be used to advantage must be understood by the analyst. Due to the limitations set by the scope of this book, only one rather elementary example of the procedure is provided. This should give the reader an idea of how the approach can be used.

There are several basic attributes of DP (66). These are that (1) the problem is divided into a series of stages, with a policy decision being required at each stage; (2) for each stage there may be any number of states associated with it; (3) the policy decision made at any given stage has the effect of changing the current state into a state associated with the next stage; and (4) given the present state, the optimal policy for the stages remaining does not depend on the policy adopted in prior stages. This is known as Bellman's principle of optimality (66).

The DP solution procedure begins with a determination of the optimal policy for each state of the last stage of the problem. A recursive equation of the form

$$f_n^*(s) = \min_{x_n} [c_{sx_n} + f_{n-1}^*(x_n)] \tag{10-68}$$

is used to march the solution backward, stage by stage, until the optimal policy associated with starting at the initial stage is found. In Equation 10-68, x_n is the decision variable, c_{sx_n} is the cost associated with moving from a state s in a given stage to another state in the next stage, $f_n^*(s)$ is the minimum value of the OBJ when starting in state s with n stages to go, and $f_{n-1}^*(x_n)$ is the optimal path through the $n-1$ remaining stages. The notation will be clarified in Example 10-6.

The stages in a DP problem may represent different points in space or they may represent occurrences in time such as an irrigation water delivery. The states associated with a particular stage in a given problem must be finite. These states describe possible conditions of the system at an associated stage. The amount of water stored in a reservoir might be likened to a state of the system, for example. A decision variable in this case might be how much water to release for some purpose. For a given release, the decision will transform the quantity of water in storage from the current amount (state) to a new amount for the next stage (point in time). These transformations of state are related to benefits or costs associated with their nature, and they are used as the basis for optimizing (where monetary measures are desired). The fact that DP can handle nonconvex as well as nonlinear OBJs and constraints makes it attractive for tackling the classes of problems for which it is well suited. Before discussing some of these applications, we shall work through a short exercise to reinforce and clarify what has been said.

Example 10-6

Consider the sketch and cost data given in Figure 10-37. Assume that the diagram represents possible waste treatment plant configurations for obtaining three successively higher levels of treatment. The influent enters on the left and can receive its first-stage processing in any of three appropriate units (states 2, 3, and 4). The second-stage processing can be accomplished by either of two units and the final process is represented by state 7. The cost data are given below the sketch. They may be interpreted as follows. Looking at the left-hand group of numbers, we can see that if we go from state 1 to state 3, the cost will be five cost units; going from state 1 to state 4 would cost four cost units. Moving to the center grouping we see that going from state 2 to state 6 would cost seven cost units and so on. The problem is to find the least-cost combination of treatment units representing each stage of treatment. The costs are then associated with going from one water quality stage to the next. The backward recursive

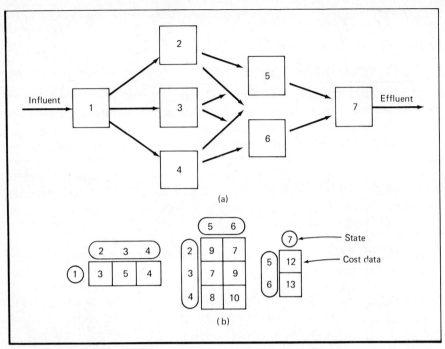

Figure 10-37 Sketch for Example 10-6: (a) waste treatment process; (b) cost data for processes.

equation of DP can be used to address this sequential decision problem as follows.

SOLUTION

1. Let us begin by considering the first stage of our problem as going from either state 5 or 6 to state 7. The procedure for this analysis is shown in Figure 10-38a. The table shows that if we are in state 5, for example, and go to state 7, the cost will be 12 units. The cost data appear in Figure 10-37. If, on the other hand, we are in state 6 and go to state 7, the cost will be 13 units. The table in part (a) of Figure 10-38 represents the solution to the first-stage problem. The left-hand column heading, s, gives the state that we are coming from in moving to the next state, which in this case is 7. The term $f_1^*(s)$ is the optimal (least cost) way of getting from state 5 or 6 to state 7. The final column heading x_1^* is the optimal destination (choice) associated with $f_1^*(s)$, which in this first-stage analysis can only be 7, irrespective of where we are coming from. What this table tells us is the following. If we were in the position of being able to choose a starting point of 5 or 6, the choice should clearly be 5 since the cost of getting from 5 to 7 (12 units) is less than that

s	$f_1^*(s)$	x_1^*
5	12	7
6	13	7

(a)

	$f_2(s, x_2) = c_s x_2 + f_1^*(x_2)$			
s	$x_2 = 5$	$x_2 = 6$	$f_2^*(s)$	x_2^*
2	9 + 12 = 21	7 + 13 = 20	20	6
3	7 + 12 = 19	9 + 13 = 22	19	5
4	8 + 12 = 20	10 + 13 = 23	20	5

(b)

	$f_3(s, x_3) = c_s x_3 + f_2^*(x_3)$				
s	$x_3 = 2$	$x_3 = 3$	$x_3 = 4$	$f_3^*(s)$	x_3^*
1	3 + 20 = 23	5 + 19 = 24	4 + 20 = 24	23	2

(c)

Figure 10-38 Tabular solution to Example 10-6: (a) solution to one-stage problem; (b) solution to two-stage problem; (c) solution to three-stage problem.

of getting from 6 to 7 (13 units). At this juncture it should be recognized that by breaking the problem up into a number of easy-to-deal-with stages, we can learn much about the optimal path.

2. Next we shall deal with stage 2. The solution is given in part (b) of Figure 10-38. What we are looking at now is the following. Suppose we are in state 2, 3, or 4 and wish to proceed to state 5 or 6 associated with the next stage; what we would like to find out is something about the costs associated with these choices. The first column of the second-stage table shows the three possible states we might have as initial values. The second column shows the cost associated with moving from any of the three initial states to state 5, and then to state 7; the third column does this for moving to state 6 and then to state 7. The equation shown above columns 2 and 3 is the recursive equation (10-68). The right-hand side of the equation has two parts. The first is the cost of going from a particular state in one stage to a new state in the following stage. For example, in going from state 2 to state 5, the cost from our cost data tabulation in Figure 10-37 gives a cost of nine units. The second part of the right-hand side of the recursive equation gives us the least-cost path from the new state and stage through the remainder of the stages in the problem. Again considering that we are going from state 2 to state 5, our first-stage solution tells us that if we

choose state 5, then the best we can do from there on is to go to 7 at an additional cost of 12 units. Thus the value of 21 shown in table (b) is the cost of going from state 2 to state 7 via state 5. The values shown under the heading $f_2^*(s)$ are the optimal choice values for moving from one state and stage to a new state and stage. If we were initially in state 2, then the table tells us that the next state to move to would be 6 at a cost of 20 units rather than to state 5 at a cost of 21 units. The final column heading x_2^* now has more meaning than it did in table (a). It shows the optimal state to move to from any given initial state.

3. The third-stage solution is given in table (c) of the figure. It is arrived at in the same way as the other two. Since the initial state in this case is 1, the choices are simply to move from state 1 to state 2, 3, or 4 in the next stage. In this case it is clear that the least cost would result in moving from state 1 to state 2.

4. The problem is now completely solved. From table (c) we see that the path should be from 1 to 2. From table (b) we see that if we are in state 2, then the optimal path is to 6. Finally, from table (a) we note that the path is then to 7 (there is no alternative in this case). Therefore we choose treatment units 1, 2, 6, and 7, in that sequence. For our objective, they will provide the degree of water treatment at the least cost.

This elementary example demonstrates the methodology of DP. It is an easy process to understand, although the development of an algorithm to address a particular problem can be complicated. By working backward through the problem (a forward recursion can also be used), it is possible to deal only with the choices that must be made at a particular stage and then combine this information with that obtained in working through previous stages. Put somewhat simply, the process tells us that once we make a decision to move from one state to another, we can immediately assess the optimal path from there on. That is what the recursive equation tells us. ∎

APPLICATIONS OF DYNAMIC PROGRAMMING

Dynamic programming has been used for various types of water resources problems (1, 88–93). It has been used to address problems of water storage, conjunctive use of ground- and surface-water supplies, watershed management, hydroelectric power generation, and waste treatment.

In reservoir system studies, the stages are often periods of time and the states represent allocations for various purposes. The objective in such a case might be to find the optimal reservoir size. Alternatively, the method might be used to evaluate reservoir operation policies. Just as in the case of LP models, stochastic considerations can be introduced. When this is done, the approach might be to evaluate the system response when it is subjected to many equally likely streamflow sequences (88). DP models have been used to size surface reservoirs intended to function conjunctively with groundwater storages. The tool has also been applied to establishing policies for the release of flows to maximize hydroelectric output. Other areas of application include aqueduct sizing, sizing of elements in urban storm drainage systems, and selection of water and wastewater treatment processes.

In closing this section on dynamic programming, it should be commented that when the number of combinations of state variables at each stage becomes large (the curse of dimensionality), it may be necessary to reduce them in order to make the solution tractable. A price is paid for gaining insights about dynamic phenomena. Most important, the size of the model must be reduced drastically compared with that for typical linear programming. There are advantages to DP, however, and these include the ability to permit the span of the planning horizon to be unbounded. Another advantage is that dynamic programming opens the way toward solving various nonlinear problems, including those that have integer-value restrictions.

10-8 STOCHASTIC MODELS

Wise use and management of water resources require estimation of future events. As has been pointed out many times, this is a hazardous undertaking at best. The problem is that the future is clouded by both uncertainty and risks.

Uncertain events are those whose probabilities of occurrence are unknown. For example, no one knows what new treatment processes will evolve in the next 30 years, or how costs of handling water will change, or how interest rates will shift, or how other factors will crop up or shift to affect water resources decision making. Such uncertainties make the task of planners difficult. To improve their lot, they must make every effort to update their findings continually, so that as new trends emerge they can be accommodated in the planning processes in the best-possible manner.

Risky events, in contrast to uncertain events, are those for which the probabilities of various outcomes are known or can be estimated. Hydrologic events are risky in this sense. We have already discussed methods for estimating their probabilities (Chapter 7 and earlier in this chapter).

With the uncertainties inherent in all futures forecasting, it should be clear that deterministic models may not always be adequate to the tasks of looking ahead. Thus it often becomes necessary to add measures of the random processes encountered in actual river basins or other systems so that the models more nearly reflect processes that may be expected to take place (synthetic generation of streamflows, for example). This new dimension does not alter the modeling rationale but it does increase the complexity of problem formulation and can significantly add to the dimensions of computation. A detailed discussion of stochastic models is beyond the scope of this book. There are many useful references, however, and in particular, the interested reader will find the book by Loucks et al. especially informative and up to date (1).

10-9 MODEL LINKAGES

It has been pointed out that there are many types of models. Some of these do one thing particularly well, while others are more suited to other tasks. In many cases the special attributes of one or more models or modeling processes can be combined for effectiveness in handling a particular problem. For example, a digital model of a surface-water system might be linked to a groundwater analog model. Simulation and optimization models are often linked as are water quantity and water quality models. The thing to remember about all of this is that when organizing to do a model analysis, it pays to consider the advantages that might be gained by employing more than one technique or model form.

10-10 THE ROLE OF MODELS IN DECISION MAKING

This chapter has emphasized the use of models to obtain information that can be used in guiding decisions about water resources issues. The types of models discussed can be used in design, management, operations, and policymaking. The use to which the model is to be put should determine both its nature and level of detail.

For technical persons in engineering design offices, complicated models may often provide useful results needing little interpretation. On the other hand, if models are to be employed in policymaking situations, their output must be structured for clear understanding by the potential users. These users may, and probably will, have little technical background. There is nothing more likely to relegate model findings to the bookshelf than mathematical jargon that few can understand. Furthermore, the model design should reflect the manner in which it is to be used. If this is done at the outset, the right questions will be answered and the desired character of interpretation ensured.

The job is not done when the model is built and run. As much work is often put into the presentation of the output as into the model itself. Decision makers do not want raw model output, they want clear, practical interpretations. Often, decision makers will find modelers' judgments useful in addition to the model output. Sensitivity analyses and the manner of presentation of results are often the difference between a model that is used and one that gathers dust on a shelf.

10-11 MODEL LIMITATIONS

Model limitations have been discussed in detail in several sections of this chapter. The details covered need not be reviewed, but because this subject is so important, some final words about it seem in order.

The most important point to remember is that all models are only approximations of the actions of a system they are supposed to represent. Large errors in model outputs can result from improper model formulation (lack of understanding of the system), lack of data for calibration and verification, and improper assumptions about future conditions. On the other hand, even where data are sparse and/or the system is not well understood, a model can provide useful insights and guidance about the next steps to take. The trick is knowing the limitations, and armed with this knowledge, making the most of the results.

It is also true that the degree of sophistication attached to any given model can be very misleading. A detailed model improperly calibrated might easily produce results less valid than a back-of-the-envelope approach. Caution and familiarity are key elements in successful model use. Where model assumptions are not clearly specified, the user must recognize that his or her use of the model is clouded by uncertainty. The bottom line is that models can be extremely useful in all levels of decision-making processes, but unless they are thoroughly understood by the user and verified by the designer, their findings may not only be erroneous but highly misleading as well.

PROBLEMS

10-1. If the mean annual rainfall of a region is 23 inches and the coefficient of variation is found to be 0.20, find (a) how often you might expect the rainfall to be less than 10 inches, (b) the 10-year rainfall, and (c) the percent of the time the rainfall would be between 13 and 23 inches.

10-2. Given the 30-year record of annual rainfall for Lakeland, Florida, determine whether these data may be fitted by the normal distribution. If such a distribution is valid, estimate the 10-year rainfall.

30-YEAR ANNUAL RAINFALL PROFILE FOR LAKELAND, FLORIDA

YEAR	RAINFALL (IN)	YEAR	RAINFALL (IN)
1946	47.05	1961	35.38
1947	60.42	1962	38.06
1948	62.80	1963	46.26
1949	46.63	1964	47.53
1950	43.81	1965	48.35
1951	49.28	1966	45.47
1952	51.45	1967	37.80
1953	59.61	1968	55.37
1954	36.30	1969	53.00
1955	44.08	1970	46.56
1956	45.12	1971	42.91
1957	62.38	1972	38.29
1958	41.74	1973	45.41
1959	70.24	1974	43.89
1960	65.42	1975	41.50

10-3. Given the following record of annual rainfall, calculate the mean, range, and standard deviation for the data. Plot a histogram relating frequency of annual rainfall to measured amount. Describe the nature of skewness in the data.

YEAR	RAINFALL (IN)
1	45
2	45
3	41
4	32
5	50
6	51
7	37
8	40
9	48
10	56
11	54
12	51
13	47
14	42
15	43
16	45
17	39
18	38
19	40
20	36

10-4. Compute the mean value of annual rainfall for the first five, second five, third five, and fourth five years of record given in Problem 10-3. Discuss the variability of these means. Compare the mean rainfalls for the first and second 10-year period. Are these more stable than the five-year means?

10-5. Calculate the coefficient of skewness for the data given in Problem 10-3.

10-6. Maximize $Z = 3X_1 + 8X_2$ subject to X_1 ranging between 1 and 5, and X_2 ranging between 3 and 7. Formulate the problem and solve graphically.

10-7. A city can draw water from two streams. Consider that there are four seasons, each with varying demands. Formulate an LP model to address this question. Make a sketch and assign appropriate variable names. Assume that each source has certain limitations and that each stream is impounded by a reservoir. Assume that the streamflows to be expected are known. Assume also that two water treatment plants will be used to process the water. Formulate the OBJ and the appropriate constraint set.

10-8. Reformulate Problem 10-7 assuming that one of the streams can be used to supply water only during the fall and winter season.

10-9. A farming operation has three sections of land that can be used for two-season crop production. The output of the operation is limited by the availability of water and land. Three crops may be grown in any combination on the available land. Using the data that follows, find the two-season crop-acreage allocation that maximizes the farm profit. Tracts 1, 2, and 3 include 500, 900, and 776 acres of land respectively. The water availability in either season is 3.8 acre-ft/acre, 3.5 acre-ft/acre, and 3.0 acre-ft/acre for tracts 1, 2, and 3 respectively. The crop types are x, y, and z. The water requirements for these are 4.0, 3.3, and 3.5 acre-ft/acre respectively. The total acreage of crop x

cannot exceed 1300 acres in season 2. Finally, the profit per acre that can be expected from crops x, y, and z is $450, $390, and $360 in that order.

10-10. Rework Example 10-9 assuming that crop x can be grown only in season 2.

10-11. Rework Example 10-9 using the added constraint of Problem 10-10 and assuming further that crop y cannot exceed a total annual acreage of 1500 acres.

10-12. Select two or more of the parameters of the model of Example 10-9 and conduct a study of how their variability would affect the optimal solution obtained by the LP model.

10-13. Consider the sketch and cost data given in the following diagram. Assume that the figure represents possible waste treatment plant configurations for obtaining three successively higher levels of treatment. Find the least-cost combination of treatment units representing each stage of treatment. Use dynamic programming.

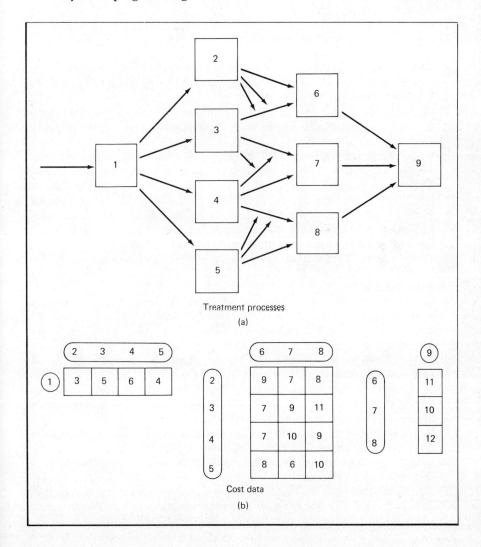

Treatment processes

(a)

Cost data

(b)

References

1. D. P. Loucks et al., *Water Resource Systems Planning and Analysis,* Prentice-Hall, Englewood Cliffs, NJ, 1981.
2. W. Viessman, Jr., et al., *Introduction to Hydrology,* Harper & Row, New York, 1977.
3. Warren Viessman, Jr., et al., *Elkhorn River Subbasin Screening Model,* Nebraska Water Resources Research Institute, Lincoln, May 1974.
4. Jared L. Cohon and David H. Marks, "A Review and Evaluation of Multiobjective Programming Techniques," *Water Resources Research,* vol. 11, no. 2, 1975.
5. Richard de Neufville and Joseph Stafford, *Systems Analysis for Engineers and Managers,* McGraw-Hill, New York, 1971.
6. Arthur Maass et al., *Design of Water Resource Systems,* Harvard University Press, Cambridge, MA, 1962.
7. Maynard F. Hufschmidt and Myron B. Fiering, *Simulation Techniques for Design of Water-Resource Systems,* Harvard University Press, Cambridge, MA, 1966.
8. Henry D. Jacoby and Daniel P. Loucks, "Combined Use of Optimization and Simulation Models in River Basin Planning," *Water Resources Research,* vol. 8, no. 6, December 1972.
9. Yacov Y. Haimes and Warren A. Hall, "Multiobjectives in Water Resources Systems Analysis: The Surrogate Worth Trade-Off Method," *Water Resources Research,* vol. 10, no. 4, 1974.
10. Yacov Y. Haimes, Warren A. Hall, and H. T. Freedman, *Multiobjective Optimization in Water Resources Systems: The Surrogate Worth Trade-Off Method,* Elsevier, New York, 1975.
11. U.S. Water Resources Council, *Guidelines for Determining Flood Flow Frequency,* Bull. No. 17 of the Hydrology Committee, Washington, D.C., 1976.
12. L. B. Leopold, *Probability Analysis Applied to a Water Supply Problem,* Geological Survey Circular 410, Washington, D.C., 1959.
13. Ven T. Chow, "Statistical and Probability Analysis of Hydrologic Data," Sec. 8–I, in V. T. Chow (ed.), *Handbook of Applied Hydrology,* McGraw-Hill, New York, 1964.
14. M. B. Fiering, *Streamflow Synthesis,* Harvard University Press, Cambridge, MA, 1967.
15. E. G. Gumbel, "The Return Period of Flood Flows," *Ann. Math. Statist.,* vol. 12, no. 2, June 1941, pp. 163–190.
16. R. K. Linsley and J. B. Franzini, *Water Resources Engineering,* 3d ed., McGraw-Hill, New York, 1979.
17. N. H. Crawford and R. K. Linsley, Jr., "Digital Simulation in Hydrology: Stanford Watershed Model IV," Dept. of Civil Engineering, Tech. Rep. No. 39, Stanford University, Stanford, July 1966.
18. Hydrocomp International, Inc., *Hydrocomp Simulation Programming Operations Manual,* 4th ed., Palo Alto, CA, January 1976.
19. L. D. James, "An Evaluation of Relationships Between Streamflow Patterns and Watershed Characteristics Through the Use of OPSET," Research Rep. No. 36, Water Resources Institute, University of Kentucky, Lexington, 1970.
20. E. Y. Liou, "OPSET: Program for Computerized Selection of Watershed Pa-

rameter Values for the Stanford Watershed Model," Research Rep. No. 34, Water Resources Institute, University of Kentucky, Lexington, 1970.

21. L. D. James, "Hydrologic Modeling, Parameter Estimation, and Watershed Characteristics," *J. Hydrology,* vol. 17, 1972.

22. V. T. Ricca, *The Ohio State University Version of the Stanford Streamflow Simulation Model, Part I—Technical Aspects,* Ohio State University, Columbus, May 1972.

23. N. H. Crawford, *Studies in the Application of Digital Simulation to Urban Hydrology,* Hydrocomp International, Inc., Palo Alto, CA, September 1971.

24. D. K. Clarke, *Applications of Stanford Watershed Model Concepts to Predict Flood Peaks for Small Drainage Areas,* Div. of Research, Kentucky Dept. of Highways, 1968.

25. G. A. Ross, "The Stanford Watershed Model: The Correlation of Parameter Values Selected by a Computerized Procedure with Measureable Physical Characteristics of the Watershed," Research Rep. 35, Water Resources Institute, University of Kentucky, Lexington, 1970.

26. *Run-off from Snowmelt,* U.S. Army Corps of Engineers, *Engineering and Design Manuals,* EM 1110-2-1406, January 1960.

27. Eric A. Anderson, *National Weather Service River Forecast System—Snow Accumulation and Ablation Model,* NOAA Tech. Mem., NWS HYDRO-17, Silver Springs, MD, November 1973.

28. L. R. Beard, "Simulation of Daily Streamflow," International Hydrology Symposium, Fort Collins, CO, September 1967.

29. U.S. Army Corps of Engineers, *HEC-1 Flood Hydrograph Package,* users and programmers manuals, HEC Program 723-X6-L2010, January 1973.

30. H. N. Holtan and N. C. Lopez, "USDAHL-73 Revised Model of Watershed Hydrology," U.S. Department of Agriculture, Plant Physiology Institute, Rep. No. 1, 1973.

31. B. J. Claborn and W. Moore, "Numerical Simulation in Watershed Hydrology," Hydraulic Engineering Laboratory, University of Texas Rep. No. HYD 14-7001, 1970.

32. U.S. National Weather Service Office of Hydrology, *National Weather Service River Forecast System Forecast Procedures,* NOAA Tech. Mem. NWS HYDRO-14, December 1972.

33. U.S. Army Corps of Engineers, *Program Description and User Manual for SSARR Model Streamflow Synthesis and Reservoir Regulation,* Program 724-K5-G0010, December 1972.

34. D. R. Dawdy et al., "A Rainfall–Run-off Simulation Model for Estimation of Flood Peaks for Small Drainage Basins," U.S. Geological Survey Professional Pap. 506-B, U.S. Gov't. Print. Off., Washington, D.C., 1972.

35. P. H. Carrigan, "Calibration of U.S. Survey Rainfall-Runoff Model for Peak-Flow Synthesis—Natural Basins," U.S. Geological Survey Computer Rep., U.S. Department of Commerce, National Technical Information Service, 1973.

36. P. H. Carrigan et al., "User's Guide for U.S. Geological Survey Rainfall-Runoff Models," U.S. Geological Survey Open-File Rep. 77884, Reston, VA, 1977.

37. J. R. Philip, "The Theory of Infiltration: The Infiltration Equation and Its Solution," *Soil Science,* vol. 83, 1957.

38. G. D. Bennett, *Introduction to Ground Water Hydraulics,* book 3, *Applica-*

tions of Hydraulics, U.S. Geological Survey, U.S. Gov't. Print. Off., Washington, D.C., 1976.

39. D. B. McWhorter and D. K. Sunada, *Ground Water Hydrology and Hydraulics,* Water Resources Publications, Fort Collins, CO, 1977.
40. D. K. Todd, *Groundwater Hydrology,* 2d ed., Wiley, New York, 1980.
41. P. W. Huntoon, "Predicted Water-Level Declines for Alternative Groundwater Developments in the Upper Big Blue River Basin, Nebraska," Resource Rep. No. 6, Conservation and Survey Div., University of Nebraska, Lincoln, 1974.
42. D. W. Peacemen and H. H. Rachford, Jr., "The Numerical Solution of Parabolic and Elliptic Differential Equations, *Soc. Indust. Appl. Math. J.,* vol. 3, 1955, pp. 28–41.
43. G. F. Pinder and J. D. Bredehoeft, "Application of the Digital Computer for Aquifer Evaluation," *Water Resources Research,* vol. 4, no. 4, 1968, pp. 1069–1093.
44. Irwin Remson, G. M. Hornberger, and F. J. Molz, *Numerical Methods in Subsurface Hydrology,* New York, Wiley, 1971.
45. T. A. Prickett and C. G. Lonnquist, *Selected Digital Computer Techniques for Groundwater Resource Evaluation,* Illinois State Water Survey Bull. No. 55, 1971.
46. R. R. Marlette and G. L. Lewis, "Digital Simulation of Conjunctive-Use of Groundwater in Dawson County, Nebraska," Civil Engineering Rep., University of Nebraska, Lincoln, 1973.
47. C. E. Jacob, "Flow of Groundwater," in Hunter Rouse (ed.), *Engineering Hydraulics,* Wiley, New York, 1950.
48. R. A. Young and J. D. Bredehoeft, "Digital Computer Simulation for Solving Management Problems of Conjunctive Groundwater and Surface Water Systems," *Water Resources Research,* vol. 8, no. 3, June 1972.
49. H. W. Crooke, "Ground Water Replenishment in Orange County, California," *Journal AWWA,* July 1961.
50. Warren Viessman, Jr., "Estimation of Lake Flushing Rates for Water Quality Control Planning and Management," *Proc. Conf. Reclamation of Maine's Dying Lakes,* University of Maine, Orono, ME, March 1971.
51. *SWMM, Volume No. 1, Final Report,* U.S. Environmental Protection Agency, Water Resources Engineers, and Metcalf and Eddy, Inc., July 1971.
52. V. Novotny and G. Chesters, *Handbook of Nonpoint Pollution, Sources and Management,* Van Nostrand Reinhold, New York, 1981.
53. A. K. Biswas (ed.), *Models for Water Quality Management,* McGraw-Hill, New York, 1981.
54. U.S. Environmental Protection Agency, *Computer Program Documentation for Stream Quality Model (Qual-II),* Environmental Research Laboratory, Athens, GA, 1977.
55. U.S. Environmental Protection Agency, *User's Manual for Stream Quality Model (Qual-II),* Environmental Research Laboratory, Athens, GA, 1977.
56. U.S. Environmental Protection Agency, *Maximum Utilization of Water Resources in a Planned Community, Application of the Storm Water Management Model,* vol. I, Municipal Environmental Research Laboratory, Cincinnati, 1979.
57. R. H. French, Fundamentals of Modeling: Concepts, Components, How to

Formulate a Model, Applicability to Water Quality Problems, lecture notes on Water Quality Modeling, Water Resources Center, Desert Research Institute, University of Nevada, Reno, 1981.

58. R. H. French, A Statistical Approach to the Modeling of Conservative and Nonconservative Substances, lecture notes on Water Quality Modeling, Water Resources Center, Desert Research Institute, University of Nevada, Reno, 1981.

59. C. W. Chen and G. T. Orlob, *Ecologic Simulation for Aquatic Environments, Final Report,* OWRR Project No. C-2044, Office of Water Resources Research, Department of the Interior, Washington, D.C., December 1972.

60. P. S. Lombardo and D. D. Franz, *Mathematical Model of Water Quality in Rivers and Impoundments,* Hydrocomp, Inc., Palo Alto, CA, December 1972.

61. P. S. Lombardo, *Critical Review of Currently Available Water Quality Models* Hydrocomp, Inc., Palo Alto, CA, July 1973.

62. Texas Water Development Board, *QUAL-I Simulation of Water Quality in Streams and Lakes, Program Documentation and Users' Manual,* National Technical Information Service, PB 202973, Springfield, VA, 1970.

63. Texas Water Development Board, DOSAG-I Simulation of Water Quality in Streams and Canals, Program Documentation and Users' Manual, National Technical Information Service, Springfield, VA, 1970.

64. L. W. Gelhar and J. L. Wilson, "Ground Water Quality Modeling," *Proc. 2d Nat. Ground Water Quality Symposium,* U.S. Environmental Protection Agency, Washington, D.C., 1974.

65. Water Resources Engineers, Inc., *Prediction of Thermal Energy Destruction in Streams and Reservoirs,* California Dept. of Fish and Game, 1967.

66. F. S. Hillier and G. J. Lieberman, *Introduction to Operations Research,* 2d ed., San Francisco, Holden-Day, Inc., 1974.

67. R. deNeufville and D. H. Marks, *Systems Planning and Design Case Studies in Modeling Optimization and Evaluation,* Englewood Cliffs, NJ, Prentice-Hall, 1974.

68. D. P. Loucks, *Stochastic Methods for Analyzing River Basin Systems,* Cornell University Water Resources and Marine Sciences Center, Ithaca, NY, August 1969.

69. A. Maas et al., *Design of Water Resources Systems,* Cambridge, MA, Harvard University Press, 1962.

70. Jon C. Liebman, Optimization Models, lecture notes, Summer Institute on Urban-Metropolitan Systems Planning, University of Nebraska, Lincoln, 1973.

71. Thomas Rachford, Notes on Non-Linear Programming and Sensitivity Analysis, lecture notes, Urban Water Systems Institute, Colorado State University, Fort Collins, CO, 1970.

72. S. K. Hoppel and W. Viessman, "A Linear Analysis of an Urban Water Supply System," *Water Resources Bulletin,* vol. 8, no. 2, April 1972.

73. M. R. Greenberg, *Applied Linear Programming,* Academic, New York, 1978.

74. *Introduction to MPSX and Its Optional Features MIP and GUB, GH20-0849,* International Business Machines Corp., White Plains, NY, 1971.

75. C. S. ReVelle et al., "A Management Model for Water Quality Control," *Journal of the Water Pollution Control Federation,* vol. 39, no. 7, July 1967.

76. R. A. Deininger, "Linear Programming for Hydrologic Analyses," *Water Resources Res.* vol. 5, no. 5, 1969.

77. G. R. Grantham, E. E. Pyatt, J. P. Heaney, and B. J. Carter, Jr., "Model for Flow Augmentation: An Overview," *J. Sanit. Eng. Div., Proc. Amer. Soc. Civil Eng.*, vol. 96, no. SA-5, 1970.

78. M. R. Greenberg and R. M. Hordon, *Water Supply Planning: A Case Study and Systems Analyses*, Center for Urban Policy Research, Rutgers University, New Brunswick, NJ, 1975.

79. J. P. Heaney, "Mathematical Programming Analysis of Regional Water Resource Systems," *Proc. Nat. Symp. Analysis Water Resour. Systems*, American Water Resources Association, 1968.

80. D. Karmeli, Y. Gadish, and S. Meyers, "Design of Optimal Water Distribution Networks," *Proc. Amer. Soc. Civil Eng.*, vol. 94, no. PL1, 1968.

81. P. H. Kirshen, D. Marks, and J. C. Schaake, Jr., *Mathematical Model for Screening Storm Water Control Alternatives*, MIT, Dept. of Civil Engineering, Cambridge, MA, 1972.

82. D. P. Loucks, "Computer Models for Reservoir Regulation, *J. San. Eng. Div.*, Amer. Soc. Civil Eng., vol. 94, no. SA-4, 1968.

83. A. S. Manne, "Product-Mix Alternatives: Flood Control, Electric Power and Irrigation," *J. Econ. Rev.*, vol. 3, no. 1, pp. 30–59, 1962.

84. C. Revelle and W. Kirby, "Linear Decision Rule in Reservoir Management and Design Performance Optimization," *Water Resources Res.*, vol. 6, no. 4, 1970.

85. C. Revelle, E. Joeres, and W. Kirby, "The Linear Decision Rule in Reservoir Management, Design," *Water Resources Res.*, vol. 5, no. 4, 1969.

86. E. T. Smith and A. R. Morris, "Systems Analysis for Optimal Water Quality Management," *J. Water Pollution Control Fed.*, vol. 41, no. 9, 1969.

87. Claire Welty, "Optimization of Water Quality Management," Masters thesis, unpublished, The George Washington University, Washington, D.C., May 1983.

88. D. D. Meredith, Dynamic Programming Concepts and Applications, lecture notes, Urban Water Systems Institute, Colorado State University, Fort Collins, 1970.

89. N. Buras, "Dynamic Programming in Water Resources Development," in V. T. Chow (ed)., *Advances in Hydroscience*, vol. 3, Academic, New York, 1966.

90. W. A. Hall and N. Buras, "The Dynamic Programming Approach to Water Resources Development," *J. Geophys. Res.*, vol. 66, no. 2, 1961.

91. W. A. Hall et al., "Optimization of the Operation of a Multi-purpose Reservoir by Dynamic Programming," *Water Resources Res.*, vol. 4, no. 3, 1968.

92. W. L. Meier, Jr., and C. S. Beightler, "An Optimization Method for Branching Multi-stage Water Resources Systems," *Water Resources Res.*, vol. 3, no. 3, 1967.

93. G. K. Young, "Finding Reservoir Operating Rules," *J. Hydraulics Div.*, Am. Soc. Civil Engrs., vol. 93, no. HY6, 1967.

Chapter 11
Water Conveyance
and Storage

To provide the water needed for cities, farms, industries, energy development, and other purposes, it is necessary to move it from its source to the
point of use. Furthermore, the seasonal and annual variations in the availability of water often make adequate storage essential to meeting water
requirements during low-flow periods (1–3). This chapter deals with these
issues and describes some of the special structural features of storage and
conveyance works.

11-1 LARGE-SCALE WATER CONVEYANCE SYSTEMS

The term large-scale water conveyance systems, as used in this book, is
intended to describe the transport mechanisms by which bulk quantities
of water are moved from points of development to locations at which
distribution to specific users is made. In the following section, dense networks typical of those used to serve urban water customers are described.

Conveyance Types

Several types of conveyances are used to move water. These may be
categorized as pipelines, tunnels, and open channels. The selection of a
particular conveyance type depends on a number of factors. These include
topography, construction costs, environmental considerations, energy
costs, and the nature of physical works along the route that must be
followed (1, 2).

PIPELINES

Pipelines are often the choice of conveyance where topographical or other conditions rule out some form of open channel. They may be buried, partially buried, or aboveground. Pipelines are designed to operate under pressure, and they are normally constructed of concrete, steel, asbestos cement, or polymer materials. Appurtenances found on pipelines include various types of valves, drains, surge control equipment, thermal expansion and insulation joints, manholes, and pumping stations. These devices are used to control flows, prevent damage to the pipeline, permit inspection and maintenance, and provide the head (pressure) needed to transport the water to its destination.

OPEN CHANNELS

Open channels operate under atmospheric pressure. Thus they do not require pumping, with its associated high costs for energy. They may be covered, if circumstances dictate that this be done, although the costs associated with such practice can be very significant. Open channels may be natural or manmade, and they may be built in a variety of shapes. Selection of an open channel as a means of conveyance depends mostly on favorable topographical conditions that permit gravity flow with minimal excavation and fill. In some cases open channels are elevated; these are usually designated as flumes. Channels may be lined or unlined. If the channel is not lined, then consideration must be given to the potential for seepage losses and for channel erosion. Linings are usually concrete, butyl rubber, vinyl, polymer, synthetic fabrics, or other similar materials. The purposes of the liners are to eliminate seepage losses, decrease the resistance to flow, and minimize channel maintenance.

TUNNELS

Where topographical conditions or other factors make surface excavation for an open channel or pipeline impossible, it may be necessary to resort to tunneling. Tunnels are often the solution to mountain or river crossings, and they may be operated as open channels or function under pressure.

Design Considerations

The design of water conveyance systems involves questions of economics, hydraulics, route selection, and structural integrity.

ROUTE LOCATION

The selection of a route for conveying water is usually based on economic, topographical, environmental, political, and social factors. In general, the source of the water supply is fixed in space, as is the destination. The choice then becomes one of evaluating alternative routes to find the one that will minimize costs subject to constraining influences. For example, rolling terrain may rule out the choice of an open channel. Often it is the case that the least-cost route, based on strict technical criteria, may not be open to selection for environmental or political reasons. What must be done is to find the best route under the circumstances and then determine the mix of conveyance types that will minimize construction and operation and maintenance costs.

ECONOMICS

Economic considerations in the design of water transport systems center on costs of construction, costs of materials, operation and maintenance costs, procurement of land, and energy costs for pumping. A relation exists between aqueduct size and the hydraulic gradient generating the flow. Given the same amount of water to be conveyed, for example, an open channel having a hydraulic gradient with a small slope would cost more than one where the slope of the gradient was steeper. For long-distance transport of water where different types of conduits pass through varied topography, it is important that conveyance type, choice of dam elevation, and selection of pumping lifts and/or power drops be coordinated to minimize total construction and operating costs of the system. This may be accomplished through the joint application of hydraulic and economic principles (1, 4, 5). The optimum combination of pumping lift and hydraulic slope is the objective.

CONVEYANCE TYPE

The size and cross-sectional shape of the water conveyance in a major transport system usually varies along the route. The selection of conveyance type is dependent on economic, environmental, construction, and topographical conditions. Sometimes construction practices may dictate a larger-than-needed facility when a structure of smaller size would be difficult to build (this is not uncommon in tunneling). The available head and limiting velocities are hydraulic determinants. Heads are affected by reservoir operations and the capabilities of pumping stations. Limiting velocities must be imposed to minimize scour of earth channels, and to protect transmission lines against excessive pressures that might develop when valves are being adjusted. When the water being transported contains suspended materials, minimum velocities must be maintained to preclude sedimentation in the conveyance. Where silt is transported, velocities should be about 2.5 ft/s or more. Maximum velocities in lined conveyances are not usually permitted to exceed about 20 ft/s, with the usual range being about 4 to 6 ft/s (6). Where power generation and pumping are involved, pumping costs and/or the value of power produced combine with conduit costs to determine conveyance size. In the special case where there is a single gravity-flow pipeline, the cross-sectional area should be large enough so that the total head available is sufficient to provide the required velocity head and to overcome friction along the route.

HYDRAULICS

The hydraulic analyses required for the design of a water transportation system are those already covered in Chapter 9. Except for sludges, which are of no concern here, most flows may be treated as if they were clean water, even though sediment loads may be large. The most extensively used equations for hydraulic design are the Manning formula (for open channel flow) and the Hazen-Williams formula for pipe flow. The application of these equations has been demonstrated in Chapter 9.

PUMPING

If water must be transported to a point higher than that of the source, pumping will be required. Even where the destination is lower, a pumping station might also be worth considering. For example, for a 50-mile-long canal with a drop in elevation of only five or six feet, the dimensions for a free-flowing system could be very large. A smaller conveyance with a pumping facility might be less expensive in this case, and would at least be worth investigating. Typical pumping facilities range from small units delivering only a few gallons per minute to large stations moving hundreds of cubic feet per second.

11-2   MUNICIPAL WATER DISTRIBUTION SYSTEMS

Municipal water distribution systems serve homes, commercial establishments, and industries and meet fire-fighting needs. These systems must be designed to meet operating requirements at adequate pressures. These requirements vary with the nature of the users being served. Components of distribution systems include pipes, storage reservoirs, pumping stations, fire hydrants, service connections to users, meters, and other adjuncts such as valves necessary to the performance and/or maintenance of the system.

Configurations

Distribution systems may be categorized principally as grid or branching or some combination of the two. Figure 11-1 illustrates their nature. The configuration selected depends mainly on the prevailing road and street pattern of the area and the location of treatment and storage works. The preferred type of system is the grid because it can furnish water to any point from two directions. Branching systems do not have this advantage, and their dead ends sometimes cause water quality problems due to lack of circulation. Combination systems have features of both systems. In general, it is desirable to have at least the main feeders looped so as to incorporate two-directional flow capability.

Where the region to be served has sectors with markedly different topographical features (lowlands and foothills, for example) it is often advantageous to divide it into several service areas. This allows provision

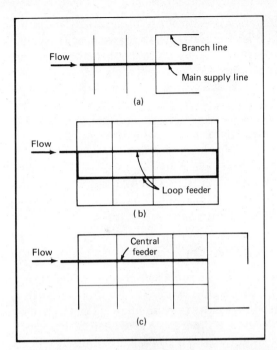

Figure 11-1 Types of water distribution systems: (a) branching system; (b) grid system; (c) combination system.

of needed pressures for the higher elevations without subjecting lower regions to greater pressures than desirable. For emergencies, these zoned service areas are usually interconnected, but the connecting links are valved off during normal operations.

General System Requirements

The design of municipal water systems is influenced by factors not encountered in the design of large-scale transportation systems. Distribution systems must accommodate great extremes in flow and be sized to handle emergency situations such as fire fighting, which the large transportation systems are not subjected to. They must also be designed to eliminate the potential for pollutants to enter at any point since the public health is at stake.

Generally, the performance of a distribution system is judged on the basis of its ability to sustain adequate working pressures while delivering a desired level of flow. The pressure distribution should be sufficient for both the consumer and fire-fighting needs to be met simultaneously. Furthermore, pressures should not be excessive, since they are costly to generate and high pressures contribute to losses (leakage) from the system. Distribution systems are expensive to build and operate, and cost-consciousness should be a primary factor in their design.

In commercial areas where there are tall buildings, pressures in excess of 60 pounds per square inch gauge pressure (psig) are usually required. Where buildings are very tall, it is sometimes necessary to provide special booster pumps to increase line pressures enough to serve the higher floors adequately. In such cases, roof storage tanks are common and distribution to the building's plumbing system is made directly from them. Most residential areas are adequately serviced by pressures in the 40 to 50 psig range.

Pipe sizes for distribution systems are determined on the basis of the water needs of those they service, plus fire-fighting demands. Generally, high velocities should be avoided. Velocities in the range of from 3 to 5 ft/s are common. The National Board of Fire Underwriters specifies criteria for distribution system design to ensure that fire flows can be maintained for various service areas (1).

Hydraulics

The hydraulic design of a water distribution network begins with a layout of the system needed to reach proposed customers. Once this has been determined, the next step is to estimate the required flows. The flows must be determined in both a spatial and a temporal sense so that the appropriate operating pressures can be established. The spatial distribution of flows reflects different water use patterns such as those of individual residences, industries, and commercial establishments. The time distribution becomes important in estimating the maximum flow rates a given sector of the system must be able to carry. If the anticipated peak requirement of a residential area is expected at about 6:30 P.M., for example, and if a local industry served by the same main had its peak water use period at midnight, then the design flow would not be the sum of the peaks but the greater of the sums of the residential peak plus the industrial flow at the time or vice versa. Determination of the water use requirements of the several sectors follows the reasoning of Chapter 4. Historically, water system designers have evaluated (a) the maximum daily rate plus fire protection and (b) the maximum hourly rate, to determine which of the two is larger. The fire flow must be provided for, but the flow in excess of this value, to be maintained during an emergency, should be carefully evaluated. Furthermore, the current trend toward demand reduction practices, at least during low-flow periods, suggests that some historical selections of pipe sizes might have been too conservative and costly.

After a determination has been made of the load (demand) to be placed on the system, it is usual practice to distribute the load at specified points on the feeder-main system. Computations to establish pipe sizes then proceed on this basis (see network analysis, Chapter 9). Ordinarily, distribution systems are designed so that reasonably uniform pressures prevail within any zone. Pressures less than about 30 psig are usually not acceptable, although during fire-fighting periods it may be permissible to let them drop to about 20 psig. Main feeder pipes should be designed for pressures in the 40 to 75 psig range unless local conditions indicate a lesser pressure would be acceptable (1). Actual pipe sizing is accomplished using standard hydraulic methods and network analyses (7–18).

Economics

Water distribution systems are costly to build, maintain, and operate. As a result, designers must be careful to avoid overconservatism, while at the same time providing for reasonable increases in water demands from the system as the area expands in population or other growth activities. Furthermore, economies may also be achieved through the development of optimal operating policies. That combination of pipe sizes, storages, and operating rules which leads to the minimum cost of providing the region's water supply should be sought. A well-thought-out operating procedure combined with a smaller pipe network might provide as much water as a larger pipe system operated in a less efficient manner. Initial construction costs must also be weighed against long-term operation and maintenance costs in determining the nature of facilities to be provided.

11-3 STORAGE SYSTEMS

Water is stored for a variety of purposes. These include flood control, water supply, water quality enhancement, recreation, navigation, and hydroelectric power generation. Both surface and subsurface storages may be used. Surface storage often requires the development of a reservoir whereas subsurface storage can take advantage of the storage capacity of underground formations.

The purpose of providing storage works is to regulate stream flows so that surplus waters can be retained for use during periods of shortage. In this way the variability of the stream is reduced, and the effects of droughts can be mitigated. Regulation is the amount of water that is stored or released from storage during a time period. The degree to which a given reservoir can regulate flow is determined by the ratio of its capacity to the volume of streamflow encountered during the time interval. In the United States, many rivers are regulated to one degree or another and considerable amounts of water have been made available through the development of storage (19). In some river basins there are opportunities for substantial gains to be made in water supply development through storage. Ultimately, however, such regulation follows a law of diminishing returns.

Through regulation, the safe yield of a stream can be made to approach its average annual flow as the level of storage approaches full development. While this ideal cannot be attained in reality, safe yields of 75 to 90 percent of the mean annual flow can be achieved through regulation. Such increases have significant implications for regional water supply.

Since the environmental movement of the 1960s, there has been widespread opposition to the construction of new reservoirs. Nevertheless, they are often the most efficient and cost-effective means for increasing water availability. Additional storage should thus be evaluated along with other options when plans are being made for meeting water requirements.

Reservoir Storage Allocations

Most modern reservoirs are multipurpose in nature. Storages are allocated for a number of functional uses. These uses are often incompatible and as such require that compromises be made. The nature of the principal functional uses is described here along with comments about the conflicts that these uses generate.

FLOOD CONTROL

Flood control was one of the earliest uses made of reservoirs. The storage allocated for this purpose is intended to be available during times of flooding and is expected to be depleted as soon after the flood event as possible in order to make space available for the next critical event. Such an operation troubles those who seek to retain as much water as possible for water supply and other purposes. Given the limitations on storage capacity at any reservoir site, it is easy to understand that those who want to store water for later use do not favor the retention of empty storage space. Although flood control storage is not compatible with other types of storage, recent advances in management techniques related to reservoir operation and hydrologic forecasting indicate that some storage allocations for flood control might be modified to better accommodate other uses. The design floods used to set storage allocations for large reservoirs are the probable maximum flood, the standard project flood, and the frequency-based flood (20). The probable maximum flood is the flood that could occur as the result of the most severe storm that is considered reasonably possible to occur. The standard project flood is obtained from analysis of severe storms that were recorded in the general vicinity of the drainage basin. Frequency-based floods are those based on studies of long records that can be expected to yield the probabilities of extreme events.

RECREATION

Many reservoirs are designed to accommodate recreation as well as the conventional uses of water supply. Most recreationists desire use of the reservoir during the summer period, a period during which withdrawal uses are usually highest. For optimal boating, swimming, and associated uses, the pool level should be maintained relatively constant. This conflicts with making withdrawals and necessitates well-controlled release policies as well as compromises to reconcile the various uses. The amount of storage dedicated to recreation depends largely on the size of the reservoir and how it is to be used. Basically, enough storage is needed to permit recreational activities even when storages for other purposes have been depleted.

MUNICIPAL AND INDUSTRIAL WATER SUPPLY (M&I)

There are many reservoirs dedicated solely to storing water for the use of cities and industries. The storage requirements for these are determined by procedures to be discussed later in this chapter. Essentially this means providing adequate capacity so that desired withdrawals can be maintained during periods when the supplying stream is unable to support them. Where water supply for M&I uses is part of a multipurpose project, the storage determination for this purpose is made in the same way except that it must be coordinated with that for all the other uses. Storage of M&I water in large reservoirs also offers some side benefits relative to water quality. The retention time in the reservoir allows suspended sediment to settle out and is also a factor in reducing the amount of bacteria in the water.

IRRIGATION

In the western United States and in other regions where irrigated agriculture is important, storage of water for use during the irrigation season (often May to September) is an important factor, and such storage may far overshadow that for any other purpose in the reservoir. Irrigation water releases are needed at a time when recreationists and other water users are also concerned about the timing and size of releases. Where irrigation use is combined with other uses, it is necessary to develop rules for reservoir operation (see the section "Estimating Storage Requirements") (21).

NAVIGATION

If the dependable flow in a river is less than that needed to sustain navigation, then the problem may be overcome by releasing water from upstream reservoirs. Such use of upstream storage conflicts with most withdrawal uses from the reservoir in question and poses several other problems. First, very large reservoir capacities are needed, since navigational flows measured in thousands of cubic feet per second are common. A second difficulty is associated with the fact that reservoirs are often far upstream of the river reaches requiring the navigational flows. This creates a problem in terms of knowing how much water to release and when, since flow times in days or longer could be involved. Finally, major rivers usually flow through multiple political jurisdictions; this situation frequently gives rise to numerous institutional problems.

HYDROELECTRIC GENERATION

Hydroelectric power may be generated in run-of-the-river plants (plants not developed with upstream storage to develop head or increase the dependability of flow), or it may be generated by providing storage above the turbines. The value of water power developments is improved when dependable flows are increased or when variability of river flows can be changed to conform more closely to the energy demands of the power system. This function is provided by reservoir storage. When the time period is about a week, this is often called pondage rather than storage (21). In any case, the storage capacity provided in the reservoir increases the dependable flow of the stream being regulated, which in turn increases the dependable capacity of the hydroelectric facilities associated with the storage. The manner in which the reservoir must be operated depends partly on whether the hydro facilities are being used to generate base load or are used for peaking purposes only (see Chapter 12). Furthermore, where multiple uses are being made of the reservoir's storage, special operating policies are required to accommodate them.

Water Quality Control

During low-flow periods, reservoirs can be operated to increase downstream flows. Such operations can be effective in diluting wastes and improving the oxygen balance for fish and other aquatic organisms. If storage is provided for this purpose, it will be in direct conflict with uses for irrigation, recreation, water supply for cities, and so on. Thus the total reservoir storage capacity must be sufficient to support all of its combined uses within acceptable limits of risk. Provision of storage for water quality control is directly analogous to providing storage to meet instream flow requirements.

Storage Period

Reservoirs are intended to regulate surface-water flows. The amount of time over which storage must be provided is a function of both the purpose (use) of the reservoir and the prevailing hydrologic conditions. Some storages are intended only to provide economy or ease of operation. These are often associated with the day-to-day operations of municipal water supply systems. The storage periods in such cases may range from hours to a few days. This subject will be covered later, in the section on equalizing and operating storages. Larger storage requirements associated with annual water supply for cities, irrigation water use, hydroelectric production and so on may, when compared with expected streamflows, necessitate reservoirs that can store water on a seasonal basis (within-year storage capacity) or over a period of years (over-year storage capacity). Methods for estimating both the time period and the needed volume will be covered later, but it is important that the time element of storage as well as the volumetric element of storage be recognized at this point.

Losses from Storage

Reservoirs for storing streamflows incur losses in water, due mainly to evaporation and seepage. Although both types of losses are undesirable, the benefits derived from use of the reservoir may offset these, and if this is the case, the potential for supplementing water supplies can be realized. Another loss, that related to siltation, does not affect water supply directly but does affect the volume available for storing it.

Once a dam has been constructed and its impoundment filled, the exposed water surface area increases significantly above what it had been before the dam was built. The result is that opportunity for evaporation greatly increases; in arid regions, an added increment of storage could be completely offset by evaporation losses. Direct precipitation on the water surface of a reservoir is captured, but there is of course no runoff from the land area flooded by the reservoir. These are known as water surface effects. Net gains usually result in humid areas, whereas losses are common in arid regions since evaporation rates are often many times greater than rates of precipitation.

The amount of water lost to seepage depends on the geology of the region. Porous underlying materials increase the seepage problem whereas impervious bottoms such as clay tend to retard seepage losses. The magnitude of these losses can be important, and an adequate understanding of the character of rocks and soils underlying the reservoir area must be acquired to evaluate them.

The sedimentation rate to be expected for a reservoir is an important factor to be evaluated (2, 21–24). The useful life of the reservoir is at issue; if it can be shown that the storage capacity of a proposed reservoir will be lost to the storage of trapped sediment within a few years, the decision on whether to go ahead with the project or not might be negative. But the rate and nature of sediment inflow to a reservoir can be controlled to a certain extent. This may be accomplished by using sedimentation basins, providing vegetative screens, and through the use of various erosion control measures (1). Dams can be designed so that some of the incoming sediment can be passed through their outlet works. A last resort is physical removal of settled material, but this is usually not feasible in an economic sense. Figure 11-2 indicates the manner in which size of reservoir and inflow rate affect the amount of sediment that a reservoir might trap.

Example 11-1

Determine the expected life of a reservoir with an initial capacity of 40,000 acre-feet and an average annual inflow of 70,000 acre-feet. A sedi-

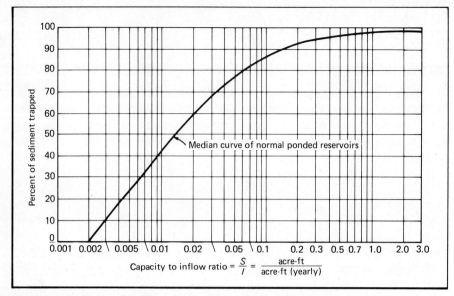

Figure 11-2 Relation between reservoir sediment trap efficiency and capacity-inflow ratio. (Developed from data in Brune, "Trap Efficiency of Reservoirs," *Trans. Am. Geophys. Union,* vol. 34, June 1953.)

ment inflow of 150 acre-feet per year is expected. Assume the useful capacity of the reservoir is exceeded when 75 percent of the original capacity is lost.

SOLUTION

The solution is given in Table 11-1. In this case the reservoir could be expected to function for many years (about 158) into the future, making the value of its construction reasonable in terms of loss of utility due to sediment loading.

This example demonstrates the procedure that could be followed in estimating sediment losses in reservoirs. In this particular case, the size of the reservoir and its anticipated sediment loading rate were of such magnitude that slow sedimentation would be expected. The reader should note from Figure 11-2 that for smaller reservoirs and higher loading rates very different results could be obtained. ■

Dams and Their Appurtenances

A reservoir is created by the construction of a dam that restricts the natural channel of the stream to be impounded. Use of the reservoir requires that certain other works (spillways, outlets, etc.) be developed to provide for flow releases and possible generation of power, and to protect the structure during times of flood (2).

Table 11-1 DETERMINATION OF RESERVOIR LIFE

(1)	(2)	(3)	(4)	(5)	(6)	(7)
RESERVOIR CAPACITY (ACRE-FT)	VOLUME INCREMENT (ACRE-FT)	CAPACITY INFLOW RATIO: (1)/70,000	PERCENT SEDIMENT TRAPPED, FROM FIG. 11-2	AVERAGE PERCENT SEDIMENT TRAPPED PER VOLUME INCREMENT	ACRE-FT SEDIMENT TRAPPED ANNUALLY: (5) × 150	NUMBER OF YEARS REQUIRED TO FILL THE VOLUME INCREMENT: (2) ÷ (6)
40,000	5000	0.57	96.0			
35,000	5000	0.50	95.7	95.9	144	35
30,000	5000	0.43	95.5	95.6	143	35
25,000	5000	0.36	95.0	95.3	143	35
20,000	5000	0.29	94.0	94.5	142	35
15,000	5000	0.21	92.0	93.0	140	35
10,000	5000	0.14	90.0	91.0	137	36
						$\overline{211}$

Number of years to fill:

Total number of years of useful life:
0.75 × 211 = 158

11-4 ESTIMATING STORAGE REQUIREMENTS

The storage of water for various functional uses requires either a surface or an underground reservoir to provide the needed capacity. The amount of storage required may be determined in any one of several ways. Records of actual streamflows or synthetic records are used to determine inflows to surface reservoirs, and the operating rules for the reservoirs are used to set the releases based on estimated demands.

The purpose of the reservoir is to stabilize the flow of the intercepted watercourse. This is accomplished by permitting impoundment of water during periods of high flow so that these flows can be saved for later release during lower-flow periods. Operation studies are conducted to determine the capacity of a proposed reservoir. These studies are actually simulations of the reservoir operation over some period of time with a prescribed set of operating rules. The period over which the performance is tested may be a critical low-flow sequence or it may be many years. Daily, monthly, annual, or other time interval data may be used. If only a critical period is evaluated, the operation study will yield only the required capacity to meet such an event if it occurs. If the evaluation period extends over a long time, then the operation study can provide information about the reliability of the reservoir for meeting specified demands or about the reliability of reservoirs of several capacities that might be constructed at a given location.

Reservoir Features

A reservoir is designed to hold water, and naturally the storage capacity is its principal characteristic. For a given location and assumed or known dam height, the volume of the reservoir created by the dam can be easily determined. Topographical surveys are conducted to provide the data for determining the surface area at any elevation. The storage contained between any two elevations is usually considered to be the product of the average surface area at the two elevations multiplied by the difference in elevation between the two levels. The total storage from the lowermost point in the reservoir to any elevation of interest is obtained by adding the storage increments between various elevations from the reference elevation to the top of the impoundment. Area v. elevation and storage v. elevation curves can be constructed from topographical data to facilitate such determinations. Such a plot is shown in Figure 11-3. By entering the graph on the left at a given elevation, the storage volume contained below that level or the surface area at that level can be determined by projecting to the right and down from the intersection with the volume curve to determine volume, or by projecting over to the area curve and projecting up from the intersection to determine the surface area.

Generally, in large multipurpose reservoirs, the total reservoir stor-

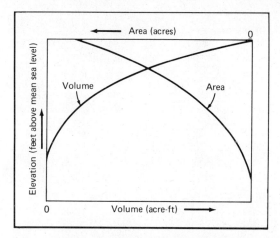

Figure 11-3 Elevation-storage and elevation-area curves.

age is considered to consist of three principal strata: (1) the active storage, which is used to regulate streamflows and provide water supply for various purposes; (2) the dead storage, which is used for sediment collection, recreational purposes, or hydroelectric production; and (3) the flood control storage capacity, which is used to reduce flood peaks downstream and thus lower the potential for damage. Because of the differences in purposes these three storages serve, they are often modeled separately and then added together to get total storage. Figure 11-4 illustrates the nature of these storages and also defines some other terms relative to the design and operation of reservoirs.

The normal pool level in a reservoir is the highest elevation of the water surface in a reservoir during normal operating conditions. As shown in Figure 11-4, this is also the top of the active storage pool. The normal pool level may be determined by the elevation of the spillway crest or it may be below the spillway crest, as shown by the diagram. In the former case, when the active storage is full and a flood occurs, flow over the spillway crest begins immediately. The minimum pool level is the lowest level to which the reservoir is to be drawn down under usual conditions of operation. In some cases there are no outlet works that permit drawing water below the minimum pool level. In other cases, this may be possible but water from dead storage would be used only under conditions of extreme stress. The storage volume contained between the minimum and the normal pool level is the active storage, which is the component that is put to water supply use. Surcharge storage, as shown in Figure 11-4, is usually uncontrolled; it is derived from the depth generated above the spillway crest to sustain the outflow during surcharge conditions. This storage will always be discharged and is not available for retention for later use.

The capacity of a reservoir is often increased above that provided by the reservoir storage volume by what is called bank storage. Since most

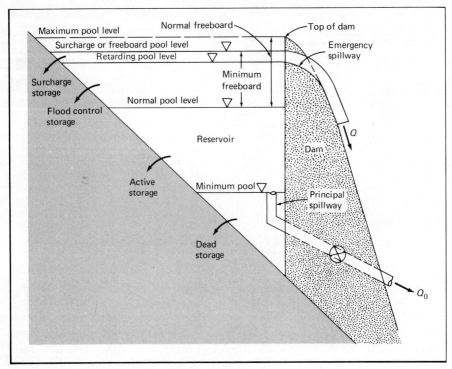

Figure 11-4   Multipurpose reservoir storage zones.

soil materials surrounding a reservoir are usually permeable, water enters these regions when the reservoir fills and drains back into the reservoir as it empties. The amount of bank storage is a function of the surrounding soil and rock materials. It may vary from insignificance to several percent of the storage capacity of the reservoir.

The actual storage volume obtained as a result of building a dam is the difference between the storage volume created by the dam and the natural valley storage provided by the stream system before development. This is of little consequence as far as the active storage is concerned, but from the flood management point of view it must be recognized that the effective flood control storage to be gained is the difference between (a) the maximum storage below the spillway crest plus surcharge storage and (b) the natural valley storage that would have existed without the reservoir.

For very large reservoirs, the water surface is often considered to be level even though this is not actually the case as long as there is an inflow. For small, narrow reservoirs, however, the water surface at high flows may be considerably sloped from the horizontal. In such cases it is necessary to compute backwater curves to determine the extent to which the reservoir creates flooding upstream. This determination is needed both for flood management purposes and for determining the lands that need to be provided with water storage if the dam is built. The relocation of highways and other manmade structures upstream of the dam site may be required as a result of backwater effects, and these must be determined in advance of construction.

Selection of a reservoir site involves many considerations. These include a topographically suitable dam site, the cost of obtaining land and relocating people and/or facilities, storage capacity available at the site, sedimentation potential at the site, and water quality. Many of the best reservoir sites in the United States have already been developed, and thus the search for new sites in a region may present many challenges. The difficulty in finding locations with suitable physical features, which at the same time do not create significant environmental or social conflicts, makes careful analyses and consideration of alternatives essential in most cases.

Yield

While the reservoir capacity is the most important physical characteristic of the facility, it is the relation between the yield that can be expected from the reservoir and its capacity that is of primary concern to those designing and operating such facilities. Yield is the amount of water that the reservoir can deliver in some prescribed interval of time. Time increments of interest vary with the purpose of the storage system. In the case of operating storage for a municipal water supply system (see Section 11-5) the appropriate time unit might be a day or less. For large reservoirs, such as those found on the Colorado River in the western United States, the time interval of concern would usually be a year or more. Obviously the yield is a function of the amount of flow reaching the reservoir as well as its capacity to store water. A term often used is the safe or firm yield. This is the amount of water that can be supplied during some critical period of streamflow. In the absence of storage, it is the lowest streamflow that might occur (the lowest flow of record is sometimes used as an estimator). Because flows less than those previously recorded may be expected to occur, firm yield should be considered probabilistic in nature, and the risk associated with it considered as a factor in reservoir design. More will be said about this later. In contrast to the safe yield, the maximum possible yield is the average streamflow less losses due to seepage and evaporation.

In most instances, a target yield based on anticipated user needs is specified for a reservoir. The problem is then to provide sufficient reservoir capacity so that the probability of not meeting the target is acceptable. For municipal water supplies the risk of not meeting the target should be low, whereas for other purposes such as irrigation, the risk to be accepted is often much higher. The water that is available above the safe yield during higher flow periods is known as secondary yield. Such yields may be used to step up hydroelectric generation, for example, but the purchasers of such energy must be aware that on a sustained basis this is not to be depended on.

Reservoir storage-yield functions define the maximum reservoir release or yield that can be delivered, at a given level of reliability, during each period of operation (3). For a sequence of known inflows, reservoir yield will depend on the amount of active storage volume provided in the reservoir. Figure 11-5 illustrates two storage-yield functions for a single reservoir. The upper curve represents yields that could be delivered with a low level of reliability and the lower curve shows the corresponding situation for greater reliability, or assurance, of achieving the target yield.

Various procedures can be followed in deriving storage v. yield functions. Several of these will be discussed later in this section. An interesting method discussed by Loucks et al. uses linear optimization (3). The model used consists of a linear objective function and linear constraints. To illustrate the method let us consider a single reservoir that must provide a uniform yield y in each time interval t for which a record of streamflows is provided. These flows may be historical or synthetic. The problem is to find the maximum level of yield y that can be obtained from a given storage capacity. The objective is

Maximize y $\qquad$ (11-1)

To complete the model, appropriate constraints are needed. These reflect the constraints on maximum yield due to water availability and reservoir capacity. Two sets of constraints are needed to define the relations among the yields, storage volumes, inflows, any excess releases, and reservoir capacity. The first set is the continuity equations, which relate the unknown final reservoir storage volume s_{t+1} in period t to the unknown initial reservoir storage volume s_t plus the known inflow i_t, minus the uniform yield y and any excess release y_t during period t. These equations take the form (3):

$$s_{t+1} = s_t + i_t - y - y_t \qquad \text{for } t = 1, 2, \ldots, T \qquad (11-2)$$

where $T + 1 = 1$

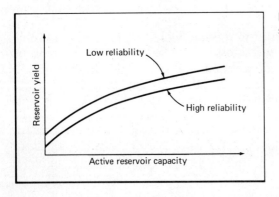

Figure 11-5 Typical reservoir storage-yield functions.

The last expression indicates that period 1 follows period T. If this reasoning is followed, it is not necessary to set a value for the initial storage volume s_1 and/or the final storage volume $s_T + 1$ (3). The solution is a steady-state one in that the entire inflow sequence repeats itself again and again. It is considered that this assumption, although not likely to occur, is as good as any other that might be followed and that the assumption would not significantly affect the model's behavior given that the streamflow sequence was relatively long. Note that in the above equations, T could be the number of time periods in a year or in some other duration.

The next set of constraints is needed to ensure that the maximum capacity of the reservoir is not exceeded. They are:

$$s_t \le K \qquad \text{for } t = 1, 2, 3, \ldots, T \tag{11-3}$$

Finally, an upper bound on yield is the mean streamflow. This is given by

$$y \le (\Sigma_t^T \, i_t)/T \tag{11-4}$$

The preceding equations are solved by linear programming to find the maximum yield for various values of the reservoir capacity K. These solutions provide the data needed to construct storage-yield curves such as those shown in Figure 11-5.

Targets and Benefit Functions

Most uses of water require withdrawals from the source. Common ones are for irrigation and for industrial, municipal, and cooling purposes. When a reservoir is involved, these uses are supplied from the active storage. Instream uses, on the other hand, do not require removal of water from the stream system, but they may require reservoir releases that will affect the timing and availability of water for other competing purposes. The instream flows may be dedicated to recreation, fish and wildlife protection, hydroelectric power production, and navigation. The allocation of flows for both withdrawal uses and instream uses requires careful management of reservoir operations. The concept of target allocations is useful in this respect.

Continuity requires that the amount of water any user can expect to receive in a specified time period must be less than or equal to the total flow available. This may be stated as

$$q_{s,t} \le Q_{s,t} \tag{11-5}$$

where $q_{s,t}$ is the quantity of water allocated to a given use at site s during period t and $Q_{s,t}$ is the total flow available at site s during the same time period. The target allocation is the amount of water a user expects to receive during the time period t. This we shall designate as T_s for an annual period of time and at a specified site s. Consider also that during some subperiod t, a fraction of T_s will be expected. If the amount of water actually allocated $q_{s,t}$ is less than the target allocation $(f_{s,t})(T_s)$, then there will be a deficit $D_{s,t}$. Note that $f_{s,t}$ is the fraction of the annual target expected during period t. On the other hand, if the allocation exceeds the target, there will be a surplus or excess $E_{s,t}$. Using this nomenclature, we can write:

$$q_{s,t} = f_{s,t}T_s - D_{s,t} + E_{s,t} \tag{11-6}$$

In the equation, it is clear that both excess and deficit cannot occur simultaneously. Thus either $D_{s,t}$ or $E_{s,t}$ will be zero. Decisions regarding the acceptance of deficits or excesses in meeting targets at a given site are dependent on the benefits or losses that would be associated with such decisions. Where the benefits derived from a particular use at a given site are not dependent on the allocations of water made to that use during other periods, the losses associated with deficits and the benefits or losses associated with excesses can be defined for each period t. The benefits from generating hydroelectric power during one time period, for example, may not be related to the benefits of producing electricity during the preceding period. The reasonableness of such assumptions must be verified in each case, however.

Where the benefits or losses associated with excesses or surpluses during any period depend on those during other periods, the benefits may be based on annual target allocations if the distribution of within-year allocations is specified and guaranteed by constraints (3). Irrigation water use is a good example where releases during one period influence benefits or losses during other periods. Providing ample water during one period following an interval in which no water was supplied might not be sufficient even to save a crop, much less produce benefits. For the case where there is dependency, the following constraint set would be needed to meet the conditions specified above:

$$q_{s,t} \geq f_{s,t}T_s \qquad \text{for all relevant } t \tag{11-7}$$

If an allocation during any period t is zero, then Equation 11-7 shows that the annual (or growing season target allocation for irrigation) would be zero.

The reason for water resources development is to provide some form of benefit to water users. In developing management models to aid in determining the best approaches to water allocation, it is common to use the target concept to relate benefits to the amount of water allocated. As previously stated, if a user expects some target allocation during a specified time period and receives it, his or her benefits will be maximized. If, however, the user receives more or less water than the target, his or her benefits may be increased or decreased. The concept of long- and short-run benefit functions is used in this regard, and some discussion of these seems appropriate at this point; they can be used directly in optimization models such as those discussed in Chapter 10.

In long-range planning, the capacities of reservoirs or other facilities and the target allocations of water are considered to be decision variables. The objective is to set their levels such as to maximize the efficiency of water use. In the short-run situation, capacities and targets are fixed by prior decisions, and allocations must be made in the best-possible manner, given those conditions.

The long-run benefits are the ones that would be obtained if capacities and targets were assigned their most efficient values (3). The approach is to set the capacities and targets so as to maximize expected net benefits. Short-run benefits are the benefits actually obtained by optimizing system operations, given that capacities and targets have been preset. If the resources available in the short run are the same as those anticipated during the long-run planning process, then it is possible for the estimated long-run benefits and the short-run actual benefits obtained to be equivalent.

The meaning of these situations can be made clear by considering the impact of meeting target allocations of water for some user. Let us consider that the long-run benefits of providing water to the user can be estimated. These benefits will be realized if the actual allocation to the user in some period equals the target allocation. Assume that the long-run benefit function is defined as $B(T)$. Consider also that for specified levels of the target T, the actual net benefits produced by various actual allocations Q can be estimated. These are the short-run benefit functions, which depend on both the target and the actual allocation. Figure 11-6 gives a relation between the long-run net benefits $B(T)$ and the short-run benefits $b(Q/T)$ for a specific target value of T.

In this figure, the long-run benefit function shows the benefits users receive when they are expecting an allocation equal to the target and they receive it. The short-run benefit function shows the benefits actually received by users when they receive more or less than the target allocation and cannot fully adjust their operations to these allocations. The short-run

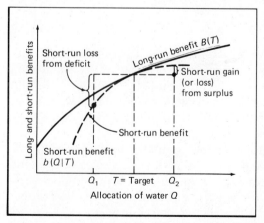

Figure 11-6 Long-run and short-run benefit functions. (After Loucks et al., reference 3.)

loss of a given allocation equals the long-run benefit associated with the target allocation minus the short-run benefit of the actual allocation. That is,

$$\text{Short-run loss} = B(T) - b(Q/T) \tag{11-8}$$

When the actual allocation equals the target allocation, the short-run loss is zero. This is obvious also from Figure 11-6. Additional information on this subject may be obtained from reference 3.

Costs associated with construction of facilities for water management are not always easily expressed as functions of targets associated with individual uses. Those costs can usually be stated in terms of the project's capacity, however. Costs must include both the amortized capital costs and annual operation, maintenance, and replacement costs. For a given facility, the annual net benefits would be determined as the long-run benefits minus the short-run losses and the capacity costs (costs of providing and operating the facility):

$$\text{Net benefits} = B(T) - L(Q/T) - C(K) \tag{11-9}$$

where $B(T)$ is the long-run benefit, $L(Q/T)$ is the short-run loss, and $C(K)$ is the capacity cost of the facility.

Mass Curve Analysis

One of the most widely used methods for determining storage requirements for reservoirs is a procedure first discussed by Rippl in 1883 (25). This procedure makes use of historical or synthetic streamflow records and uses a period of the record considered to be critical. This might be the most severe drought on record. Once the critical period is selected, storage requirements are calculated analytically or graphically by evaluating the cumulative difference between inflow to the reservoir and release. The maximum cumulative value is the required storage. This may be stated as

$$K_a = \text{maximum } \Sigma (R_t - Q_t) \tag{11-10}$$

where K_a is the required active storage capacity, R_t is the reservoir release during time interval t, and Q_t is the reservoir inflow during period t. This procedure will give results only if the sum of the releases does not exceed the sum of inflows during the period of record. Figures 11-7 and 11-8 illustrate a graphical approach to determining reservoir capacity in this manner and Example 11-2 gives an analytical solution.

Figure 11-7 illustrates Rippl's original approach to the reservoir capacity problem. The cumulative inflow during the selected critical period is plotted v. time. Assuming a constant reservoir release during each time period t, a line with a slope representing this constant release rate is plotted so that it is tangent to the cumulative inflow curve (point A on the figure). To the right of point A and until time period 9, the reservoir

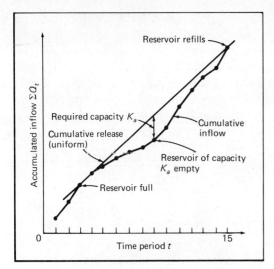

Figure 11-7 Mass diagram analysis for estimating active reservoir storage capacities.

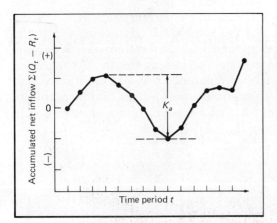

Figure 11-8 Alternative mass diagram analysis using accumulated net inflows.

release exceeds the inflow. After time period 9 the inflow exceeds the release and the reservoir begins to fill. By time period 15 the reservoir is full. The maximum vertical difference between the inflow and release curves is the maximum deficit, and thus the storage requirement necessary to meet the constant demand is determined.

The graphical approach just discussed works very well if the reservoir releases are constant during the period of analysis. For cases in which the releases vary, however, it is often easier to plot the cumulative difference between the inflows and releases, as shown in Figure 11-8. When this is done, the maximum vertical distance between the highest peak of the cumulative difference curve and the lowest dip that occurs to the right of the maximum peak is the measure of the needed active storage capacity. Note that the procedures outlined can be used to determine yield v. capacity for a given reservoir site.

Figure 11-7 illustrates a method that will yield the amount of active storage required for a particular water demand for a specific low-flow sequence. The reader should understand that a more severe low-flow period would require greater storage to meet the same demand. Thus it is easy to see that unless the frequency of the flow conditions is known, little can be said about the short- or long-term adequacy of the determined active storage capacity to meet the water supply needs of the prospective users. Procedures for dealing with the associated risk will be addressed later in this section.

Finally, before making calculations regarding needed storage capacity, it is important to consider the magnitude of possible seepage and evaporation losses from the reservoir. Once a reservoir is filled, the evaporation opportunity increases due to the large exposed surface area of water that results. Usually this produces a net loss of water from storage. In dry localities, such as the southwestern United States, these losses may be great enough to cancel the positive effects of impounding the water. The evaporation that occurs can be estimated by calculating the approximate free-water surface evaporation from the average expected pool level and diminishing it by the amount of natural evapotranspiration that would have occurred from the area that the reservoir floods. Seepage from the reservoir may also be significant. The losses associated with it may be estimated by using the procedures for determining flow in soils presented in Chapter 7. Where there is a large difference between the surface area of the average pool level and the maximum pool level, it may be necessary to compute evaporation losses for each period of reservoir operation in order to get the best estimate of cumulative evaporation losses.

Example 11-2

Table 11-2 gives the monthly inflows during a critical flow period at the site of a proposed dam. In addition, monthly evaporation loss estimates are given, as are monthly amounts of net precipitation on the mean pool level. Note that these values are already adjusted to show the gain to the reservoir above that which would have occurred from precipitation over the area occupied by the mean pool level without the reservoir. A local instream flow requirement is for a uniform release of 40 acre-feet per month. The water supply requirements to be met from the active storage capacity are also tabulated in the table. Using Equation 11-10, find the required active storage capacity of the reservoir.

SOLUTION

The required storage is gotten by accumulating the values in column 8. This results in a required storage capacity of 7305 acre-feet to meet the imposed demands.

This example illustrates the use of an analytic approach to mass

Table 11-2 STORAGE REQUIREMENT COMPUTATIONS FOR EXAMPLE 11-2

(1) MONTH	(2) INFLOW Q_t	(3) DEMAND R_t	(4) IN-STREAM FLOW RELEASE	(5) EVAPO-RATION	(6) PRECI-PITA-TION	(7) ADJUSTED FLOW Q_{ta}	(8) DEFI-CIENCY $(Q_{ta}-R_t)$
F	2000	1800	40	200	280	2040	0
M	2500	2300	40	300	290	2450	0
A	2700	2600	40	350	310	2620	0
M	3800	3500	40	370	370	3760	0
J	4600	4700	40	410	400	4550	150
J	4000	4500	40	400	390	3950	550
A	2100	4300	40	390	205	1875	2425
S	1800	4000	40	300	200	1660	2340
O	1600	3000	40	280	195	1475	1525
N	2500	2800	40	250	275	2485	315
D	3000	2500	40	225	280	3015	0
J	2100	2000	40	210	250	2100	0
F	1900	1800	40	195	210	1875	0

Note that all values in columns 2 through 8 are in acre-feet. The adjusted flow, column 7, is obtained by combining the values in the designated columns in the following manner: (col. 2) − (col. 4) − (col. 5) + (col. 6). The values in column 8 are gotten by subtracting the values in column 3 from those in column 7 whenever the result is negative.

analysis for determining active reservoir storage. Note that the answer obtained is valid for the inflow sequence given but that it does not give any expression of the probabilities of the shortages that might result from such a design if more critical low-flow periods were encountered. ■

Sequent-Peak Analysis

The mass diagram analysis just presented is easy to use when brief periods of data are to be analyzed. When long traces such as those generated synthetically are to be evaluated, a modification of the procedure called sequent-peak analysis is often used (26). This approach is especially suited to computer studies. The cumulative sum of inflows Q_t minus releases R_t is computed (this calculation should include any needed adjustments for seepage or evaporative losses). The first peak (see Figure 11-9) and the sequent peak (the next peak that is greater than the first) are noted. The required storage for the interval is the vertical difference between peak 1 and the low point before the sequent peak as illustrated in the figure. This process is repeated for at least twice the length of the time interval under study. The largest value of storage is selected as the design value. In Figure 11-9 this is designated as the maximum storage. As is apparent from the figure, the method can be applied graphically if desired.

An analytical solution to the sequent-peak method makes use of the following equation:

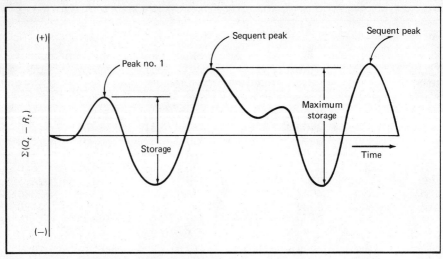

Figure 11-9   Application of the sequent-peak algorithm.

$$K_t = \begin{cases} R_t - Q_t + K_{t-1} & \text{if positive} \\ 0 & \text{otherwise} \end{cases} \qquad (11\text{-}11)$$

where K_t is the required storage capacity at the beginning of period t, R_t is the release during period t, and Q_t is the inflow to the reservoir during the period. The initial value of K_t is set at zero, and then Equation 11-11 is used to calculate values of K_t consecutively for up to twice the length of the recorded time span. This assumes that the record repeats to take care of the case when the critical sequence of flows occurs at the end of the streamflow record. The maximum of all the calculated values of K_t is the required reservoir storage capacity for the specified inflows and releases. Example 11-3 illustrates the method.

Example 11-3

For the data on inflow and releases given in Table 11-3, find the required reservoir capacity K_t using the sequent-peak approach. The procedure and calculations are indicated in the table. The required storage capacity is 13 units. ■

Optimization Analysis

The mass diagram and sequent-peak methods can be used to evaluate a variety of circumstances relative to the determination of reservoir capacity or for developing reservoir yield v. capacity curves. Mathematical

Table 11-3 CALCULATION OF STORAGE CAPACITY FOR EXAMPLE 11-3

PERIOD t	RELEASE $[R_t$	INFLOW $-\quad Q_t$	PREVIOUS REQUIRED CAPACITY $+\quad K_{t-1}]$	PRESENT[a] REQUIRED CAPACITY $=\quad K_t$
1	6	6	0	0
2	6	8	0	0
3	6	9	0	0
4	6	6	0	0
5	6	4	0	2
6	6	4	2	4
7	6	3	4	7
8	6	2	7	11
9	6	4	11	13
10	6	7	13	12
11	6	9	12	9
12	6	10	9	5
13	6	4	5	7
14	6	5	7	8
15	6	10	8	4
16	6	6	4	4
17	6	8	4	2
18	6	9	2	0
19	6	6	0	0
20	6	4	0	2
21	6	4	2	4
22	6	3	4	7
23	6	2	7	11
24	6	4	11	13
25	6	7	13	12
26	6	9	12	9
27	6	10	9	5
28	6	4	5	7
29	6	5	7	8
30	6	10	8	4

[a]K_t is the larger of zero or the quantity in brackets.

programming methods can extend the utility of this method, especially for problems involving more than one reservoir (3). These procedures also facilitate the incorporation of evaporation and seepage loss components.

The applicable optimization methods are based on the use of mass balance equations for routing water through a reservoir. These continuity equations explicitly define storage volumes at the outset of each time period t. Information about reservoir storage volumes at a given site must be available to permit estimation of evaporation and seepage losses and to analyze recreational and electric power generating alternatives. Such data are usually recorded in the form of area v. elevation and area v. volume curves of the type shown in Figure 11-3.

Risk Associated with Reservoir Yield

For any draft imposed on a reservoir, there is a risk associated with meeting it over a given interval of time. The time period of concern is usually the economic life of the reservoir, often between 50 and 100 years. Such risks can be estimated by various procedures analogous to those discussed in Chapters 7 and 10.

When water supply is the issue, low-flow sequences are of particular interest to the designers of reservoirs. For flood control capacity determination, it is the high-flow sequences that are of concern. Basically, the procedures used in dealing with either of these are similar.

In designing a reservoir to supply a given flow of water on a sustained basis, certain data must be developed. Required are the duration of the critical low-flow sequence, its magnitude, and its frequency of occurrence. Critical periods can be identified from either historical or synthetic records. Their frequency of occurrence can then be estimated by the use of the statistical methods already presented. An example will serve to illustrate one approach that can be taken.

Example 11-4

Let us assume that we are investigating the reliability of a reservoir that is expected to have an economic life of 50 years. We begin by synthetically generating 1000 years of streamflow record based on a historical record of 75 years. This can be done with the methods discussed in Chapter 10. The streamflow traces we shall be working with are equal in length to the project's life of 50 years and thus there are 20 of them. Each trace can be treated as an equally likely record of 50 years of streamflows for the system to be developed by storage. Now if the storage to be developed in order to meet a prescribed demand is determined for each trace, these storage levels (active storage requirements) can be ranked and analyzed with the frequency methods we have discussed before. The result will be a frequency curve indicating the probability of meeting the demand for a given storage capacity (Figure 11-10).

Using the frequency curve shown in the figure, we can then determine the risk associated with meeting the projected demand. For example, the probability of meeting the prescribed demand over the life of the reservoir with no shortfall is 95 percent if the storage capacity is 300,000 acre-feet and 99 percent if an active capacity of 350,000 acre-feet is provided. Note that the case of zero risk is impossible to achieve since there is always some probability, no matter how slight, of encountering a more critical period than that experienced in the synthetic (or observed) record. In this sense, the traditional concept of safe or firm yield (the lowest streamflow or sequence of flows recorded) is erroneous if considered as a fully dependable supply. For long historical or synthetic records, the old

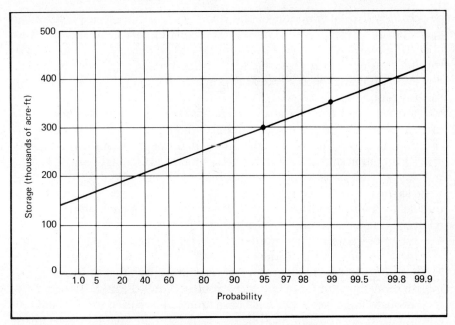

Figure 11-10   Graphical determination of reservoir reliability.

notion of safe yield would, however, serve as the basis for estimating a level of supply that would very infrequently be deficient. ∎

In addition to the active storage capacity provided to meet with water supply requirements, reservoirs are designed with additional capacity to retard flood flows and thus reduce the damages from them downstream. In contrast to water supply determinations for large reservoirs, where monthly or annual flows are considered, the flood control component of reservoir storage requires dealing with flows that may be generated in hours, days, or sometimes weeks. This condition makes the approach to flood storage capacity determination somewhat different than that for water supply. Generally, flood routing procedures, combined with (a) knowledge of, or assumptions about, a flood control operating policy for the reservoir and (b) information on channel storage characteristics between the reservoir and some downstream site to be protected, provide the basis for estimating the influence on peak flows downstream of various levels of upstream reservoir storage capacity.

The probability of a flood peak of given magnitude is commonly defined in terms of its return period. The return period (Chapter 7) of a flood is the expected number of years between the occurrence of a flood of the same or greater size. The probability that this T-year flood will be exceeded in any particular year is $1/T$. It is easy to see that the annual flood damage expected at a potential damage site is related to this probability. The peak flow Q_{pT} at a damage site that results from a flood of return period T will be a function of the flood control storage capacity of an upstream reservoir K_f and the operating policy for the reservoir. If an operating policy is assumed, this function can be defined by routing flows through the upstream reservoir for various storage capacities K_f to the downstream damage site. A flood routing simulation model is needed for this purpose (20, 27).

For any peak flow Q_{pT} at a potential damage site, there is a flood stage (depth of flow). The flood stage along with the flow will determine the extent of damages that will result. Flood damage functions can be developed by conducting field surveys at a potential damage site (28). The probability that some level of flood damage will be exceeded is exactly the same as the probability that the peak flow Q_{pT} will be exceeded. A detailed discussion of an analytical method for flood storage capacity determination is given in reference 3.

Expected annual flood damages can be derived graphically using a procedure developed by Loucks et al. (3). Figure 11-11 illustrates their method. Figure 11-11a shows, for three different return periods T, the information that can be obtained by routing flows through the reservoir for various storage capacities K_f. These functions are used next to facilitate computation of expected flood damages at the potential damage site.

The relations between flood stage and flood damage and between flood stage and peak flow must be determined by field surveys and hydraulic calculations. These relations are illustrated in quadrants 1 and 2 of Figure 11-11b. The relation displayed in quadrant 3 is derived from a determination of the exceedance probabilities of the peak flows and from information of the nature shown in part (a) of the figure. With all of this data plotted as shown, it is then possible to determine the probability of exceeding a particular level of flood damage (quadrant 4). The graphical procedure for developing the curves in quadrant 4 is shown in Figure 11-11b.

The areas under the exceedance probability distributions shown in quadrant 4 are the flood damages expected for the three storage capacities shown in quadrant 3. The data from these probability distributions for the three capacities then yield three points on the damage reduction–capacity curve shown in Figure 11-11c. This function is the difference between the amount of damages expected at the potential damage site with no upstream management and with the various levels of flood storage that might be provided. The tradeoff to be made is between the benefits to be gained by flood damage reduction and the costs associated with achieving these benefits.

Stochastic Models

Deterministic reservoir and other water resources planning models are based on mean values of inputs such as streamflows. Such models often

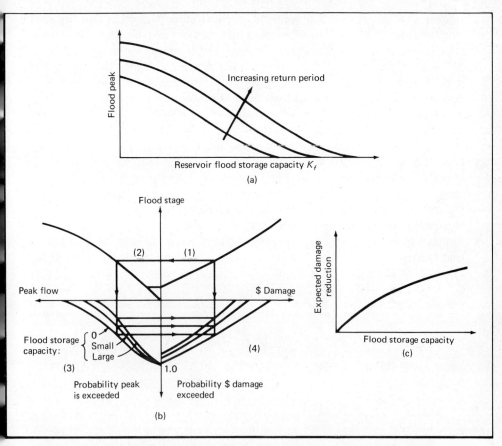

Figure 11-11   Loucks' approach to determining flood damage reduction: (a) determination of effects of upstream storage capacity on downstream flood peak by simulation; (b) method of calculating the probability of flood damage exceedance as a function of reservoir flood storage capacity; (c) expected damage reduction for specified levels of flood storage capacity as derived from quadrant 4 in part (b). (After Loucks et al., reference 3.)

tend to underestimate costs and overstate benefits (3). These limitations can be reduced by the use of stochastic models, that is, models accounting for hydrologic uncertainty. Probability theory is the underpinning for most of the stochastic models that have been developed. Generally, these models are considerably more complex than their deterministic counterparts. A detailed treatment is beyond the scope of this book.

Reservoir Operating Rules

Operating policies or rules for reservoir operation are intended to guide those managing such systems so that the releases made are in the best interests of the system's objectives, consistent with certain inflows and existing storage levels. There are several types of rules, but they all specify releases to be made or storage volumes to be maintained at any given time of the year. One type of rule specifies the storage volumes that are to be maintained if this is possible. Another type identifies storage zones (active, flood control, and so on) and associates them with a particular policy for releasing flows. The latter type of rule can be developed by considering storage-yield relations (3).

Rule curves are diagrams indicating storage requirements during the year or some other period of time. These curves serve to guide day-to-day operation of the reservoir and can be incorporated into detailed instructions for reservoir regulation. To illustrate this concept, we shall discuss the development of a rule curve for flood control operation of a reservoir.

Referring to Figure 11-12, let us assume that the reservoir is designed to provide water supply and to reduce downstream damages due to flooding. During normal periods of river flow, the reservoir will be maintained

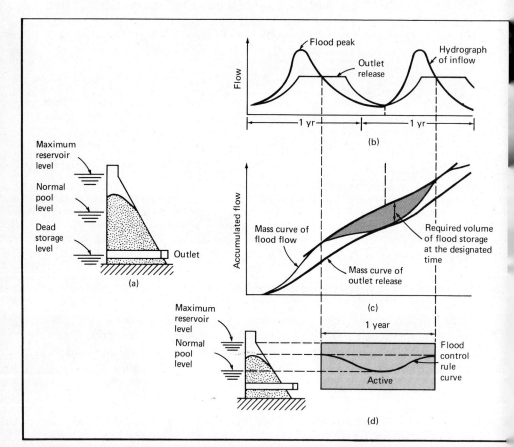

Figure 11-12 Flood control rule curve. (After Kuiper, reference 21.)

at the normal pool level (maximum elevation of the active storage component). In general, the storage volume below the normal pool level is available for water supply purposes, while that above the normal pool level is available for flood control. If a flow-forecasting system is in operation, all or part of the active storage volume can also be made available for flood control. Once a prediction has been made that high flows are to be expected, the normal pool level can be drawn down to such an elevation that the minimum anticipated flood flow will be sufficient to restore the active storage to its maximum level. When snowmelt is the cause of flooding, forecasts can usually be prepared well in advance of the floodwaters reaching the reservoir. In such cases there is often time to empty the full contents of the active pool prior to the arrival of the flood flows. This volume can then be refilled during the passage of the flood flow and an added increment of flood storage capacity provided at the same time.

For operation of the active storage, with information available on the volume available and on the nature of expected flows, it is possible to determine a yield that can be depended on with a high level of confidence. Whenever the inflow to the reservoir exceeds this amount but is below flood magnitude, the maximum pool level is maintained. Whenever the inflow to the reservoir falls below the yield specified, water is released from storage to cover the deficiency.

For the reservoir shown in Figure 11-12 it can be seen that there is a conduit through the dam whose invert is at the top of the dead storage pool elevation. There is also a spillway at the top of the dam. If a mass curve of the design flood is plotted (Figure 11-12c), and in addition a mass curve of the release from the conduit is plotted, then the difference between the two curves is the amount of water entering storage. Now if the mass curve of conduit discharge is shifted upward (Figure 11-12c), so that it becomes tangent to the mass curve for the flood flow, the ordinates that indicate the needed volume of flood storage at any time are obtained. Converting these ordinates to represent volume of flood storage required, and plotting them as shown in Figure 11-12d (downward from the spillway crest), a rule curve for flood control operation is produced. This rule curve is designed to ensure that there will always be adequate storage capacity available to accommodate the design flood (21). Actually the design flood could come at various times and thus under varying conditions of initial storage in the reservoir. The procedure outlined above could be followed for several alternatives, and rule curves could be developed for each. An enveloping curve below these different curves could be constructed and then used as the rule curve for the reservoir. The rule curve provides for flood damage reduction as well as enhancing the availability of water for water supply purposes.

Using the rule curve developed, we can see how the reservoir would be operated. During normal flow conditions, the reservoir level is maintained at the rule curve elevation. When minor floods occur, the water level in the reservoir will rise above the rule curve. When major floods are predicted, the reservoir will be drawn below the level of the rule curve as previously discussed. During low-flow conditions, the reservoir will be drawn down below the rule curve to provide the required yield. When a reservoir is operated for auxiliary purposes beyond the usual ones of water supply and flood control, the development of rule curves is somewhat more complex but still follows the rationale just presented (21).

11-5 EQUALIZING AND OPERATING STORAGE

Most of the discussion on storage so far has related to large reservoirs. There are many small storage systems, however, mostly related to municipal water supply operations. Such storage works are designed to permit uniform operation of treatment units and pumping equipment. Often these storages are designed to fill and empty in periods of one day or less. The procedures for estimating storage requirements are analogous to those for large reservoirs but their scale is much different.

In a municipal water supply system, distribution reservoirs meet the fluctuating demands imposed on the distribution system to provide storage for fire fighting and emergencies, and to provide more uniform operating pressures in the system (1, 2, 29–31). Most such storage works are elevated or are just below ground level. They are usually classified as surface reservoirs, elevated tanks, or standpipes. The elevated tank or standpipe is employed where a surface reservoir would not be at a high enough elevation to provide the head needed for operation of the system.

Ordinarily, distribution reservoirs should be located as near the center of use as possible. Often it is necessary to have a number of these placed strategically throughout the area that is to be served by them. Where the reservoir is expected to provide service storage (storage on line that directly furnishes users), it must be at an elevation sufficient to ensure adequate operating pressures. Central locations reduce the frictional losses in supplying pipelines. In addition, such locations facilitate equalization of pressures. For example, an elevated tank placed at the extremity of an area to be served (service area) would have to be high enough to provide satisfactory pressure at the farthest point it is to serve. If this is done, the outcome could be excessive pressures at those locations close to the tank. By placing the tank more centrally, a greater uniformity of pressures can be maintained without overpressuring or underpressuring any specific area.

The storage requirements of distribution facilities are a function of the capacity of the distribution network (pipe system), the location of the service storage, and the use to which it is to be put. When water treatment facilities are part of the system, it is usually the practice to operate them at uniform rates such as the average daily rate. It is also desirable to operate pumping equipment at constant rates. Demands on the system in excess of these rates are then met by operating storage. Requirements for fire fighting are such that water must be available to provide fire flows for periods of 10 to 12 hours in large communities and for at least two or more hours in smaller ones (1). Emergency storage requirements are associated with providing enough capacity to supply users for some reasonable period if the reservoir inflow is shut off by a fortuitous event such as failure of pumping units. It is common to provide enough emergency storage to last for several days.

To compute the required equalizing or operating storage, a mass diagram or hydrograph showing the hourly rate of water use is required. The method used to determine the necessary storage volume is then:

1. Obtain a hydrograph of hourly demands that reflects the conditions of interest. Often this is the maximum day.
2. Tabulate the hourly demand.
3. Find the required storage by using a mass diagram or a demand hydrograph.

Note that unless pumping follows the demand curve for a municipal water supply system, storage will be required to offset the deficiencies. It is common to operate pumping units at constant rates for economic reasons. Usually the rate chosen is the average rate for the maximum day. When the demands are less than this, some pumping units will stand idle. Alternatively, pumping units may be operated at the average rate for the average day, with storage being provided to meet greater requirements. When this is the mode of operation, reserve pumping units are usually provided and put on line during peak periods as a supplement. It is usually unwise to provide sufficient pumping and storage capacity to meet demands that might materialize for only several hours every few years. Under such circumstances the available pumping units might be operated under overload conditions for short periods of time.

11-6 GROUNDWATER STORAGE

As has been discussed in Chapters 7 and 10, in many locations there is significant storage volume available underground that can be used to supplement surface-water storage systems (32–36). The approach is generally one of joint use of surface-water and groundwater resources so that the availability and properties of each system can be capitalized on. Concurrent use is founded on the premise of transference of impounded surface water to groundwater storage at optimum rates. Annual water requirements are usually met by surface storage whereas groundwater storage is used to meet cyclic requirements covering periods of drought. The operation involves drawing down groundwater supplies (reducing underground storage) during dry years and replenishing these supplies during wet years. Various methods of artificial recharge are used to effect the transfers (see Chapters 7 and 8). These include spreading, ponding, injecting, returning flows from irrigation, and other techniques. Storage of water in underground systems makes use of natural storage capacity and all but eliminates major losses from evaporation. Where underground storage capacity can be managed and used, there is much to be gained. However, the problems of recharge and ownership of these stored waters must be dealt with (see Chapter 3); depending on the locality, they may be severe.

PROBLEMS

11-1. What would the maximum continuous constant yield be from a reservoir having a storage capacity of 750 acre-ft? Give your results in acre-ft/yr and m^3/yr.

11-2. If a constant annual yield rate of 1500 gal/min was required, what reservoir capacity would be needed to sustain it? Give the capacity in acre-ft/yr.

11-3. You are given the following data on reservoir inflows and outflows. Assume that at 8 A.M. the reservoir contains 6.5 acre-ft of water. What storage will exist at 9 P.M.?

TIME	INFLOW (ft^3/s)	OUTFLOW (ft^3/s)
8 A.M.	27	21
10	29	28
12 NOON	36	43
2 P.M.	39	47
4	43	50
6	41	40
8	37	35
10 P.M.	30	25

11-4. A mean draft of 100 mgd is to be developed from a 150 mi^2 catchment area. At the flow line the reservoir is estimated to be 4000 acres. The annual rainfall is 38 in, the mean annual runoff is 13 in, and the mean annual evaporation is 49 in. Find the net gain or loss in storage that this represents. Compute the volume of water evaporated. State this figure in a form such as the number of years the volume could supply a given community.

11-5. Find the expected life of a reservoir having an initial capacity of 48,000 acre-ft. The average annual inflow is 63,000 acre-ft, and a sediment inflow of 180 acre-ft/yr is reported. Consider the useful life of the reservoir to be exceeded when 80 percent of the original capacity is lost. Use 5000-acre-ft volume increments. Obtain values of percent sediment trapped from Figure 11-2.

11-6. What precautions might be taken to avoid or minimize silting when planning a reservoir?

11-7. Given the following average hourly demand rates in gal/min, find the uniform 24-hour pumping rate and the required storage.

12	P.M.	0	12	A.M.	6300
1	A.M.	1900	1	P.M.	6500
2		1800	2		6460
3		1795	3		6430
4		1700	4		6500
5		1800	5		6700
6		1910	6		7119
7		3200	7		9000
8		5000	8		8690
9		5650	9		5220
10		6000	10		2200
11		6210	11		2100
			12		2000

11-8. Solve Problem 11-7 if the period of pumping is from 6 A.M. to 6 P.M. only.

References

1. J. W. Clark, et al., *Water Supply and Pollution Control*, 3d ed., Harper & Row, New York, 1977.
2. R. K. Linsley and J. B. Franzini, *Water Resources Engineering*, 3d ed., McGraw-Hill, New York, 1979.
3. D. P. Loucks, et al., *Water Resource Systems Planning and Analysis*, Prentice-Hall, Englewood Cliffs, NJ, 1981.
4. J. M. Edmonston and E. E. Jackson, *The Feather River Project and the Establishment of the Optimum Hydraulic Grade Line for the Project Aqueduct*, Los Angeles, 1964.
5. J. Hinds, "Economic Water Conduit Size," *Eng. News Record*, January 1937.
6. N. Joukowsky, "Water Hammer," O. Simin (tr.), *Proc. Am. Water Works Assoc.*, vol. 24, 1904.
7. M. B. McPherson, "Generalized Distribution Network Head Loss Characteristics," *Proc. Am. Soc. Civil Engrs., J. Hydraulics Div. 86*, no. HY1, January 1960.
8. C. W. Reh, *Hydraulics of Water Distribution Systems*, University of Illinois Experiment Station Circular No. 75, February 1962.
9. M. B. McPherson, *Applications of System Analyzers: A Summary*, University of Illinois Engineering Experiment Station Circular No. 75, February 1962.
10. H. Cross, *Analysis of Flow in Networks of Conduits or Conductors*, University of Illinois Bull. No. 286, November 1936.
11. R. G. Kincaide, "Analyzing Your Distribution System," *Water Works Engr.*, vol. 97, nos. 2, 6, 10, 16, 21, January, March, May, August, October 1944.
12. M. S. McIlroy, "Direct Reading Electric Analyzer for Pipeline Networks," *J. Am. Water Works Assoc.*, vol. 42, no. 4, April 1950.
13. V. A. Appleyard and F. P. Linaweaver, Jr., "The McIlroy Fluid Analyser in Water Works Practice," *J. Am. Water Works Assoc.*, vol. 49, no. 1, January 1957.
14. M. B. McPherson and J. V. Radziul, "Water Distribution Design and McIlroy Network Analyzer," *Proc. Am. Soc. Civil Engrs.*, vol. 84, Pap. 1588, April 1958.

15. R. W. Jeppson, *Steady Flow Analysis of Pipe Networks*, Utah State University, Dept. of Civil Engineering, Logan, Utah, September 1974.

16. J. L. Gerlt and G. F. Haddix, "Distribution System Operation Analysis Model," *J. Am. Water Works Assoc.*, July 1975.

17. R. DeMoyer, Jr., and L. B. Horwitz, "Macroscopic Distribution System Modeling," *J. Am. Water Works Assoc.*, July 1975.

18. D. J. Wood and C. O. A. Charles, "Hydraulic Network Analysis Using Linear Theory," *Proc. Am. Soc. Civil Engrs.*, Hydraulics Div., vol. 98, no. HY7, July 1972.

19. W. B. Langbein, *Water Yield and Reservoir Storage in the United States*, U.S. Geological Survey Circular, U.S. Gov't. Print. Off., 1959.

20. W. Viessman, et al., *Introduction to Hydrology*, 2d ed., Harper & Row, New York, 1977.

21. E. Kuiper, *Water Resources Development: Planning, Engineering, and Economics*, Butterworth and Co., Washington, D.C., 1965.

22. G. M. Brune and R. E. Allen, "A Consideration of Factors Influencing Reservoir Sedimentation in the Ohio Valley Region," *Trans. Am. Geophys. Union*, vol. 22, 1941.

23. G. M. Brune, "Trap Efficiency of Reservoirs," *Trans. Am. Geophys. Union*, vol. 34, June 1953.

24. L. C. Gottschalk, "Reservoir Sedimentation," in V. T. Chow (ed.), *Handbook of Applied Hydrology*, McGraw-Hill, New York, 1964.

25. W. Rippl, "The Capacity of Storage Reservoirs for Water Supply," *Proc. of the Institute of Civil* Engineers (Brit.), vol. 71, 1883.

26. H. A. Thomas, Jr., and R. P. Burden, *Operations Research in Water Quality Management*, Harvard Water Resources Group, Cambridge, MA, 1963.

27. E. A. Lawler, "Flood Routing," in V. T. Chow (ed.), *Handbook of Applied Hydrology*, McGraw-Hill, New York, 1964.

28. L. D. James and R. R. Lee, *Economics of Water Resources Planning*, McGraw-Hill, New York, 1971.

29. H. E. Babbitt, J. J. Doland, and J. L. Cleasby, *Water Supply Engineering*, McGraw-Hill, New York, 1962.

30. J. E. Kiker, "Design Criteria for Water Distribution Storage," *Public Works*, March 1964.

31. W. G. Yeh, L. Becker, and W. S. Chu, "Real-Time Hourly Reservoir Operation," *Journal of the Water Resources Planning and Management Division, ASCE*, vol. 105, no. WR2, 1979.

32. M. E. Harr, *Groundwater and Seepage*, New York, McGraw-Hill, 1962.

33. N. Buras, "Conjunctive Operation of Dams and Aquifers," *Proc. Am. Soc. Civil Engrs., J. Hydraulics Div.*, vol. 89, no. HY6, November 1963.

34. F. B. Clendenen, "A Comprehensive Plan for the Conjunctive Utilization of a Surface Reservoir with Underground Storage for Basin-wide Water Supply Development: Solano Project, California" D. Eng. thesis, University of California, Berkeley, 1959.

35. *Ground Water Basin Management*, Manual of Engineering Practice No. 40, New York, American Society of Civil Engineers, 1961.

36. D. K. Todd, *Ground Water Hydrology*, 2d ed., New York, Wiley, 1980.

Chapter 12
Water Management Methods and Facilities

In this chapter we shall use the term water management facilities in a broad sense that includes both structural and nonstructural methods of achieving water allocation and water quality control. Irrigation, municipal and industrial water supply, hydroelectric power, waterways, flood damage reduction, wastewater treatment and management, and recreation facilities are discussed.

Construction of individual water management facilities is one of the last steps in the long, complex process of planning and designing water resources systems. Only after assessing the various factors affecting water resources development, and resolving conflicts encountered, can needed water management projects or approaches be proposed.

Of important note is that many of the physical facilities needed for water management have been completed in the past 30 years, lessening the demand for new facilities in today's society. As these facilities have grown older, however, many have become in such dire need of repairs that they are inefficiently used, resulting in higher costs. There are also pressures to build new, bigger, and better facilities to replace the older ones. In times of federal funding cutbacks in an area that has traditionally been publicly funded, there is also pressure to minimize large new structural undertakings. This presents a major challenge for water managers of the future. They should recognize that there are many opportunities to make in-place systems more efficient, thereby avoiding or delaying the construction of new facilities. The reader should keep this in mind, but observe also that additional water management structures will be required in the future. Figures 12-1 and 12-2 illustrate several large multiple-purpose facilities.

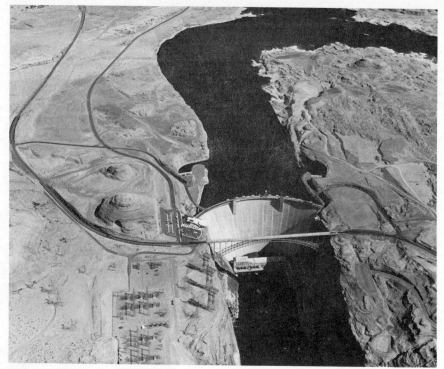

Figure 12-1 Glen Canyon Dam, Arizona. (Courtesy of the U.S. Bureau of Reclamation.)

12-1 IRRIGATION

As was shown in Chapter 4, irrigation water use accounts for the second-largest withdrawal of water in the United States. Moreover, irrigation accounts for the greatest portion of consumptive use, as water taken up by plants is lost from the surface- and groundwater budget to the atmosphere. The use of irrigation in agriculture since World War II has accounted for the fact that agricultural productivity has increased tremendously with virtually no increase in total acreage used for crops. Irrigated land accounts for only one-seventh of the nation's cropland but produces over one-fourth of the nation's crops (1).

In this section we shall take a look at how to determine the amount of water needed for an irrigation project, methods of irrigation, the impact of irrigation practices on water quality and quantity, irrigation trends in the United States, and finally, methods for improving the efficiency of existing irrigation systems.

Determination of Water Requirements

The amount of water needed for a particular irrigation project depends on a number of factors, including the type of crops, the stage of their

Figure 12-2 Canyon Ferry Dam, Montana. (Courtesy of the U.S. Bureau of Reclamation.)

development, the availability of water from other sources, the temperature and humidity of the air, wind movement, intensity and duration of sunlight, the quality of available water, the length of the growing season, and the efficiency of the irrigation system.

CROP REQUIREMENTS

The major crops irrigated in the United States are corn, alfalfa, hay, cotton, barley, soybeans, potatoes, other vegetables, and fruits. Several formulas have been developed that can be used to determine crop water requirements or *consumptive use.* Two of the most commonly used equations were developed by Penman and by Blaney and Criddle. Hansen et al. present a comparison of calculated results for one data set using these two methods as well as two others commonly used: the Jensen-Haise method and the Hargreaves equation (2).

The Blaney-Criddle equation was introduced in Chapter 7 as

$$U = k_s B \tag{7-8}$$

If monthly values for the consumptive use coefficient k are available, monthly consumptive use can be found as follows:

$$u = ktp/100 \tag{12-1}$$

where u is the monthly consumptive use (in inches) and the other terms are as described in Chapter 7. Table 12-1 provides values of k_s and k. The use of the Blaney-Criddle equation for estimating consumptive use is illustrated in Example 12-1.

Table 12-1 SEASONAL CONSUMPTIVE USE CROP COEFFICIENTS (k_s) FOR IRRIGATED CROPS, FOR USE IN EQUATION 7-8

CROP	LENGTH OF NORMAL GROWING SEASON OR PERIOD[a]	CONSUMPTIVE USE COEFFICIENT k_s[b]	MAXIMUM MONTHLY k[c]
Alfalfa	Between frosts	0.80–0.90	0.95–1.25
Bananas	Full year	0.80–1.00	—
Beans	3 months	0.60–0.70	0.75–0.85
Cocoa	Full year	0.70–0.80	—
Coffee	Full year	0.70–0.80	—
Corn (maize)	4 months	0.75–0.85	0.80–1.20
Cotton	7 months	0.60–0.70	0.75–1.10
Dates	Full year	0.65–0.80	—
Flax	7–8 months	0.70–0.80	—
Grains, small	3 months	0.75–0.85	0.85–1.00
Grain, sorghums	4–5 months	0.70–0.80	0.85–1.10
Oilseeds	3–5 months	0.65–0.75	—
Orchard crops:			
Avocado	Full year	0.50–0.55	—
Grapefruit	Full year	0.55–0.65	—
Orange and lemon	Full year	0.45–0.55	0.65–0.75[d]
Walnuts	Between frosts	0.60–0.70	—
Deciduous	Between frosts	0.60–0.70	0.70–0.95
Pasture crops:			
Grass	Between frosts	0.75–0.85	0.85–1.15
Ladino white clover	Between frosts	0.80–0.85	—
Potatoes	3–5 months	0.65–0.75	0.85–1.00
Rice	3–5 months	1.00–1.10	1.10–1.30
Soybeans	140 days	0.65–0.70	—
Sugar beets	6 months	0.65–0.75	0.85–1.00
Sugarcane	Full year	0.80–0.90	—
Tobacco	4 months	0.70–0.80	—
Tomatoes	4 months	0.65–0.70	—
Truck crops, small	2–4 months	0.60–0.70	—
Vineyard	5–7 months	0.50–0.60	—

SOURCE: From *Irrigation Water Requirements*, Technical Release no. 21, Soil Conservation Service, USDA, September 1970.

[a]Length of season depends largely on variety and time of year when the crop is grown. Annual crops grown during the winter period may take much longer than if grown in the summertime.

[b]The lower values of k_s for use in the Blaney-Criddle formula, $U = k_s B$, are for more humid areas and the higher values are for more arid climates.

[c]Dependent on mean monthly temperature and crop growth stage.

[d]Given by Criddle as "citrus orchard."

Example 12-1

Determine the seasonal consumptive use of a tomato crop grown in New Jersey if the mean monthly temperatures for May, June, July, and August are 61.6°F, 70.3°F, 75.1°F, and 73.4°F respectively and the percent daylight hours for the months May to August are 10.02, 10.08, 10.22, and 9.54 as percent of the year, respectively.

SOLUTION

1. From Table 12-1, the growing season for tomatoes is four months and the range of the consumptive use coefficient is 0.65 to 0.70. Since New Jersey is a humid area, choose the lower value of k_s = 0.65.

2. The term B is calculated using Equation 7-9 as:

$B = (61.6 \times 10.02/100) + (70.3 \times 10.08/100) + (75.1 \times 10.22/100) + (73.4 \times 9.54/100) = 27.9$

3. The seasonal consumptive use can then be determined from Equation 7-8:

$U = k_s B$
$= 0.65 \times 27.9 = 18.1$ in of water for the four-month growing season. Note that the total amount of water to be supplied to an irrigated plot must include consumptive use plus conveyance losses, and so on. Thus it may be considerably more than the consumptive use figure. ∎

WATER SOURCES

The major sources of irrigation water in the United States are surface water and groundwater. To a very minor extent, reclaimed wastewater is also used for this purpose. With the continuing institutional problems tying up water supplies in some parts of the country, reclaimed water as a source for irrigation is likely to become more important in the future. In 1970, surface-water withdrawals accounted for about 66 percent of all water used for irrigation and groundwater withdrawals accounted for about 34 percent.

In many areas of the country, periods of high surface-water flow occur in winter months, whereas the need for irrigation water is most critical in dry summer months when the river water levels are correspondingly low. It is often possible to circumvent this problem by diverting and storing a portion of the high-flow waters in surface impoundments for summer irrigation use. In arid areas, generating water through storage is adversely affected, however, due to high evaporation rates. (See Figure 7-6 for annual evaporation rates in the United States.)

An attractive approach to storing surface water in arid areas is to use surface-water and groundwater sources and storages conjunctively (see

Section 7-5). By diverting surface waters to irrigation fields during winter months to recharge aquifers, for example, excess winter waters can be stored without encountering the problem of summer evaporation, while at the same time replenishing groundwater supplies. Irrigators can later withdraw water from aquifers during low-flow periods. This approach is particularly attractive where irrigators are considering abandoning their in-place irrigation wells and center pivot distribution systems due to severe groundwater depletion.

IMPORTANCE OF WATER QUALITY

Human activities are often responsible for imparting characteristics to water that may make it unsuitable for irrigation use. Surface-water contamination may result from upstream sources such as discharge from municipal wastewater treatment plants or industrial operations, runoff from agricultural activities containing excess dissolved salts and pesticides, or acid drainage from mining operations. Groundwater contamination may result from septic field leachate, land disposal of municipal and industrial wastes, drainage from agricultural and mining operations, or saltwater intrusion in coastal areas. Excess levels of chemical and biological constituents in water intended for irrigation use may cause a number of water quality problems.

A major contributor to poor water quality in irrigation is *salinity,* or total dissolved solids (TDS). The dissolved salts consist primarily of the cations sodium, calcium, and magnesium and the anions chloride and sulfate. Other salts occurring in minor amounts are the cation potassium and the anions bicarbonate, carbonate, and nitrate. Water having a high salinity content when applied to land increases the osmotic pressure of the soil solution, which has the effect of withholding water from plant uptake. Depending on the type of crop, such conditions can cause plant wilt even when soil moisture conditions appear to be adequate.

Salinity is commonly measured by determining the electrical conductivity (EC) of a solution. The EC, expressed as millimhos (mho $\times$ 10^{-3}) per centimeter, is a measure of the ability of the salts in solution to conduct electricity. Waters with total dissolved solids (TDS) of less than 500 mg/L (EC < 0.75 mmho/cm) can be used for irrigation without concern for any salinity problem unless there is an unusually high water table. Waters with a salinity level greater than 5000 mg/L (EC > 7.50 mmho/cm) are generally not acceptable for irrigation use. Within these limits the value of the water decreases as salinity increases (3). Table 12-2 is a suggested classification of irrigation waters for salinity hazard.

In addition to causing a wilting problem, certain of the dissolved ions that constitute TDS, such as boron, chloride, and sodium, are toxic to plants at some levels. High sodium concentrations can be damaging to some soils. Also, trace metals and synthetic organic chemicals can have deleterious effects on plants. Herbicides, which may get into the irrigation

Table 12-2 SUGGESTED CLASSIFICATION OF IRRIGATION WATERS FOR SALINITY HAZARD

	TDS (mg/L)	EC (mmho/cm)
Water for which no detrimental effects are usually noticed	<500	0.75
Water that can have detrimental effects on sensitive crops	500–1000	0.75–1.50
Water that can have adverse effects on many crops; requires careful management practices	1000–2000	1.50–3.00
Water that can be used for tolerant plants on permeable soils with careful management practices	2000–5000	3.00–7.50

SOURCE: National Academy of Sciences–National Academy of Engineering, *Water Quality Criteria 1972: A Report of the Committee on Water Quality Criteria*, EPA-R3-73-033, U.S. Environmental Protection Agency, Washington, D.C., 1973.

water, are harmful to crops in very small quantities. An additional health effect of certain heavy metals, for example, molybdenum and possibly cadmium, is that they are concentrated by some plants in levels high enough to be toxic to animals that eat the plants. Recommended limits by the EPA for metals and other constituents in irrigation water are listed in Table 12-3.

A final consideration in irrigation water quality is possible biological contamination by bacteria and viruses. This is of particular concern if water reclaimed from sewage is applied to crops. The EPA recommends that wastewater which has received solely primary treatment should not be used on crops for human consumption, but that wastewater which has received secondary treatment may be used to irrigate crops that are canned or processed before being sold. For unrestricted irrigation use, the EPA has recommended that the irrigation water contain no more than a maximum of 1000 fecal coliforms per 100 milliliters.

Several western states trying to increase wastewater reuse have set stringent bacteriological standards for irrigation use due to public fears that direct reuse of the water poses a health hazard to the population. As an example, California has specified that tertiary-treated wastewater used to spray-irrigate food crops must contain less than 2.2 fecal coliforms per 100 milliliters as a weekly median count (4). This very low limit is based on the possibility of aerosolization of bacteria during the spraying process, which could pose a hazard to workers through inhalation or ingestion.

Irrigation Methods

Four methods are used primarily in the United States for irrigation. These are surface, subsurface, sprinkler, and trickle (drip) irrigation. Surface irrigation includes flood, strip, and furrow methods. The main types of

Table 12-3 RECOMMENDED MAXIMUM CONCENTRATIONS OF TRACE HEAVY METALS IN IRRIGATION WATER

CONSTITUENT	LONG-TERM USE[a] (mg/L)	SHORT-TERM USE[b] (mg/L)	REMARKS
Aluminum	5.0	20.0	Can cause nonproductivity in acid soils, but soils at pH 5.5 to 8.0 will precipitate the ion and eliminate toxicity.
Arsenic	0.10	2.0	Toxicity to plants varies widely, ranging from 12 mg/L for Sudan grass to less than 0.05 mg/L for rice.
Beryllium	0.10	0.5	Toxicity to plants varies widely ranging from 6 mg/L for kale to 0.5 mg/L for bush beans.
Boron	0.75	2.0	Essential to plant growth, with optimum yields for many obtained at a few tenths mg/L in nutrient solutions. Toxic to many sensitive plants (e.g., citrus plants) at 1 mg/L.
Cadmium	0.01	0.05	Toxic to beans, beets, and turnips at concentrations as low as 0.1 mg/L in nutrient solution. Conservative limits recommended.
Chromium	0.1	1.0	Not generally recognized as essential growth element. Conservative limits recommended due to lack of knowledge on toxicity to plants.
Cobalt	0.05	5.0	Toxic to tomato plants at 0.1 mg/L in nutrient solution. Tends to be inactivated by neutral and alkaline soils.
Copper	0.2	5.0	Toxic to a number of plants at 0.1 to 1.0 mg/L in nutrient solution.
Fluoride	1.0	15.0	Inactivated by neutral and alkaline soils.

Table 12-3 *(Continued)*

CONSTITUENT	LONG-TERM USE[a] (mg/L)	SHORT-TERM USE[b] (mg/L)	REMARKS
Iron	5.0	20.0	Not toxic to plants in aerated soils, but can contribute to soil acidification and loss of essential phosphorus and molybdenum.
Lead	5.0	10.0	Can inhibit plant cell growth at very high concentrations.
Lithium	2.5	2.5	Tolerated by most crops at up to 5 mg/L; mobile in soil. Toxic to citrus at low doses; recommended limit is 0.075 mg/L.
Manganese	0.2	10.0	Toxic to a number of crops at a few tenths to a few mg/L in acid soils.
Molybdenum	0.01	0.05	Not toxic to plants at normal concentrations in soil and water. Can be toxic to livestock if forage is grown in soils with high levels of available molybdenum.
Nickel	0.2	2.0	Toxic to a number of plants at 0.5 to 1.0 mg/L; reduced toxicity at neutral or alkaline pH.
Selenium	0.02	0.02	Toxic to plants at low concentrations and to livestock if forage is grown in soils with low levels of added selenium.
Tin, tungsten, titanium	—	—	Effectively excluded by plants; specific tolerance levels unknown.
Vanadium	0.1	1.0	Toxic to many plants at relatively low concentrations.
Zinc	2.0	10.0	Toxic to many plants at widely varying concentrations; reduced toxicity at increased pH (6 or above) and in fine-textured or organic soils.

SOURCE: Reference 3.
[a]For water used continuously on all soils.
[b]For water used for a period of up to 20 years on fine-textured neutral or alkaline soils.

sprinkler systems employed are tow line, traveler, and center pivot. The best method for a particular location depends on many factors such as type of crop grown, availability and cost of water, topography of the land, and soil characteristics.

SURFACE IRRIGATION SYSTEMS

Surface irrigation is used on about 75 percent of the irrigated land in the United States. Basically, water is delivered to farms via canals (see Figure 12-3) and then distributed to individual fields via "laterals" (small canals). Water is allowed to flow over the fields by gravity wherever possible (see Figure 12-4). Pumping, if required, increases operating costs proportionally. The manner in which the water is distributed over a field distinguishes the type of surface method involved. Furrow irrigation is used on crops grown in rows, with the water confined to running laterally between the raised (mounded) rows of crops. Flood irrigation is used on close-growing field crops (for example, rice) where the field or part of the field is surrounded by shallow levees so that the entire field can be flooded. Flood irrigation is the least efficient of the surface irrigation methods because the rate of application is difficult to control.

Figure 12-3   Palo Verde Canal, California. (Courtesy of the U.S. Bureau of Reclamation.)

Figure 12-4   Surface irrigation of lettuce in Palo Verde Mesa, California.
(Courtesy of the U.S. Bureau of Reclamation.)

SUBSURFACE IRRIGATION SYSTEMS

In subirrigation, water is applied to soils directly under the surface. Subsurface irrigation may be one of two types: that which is controlled by lateral supply ditches, or that which is uncontrolled, where excess application of water to adjacent or higher lands is the source of irrigation water. Five conditions necessary for successful subirrigation, as listed by Hansen et al., include (1) an impervious subsoil at a depth of two meters or more, (2) a very permeable upper subsoil, (3) a permeable loam or sandy loam surface soil, (4) uniform topographical conditions, and (5) moderate slopes (2). The main advantage of subirrigation is the saving of water that would otherwise be lost to evaporation. Other benefits include low labor costs and high crop yields (2).

SPRINKLER SYSTEMS

Sprinkler systems have the advantage of a more controllable application rate than surface irrigation systems. Although sprinkler systems have become very popular since the 1960s, there is concern about their cost of operation due to rising energy costs.

A *tow-line irrigation system* consists of a main water line positioned in the center of a field with a sprinkler attached to it by means of a flexible joint. The water is delivered to the crop through lateral sprinkler lines that are towed over the main line by a tractor from one side of the field to the other. This system best suits rectangular fields with a level to mild sloping terrain, on soils of medium to low soil moisture absorbancy. Shallow sandy soils, which require frequent irrigation (every three to five days), are not amenable to this type of irrigation, due to the excessive pipe wear that would result.

Traveling sprinklers are high-pressure, self-propelled portable units that travel across a field with the water supply hose attached by cable. Although advantageous due to portability, they require considerable energy to operate, and this contributes to high operating costs.

Center pivot systems consist of a sprinkler system that rotates continuously around a pivot point. Multiple pivot systems may be used to further increase the irrigated acreage. These systems are operated by electricity, water, or oil hydraulic drive. Electric units are more expensive but have the advantage of being able to reverse instantly and to be operated dry or without applying water. This means that the system can bypass a crop not needing water in order to irrigate another crop. Center pivot systems are well suited to irrigating tall crops such as corn and work well on uneven terrain and rolling hills.

TRICKLE IRRIGATION SYSTEMS

In trickle irrigation systems, water is delivered via plastic pipe through openings (emitters) that are located along water delivery lines. Water is applied very slowly in order to limit runoff and thus waste. These systems are particularly well suited to fruit and vegetable crops where a relatively small amount of water is needed, and careful application can provide substantial cost savings. The initial capital costs of installing such a system are quite high, as a large amount of pipe is needed to deliver the water directly to the plants. The method is highly regarded as a method to conserve water and thus save money in water costs, and so the capital outlay must be balanced against the savings that could be realized in reduced water bills.

Impact on Water Quality

Plants take up and evapotranspire water in a relatively pure form, leaving dissolved salts behind in the soil. Enough excess water must be applied to the irrigated land to flush out these residues. In humid areas, there is generally adequate rainfall to leach the salts from the soil to the groundwater and carry them ultimately to the oceans. In the arid west, on the other hand, temperatures and accompanying high evaporation rates inhibit the natural leaching process, resulting in salt buildup in the soil. Runoff or irrigation return flow from the irrigated lands may then dissolve these salts and carry them to surface waters, which can have an adverse effect on stream life and on downstream water use. In places where water from a stream is withdrawn, used for irrigation, and returned to the stream several times along its course, the result can be a marked increase in salinity by the time the water reaches the stream's mouth. Downstream irrigators are essentially using the irrigation return flows from upstream farms and returning them in a more polluted state to the surface-water source.

Impact on Water Quantity

Because irrigation practices withdraw and consume large quantities of water, any change in the percentage of water used for irrigation has a significant impact on the availability of water for other uses.

There is little doubt that in several areas of the country increased use of water for irrigation has led to critical local water supply situations. As a result, development of surface-water supplies for irrigation use has slowed. Competition from nonfarm uses and the low availability of undeveloped water supplies in the areas most suitable for irrigation are contributing factors (1). Instead, irrigators have turned to groundwater sources for water. Table 12-4 shows how the percentage of groundwater used for irrigation has dramatically increased since the mid-1950s. This practice has led to groundwater mining in many areas and has caused concern about depletion of the resource. Of particular note is the practice in the Southern Plains, where groundwater used for irrigation increased from 37 percent of the total irrigation water use in 1950 to 80 percent in 1975.

Although depletion of groundwater resources was a recognized problem in the early 1970s, more recently the problem has been compounded in high-groundwater-use areas due to the costs associated with pumping. The problem of rising energy costs is exacerbated in areas of groundwater mining because of the increased amount of energy that must be expended to withdraw the water from greater and greater depths.

Irrigation Trends in the United States

While irrigation is widely used in the western states, it is becoming more costly due to rising water costs and limited supplies. Predictions are that there will be enough water for most irrigation needs until about the end of the century, but that prices will increase significantly (5). In view of this, it is expected that farmers will increase the efficiency of their irrigation systems to combat price increases in water and energy. Requirements for additional supplies of irrigation water are likely to be reduced as well.

Although the west continues to be the largest user of water for irrigation, eastern irrigation water use is expanding rapidly. Several factors have contributed to this situation. First, water is often still available in the east. Second, as land continues to become increasingly scarce in the east, the demand for cropland to produce feed grains and soybeans has risen. Third,

Table 12-4 GROUND- AND SURFACE-WATER WITHDRAWN FOR WESTERN IRRIGATION, 1950–1980 (THOUSANDS OF ACRE-FEET)

REGION IS THE 17 WESTERN STATES, I.E., ALL STATES WEST OR PARTLY WEST OF THE 100TH MERIDIAN	1950	1955	1960	1965	1970	1975	1980
Groundwater	18,191	31,014	35,892	41,598	46,186	56,019	58,043
Surface water	66,550	88,025	78,047	79,520	87,660	88,400	94,730
Total	84,741	119,039	113,939	121,118	133,846	144,419	152,773
Groundwater as percent of total	21	26	32	34	35	39	38

SOURCE: Data from U.S. Geological Survey Circulars, "Estimated Use of Water in the United States," Circular 115, 1950; Circular 398, 1955; Circular 456, 1960; Circular 556, 1965; Circular 676, 1970; Circular 765, 1975; Circular 1001, 1980.

the development of new technologies, such as sprinkler irrigation, has expanded the amount of land suitable for irrigation, such as moderately rolling terrain, which was previously uneconomical to irrigate (6). Although the west will continue to dominate the irrigation scene in volume of water used, it may soon be replaced by the east in terms of rate of irrigation growth (6).

Increasing the Efficiency of Existing Systems

The popularity of irrigated agriculture has increased over the past several decades because water has historically been treated as a free good, and because irrigators have been provided with federal subsidies to continue operations. However, this explosive use has taken its toll in many midwestern areas that have depended largely on groundwater reserves for irrigation, in that many groundwater aquifers have been extensively and sometimes irreversibly depleted. Due to this phenomenon plus higher energy costs, poor water management, and institutional constraints, water no longer runs as freely in these areas as it once did. Given these factors, the 1980s and beyond will most likely be a period that sees a concerted effort at increasing the efficiency of existing systems in the face of more costly water.

The USDA has offered several suggestions for cutting consumption and costs, resulting in improved efficiency of irrigation systems (5). In general, the first step toward improved irrigation efficiency is to cut out unnecessary irrigation. Often, however, irrigators do not have adequate information to determine whether they are overwatering. The USDA has shown by field experiments that some irrigation has little effect on crop yield or quality.

To conserve water, better scheduling of water application can be implemented. The use of soil moisture detection devices can serve as an aid to irrigators to determine the optimum timing for irrigation. A highly sophisticated system involves the use of computers to interpret the soil moisture data and calculate the optimum water application time and rate. For both surface- and groundwater irrigation systems, a savings in energy may be realized by modifying tillage and land management practices to reduce rainfall runoff from sloping fields so that the pumped water requirement is decreased.

The General Accounting Office has reported that less than half of the water delivered to farms for irrigation is actually used by crops (7). These water losses can be at least in part attributed to seepage from inefficient irrigation delivery systems. The Department of Agriculture has estimated that 20 to 25 percent of the water diverted from streams and reservoirs for agriculture does not reach farms (8). Seepage can be reduced, and thus water conveyance efficiency increased, by transporting water through closed pipes or by lining canals or laterals with compacted earth or an impervious material such as asphalt or concrete. Advantages of piped or lined systems include lower maintenance and repair costs, as well as eliminated bank erosion. The use of closed-conduit distribution systems has the additional advantages of reducing losses by evaporation, making the overlying land available for use, and eliminating the potential hazard of canal drownings (9).

Irrigation systems can also be made more efficient by reducing pumping and thus energy costs where feasible. For example, a surface-water diversion system employing pumps to move stream water to fields may be converted to a gravity flow system by changing the location of the diversion. This would provide an energy and cost savings by reducing pumping requirements.

Furthermore, small surface impoundments can be employed to catch runoff for pumping back to fields for reuse. The pumping costs for such operations are usually only a fraction of the costs of pumping the same quantity of water out of the ground.

For sprinkler systems, another method that may be used to save energy is to convert from high-pressure operation to low-pressure operation. Finally, users of pumped groundwater/sprinkler systems may consider converting to modern, well-designed surface irrigation systems. Where practicable, energy use and costs may be significantly reduced by such conversions.

12-2 MUNICIPAL AND INDUSTRIAL SYSTEMS

Municipal and industrial water systems include components of water source development, conveyance from the source to the point of use or treatment, water treatment, and distribution to the customer. The facilities required to develop water sources, wells, dams, and so on have been covered extensively in other sections of the book. Water distribution systems have also been discussed. The remaining component of municipal and industrial water systems is treatment, and that is the focus of this section.

Water Requirements

Urban water systems usually are characterized by several classes of use. These are households, industry, commercial establishments, and public facilities. The nature of treatment facilities required to process water for these various uses depends partly on the quality of the water available for use, partly on the special requirements of the user, and partly on the quantities of water that are to be processed.

QUANTITY
The quantities of water used in municipal and industrial sectors vary with climate, economic conditions, availability of water, time of day, and other

factors. Household water use varies from about 40 to 90 gpcd, commercial and public uses are on the order of 15 to 25 gpcd, and industrial water use varies widely. Commercial uses are those for office buildings, stores, and so on; whereas, public water uses include uses by schools, hospitals, parks, golf courses, and other public facilities. In 1980, municipal public water systems supplied about 180 gpcd nationally for domestic, commercial, and some industrial use.

QUALITY

Water use for cities and industries requires treatment of some type or another. The degree of treatment required is a function of the quality of the water source and the use to which the water is to be put. Water used for cooling in industry does not have to meet drinking water standards. On the other hand, water used by industries making soft drinks and other products must often be of a quality even better than that generally required for human consumption. Water treatment costs money and thus it is easy to understand that water users are concerned about the quality of their source waters. In some cases, it is more economical to transport water into an area from a distant source than to treat the local water supply. In making decisions about expanding water supplies or developing new ones, the quality dimension must be carefully evaluated along with the water quantity aspects.

Water to be used for public water supplies must be potable (drinkable), that is, not contain pollution. Pollution may be defined as the presence of any foreign substance (organic, inorganic, radiological, or biological) that tends to degrade the water quality and constitutes a hazard or impairs the usefulness of the water. Analyses of water sources are made to determine the acceptability of the water for domestic and industrial uses. The results of these analyses are also instrumental in determining the types of treatment required. A complete analysis of a source water includes a sanitary survey and physical, chemical, and biological analyses. In the United States, the procedures used in examining water sources are prescribed by *Standard Methods for the Examination of Water and Wastewater* (10, 11).

DRINKING WATER STANDARDS

Drinking water standards of some form or another have existed in the United States since about 1914. The current standards were developed following the passage of the National Safe Drinking Water Act in 1974. They appeared as the National Interim Primary Drinking Water Regulations. Secondary regulations related to taste, odor, and aesthetics are under development.

The maximum contaminant levels for inorganic chemicals are shown in Table 12-5a. They are generally based on the possible health effects that might occur after a lifetime exposure of about two liters of water per day. Table 12-5b displays similar limits for organic chemicals. The permissible

Table 12-5(a) MAXIMUM
CONTAMINANT LEVELS FOR
INORGANIC CHEMICALS OTHER
THAN FLUORIDE FOR PUBLIC
WATER SUPPLIES

CONTAMINANT (INORGANIC CHEMICALS)	LEVEL (mg/L)
Arsenic	0.05
Barium	1
Cadmium	0.010
Chromium	0.05
Lead	0.05
Mercury	0.002
Nitrate (as N)	10
Selenium	0.01
Silver	0.05

Table 12-5(b) MAXIMUM CONTAMINANT LEVELS FOR ORGANIC
CHEMICALS FOR PUBLIC WATER SUPPLIES

CONTAMINANT (ORGANIC CHEMICALS)	LEVEL (mg/L)
(a) Chlorinated hydrocarbons:	
Endrin (1,2,3,4,10,10-hexachloro-6, 7-epoxy-1,4,4a,5,6,7,8,8l-octahydro-1,4-endo, endo-5,8-dimethanonaphthalene)	0.0002
Lindane (1,2,3,4,5,6-hexachlorocyclohexane, gamma isomer)	0.004
Methoxychlor (1,1,1-trichloro-2,2-bis[p-methoxyphenyl]ethane)	0.1
Toxaphene ($C_{10}H_{10}Cl_8$-technical chlorinated camphene, 67–69 percent chlorine)	0.005
(b) Chlorophenoxys:	
2,4-D (2,4-dichlorophenoxyacetic acid)	0.1
2,4,5-TP (2,4,5-trichlorophenoxypropionic acid)	0.01
(c) Total trihalomethanes (sum of the concentrations of bromodichloromethane, dibromochloromethane, tribromomethane (bromoform), and trichloromethane (chloroform))	0.10

contaminant levels shown in the tables indicate to the engineer the quality of water that must be achieved by treatment. The selection of treatment processes is affected by the nature of the raw water entering the plant.

Water Treatment Processes

The purpose of water treatment is to provide potable water that is chemically and biologically safe for human consumption or is fit for industrial uses. For domestic use, water should be free of tastes and odors in addition to its potability. Contaminants that must be dealt with in treating water supplies include pathogenic bacteria, viruses, organic and inorganic compounds, turbidity and suspended solids, color, tastes and odors, and hardness. Figure 12-5 depicts a common treatment plant sequence. Additional

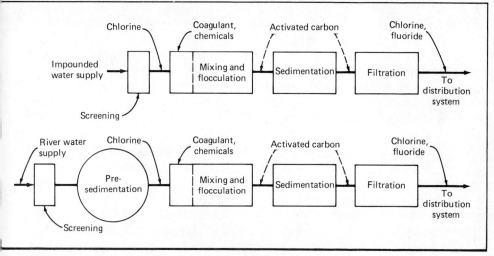

Figure 12-5 Typical water treatment plant flow diagrams.

specialized treatment may be required if the source water contains constituents not usually removed by conventional processes (10).

The types of water treatment processes discussed here may be divided into two categories, physical and chemical. Biological processes are usually used in conjunction with wastewater treatment. They are described in Section 12-6. Furthermore, the processes described are those customarily found in treatment plants designed to provide drinking water for cities. Industries often use processes that are specifically required for their operations. The interested reader should consult references 12 to 14.

PHYSICAL PROCESSES

The commonly used physical treatment processes include screening, aeration, mixing, flocculation, sedimentation, and filtration.

• *Screening.* The first operation encountered in most treatment plants is screening. Source waters tapped often contain large suspended or floating materials varying in size from logs to small bits of paper and rags. This material is objectionable because of its potential for damaging plant equipment, fouling pumps, and so on. In designing screening systems, care must be taken to see that the approach velocity is great enough to preclude sedimentation of suspended materials in the screening channel while at the same time preventing the dislodgment of material trapped by the screen. In addition, head losses resulting from screening must also be controlled so that backwater will not become a problem.

• *Aeration.* Aeration is widely practiced in water and wastewater treatment operations. It is a physical process in which oxygen is added to the water being treated to accomplish such objectives as oxidation of iron and manganese, aid in removing tastes and odors, removal of carbon dioxide, and removal of noxious substances such as those released by some types of algae and microorganisms. Aeration may be accomplished by using mechanical equipment that agitates the water and thereby promotes air transfer or with sprays, cascades, or diffusers that introduce air bubbles into the water being treated. The choice of method is based on the objective of the aeration and on the cost of accomplishing it.

• *Mixing.* Mixing and agitation are common to most water treatment facilities. Mixing is the blending of constituents to some desired state of uniformity. Agitation is an operation whose major function is to promote fluid turbulence. A primary example of the application of agitation is the promotion of floc growth in suspensions (flocculation). Mixing processes are employed to disperse a variety of chemicals and gases in fluids. The design of mixing systems is usually based on the use of a simplified mixing model (15–18).

Various devices have been employed in mixing operations. Common equipment includes pumps, venturi flumes, air jets, and rotating impellers (paddles, turbines, propellers). Of all the devices listed, the vertical shaft, turbine-type impeller is the most widely used device. It is composed of a vertical shaft driven by a motor on which one or more straight or curved turbine blades are mounted. These turbines are designed to provide both horizontal and vertical mixing. Flow through the mixing tank is usually from bottom to top. Mixing-tank diameters commonly range from three to 10 feet. Detention periods are usually less than one minute, although longer periods have been used.

• *Flocculation.* Flocculation is an operation designed to promote agitation in a fluid for the purpose of inducing coagulation. In this manner, very small suspended particles are caused to collide and agglomerate into larger, heavier particles or flocs, and settle out. Flocculation is a principal mechanism in the removal of turbidity from water. Floc growth depends on two factors: intermolecular chemical forces and the physical action induced by agitation. It is promoted by the use of diffused air, baffled tanks, transverse or parallel shaft mixers, vertical turbine mixers, and walking-beam-type mixers (10).

The commonest type of flocculator is the paddle flocculator. Paddle wheels may be mounted on vertical or horizontal shafts, although for a series of units, vertically mounted paddle wheels have been found to be more expensive (18). Horizontally mounted units may be located transverse to the flow or parallel to the flow. The orientation does not seem to have any appreciable effect on the results. A paddle flocculator consists mainly of a shaft with protruding steel arms on which are mounted a number of wood or metal blades. The shaft slowly rotates (on the order of 60 to 100 revolutions per hour), causing gentle agitation of the fluid. This results in the collision of floc particles with one another and with suspended matter in the raw water. The end result is the promotion of flocs incorporating finely divided suspended solids and colloidal particles, which can be removed by sedimentation.

Flocculation begins with dissolving chemicals in a rapid mixer. Initial collisions between colloidal particles result from brownian motion and contacts brought about due to the differences in settling velocities of heavier and lighter particles. In a quiescent vessel, floc growth is slow, and gentle agitation or turbulent mixing is therefore necessary to hasten the process. Floc production is directly proportional to the velocity gradients that are established in the water being treated. Stirring is responsible for establishing these gradients and is fundamental to the process. The number of contacts between particles in a unit time has also been shown to vary with the number and size of the particles (10, 19).

• *Sedimentation.* Sedimentation is the removal of solid particles from a suspension through gravity settling. Other terms used to describe this process are clarification and thickening.

In water treatment, sedimentation is used to remove granular materials, flocculated impurities (usually color and turbidity), and precipitates that are formed in operations such as water softening or iron removal. In sewage and industrial water treatment operations, sedimentation is used to remove both inorganic and organic materials that are settleable or that have been converted into settleable solids. Most modern sedimentation basins are operated on a continuous-flow basis.

Settling operations may be classified approximately as falling into four separate categories. These classifications are termed type I, type II, zone, and compression; all are dependent on the concentration of the suspension and the character of the particles (16). Type I and type II clarifications both deal with dilute suspensions, the difference being that type I consists of essentially discrete particles, whereas type II deals with flocculent materials. Zone settling describes a mass settling process in intermediate-concentration suspensions of flocculent materials, and compression results when the concentration increases to the point where particles are in physical contact with one another and are supported partly by the compacting mass.

Type I sedimentation is concerned with the removal of nonflocculating discrete particles in a dilute suspension. Under such circumstances the settling may be said to be unhindered and is a function only of fluid properties and the characteristics of the particles. The settling of heavy, inert materials would be an example of type I sedimentation.

The settling properties of dilute suspensions of flocculating particles differ from those of nonflocculating particles in that the flocculating properties of the suspension must be considered along with the settling characteristics of the particles (16). In this case, heavier particles having large settling velocities overtake and coalesce with smaller, lighter particles to form still larger particles with increased rates of subsidence. The opportunity for particle contact increases as the depth of the settling vessel increases. As a result, the removal of suspended matter depends not only on the clarification rate but on depth as well. This is the important difference between type I and type II clarification. The detailed mechanics of the various sedimentation models are beyond the scope of this book. The interested reader should consult references 10, 16, and 20 to 25 for this information.

Sedimentation basins are important components of most water treatment systems. Poor design or operation of them will result in the passage of inadequately conditioned water to the next unit process. Such an occurrence may adversely affect the outcome of the entire remaining treatment sequence.

Physically, a sedimentation basin may vary from an excavation in the ground (often for presedimentation of very turbid waters) to a structure of concrete or steel. Basins may be rectangular, square, or round. Some are deep, others shallow, and they may be covered or uncovered. Sludge-removal equipment may be provided or hand-cleaning methods may be employed. Most modern sedimentation basins are concrete and are not covered.

• *Filtration.* Filtration is an operation in which water and suspended matter are separated by passing the water through a porous material. The medium used may be sand, anthracite coal, diatomaceous earth, a fine-mesh fabric, or similar material.

The commonest types of granular filters used in water treatment plants employ sand as the filter medium. There are two basic types of sand filters: the rapid filter and the slow filter. The slow sand filter is usually about half an acre in size and consists of a bed of unstratified sand resting on a gravel bed. Rates of operation of these filters range from about 2 to 10 mgd. Solids that accumulate at the surface must be removed periodically (about every 30 days) to preclude clogging of the filter. Today, slow sand filtration is normally prescribed only for secondary or tertiary treatment of sewage. Reasons for the declining use of these filters in drinking water treatment include their high cost of construction combined with the need for considerable land area and the difficulties encountered in cleaning.

Rapid sand filters may be either of the free-surface type or the pressure type. Most filtration of water supplies is accomplished by the use of such filters. In a free-surface filter the water is passed downward through the filter medium by gravitational action. Filtration rates are usually about 2 to 3 gal/min/ft² although more recent trends are toward higher rates (5 to 10 gal/min/ft²), depending on the nature of the process water. Pretreatment by coagulation is essentially a necessary requirement where rapid filters are used. This is so that much of the suspended matter will be removed by sedimentation. Rapid sand filters consist of beds of stratified sand and are ordinarily about 500 ft² in size. Filter cleaning is accomplished by reversing the flow through the filter. This process is known as backwashing.

Pressure filters are built into steel cylinders or tanks and are operated under pressure to produce flow rates of about 2 to 4 gal/min/ft². These filters are also cleaned by reversing the flow. Because of size limitations, pressure filters are not generally employed in large-scale treatment works.

Diatomaceous-earth filters are pressure-operated filters that make use of a processed diatomaceous earth as the filter medium. They were first used extensively during World War II to provide water for military units in the field. The filter medium is supported on a fine metal screen, a porous ceramic material, or a synthetic fabric known as a septum.

Microstraining is a form of filtration whose primary objective is the removal of microorganisms (various forms of phytoplankton, zooplankton, and other general microscopic debris) and other suspended solids. A filtering medium consisting of a finely woven stainless steel fabric is normally used. This fabric supports a thin layer or mat of removed materials, which further improves the ability of the filter to effect removals. Microstrainers usually have high flow ratings corresponding to low hydraulic resistance. Fabrics become matted rapidly, and for this reason they must be backwashed almost continuously. Most microstrainers are of the rotating drum type where the fabric is mounted on the periphery of the drum and the raw water passes from the inside to the outside of the drum. Backwashing is usually accomplished through the utilization of wash water jets.

Microstrainers have been successfully employed in the primary clarification of water preceding filtration, in the preparation of water prior to its use for groundwater recharge, in the final clarification of sewage effluents, in the treatment of industrial waters and wastes, and in other applications.

The effectiveness of the filtration process (when granular materials are used) is a function of several mechanisms. These are straining (the primary process), sedimentation, flocculation, and, under certain conditions, biological activity.

The straining process occurs principally at the interface between the filter medium and the water to be filtered. Initially, materials are strained out that exceed in size the pore openings at the interface. During the filtration process the amount of material deposited as mat at the filter surface builds up. This mat further enhances the straining process and tends to further restrict the removal of impurities to the interface. When the raw water contains considerable organic matter (such as in the filtration of sewage), bacteria grow within the surface mat and utilize the accumulated deposits for food. As the organisms multiply, the mat becomes slimy. This improves the effectiveness of the mat in removing objectionable materials. Such biological activity is important, however, only where the mat is left intact for relatively long periods of time.

Hazen has stated that a filter medium acts in part in a manner similar to that of a sedimentation basin with a very large number of trays or false bottoms (25). When particles smaller than the pore spaces are introduced into the filter, they are given the opportunity to settle out on the surface of the filter material while they are passing through the filter bed. In this respect, each pore space acts as a tiny sedimentation basin. With spherical sand grains 5×10^{-2} cm in diameter, it has been noted that the settling velocity of removable particles is approximately $1/400$ that of particles that can be removed effectively in a sedimentation basin of equal loading (26).

As was pointed out earlier, floc growth is dependent on the opportunity for particle contacts to be made. In the filtration process, conditions are such that within the pores of the filter bed, flocculation is promoted. Particles grow in size and become trapped in the interstices, enhancing removal. Furthermore, biological metabolism may play a significant role in the slow sand filtration process or where a filter is operated intermittently, as in the case of sewage disposal.

Broadly speaking, a filter medium should possess the following qualities: (1) It should be fine enough to retain large quantities of floc, (2) it should not permit floc to pass through the filter, (3) it should allow relatively long filter runs, (4) it should be easily cleaned, and (5) it should be clean and free of foreign materials. These attributes are not all compatible. An obvious example is that very fine sand will retain floc but will tend to shorten the filter run, while for a coarse sand the opposite would be true. Design trends are now toward coarser sands so that higher rates of filtration can be obtained. Care must be exercised, however, because the efficiency of bacterial removal will be reduced if the sand is too coarse. In general, coarse filter beds should be of greater depth than fine ones.

The hydraulics of granular filters derive from the basic concepts of the flow of fluids through porous media. An analogy may be drawn to the flow of fluids through small pipes when filtration is the subject of interest. When backwashing or the expansion of the filter bed is of concern, an analogy may be drawn to the settling of particulate matter. Studies of the filtration process have indicated that the head lost through a filter medium can be expressed by the following functional relation:

$$H_f = f(e, l, d, v, \nu, \rho, g) \tag{12-2}$$

where $H_f =$ head lost in a depth of filter l
$e =$ porosity of the bed
$d =$ diameter that characterizes the filter medium grains
$v =$ velocity of flow moving toward the filter medium
$\nu =$ dynamic viscosity

$\rho =$ mass density of the fluid
$g =$ acceleration due to gravity

Evaluation of head loss is important in the hydraulic design of a filter unit. In clean filters, initial head losses commonly range from about 1.5 to 2.5 ft. Terminal head losses of about 9 ft are common. These head losses have an important bearing on the overall design of a water treatment plant. This is so because it is common practice to have gravity flow from the filters to the next plant unit, which is generally a clear-well (a clear water storage area). The elevation of the clear-well is thus controlled to a great extent by the loss of head through the filter and the connecting transportation system.

Two general equations, one proposed by Rose and one by Carmen-Kozeny, are used to compute the head loss resulting from the passage of water through the filter medium. The results obtained using either equation are essentially equivalent. Details of the development and use of these equations may be found in references 10 and 26.

After a filter has been in operation for a period of time, the operating head loss increases due to the suspended matter that has been collected. When the head loss has reached the point (usually 8 to 10 ft) where the flow controller from the filter to the clear well is wide open, an additional loss of head would produce a reduction in flow. To prevent this, it becomes necessary to remove the particles that have been trapped in the filter bed. This removal may be accomplished by scraping off the clogged portion of the bed or by reversing the flow through the bed so that it is expanded and the trapped particles can be washed out. This latter procedure, known as backwashing, is the method used to cleanse rapid sand filters.

The backwashing process is carried out by reversing the flow in the underdrainage system so that it moves upward through the filter bed. For very low upflow velocities the bed remains fixed, but as the velocity is increased the lighter particles begin to be moved upward. The velocity at which a given size particle is suspended or "fluidized" is known as the critical velocity. As the velocity is further increased, the particles become more widely separated and behave in an unhindered manner. The lighter soiled materials that have been previously trapped are then freed and pass to waste with the wash water. During the expansion of the bed the trapped particles are dislodged by the shearing action of the water or by the abrasive action resulting from contacts made between the rising bed particles. This scouring action is an important phase of the cleansing operation, and it can be enhanced by agitating the expanded filter bed. Hydraulic jets are often used to accomplish this, although mechanical rakes and compressed air have also been employed.

In designing a filter unit, consideration must be given to the capacity of the filter unit, the volumetric dimensions of the unit, the placement of wash water troughs, the depth of the filter medium and gravel layer, the underdrainage system, and various associated equipment or filter appurtenances.

CHEMICAL PROCESSES

The chemical treatment processes that will be discussed here are those most commonly found in water treatment plants. They include coagulation, disinfection, softening, adsorption, oxidation, and taste and odor removal.

• *Coagulation* Coagulation involves the formation of chemical flocs that adsorb, entrap, or otherwise bring together suspended matter. This material may vary in size from 10^{-7} to 0.1 mm, a range of 1 to 1,000,000. Particle sizes of 10^{-4} mm and larger produce turbidity, whereas smaller particles (primarily colloids) impart color, tastes, and odors.

The colloidal state is defined as a heterogeneous state in which one phase of matter is finely scattered throughout a second, continuous phase. The continuous phase is water. The actual boundaries of the colloidal state are indefinite. If the dispersed phase is divided finely enough, the properties of a colloidal dispersion merge gradually into those of a true solution. This occurs at a particle size of about 10^{-6} mm. If the particles of the dispersed phase increase in size, the colloidal dispersion takes on the properties of an impermanent suspension. This occurs at a particle size of about 10^{-3} mm. Not all particles of this approximate size form stable colloidal systems, since factors other than size must be taken into account.

In order to bring about the coagulation of a colloidal suspension it is necessary to offset the various factors that account for its stability. Much of the behavior of colloidal particles is associated with surface phenomena.

Coagulation results when ions of a charge opposite to the charge of the colloidal system are added to the solution. The diffused layer surrounding each particle is reduced as the added ion is increased. This diffused layer is reduced until a point is reached when the Van der Waals attractive forces are stronger than the repulsive forces of the zeta potential and coagulation results. The valence of the ion of opposite charge is important and the observed effects, in general, follow the Schulze-Hardy rule (27). This rule states that a bivalent ion is 50 to 60 times more effective than a monovalent ion and that a trivalent ion is 700 to 1000 times more effective than a monovalent ion.

The two coagulants most used in sanitary engineering are aluminum sulfate (alum), $Al_2(SO_4)_3$, and ferric sulfate, $Fe_2(SO_4)_3$. These both possess positive zeta potentials and have the ability to precipitate negatively charged color or turbidity by mutual coagulation. Alum reacts with the natural alkalinity of the water or, if the alkalinity is insufficient, with the added alkalinity in the form of lime or soda ash. The precipitate is usually considered to be aluminum hydroxide. When there is natural alkalinity in the water to react with the coagulant, the reaction is as follows:

$$Al_2(SO_4)_3 \cdot 14.3H_2O + 3Ca(HCO_3)_2 \longrightarrow \qquad (12\text{-}3)$$
$$2Al(OH)_3 \downarrow + 3CaSO_4 + 14.3H_2O + 6CO_2$$

When natural alkalinity is not present in sufficient amounts, lime is added to facilitate the chemical reaction (10). Waters vary widely in quality, and thus the chemical reactions such as that indicated by Equation 12-3 are complex and often not subject to exact calculation. Optimum dosages of chemicals must usually be determined by laboratory testing using samples of the water that is to be treated.

Coagulation in water treatment is usually carried out prior to sedimentation and filtration. The coagulant is applied in a fast-mixing operation to disperse the chemicals uniformly throughout the water. After flash mixing, the water is gently agitated for a period of time sufficient to promote good floc growth. Once the flocs have been formed, the water is passed through a settling basin and then filtered.

• *Disinfection.* Potable water must be free of two groups of living organisms: (1) the pathogenic microorganisms, which may infect humans through their use of contaminated water; and (2) the algae and other aquatic growths, which may render water aesthetically unfit for human consumption. Tastes and odors are, at times, associated with the destruction of these organisms. It is thus necessary to operate treatment plants with a high degree of odor control.

The purpose of disinfecting water supplies is to kill pathogenic organisms and thus prevent the spread of waterborne disease. Most pathogenic bacteria and many other microorganisms are destroyed or removed from water in varying degrees by most of the conventional treatment processes. The destruction and removal is brought about in several ways: (1) physical removal through coagulation, sedimentation, and filtration; (2) natural die away of organisms in an unfavorable environment during storage; and (3) destruction by chemicals introduced for treatment purposes other than disinfection.

Although the number of microorganisms in polluted waters is reduced by treatment processes and natural purification, the term disinfection is used in practice to describe treatment processes that have as their sole objective the killing of pathogenic organisms. Strictly defined, disinfection is the destruction of all pathogenic organisms, whereas sterilization is the total destruction or removal of all microorganisms. These two terms are similar but quite different. Disinfection is usually brought about by heating, ultraviolet irradiation, chlorination, and the like. These methods and materials can be used to sterilize water, but it is usually impractical to do so from an economic point of view. Disinfection is far more practical.

Chlorine and chlorine derivatives are the commonest disinfectants used in environmental control. Chlorination of water supplies on an emergency basis has been used since about 1850. The continuous chlorination of a public supply was first attempted in England during 1904. The first use of chlorine on a continuous basis for a public supply in the United States was in 1908 when George A. Johnson and John L. Leal employed chloride of lime for the disinfection of the water supply of Jersey City, New Jersey (10). This led to a celebrated court case in which the judge upheld the right of the city to chlorinate the water supply in the best interest of public health. From that time, chlorination of public water supplies has become routine practice.

When chlorine is added to water, two reactions take place. These are known as hydrolysis and ionization. The reactions are:

$$Cl_2 + H_2O \rightleftharpoons HOCl + Cl^- + H^+ \tag{12-4}$$

$$HOCl \rightleftharpoons OCl^- + H^+ \tag{12-5}$$

The hypochlorous acid, HOCl, and the hypochlorite ion, OCl^-, are known as the free available chlorine. These are the agents that are responsible for disinfection.

The quantity of chlorine required to treat a water supply depends on the amount of reducing organic and inorganic material present in the water and on public health considerations (see Section 12-6 on disinfection). Usually, a free-chlorine residual of 0.2 mg/L, 10 minutes after chlorination, is considered satisfactory. In most water treatment plants, chlorine is applied at the end of the treatment sequence, but it may also be used at other stages to improve coagulation, to prevent the growth of algae, and for other purposes.

• *Softening.* Water is softened to remove hardness. Hardness in water is associated with the ions of calcium, magnesium, iron, manganese, strontium, and aluminum. Most of these hardness-producing elements can be found in natural waters in some concentrations. However, in most waters only the ions of calcium and magnesium are present in objectionable quantities.

There are various methods for reducing the hardness of water for home and industry. The water may be centrally softened at the treatment plant prior to being introduced into the distribution system, or it may be softened at the point of use. Softening at the treatment plant is usually with one of the two following methods:

1. Softening with lime and soda ash
2. Softening with ion-exchange resins

Softening at the point of use at the home or industry is usually by one of the three following methods:

1. Softening with ion-exchange resins
2. Softening with lime and soda ash
3. Softening with detergent additives

In the lime–soda–ash process, lime, $Ca(OH)_2$, and soda ash, Na_2CO_3, are added to the water. The equations expressing the reactions occurring when lime is added to remove the calcium and magnesium bicarbonates are

$$Ca(HCO_3)_2 + Ca(OH)_2 \longrightarrow 2CaCO_3\downarrow + 2H_2O \qquad (12\text{-}6)$$

$$Mg(HCO_3)_2 + 2Ca(OH)_2 \longrightarrow 2CaCO_3\downarrow + Mg(OH)_2\downarrow + 2H_2O \quad (12\text{-}7)$$

$$MgSO_4 + Ca(OH)_2 \longrightarrow Mg(OH)_2\downarrow + CaSO_4 \qquad (12\text{-}8)$$

$$CaSO_4 + Na_2CO_3 \longrightarrow CaCO_3\downarrow + Na_2SO_4 \qquad (12\text{-}9)$$

The lime reduces carbonate hardness and replaces calcium salts with magnesium salts. The sodium salts that are formed in the softening process are usually not objectionable. The precipitates of $CaCO_3$ and $Mg(OH)_2$ that are formed are mostly removed by sedimentation. Residuals of these precipitates that may deposit on pipes or other equipment can be a problem, however, and to prevent this from occurring, the water may be recarbonated to stop further precipitation (10).

The amounts of chemicals required in softening are determined by the quality of the water coming into the plant. As in the case of coagulation, laboratory tests are usually run to determine optimal dosages. In most treatment plants, once the softening process has been completed, the water is settled and filtered. Problems associated with lime-soda softening are the large quantities of sludge produced, the need for a high degree of control, and the problem associated with the possible postprecipitation in pipes and treatment units.

Ion exchangers are also used to soften water, to selectively remove specific impurities, and to recover valuable chemicals lost in industrial waste discharges. In very dilute ionized solutions, such as natural waters, the ion-exchange process is an economical method of producing water free of all ions.

• *Adsorption.* The chemical treatment processes just discussed are not effective in removing some of the many organic compounds that find their way into watercourses from industrial and other operations. Adsorption has been found to be an effective method of removing them, however, with activated carbon being the principal material used. Activated carbon has the properties needed to foster adsorption processes. These processes are associated with large surface areas and freedom from adsorbed materials. Generally, activated carbon is used in powder form, and after its adsorption capacity has been exceeded, it is regenerated for further use (10). To be most effective, adsorption should follow normal filtration of water. This ensures that there will be few carryover suspended solids to compete for removal with those constituents the activated carbon is intended for.

• *Oxidation.* Oxidation is sometimes used in water treatment to effect conversion of undesirable chemical constituents into forms that are harmless or at least less undesirable. In the process, the oxidation state of a substance is changed (increased) by means of a chemical reaction. Oxidation has been found effective in treating waters containing iron and manganese, phenols, humic acids, taste and odor producers, bacteria, and algae.

• *Taste and Odor Control.* Undesirable tastes and odors in waters make them unpalatable to humans and undesirable for many manufacturing processes, especially those to do with foods and beverages. Most tastes and odors are caused by (1) dissolved gases, (2) algae, (3) decaying organic matter, (4) chlorine, and (5) various industrial wastes.

The commonest control measures in use for taste and odor control are the application of activated carbon, free-residual chlorination, combined residual chlorination, chlorine dioxide, ozone, and aeration. Activated carbon treatment has been widely used. Activated carbon removes organic contaminants from water by adsorption. Adsorption is the attraction and accumulation of one substance on the surface of another. Adsorption is primarily a surface phenomenon—the greater the surface area of the adsorber, the greater its adsorptive power. Carbon for water treatment is rated in terms of square meters of surface area per gram. It has been estimated that one pound of activated carbon has more than 100 acres of surface area. Excessive dosages of carbon do not harm the water, as it is easily removed by filters. Besides controlling tastes and odors, carbon has been reported to stabilize sludge, improve floc formation, and remove organic material.

Carbon is fed to water either as a dry powder or as a wet slurry. Special equipment is available for feeding carbon. Slurry feeding has the advantage of being cleaner to handle, and the slurry ensures that the carbon is thoroughly wet, which increases its effectiveness. The points of application of carbon will vary with local conditions and water problems. Carbon may be added to the water at any point prior to filtration. The adsorption is nearly instantaneous, although a contact time is normally helpful. The amount of carbon needed will vary with the type of carbon used and water conditions. A few milligrams per liter of carbon is the usual dosage, but concentrations up to 100 mg/L may be needed at times.

The application of carbon is normally most effective at the lowest pH value of the raw water and, if suitable mixing is available, the addition of the carbon to the raw water intake is desirable. Carbon may also take up some of the materials that have a chlorine demand and hence a saving in chlorine is effected.

The oxidative methods for taste and odor control include chlorination, ozonation, and aeration. Marginal chlorination consists of the application of enough chlorine to secure a residual without satisfying the potential demand (combined residual). It is common practice to maintain this residual through part or all of the treatment plant and distribution system. This treatment tends to develop tastes and odors with phenolic compounds and certain other pollutants. Some tastes and odors may, however, be removed by combined residual chlorination.

Free-residual chlorination is the application of chlorine to water to produce, directly or through the destruction of ammonia or nitrogenous compounds, a free available chlorine residual. Tastes and odors from phenolic compounds are usually controlled by this treatment. Many other taste and odor materials are also destroyed or rendered less obnoxious. Complete reduction is not universal, and free-residual chlorination may have to be supplemented by other treatment, such as improved coagulation, algae control, and activated carbon.

Free-residual chlorination followed by chlorine dioxide addition has been found effective in stubborn taste and odor control problems. The action of chlorine dioxide is very rapid and therefore does not initially show a residual. Further addition of chlorine dioxide should result in an increased residual. All of the chlorine practices have merits and can, under appropriate conditions, provide a means of control for taste and odor.

Ozone has been widely used in Europe and to a limited extent for taste and odor control in the United States. Ozone does not form objectionable tastes and odors by reaction with phenolic compounds. The high capital investment required for generation equipment for ozone and the speed with which it dissipates from water have retarded its use.

Aeration has been successfully used for the control of tastes and odors. This method has been particularly effective in the removal of sulfides and volatile chemicals. It has been estimated that spray aeration with 100 lb/in^2 pressure at the nozzles is equivalent in cost to treatment with 17 mg/L of activated carbon.

Raw water storage tends to improve taste and odor qualities, although few plants are in a position to provide it. The location or position of the intakes may be quite significant in procuring a good water quality. This is especially important where industrial wastes are concerned.

SLUDGE DISPOSAL

The handling and disposal of sludges from water treatment plants is a significant problem. In the past, the custom was to discharge these sludges into receiving waters with no treatment. This practice is no longer tolerable, and provisions must be made to further process these semisolid wastes. Some of the methods used in handling sludges are gravity thickening, lagooning, drying beds, centrifugation, discharge into sewers, heat treatment, freezing, vacuum filtration, and operations designed to recover certain constituents such as alum and magnesium from the sludge. The methodology of sludge processing is complex and will not be described further here. It is a significant problem in the operation of a water treatment plant, however, and deserves careful attention in design. For the interested reader, references 10, 26, and 28 are recommended.

Treatment Plant Design

The design of a water treatment plant must take into consideration (1) the quality of the source water, (2) the quality of the finished product water (this will depend on the use to which the water is to be put); and (3) the nature of the treatment processes and operations available for use. The final design should reflect the ability to transform source water into product water in the most efficient and economical manner. Figure 12-5 illustrates a typical flow diagram for a conventional water treatment plant.

Prior to processing in a water treatment plant, a number of pretreatment processes are often employed. These include presedimentation, chemical addition, and aeration. Screening is used to remove debris and large objects from the water to be processed. Chemical treatment prior to in-plant coagulation is sometimes used to improve sedimentation, to facilitate the removal of tastes and odors, and to reduce bacterial loads. Aeration is commonly the first step in treating well waters for the removal of iron and manganese.

The selection of specific chemicals for water treatment depends on their effectiveness and cost. For example, activated carbon, chlorine, chlorine dioxide, and potassium permanganate are all used for taste and odor control. Superchlorination is usually the least expensive, but activated carbon is more effective. Equipment for introducing several taste and odor removal chemicals is usually provided, and so the operator can select the best and least costly application. There is no general solution to color removal problems that is applicable to all waters. Alum coagulation with adequate pretreatment and the use of oxidizing chemicals or activated carbon may work. On the other hand, a more expensive coagulant might be more effective and reduce overall chemical costs. Such tradeoffs should be carefully evaluated.

An important consideration in designing water treatment processes is flexibility. Plant operators should have the means to change the points of application of chemicals. Multiple chemical feeders and storage tanks should be supplied so that chemicals can be employed in the treatment sequence as desired. Changes in raw water quality, or changes in costs of chemicals, may dictate a change in coagulant or auxiliary chemicals used in coagulation. In the case of surface-water treatment plants, it is often desirable to provide space for additional pretreatment facilities. River flows often change in character due to the construction of dams, channel improvements, or upstream water uses. Details of process designs may be found in references 10, 16, 26, and 29.

12-3   HYDROELECTRIC POWER

In 1882 the world's first hydroelectric power plant generated electricity, providing illumination to Appleton, Wisconsin. Throughout the first part of the twentieth century, hydropower continued to be a major source of electric power, and by the end of World War II, it accounted for about 35 percent of the nation's electrical capacity (30, 31).

Today, this percentage has dropped to about 14. Fewer prime sites and concern about the environmental impact of impoundments have been largely responsible for this relative decline, but rising energy costs may stimulate the expansion and development of hydroelectric facilities.

An advantage of conventional hydroelectric projects is that they do not consume fuel and they are nonpolluting. Hydroplants have long lives, low operating expenses, and low outage rates. They can assume load rapidly and are especially suited to providing peak and reserve capacity for electrical systems. In addition, hydroelectric facilities may be coordinated with the development of water resources for many other purposes, such as recreation, water supply, and flood control.

Hydroelectric Capacity in the United States

At the beginning of 1976, the total conventional hydroelectric power developed in the United States (including Alaska and Hawaii) amounted to about 57,000 megawatts of capacity or approximately 271 billion kilowatt-hours. This accounted for about 14 percent of the total electric generation in 1976 but represented only about 4 percent of the total energy consumed for all purposes in the United States (31).

The total hydroelectric potential of the United States can be estimated on the basis of the average flow of all streams and their change in elevation. A theoretical limit for the contiguous United States has been determined as 390,000 megawatts electrical capacity (MWe) (32). Technical constraints such as difficulties in taking advantage of low heads reduce this figure to about 179,000 MWe, and other reductions resulting from economic, political, and environmental constraints are likely. Large undeveloped potentials in Alaska (about 33,000 MWe) and in the North Pacific Region (about 39,000 MWe) constitute about 64 percent of the remaining undeveloped capacity in the United States (39).

Advantages and Disadvantages of Hydroelectric Facilities

Hydropower is an attractive energy source for many reasons. It utilizes a renewable resource and is based on reliable technology. It consumes no fuel and creates no air pollution. Advantages over coal-fired and nuclear plants include: (1) hydropower plants are virtually inflation-proof over their service lives because operating costs for existing facilities are minimal, and (2) hydropower plants can be brought on line much faster than the usual 10-to-15-year wait for conventional power plants. Hydropower is particularly suited to meeting reserve and peak demand power needs in some regions of the country, such as the northeast.

Hydropower also has its disadvantages, some of which can be stumbling blocks during development stages. Challenges or problems that must be met in developing hydroelectric facilities include:

Compliance with environmental damage mitigation requirements, which can be particularly challenging because of water use related issues

The delivery of streamflow, which may be intermittent

High initial costs and financing problems

The costs of transmission facilities, substations, and monitoring equipment

Absorbing cost overruns that are characteristic of small-scale hydropower developments

Cost and time of the permit and licensing process

Assurance of the safety of the dam structure

Time and expense for land acquisitions at the site as well as right-of-way and compliance with other property and water laws

The compatibility of hydroelectric facilities with other current or proposed uses of an impoundment is often at issue. Flood control and recreation are two aspects of multipurpose reservoirs that are particularly incompatible with using them for hydroelectric energy generation.

Constraints on Achieving Hydroelectric Potential

Economic, environmental, and legal factors may preclude the development of many potential hydroelectric sites. Federal statutes that have an impact on hydropower development are the Colorado River Basin Project Act and the Wild and Scenic Rivers Act (33). The former prohibits the Federal Power Commission from issuing licenses for projects on the Colorado River between the Glen Canyon and Hoover Dam projects. This preempts a power potential of about 3500 megawatts. The Wild and Scenic Rivers Act prohibits the commission from licensing the construction of power facilities affecting rivers included in the national wild and scenic rivers system. The 37 river reaches proposed for inclusion in that system or to be studied for possible inclusion in the system contain sites that could provide about 9000 megawatts of hydroelectric capacity.

RESOURCE BASE LIMITATIONS

An important constraining element in hydropower development is the conflict between expanding electric energy demands and the concern for environmental quality. All levels of government, the electrical industry, and various citizens' groups are concerned with this issue. Institutional changes have been made to require utilities and construction agencies to be more sensitive to environmental impacts and to explore a wider range of project alternatives. Unfortunately, developing such information and processing it through the review and decision-making levels of government is complex and often results in inordinate delays.

The degree to which hydroelectric facilities affect air, land, and water quality depends on site, design, mode of operation, and other factors. There are also effects during the period of construction as well as after the facilities are in place (32). The environmental and social costs of expanded hydroelectric facilities are tied primarily to the impoundment of flowing streams. In this process, there is an irretrievable commitment of the land that is inundated by the formation of a reservoir. Losses include prime farmlands, mineral deposits, forests, wildlife habitats, and scenic and recreational opportunities on free-flowing streams. It is common to have to relocate individual houses, communities, and industries. This may exact severe hardships on those displaced, especially the aged or those dependent on the original location or community for employment.

Water quality changes resulting from a shift of the stream's flow regime are also common and may have a significant impact on local ecosystems.

TECHNOLOGICAL CONSTRAINTS

Technological constraints related to site development and facilities for locations where heads are less than about 20 feet reduce the theoretical potential for hydroelectric development by about 50 percent (32). In general, where heads are less than 30 feet, development is often uneconomical, but aside from this, acceptable locations are also limited. Providing 30 feet of head on a river flowing through flat terrain might entail flooding of large areas of land or construction of miles of levees. Where substantial benefits to navigation and flood control are possible, low-head units are sometimes justified and sites with very low heads have been developed. Advances in low-head turbine technology could signal the beginning of a much greater exploitation of river flows.

ECONOMIC CONSTRAINTS

Hydroelectric facilities usually require large outlays of capital for long periods of time. The pre-1974 low costs of fuels and fossil fuel electric plants also made hydroelectric development less attractive. With rising fuel costs and scarcity, this may not continue to be the case, however.

Facility construction costs are variable and depend on the size, type, and location of the dam. Land procurement and relocation of people, buildings, and facilities can be very costly. For example, the 1971 cost of a dam for a small Pennsylvania hydroelectric facility was $15 million, but relocation and property adjustment added $100 million to the total facility cost (32).

An important consideration in determining the cost per unit of power is the annual capacity factor or percent of time the facility is generating electricity. This factor has been decreasing because the trend in hydroelectric facilities use is to satisfy peak demands rather than to serve the base load. In 1970, the annual operating factor averaged 55 percent for United States hydroelectric facilities but an annual capacity factor of 20 percent is more typical of new sites (32, 34).

Capital costs of the powerhouse and equipment decrease with an increase in the operating head. Average costs for hydroelectric facilities have varied between $200 and $400 per kW (32). New economies are being realized, however, through improved design and construction practices for dams and as the result of new tunneling practices and improved underground excavation equipment.

TIME LAG IN DEVELOPMENT

From the time a hydroelectric project is conceived until it is on line, a period of 20 years or more may pass. The sequence of events that transpire in the process must thus be considered, and efforts made to reduce delays when this can be accomplished (35).

Terminology

The unit of electric power is the kilowatt. It is equivalent to 1.34 horsepower. The electrical energy unit is the kilowatt-hour, which is one kilowatt of power delivered for a period of one hour. Sometimes electrical energy is expressed in terms of kilowatt-days or kilowatt-years. The conversion from one of these measures to another is straightforward.

Hydroelectric power is derived from the conversion of mechanical power—falling water—to electricity through the use of turbines and generators. Consequently, the head differential between the upstream water surface and the downstream water surface after passage through the hydroelectric plant is very important. Terms commonly used in describing head are gross head and net, or effective, head. The gross head is the difference in elevation between the upstream water surface and the water surface downstream at the point at which the water passing through the hydroelectric plant is returned to the stream after passing through the turbines. The net, or effective, head is the head actually available for the generation of electricity. That is, it is the gross head reduced by losses resulting from friction, entrance conditions, transitions in conveyances, and other hydraulic losses such as those described in Chapter 9. The hydraulic efficiency of a hydroelectric plant is defined as the ratio of the net head to the gross head. On the other hand, the overall efficiency of a hydroelectric plant is the hydraulic efficiency multiplied by the efficiency of the generating machinery (turbines and generators). Usually, the overall efficiency of a hydroelectric plant is in the range of 60 to 70 percent (36). The maximum power that can be realized at a hydroelectric plant is determined by what the generators can produce under conditions of normal head and full flow. This is known as the plant capacity.

The measure of hydroelectric generation is commonly based on the output of the plant during a period of low streamflow. When a single plant is being considered, this means minimum conditions of water availability, including storage. The plant capability under these conditions is known as dependable power or firm power. It is defined in this way because it is expected that this level of power can be depended on with minimum risk. During most years, however, hydroelectric plants usually produce substantially more than firm power; the difference between the firm power and that actually produced is known as surplus, secondary, or interruptible power. Secondary power cannot be depended on, however, and thus it is usually marketed at a rate well below that of firm power. On occasion, however, surplus power is available at a generating station, and where this is the case it may be sold at rates not very different from those charged for firm power.

Two basic terms are used in defining power: base load and peaking. Because the daily demand for power varies over the course of a day, reflecting society's needs, it is commonly divided into "base load," which is the constant 24-hour-a-day part of the load, and "peak load," which is the variable part of the load that is greatest during the hours when people are most active (see Figure 12-6).

Hydroelectric facilities are usually used to complement other electrical energy producing facilities. For example, thermal plants usually assume a greater portion of the base load in a region. The most economical way to operate these thermal plants is to run them at full capacity as much as possible. When this is done, the complementary hydroelectric plants

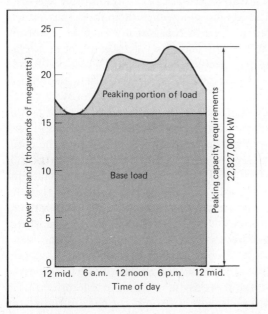

Figure 12-6   Daily power load shape—energy and capacity. Northwest Power Pool, January 25, 1972. (After O. W. Bruton, "Hydropower and Pumped Storage of the Northwest," reference 37.)

are used to meet peaking loads. Finally, expanding existing hydroelectric plants adds very little energy to a power-producing system (37). The added generating units permit "reshaping" of the energy produced, however, and larger loads can often be carried during the peak hours whereas the output is lowered during slack times (37). This reshaping is useful, since if the peaking is not handled by the hydroelectric facilities, it will have to be assumed by more costly combustion turbine plants or other thermal facilities.

Power Systems

Hydroelectric facilities are usually only one component of most regional power systems. Thus it is important to consider how these facilities should be used to most effectively complement other system components. Furthermore, in planning to meet future electrical generating needs, it is necessary that the development of hydroelectric facilities be compared with the development of other facilities such as nuclear plants so that the most economical and environmentally sound development will result.

In planning to develop a power system involving the possible use of hydroelectric power plants, numerous studies must be made. These include estimating the future needs for electricity (see Chapters 1 and 4); exploring alternative means of producing power (steam, nuclear, and hydro); conducting analyses to determine the least costly alternative; and undertaking final designs, scheduling construction, and providing for financing of the project. Since the size of the facility or facilities to be built must be based on projected needs for electricity, it follows that all the cautions previously presented relative to forecasting must be carefully considered. Again, flexibility in project planning and staging of construction should be promoted if at all possible.

In most modern power systems of any scale, there will be several plants, often of different character. Furthermore, many power systems are linked together so that they aid one another in times of stress or as conditions require. In such cases, the operating procedures for managing these interconnected systems are an important consideration and must be carefully designed. Often, the greatest economy and reliability can be obtained if there is an "optimal" mix of water and steam power stations. Hydroelectric plants require almost no start-up time and can thus be brought on line very quickly to respond to peak loads. Steam plants, on the other hand, usually require at least 30 minutes or more for start-up, and keeping them on standby is costly. As was stated earlier, the usual procedure is to operate steam plants continuously to supply base load and to use the hydroelectric facilities to handle the peaks. If the only power station in a region is hydroelectric, it is easy to see that problems could be encountered in meeting electrical demands if the plant has limited water storage capacity or if unregulated river conditions were such that the net head was reduced.

The demands for electrical energy fluctuate just as those for water do. Water use rates in residential areas often show peaks in the late morning and early evening, with little use during the middle of the night. Industrial fluctuations are less pronounced, especially where there are around-the-clock operations. There are also seasonal fluctuations, which are related to both the weather and the nature of the use. Irrigation water use is usually seasonal, for example, and so are the energy requirements to sustain it. Residential electrical energy needs also vary with heating and cooling needs as well as length of daylight period. Consequently, the demands for electrical energy show variations such as those indicated in Figure 12-7 for a typical residential area.

The load on the system that is imposed during the peak day of the year determines the amount of generating capacity that must be provided. This is analogous to providing water delivery capacity to meet peak-day or related requirements. Note that the same concepts in conservation and scheduling can also be used to either curtail the needs for electrical energy or to shift some of the peak periods of use so that they do not coincide with other intensive use periods. By scheduling irrigation deliveries for the night, for example, electric power needs for that purpose would be moved to a time less demanded by other users. And while the daily peak loads determine capacity, weekly and monthly peaks are the ones that set the requirements for storage of fuel or water needed to derive the required power. A term commonly used to evaluate system generating needs is the load factor. The load factor is the ratio of the average load for a defined time period to the peak load for that period. In Figure 12-7 it is shown to be 46.5 percent for the sample residential area. Daily, weekly, monthly,

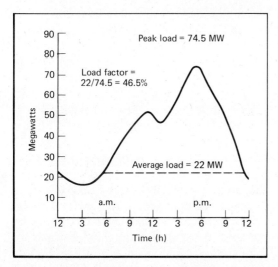

Figure 12-7 Representative residential load curve for 24 hours.

and yearly load factors are used. Load factors vary in magnitude with the nature of the region for which they are applicable. Residential area load factors are often as low as 30 to 40 percent whereas those for industrial regions are usually much higher, sometimes reaching 80 percent or more. From the point of view of the power company, high load factors are the most desirable since they permit operating generating units at near-capacity levels, a condition under which efficiency tends to be maximized. It should be clear that where load factors are very low, there will always be much idle capacity in the generating system.

The operation of electric generating systems is complex and requires careful coordination of all power-producing units. As has been pointed out earlier, where a generating system includes both hydroelectric plants and steam plants, it is the usual practice to operate the steam units so that they provide the base load while the hydroelectric units are used to respond to the peaks. Sometimes during periods of high flow, however, this procedure may be reversed. In such cases, the hydroelectric units can often carry the base load, and thus permit the more-costly-to-operate steam units to be used only to meet some peaks. This can, given the right conditions, result in significant fuel and thus dollar savings. The lesson is that an operating policy should be set to maximize the efficiency of the whole system and to obtain the greatest advantage possible from the special characteristics of each of the individual generating facilities.

Types of Hydroelectric Facilities

Power available from a river is directly proportional to the quantity of water that passes through the turbines and the head available for operation of the turbines. When expressed as horsepower (hp), the following relation is obtained:

$$\mathrm{hp} = \frac{Q \gamma h}{550} \tag{12-10}$$

where Q = discharge (ft^3/s)
γ = specific weight of water (lb/ft^3)
h = head (ft)

Adjustments must be made in values obtained by Equation 12-10 to account for efficiency.

The prime feature of water control for power development is the production and maintenance of the maximum possible head at the power plant. Any flow releases from the reservoir will reduce the pool level and thereby affect the power potential. For example, if the water level is reduced by 50 percent, the power output of the plant will also be cut by 50 percent for the same rate of flow. Where the storage of water is intended to satisfy uses other than power production, an operating schedule must be designed to provide for maximum efficiency of power production under the circumstances.

There are actually three categories of hydroelectric plants: run of the river, storage, and pumped storage. Each of these will be described in the following sections. A fourth classification, low-head (small-scale) hydroelectric power generation, will also be addressed since a revived interest in this country related to the refurbishing of abandoned historical low-head facilities and the development of new ones has been spawned by the energy crisis.

RUN OF THE RIVER

Run-of-the-river plants are characterized by very limited storage capacities. They use the river as it flows and generally have little or no upstream storage. In some cases, run-of-the-river plants have enough storage to permit saving water during off-peak hours for use during the same day. This storage is designated as pondage, and it does not have any carryover capacity beyond 24 hours or so, at most. Obviously, run-of-the-river plants are not suited to streams subjected to dry periods unless other upstream storages can counteract the situation.

STORAGE

Storage plants have adequate reservoir capacity to impound wet-season flows for use during dry periods. As a result, they can develop firm flows that are substantially greater than those of the undeveloped stream that they impound. The heads that can be developed at storage sites are a function of the heights of their associated dams. Often these heads are classified as low-head, medium-head, and high-head plants. The distinction is as follows. Low-head plants are usually designated as those having heads less than 50 feet (see also the section on low-head hydro). Medium-head plants may range from about 50 to 200 feet and high-head plants may range in head from 200 to 5000 feet (38).

PUMPED STORAGE

Pumped storage plants are used to produce power during peak load periods. Basically, pumped storage involves storing energy by pumping water into a storage reservoir when surplus power is available at night, on weekends, or during high-flow periods and then releasing it when the power is needed. The object is to convert surplus off-peak energy into valuable peaking energy by pumping water and storing it in higher level reservoirs.

Pumped-storage operation is costly. It takes about 1½ kilowatt-hours of pumping energy for every kilowatt-hour of energy delivered. This is because of losses and system inefficiencies. Nevertheless, the operation is often worthwhile because peak energy has a much higher value than off-peak energy—as high as five times as much (37).

Off-peak pumping energy may come from base load thermal plants.

Such plants are most efficient and economical when they are operated continuously at near-full output; however, the demand for power usually declines at night and on weekends, and thermal plants normally reduce their power output during these periods. Consequently, an unused source of energy can be made available for pumping, for only the cost of the fuel. In other words, low-cost surplus energy from base load plants is used during off-peak hours to provide more valuable capacity and energy during peak-load hours.

Pumped storage does more than provide a source of peaking power. It is also an excellent source of emergency reserve generation, which can be brought on line very quickly in the event of a large generating plant or transmission line in a power system breaking down. By providing additional system flexibility, conventional hydro resources can often be used more efficiently. They can also improve the economics of large-base-load thermal plants by keeping them fully loaded during the off-peak hours. Finally, pumped storage directly saves oil or petroleum products because the power produced would otherwise have to be generated by oil-fired peaking plants (37). Pumped storage is not a primary energy source, however, and should not be counted as such.

Because remaining favorable sites for conventional hydroelectric development are limited, construction of pumped-storage projects for peak load has increased. The development of reversible equipment that can be used for both pumping and generating has facilitated this trend. Unit costs of constructing pumped-storage projects are usually low because the needed reservoirs are relatively small. Operating expenses include the cost of pumping energy, which amounts to about three kilowatt-hours for each two kilowatt-hours generated (31). On the positive side, pumping is accomplished during off-peak hours when idle thermal capacity is usually available, and since pumping energy is usually generated from the more efficient plants on the system, there may be little if any increase in use of system fuel as the result of pumped storage installations. Further, the pumping energy can be provided by coal-fired or nuclear-fueled plants, while pumped storage generation could replace the peak-load output of combustion turbine plants using distillate oil.

As of May 1974, the total developed pumped storage capacity in the contiguous United States amounted to about 8000 megawatts with about 6000 additional megawatts in pumped storage hydroelectric plants under construction. In contrast to locations of conventional hydroelectric developments, which have the greatest potential in the Pacific northwest, over 80 percent of the developed and emerging pumped storage capacity is in the central and eastern sections of the United States.

LOW HEAD
The energy crisis of the late 1970s has rekindled interest in new hydroelectric facilities and in the improvement of existing ones. In particular,

the idea of installing small electric generating units on minor rivers and tributaries has become popular. Many previously developed sites, now abandoned, offer possibilities for modestly augmenting electrical energy needs because they pose few environmental and social risks (40,41).

Low-head hydro projects may be classified into categories of high flow, low head, and low flow, high head. The first classification involves flows exceeding 500 ft^3/s and heads of less than 50 ft. The second category involves flows of less than 500 ft^3/s and heads greater than 50 ft. Sites having low dams and irrigation canals are typical of the first category whereas the second classification is usually associated with high-pressure water systems such as those serving urban water needs. An example of a low-head, high-flow system is given in Figure 12-8.

The components of a typical high-head, low-flow hydro project normally include a principal water supply reservoir where runoff is collected and stored for use by municipalities and industries. The conduit that transmits water from the reservoir to the treatment works serves to house the generating equipment. The location of the hydro stations is usually at the low point of the conveyance prior to its discharge into an equalizing reservoir or before its discharge into a water treatment plant. Power transmission lines convey the power generated to power company grids or to the power plant owner's facilities.

The technical aspects of small-scale hydro development that need consideration include variation in flow rate of the water, pressures in conveyances, operating hours for the generating and conveyance facilities, and the nature of the electromechanical equipment available (42). The single most important criterion for developing a hydroelectric project is its economic feasibility. Included in economic analyses must be consid-

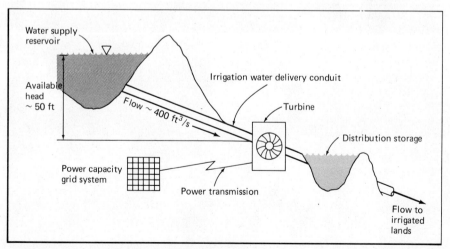

Figure 12-8 Typical components of a high-head, low-flow hydroelectric development coupled with an irrigation system.

erations of construction and engineering costs; operating, maintenance, and replacement costs; the market value of the power generated; and effects of inflation on estimated costs.

Components of Hydroelectric Plants

Most large hydroelectric facilities include a structure for diverting flows from the source to the plant. From the reservoir or diversion structure to the turbines, a conduit (called a penstock) carries the flow (Figures 12-9 and 12-10). It is sometimes necessary to install trash racks at penstock entrances to combat problems of debris. Because sudden load changes in penstocks might occur, water hammer must often be guarded against. This is done by the installation of surge tanks, a practice generally required where penstocks are very long. Sometimes a forebay is required to temporarily store water when plant loads are reduced or to provide water for increasing the load prior to stepping up releases from the impoundment. Forebays are in reality regulating reservoirs. They are located, when they are needed, at the end of the diversion canal or conduit and

Figure 12-9 Shasta Dam on the Sacramento River north of Redding, California. (Courtesy of the U.S. Bureau of Reclamation.)

Figure 12-10   Davis Dam, Arizona. (Courtesy of the U.S. Bureau of Reclamation.)

before the entrance to the plant. When the outflow from the power plant cannot be discharged directly into the receiving stream or river, a tailrace (channel) is used to connect the powerhouse and the stream. Other equipment associated with hydroelectric facilities includes turbines, generators, transformers, and electric transmission lines.

The design of each hydroelectric facility, although having certain common elements, will have its own features, which relate to hydrologic conditions, topography, geology, and the quantity and timing of electrical energy needs. For low-head installations, the powerhouse is often located at one end of or just downstream of the dam. This situation is usually considered to be one of concentrated fall. Divided-fall hydroelectric facilities, on the other hand, are characterized by long distances between the impoundment and the power plant. In such cases, water is conveyed to the plant through canals, tunnels, or penstocks, which often discharge into a forebay. Depending on the topography, a divided-fall facility may be able to incorporate a high head even if the dam is low. The head is developed by the decrease in elevation from the dam outlet to the location of the power plant. When a substantial head can be developed by locating the generating facility some distance from the dam, it is often possible to operate turbines near the maximum head (and thus near peak efficiency) continuously. This is because fluctuations in water surface elevation behind the dam are small compared with the total drop in elevation between the reservoir water surface elevation and the elevation of the turbines.

12-4 WATERWAYS

Introduction

A waterway is a river, canal, channel, or other navigable body of water used for travel or transport. In the United States, waterways have played an important role in the development of the nation from early settlement to modern-day commerce. Navigable rivers first served as routes for inland exploration, and later major cities were founded along these waterways, as trade and travel by water was the most efficient and least costly mode of transport. Early navigation on rivers was limited, however, by natural obstructions including sandbars, turbulent water, seasonal flows, and flooding. As a result, construction of extensive systems of canals having controlled water velocities and depths and dependent on animal power became popular for barge transport in the 1820s.

At that time, canal construction was justified based on the economics of prevailing transport alternatives: a horse drawing a wagon on a rough road could haul about 1200 pounds; for the same amount of work, about 50 tons could be pulled by horse-drawn barge. The success of the Erie Canal connecting the Hudson River to the Great Lakes stimulated a subsequent "canal craze." This unfortunately led to many quickly conceived, poorly planned, costly projects that could not be justified on economic grounds.

The growth of the railroad system with its fast-moving cars soon eclipsed the previous advantages displayed by canals; as a result, many canals in the planning stages in the late 1800s were never completed, and others ceased to be used. However, by the end of the great canal era in the late 1800s, waterway engineering technology had advanced to the point where rivers could be looked to once again to support waterway commerce. The federal government committed large amounts of resources to tame the rivers, capitalizing on advanced technology. Methods such as dredging, channelization, and building of lock and dam systems promised to make waterways more dependable and available for safe navigation, with canals relegated to the function of interconnecting structures for existing water bodies.

As a result of modern technology, today the United States enjoys many navigable waterways that are maintained to provide virtually uninterrupted use. This section describes the existing waterways in the United States, the factors that govern the suitability for the use of a water body as a navigable waterway, and the engineering methods for construction and maintenance of these systems.

Waterways in the United States

The waterways system of the United States consists of seven major groups of waterway routes that total 25,543 miles of navigable length, with an additional 3675 miles authorized for improvement by the U.S. Congress as of 1981 (43). The seven systems include the Atlantic Coast Waterways, the Atlantic Intracoastal Waterway, the Gulf Coast Waterways, the Gulf Intracoastal Waterway, the Mississippi River System, the Pacific Coast Waterways, and the Great Lakes System. The extent of these waterways is shown in Figure 12-11. These systems together enable commercial water transportation to serve 38 states, or about 95 percent of the nation's population (44). Petroleum, coal, building materials, grain, chemicals, iron and steel products, and manufactured goods account for the greatest volume of freight moved by water (43). A typical barge tow of freight is pictured in Figure 12-12.

Navigation Requirements

ECONOMIC FACTORS

A basic criterion for waterway construction is that it provide a more beneficial alternative to transport or travel than other available means. When this ceases to be the case, people will choose the more desirable alternative, and the demand for water transport will fall, as the great canal systems of the nineteenth century fell to the alternative of more economical rail transport.

With the notable exception of oil transport by pipeline, water continues to be the cheapest mode of transport per ton-mile*. In 1977, freight costs were 0.3 cents per ton-mile by barge; as a comparison, it cost 1.6 cents to ship the same amount of freight by rail, 8 cents by truck, and 22.5 cents by air (44). Waterway transport has the advantage of being more energy conserving and efficient than rail and truck transport. One gallon of fuel will allow a barge to move 514 ton-miles of freight, whereas the same amount of fuel would move the freight 202 ton-miles by rail, or 59.2 ton-miles by truck. Water transport is more efficient than other modes of transport due to economy of size. One barge can carry as much as 15 rail cars or 58 trucks. A 35-barge tow of freight would be equivalent to 525 rail cars or over 2000 trucks (43, 45).

Transport by waterway has the disadvantage of being slower than transport by rail or truck, and it is limited to serving cities located along the waterway; other modes of transport must be depended on to complete

---

*A ton-mile is the movement of 1 ton (2000 pounds) of freight over the distance of one mile.

NAVIGABLE LENGTHS AND DEPTHS[a]
OF UNITED STATES WATERWAY ROUTES

LENGTH IN MILES OF WATERWAYS

GROUP	UNDER 6 FT	6 TO 9 FT	9 TO 12 FT	12 TO 14 FT	14 FT AND OVER	TOTAL
Atlantic Coast Waterways (exclusive of Atlantic Intracoastal Waterway from Norfolk, Va., to Key West, Fla.) but not including New York State Barge Canal System	**1426** 1487	**1241** 1445	**584** 589	**938** 965	**1581** 1544	**5768** 6030
Atlantic Intracoastal Waterway from Norfolk, Va., to Key West, Fla.	**–** –	**65** 160	**65** 65	**1104** 1104	**–** –	**1234** 1329
Gulf Coast Waterways (exclusive of Gulf Intracoastal Waterway from St. Marks River, Fla., to Mexican border)	**2055** 2174	**647** 812	**1135** 2095	**79** 269	**378** 388	**4292** 5738
Gulf Intracoastal Waterway from St. Marks River, Fla., to Mexican border (including Port Allen-Morgan City alternate route)	**–** –	**–** –	**–** –	**1137** 1180	**–** –	**1137** 1180
Mississippi River System	**2020** 4365	**969** 1457	**4957** 5062	**740** 755	**268** 268	**8954** 11,907
Pacific Coast Waterways	**597** 700	**498** 515	**237** 237	**26** 27	**2367** 825	**3825** 2554
Great Lakes	**45** 100	**89** 148	**–** 14	**8** 8	**348** 369	**490** 639
All other Waterways (exclusive of Alaska)	**76** 76	**7** 7	**–** –	**1** 1	**7** 7	**91** 91
GRAND TOTAL	**6352** 8935	**3516** 4544	**6976** 8062	**4033** 4309	**4666** 3368	**25,543** 29,218

[a] The mileages shown in this table in bold type represent the lengths of all navigable channels of the United States including those improved by the federal government, other agencies, and those that have not been improved but are usable for commercial navigation.

The mileages shown in this table in light type represent the lengths authorized for improvement by the Congress of the United States in legislation known as Rivers and Harbors Acts.

The source for these tabulations are publications of the Corps of Engineers, United States Army.

Figure 12-12 Typical barge tow of freight. (Courtesy of the American Waterways Operators, Inc.)

delivery to inland points. Obviously, however, transport by waterway is advantageous to enough suitably located industrial and agricultural interests to make it highly competitive with rail and truck transport.

Our economy is, in fact, highly dependent on transport of goods by waterway. In 1981, freight transport by waterway accounted for about 12

Figure 12-11 Waterways of the United States. (Courtesy of the American Waterways Operators, Inc.) (See facing page.)

percent of the nation's freight volume or 302 million ton-miles, at only 2 percent of the national outlay for freight transport (43). The barge and towing industry experienced growth in the early 1980s, and the prospects for future growth look good, particularly in transporting energy-related products and grain. In 1979, petroleum and petroleum products accounted for almost 40 percent of total barge traffic. Increased overseas demand for coal raised coal's share of barge tonnage to 20 percent in the same year. In 1981, the St. Lawrence Seaway Development Corporation reported a record coal transit of more than 1.6 million metric tons through the Montreal–Lake Ontario section of the seaway, which was more than double the previous all-time record of 643,157 metric tons set in 1959 (46).

United States waterways have been traditionally constructed and maintained by the federal government and equally available to commercial users free of charge. As the nation's many waterways grow older, however, they are in need of substantial repair in many locations. To provide a source of funds for keeping them operable in times of federal spending cutbacks, Congress for the first time instituted a waterway user charge in the form of a fuel tax for commercial traffic on inland waterways (Inland Waterways Revenue Act of 1978) (47). The tax schedule is levied at the rate of four cents per gallon beginning October 1, 1980, rising to six cents beginning October 1, 1981, eight cents beginning October 1, 1983, and 10 cents beginning October 1, 1985. The revenue generated by the tax provides monies to repair and maintain the inland waterways system and partially recover federal construction expenditures. The 10-cents-per-gallon level reflects an overall cost recovery of approximately 20 to 25 percent of navigation costs subject to recovery. Once the impact of this tax is assessed, Congress hopes to increase the tax rate to make possible 100 percent cost recovery. The barge and towing industry is concerned that such large tax increases may have a profound effect on the competitiveness of barge transportation with transport by truck and rail.

PHYSICAL REQUIREMENTS
Once it has been determined that waterway transport is economically justified based on potential commodity flows and costs of alternative transport methods, the problem is to determine the dimensions and auxiliary features of channels necessary to most economically support the required cargo fleet. A waterway must be of sufficient depth, width, and velocity to accommodate transport vessels. Where a natural water body does not have the dimensions to handle the desired cargo fleet, three basic strategies may be used. Each requires a different amount of water to make navigation possible. In order of increasing costliness, these are river regulation, canalization, and construction of artificial canals.

River regulation encompasses a number of engineering methods used to improve natural channels (their depth, width, slope, degree of meandering) that are subject to shifting or siltation due to floods, or that are subject to low water levels due to low seasonal flows. River regulation includes contraction works (a series of dikes and jetties designed to deepen and stabilize the location of the channel), river straightening, dredging, bank stabilization, removal of obstructions ("snags") such as trees or stumps, and upstream release of impounded water to increase the depth of flow downstream. *Canalization* is the construction of a series of dams along the length of a natural river too shallow for navigation vessels, for the purpose of converting the river into a string of navigable pools, which are bypassed by locks. Construction of *artificial canal systems* to either join existing water bodies or to parallel otherwise unnavigable waterways is a third means of facilitating navigation.

Components of Waterway Systems

NATURAL CHANNELS

In most cases, only the lowermost reaches of a channel are sufficiently deep and wide to permit navigation vessels to freely pass through. To provide a continuous navigable waterway, usually a combination of river regulation methods is employed to improve the channel. These include dredging, construction of contraction works, bank stabilization, and channel straightening.

Dredging is the act of cleaning, deepening, or widening a channel with any one of a number of types of mechanical or hydraulic *dredges*—machines equipped with scooping or suction devices for the purpose of removing channel-bed material. Dredging is commonly employed to initially improve a channel where navigation is impeded by sandbars or heavy deposits of silt. Yearly maintenance dredging is usually necessary for waterways that are subject to heavy siltation from flood flows.

Contraction works are constructed for the purpose of forcing water into a channel of predetermined depth, width, and location, both to maintain a minimum depth of flow and to prevent migration of the channel over the years. Contraction works consist of a series of *spur dikes* (jetties) and *longitudinal dikes* built to direct the flow into a main channel, as illustrated in Figure 12-13. *Permeable* spur dikes made of pile clumps or brush fences are used to promote sedimentation and filling between parallel dikes in channels carrying a heavy sediment load. *Impermeable* spur dikes made of rock piles or other heavy material are usually used for channel flows carrying a light sediment load. Where the design of the works calls for very short spur dikes, a longitudinal dike or riverbank revetment can be instead used, as shown in Figure 12-13. The initial impact of construction of a contraction works is to cause sediment deposit upstream of the works and an initial increase in water level in the channel. Over time the project will have its intended effect of increasing the water velocity so as to scour out the channel bed, and thus deepen the channel.

Bank stabilization is desirable to prevent channel bank erosion and subsequent downstream sedimentation and riverbed meandering. Com-

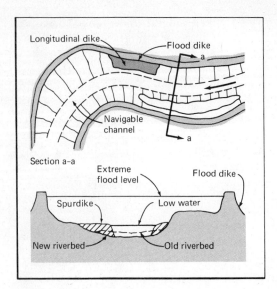

Figure 12-13 River contraction works.

mon types of revetments used to stabilize banks are *articulated concrete matresses* consisting of concrete blocks connected by wire mesh, lightly reinforced *asphalt cement mattresses,* and *willow mattresses* covered with riprap. Criteria for successful riverbank stabilization are: (1) the bank slope must be sufficiently mild that sliding will not occur, (2) the revetment must be tight enough to prevent soil from washing through it, (3) the revetment must extend from the top of the bank to the bottom of the river so that undermining of the toe is prevented, and (4) the revetment must be flexible enough to adapt to the contour of the bank as it exists, and as it may change over time (36, 38).

Some *channel straightening* may result from construction of contraction works or from bank stabilization. In cases where a natural channel has many bends resulting from meandering, it may be desirable to shorten the waterway by cutting off the bends, as shown in Figure 12-14. Once an initially narrow cut is made with dredging equipment, the scouring action of the water will widen the channel to match the width of the natural sections.

RESERVOIR RELEASES
It is possible to deepen the lower reaches of a channel by releasing upstream impounded water during low-flow periods. There are several limitations to this approach, however. First, the quantities of water needed to augment river flow usually would require constructing huge reservoirs containing on the order of up to several million acre-feet of water. Second, significant quantities of water could be lost to seepage and evaporation by the time the released water reached the desired location, which is usually quite far downstream. Another problem with this approach is that

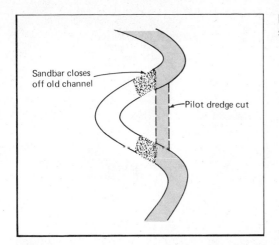

Figure 12-14   River straightening.

it competes with other water uses, particularly irrigation, hydroelectric power, and recreation, which would be in high demand at the time the releases are most needed—during the dry summer months. Usually the use of such large quantities of impounded water solely for navigation cannot be economically justified when compared to the benefits that would be derived by use of the same water for irrigation or hydroelectric power. More commonly, *multipurpose reservoirs* are built for flood control, irrigation, recreation, hydroelectric power, and limited releases for navigation. Such multipurpose reservoirs can be found on the Missouri River, where five reservoirs with a storage capacity of 75 million acre-ft have been built to release 20,000 ft³/s to augment the Missouri River's summer low flow of about 5000 ft³/s (38). An important consideration in the release of water for navigation is determining the time required for flow to reach the desired location.

LOCK AND DAM SYSTEMS

Where the channel flow is too shallow for navigation due to steep channel slopes, or where there is an abrupt change in channel-bed profile, a *dam* may be constructed so that a sufficiently deep navigable pool of water is created behind it. A dam is usually designed to provide the minimum depth of water to make a channel stretch navigable, but if other uses are to be made of the dam, such as flood control or hydroelectric power generation, additional storage must be provided. Where it is desirable to make a long stretch of a channel navigable, a series of several dams is used. A simplified profile of a river converted into a navigable waterway by a series of dams is shown in Figure 12-15.

Several types of dams may be used in waterway construction, namely *navigable, nonnavigable,* or *fixed. Navigable* dams allow the free passage of vessels without the use of locks during periods of high flow. *Non-*

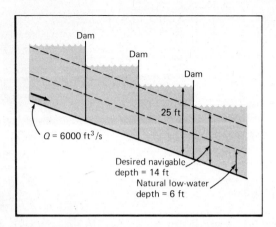

Figure 12-15   Profile of a dammed river.

navigable dams have gates that can be partially lowered to allow flood flows or ice to pass but cannot be crossed by vessels. *Fixed dams* are usually built in conjunction with power plant operation, are often greater than 30 ft in height, and are typically of the gravity, earth, or rock-fill type. Movable dams are advantageous in that they minimize flood hazards by allowing flood flows to freely pass through. Fixed dams, on the other hand, cause flood water levels to be raised to greater elevations than the natural flood elevations that would occur without the dams.

A dam is bypassed by a *lock,* which is a longitudinal chamber aligned with the flow of the river and closed off by gates that allow a navigation vessel to be raised or lowered from one water surface elevation to another by filling and emptying of the lock chamber (see Figure 12-16). The operation of a lock is illustrated in Figure 12-17.

Modern locks are built of concrete. On large waterway systems, older locks are typically 600 ft long and 110 ft wide; the newer locks are usually 1200 ft long and 110 ft wide. Typical standard barge sizes that must pass through the locks are 175 ft long by 26 ft wide for a 1000-ton capacity, 195 ft by 35 ft for a 1500-ton capacity, and 290 ft by 50 ft for a 3000-ton capacity. The height of the lock is dictated by the difference between the lower and upper water surface elevations.

It is desirable to fill and empty the lock in as short a time as possible in order to avoid barge traffic backups; however, the lock must not be filled too quickly because the surge wave created by inflowing water can cause stress on the vessel's mooring hawsers and create a risk of breaking the tow loose. Typical lock filling time is 15 minutes (36).

CANAL SYSTEMS
Canals are constructed for three basic purposes: (1) to connect two existing water bodies, (2) to connect an inland city with a port, and (3) to circumvent unnavigable portions of a river, for example, steep rapids or falls. All involve significant excavation and building of locks and are consequently

Figure 12-16 Illustration of a river lock. (Courtesy of the U.S. Army Corps of Engineers.)

Figure 12-17 Lock operation.

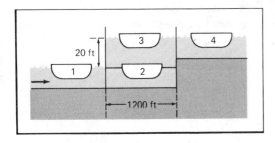

very costly to construct. In addition, canals are subject to water losses from evaporation, seepage, and locking operations. Careful consideration must be given to determine the most economical location and cross section of the canal, and an adequate water supply must be guaranteed in order to make its operation economically viable.

To minimize costs in completing a canal, the following factors should be considered in determining the most economical location: (1) the alignment should be as close to straight as possible, (2) the minimum number of locks should be built, (3) the total amount of earth movement should be minimized, and (4) the canal water level should not be lower than the groundwater level, otherwise significant lowering of the water table could result from the canal acting as an infiltration gallery (see Chapter 7) (38).

To construct a satisfactory canal cross section, Kuiper gives the following empirical criteria for inland, quiescent canals: (1) the shape should be trapezoidal, (2) the slope of the sides should be 1 vertical to 3 horizontal, (3) the largest vessels should be able to pass one another with a clearance of 10 ft, (4) the clearance of the vessel bottom with the canal bottom should be 2 ft for vessels up to 500 tons and 3 ft for vessels over 1000 tons, and (5) the ratio of the wetted cross-sectional area of the canal to the wetted cross-sectional area of the largest vessel should be at least 6 (38). These criteria are illustrated by a sketch in Figure 12-18.

Relation to Other Water Uses

Construction of waterway systems may compete with other water uses when a particular waterway component is built solely for navigational purposes. As mentioned above, reservoirs can rarely be economically justified when constructed only for navigational releases, but they do become very attractive when planned for multiple uses including flood control, irrigation, hydroelectric power generation, water supply, and recreation. Waterway training works such as dikes and levees serve to deepen and stabilize a channel while at the same time providing flood control and land reclamation in the surrounding floodplain. River dam and lock systems built for navigational purposes also provide flood control for the surrounding area. In addition, dams prevent stretches of rivers from drying up during periods of low precipitation and protect fish and other wildlife from killing droughts and floods.

12-5 FLOOD DAMAGE REDUCTION

Historically, lands bordering on waterways have been attractive places to settle, as these locations provide fertile land for agriculture and easy access to transport, hydropower, water supply, and recreation. Time and again a price has been paid for these benefits by those choosing riverside or

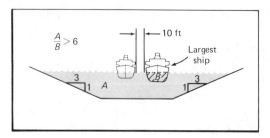

Figure 12-18 Standard canal cross section. (After E. Kuiper, *Water Resources Development: Planning, Engineering, and Economics,* Butterworth and Co., London, 1965.)

coastal dwellings. Every year severe storms cause inland and tidal waters to overflow their boundaries and inundate normally dry areas. This phenomenon, *flooding*, causes yearly loss of life and billions of dollars worth of property damage to inhabitants of the inundated areas, and millions are spent on cleanup and rehabilitation of the damaged land. Traditionally, effort has been expended in finding more effective ways to modify flood behavior by building progressively larger and stronger flood control structures—dams, dikes, levees, or channel enlargements—to restrict the movement of waters to land immediately adjacent to the flood prone areas. This approach, coupled with increased urban development (and increased amounts of impervious area) along waterways, has only served to exacerbate the problem by causing faster and larger floods to occur downstream. It has not been until within the past 20 years that the concept of nonstructural approaches to flood damage reduction has taken hold in this country. The nation has come to realize that floods will continue to take lives and destroy property as long as people are living in floodplains who are unaware that these events will reoccur. One approach to nonstructural flood damage reduction has been the dissemination of information on flood hazards to those living in flood-prone areas. Other nonstructural approaches include land use planning, zoning, flood warning systems, flood insurance, floodproofing, evacuation, and relocation. This section describes the trends of flood damages in the United States and both structural and nonstructural methods for their reduction.

Definitions

The Water Resources Council has defined a *flood* or *flooding* as a general or temporary condition of partial or complete inundation of normally dry areas from the overflow of inland or tidal waters and/or the unusual and rapid accumulation or runoff of surface waters from any source. The *floodplain* is the lowland and relatively flat areas adjoining inland and coastal waters, including flood-prone areas of offshore islands. Usually the floodplain is also considered to be the area subject to a flood having a recurrence interval of 100 years (see Section 7-2) (48).

Perspective on Flood Losses in the United States

COST TRENDS
Despite modern flood damage reduction technology, flood losses continue to increase in the United States. Figure 12-19 shows the trend of United States flood loss estimates from 1903 to 1974. The National Oceanic and Atmospheric Administration has calculated that the trend has been about a 4 percent per year increase in this century. The Water Resources Council estimated that flood losses were $3.4 billion for 1975 (49). A partial list

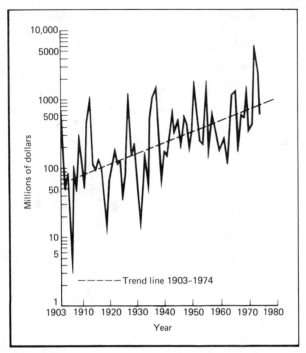

Figure 12-19   Flood loss estimates for the United States. Actual damages for each year have been converted to 1975 dollars with the Wholesale Price Index.

of federal expenditures for flood damage reduction for fiscal year 1980 is given in Table 12-6. This table also illustrates the variety of federal agencies that are involved in these activities.

AREAS PRONE TO FLOODING

Many localities in the United States are subject to flooding along streams or in coastal areas. In 1975 the WRC estimated the following distribution of flood losses: 48 percent agricultural areas, 22 percent urban areas, and 19 percent other areas, including public lands, public buildings, mining, utilities, and rural industries. The WRC predicted that with the current trend of migration toward urban areas, construction in floodplains, and increased replacement of pervious soils with impervious areas, that by the year 2000 flood losses in urban areas would increase to 36 percent of the total, agricultural losses would decrease to 40 percent of the total, and other losses would account for 23 percent.

Structural Approaches to Flood Damage Reduction

The traditional approach to flood damage reduction has been one of attempting to reduce the flood hazard by physical means, including con-

Table 12-6 PARTIAL LIST OF FEDERAL COSTS FOR FLOOD LOSSES IN FISCAL YEAR 1980

National Weather Service	
Flood forecasting and warning	$14.7 million
Corps of Engineers	
Construction: $775 million	
Operations: 204 million	
Flood fighting: 32 million	$991 million
Federal Highway Administration	
Repair and restoration	$100 million
Federal Insurance Administration	
Claims incurred	$483 million
Office of Disaster Response and Recovery	
Individual assistance: $197 million	
Repair and restoration of public facilities: $482 million	$679 million
Red Cross	
Assistance to victims	$12 million
Total	$2.28 billion

SOURCE: National Science Foundation, *A Report on Flood Hazard Mitigation,* Washington, D.C., 1980.

struction of dams and levees, channel improvement, and watershed improvement. But the trend of increasing flood losses will not be leveled off or reversed unless floodplain development is controlled.

DAMS AND RESERVOIRS
Dams with controlled outlets may be constructed across streams to create reservoirs to store floodwaters as they flow into the channel, and to provide controlled release in order to decrease peak flood stage downstream. Design storage capacity is determined from historical flood records and from requirements for other planned uses of the impounded water. Floodwater storage reservoirs may be used to provide water for irrigation, water supply, hydroelectric power generation, recreation, and navigation.

ON-SITE DETENTION MEASURES
Small dams, embankments, or excavations may be employed to create detention basins. Detention basins are small impoundments with uncontrolled outlets used to intercept and collect runoff before it reaches the stream channel, and thus to reduce downstream peak flood stages. These structures are suitable in urban areas for controlling runoff. Detention basins may act as recharge areas for groundwater aquifers, and they provide water quality control measures by settling suspended sediment, thereby reducing the amount of sediment flowing into the channel.

LEVEES AND FLOOD WALLS
Levees are earthen walls or embankments constructed in the floodplain parallel to rivers or coastal areas to prevent the encroachment of floodwaters on inland points. They are typically designed with an interior drain-

age system so that any water flowing from inland points can be ponded or removed by pumping. Flood walls are reinforced concrete structures built along channel banks. They are designed to confine floodwaters to the stream channel in areas where it is undesirable to permit any overflow of water onto the floodplain.

CHANNEL MODIFICATIONS

Modifications of channels in the form of deepening, widening, or straightening are carried out in order to reduce peak flows and to carry off floodwaters more quickly in a particular location. Unfortunately this has the undesirable side effect of increasing the magnitude of flooding downstream and also of reducing the natural recharge potential to channelized areas. In addition, channel modification may have adverse environmental effects on the natural flora and fauna inhabiting the channel.

HIGH-FLOW DIVERSIONS AND SPILLWAYS

These structures are naturally or artificially constructed bypass channels or conduits that have limited use in redirecting excess flows away from developed areas. Use of diversions and spillways for this purpose is limited by the few opportunities to locate them in existing developed areas.

WATERSHED IMPROVEMENT

Whereas detention basins are appropriate for controlling runoff in urban areas, in nonurban areas larger-scale methods can be used to control runoff before it reaches the channel. Physical measures can be taken to alter the land in a watershed to increase infiltration and decrease or delay runoff; they have the effect of decreasing impacts of flooding downstream. These techniques include improving vegetative cover, regrading, terracing, and forest and open-range management. Only sustained very high flows are ineffectively dealt with by this method. Watershed improvement usually has the side benefits of improving infiltration and groundwater recharge and of reducing erosion and the amount of sediment washed into the river.

EMERGENCY STRUCTURAL MEASURES

Few structural measures can be taken on an emergency basis because time is too short for gathering of materials and construction. Sandbagging, or the stacking of sandbags to increase the height of levee walls or to provide floodwater diversion, is an effective emergency structural flood protection tool. Emergency pumping can be used to remove water from behind levees or from basements. In both cases, it is useful to have on hand a flood plan that outlines where the emergency equipment and provisions are stored so that they may be quickly and easily accessible in the event of a flood.

Nonstructural Approaches to Flood Damage Reduction

The "nonstructural approach" generally refers to all other adjustments employed to modify the exposure of people to floods. This includes both measures to modify the susceptibility to flood damage and disruption and measures to modify or reduce adverse impacts of floods on the individual or the community.

FLOODPLAIN REGULATIONS

One method of nonstructural floodplain management is the passage of regulations and ordinances by state and local governments affecting land use and development within channel and floodplain areas. State regulations may typically take the form of basic guidelines with provisions for local implementation, so that local regulations are compatible with one another and with statewide objectives and standards. Local regulations principally include zoning ordinances, subdivision regulations, building and housing codes, encroachment line statutes, open-area regulations, and sanitary codes with specific flood hazard provisions.

DEVELOPMENT AND REDEVELOPMENT POLICIES

Nonregulatory action may be taken on the part of federal, state, or local government to guide development in a manner that reflects the flood hazard and the natural characteristics of the floodplain. Such actions include promoting the design and location of utilities and services in low-risk areas, open-space acquisition, promoting redevelopment activities such as urban renewal in low-risk areas, and encouragement of permanent evacuation out of flood-prone areas.

FLOOD INSURANCE

The concept of flood insurance in the United States dates back to the 1920s. But when insurance companies suffered huge financial losses due to payments for severe flooding, most of them eliminated or reduced the scope of their flood insurance programs. In 1956 flooding in the northeastern United States prompted Congress to authorize a major flood insurance program, but it was never funded. Finally in 1968, after extensive study of the national flood problem and formal recommendations by the Department of Housing and Urban Development, Congress passed the National Flood Insurance Act, which required local floodplain regulation before communities could obtain flood insurance and a dual insurance rate structure where existing buildings were insured at subsidized rates and new buildings at actuarial rates based on the actual extent of the hazard to which they were exposed. This program really never took off, due to lack of public awareness, failure of communities to apply for eligibility, and lack of marketing on the part of insurance companies. Part of the cause of lack of public awareness was the lack of availability of flood zone maps and accompanying flood insurance rate maps for people to use to determine whether they were eligible for the insurance.

In 1973 Congress strengthened the act by passing the Flood Disaster Protection Act, which required communities to participate in the flood insurance program in order to obtain any form of federal financial assistance for land acquisition or construction in any designated flood area, or federally funded relief for flood victims. Congress has waived these mandatory requirements in certain cases by special congressional actions to help ineligible victims who would otherwise not receive funds.

Nonetheless, the flood insurance program has slowly grown over the past decade, due to the requirement that flood victims purchase policies in order to obtain federally funded relief or disaster loans. In addition, with the completion of more extensive flood zone and insurance rate maps, insurance companies are taking a more active role in marketing the insurance.

FLOODPROOFING

Floodproofing is the modification of individual structures and facilities, their sites, and their contents to protect against structural failure, to keep water out, or to reduce the effects of water entry (49). A primary purpose of floodproofing structures is to reduce property losses and provide early return to normal occupation soon after the floods have receded, *not* to provide self-contained structures for occupancy during a flood. Floodproofing may be permanent or contingent on some action at the time of flood. The method includes construction of flood walls or levees around buildings, waterproofing, or elevating structures so that they are above the elevation of a severe-magnitude flood.

Floodproofing walls or levees are designed to protect one or several buildings, as opposed to flood walls and levees constructed along rivers for more general protection. They are usually less than six feet high and are built to blend in with the architecture and landscape of the surrounding buildings and grounds. Walls may be constructed of brick, stone, concrete, or other material that will resist the lateral uplift pressures of floodwaters. Levees may be constructed of an impervious inner core to prevent seepage and with slope protection if needed.

Structures may be elevated by the use of materials such as earth fill, concrete walls, wood, steel, concrete or masonry posts, piles, or piers. The choice of material of construction depends on the flood hazard involved.

Floodproofing has been used as a provision of the National Flood Insurance program that requires new structures built in flood hazard areas to floodproof utility and sanitary facilities and to elevate the lowest floor, including the basement, to a height at or above the 100-year flood level.

FLOOD FORECAST WARNING AND RESPONSE SYSTEMS

Once the physical response of a drainage basin is understood, data on rainfall levels from rain gauges placed throughout the basin enable designated officials to make certain predictions concerning the time of occurrence and the magnitude of flows downstream. The larger the watershed, the more advance notice that can be given to those in danger of downstream flooding; for example, on major rivers where the flood peak moves slowly, forecasts can be given several days to a few weeks in advance. The National Oceanic and Atmospheric Administration is primarily responsible for collecting data by means of a predetermined communication system during the time of heavy rains and using the information for flood predictions. With this data, local officials can determine whether it is necessary to issue a warning to evacuate an area until the floodwaters have passed. Flood forecasting systems have been established for the major rivers in the United States.

DISASTER PREPAREDNESS
A flood warning and forecast system is of little use unless the community is prepared to respond to such warnings. Disaster preparedness in the form of evacuation plans, relief plans, and forecast-response plans ensures that a flood warning and forecast system is explained so that people know what to do in case of an emergency. Essential to all disaster preparedness plans is training and public information activities. Typically the response to flood forecasts is carried out by state and local civil defense and emergency service organizations. Also included as part of a disaster preparedness plan should be assurance that adequate flood insurance coverage is obtained.

RELIEF AND REHABILITATION
A plan for financial and other relief is an essential part of planning for postflood recovery. Relief from donating organizations is usually in the form of food and clothing or may be grants or loans for reconstruction. Tax adjustments are another means of relief to those suffering from flood damages. Plans should provide for encouragement of reconstruction in a manner that will minimize future flood exposure, which may mean relocating people out of the flood-prone area, if possible.

12-6   WASTEWATER TREATMENT AND MANAGEMENT

Ever since it was conclusively demonstrated that fecal pollution was connected with disease transmission, man has been concerned with removing pathogens from wastewater that may subsequently contact humans or animals. Since the industrial revolution, the concern for wastewater contaminants has expanded to include metals, toxic organic chemicals, and pesticides whose presence in wastewater could result in impaired recreational use of receiving waters, death of aquatic organisms, or fouling of water supplies. The goal of water pollution control is to deactivate, destroy, or remove harmful substances from wastewater to avoid disease or death of humans or animals who may be downstream users of the treated wastewater. This section will discuss the sources and characteristics of wastewater, the desirable final water quality characteristics, the legal requirements for treatment, and the methods of treatment commonly used. Also presented are methods for managing wastewater treatment sludges.

Sources and Quantities of Wastewater

DEFINITIONS

Wastewater is the combination of liquid and water-carried wastes from residential, commercial, and institutional buildings and industrial plants together with ground-, surface, or storm water that may enter the system. Wastewater is typically 99 percent pure water; contaminants are usually found in concentrations of 1000 mg/L or less.

The term *sewerage* was formerly used to denote sewage. The modern use of the term is taken to mean the collection system (network of underground pipes) designed and constructed for the purpose of carrying the sewage from its source to its treatment point.

Sanitary or *municipal sewage* refers to wastewater from domestic, commercial, and institutional sources, whereas *industrial wastewater* is the water-carried waste from exclusively industrial sources. These two sources of wastewater are frequently discharged and carried together in the municipal sewer system for treatment by the town or city wastewater treatment plant. When industrial wastes are disposed of in this manner, local ordinances often require some degree of pretreatment before discharge into the municipal sewer in order to make the characteristics and treatment of the industrial wastewater compatible with the treatment of the municipal sewage. Frequently, because of unique and difficult-to-treat characteristics of industrial wastes, industrial sources choose to treat their wastewater separately and completely in privately owned, on-site treatment plants.

Other water entering the sewer is designated as infiltration and inflow. *Infiltration* is groundwater entering the sewer through cracks in pipes, joints, and manhole walls. *Inflow* is surface and storm water reaching the sewer from sources including roof and foundation drains, outdoor paved areas, holes in manhole covers, and cooling water discharges.

Storm water may be collected together with or separately from the sanitary sewage and industrial wastewater. A *combined sewer* is a sewer used for collection of storm water plus sanitary (and industrial) wastewater. Under dry weather conditions, a combined sewer carries the sanitary and industrial wastewater to the treatment plant. Under storm conditions, the storm water is diverted to the same sewer and the combined flow is carried to the treatment plant. When the capacity of the treatment plant is exceeded under these conditions, the excess combined flow is discharged into the receiving body of water, untreated or partially treated. This can result in significant levels of surface-water pollution during wet weather flows, which may have a serious impact on the quality of water provided for downstream users.

Unfortunately, from a pollution control viewpoint, many cities in the United States are served by combined sewers, since the original purpose of many of these sewers was to carry storm water, and later they were used to carry sanitary sewage in addition. An obvious solution is to replace the combined sewers with sanitary sewers; however, such construction could be prohibitively expensive. Realizing the advantages of separate sewers, many cities have made provision for new developments to be served by separate systems. The pollution caused by combined sewer overflow is a problem that has received a great deal of attention in recent years since it has become obvious that more stringent controls placed on wastewater treatment plants are not solving the receiving water pollution problems that are in part being caused by combined sewer overflows (50). The nature and sources of pollution caused by urban runoff and appropriate management and treatment methods are discussed in Section 12-7.

Estimating Quantities of Wastewater

The sources of wastewater in sanitary sewers are domestic households, commercial buildings, industrial plants, infiltration of groundwater through pipe and manhole cracks, and inflow from storm runoff. Some of these fractions of the total flow can be estimated quite easily, whereas others are very much dependent on the type of activities engaged in by the source.

The amount of domestic wastewater entering a sewerage system is directly dependent on the amount of water used in a nonconsumptive fashion by the source. Approximately 70 percent of the water used domestically is used nonconsumptively. Since on the average, per capita household water use rates vary from about 40 to 90 gpcd, approximately 30 to 65 gpcd enters the wastewater system. Therefore, estimates of quantities of domestic wastewater can reasonably be based on population projections. Such methods for estimating water use are discussed in Chapter 4.

Because commercial and industrial water use varies widely, estimates of wastewater flows generated by these sources are more difficult to derive. For example, a 100-ton-per-day paper mill may use 20 mgd of water, whereas a warehousing operation may use only 15,000 to 35,000 gpd. This could mean that a small town's water use and thus wastewater flow could be significantly affected by the start-up or shutdown of one large industrial operation. To arrive at accurate estimates of flow from these sources, the source should be metered.

Estimates of storm water flow entering a combined or storm sewer are commonly derived by the use of the Rational Method and intensity-duration-frequency curves. For very large areas, hydrograph methods may be employed. These methods are discussed in Section 12-7.

COMPONENTS OF A SEWERAGE SYSTEM

The sewerage system consists of the network of pipes collecting wastewater from various sources, any necessary pumping stations, the treatment plant, and the pipes used to convey the treated water to the point of ultimate discharge. The collection system consists of a system of increasingly large pipes: the house or building sewers are connected to collector sewers, which feed into mains or trunk sewers. *Interceptors* connect the trunk sewers to the wastewater treatment plant. After treatment, the discharge from the wastewater treatment plant is carried by large pipes (the *outfall* sewer) to the point of disposal—either to a surface-water body or, alternatively, to disposal fields (where groundwater recharge and/or irrigation may also be intended).

The primary materials used in the manufacture of sewer pipes include vitrified clay, concrete, plastic, asbestos-cement, ductile iron, or corrugated steel alloy. Specifications for pipe strength and design and a list of manufacturers of various pipe materials can be found in the annual *Public Works Manual* (for example, see reference 51).

Ideally, a wastewater collection system is designed so that the wastewater flows by gravity to the wastewater treatment plant, to avoid the costs that would be associated with the pumping needed otherwise. In reality, however, pumping stations are often required to carry the wastewater over uneven terrain and unavoidable increases in elevation between points of collection and treatment. For gravity flow, collection pipes must be laid at a slope to ensure that a minimum wastewater velocity is maintained in order to avoid solids deposition and septic conditions, which can lead to generation of odorous gases.

An interesting problem has arisen in recent years where communities have implemented strict water conservation measures due to increased demands placed on the water supply: the flow to the sewer in certain instances has become so drastically reduced that minimum velocities are not maintained by the system design slope. Solids deposition and septic conditions are often the result.

Collecting sewers are typically located under the street pavement, offset to one side, with the storm sewer (if separate) being centered and the water supply main located on the opposite side of the road.

Manholes are constructed at intervals along sewers to provide access to the system for inspection, cleaning, and maintenance. They are located at changes in flow velocity, direction of flow, and pipe size and at sewer intersections. For small sewers (< 24 in), manholes should be spaced no farther than about 350 ft apart. For larger sewers (27 to 48 in), the recommended maximum interval is 400 ft. For sewers larger than 48 in, no maximum interval is prescribed; the interval necessary for cleaning and maintenance will vary depending on local conditions.

Sewer appurtenances is a term that refers collectively to manholes, house connections, inlets to storm or combined sewers, catch basins, sewer flushing devices, flow regulators, junctions, overflow structures, inverted siphons, sewer crossings, pumps and pumping stations, and outlets. Detailed descriptions and design considerations of these structures may be found in references 52, 53, and 54.

FLOW VARIABILITY

Wastewater flow for a given community varies throughout the day, from week to week, and seasonally. For design purposes, both peak flow rates and average flow rates are needed. Peak flows are used in sizing collector and interceptor sewers; average flows are used to design treatment facilities. It is desirable to determine peaking factors—the ratio of peak to average flow—for each contribution to the sewer, and then to determine the maximum possible peak flow that could occur by summing the peak flows.

WASTEWATER FLOW MEASUREMENT

For effective operation and process control at a wastewater treatment plant, it is essential to accurately measure the flow entering the plant. Measuring devices for open-channel flow regimes are applicable. Because in channel sections where critical flow occurs (see Section 9-1 for definitions) the relation between depth and discharge is independent of roughness and other uncontrollable factors, devices creating critical-flow regimes have been developed for placement in the channel for the purpose of measuring critical depth and thus making possible calculation of the flow. These devices are called critical-flow flumes. The critical-flow flume most commonly used in the United States in wastewater flow measurement is the Parshall flume (see Figure 12-20). By utilizing this device, critical flow is created in the cross section. The depth of critical flow is

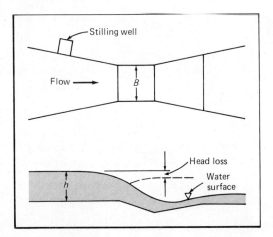

Figure 12-20 Parshall measuring flume.

measured upstream of the cross section and then the discharge may be directly determined.

Wastewater Quality and Treatment Objectives

WHAT IS POLLUTION?
Pollutional strength of wastewater is defined in terms of measurements of a number of physical, chemical, and biological characteristics. The primary physical characteristics of concern are solids content, odors, temperature, and color. In general, organic matter (proteins, carbohydrates, fats, oils, greases, synthetic organic chemicals, pesticides), inorganic matter, and gases are the chemical constituents in wastewater. The biological characteristics that give rise to pollution are certain microorganisms, in particular, pathogenic microorganisms. Typical compositions of strong, medium, and weak wastewaters based on these characteristics are given in Table 12-7.

Table 12-7 TYPICAL COMPOSITION OF UNTREATED DOMESTIC WASTEWATER[a]

	CONCENTRATION		
CONSTITUENT	STRONG	MEDIUM	WEAK
Solids, total	1200	720	350
Dissolved, total	850	500	250
Fixed	525	300	145
Volatile	325	200	105
Suspended, total	350	220	100
Fixed	75	55	20
Volatile	275	165	80
Settleable solids, ml/L	20	10	5
Biochemical oxygen demand, 5-day, 20°C (BOD$_5$, 20°C)	400	220	110
Total organic carbon (TOC)	290	160	80
Chemical oxygen demand (COD)	1000	500	250
Nitrogen (total as N)	85	40	20
Organic	35	15	8
Free ammonia	50	25	12
Nitrites	0	0	0
Nitrates	0	0	0
Phosphorus (total as P)	15	8	4
Organic	5	3	1
Inorganic	10	5	3
Chlorides[b]	100	50	30
Alkalinity (as CaCO$_3$)[b]	200	100	50
Grease	150	100	50

SOURCE: Metcalf and Eddy, Inc., *Wastewater Engineering: Treatment, Disposal, Reuse*, McGraw-Hill, New York, 1979. Reprinted with permission of McGraw-Hill Book Company.
[a]All values except settleable solids are expressed in mg/L = g/m^3. Note that 1.8(°C) + 32 = °F.
[a]Values should be increased by amount in domestic water supply.

DEFINITIONS OF WASTEWATER QUALITY PARAMETERS

The purpose of design of wastewater treatment processes is to remove certain amounts of the constituents from wastewater that are listed in Table 12-7. Therefore, it is essential that the sanitary engineer fully understand the parameters involved and the means by which they are measured. The wastewater characteristics identified in Table 12-7 are discussed briefly here to acquaint the reader with their meaning and significance. Discussion of test methods for wastewater characteristics goes beyond the scope of this book; two sources of information on test methods for evaluating these parameters are *Chemistry for Environmental Engineering* and *Standard Methods for the Examination of Water and Wastewater* (56, 57).

• *Solids.* The definitions of solids are arbitrary and are tied directly to test methods for determination. In making comparisons of data, it is essential that standard procedures for analyses are followed so that such comparisons are valid.

> *Total solids* is defined as the residue remaining after evaporation and drying of a sample (of wastewater) at 103 to 105°C.
>
> *Suspended solids* is defined as the portion of total solids that is not filterable.
>
> *Volatile solids* is the measure of organic material present in a sample. The loss of organic matter on ignition of a dried sample at 550±50°C is considered to be a measure of volatile solids (56).
>
> *Fixed solids* represents the inorganic or mineral fraction of a solids sample. When a dried sample is ignited, the fixed solids are considered to be the the weight that remains after ignition.
>
> *Settleable solids* is that portion of suspended solids that will settle under quiescent conditions under the influence of gravity (56).

In analyzing raw wastewater and effluent samples from primary treatment (defined in the next section), the suspended solids concentration is the solids parameter of concern for use in evaluating the strength of the wastewaters and determining the efficiency of treatment units. Since dissolved solids would be a source of error in a total solids determination due to the large and varying amount present in a raw waste, total solids determinations are not made on raw wastes (56). (Total solids determinations are more appropriate for thicker wastes, that is, sludges). Suspended solids is the parameter that must be reduced to meet effluent standards. The determination of settleable solids in raw wastewater is also important because it is an indication of the quantity of sludge that will be removed by sedimentation.

For wastewater treatment sludges, total solids tests are appropriate because the solids content of sludges is very high compared with the quantity of dissolved species. Sludges are usually 2 to 3 percent solids by weight (dry). The total volatile content of a sludge is of interest because it is an indication of the total mass of bacteria (organics) in the sludge. Knowledge of it is used in setting return sludge levels that ensure adequate biological activity in activated sludge units.

· *Biochemical Oxygen Demand (BOD).* BOD is a measure of the amount of oxygen required by bacteria while stabilizing decomposable material under aerobic conditions (56). The quantitative reaction can be represented as follows:

$$C_n H_a O_b N_c + (n + a/4 - b/2 - 3c/4)O_2 \longrightarrow$$
$$n CO_2 + (a/2 - 3/2c)H_2O + cNH_3 \quad (12\text{-}11)$$

where $C_n H_a O_b N_c$ = decomposable material under consideration
n = number of carbon atoms
a = number of hydrogen atoms
b = number of oxygen atoms
c = number of nitrogen atoms

The reaction is considered to be complete in 20 days, but the five-day BOD is used as a standard since a large percentage of the reaction is completed in five days.

BOD is an especially important determination of the organic strength of a waste because it is an indication of the rate at which oxygen is consumed. For this reason it is one of the most important quantities in determining the pollution potential of a waste.

The rate at which oxygen is consumed is depicted by the curve in Figure 12-21. The curve represents the first-order kinetics displayed by carbonaceous BOD. The rate at which organic polluting matter is destroyed is represented by the expression:

$$-dL/dt = k'L \quad\quad\quad (12\text{-}12)$$

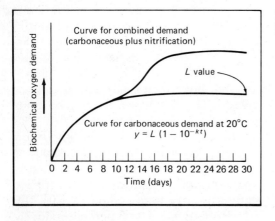

Figure 12-21   Progress of biochemical oxygen demand.

where L = ultimate demand for oxygen
  t = time (days)
  k' = the rate constant for the reaction

Integration of the expression yields

$$L_t/L = e^{-k't} \qquad\qquad (12\text{-}13)$$

Or, since $y = L - L_t$,

$$y = L(1 \quad e^{-k't}) \qquad\qquad (12\text{-}14)$$

where y is the BOD at time t with known k' and L .

The theoretical oxygen demand can be calculated using Equation 12-11; this will never be the same as the ultimate carbonaceous BOD, however, due to the fact that a certain amount of the organic matter is used as food for the synthesis of cell organisms. For example, the theoretical oxygen demand of 300 mg/L of glucose ($C_6H_{12}O_6$) is 320 mg/L, but only 250 to 280 mg/L will be measured as ultimate BOD. This means that 250 to 280 mg/L is used for cell respiration, while 40 to 70 mg/L is used for cell synthesis.

• *Significance of BOD$_5$.* The dissolved oxygen of a water body must remain sufficiently high to support the oxygen requirements of aquatic life. Severe oxygen depletion will occur if a water body receives a wastewater that has a high BOD$_5$. For this reason, BOD$_5$ is a primary consideration in evaluating the strength of a wastewater and the impact that it will have on a receiving body of water. It is the goal of wastewater treatment to reduce the oxygen demand of effluents before discharge so that the oxygen levels of receiving waters will not be depleted below a level that supports fish life (4 mg/L). The BOD parameter is thus an important parameter in determining the design and types of units for a wastewater treatment plant. After a plant is built, BOD is an important parameter in determining the operating efficiencies of the units.

• *Chemical Oxygen Demand (COD).* COD is a measure of the total oxygen required for oxidation of organic matter in water and wastewater to end products. The reaction is represented by Equation 12-11. COD is an indirect measure of the strength of a wastewater in terms of oxygen, although COD does not yield information on the *rate* at which oxygen is demanded. COD does not measure what actually will occur in nature, since many organic chemicals from industrial sources, which are included in COD results, are highly resistant to biological oxidation.

COD will normally have a higher value than BOD since COD measures the oxygen demand of many materials that cannot be biologically oxidized. The difference between BOD and COD is an indication of biologically resistant material present in the wastewater.

Although the BOD_5 test yields useful information on the rate of oxygen demand, it has the disadvantage of taking five days to complete. The BOD_5 can be correlated with the COD if a waste stream is fairly consistent in its oxygen demand. For typical untreated domestic wastes the BOD_5/COD ratio varies from 0.4 to 0.8 (55). It is advantageous to determine the BOD_5/COD ratio for a waste stream at a treatment plant so that the BOD_5 can quickly be determined by running the shorter COD test (several hours) for use in operation and control of the wastewater treatment plant.

• *Total Organic Carbon (TOC).* TOC is a measure of the organic carbon oxidized to carbon dioxide in a high-temperature furnace. The test method for TOC is most suitable for determining small quantities of organic carbon in water (55, 56). Because certain resistant compounds may not be oxidized, the measured TOC will fall short of the actual total carbon value. As is the case for COD/BOD_5 relations, if a long-term TOC/BOD_5 relation can be established for a given wastewater, TOC measurements, which take a shorter amount of time to complete, may be used to deduce the BOD_5 content of a sample.

• *Nitrogen.* Nitrogen may be present in wastewater in several forms: organic nitrogen, ammonia nitrogen, nitrite nitrogen, or nitrate nitrogen. In raw domestic wastewater, virtually all nitrogen is present in the organic and ammonia forms. Usually about 40 percent is organic nitrogen and 60 percent ammonia nitrogen. In nature, the organic nitrogen and ammonia nitrogen are converted into nitrite (NO_2^-) and then to nitrate (NO_3^-) by microorganisms. This two-step reaction can be written as

$$NH_3 + \tfrac{3}{2}O_2 \xrightarrow{\textit{Nitrosomonas}} NO_2^- + H^+ + H_2O \tag{12-15}$$

$$NO_2^- + \tfrac{1}{2}O_2 \xrightarrow{\textit{Nitrobacter}} NO_3^- \tag{12-16}$$

with the overall reaction being

$$NH_3 + 2O_2 \longrightarrow NO_3^- + H^+ + H_2O \tag{12-17}$$

From the overall reaction it can be seen that discharge of raw wastewater containing organic and ammonia nitrogen would exert an oxygen demand on the receiving waters. (This is often called the nitrogenous oxygen demand; see the upper curve in Figure 12-21). For this reason it is desirable to convert the nitrogen present in the raw wastewater into nitrate nitrogen before discharge, or to remove the nitrogen from the wastewater altogether, since nitrates contribute to eutrophication and are toxic at high concentrations to some aquatic species.

• *Phosphorus.* Phosphorus is necessary to all forms of life. It is a component of ATP (adenosine triphosphate), which is a basic source of energy for living cells. Phosphorus may be contributed to natural water bodies in small amounts from natural sources, including rocks and minerals. Most relatively uncontaminated lake districts are known to have surface waters that contain 10 to 30 mg/L of elemental phosphorus (58).

Large amounts of phosphate (PO_4^-) may be contributed to surface waters in phosphate mining areas and from agricultural land where phosphate-containing fertilizer is solubilized in runoff. Phosphates are contributed to municipal wastewater from the use of phosphate-containing detergents. If adequate phosphorus removal is not provided, wastewater treatment plant effluents are an additional source of phosphorus to surface waters.

Sometimes phosphates are added to a water source for scale control in water supply systems. Also, phosphorus (phosphoric acid) is sometimes added to industrial wastes low in phosphorus for proper functioning of biological treatment, since phosphorus is an essential element for microorganism growth.

Sludges from municipal wastewater treatment have about a 1 percent phosphorus content and therefore have value as a fertilizer. Since commercial phosphate fertilizers are abundant, the phosphate content of sludges for use as a fertilizer usually receives little attention.

Because large amounts of phosphate can cause algal blooms and subsequent eutrophication of natural water bodies, it is desirable to maintain a phosphorus level of < 0.01 mg/L in receiving water bodies to control algal growth. For this reason, strict effluent standards for phosphorus control are often common.

• *Chlorides.* Chlorides are usually present in natural waters in proportion to the mineral content of the water. In mountain areas, the chloride levels in natural waters are quite low, whereas the levels in rivers and groundwater are much higher. At sea level, where salt water mixes with surface water and in many cases intrudes on groundwater, chloride levels in natural waters are quite high. The concentration of chloride in wastewater depends on the concentration found in the water supply, as well as on contributions from more concentrated sources, such as industrial wastes and salt brines.

• *pH.* pH is a measure of the hydrogen ion activity $[H^+]$ in a solution, where $pH = -\log[H^+]$. The pH scale ranges from 0 to 14. Liquids having a pH < 7 are in the acid range, whereas liquids having a pH > 7 are in the basic range. A pH of 7 is considered to be neutral. Knowledge of the pH of a water or wastewater is essential in determining the proper treatment needed to make the water suitable for consumption or discharge. For example, in water treatment, if the pH is not in the range of about 5.0 to

9.0, treatment by coagulation, sedimentation, filtration, and chlorination will not be optimal. In addition, if the pH is not properly adjusted for a domestic water supply, the water may be corrosive to water or wastewater treatment processes.

The pH is not an indication of how well water will neutralize acids or bases. The ability of water to neutralize acids or bases depends on its alkalinity and acidity content.

• *Alkalinity.* Alkalinity is the measure of the ability of water to consume acids, and it is commonly expressed as mg/L of $CaCO_3$. Alkalinity in water arises from the salts of weak acids: it consists primarily of hydroxides, bicarbonates, and carbonates and, to a minor extent, of phosphates, borates, and silicates from natural sources. Polluted water may contribute salts of weak acids such as acetic, propionic, and hydrosulfuric acids. Extensive algal growth in surface-water bodies contributes to alkalinity by raising the pH of water in the removal of CO_2.

Alkalinity is not normally a problem from a health standpoint. When water supplies have high alkalinity, the water is so unpalatable that the population will not consume it.

The EPA has set a water quality criterion of 20 mg/L or more of alkalinity as $CaCO_3$ for freshwater aquatic life except where natural concentrations are less (58). The EPA's rationale for setting this criterion is that the alkalinity is necessary to "buffer the pH changes that occur naturally as a result of photosynthetic activity of chlorophyll-bearing vegetation" (58). An additional benefit of alkalinity is that carbonate and bicarbonate ions form complexes with certain toxic heavy metals, thereby reducing the toxicity of certain chemical species present in the water (58).

Since alkalinity is a measure of the capacity of water to neutralize a base, alkalinity is used as an index of the buffering capacity of water. Alkalinity measurements are important in determining water and wastewater treatment needed to make water suitable for consumption or discharge. In treatment by chemical coagulation, alkalinity must be present not only to react with acid produced by the coagulant and also to maintain proper pH of the water being treated. Alkalinity must also be known for determining amounts of lime and soda ash needed to soften a given water. Industrial wastes must be sufficiently treated to reduce alkalinity such that they are not corrosive, before discharge or disposal.

• *Acidity.* Acidity is a measure of the ability of water to neutralize a base, and it is expressed as mg/L $CaCO_3$. Acidity of water consists of two portions: mineral acidity and CO_2 acidity (which is actually CO_2 plus other weak acids). Mineral acidity arises from both natural sources (for example, sulfuric acid contributed to surface waters by acid mine drainage) and industrial sources (for example, discharge of highly acidic waste).

Mineral acidity is responsible for contributing acidity in water up to a pH of about 4.5. CO_2 acidity in water arises from the equilibrium of CO_2 in water established with the atmosphere in surface waters and as a product of biological activity in groundwater or in lower levels of a stratified lake. CO_2 is responsible for contributing acidity to water at a pH from about 4.5 to 8.3.

Acidity in drinking water is not normally a problem from a health standpoint. The CO_2 levels in groundwater can be quite high (up to 120 mg/L), but this is less than the concentration found in carbonated beverages. CO_2 acidity can be corrosive, however, to pipes in water supply systems.

Determination of CO_2 acidity in water is important in order to determine any necessary wastewater or water treatment. For example, underground supplies that contain high levels of CO_2 must be treated to remove corrosivity before use in a water supply. Similarly, industrial wastes must often be treated to remove acidity before discharge to reduce the corrosivity of the effluent. The acidity must be known in order to calculate the quantities of chemicals that must be added to the wastewater for treatment.

• *Grease.* Large quantities of grease disposed of to the sewer can cause clogging problems in sewer lines, since grease readily separates from an aqueous solution. Sources include rendering operations and commercial food preparation facilities. Determinations of the grease content of wastewater are important for determining the efficiency of various operations in removing grease and the grease content of wastewater treatment sludge.

• *Taste, Odor, and Color.* Removal of offensive tastes, odors, and colors is one of the goals of wastewater treatment. Of course, these parameters are not removed by conventional treatment processes to the degree that would be required to make the wastewater effluent acceptable for potable use. If this is to be done, extra treatment steps over and above conventional treatment (that is, "advanced treatment") must be employed in order to achieve the desirable quality of effluent.

• *Biological Quality.* The chief microorganisms of concern in wastewater treatment are pathogenic, or disease causing, microorganisms, including pathogenic bacteria, viruses, and parasites. They commonly are removed by one of a number of disinfection methods. To determine the effectiveness of the disinfection process, typically the survival of *Escherichia coli* is determined. *E. coli* is a nonpathogenic bacterium present in the human gut that is found in much larger quantities than pathogenic microorganisms from the same source. Because it is more resistant to disinfection than most pathogens present in wastewater, the detection of its presence in very low numbers in wastewater effluent is an indication that the desired level of pathogen kill has been achieved.

WASTEWATER TREATMENT OBJECTIVES

The impetus for wastewater treatment in this country has its roots in the federal Water Pollution Control Act and its amendments. Although the act was originally passed in 1956, when the effects of disposal of increased quantities of sewage resulting from post–World War II growth became apparent, it was not until the 1972 amendments were enacted (P.L. 92-500) that the foundations for today's programs in wastewater treatment were laid in the United States.

Degrees of removal of pollutants from wastewater are achieved by various levels of treatment. Conventional treatment processes consist of preliminary, primary, and secondary treatment steps.

Preliminary treatment processes are designed to remove large pieces of debris, sand, and other coarse material, for the purpose of protecting equipment and processes in the wastewater treatment plant from damage. Preliminary processes include bar racks, screens, comminutors, flow measurement devices (for example, Parshall flumes) grit removal, pumping, preaeration, and flow equalization. In addition, where industrial discharges into the municipal sewer have not been adequately pretreated, flotation, flocculation, or chemical treatment may be also used. These processes are defined and described later in this section.

Primary treatment (or *sedimentation*) consists of physical operations to remove heavy solids (by settling), and floatable materials (by skimming), commonly in slowly stirred tanks. The term primary treatment is also often used to include the above-described preliminary treatment units. In terms of the pollution parameters listed in Table 12-7, primary wastewater treatment typically removes 35 percent of the BOD and 30 to 50 percent of the suspended solids in the raw wastewater.

Secondary treatment, achieved by biological and chemical treatment processes, is employed to metabolize and flocculate colloidal and dissolved organics. Biological processes used in secondary treatment include activated-sludge processes, trickling filters, rotating biological disks, and stabilization ponds, among others. The biological products of activated-sludge processes, trickling filters, and rotating biological disks must be settled from the process effluent. This is typically accomplished by the addition of chemicals that promote coagulation of the biological products followed by settling in a clarification basin. Since both biological treatment and settling are achieved with stabilization ponds, the effluent from stabilization ponds is discharged directly into the next treatment step.

Secondary treatment processes must remove the pollutants remaining in the wastewater after primary treatment in order to meet, at minimum, the EPA standards for secondary treatment delineated in Table 12-8. The addition of oxidizing chemicals to disinfect the secondary efflu-

Table 12-8   EPA STANDARDS FOR SECONDARY TREATMENT

PARAMETER	MINIMUM LEVEL OF EFFLUENT QUALITY
BOD_5, suspended solids	30 mg/L: For the arithmetic mean for effluent samples collected over a period of 30 consecutive days.
	45 mg/L: For the arithmetic mean for effluent samples collected over a period of 7 consecutive days.
	85% removal: The arithmetic mean for effluent samples collected in a period of 30 consecutive days shall not exceed 15% of the arithmetic mean of the values for influent samples collected at approximately the same times during the same period.
pH	6.0–9.0: Must be maintained in effluent unless the publically owned treatment works can demonstrate that inorganic chemicals are not added to the waste stream as part of the treatment process, and contributions from industrial sources do not cause the pH of the effluent to be less than 6.0 or greater than 9.0.

ent is necessary to kill pathogenic microorganisms when the wastewater treatment effluent is to be discharged into a receiving water body.

Concentrated solids (sludge) produced by all treatment processes must be collected and treated for disposal. A typical schematic of a conventional wastewater treatment plant is given in Figure 12-22.

If additional levels of constituents must be removed beyond the capabilities that a conventional treatment sequence can provide, more physical, chemical, and biological treatment processes may be added to achieve the desired treatment. These extra processes together are called tertiary or advanced treatment.

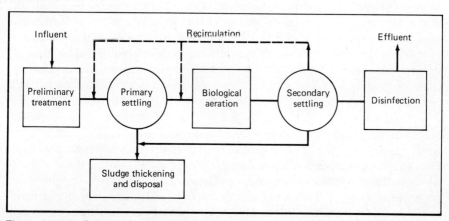

Figure 12-22   Schematic diagram of conventional wastewater treatment.

The goal of municipalities meeting the requirement of secondary treatment was initially written into the 1972 amendments of the Water Pollution Control Act. By 1977, when it became apparent to Congress and the EPA that not only was the goal of secondary treatment not going to be met by the original deadline but that installation of a conventional secondary wastewater treatment plant was not the answer to every community's wastewater problems, the deadline for meeting the EPA requirements for secondary treatment was extended to 1983, and financial incentives were provided for communities to explore innovative and alternative wastewater treatment technologies to the conventional secondary treatment processes. In 1980, when it became obvious that the 1983 deadline would not be met, and a number of administrative problems continued to menace the program, Congress passed the Municipal Wastewater Treatment Construction Grant Amendments of 1981 (P.L. 97-117). These amendments extend the compliance date for secondary treatment to mid-1988, and deem oxidation ponds, ditches, lagoons, and trickling systems equivalent to secondary treatment when water quality will not be adversely affected (59).

The EPA standards for secondary treatment are issued in volume 40, part 133, of the *Code of Federal Regulations* (60). In these rules, the EPA has placed limitations on BOD_5, suspended solids, and pH, with special considerations given to combined sewer flow and industrial wastes. These standards are summarized in Table 12-8. It should be kept in mind that local standards may be, and often are, more stringent than the federal requirements.

Methods of Wastewater Treatment

PHYSICAL TREATMENT PROCESSES
In preliminary treatment, separate physical operations can be identified and described. In other parts of the treatment plant, physical treatment is an integral part of chemical and biological treatment processes, examples being the mixing of chemicals and agitation of biological floc in secondary wastewater treatment. These processes necessitate physical operations, yet it is the biological nature of the system that dictates the operating parameters of the physical method.

• *Screening Devices.* Screening devices are classified as coarse, medium, or fine, depending on the size of the openings in the screening material. Coarse screens or bar racks are usually placed at the inlet of the wastewater treatment plant to remove large debris as a measure to protect the wastewater pumps. This is especially important in plants receiving combined sewer water, due to the large objects that can be washed into the sewer during severe storms. Coarse screens are constructed of steel bars usually not more than 2.5 in apart, and they are installed in the wastewater channel at an angle of 30° to 45° to the horizontal to enable hand or mechanical cleaning.

Medium screens with clear bar openings of 5/8 to 1.75 in also find application in preliminary treatment. A minimum velocity of about 1 ft/s must be maintained to avoid sedimentation, but the velocity should not exceed 2.5 ft/s in order to avoid forcing large objects through the openings.

Fine screens (microscreens) with openings as small as 15 to 60 μ may be employed after secondary treatment to remove residual suspended solids. They are often used in the pretreatment of industrial wastes to remove suspended and settleable solids.

The rakings from screens are high in organics, odorous, and difficult to dispose of. Options for disposal include grinding and return to the wastewater flow for downstream treatment, incineration, or disposal in a sanitary landfill.

• *Comminutors.* A comminutor is a device designed to pulverize solids in raw wastewater to about ¼ to ⅜ in in size to protect pumps delivering the raw wastewater to other parts of the plant. They are installed directly in the wastewater flow channel and are provided with an emergency bypass containing a fixed bar screen, so that the channel section containing the unit may be drained for cleaning and maintenance.

• *Grit Removal.* Grit is defined as fine-sand, 0.2-mm-diameter particles with a specific gravity of 2.65 and a settling velocity of 0.075 ft/s. In wastewater, this size range of particles includes material such as coffee grounds, corn kernels, bone chips, and eggshells. Grit removal protects mechanical equipment and pumps from abnormal wear, prevents deposition and thus clogging of pipes, and reduces sediment accumulation in settling tanks and digesters.

Several types of grit removal units are used in wastewater treatment. The kind selected depends on the amount of grit in the wastewater, the size of the plant, convenience of operation and maintenance, and costs of installation and operation. Standard types are channel-shaped settling tanks, aerated tanks of various shapes with hopper bottoms, clarifier-type tanks with mechanical scraper arms, and cyclone grit separators with screw-type washers.

In channel-shaped settling tanks, the horizontal velocity of the wastewater is controlled by means of a weir or an open slot at the end of the channel to reduce the velocity of flow to about 1 ft/s. This will have the effect of allowing most materials greater than 0.25 mm in diameter to settle out by gravity. The design length of the tank depends on the size of particle removal desired.

Aerated grit chambers have become quite popular because they produce a relatively clean grit (not requiring separate grit washing facilities) and because of the ease of controlling the grit size removed. Air is introduced into the grit chamber by means of diffusers; this causes spiral circulation of the wastewater from one end of the grit chamber to the other, accompanied by gravity removal of the grit particles.

• *Flow Equalization.* Flow equalization is employed in the headwaters of a treatment plant to dampen diurnal and storm variations in the quantity of flow entering the plant. The size of the drainage basin and the length of the sewer will directly affect these variations in flow. The larger the drainage basin and the longer the sewer contributing to the system, the smaller will be the variations in flow. The result of reducing variations in flow will be to stabilize plant operations.

Two basic types of flow equalization techniques are used in wastewater plants: on-line and off-line systems. These are illustrated in Figures 12-23 and 12-24 respectively. The equalization basin is essentially a storage basin enabling storage of high flows to be released to augment low flows, thereby allowing a steady flow level to subsequent treatment units. On-line equalization basins also have the advantage of being able to dampen pollution loads.

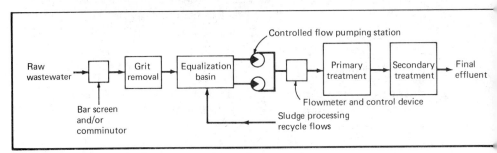

Figure 12-23 Example of in-line flow equalization.

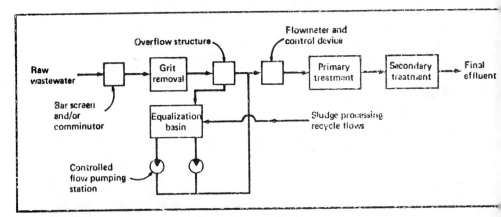

Figure 12-24 Example of off-line flow equalization.

• *Mixing.* Mixing is employed to achieve a desired dispersal of chemicals or gases in wastewater. Generation of turbulent flows is a means of promoting wastewater mixing through the erratic displacement of fluid particles. Of the devices used in wastewater treatment for rapid mixing, the commonest is the vertical shaft, turbine-type, rotating impeller.

The flow pattern generated by an impeller affects the results of the mixing operation being performed. The pattern is a function of the size, shape, and speed of the impeller and baffle and the nature of the mixing tank (61). The turbulence produced in mixing vessels is principally derived from contact between low- and high-velocity flow streams.

• *Flocculation.* In chemical precipitation processes, chemicals are added to the wastewater to promote collision and agglomeration of very small particles into larger, heavier particles or floc, for the purpose of causing them to settle out. Flocculation depends on intermolecular chemical forces and on the physical action induced by gentle agitation of the wastewater. Therefore, agitation of wastewater is a physical treatment operation that is very much a part of the chemical precipitation process.

• *Sedimentation.* Sedimentation is employed in preliminary treatment for grit removal, in primary treatment to remove influent suspended solids from raw wastewater, after secondary biological treatment to remove biological floc from secondary effluent, and in chemical precipitation to remove chemical floc. The units used for sedimentation are called a variety of names, including clarifiers, sedimentation tanks or basins, and settling tanks or basins.

Sedimentation tanks may be rectangular or circular in design and are supplied with influent either from the center or the periphery. The sludge —the settled particles—accumulates in the bottom of the tank and is removed by scraping or pumping. The effluent flows over weirs at the water surface of the tank into collection channels. The effluent from secondary sedimentation is a clear supernatant, and after subsequent disinfection, it is suitable for discharge in areas requiring a minimum of secondary treatment. Figure 12-25 is a photograph of a series of sedimentation basins at the Orange County District Water Factory 21 in Fountain Valley, California.

• *Flotation.* Particles may be removed from wastewater by releasing air or supersaturated air (dissolved air flotation) under pressure into the bottom of a tank so that fine bubbles carry flotable materials to the surface, where they are removed by skimming. This process finds the most application in preliminary treatment of wastewater and in sludge treatment.

• *Filtration.* Filtration is an operation to separate suspended material from wastewater by passing it through a porous material. Although used primarily in treatment of water for potable use, filtration has been increas-

Figure 12-25 Clarification basin at the Orange County Water District's Water Factory 21. (Courtesy of the Orange County Water District, California.)

ingly employed in wastewater treatment to provide additional levels of removal of suspended solids from treatment plant effluent, where strict effluent standards have been set in place. Granular bed filtration is the method that is most often applied to this use. The granular beds may consist of one, two, or three media. The commonest single-layer medium is sand; a combination of anthracite and sand is often used for two layers, and anthracite-sand-garnet is a typical three-bed combination. The parameters that affect the efficacy of a filtration unit include the characteristics of the suspended solids (total suspended solids, particle size, particle distribution, and floc strength), filter medium characteristics (grain size, grain distribution, density of materials in multimedia filtration), and the filtration rate. A filtration loading rate of 2 to 4 gal/min/ft^2 is common.

CHEMICAL TREATMENT PROCESSES

The most important chemical treatment processes in wastewater treatment are chemical precipitation and disinfection. Chemical precipitation is employed in conventional treatment processes to aid settling of colloidal particles in sedimentation basins, since particles in this size range cannot be removed by quiescent gravity settling. Disinfection is a necessary final step to ensure that pathogens are destroyed to an acceptable level in the effluent.

• *Chemical Precipitation.* In order to remove colloidal particles from wastewater, they must first be destabilized and aggregated. The term *coagulation* is used to describe the reduction in net electrical repulsive forces at particle surfaces by electrolytes in solution. *Flocculation* is aggregation by chemical bridging between particles. Although coagulation and flocculation are dependent on chemical processes, the choice of chemical dosage, pH, and coagulant aids are very much dependent on the physical process of mixing that promotes the aggregation of the destabilized colloids.

The chemicals used in wastewater treatment for precipitation are alum (aluminum sulfate), ferrous sulfate (copperas), lime, ferric chloride, and ferric sulfate. The choice of a coagulant depends on the chemical properties of the wastewater, which affect the solids removal efficiency of the coagulant. Laboratory tests should be run on samples of wastewater to determine the performance of various coagulants and the dosages required. Final choice of a coagulant will depend on these two factors and on the overall economics involved. The reactions involved with several coagulants in forming floc are given below.

Alum

The commercial strength of filter alum contains 15 to 22 percent Al_2O_3 with a hydration of about 14 moles of water. The material is usually shipped and fed in dry granular form, although it is also available as a powder or an alum syrup.

The aluminum sulfate reaction with the natural alkalinity present in wastewater to form aluminum hydroxide floc can be represented as:

$$Al_2(SO_4)_3 \cdot 14.3H_2O + 3Ca(HCO_3)_2 \longrightarrow$$
$$2Al(OH)_3\downarrow + 3CaSO_4 + 14.3H_2O + 6CO_2 \quad (12\text{-}3)$$

The addition of alum has the side effect of increasing the concentration of carbon dioxide, which is undesirable, since this increases the corrosivity of the wastewater. If the wastewater does not contain enough alkalinity to react with the alum, then lime may be added to the solution.

The lime and alum reaction is represented as:

$$Al_2(SO_4)_3 \cdot 14.3H_2O + 3Ca(OH)_2 \longrightarrow$$
$$2Al(OH)_3\downarrow + 3CaSO_4 + 14.3H_2O \quad (12\text{-}18)$$

Ferrous Sulfate

Commercial ferrous sulfate has a strength of 55% $FeSO_4$ and is supplied as a green crystal or granule for dry feeding. Ferrous sulfate reacts with natural alkalinity much slower than does alum with natural alkalinity, and therefore lime is generally added to raise the pH to the point where the ferrous ions are precipitated as ferric hydroxide by the caustic alkalinity. The reactions with and without lime are represented respectively as:

$$2FeSO_4 \cdot 7H_2O + 2Ca(HCO_3)_2 + 0.5O_2 \longrightarrow$$
$$2Fe(OH)_3\downarrow + 2CaSO_4 + 4CO_2 + 13H_2O \quad (12\text{-}19)$$

$$2FeSO_4 \cdot 7H_2O + 2Ca(OH)_2 + 0.5O_2 \longrightarrow$$
$$2Fe(OH)_3\downarrow + 2CaSO_4 + 13H_2O \quad (12\text{-}20)$$

Ferric Salts

Ferric sulfate and ferric chloride are additional chemicals that may be used to react with natural alkalinity or lime and act as wastewater coagulants. Ferric coagulants have an advantage over ferrous coagulants in that coagulation is possible over a wider pH range and the precipitate produced is a heavy, quick-settling floc.

Ferric sulfate is available in crystalline form and may be fed using dry or liquid feeders. Ferric sulfate is quite corrosive and requires handling with corrosion-resistant equipment. The reactions for these two coagulants with the addition of lime may be represented by the following equations:

Ferric chloride:

$$2FeCl_3 + 3Ca(OH)_2 \longrightarrow 2Fe(OH)_3\downarrow + 3CaCl_2 \quad (12\text{-}21)$$

Ferric sulfate:

$$Fe_2(SO_4)_3 + 3Ca(OH)_2 \longrightarrow 3CaSO_4 + 2Fe(OH)_3\downarrow \quad (12\text{-}22)$$

• *Coagulant Aids.* Acids and alkalies may be added to wastewater to adjust the pH for optimum coagulation. Common chemicals used are sulfuric and phosphoric acids to lower the pH, and lime to raise the pH when needed. Various polyelectrolytes are used as coagulant aids to increase the rate and degree of flocculation by various chemical phenomena, including adsorption, interparticle bridging, and charge neutralization.

• *Disinfection.* Disinfection, or selective destruction of pathogenic organisms in wastewater, is desirable in order to reduce spread of waterborne disease. A number of chemical and physical means can be used to disinfect wastewater; chemicals are the commonest, with chlorine being the most widely used. Other chemicals that can be used for disinfection include bromine, iodine, ozone, certain heavy metals at very low concentrations (mercury, silver, copper), dyes, soaps and detergents, quaternary amines, hydrogen peroxide, alkalies at pH > 11, and acids at pH < 3. Physical methods that have been used include heat, ultraviolet radiation, gamma radiation, electron beam radiation, and photon beam radiation. Because chlorine is still the most widely used disinfecting agent, its chemistry and significance will be discussed here.

Chlorine works as a disinfectant by oxidizing organic matter and by interference with the enzyme action in the microorganisms that it contacts. The effectiveness of chlorination can be tested by the use of an indicator organism *(E. coli)* on the treated wastewater to test for the presence of pathogenic microorganisms. Adequate disinfection of secondary effluent is considered to be reached when an average coliform count of less than 200 per 100 milliliters remains in the final effluent.

The reactions of chlorine with water are as follows:

$$Cl_2 + H_2O \rightleftharpoons HOCl + Cl^- + H^+ \tag{12-4}$$

$$HOCl \rightleftharpoons OCl^- + H^+ \tag{12-5}$$

The concentration of HOCl plus the concentration of OCl^- is called the *free available chlorine.* The dependence on pH and temperature for one form or the other to dominate is illustrated by Figure 12-26. HOCl is 40 to 80 times more effective than OCl^- as a disinfectant, and so a pH favoring HOCl formation would be desirable. From Figure 12-26 it can be seen that a pH below 8 is preferable.

In addition to free available chlorine, other chlorine compounds are formed when chlorine is added to water that are also good disinfectants.

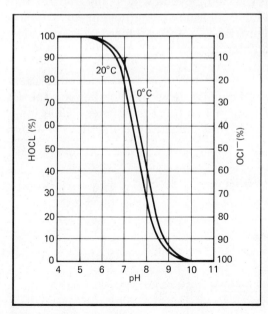

Figure 12-26 Relation between HOCl, OCl^-, and pH.

Specifically, these compounds are the ones that are formed when chlorine reacts with ammonia nitrogen, which is typically present in wastewater. These reactions are represented as follows:

$$NH_3 + HOCl \longrightarrow NH_2Cl + H_2O \text{ (monochloramine)} \qquad (12\text{-}23)$$

$$NH_2Cl + HOCl \longrightarrow NHCl_2 + H_2O \text{ (dichloramine)} \qquad (12\text{-}24)$$

$$NHCl_2 + HOCl \longrightarrow NCl_3\uparrow + H_2O \text{ (nitrogen trichloride)} \quad (12\text{-}25)$$

These reactions occur simultaneously and are very much a function of pH, temperature, duration of reaction, and concentration of reactants. At a low pH, there is a high ratio of chlorine to ammonia, and the formation of dichloramine is favored. At pH > 8, mostly monochloramines will be formed, regardless of the chlorine/ammonia ratios present. If the pH is less than 4.0, almost all nitrogen trichloride is formed. This situation is to be avoided because nitrogen trichloride is a highly odorous, corrosive gas and provides no disinfection. At a pH between 5 and 8, significant amounts of both mono- and dichloramines are present. Both mono- and dichloramines are good disinfectants, but neither is as effective as free available residual chlorine.

The sum of monochloramine and dichloramine is referred to as the *combined chlorine residual.* The total chlorine residual is the sum of the free available chlorine residual and the combined chlorine residual. In a typical wastewater, as chlorine is added the chlorine species present will change until the *breakpoint* is reached, beyond which only free chlorine residual will increase with added chlorine. This situation for a typical wastewater is depicted in Figure 12-27. Most wastewaters are satisfactorily disinfected when a free chlorine residual of about 0.2 mg/L is obtained after chlorination.

One side effect of chlorination that has received considerable attention in recent years is the reaction of chlorine with other chemical species in wastewater to produce carcinogenic and toxic substances. Chlorine is capable of reacting with any unsaturated linkage in an organic compound.

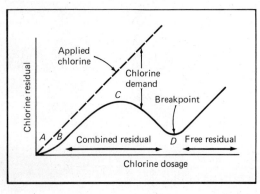

Figure 12-27 Chlorine-residual curve for breakpoint chlorination.

For example, chlorine in the form of HOCl can react with phenols to form mono-, di-, or trichlorophenols, which are toxic substances as well as medicinal tasting in very small quantities. In drinking water supplies chlorine may react with humic acid or low-molecular-weight organic compounds to produce chlorinated methanes, which are carcinogenic. Such discoveries have caused sanitary engineers to take a hard look at chlorine dosages to ensure that an unnecessary excess of chlorine is not entering receiving waters or the water supply. In many instances, wastewater is now dechlorinated before discharge into receiving water bodies.

BIOLOGICAL TREATMENT PROCESSES

Biological treatment systems are living systems that rely on mixed biological cultures to break down waste organics and remove organic matter from solution. Domestic wastewater supplies the biological food, growth nutrients, and inoculum. A treatment unit provides a controlled environment for the desired biological process.

Numerous bacteria, fungi, algae, and protozoans found in wastewater take part in the process of metabolizing the wastewater as food. The number and types present depend on environmental conditions such as the amount of oxygen available, temperature, the availability of nutrients, the presence of toxins, and the type of substrate (food) available. In addition, microorganisms compete with one another for food, and certain species become dominant under a given set of conditions. In biological wastewater treatment, identification of the various types of microorganisms for the different treatment processes has been established, and it is well known which types of microorganisms should be present in a properly operating system. The complete microbiology associated with biological wastewater treatment goes far beyond the scope of this discussion; references 52, 53, and 55 provide good summaries of the life cycles and population dynamics of the microorganisms involved. Pertinent facts relating to the microorganisms associated with each biological wastewater treatment process discussed below will be given where appropriate.

• *Activated Sludge.* Activated-sludge processes are used for secondary treatment and for complete aerobic treatment without primary sedimentation. The primary microbial feeders in activated sludge are bacteria; secondary feeders are protozoans that consume the bacteria. As shown in Figure 12-28, in the activated-sludge process wastewater is fed continuously into an aerated tank, where a mixed culture of microorganisms (activated sludge) contacts the waste for a sufficient period of time to permit synthesis of waste organics into biological cells. The microorganisms are settled from the aerated mixed liquor under quiescent conditions in the secondary settling tank, removed from the bottom of the tank, and a portion is returned to the aeration tank to metabolize additional waste organics. Clear supernatant from the secondary clarifier is the plant efflu-

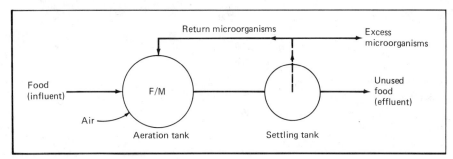

Figure 12-28   Schematic diagram of a continuous-flow activated-sludge process.

ent. Unused food, the nonsettleable and dissolved fraction of the aeration plant effluent, passes out in the system effluent. Metabolism of the organic matter results in an increased mass of microorganisms in the system. Excess microorganisms are removed (wasted) from the system to maintain proper balance between food supply and mass of microorganisms in the aeration tank. This balance is referred to as the *food-to-microorganism ratio* (F/M).

The F/M ratio maintained in the aeration tank defines the operation of an activated-sludge system. Maintenance of a low F/M ratio is desirable to promote a low growth rate yet nearly complete metabolism of the organics, causing the microorganisms to subsequently flocculate rapidly and settle out of solution by gravity.

A flow diagram for a conventional activated-sludge process is shown in Figure 12-29. The aeration basin is a long rectangular tank with air diffusers on one side of the tank bottom to provide aeration and mixing. The cross-section of a typical tank is illustrated by Figure 12-30. The standard activated-sludge process uses fine air bubble diffusers set at a depth of 8 feet or more to provide adequate oxygen transfer and deep mixing. An air supply is tapered along the length of the tank to provide a greater amount of diffused air near the inlet, where the rate of biological

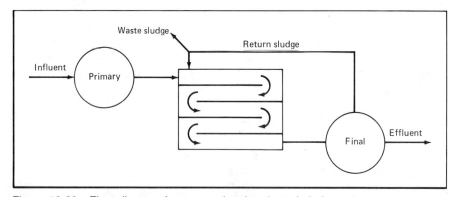

Figure 12-29   Flow diagram for conventional activated-sludge process.

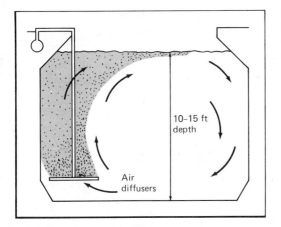

Figure 12-30   Cross section of a typical diffused-air, spiral-flow, conventional activated-sludge aeration tank.

metabolism and resultant oxygen demand is greatest. Settled raw wastewater and return activated sludge enter the inlet of the tank and flow down the length in a spiral pattern.

Operation of an activated-sludge treatment plant is controlled by regulating (1) the quantity of air, (2) the rate of activated-sludge recirculation, and (3) the amount of sludge wasted from the system. A conventional activated-sludge process typically removes 95 percent of the influent BOD.

· *Trickling Filters.* Trickling filters are a second type of biological treatment that can be used for secondary treatment of municipal wastewater. In the trickling filter system, primary effluent is sprayed on a bed of crushed rock, or another medium, coated with biological films. The biological slime layer consists of bacteria, protozoans, and fungi. Sludge worms, filter-fly larvae, rotifers, and other higher animals frequently find the environment suitable for growth. The surface of the bed may support algal growth when temperature and sunlight conditions are optimum. The lower portion of a deep filter frequently supports populations of nitrifying bacteria, that is, bacteria that convert ammonia nitrogen into nitrite, or nitrite into nitrate nitrogen.

Although classified as an aerobic-treatment device, the microbial film on the filter medium is aerobic to a depth of only 0.1 to 0.2 mm (see Figure 12-31). The zone next to the medium is anaerobic. As the wastewater flows over the microbial film, the soluble organics are rapidly metabolized and the colloidal organics adsorbed onto the surface.

Microorganisms near the surface of the bed, where food concentration is high, are in a rapid-growth phase, whereas the lower zone of a bed is in a state of starvation. Overall operation of a trickling filter may be considered in the *endogenous* growth phase, where large masses of microorganisms are competing for the small amount of food available, resulting in near-starvation conditions for the majority of microorganisms

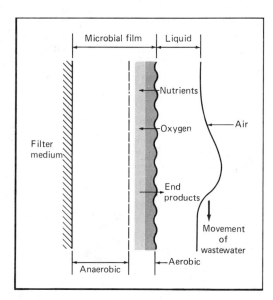

Figure 12-31 Schematic diagram showing the form of the biological process in a trickling filter.

within a short period of time. As mentioned for activated sludge, this overall condition produces nearly complete metabolism of the organics.

Dissolved oxygen extracted from the liquid layer is replenished by reoxygenation from the surrounding air. Undesirable anaerobic conditions can be created in a trickling filter if aeration of the bed is inhibited. Plugging of the air passages with excess microbial growth, as a result of organic overload, can create anaerobic conditions and foul odors.

A sketch of a cutaway view of a trickling filter is shown in Figure 12-32. Major components are the filter media, underdrain system, and rotary wastewater distributor. The filter media provide a surface for growth and voids for the passage of liquids and air. The commonest filter

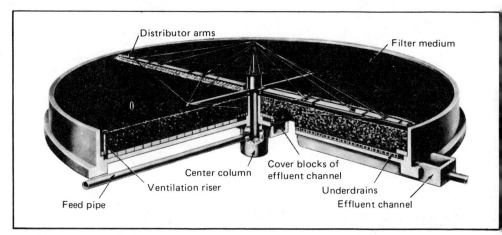

Figure 12-32 Cutaway view of a trickling filter. (Courtesy of Dorr-Oliver.)

media in existing filters are crushed rock, slag, or field stone, because these materials are durable, insoluble, and resistant to chipping. The preferred size for the stone media is 3 to 5 in in diameter. Several forms of manufactured plastic media are also used, their main advantages being light weight, chemical resistance, and high specific surface (area/volume) with a large percentage of free space.

The underdrain system carries away the effluent and permits circulation of air through the bed. A rotary distributor consisting of two or more arms mounted on a pivot in the center of the filter bed provides a uniform hydraulic load of wastewater on the filter surface. The most prevalent kind is driven by dynamic reaction of the wastewater flowing out of the distributor nozzles. This generally requires a minimum pressure head of 24 in measured from the center of the arms.

A trickling filter secondary treatment system includes a final settling tank to remove biological growths that are washed off the filter media. These sloughed solids are commonly disposed of through a drain line from the bottom of the final clarifier to the head of the plant. This return sludge flow is mixed with the raw wastewater and settled in the primary clarifier.

• *Biological Disc Process.* A biological disc unit consists of a shaft of rotating circular plates immersed approximately 40 percent in a contour-bottomed tank. The discs are spaced so that during submergence, wastewater can enter between the surfaces. When rotated out of the tank, air enters the voids while the liquid trickles out over the films of fixed biological growth attached to the medium. Alternating exposure to organics in the wastewater and oxygen in the air is similar to dosing a trickling filter with a revolving distributor. Excess microbial solids slough from the medium and are carried out in the process effluent for gravity separation in a final clarifier. Advantages over other biological processes include lower power consumption, greater process stability, and a smaller quantity of waste sludge than with activated sludge. Efficient aeration and increased contact time between the biomass and wastewater yields better treatment than by trickling filtration.

• *Stabilization Ponds.* Domestic wastewater may be effectively stabilized by the natural biological processes that occur in shallow ponds. Those suitable for treating raw or partially treated wastewater are referred to as *stabilization ponds, lagoons,* or *oxidation ponds.*

Stabilization ponds have light BOD loadings, in the range of 0.2 to 0.5 $lb/100 ft^3/day$, and long liquid retention times of 20 to 120 days. A wide variety of microscopic plants and animals find the environment a suitable habitat. Waste organics are metabolized by bacteria and saprobic (nonliving-matter or decaying-matter feeders) protozoans as primary feeders. Secondary feeders include protozoans and higher animal forms, such as rotifers and crustaceans.

At the liquid depth commonly used in stabilization-plant design, bottom waters may become anaerobic while the surface remains aerobic. In terms of general oxygen conditions, these lagoons are commonly referred to as facultative lagoons. During periods when the dissolved oxygen is less than the saturation level, the surface water is aerated through wind action. During the winter both bacterial metabolism and algal synthesis are slowed by cold temperatures. The lagoon generally remains aerobic, even under a transparent ice cover. If the sunlight is blocked by snow cover, the algae cannot produce oxygen and the lagoon becomes anaerobic. The result is odorous conditions during the spring thaw until the algae become reestablished. This may take from a few days to weeks, depending on climatic conditions and the amount of organic matter accumulated in the lagoon during the winter.

The BOD removal provided by a stabilization pond depends on the climatic conditions described above. During warm, sunny weather BOD reductions usually exceed 95 percent. Under winter ice cover, the lagoon treatment process is essentially reduced to sedimentation, and BOD reductions are generally 50 percent.

Physically, a stabilization pond is a flat-bottomed pond enclosed by an earthen dike, as depicted in Figure 12-33. It may be of round, square, or rectangular design with a length not greater than three times the width.

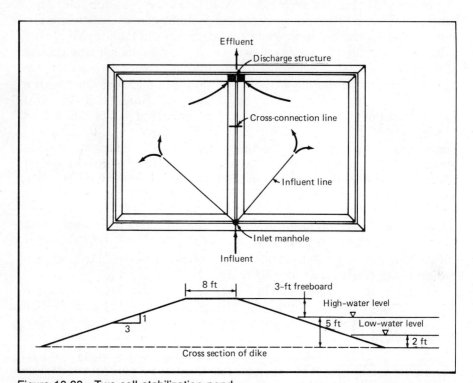

Figure 12-33 Two-cell stabilization pond.

Operating liquid depth is in the range of 2 to 5 ft with 3 ft of dike freeboard. A minimum of about 2 ft is required to prevent growth of rooted aquatic plants. Operating depths greater than 5 ft can create odors because of anaerobic conditions on the bottom.

Influent lines discharge near the center of the pond, and the effluent usually overflows in a corner on the windward side to minimize short circuiting, that is, deviation from design detention time. The overflow is generally a manhole or box structure with multiple-valve draw-off lines to offer flexible operation. Where the lagoon area required exceeds six acres, it is good practice to have multiple cells that can be operated individually, in series, or in parallel. If the soil is pervious, the bottom and sides should be sealed to prevent groundwater contamination. A commonly used sealing agent is bentonite clay. Dikes and the area surrounding the ponds should be seeded with grass to prevent runoff from entering the ponds and fenced to keep out livestock and discourage trespassing.

During winter months and under ice conditions, operation of overloaded stabilization ponds may be augmented by mechanical aeration and mixing to promote a higher level of BOD removal. A common system employed is air diffusion through a plastic hose dispensing network fixed to the bottom of the pond. Compressed air is introduced through rows of plastic tubing strung across the pond bottom. Streams of bubbles rising to the surface induce vertical mixing and oxygenation of the water (see Figure 12-34). Alternatively, floating surface aerators and air diffusers may be used if ice formation does not impair their operation.

• *Complete-Mixing Aerated Lagoons.* Mechanically aerated ponds for pretreatment of industrial wastes or for first-stage treatment of municipal wastewaters are commonly completely mixed lagoons 8 to 12 ft deep with

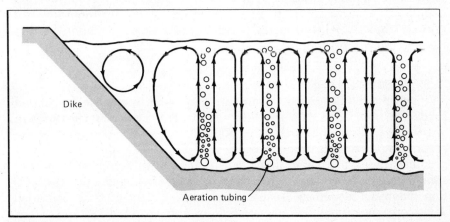

Figure 12-34 Stabilization pond aerated and mixed by compressed air emitting from plastic tubing laid on the lagoon bottom.

floating or platform-mounted mechanical aeration units. A floating aerator consists of a motor-driven impeller mounted on a doughnut-shaped float with a submerged intake cone. Inspection and maintenance is performed using a boat or by disconnecting the restraining cables and pulling the unit to the edge of the lagoon. Platform-mounted aerators are placed on piles or piers extending to the pond bottom. The impeller is held beneath the liquid surface by a short shaft connected to the motor mounted on the platform. A bridge may be constructed from the lagoon dike to the aerator for ease of inspection and maintenance.

Complete mixing and adequate aeration are essential environmental conditions for lagoon biota. Organic stabilization depends on suspended microbial floc developed within the basin since there is no provision for settling and return of activated sludge. BOD removal is a function of detention time, temperature, and nature of the waste, primarily biodegradability and nutrient content.

Advanced Treatment of Wastewater

In areas where limitations on the mass of constituents allowable in wastewater discharges are very much more stringent than the federal requirements for secondary treatment, or where high-purity quality effluent is desired for reuse, conventional wastewater treatment processes often are not sufficient to achieve the desired level of removal of many of the remaining wastewater constituents. Of particular interest in many applications is the removal of nitrogen, phosphorus, total dissolved solids, and refractory organics, over and above removal achieved by the conventional processes. In such instances, additional units or processes are added to the wastewater treatment train to achieve removal of the constituents of concern. In many cases these processes are quite costly to operate and maintain to achieve the relatively small increment of constituent removal desired. Table 12-9 lists selected treatment processes that can be used to remove these constituents.

SUSPENDED SOLIDS REMOVAL

Granular-media filtration is commonly employed to remove suspended solids (SS) remaining after secondary treatment. The salient features of gravity flow filters employed in the United States were described in the section on physical treatment processes. Of particular importance in using granular filters to treat wastewater is the varying rate of flow and the simultaneous occurrence of hydraulic and solids loadings, since clarification following secondary treatment is least efficient at peak overflow. Therefore, the critical design condition for granular media filters is often based on the maximum 4-h flow rate at the worst expected suspended solids concentration. Experience indicates that filtration following secondary treatment can reduce suspended solids to a level of 4 to 9 mg/L, so

Table 12-9 SELECTED ADVANCED
WASTEWATER TREATMENT PROCESSES

Suspended-solids removal
  Filtration through granular beds
  Microscreening
  Chemical coagulation and clarification
Organic removal
  Adsorption on granular activated carbon
  Extended biological oxidation
Phosphorus removal
  Biological-chemical precipitation and clarification
  Chemical coagulation and clarification
  Irrigation of cropland
Nitrogen removal
  Biological nitrification-denitrification
  Ammonia reduction by air stripping
  Breakpoint chlorination
  Ion-exchange extraction
  Irrigation of cropland

that the expected performance of a well-designed and properly operating system is an effluent with SS and BOD_5 concentrations of less than 10 mg/L. Chemical treatment prior to filtration is required to consistently produce an effluent with 5 mg/L SS and 5 mg/L BOD_5 (52).

Microscreens, described previously in the section on physical treatment methods (screening), may alternatively be used to remove suspended solids from secondary effluent. The efficacy of treatment depends on the nature and concentration of suspended solids, hydraulic loading, mesh size, and drum speed.

The filters, typically 10 ft in diameter, operate under gravity conditions with peripheral drum speeds up to 150 ft/min in normal operation. The drums should be operated at the slowest rate possible given the feed flow to provide a head differential across the filter fabric of typically 3 to 6 in. Fabrics made of finely woven stainless steel with mesh openings of 20 to 25 μm are fitted onto rotating drum filters. Influent enters the open end of the drum and flows out through the rotating fabric. Solids collected on the screen form a mat that strains out suspended particles having dimensions smaller than the screen openings. High-pressure water jets, located outside at the top of the drum, continuously backwash the sludge mat into an effluent trough within the drum. Hydraulic loadings vary from 5 to 10 gal/min/ft^2 of submerged surface area. A major operating problem is the buildup of biological slime on the filter fabric. An effluent suspended solids content varying from 5 to 15 mg/L can be produced by microstraining, which fluctuates due to fluctuating influent loading.

ORGANICS REMOVAL
Low concentrations of organics can be effectively removed from wastewater by *activated carbon*. Activated carbon is bituminous or lignite coal that

is processed to increase its porosity, and thus surface area, by burning off volatile materials. The surface area in coal is typically 1 to 5 m^2/g. This is increased to $1000 \, m^2/g$ by the activation process. Organics are removed by adsorption onto the surface area of activated carbon, primarily in the micropores of the structure. Microbial action also contributes to the degradation of the organics in packed beds of activated carbon.

Adsorption of the organics eventually results in exhaustion of the carbon, which can then be thermally treated in order to render it reusable. This process is called regeneration. Thermal regeneration involves drying, gasifying of the adsorbed volatile organic material, and reactivation of the carbon. This is accomplished by heating the exhausted activated carbon in a multiple-hearth furnace with a low-oxygen steam atmosphere. Adsorbed organics are volatilized and released in a gaseous form at about 1700°F. The time required for regeneration is about 30 minutes. With proper control, granular carbon can be restored to near-virgin adsorptive capacity with only 5 to 10 percent weight loss (52).

PHOSPHORUS REMOVAL

The significance of phosphorus in wastewater and its impacts on receiving waters were discussed under the section on definitions of wastewater quality parameters. Conventional biological treatment of wastewater removes a portion of the phosphorus present in it; the amount assimilated by the biological floc is equal to about 1 percent of the BOD applied (52). The removal in the treatment of a typical wastewater with 200 mg/L BOD would therefore be 2 mg/L of phosphorus, or a 20 percent reduction. Disposal of the biological sludge is an important consideration in determining effective phosphorus removal. Vacuum filtration of the sludge followed by land burial of solids results in maximum phosphorus removal. Conventional sludge digestion by anaerobic or aerobic digestion generates a supernatant containing phosphorus that is returned to the influent of the treatment plant.

Chemical addition is a common practice to aid in the removal of phosphorus by biological systems. Three popular systems of chemical addition are depicted in Figure 12-35. In Figure 12-35a, coagulant is added before secondary treatment. Either alum or ferric chloride may be used for this purpose, with lime or polyelectrolytes occasionally added as coagulant aids. The theoretical chemical reaction between alum and phosphate is

$$Al_2(SO_4)_3 \cdot 14.3H_2O + 2PO_4^{3-} \longrightarrow$$
$$2AlPO_4\downarrow + 3SO_4^{2-} + 14.3H_2O \quad (12\text{-}26)$$

The molar ratio of aluminum to phosphorus is 1:1, equivalent to a weight ratio of 0.87:1.00. Since alum contains 9.0 percent Al, 9.7 lb of coagulant is theoretically required to precipitate 1.0 lb of P.

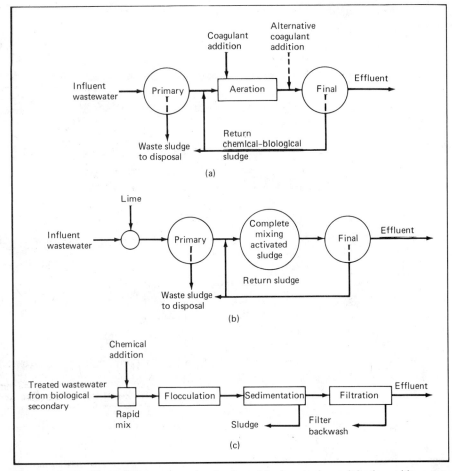

Figure 12-35 Phosphorus removal schemes: (a) chemical precipitation with activated-sludge treatment; (b) lime precipitation in primary sedimentation followed by secondary complete mixing of activated sludge; (c) tertiary treatment by chemical precipitation.

The theoretical chemical reaction between ferric chloride and phosphorus is

$$FeCl_3 + PO_4^{3-} \longrightarrow FePO_4\!\downarrow + 3Cl^- \tag{12-27}$$

The molar ratio of iron to phosphorus is 1:1, equivalent to a 1.8:1 weight ratio. Theoretically, 5.2 lb of $FeCl_3$ would be required to precipitate 1 lb of P since ferric chloride is 34 percent Fe. For 85 to 95 percent removal, the actual dosage is usually greater, with lime commonly applied to maintain optimum pH and aid coagulation.

Coagulants are sometimes added to raw wastewater to precipitate phosphates in primary sedimentation. The primary advantage of additional primary settling is to increase suspended solids removal and reduce the organic load for biological secondary treatment.

As depicted in Figure 12-35b, lime can be added before primary treatment to precipitate phosphate, in addition to precipitating organic suspended solids. The lime combines with alkaline substances present in the wastewater to produce calcium carbonate residue, which aids in settling the suspended solids. This can be represented by the following equation:

$$Ca(HCO_3)_2 + Ca(OH)_2 \longrightarrow 2CaCO_3\downarrow + 2H_2O \qquad (12\text{-}28)$$

Calcium ion also combines with orthophosphate in an alkaline solution to form calcium hydroxyapatite, which is also precipitated:

$$5Ca^{2+} + 4OH^- + 3HPO_4^{2-} \longrightarrow$$
$$Ca_5(OH)(PO_4)_3\downarrow + 3H_2O \quad (12\text{-}29)$$

A dosage of 100 to 200 mg/L of lime is typically required to remove 80 percent of the phosphate (52). This will vary depending on the amount of phosphorus present and the alkalinity of the wastewater.

Use of excess lime in chemical treatment poses the problems of scale formation in wastewater treatment plant equipment and generation of a large quantity of lime sludge, which can add significantly to the sludge disposal costs.

A third method of removing phosphorus, as depicted by Figure 12-35c, is the addition of chemicals after secondary treatment. The mixing, flocculation, and sedimentation systems can be separate units in series, or the processes can be performed in a single tank. Filters are usually multimedia beds operated by pressure or gravity flow. Chemical additives may be lime, alum, ferric chloride, and ferric sulfate, with polyelectrolytes as flocculation aids. A major design consideration of tertiary treatment is processing and disposal of settled sludge and filter backwash water.

NITROGEN REMOVAL

Ammonia nitrogen is the primary form of nitrogen found in domestic wastewater. It can be removed from wastewater by nitrification-denitrification processes, air stripping, breakpoint chlorination, or ion exchange.

In biological nitrification, nitrifying bacteria convert ammonia into nitrite and nitrite into nitrate under aerobic conditions. This eliminates the problem of ammonia-nitrogen toxicity to fish and reduces the nitrogenous oxygen demand for streams. Temperature, pH, and dissolved oxygen concentration are important parameters in nitrification kinetics. The rate of nitrification is a function of time and independent of ammonia concentration. Because biological nitrification destroys alkalinity, it may be desirable to add chemicals to the reaction.

Biological denitrification can be employed to convert nitrate and nitrite nitrogen into nitrogen gas. This is accomplished by denitrifying bacteria in an anaerobic environment. An organic carbon source such as acetic acid, acetone, ethanol, methanol, or sugar is needed to act as a hydrogen donor and to supply carbon for biological synthesis. Methanol is preferred because it is the least expensive synthetic compound available that does not have the effect of leaving a residual BOD in the process effluent. Methanol first reduces the dissolved oxygen present, and then denitrifying bacteria convert the nitrite and nitrate into nitrogen gas:

$$3O_2 + 2CH_3OH \longrightarrow 2CO_2\uparrow + 4H_2O \tag{12-30}$$

$$6NO_3^- + 5CH_3OH \longrightarrow$$
$$3N_2\uparrow + 5CO_2\uparrow + 7H_2O + 6OH^- \tag{12-31}$$

$$2NO_2^- + CH_3OH \longrightarrow N_2\uparrow + CO_2\uparrow + H_2O + 2OH^- \tag{12-32}$$

The amount of methanol required for complete denitrification can be estimated from the following empirically derived equation (52):

$$CH_3OH = 0.7DO + 1.1NO_2\text{--}N + 2.0NO_3\text{--}N \tag{12-33}$$

where CH_3OH = methanol, mg/L
$\qquad\quad DO$ = dissolved oxygen, mg/L
$\qquad NO_2\text{--}N$ = nitrate nitrogen, mg/L
$\qquad NO_3\text{--}N$ = nitrite nitrogen, mg/L

Since an excess of approximately 30 percent is needed for synthesis, Equation 12-33 can be rewritten as

$$CH_3OH = 0.9DO + 1.5NO_2\text{--}N + 2.5NO_3\text{--}N \tag{12-34}$$

to satisfy both energy and synthesis requirements (52).

Ammonia stripping is the process by which ammonia nitrogen is converted into ammonia gas. Equilibrium of ammonium ion and dissolved ammonia gas in water is controlled by both pH and temperature. Only NH_4^+ ions are present in neutral solution at ambient temperatures, while at pH 11, essentially all of the ammonia appears as gas. The process of ammonia stripping takes advantage of this distribution. The process consists of (1) raising the pH of the wastewater to 10.8 to 11.5, with lime applied for preceding phosphorus precipitation; (2) formation of wastewater droplets in a stripping tower; and (3) providing air-water contact and droplet agitation by circulation of large quantities of air through the tower. The rate of gas transfer from liquid to air is influenced by pH, temperature, relative ammonia concentrations, and agitation at the air-water interface.

Advantages of air stripping for nitrogen removal are simplicity of operation, ease of control, and low cost relative to that of other extraction processes. Disadvantages are the inability to operate at an ambient temperature below 32°F and deposits of calcium carbonate scale on the tower packing.

Breakpoint chlorination is the third process commonly employed for nitrogen removal. Addition of excess chlorine oxidizes the ammonia nitrogen to form, among other products, nitrogen gas. The reaction may be represented by the following unbalanced equation:

$$NH_3 + HOCl \longrightarrow N_2\uparrow + N_2O\uparrow + NO_2^- + NO_3^- + Cl^- \quad (12\text{-}35)$$

In a pH range of 6 to 7, conversion of ammonia into nitrogen gas is 90 to 95 percent complete. The rate and extent of the reaction depends on pH, temperature, contact time, and initial chlorine/ammonia ratio. In practice, a weight ratio of eight to 10 chlorines to one ammonia nitrogen is needed. Problems with this method of nitrogen removal include a substantial increase in total dissolved solids and difficulties caused by discharge of excess chlorine. Excess chlorine can be toxic to fish and can react with organics to form trihalomethanes, and therefore dechlorination of the effluent may be required.

A fourth method for ammonia nitrogen removal is ion exchange. *Ion exchange,* in general, is a type of sorption process by which ions are held by electrostatic forces to charged functional groups on the surface of a solid and are exchanged for ions of similar charge in a solution in which the solid is immersed. Materials used for ion exchange may be either natural (clays, other soils, coal) or synthetic. For nitrogen removal, the natural ion-exchange resin clinoptilolite is used, which has a high selectivity for ammonium ion. The effectiveness of the ion exchange depends on the initial ammonium ion content, competing cation concentrations, hydraulic loading of the bed, and method of regeneration. After 150 to 200 bed volumes are passed through the resin, it must be regenerated, that is, the adsorbed ammonium ions must be removed. Clinoptilolite is regenerated by using a solution of NaCl or CaCl.

Land Treatment of Wastewater

Land disposal is one option for treatment of domestic wastewater, where large tracts of suitable land are available. The soil acts as a natural filter for suspended solids, soil microorganisms biologically treat the waste, and any vegetation grown in the disposal area may utilize the nutrients in the wastewater as food. Another benefit may be recharge of underlying groundwater aquifers. This method is attractive in that nutrients are recycled to the land instead of polluting receiving waters; however, in densely populated areas, and in areas with freezing climates or high annual average precipitation, the use of this method may be limited.

Figure 12-36 illustrates the three techniques most commonly used for spreading wastewater onto the land: irrigation, overland flow, and infiltration-percolation. Selecting the appropriate system depends primarily on the drainability of the soil, which determines the allowable hydraulic loading rate and the required degree of pretreatment. Wastewater quality, climate, and land availability are also interrelated factors that must be considered in selecting a system. The comparative characteristics of the

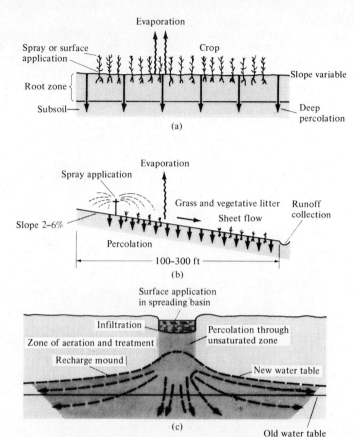

Figure 12-36   Three types of land treatment systems: (a) irrigation; (b) overland flow; (c) infiltration-percolation. (From *Process Design Manual for Land Treatment of Municipal Wastewater,* U.S. Environmental Protection Agency, October 1981.)

three types of systems are given in Table 12-10. Much smaller areas of land are required for infiltration-percolation, but this method poses the threat of ground water contamination. For the purpose of wastewater treatment, irrigation is the process most widely used in the United States, while overland flow is still in the experimental stages. Rapid infiltration is used for groundwater recharge and aquifer injection as a barrier to saltwater intrusion.

Sludge Treatment and Disposal

The importance of accounting for generation, handling, and disposal of sludges in planning and designing a wastewater treatment plant cannot be overemphasized. The sludge from wastewater treatment is only a small portion of the volume of material passing through the treatment plant, but it contains the most offensive substances found in the raw wastewater. In

Table 12-10 COMPARATIVE CHARACTERISTICS OF IRRIGATION, OVERLAND FLOW, AND INFILTRATION-PERCOLATION SYSTEMS

PARAMETER	IRRIGATION	OVERLAND FLOW	INFILTRATION-PERCOLATION
Liquid loading rate	0.5–4 in/week	2–5.5 in/week	4–120 in/week
Annual application	2–8 ft/yr	8–24 ft/yr	18–500 ft/yr
Land required for 1-mgd flow	140–560 acres plus buffer zones	46–140 acres plus buffer zones	2–62 acres plus buffer zones
Application techniques	Spray or surface	Usually spray	Usually surface
Soils	Moderately permeable soils with good productivity when irrigated	Slowly permeable soils, such as clay loams and clay	Rapidly permeable soils, such as sands, loamy sands, and sandy loams
Probability of influencing groundwater quality	Moderate	Slight	Certain
Needed depth to groundwater	About 10 ft	Undetermined	About 15 ft
Wastewater lost to:	Predominantly evaporation or deep percolation	Surface discharge dominates over evaporation and percolation	Percolation to groundwater

SOURCE: C. E. Pound and R. W. Crites, *Wastewater Treatment and Reuse by Land Application,* vol. I, Environmental Protection Agency, Office of Research and Development, August 1973.

addition, sludge handling and disposal can account for 25 to 50 percent of the costs of wastewater treatment (the proportion tends to be higher for larger plants). If for no other reason, sludge handling and disposal must be given due consideration because of the high costs involved.

One objective of sludge treatment is to obtain a higher solids content in order to reduce the volume that must ultimately be disposed of. In addition, the sludge may be treated to reduce the pathogen content to make it safer for handling and land disposal.

The primary sources of sludges in a wastewater treatment plant include:

1. Skimmings and screenings removed during pretreatment that have been ground and returned to the wastewater

2. Suspended solids collected in primary sedimentation
3. Colloidal and dissolved solids converted into biomass and settled out during secondary sedimentation
4. Reaction products from coagulant chemicals added during treatment.

Sludges from different sources have varying characteristics (for example, fuel value) that may affect the choice of treatment processes.

The total solids in raw wastewater is typically 500 mg/L or 0.05 percent solids, with the total solids contained by the combined raw sludges being on the order of 8000 mg/L or 0.8 percent solids. A wastewater sludge that has undergone treatment through several steps including dewatering is typically 0.2 percent of the volume of the raw wastewater and contains 300,000 mg/L or 30 percent solids.

There are a number of treatment steps that may be used, depending on treatment objectives and characteristics of the raw sludges. Treatment options include thickening, stabilization, conditioning, disinfection, dewatering, drying, composting, and thermal reduction. Not all steps are used at every plant; the chosen combination will depend on a number of variables including the composition and quantity of the sludges, space requirements for the treatment processes, and the costs involved. These various processes are described briefly here. For detailed information, reference 53 may be consulted.

Thickening is usually accomplished by gravity settling for primary sludges and by dissolved air flotation for secondary sludges. These operations were described previously in this section under physical treatment processes.

Sludge stabilization processes are intended to reduce bacterial and viral activity and odors in sludges. Methods to achieve stabilization include (1) dosage with chlorine, (2) dosage with lime, (3) pasteurization with heat at 500°F at 400 pounds per square inch gauge (psig), (4) aerobic digestion, and (5) anaerobic digestion.

Sludge conditioning refers to processes for improving the sludge dewatering characteristics. The commonest method is the addition of coagulant chemicals (alum, ferric chloride, lime, or polyelectrolytes); others include elutriation (washing primarily to remove alkalinity), heat treatment, freezing, and irradiation.

Whereas the intent of sludge stabilization is to *reduce* the pathogen content, the purpose of disinfection is to destroy pathogens. Techniques for disinfection include (1) pasteurization for 30 minutes at 70°C, (2) high pH (lime) treatment for 12 hours at pH > 12, (3) long-term storage of liquid-digested sludge, (4) composting at 55°C and curing for 30 days, (5) use of gaseous chlorine or other chemicals, and (6) beta or gamma irradiation (53).

The purpose of sludge dewatering is to reduce the volume and weight of the sludge, reduce the fuel and heat required for subsequent heat treatment, and remove the excess liquids from previous sludge treatment processes. Unit operations for dewatering include several mechanical ones —vacuum filters, centrifuges, filter presses, belt filters—and two nonmechanical ones, sand beds and sludge lagoons. The latter are typically used for smaller plants. The sheer volume of sludge generated by larger plants and thus the land area required for nonmechanical dewatering usually precludes this option for large plants.

Heat-drying operations reduce the water content of sludges by vaporizing the water content into the air and are used to prepare sludge for incineration or for use as a fertilizer. Unit operations include flash dryers, spray dryers, rotary dryers, cement kilns, and multiple-hearth furnaces.

Composting is a process in which organic material undergoes biological degradation into end products. Typically sludge composting involves piling dewatered sludge loosely, sometime mixed with bulking agents such as wood chips, and drawing air through the piles. Within a few days, biological action causes the pile to reach temperatures in excess of 55°C, with 20 to 30 percent of the volatile solids converted into water and carbon dioxide. The product is useful as a soil conditioner.

Thermal reduction may be achieved by incineration, pyrolysis, or wet air oxidation. Incineration is defined as the complete oxidation of volatile solids to CO_2, H_2O, and N_2. The commonest unit used for this purpose in the United States is the multiple-hearth furnace; others that are appropriate include the fluidized bed furnace, the cyclone furnace, and the rotary kiln.

Pyrolysis is the heating in the absence of air to break down volatile organic material in sludge. The products are a number of liquid, gaseous, and solid components, all of which have significant fuel value. There are few pyrolysis installations in the United States because the operating experience to date with sludge has not been good.

Wet air oxidation is the wet oxidation of untreated sludges at high temperatures and pressures. The process is similar to thermal conditioning, except that higher temperatures and pressures and much more air are used to achieve complete oxidation.

Although thermal reduction is very effective at reducing the volume of solids to be disposed of, problems may be encountered with volatilization of certain species. This may cause air pollution problems, and retention of heavy metals in the ash can cause leaching problems when the ash is land disposed.

Options for ultimate disposal include landfilling, lagooning, land spreading, and ocean disposal. The choice depends on land availability, cost of transportation, and proximity to the ocean, among other factors.

CASE STUDY *District of Columbia Wastewater Treatment Plant at Blue Plains*

The wastewater treatment plant at Blue Plains is designed to treat sewage generated by the District of Columbia and parts of suburban Maryland and Virginia. The flow to the wastewater treatment plant is generated by a population of approximately two million and an area of 725 mi^2 (see Figure 12-37). In the older sections of the city, combined sewers collect storm water that also flows to the Blue Plains plant for treatment before discharge into the Potomac River. The primary pollutants of concern in the raw wastewater are BOD_5 (215 mg/L), total phosphorus (8.5 mg/L), and total nitrogen (21.9 mg/L). The wastewater delivered to Blue Plains can therefore be classified as a medium-strength wastewater, based on Table 12-7. The National Pollutant Discharge Elimination System (NPDES) permit for the District of Columbia requires an effluent quality of 4.95 mg/L BOD_5, 0.22 mg/L total phosphorus, and 2.39 mg/L total nitrogen in water discharged into the Potomac River. In order to achieve these very strict limitations for discharge of pollutants, removals of 97.7, 97.4, and 89.1 percent for BOD_5, total P, and total N, respectively, must be achieved. Toward this end, advanced wastewater treatment methods are necessarily part of the treatment train at Blue Plains.

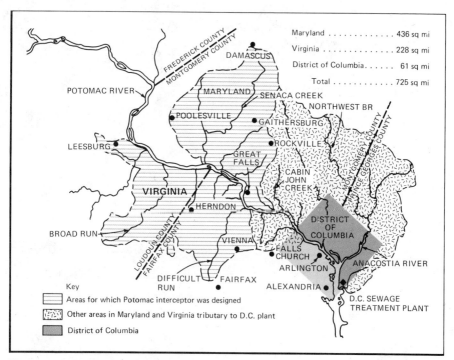

Figure 12-37 District and suburban areas tributary to the District of Columbia sewer system. (Courtesy of the District of Columbia Department of Environmental Services, Water Resources Management Administration.)

The Blue Plains plant is designed to treat an average dry weather flow of 309 mgd, with a maximum flow capacity of 650 mgd. Primary treatment followed by disinfection is also provided for an additional wet weather flow of 289 mgd that can be expected to occur 100 times per year for a total of 100 hours (62). By all standards, this is a large plant; in fact, it is one of the largest in the United States. The physical layout of the plant and a wastewater flow schematic are shown in Figures 12-38 and 12-39, respectively.

PRELIMINARY TREATMENT

Preliminary treatment consists of chlorine addition for odor control and screening by bar racks to remove debris that could clog pumps. The raw wastewater is then pumped by one of two pumping stations to aerated grit chambers for grit removal. The grit—mainly silt and sand—is contributed to the flow primarily by the storm water entering combined sewers. The screenings and grit removed in preliminary treatment operations are transported to a landfill for disposal.

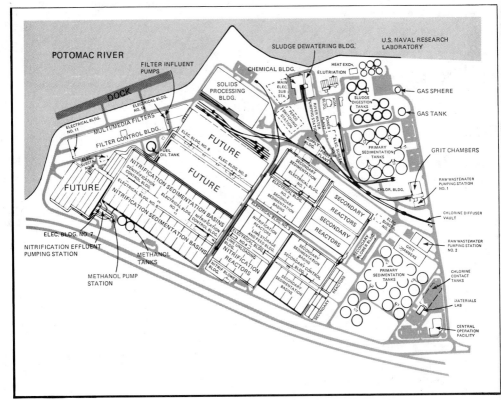

Figure 12-38   Blue Plains Wastewater Treatment Plant, District of Columbia. (Courtesy of the District of Columbia Department of Environmental Services, Water Resources Management Administration.)

PRIMARY TREATMENT

Following grit removal, chemical coagulants are added to the wastewater to enhance phosphorus removal. The water then flows to 36 primary sedimentation tanks, 16 tanks each of which is 106 ft in diameter and 13.7 feet deep, and 20 tanks each of which is 120 ft in diameter and 14.3 ft deep. The settleable solids are removed by gravity settling. The settled material—the raw primary sludge—is removed from the primary sedimentation tanks and pumped to gravity thickeners. Six gravity thickeners, each 65 ft in diameter and 10 ft deep, concentrate the sludge to 7.5 to 10 percent solids. The effluent from the primary sedimentation basins, containing nonsettleable and dissolved materials, overflows into the secondary treatment units.

SECONDARY TREATMENT

Secondary treatment consists of a modified activated sludge process. Four aeration tanks each having four channels 29 ft wide, 460 ft long, and 15 ft deep, in addition to two aeration tanks each having two channels 20 ft wide, 119 ft long, and 15 ft deep, are used to mix wastewater with air from the secondary blower building and sludge returned from the secondary sedimentation tanks. The microorganisms in the return sludge assimilate the organic material in the wastewater, thereby providing removal of nonsettleable and dissolved organic material. A detention time of 2.0 h is provided for an average flow of 309 mgd.

Following treatment in the secondary reactors, chemicals are again added to the wastewater to enhance phosphorus removal. Either alum or ferric chloride is used for this purpose. In addition, polymers are added to aid flocculation of the biomass in the secondary sedimentation tanks.

Twenty-four basins are provided for sedimentation to remove the biological growths generated by the secondary reactors. Each tank is 80 ft wide, 260 ft long, and 12 ft deep. An average detention time of 2.7 h is provided. Part of the sludge is returned to the secondary reactors to provide the necessary microorganisms for continued growth, and the remainder of the sludge is pumped to flotation thickeners. Eighteen flotation thickeners each 20 ft wide, 59 ft long, and 14 ft deep thicken the waste activated sludge to 4 to 6 percent solids.

ADVANCED TREATMENT

Following secondary sedimentation, a sequence of advanced treatment operations (biological nitrification, multimedia filtration, and disinfection) is employed to meet the strict effluent standards. Prior to biological nitrification, lime is added to maintain the proper pH and to compensate for alkalinity lost as a result of previous chemical addition. There are 12 nitrification reactors, each 80 ft wide, 249 ft long, and 30.9 ft deep. In these tanks, return sludge from the nitrification settling tanks is mixed with wastewater from the secondary sedimentation basins and air from the nitrification blower building to promote conversion of ammonia nitrogen into nitrate nitrogen by nitrifying bacteria. The effluent from the nitrification basins flows to 28 nitrification tanks, each 80 ft wide, 249 ft long, and 30.9 ft deep, for removal of the biomass generated by the nitrification process. An average detention time of 4 h is provided. Chemicals are

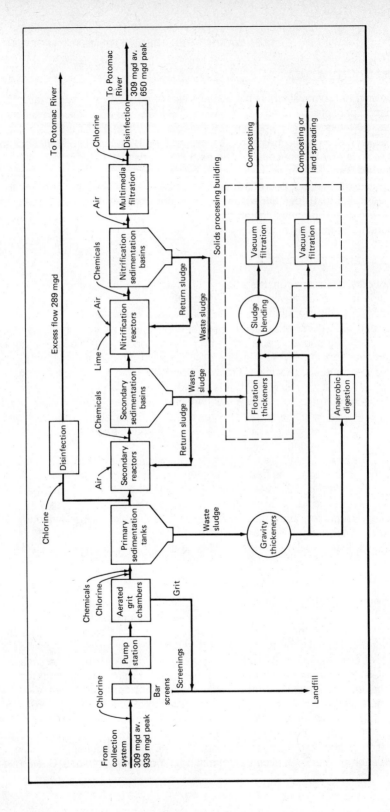

added to the flow entering the sedimentation basins to aid in the sedimentation process. A portion of the sludge is returned to the nitrification reactors to maintain the desired microbial population. The excess sludge is pumped to 28 flotation thickeners each 79 ft wide, 242 ft long, and 15.5 ft deep for an average detention time of 4.5 h.

Effluent from the nitrification sedimentation basins is pumped to the filter control building for multimedia filtration and disinfection. Thirty-six multimedia gravity flow filters having a total surface area of 75,000 ft^2 and four disinfection tanks each with a volume of 364,000 ft^3 are provided for these purposes. Chlorination is presently used for disinfection, with the chlorine contact tanks providing a detention time of 48 min at average flow. After chlorination, the wastewater effluent is discharged through the outfall to the Potomac River.

SLUDGE TREATMENT AND DISPOSAL

A portion of the sludge from the gravity thickeners is pumped to anaerobic sludge digesters. In the digesters, anaerobic bacteria use the sludge as food to produce carbon dioxide and methane gas, reduce the amount of solids, and reduce the moisture content of the sludge. Twelve fixed-cover digesters with a capacity of 1,710,000 ft^3 are provided for this purpose. At Blue Plains, the methane gas produced by digestion is used as fuel to produce power and heat at the plant. For example, the 3 million Btu capacity heat exchangers used to maintain the sludge digesters at 95°F are fueled by the methane gas. Stabilized sludge produced by the digesters is pumped to the solids process building for elutriation, followed by dewatering by vacuum filtration.

Elutriation of the digested sludge is necessary to remove the alkaline byproducts produced by the digestion, since alkalinity can interfere with subsequent solids compaction and impose a requirement for high chemical addition prior to vacuum filtration. Elutriation reduces the alkalinity of the digested sludge from 4000 ppm (as $CaCO_3$) to 600 ppm.

The elutriated, digested sludge is pumped to chemical conditioning tanks for ferric chloride and polymer addition. The undigested sludge from the gravity thickeners and the sludge from the flotation thickeners are blended and chemically conditioned with lime, ferric chloride, and polymer. The chemically conditioned sludges flow into cloth-covered vacuum filters, where water is removed by centrifugal force. The remaining sludge filter cake is carried by conveyor belt to trucks that remove it to a composting area or transport it off-site for land spreading. The vacuum filters are designed to ultimately produce up to 2400 tons per day of sludge cake containing 15 to 20 percent solids.

Sludge disposal in the District of Columbia continues to be a pressing problem, due to the limited availability of land for disposal and the high costs of transporting the sludge long distances to remote areas for disposal. At one point incineration was being considered as an option for sludge disposal, but serious opposition was raised due to the potential for air pollution. Other options such as pyrolysis and wet air oxidation are being explored as a means of solving this problem.

Figure 12-39   Wastewater flow schematic at Blue Plains Wastewater Treatment Plant. (See opposite page.)

12-7 URBAN RUNOFF

Urban runoff is defined as surface runoff from an urban drainage area that reaches a stream or other body of water or a sewer (63). In this section we shall consider the impact of urban runoff on the quality of receiving surface waters. Also discussed is a subject of great importance to the engineer: estimating the quantity of water generated by storms of various magnitudes in urban areas for the purpose of designing urban drainage systems. Finally, the best management practices for treating urban storm water will be covered.

Impact of Urban Runoff on Water Quality

Second only to agriculture, urban activities that disturb the natural environment are the primary contributors to surface-water pollution in the United States. With about 2000 hectares of United States rural land being converted daily to urban use, accelerated urbanization has led to increased nonpoint pollution loadings from urban runoff in the past 30 years (64).

The primary sources of the pollution are fertilizer from lawns and gardens, animal and bird feces, oil drippings, street litter, herbicide residues, atmospheric fallout of air pollutants, and dead animals and vegetation that have been either purposely or incidently placed on the land. In suburban areas, soil erosion and soil-adsorbed pollutants are also sources of nonpoint pollution. As runoff from precipitation travels over the land, the wastes and residues are entrained by the flow and carried to receiving surface-water bodies. These residues contribute significant amounts of suspended solids, BOD, nitrates, phosphates, fecal coliforms, and toxic metals to receiving waters. A summary of the pollutant characteristics imparted to urban runoff by urban residues is given in Table 12-11 (64).

The magnitude of the pollution load transported by urban runoff to receiving water bodies is comparable to that of treated sewage or even untreated sewage in some cases. The highest concentration of pollutants in storm water is measured during the initial stages of storm runoff, during which the storm water exhibits a so-called first flush effect by initially cleansing away the bulk of pollutants deposited during the preceding dry weather period.

The concentration of pollutants in storm water depends on whether the storm water reaches the receiving water by overflow from combined sewers, flow from storm sewers or nonsewered overland flow, or municipal sewer overflow. A *combined sewer* is designed to receive both intercepted surface runoff and municipal sewage. *Combined sewer overflow* is the flow from a combined sewer in excess of the interceptor capacity that is discharged into a receiving water. A *storm sewer* carries intercepted surface runoff, street wash and other wash waters or drainage but excludes domes-

Table 12-11   SOURCES OF NONPOINT POLLUTION FROM URBAN RESIDENTIAL AND COMMERCIAL AREAS

CATEGORY	PARAMETERS	POTENTIAL SOURCES
Bacterial	Total coliforms, fecal coliforms, fecal streptococci, other pathogens	Animals, birds, soil bacteria (humans)
Nutrients	Nitrogen, phosphorus	Lawn fertilizers, decomposing organic matter (leaves and grass clippings), urban street refuse, atmospheric deposition
Biodegradable chemicals	BOD, COD, TOC	Leaves, grass clippings, animals, street litter, oil and grease
Organic chemicals	Pesticides, PCBs	Pest and weed control, packaging, leaking transformers, hydraulic and lubricating fluids
Inorganic chemicals	Suspended solids, dissolved solids, toxic metals, chloride	Erosion, dust and dirt on streets, atmospheric deposition, industrial pollution, traffic, deicing salts

tic sewage and industrial wastes. *Nonsewered urban runoff* is that part of the precipitation which runs off the surface of an urban drainage area and reaches a stream or other body of water without passing through a sewer system. It is of about the same strength as water collected by a storm sewer. Storm water enters the municipal sanitary sewer system to a certain degree; if infiltration to the system is severe enough, the storm water may cause the municipal system to overflow (63).

The most significant characteristic of urban runoff is the suspended solids content. On average, the suspended solids concentration of combined sewer overflow is greater than twice, and for surface runoff three times, the concentration of suspended solids in *untreated* sewage. For this reason, physical and chemical treatment of storm water to remove suspended solids are usually the principal treatment methods employed.

The BOD_5 content of combined sewer overflow and municipal sewer overflow is approximately equivalent—about half the concentration of untreated sewage. Surface runoff and storm sewer flow have about the same BOD_5 strength as secondary municipal effluent. The bacterial content of combined sewer overflow has been found to be typically one order of magnitude lower than that of untreated municipal sewage, whereas the bacterial content of surface runoff is two to four orders of magnitude lower than that of untreated sewage (63). The bacterial concentrations in urban surface runoff, however, can be two to five orders of magnitude higher than those considered safe for water contact activities. Table 12-12 sum-

Table 12-12 GENERALIZED QUALITY COMPARISONS OF WASTEWATERS[a]

TYPE	BOD$_5$ (mg/L)	SS (mg/L)	TOTAL COLIFORMS (MPN/100 ML)	TOTAL NITROGEN (mg/L AS N)	TOTAL PHOSPHORUS (mg/L AS P)
Untreated municipal	200	200	5×10^7	40	10
Treated municipal					
Primary effluent	135	80	2×10^7	35	8
Secondary effluent	25	15	1×10^3	30	5
Combined sewage	115	410	5×10^6	11	4
Surface runoff	30	630	4×10^5	3	1

SOURCE: Reference 63.
[a]Values based on flow-weighted means in individual test areas.

marizes a comparison of the quality of untreated and treated sewage and urban runoff (63).

Realizing that water pollution from urban runoff is a problem of increasing magnitude, researchers have devoted considerable resources in attempting to quantify the nature and source of the problem and determining methods for its control (see references 63–65). For example, Novotny and Chesters have shown that the factors for determining pollutant loads from residential areas include (1) degree of imperviousness of land surfaces, (2) street refuse accumulation and cleanliness of impervious surfaces, (3) street sweeping practices, (4) curb heights, and (5) type of storm water drainage system (64).

Best Management Practices for Urban Runoff

Best management practices (BMPs) for urban runoff are nonstructural or low structurally intensive alternatives for the control of urban runoff pollution at its source (65). BMPs are less costly and more efficient than the alternative—the use of unit processes (see Section 12-6) to reduce pollutant loads—and include the benefits of soil erosion and flood control and cleaner neighborhoods. The success of such measures in controlling urban runoff pollution is very much dependent, however, on educational programs and passage of legislation or ordinances to encourage or force people to comply with the intended BMPs. The EPA has delineated the following preventive measures, construction controls, and corrective maintenance and operation practices as suggestions for BMPs (65):

Preventive Measures

1. Utilization of greenways and detention ponds
2. Utilization of pervious areas for recharge

3. Avoidance of steep slopes for development
4. Maintenance of maximum land area in a natural, undisturbed state
5. Prohibiting development on floodplains
6. Utilization of porous pavements where applicable
7. Utilization of natural drainage features

Soil Erosion Controls at Construction Sites

1. Minimizing area and duration of soil exposure
2. Protecting soil with mulch and vegetative cover
3. Increasing infiltration rates
4. Construction of temporary storage basins or protective dikes to limit storm runoff

Corrective Maintenance and Operation Practices

1. Control of litter, debris, and agricultural chemicals
2. Regular street sweeping and repair
3. Improved roadway deicing and materials storage practices
4. Proper use and maintenance of catch basins and drainage collection systems
5. On-site retention or detention of storm water runoff

Treatment Processes for Urban Runoff

The alternative (or supplement) to BMPs is treatment of storm water pollution by storage, physical or chemical treatment, biological treatment, or disinfection (65). Unit processes may be used separately or in sequence to achieve the desired level of treatment.

STORAGE

The EPA has demonstrated that some form of storm water flow equalization or storage reduces the size, number, and cost of downstream treatment facilities required due to the high volume and variability of storm water flows (63, 68). *In-line storage* is the use of the unused volume in interceptors and trunk sewers for storing storm runoff. This often includes installation of flow regulators, level sensors, tide gates, rain gauge networks, sewage and receiving water quality monitors, overflow detectors, and flowmeters to permit effective operation as storage systems. Data from such devices can be automatically fed into a computer, which can then provide control of the system. *Off-line storage* facilities are designed for (1) flow containment to reduce the magnitude of peak flows before the flows reach downstream treatment facilities, or (2) storm water detention and sedimentation before discharge into receiving waters. Basic appurtenances usually include flow regulators, coarse screens, storage overflow basins, and sludge dewatering facilities. Typical flow schematics for off-line storage are shown in Figures 12-40 and 12-41. Storage/detention facilities that are designed to provide primary treatment also usually include fine

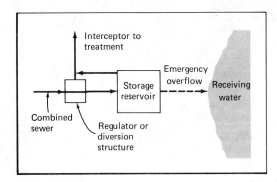

Figure 12-40 Flow schematic of off-line storage used for containment.

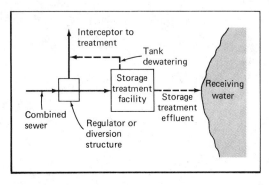

Figure 12-41 Flow schematic of off-line storage/treatment facility.

screening of the influent and/or effluent, disinfection, and sludge/solids collection and removal (65).

PHYSICAL AND CHEMICAL TREATMENT

Physical treatment operations, which are primarily designed to remove suspended solids, are particularly important in storm water treatment, since the high solids content of storm water is the primary pollutant of concern. Typical physical treatment units include screening, sedimentation, flotation, and filtration. Coagulating chemicals such as alum, ferric chloride, and polymers may be added as part of the treatment sequence to achieve additional removal levels.

Physical treatment units for storm water may be constructed as adjuncts to existing wastewater treatment facilities or can function alone as separate facilities. The principal disadvantage in constructing physical treatment units as separate facilities is that they sit idle during dry weather periods. By constructing them as part of a larger wastewater treatment plant, they can be used as pretreatment or effluent polishing units for conventional wastewater flows, which often provides reduced capital investment for the storm water treatment units (65).

Typical physical treatment units and the levels of pollutant removals they provide are summarized in Table 12-13. Of particular importance in the application to storm water treatment is the swirl concentrator/regula-

Table 12-13 COMPARISON OF PHYSICAL TREATMENT SYSTEMS

PHYSICAL UNIT PROCESS	PERCENT REDUCTION						AVERAGE CAPITAL COST ($/mgd)[a]
	SUSPENDED SOLIDS	BOD$_5$	COD	SETTLEABLE SOLIDS	TOTAL PHOSPHORUS	TOTAL KJELDAHL NITROGEN	
Sedimentation							
Without chemicals	20–60	30	34	30–90	20	38	23,000
Chemically assisted	68	68	45	....	..	..	23,000
Swirl concentrator/flow regulator	40–60	25–60	..	50–90	..	..	4500
Screening							
Microstrainers	50–95	10–50	35	....	20	30	19,500
Drum screen	30–55	10–40	25	60	10	17	19,300
Rotary screens	20–35	1–30	15	70–95	12	10	19,900
Disc screens	10–45	5–20	15	....	..	..	....
Static screens	5–25	0–20	13	10–60	10	8	17,600
Dissolved air flotation[b]	45–85	30–80	55	93[c]	55	35	34,000
High-rate filtration[d]	50–80	20–55	40	55–95	50	21	58,000
High-gradient magnetic separation[e]	92–98	90–98	75	99	..	..	......

[a]ENR Construction Cost Index 2000.
[b]Process efficiencies include both prescreening and dissolved air flotation with chemical addition.
[c]From pilot plant analysis (69).
[d]Includes prescreening and chemical addition.
[e]From bench-scale pilot plant operation, 1 to 4 L/min (0.26 to 1.06 gal/min).

tor, which has proved to have a steady removal performance over a wide range of hydraulic loading rates (65). Typical process flow diagrams for sedimentation, dissolved air flotation, and advanced physical/chemical treatment systems are given in Figures 12-42, 12-43, and 12-44, respectively. These are the commonest treatment sequences used for storm water.

BIOLOGICAL TREATMENT

Biological treatment is designed to remove organic pollutants from wastewaters, and it can be achieved aerobically or anaerobically. Several biological treatment processes that have been successfully used on combined sewer overflow include contact stabilization, trickling filters, rotating biological contactors, and treatment lagoons. However, because biological treatment processes depend on continuous operation or access to a system that is operating continuously for a source of active biomass, this coupled with high capital costs presents major drawbacks in using biological processes to treat storm water.

In conventional wastewater treatment, biological treatment removes 70 to 90 percent of the BOD_5 and suspended solids from the flows. These efficiencies are lower for storm water treatment, and they are controlled to a large degree by hydraulic and organic loading rates. Because most biological treatment systems are easily upset by overloading conditions and shock loads, application to storm water treatment often presents difficulties. Usually biological treatment is coupled with final clarification to

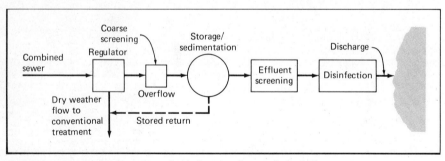

Figure 12-42 Typical process flow diagram for sedimentation.

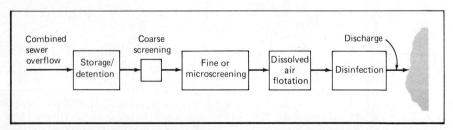

Figure 12-43 Typical process flow diagram for dissolved air flotation.

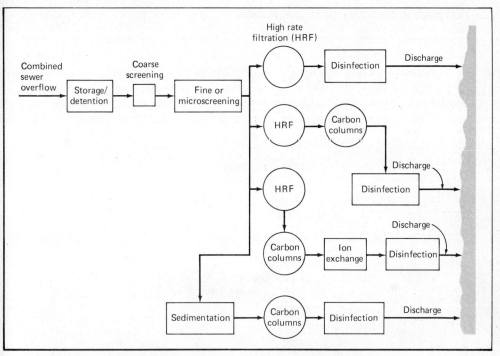

Figure 12-44   Typical process flow diagram for several advanced physical/chemical treatment systems.

remove the biological solids generated by the process. Table 12-14 summarizes typical pollutant removal levels for wet weather loading conditions of combined sewer overflow for three types of biological treatment processes. The example treatment sequences include primary and final clarification (65).

LAND TREATMENT
Land treatment of storm water is limited by the land requirements needed for the hydraulic application rates. Wetlands development, rapid infiltration methods, and overland flow processes are currently being investigated for their potential applicability (65).

Table 12-14 TYPICAL WET WEATHER BOD AND SUSPENDED SOLIDS REMOVALS FOR BIOLOGICAL TREATMENT PROCESSES

	EXPECTED RANGE OF POLLUTANT REMOVAL (%)	
BIOLOGICAL TREATMENT PROCESS	BOD	SUSPENDED SOLIDS
Contact stabilization	70–90	75–95
Trickling filters	65–85	65–85
Rotating biological contactors[a]	40–80	40–80

[a]Removal reflects flow ranges from 30 to 10 times dry weather flow.

Estimating Quantity of Urban Runoff

In order to design storm water drainage systems, an estimate must be made of the amount of storm water that the sewer is to receive. All such design methods are based on precipitation input. A standard method of determining peak runoff rates for urban storm drainage design today is the Rational Method. This method makes use of intensity-duration-frequency curves derived from frequency analysis of rainfall data (see Figure 12-45).

RATIONAL METHOD

The Rational Formula was introduced in the United States by Emil Kuichling in 1889 (66). Since then it has become the most widely used method for designing drainage facilities for small urban areas and highways. Peak flow is found from the equation

$$Q_p = CIA \tag{12-36}$$

where Q_p = peak runoff rate (ft^3/s)
  C = runoff coefficient (assumed to be dimensionless)
  I = *average* rainfall intensity (in/h), lasting for a critical period of time t_c
  t_c = time of concentration
  A = size of drainage area (acres)

The runoff coefficient C can be assumed to be dimensionless because 1.008 acre-in/h is equivalent to 1.0 ft^3/s. Typical values of C for storms of five- to 10-year return periods are given in Table 12-15.

The basis for the Rational Method is the concept that application of steady, uniform rainfall intensity will cause runoff to reach its maximum rate when all parts of the watershed are contributing to the outflow at the point of design. That condition is met after the time of concentration t_c has been reached, which is usually taken as the time for water to flow

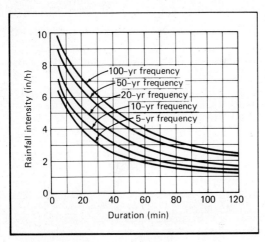

Figure 12-45   Typical intensity-duration-frequency curves.

Table 12-15 TYPICAL C COEFFICIENTS
FOR 5- TO 10-YR FREQUENCY DESIGN

DESCRIPTION OF AREA	RUNOFF COEFFICIENTS
Business	
Downtown areas	0.70–0.95
Neighborhood areas	0.50–0.70
Residential	
Single-family areas	0.30–0.50
Multiunits, detached	0.40–0.60
Multiunits, attached	0.60–0.75
Residential (suburban)	0.25–0.40
Apartment dwelling areas	0.50–0.70
Industrial	
Light areas	0.50–0.80
Heavy areas	0.60–0.90
Parks, cemeteries	0.10–0.25
Playgrounds	0.20–0.35
Railroad yard areas	0.20–0.40
Unimproved areas	0.10–0.30
Streets	
Asphaltic	0.70–0.95
Concrete	0.80–0.95
Brick	0.70–0.85
Drives and walks	0.75–0.85
Roofs	0.75–0.95
Lawns, sandy soil:	
Flat, 2%	0.05–0.10
Average, 2–7%	0.10–0.15
Steep, 7%	0.15–0.20
Lawns, heavy soil:	
Flat, 2%	0.13–0.17
Average, 2–7%	0.18–0.22
Steep, 7%	0.25–0.35

from the most remote part of the watershed to the point of design. This rainfall/runoff relation is illustrated in Figure 12-46.

In Figure 12-46, the *IDF* curve is the intensity-duration-frequency relation for the area and the peak runoff is $Q/A = q$, which is proportional to the value of I defined at t_c. The constant of proportionality is thus the runoff coefficient, $C = (Q/A)/I$. One limitation of the Rational Method is that Q/A is a point value and as such, the relation yields nothing of the nature of the rest of the hydrograph.

Most applications of the Rational Formula in determining peak flow rates utilize the following steps:

1. Estimate the time of concentration of the drainage area.
2. Estimate the runoff coefficient from a table such as 12-15.
3. Select a return period T_r and find the intensity of rain that will be equaled or exceeded, on the average, once every T_r years. To

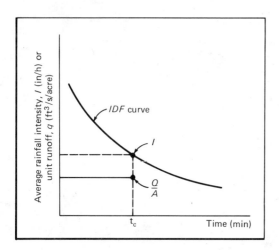

Figure 12-46   Rainfall runoff relation for the Rational Method.

produce equilibrium flows, this design storm must have a duration equal to t_c. The desired intensity can be read from an *IDF* curve derived from local precipitation input such as that in Figure 12-45, by using a rainfall duration equal to the time of concentration.
4. Determine the desired peak flow Q_p using Equation 12-36.
5. Some design situations produce larger peak flows if design storm intensities for durations less than t_c are used. Substituting intensities for durations less than t_c is justified only if the contributing area term in Equation 12-36 is also reduced to accommodate the shortened storm duration.

One of the principal assumptions of the Rational Method is that the predicted peak discharge has the same return period as the rainfall *IDF* relation used in the prediction. Another assumption is the constancy of the runoff coefficient C during individual storms and from storm to storm. In practice, a composite, weighted runoff coefficient is computed for various surface conditions by estimating the percentage that is covered by the various types of surfaces, multiplying each fraction by the appropriate coefficient, and then summing the products. Times of concentration are determined from the hydraulic characteristics of the principal flow path, which typically is divided into two parts, overland flow and flow in defined channels. The times of flow in each segment are added to obtain t_c.

The Rational Method is used for the design of urban storm drainage systems serving areas of up to several hundred acres in size. For areas larger than 1 mi^2, hydrograph techniques are generally warranted (see Chapter 7) (67).

RUNOFF SIMULATION
The use of simulation models, particularly digital computer models, to analyze urban watersheds for the hydrologic design of storm drainage

systems has become popular in recent years. These models are characterized by an attempt to quantify all pertinent physical phenomena
from the input (rainfall) to the output (runoff). This usually involves the
following steps: (1) determine a design storm, (2) deduct losses from the
design storm to arrive at an excess-rainfall rate, (3) determine the flow to
the gutter by overland flow equations, (4) route the gutter flow, (5) route
the flow in pipes, and (6) determine the outflow hydrograph (67). A
widely used storm water runoff model that assesses quantity as well as
quality of urban runoff is the EPA Storm Water Management Model
(SWWM). A detailed discussion of this model and other models is presented in Chapter 10.

12-8 RECREATION

Water requirements for recreation are highly seasonal, with summer
being the peak demand time during the year. Because many other water
uses also require the greatest monthly quantities at this time of year,
recreation water uses often compete with other water uses such as irrigation and navigation. This pattern is an important consideration when
developing multiple-use water projects such as storage reservoirs where
recreation is planned. For example, if recreation facilities such as docks
and beaches are developed on reservoirs, large drawdowns resulting in
lowering of the surface-water elevation from other uses during peak demand periods could hamper the intended recreation uses.

Water Quality for Recreation

Of historical concern is the quality of water to be used for recreation.
Contamination with any substance that may pose a hazard to human
health through ingestion, skin absorption, or entrance through body openings such as the ear is due cause for public health authorities to restrict the
use of a water body to nonswimming recreation or, in severe cases, to
prohibit the use of a water body for recreation altogether. Pathogens
contributed to water by inadequately treated sewage are a common problem in waters that may otherwise be suitable for recreation.

The California State Water Pollution Control Board has designated
three general water quality criteria for waters to be used for recreation:
(1) they must be free from obnoxious floating or suspended substances,
color, or odors; (2) they must be reasonably free of toxic substances; and
(3) they must have a low probability of contamination with pathogenic
organisms (68). The EPA recommends two specific criteria for recreation
waters as follows:

1. *Fecal coliform bacteria (bathing waters).* Based on a minimum of
   five samples taken over a 30-day period, the fecal coliform bacterial level should not exceed a log mean of 200 per 100 ml, nor

should more than 10 percent of the total samples taken during any 30-day period exceed 400 per 100 ml (58).

2. *pH.* For most bathing and swimming waters, eye irritation is minimized and recreational enjoyment enhanced by maintaining the pH within the range of 6.5 to 8.3 except for those waters with a low buffering capacity where a range of pH between 5.0 and 9.0 may be tolerated (3).

Wastewater Reuse for Recreation

In many water-short western states, there has been an emphasis on increased water reuse for nonpotable applications. Recreation is one reuse that the State of California has deemed acceptable for wastewater that has been treated by specified advanced (tertiary) methods. Specifically, wastewater that has been oxidized and disinfected and has a bacteriological quality of ≤ 2.2 coliforms per 100 ml may be impounded for restricted recreational use. For nonrestricted use, wastewater must be oxidized, coagulated, clarified, filtered, disinfected, and have an average coliform count of $\leq 2.2/100$ ml (with a maximum of 23 coliforms per 100 ml in any sample). In some cases, reuse of wastewater for recreation may be coincident with reuse for other purposes such as irrigation (4).

PROBLEMS

12-1. Determine the monthly consumptive use of a cotton crop grown in South Carolina if the mean monthly temperature is 65°F and the latitude is 32° N. Assume that the percent daylight hours for 32° N are as follows: April, 8.76; May, 9.62; June, 9.59; July, 9.77; August, 9.27; September, 8.34; October, 7.95.

12-2. What percentage of the total amount of water used in your state is used for irrigation? How many gallons per year would be saved by a 1 percent reduction in irrigation water use? How does this saving compare with the total quantities used for other purposes in your state? (See Chapter 4 for references to data.)

12-3. What are the causes for wasteful water use in irrigation? What are some simple methods for improving the efficiency of existing systems?

12-4. Discuss how you would go about designing a rectangular sedimentation basin. What information would you need? How would you use this information?

12-5. A rectangular sedimentation basin(s) is to be used to treat 5 mgd of a waste containing granular solids. The basin depth must be 10 ft and the recommended surface loading is not to exceed 1500 gal/day/ft^2. What will be the basin dimensions and theoretical retention time?

12-6. A water treatment plant is to process approximately 23 mgd. About how many slow sand filters would be required? How many rapid sand filters? What would be the size of each unit and the surface loading?

12-7. Write a paper describing a modern water filtration plant that is now in operation. Sketch the flow sequence and unit processes. Label all operations.

12-8. Discuss the factors that should be considered before selecting any of the unit operations in this chapter for inclusion in a treatment plant design.

12-9. For a 15-ft-deep, square rapid sand filter, determine the amount of backwash that would be required if the design rate of wash water rise is 20 ft per minute. If the reservoir supplying wash water is 43 ft above the filter underdrains, the operating pressure needed at the entrance to the filter is 15 lb/in^2, and 230 ft of cast iron pipe are needed to supply the wash water, what diameter pipe would be required? Since you are not given the details of the piping, neglect losses in bends and fittings.

12-10. Obtain data from your local power company on the growth of electrical energy use in your area since 1960. Obtain similar data on the trends in water use for the same period. Are the percentage increases similar? Explain any variances you find in the two trends.

12-11. Construction of a 100,000 kW power plant is being considered. Figures have been obtained for both thermal and hydroelectric facilities. Using the data given below and a return rate of 10 percent, determine which facility you would propose.

	THERMAL PLANT	HYDRO PLANT
First cost	$11,000,000	$26,000,000
Estimated life	25 yr	50 yr
Taxes and insurance	4.1%	3.4%
Annual fuel costs	$1,800,000	$0
Labor, maintenance	$400,000	$140,000
Additional transmission facilities	$0	$500,000

12-12. A hydropower plant will have an average flow of 150 ft^3/s available with a gross head of 700 ft. The efficiency of the turbine and generator units is estimated to be 80 percent. The penstock can be constructed over one of two routes. The first of these is 1.6 mi and would be built using 60-in steel pipe. The second route would be shorter, 1.3 mi, but would require a tunnel of 1500 ft. The tunnel would be 72 in in diameter. If the costs installed for the pipeline were $38 per foot and the costs installed for the tunnel were $50 per foot, which route would you choose? Assume that a 60-in pipe would be used in conjunction with the tunnel route, that the energy produced by the plant would be worth 1¢ per kWh, and that the interest rate would be 9 percent.

12-13. Define a waterway. What are the criteria for using a natural water body for navigation purposes?

12-14. Describe the navigable waterways for the river basin in which you live. Using the references at the end of the chapter or other library sources, determine the types of goods transported on these waterways and the total tonnages per year.

12-15. What is a waterway user tax? How might this affect the competitiveness of water transport with rail and truck transport?

12-16. Describe the methods by which natural channels can be improved to make them navigable.

12-17. What are the types of dams that can be used in lock and dam systems? What advantages does each type offer?

12-18. Why can reservoir construction rarely be economically justified for navigation only? What are some of the other uses for reservoirs that could make multiple use, including navigation, viable?

12-19. What is the difference between structural and nonstructural flood damage reduction? Why, despite increased efforts expended on flood control, do flood damages continue to increase? Why is it expected that the percentage of urban flood damages will increase while agricultural damages will decrease in the future?

12-20. Describe how structural measures reduce flood damages.

12-21. Describe how nonstructural measures reduce flood damages.

12-22. Using library resources, determine whether you live in a floodplain. If so, what types of structural and nonstructural measures have been taken to mitigate future flood damages?

12-23. Define the following terms: sewerage, sanitary sewage, combined sewage, infiltration, inflow, and combined sewer.

12-24. Define BOD_5 and explain its significance as a measure of pollution strength.

12-25. Determine the ultimate BOD for a wastewater having a BOD_5 of 250 mg/L where $k' = 0.5$.

12-26. How can COD be used to estimate BOD_5? Why is it easier to measure COD than BOD_5? What precautions must be taken in correlating the two parameters?

12-27. Determine the theoretical COD for stearic acid ($C_{18}H_{36}O_2$). How will the measured COD differ from the theoretical COD? Explain why this is so.

12-28. What are the primary objectives in treating wastewater?

12-29. For the community in which you are living, contact the municipal wastewater authority and obtain the following information: (a) the quantity of wastewater flowing to the wastewater treatment plant; (b) a complete characterization (pollutant parameters) of the raw wastewater; (c) state and local effluent limitations that must be met for discharge; (d) the entire treatment train used at the plant, including number and types of units, design parameters for each, quantities and types of chemicals used, and levels of pollutants removed by each, and (e) sludge treatment and disposal methods employed at the plant. From this information draw a plant wastewater flow schematic. Be certain to account for sludge generated by all processes.

12-30. Under what conditions are advanced treatment processes employed at a wastewater treatment plant?

12-31. Define urban runoff. Explain how it contributes to surface-water pollution.

12-32. What types of treatment processes are best suited to treat combined sewer overflow? To treat storm water?

12-33. Referring to Figure 12-45, find the 50-year design storm using the *IDF* curves given in Figure 12-45 and $A_1 = 4$ acres, $C_1 = 0.5$, $t_1 = 15$ min, $A_2 = 3.5$ acres, $C_2 = 0.4$, and $t_2 = 10$ min.

13-34. Explain the significance of water quality for a body of water that is to be used for recreation.

References

1. K. D. Frederick with J. C. Hanson, *Water for Western Agriculture,* Resources for the Future, Inc., Washington, D.C., 1982.
2. V. E. Hansen, O. W. Israelson, and G. E. Stringham, *Irrigation Principles and Practices,* 4th ed., Wiley, New York, 1980.
3. National Academy of Sciences–National Academy of Engineering, *Water Quality Criteria 1972: A Report of the Committee on Water Quality Criteria,* EPA-R3-73-033, U.S. Environmental Protection Agency, Washington, D.C., 1973.
4. California Department of Health, *Wastewater Reclamation Criteria,* California Administrative Code, Title 22, Div. 4, Water Sanitation Sec., Berkeley, CA, 1975.
5. M. E. Jensen and E. J. Kruse, "Cheaper Ways to Move Irrigation Water," in *1980 Yearbook of Agriculture,* USDA, Washington, D.C., 1980.
6. U.S. EPA, *Trends in U.S. Irrigation: Three Regional Studies,* draft rep., Athens, GA, June 1971 (unpublished).
7. U.S. GAO, Report to Congress, *Better Federal Coordination Needed to Promote More Efficient Farm Irrigation,* RED-76-116, Washington, D.C., June 22, 1976.
8. USDA, *Crop Consumptive Irrigation Requirements and Irrigation Efficiency Coefficients for the United States,* Washington, D.C., June 1976.
9. U.S. GAO, Report to Congress, *More and Better Use Could Be Made of Billions of Gallons of Water by Improving Irrigation Delivery Systems,* CED-77-117, September 2, 1977.
10. J. W. Clark, W. Viessman, and M. J. Hammer, *Water Supply and Pollution Control,* 3d ed., Harper & Row, New York, 1977.
11. *Standard Methods for the Examination of Water and Wastewater,* 15th ed., American Public. Association, New York, 1980.
12. P. Hamer, J. Jackson, and E. F. Thurston, *Industrial Water Treatment Practice,* Butterworth and Co., London, 1961.
13. E. Nordell, *Water Treatment for Industrial and Other Uses,* 2d ed., Reinhold Publishing Corp., New York, 1961.
14. S. T. Powell, *Water Conditioning for Industry,* McGraw-Hill, New York, 1954.
15. R. E. Greenhalgh, Ronald L. Johnson, and Howard D. Nott, "Mixing in Continuous Reactors," *Chem. Eng. Progr.,* vol. 55, February 1959, pp. 44–48.
16. Linvil G. Rich, *Unit Operations of Sanitary Engineering,* Wiley, New York, 1961.
17. *Mixers and Mixing,* Infilco Inc., Bull. 730-5430.
18. S. L. Tolman, "The Mechanics of Mixing and Flocculation," *Public Works,* December 1962.
19. T. R. Camp, "Flocculation and Flocculation Basins," *Trans. Am. Soc. Civil Engrs.,* vol. 120, 1955.
20. J. A. Salvato, Jr., *Environmental Engineering and Sanitation,* 2d ed., Wiley, New York, 1972.
21. S. L. Tolman, "Sedimentation Basin Design and Operation," *Public Works,* June 1963.
22. T. R. Camp, "Studies of Sedimentation Basin Design," *Sewage Ind. Wastes,* vol. 25, no. 1, January 1953.

23. E. B. Fitch, "The Significance of Detention in Sedimentation," *Sewage Ind. Wastes*, vol. 29, no. 10, 1957.
24. Arthur B. Morrill, "Sedimentation Basin Research and Design," *J. Am. Water Works Assoc.*, vol. 24, 1932.
25. A. Hazen, "On Sedimentation," *Trans. Am. Soc. Civil Engrs.*, vol. 53, 1904.
26. G. M. Fair and J. C. Geyer, *Water Supply and Wastewater Disposal*, Wiley, New York, 1961.
27. Jack E. McKee, C. J. Brokaw, and R. T. McLaughlin, "Chemical and Colloidal Effects of Halogens in Sewage," *J. Water Pollution Control Federation*, vol. 32, no. 8, 1960, pp. 795–818.
28. H. E. Babbit, J. J. Doland, and J. L. Cleasby, *Water Supply Engineering*, 6th ed., McGraw-Hill, New York, 1962.
29. *Water Treatment Plant Design*, American Water Works Association, New York, 1969.
30. Federal Power Commission, *Staff Report on the Role of Hydroelectric Developments in the Nation's Power Supply*, Washington, D.C., June 13, 1974.
31. U.S. Water Resources Council, *Water Requirements, Availabilities, Constraints, and Recommended Federal Actions*, Project Independence, U.S. Gov't. Print. Off., Washington, D.C., November 1974.
32. U.S. Council on Environmental Quality, *Energy Alternatives: A Comparative Analysis*, Washington, D.C., May 1975.
33. Federal Power Commission, *The 1970 National Power Survey*, U.S. Gov't. Print. Off., Washington, D.C., December 1971, 4 pts.
34. National Petroleum Council, Committee on U.S. Energy Outlook, Other Energy Resources Subcommittee, New Energy Forms Task Group (1973), *U.S. Energy Outlook: New Energy Forms*, Washington, D.C., 1973.
35. Federal Energy Administration, *Hydroelectric Generating Facilities Report*, Washington, D.C., September 1974.
36. R. K. Linsley and J. B. Franzini, *Water-Resources Engineering*, 3d ed., McGraw-Hill, New York, 1979.
37. O. W. Bruton, "Hydropower and Pumped Storage in the Northwest," *Proc. Spring Seminar, Energy and Water Resources*, Water Resources Research Institute, Oregon State University, Corvalis, OR, January 1977.
38. E. Kuiper, *Water Resources Development: Planning, Engineering, and Economics*, Butterworth and Co., London, 1965.
39. U.S. Army Corps of Engineers, *National Hydroelectric Power Resources Study, Preliminary Inventory of Hydropower Resources*, July 1979.
40. U.S. General Accounting Office, *Hydropower—An Energy Source Whose Time Has Come Again*, EMD-80-30, January 11, 1980.
41. J. M. Newcomb, "Small-Scale Hydropower: Renewed Interest in a Renewable Resource," Rep. No. 82-130S, Congressional Research Service, Library of Congress, Washington, D.C., August 1982.
42. D. V. MacDonald, "Energy Recovery on High Pressure Water Conduits," *Public Works*, January 1981.
43. The American Waterways Operators, Inc., *Annual Report 1981–82*, Arlington, VA, 1982.
44. "The U.S. Inland Waterways," *Marine Engineering/Log*, vol. 82, no. 8, August 1977.
45. The American Waterways Operators, Inc., *1979 Inland Waterborne Commerce Statistics*, Arlington, VA, 1982.

46. St. Lawrence Seaway Development Corporation, *1981 Annual Report,* Washington, D.C., 1981.
47. U.S. Congress, *The Inland Waterways Revenue Act of 1978,* Title II, P.L. 95-502, 92 Stat. 1693, Washington, D.C., October 21, 1978.
48. U.S. Water Resources Council, "Floodplain Management: Guidelines for Implementing Executive Order 11988," *Federal Register,* vol. 43, FR 6030–6055, February 10, 1978.
49. National Science Foundation, *A Report on Flood Hazard Mitigation,* Washington, D.C., 1980.
50. *Eleventh Annual Report of the Council on Environmental Quality, 1980,* U.S. Gov't. Print. Off., Washington, D.C., 1980.
51. 1982 Public Works Manual, *Public Works,* Public Works Journal Corp., Ridgewood, NJ, 1982.
52. J. W. Clark, W. Viessman, Jr., and M. J. Hammer, *Water Supply and Pollution Control,* 3d ed., Harper & Row, New York, 1977.
53. E. W. Steel and T. J. McGhee, *Water Supply and Sewerage,* 5th ed., McGraw-Hill, New York, 1979.
54. Metcalf and Eddy, Inc., *Wastewater Engineering: Collection and Pumping of Wastewater,* McGraw-Hill, New York, 1981.
55. Metcalf and Eddy, Inc., *Wastewater Engineering: Treatment, Disposal, Reuse,* 2d ed., McGraw-Hill, New York, 1979.
56. C. N. Sawyer and P. L. McCarty, *Chemistry for Environmental Engineering,* 3d ed., McGraw-Hill, New York, 1978.
57. APHA, AWWA, and WPCF, *Standard Methods for the Examination of Water and Wastewater,* 15th ed., APHA, Washington, D.C., 1981.
58. U.S. EPA, *Quality Criteria for Water,* Washington, D.C., 1976.
59. *Twelfth Annual Report of the Council on Environmental Quality, 1981,* U.S. Gov't. Print. Off., Washington, D.C., 1981.
60. U.S. Environmental Protection Agency, "Secondary Treatment Information," in *Code of Federal Regulations,* vol. 40, pt. 133, U.S. Gov't. Print. Off., Washington, D.C., 1982.
61. L. G. Rich, *Unit Operations of Sanitary Engineering,* Wiley, New York, 1961.
62. District of Columbia Department of Environmental Services, *By Broad Potomac's Shore: The Water and Sewerage Systems of the District of Columbia,* Washington, D.C., February 1979.
63. J. A. Lager and W. G. Smith, *Urban Stormwater Management and Technology: An Assessment,* U.S. EPA Rep. No. EPA-670/2-74-040, Washington, D.C., 1975.
64. V. Novotny and G. Chesters, *Handbook of Nonpoint Pollution: Sources and Management,* Van Nostrand Reinhold, New York, 1981.
65. J. A. Lager et al., *Urban Stormwater Management and Technology, Update and Users Guide,* U.S. EPA Rep. No. EPA-600/8-77-014, Washington, D.C., 1977.
66. E. Kuichling, "The Relation Between the Rainfall and the Discharge of Sewers in Populous Districts," *Trans. ASCE,* vol. 20, 1889.
67. W. Viessman, J. W. Knapp, G. L. Lewis, and T. E. Harbaugh, *Introduction to Hydrology,* 2d ed., Harper & Row, 1977.
68. J. E. McKee and H. W. Wolf, *Water Quality Criteria,* California State Water Pollution Board Pub. No. 3-A, 1963.

Chapter 13
Case Studies of Water Resources Systems

We have discussed the principal components of water resources systems and some techniques that might be used to analyze them. In this chapter a number of case studies are summarized to illustrate how the previously presented methods have been applied to actual analyses. They illustrate combinations of system elements, types of objectives, and analytical approaches that one might encounter or employ in practice.

The first study discussed is related to water supply enhancement in the Potomac River Basin. It is interesting because it clearly shows the potential of modern problem-solving techniques for producing innovative alternatives and for guiding future water policies. Following this, there is tabulated a series of examples of model applications to a variety of water resources problems around the world.

13-1 WATER SUPPLY FOR THE WASHINGTON, D.C., METROPOLITAN AREA

Since the early 1600s, when man first settled in the Potomac River Basin, there has been a continuing concern with the river and its use. For about the first 200 years, this focus was mainly on transportation and communication. Following that era of early western movement, attention shifted to issues surrounding water supply, and later pollution control. The generator for this shift was the ever increasing population in the basin, especially in the Washington metropolitan area (WMA).

Shortly after the turn of the century, water planning of various sorts became commonplace. Hundreds of studies emerged, some by the Army

Corps of Engineers, others by state and local levels of government. Perhaps unfortunately, perhaps not, most of these plans became library showpieces rather than blueprints for action. The reasons for this have been many, but a principal determining factor has been the enormous number of institutions having influence over decisions about water management in the basin. Dr. Abel Wolman aptly put it: "An orderly management of the array of functions . . . is distinguished by its absence. That it is needed has generally been agreed upon [but] suspicion of an overlying authority, by whatever name, has characterized public and private reactions."(1)

Institutional tug-of-war well describes most previous attempts to implement proposals for Potomac River Basin development and/or management. The result was a general stagnation of effort. But concurrent with this inactivity was the building of pressure to "do something" as the metropolitan area population grew and periodic low flows in the river became more troublesome. It is axiomatic that crisis generates action. That was true for the Potomac.

Since the late 1970s a unique amalgam of institutional cooperation and technological expertise regarding water supply issues in the Potomac River Basin has taken place. The Corps of Engineers, the states of Maryland and Virginia, the Interstate Commission on the Potomac River Basin, the Fairfax County Water Authority, the Washington Surburban Sanitary Commission, the Metropolitan Washington Area Council of Governments, and other key actors worked hard and diligently to provide a setting for coordination of river management policies that would work to the benefit of all. An exercise in mutual cooperation was complemented by a fresh new technical approach to solving the Potomac's water supply problems. The direction taken was that of improved systems management rather than structural development. The principal elements of the approach taken include (2):

Combination of optimization and simulation techniques to provide practical rules for operation of the water supply system

Large-scale use of the National Weather Service River Forecast System based on a soil moisture accounting model and its direct integration with reservoir operations

Development and implementation of a technique to predict water demand and the application of that technique in water resource system design and operation

Combination of distribution analysis and hydrologic modeling to develop operating procedures for a complex water distribution system including many independent water suppliers

Use of risk analysis to identify the start of potential droughts and to quantify the risks of continued drought

Use of "drought games" to test and improve water supply operating procedures and to illustrate the use of those procedures to decision makers

The benefits of coordinated water management were found to be quite large. If all the facilities of the WMA water supply were independently operated, the sum of the yield would be about 620 mgd. The analysis showed, however, that joint operations could achieve yields of better than 825 mgd from the same system. This is more than a 25 percent increase in yield and about equivalent to the combined yields of several additional reservoirs that were under consideration. Construction costs for these two reservoirs, close to a quarter of a billion dollars, could thus be saved and many heated environmental fights over additional reservoir construction avoided.

It was not an easy task to implement a plan to provide the needed additional water supply for the Washington metropolitan area. Complex engineering, social, economic, environmental, and political problems had to be solved. For years, structural proposals of various sorts had been suggested, but these were found to be unacceptable on many grounds. The fresh approach presented here was needed; it broke away from tradition and focused on what could be done in the face of prevailing constraints. It grew out of advances in water resources engineering analysis that had developed since the early 1960s.

Modern techniques of systems analysis—linear programming, synthetic hydrology, statistical analysis, hydrologic modeling, and computer simulation—were merged to produce a predominantly nonstructural solution to the water supply problem. As a result, a problem that had been without resolution for almost 30 years was taken in stride. What had appeared to be an impasse in regional cooperation was obliterated. Furthermore, between $200 million and $1 billion were potentially saved compared with the costs of previous alternatives. The environmental impact of the solution was also minimal.

An important aspect of this example is the proof it provides that nonstructural engineering alternatives, including better management of existing facilities, can be devised to solve difficult technical/institutional water resources problems at low economic and environmental cost. Since the replacement value of existing facilities is much greater than the present value of expenditures on new facilities at current discount rates, the potential benefits of widespread application of the types of engineering analyses used for the Potomac are enormous. The "coming of age" of the use of modern systems analysis techniques for solving water resources problems is exemplified in the Potomac example.

13-2 A SUMMARY OF WORLDWIDE MODEL APPLICATIONS

Table 13-1 summarizes the application of modeling approaches to water resources problems in many areas of the world. A review of the results column shows that not all applications were put into practice, nor were they all favorably received. The evidence is strongly suggestive, however,

Table 13-1 MODEL APPLICATIONS TO WATER RESOURCES PROBLEM SOLVING[a]

CASE STUDY	PURPOSE	PROBLEM ATTRIBUTES	OBJECTIVES	MODELS USED	RESULTS
1. Delaware River Basin, U.S., 1968 (3)	To develop, test, and apply screening models in a multipurpose river basin setting and to evaluate alternative development plans.	Small but economically important river basin. 29 potential and 6 existing multipurpose reservoirs. Water supply, hydropower production, and recreation functions. Flow augmentation for water quality control.	Economic net benefits, regional development, environmental quality.	Deterministic and stochastic LP, dynamic programming, simulation.	Deterministic mean flow models were found to be ineffective. Stochastic mean-flow models were found to be very effective but complex. Part of the study results was implemented by the Corps of Engineers.
2. Ganges-Brahmaputra Basin, India and Pakistan, late 1960s (4)	To improve the quality of data and methodology for river basin planning and to resolve international conflicts.	Large land area and population affected. Irrigation, hydropower, flood control, and salinity control functions.	Economic efficiency, equity, regional development.	LP, simulation, economic input-output, game theory.	Some methodological advances, but India-Pakistan conflict resulted in India withdrawing from the study.
3. Texas Water Resources Development, late 1960s (5)	To develop computer programs for planning and operation of water resources systems and for evaluating plans for water resources investments.	A potential network of 18 reservoirs, 30 canals, 12 river reaches, and 24 demand points encompassing a distance of 500 miles.	Cost-effectiveness, reliability.	LP, simulation, data management programs.	Results were considered preliminary in nature. Models were used for sensitivity analysis and as a guide for additional data collection. Models were modified and applied elsewhere successfully.

[a]Data for this table were provided by D. P. Loucks, Cornell University.

Table 13-1 *(Continued)*

CASE STUDY	PURPOSE	PROBLEM ATTRIBUTES	OBJECTIVES	MODELS USED	RESULTS
4. Vistula River Basin, Poland, early 1970s (6)	Comprehensive planning for water supply, flood control, navigation, and water quality management. Training in systems analysis.	Large river basin covering half of Poland with little storage capacity. One of the first such modeling efforts in a planned economy.	Cost-effectiveness in meeting water supply, recreation, water quality targets.	LP, stochastic dynamic programming, simulation.	Many alternatives were presented to the government. The methodology was expanded and used for planning. Considerable personnel training accomplished.
5. North Atlantic Regional Water Study, U.S., late 1960s (7)	To develop a framework for optimizing the development of water and related land resources.	Study area encompassed 13 states and the District of Columbia. There were 39 water-using sectors. Interbasin transfers were considered.	Economic development, regional development, environmental quality.	LP for supply predictions, input-output for demand prediction and statistical regressions.	Systems methods were found to be useful but the trend away from multistate coordination caused limited applicability.
6. Upper Mures River Basin, Rumania, early 1970s (8)	To aid in developing agricultural and flood control measures and for improving water supply and water quality management plans.	Study resulted from history of flooding. Emphasis was on flood damage reduction and agricultural land use.	Economic efficiency, cost-effectiveness, flood warning.	Simulation and stochastic LP.	Data acquisition was hampered by internal security. Conflicts between sponsor and the government constrained effective use of analyses.

Case	Objective	Description	Criteria	Methods	Results
7. Saint John River, Canada, early 1970s (9)	To evaluate the potential of mathematical modeling for water quality management. To predict impacts of alternative plans for basin development and wastewater treatment.	River basin used for water supply and hydropower production. Significant waste loads from pulp and paper industry and potato processing.	Water quality improvement, cost-effectiveness.	Simulation and LP.	Model results had great influence on debate but model and data reliability were questioned. Modeling served to coordinate project activities.
8. National Water Management in Israel, continuing since late 1960s (10)	To develop a comprehensive multipurpose design and management system.	Demand exceeds supply, necessitating wastewater reuse and desalination. One of the most intensively managed water systems in the world.	Efficient water use, economic net benefits, regional development, national security.	Simulation and various optimization models.	The modeling results form the basis for most investment and operating policy decisions. Analysts are in important government advisory positions.
9. Elkhorn River Basin, Nebraska, U.S., mid-1970s (11)	Multipurpose development emphasizing flood control, water supply, irrigation, and recreation.	Large number of potential reservoir sites were involved. Some method of screening options was considered essential.	Economic efficiency, regional development, flood protection.	LP and simulation.	Significant planning time was saved by model development and use. Slight improvement in economic efficiency determinations was noted. Sensitivity analyses aided debate.

Table 13-1 *(Continued)*

CASE STUDY	PURPOSE	PROBLEM ATTRIBUTES	OBJECTIVES	MODELS USED	RESULTS
10. Seversky Donnets River Quality, U.S.S.R., late 1970s (12)	Exchange of information on systems analysis approaches for water quality management between the U.S. and the U.S.S.R.	Highly polluted river in the southern Ukraine was chosen for testing the application of U.S. water quality prediction models.	Cost-effectiveness, environmental quality.	Simulation and optimization, multiconstituent water quality prediction.	Numerous alternative management strategies were identified. The methodology was adopted by the U.S.S.R. for further study and application. There was some resistance to adapting theory to practice.
11. Rio Colorado River Basin, Argentina, late 1970s (13)	Application of modern planning technologies to water resources in Argentina. Training of professionals.	River initiates in the Andes and flows through arid lands. Irrigation and hydropower potential exists.	Economic efficiency, regional development.	Multiobjective deterministic LP and simulation.	Training was accomplished. Future use of model study is uncertain.
12. Irrigation Planning and Development, Algeria, late 1970s (14)	To aid in preparing a master plan for staged development of surface-water supply infrastructure for irrigation and for developing an irrigation program for self-sufficiency.	Many subsystems of potential reservoirs, canals, pumps, and treatment facilities were to be evaluated. It was desired to reuse the fresh water extensively.	Cost-effectiveness and to improve water yields and reliabilities and irrigation yields.	LP and irrigation model.	A complete plan of development was submitted to the government. The plan was incorporated into the country's Charte Nationale.

	Objective	Description	Benefits	Method	Results
13. National Water Management, Netherlands, late 1970s (15)	To yield information for improved water management, to develop procedures for impact assessment, and to provide training.	Surface-water, groundwater, and water quality problems existed. Considered was a national network of reservoirs, lakes, aquifers, canals, pipes, pumps, irrigation areas, and treatment plants.	Economic efficiency, improved understanding of quantity-quality impacts of alternative water and land use.	Optimization and simulation.	Documentation of model study not complete, but models are being run in the Netherlands.
14. Chao Phraya River Basin, Thailand, late 1970s (16)	To increase irrigation water use efficiency and to improve on data collection and prediction of crop water needs.	Large river basin with all regulated water fully allocated. Irrigation is the major use. Reservoirs fully control streamflows.	Water use efficiency, irrigation productivity, salinity control.	LP and simulation.	Models have been implemented and used weekly since 1979. Improved water use efficiencies.
15. Operation of High Aswan Dam, Egypt, late 1970s (17)	To develop better reservoir operating policies for increased irrigation, hydropower, and flood control. To provide training in systems analysis.	Irrigation is top priority. Dam fully controls the Nile's downstream flow. The dam provides for about 70 percent of all electrical energy in the country.	Economic efficiency, hydropower production, irrigation yield and expansion.	Stochastic optimization (dynamic programming) and simulation for reservoir operation. Deterministic optimization for irrigation planning and operation.	Optimizing to meet needs permits 11–20 percent increase in firm hydropower production and an annual savings of $20 to $30 million in fuel for thermal power. Operating rules have been implemented.

of the role that models can play in the future and the wide use to which they are already being put. Problems addressed vary from those of small river basins to large ones, and from narrowly defined proposals to those encompassing many objectives. References to the case studies are indicated following the title in column 1.

The case studies presented in this chapter, although few in number, show that models, in spite of their limitations, can be very useful in the day-to-day world of planning and decision making. Used appropriately, and tempered with good judgment and an understanding of the physical and institutional dimensions of the problems being attacked, models can serve to provide insights that would be difficult to obtain in any other way.

References

1. U. S. Congress, Senate, "A 1980's View of Water Management in the Potomac River Basin," *Report of the Committee on Governmental Affairs*, 97th Cong., 2d Sess., U.S. Gov't. Print. Off., Washington, D.C., November 12, 1981.
2. Anon., "Water Supply," *Civil Engineering*, vol. 53, no. 6, June 1983.
3. H. D. Jacoby and D. P. Loucks, "Combined Use of Optimization and Simulation Models in River Basin Planning," *Water Resources Research*, vol. 8, no. 6, December 1972.
4. Meta Systems, Inc., *Systems Analysis in Water Resources Planning*, Cambridge, MA, July 1971.
5. Texas Water Development Board, "Systems Simulation for Management of a Total Water Resource," Rep. 118, Austin, TX, May 1970.
6. G. T. Orlob et al., "Mathematical Models for Planning the Future Development and Management of the Vistula River System, Poland, Final Report," Water Resources Engineers, Inc., Walnut Creek, CA, December 1971.
7. H. E. Schwarz et al., "The NAR Study . . . ," series of four articles in *Water Resources Research*, vol. 8, no. 3, June 1972.
8. D. P. Loucks, personal communication, 1983.
9. A. K. Biswas, *Models for Water Quality Management*, McGraw-Hill, New York, 1981.
10. U. Shamir, "Application of Operations Research in Israel's Water Sector," *Third European Congress on Operations Research*, Amsterdam, April 1979.
11. W. Viessman, Jr., et al., "A Screening Model for Water Resources Planning," *Water Resources Bulletin*, vol. 11, no. 2, April 1975.
12. D. P. Loucks, "Water Quality Management in the Soviet Union," *Journal of the Water Pollution Control Federation*, vol. 49, no. 8, August 1977.
13. D. C. Major and R. L. Lenton, *Applied Water Resource Systems Planning*, Prentice-Hall, Englewood Cliffs, NJ, 1979.
14. D. W. Meyers, *Preliminary Design Studies of Surface Water Resource Systems in Northern Algeria*, Cornell University, Ithaca, NY, May 1976.
15. B. F. Goeller et al., *Policy Analyses of Water Management for the Netherlands*, vols. I–XX, Rand Corp., Santa Monica, CA, 1981.
16. J. E. Crowley et al., "A Water Operations System for the Chao Phraya Basin,

Thailand," *Second Congress of the Asian and Pacific Regional Division of IAHR,* Taipei, Taiwan, May 1980.

17. K. Oven-Thompson et al., "Agricultural vs. Hydropower Tradeoffs in the Operation of the High Aswan Dam," *Water Resources Research,* vol. 18, no. 6, December 1982.

Chapter 14
Outlook for Tomorrow

It is difficult to look ahead in an attempt to foresee the future and thereby plan for events that have yet to occur. Nevertheless, that is the task facing planners and managers, whether their concern is water resources, education, highways, housing, defense, health, or other areas. The task is much more difficult today than it was 50 or even 20 years ago. The rapid rates of growth of population and technology, an almost instantaneous worldwide communication capability, and rapidly shifting social and political objectives have made it nearly impossible for planners to project even a few years ahead with any degree of certainty. But look ahead we must, or suffer the consequences of falling far short of the needs of future generations.

This book was written recognizing that the problems indicated above must be understood and dealt with directly by the scientific and engineering community as well as by those concerned with social and political forces. The thoughts presented in this final chapter are intended to tie the elements of the book together and to place its sections in perspective. It summarizes the factors that planners, managers, engineers, environmental scientists, and others must deal with and considers some approaches that they may take in developing plans and programs and in reconciling conflicts.

14-1 TRENDS IN WATER USE

Fundamental to water resources planning and management is an understanding of the availability of water and a notion of how much of it will be needed, in what quality, for how long, and for what purposes. This requires an evaluation of the regional resource base (data) coupled with projections of population change, agricultural and industrial activity, economic growth or decline, and so on. Furthermore, an understanding of influencing customs, laws, organizations, and regulations must be acquired.

Historically, those making projections of future water needs based their estimates on single projections flowing from past histories. More often than not, those projected trends included increases based on population growth and the idea that future water users would somehow always develop water-using methods that were more water intense than those of the past. In some cases this has led to overdevelopment and wasteful practices. In other cases it has stimulated regional growth that might not have taken place otherwise, and that in retrospect might not be looked on with favor. In any event, history indicates that the concept of growth, and generally accelerating growth, seems to have been strongly implanted in the minds of most agencies concerned with providing water. Some years ago there was a rationale behind this approach; in many areas water was less committed to use than it is now, and it was often of a better quality. When a resource is easy to obtain and inexpensive to handle and process, it is hard for many to think in conservative terms. Today, however, many regions are facing water supply problems of one form or another, and the idea that future needs will have to be (on a per capita basis) much greater than those of today is costly, wasteful, and founded on historical attitudes rather than on the realities unfolding. The lesson here is that water resources planners and managers should balance their projections of future needs with an understanding that per capita water use can sometimes be decreased without adverse effects on standard of living. What must be done is to seek out the optimal patterns of water use and to implement the most effective schemes for management. This will often require technological and institutional reforms, and when they are needed, they should be striven for, if not fully, at least in a stepwise manner. Options for change will have to be carefully evaluated and laid out to those responsible for making the decisions about providing funds, enacting laws, setting up or revising regulations, and fostering intergovernmental and interagency cooperation and coordination. In many cases it seems likely that we can do more with less, or at least more with the same amount. The challenge to the planner is to attempt to foresee the future in terms of the number of people to be served and the level of water-using activity to be accommodated, and then to seek approaches for meeting the water needs of this mix in the most efficient manner. In some cases, shifts in past practices or revised facilities will be required. In other cases, implementation of methods for making the transfer of water among various users attractive and legal might be a requirement. In any event, there are many possibilities for increasing the availability of water, short of developing new supplies, and it is time that these be thoroughly investigated. The water use trends of the future will always have a link to the past, but they can be shaped by many innovative practices. It is important that these be identified and capitalized on.

14-2 CRITICAL ISSUES AND THE POTENTIAL FOR THEIR RESOLUTION

There are many water resources problems facing the United States and other nations. These include traditional ones such as flood damage reduction, navigation, and providing water for various purposes. In recent years the emphasis in the United States has shifted significantly from its historical concern with water supply to problems related to environmental protection and management. Furthermore, it is now widely recognized that the institutional issues surrounding both water quality and water quantity are often more influential in matters of water availability than are the physical realities of the resource.

Issues of concern in the 1980s, and ones that will be around for some time to come, include nonpoint source pollution; acid precipitation; groundwater quality and overdraft; water quality management; provision of safe drinking water; water allocation among competing uses; groundwater management; floodplain management; provision of instream flows for fish and wildlife protection; hydroelectric development; providing water for energy resource development; rural water supply and wastewater disposal; management, repair, and replacement of elements of urban water systems (decaying infrastructures); providing water for agriculture and meeting the challenge of increasing water use for this purpose in humid regions; and developing and implementing comprehensive water management programs that will permit the most efficient use of a region's water resources. Some of these problems have been of concern to water resources planners and managers for many years, others are of more recent origin, and others have been around but were not identified as of importance or have been skirted because of their political and social sensitivities. For the most part, however, they are interrelated and the institutional aspects are common to most, if not all, of the technical issues. As has been pointed out many times in earlier chapters, solution of most of the nation's water problems will not be achieved without recognition and taking on of all of the related elements—political, social, economic, and technical.

The opportunity to solve water problems exists in almost all cases. Sometimes there are many options, in other cases there are few. But in general, if all of the actors involved can be brought to a state of cooperation, the chances of providing additional water, making it cleaner, and sharing it among competing users will be enhanced. The options for addressing water problems include surface- and groundwater development, implementation of conservation measures, interbasin transfers, reusing wastewaters, desalination, phasing out marginal water uses, weather modification, development of new and innovative technologies, development of cooperative and/or consolidated water management approaches, and considering the system-wide features of water management and applying these to overcome the limitations on water use or control that are imposed by single-purpose or boundary-restricted approaches to water management. The case study of the Potomac River Basin (see Chapter 13) illustrates what can be achieved by assessing the potential of existing facilities in a region so that thcy function jointly in a different, more efficient manner than prevailing agency or governmental unit restrictions would ordinarily consider or possibly permit.

Given the technology that we already have, it seems clear that innovative planners and managers will be able to develop options for ensuring adequate water supplies for future generations if they can break away from the mold of tradition, circumvent existing constraints, and seek the best solutions available. Armed with this knowledge they will then be in a strong position to suggest reforms, where needed, and to demonstrate the payoffs to be achieved through making the needed changes. The technical and nontechnical aspects of water resources management have all been discussed in this book. It is the bringing together of all these parts in a meaningful manner that will be needed to solve the most troublesome issues. The threat that we are running out of water is mostly false, but the threat that there may be widespread water shortages resulting from mismanagement, lack of good decision making, unwillingness to pay the costs for needed programs, and political sensitivity about bringing about needed change is real. Only through an aggressive analysis of water problems and the design of workable options (workable in the sense that they will be accepted) can we expect to overcome past practices and traditions and bring about the modernization of laws, regulations, and organizations that will have to accompany improvements if we are to wisely allocate and use the nation's waters.

14-3 CHANGING SOCIAL GOALS AND THEIR IMPACT ON WATER POLICY

The concerns of United States citizens have shifted significantly over the past 50 years from issues related to navigation and flood control to matters of clean water, preservation of wilderness streams, fish and wildlife protection, and other environmental protection subjects. Often these changes in social awareness and concern are not followed immediately by action programs of the various levels of government, but eventually they are. Sometimes the results are a sweeping reform, with little thought given to the practicality of the proposed actions. In other cases, programs are clearly thought out. Irrespective of which path is followed, it is not uncommon for the new program or approach to be layered over the old with little concern for the conflict this may create. For example, the Reclamation Act of 1902 still stands, and thus continues in a statutory, if not in a contemporary, sense as a national policy intended to further western development through the irrigation of dry lands. This statement of policy is in conflict with new directions in water policy that favor nonfederal programs for irrigation and other aspects of water supply and also favor the commitment of federal funds to pollution control and other environmental objectives.

The problem is that as new directions for water policy unfold, these must be accommodated within a myriad of outdated programs and laws that have never been revised. Thus conflicts are created that are sometimes very difficult to deal with. The institutional reforms needed in the water policy field relate strongly to the layering-on process that has typified national actions on water matters over the years. The challenge for water resources planners and managers is to identify the areas of greatest conflict and to work unceasingly to bring about the needed legislative or regulatory reforms. Beyond this, there is still the dimension of conflict between broad national movements toward environmental protection, for example, and local interests still favoring traditional forms of water resources development and use. The problem the planner faces here is one of attitude and accommodation. If an alternative or alternatives can be laid out that permit a reasonable compromise in interests, then positive progress in solving the issue at hand is likely. On the other hand, if a one-sided proposal is carried forward, it is likely to stem all progress, regardless of the beneficiary.

Water resources planners and managers must continually be aware of shifts in public attitude and desires regarding the allocation and use of the nation's waters. By recognizing these, it is possible to prepare in advance for changes that will have to be made and, more importantly, to determine the nature of, and options for, resolving the conflicts that are sure to follow. As time goes on, our social goals will always be shifting, and these must be incorporated in our plans and programs. The concept of the dynamic planning process that was discussed in Chapter 4 fits the need to be flexible in all decisions about the future.

14-4 TOTAL WATER MANAGEMENT: THE WAY OF THE FUTURE

The theme of this book is water management. The term is defined broadly so that it includes developing new facilities when they are needed in addition to "managing" those already in place. It can be said that as a nation matures, it passes through stages of early growth and exploitation of resources, to more accelerated growth and higher technological development, to a point where management of the systems that have evolved becomes exceedingly important, and often offers the only real opportunity for change.

The water programs of the United States have gone through several phases, as was pointed out in Chapter 2. The early years of this century were ones of construction of dams, waterways, water treatment plants, and wastewater treatment facilities. Irrigation works helped open up and settle the west. Waterways improvements encouraged commerce and industry in populous areas of the east, south, and midwest. Municipal water and waste systems provided the means for increasing urbanization and industrial growth in many localities. But now many of the nation's rivers have been subjected to engineering controls, and the reasons for some of the old programs of construction are no longer valid, or at least are less valid than they were 20 or 30 years ago. In addition, many of the facilities that have been constructed are now reaching their design life, and questions of how to handle the rehabilitation of these systems are being raised. Furthermore, many water supply or treatment systems have been developed in isolation from other similar undertakings, often within the same river basin or subbasin. It is well known that the deficiencies of some of these systems could be overcome by linking them with neighboring systems or by operating them in a different manner. All of this falls within the realm of water management.

The concept of total water management is not new. It means considering all aspects of the resource—quantity and quality—in concert, and formulating a program to maximize the utility of the resource in its region for whatever purposes it is to be dedicated. It also means considering the interconnections between surface- and groundwater bodies and making use of these linkages to enhance storage and minimize costs. Conceptually total water management is simple; the complete system is analyzed and an "optimal" way to control discharges and withdrawals is struck. The system is then operated according to this plan—subject of course to revision as uses change or new policies unfold. The trouble is that the boundaries of the physical systems that are being dealt with are usually different than the political boundaries that affect how water is used or developed in a region. Furthermore, agency and other interest group boundaries are imposed, and these create additional fragmentation. Thus while it is clear that the idea of total water management has much to recommend it, it is difficult to implement such an approach short of forming a regional authority that actually controls the water resource and can make decisions on how allocations and transfers are to be made at any point in time.

Few would argue that the time is right for proposing a system of comprehensive regional water authorities in the United States, but this does not mean that the concept of total water management should be abandoned. Far from it. The case study of the Potomac showed that at least a partial regional water management plan could be put into effect using existing regional authorities acting cooperatively to face a specific issue. This approach can be extended to other river basins and for other reasons. Again, the point to be made is that if the merits of coordinated action can be clearly demonstrated, the opportunity to move in the direction of total water management will be enhanced. Many regions in the United States have reached the point where developmental opportunities are limited for one reason or another. This suggests that the time for innovative and effective programs of water management is at hand. Implementation of such schemes requires broad and imaginative approaches not bounded by traditions or other institutions of the past. Total water management is the way of the future, and if it cannot be put into effect in its entirety, then it should be approached in a stepwise fashion and its best features continually exposed and documented.

14-5 THE TECHNOLOGICAL ROLE

Much has been said in this book about the importance of institutions. It is true that many of the greatest water issues involve institutions rather than technology. The fact remains, however, that the changes that must be made institutionally can only be brought about if they are supported by strong technical studies. For example, the cooperative water management program developed for the Potomac River Basin would never have come about if it had not been for the technical studies done by the modelers, which proved that the proposed way of operation could save construction costs and result in added availability of water during low-flow periods. Furthermore, research and development work are still needed on many issues such as the health effects of various constituents in drinking water, more economical methods for wastewater renovation, and groundwater quality modeling, to name only a few. It seems that what must change, however, is the attitude of technical people toward those who are involved in making investment or other water management decisions or who are simply concerned with their environment and the quality of the water that they drink. Technicians must become more responsive to the needs of society and must be willing and capable of demonstrating how their technical achievements can be applied to practical advantage by those who must supply, treat, and manage water for the citizens, industries, and farms of this and other nations.

Appendix Tables

Appendix A
Conversion Factors
and Constants

CONSTANTS

GAS CONSTANTS (R)	HEAT OF VAPORIZATION OF WATER AT 1.0 ATM
$R = 0.0821$ (atm)(liter)/(g-mol)(°K) $R = 1.987$ g-cal/(g-mol)(°K) $R = 1.987$ Btu/(lb-mol)(°R)	540 cal/g = 970 Btu/lb
ACCELERATION OF GRAVITY (STANDARD)	SPECIFIC HEAT OF AIR
$g = 32.17$ ft/s² $= 980.6$ cm/s²	$C_p = 0.238$ cal/(g)(°C)
HEAT OF FUSION OF WATER	DENSITY OF DRY AIR AT 0°C AND 760 MM MERCURY
79.7 cal/g = 144 Btu/lb	0.001293 g/cm³

CONVERSION FACTORS

1 foot	=	0.3048 meter
1 mile	=	1.609 kilometers
1 acre	=	0.4047 hectare
	=	4047 square meters
1 square mile (mi²)	=	259 hectares
	=	2.59 square kilometers (km²)
1 acre foot (acre-ft)	=	1233 cubic meters
	=	325,851 gallons
	=	43,560 cubic feet
1 million gallons	=	3.07 acre-feet
1 cubic foot	=	7.48 gallons
1 million cubic feet (mft³)	=	28,320 cubic meters
1 cubic foot per second (ft³/s)	=	0.02832 cubic meters per second
	=	1.699 cubic meters per minute
1 second-foot-day (ft³/s/day)	=	2447 cubic meters
1 million gallons (MG)	=	3785 cubic meters
	=	3.785 million liters
1 million gallons per day (mgd)	=	694.4 gallons per minute (gal/min)
	=	2.629 cubic meters per minute
	=	3785 cubic meters per day
	=	1.55 cubic feet per second
	=	1120 acre-feet per year
1 billion gallons per day (bgd)	=	1.12 x10⁶ acre-feet per year
1 second-foot-day per square mile	=	0.03719 inch
1 inch of runoff per square mile	=	26.9 second-foot-days
	=	53.3 acre-feet
	=	2,323,200 cubic feet
1 cubic foot per second	=	0.9917 acre-inch per hour
	=	1 s-ft = 1 ft³/s
	=	1.98 acre-feet per day
1 horsepower	=	0.746 kilowatt
	=	550 foot-pounds per second
e	=	2.71828
$\log_{10} e$	=	0.43429
$\log_e 10$	=	2.30259

BASE AND SUPPLEMENTARY UNITS IN SI MEASUREMENT

QUANTITY	UNIT	SI SYMBOL
Base Units		
Length	meter	m
Mass	kilogram	kg
Time	second	s
Electric current	ampere	A
Thermodynamic temperature	kelvin	K
Amount of substance	mole	mol
Luminous intensity	candela	cd
Supplementary Units		
Plane angle	radian	rad
Solid angle	steradian	sr

COMMONLY USED EQUIVALENT UNITS IN WATER RESOURCES[a]

A. LENGTH

UNIT	EQUIVALENT[b, c]					
	MILLIMETER	INCH	FOOT	METER[d]	KILOMETER	MILE
Millimeter	1	0.03937	0.003281	0.001000	1 E-6	0.6214 E-6
Inch	25.40	1	0.0833	0.02540	25.40 E-6	15.78 E-6
Foot	304.8	12	1	0.3048	304.8 E-6	189.4 E-6
Meter[d]	1000	39.37	3.281	1	0.001	621.4 E-6
Kilometer	1,000,000	39,370	3281	1000	1	0.6214
Mile	1,609,000	63,360	5280	1609	1.609	1

B. AREA

UNIT	EQUIVALENT[b, c]						
	SQ. INCH	SQ. FOOT	SQ. METER[d]	ACRE	HECTARE	SQ. KILOMETER	SQ. MILE
Sq. inch	1	0.006944	645.2 E-6	0.1594 E-6	64.52 E-9	645.2 E-12	249.1 E-1
Sq. foot	144	1	0.09290	22.96 E-6	9.290 E-9	92.90 E-9	35.87 E-9
Sq. meter[d]	1550	10.76	1	247.1 E-6	1 E-4	1 E-6	386.1 E-9
Acre	6,273,000	43,560	4047	1	0.4047	0.004047	0.001563
Hectare	15,500,000	107,600	10,000	2.471	1	0.01	0.003861
Sq. kilometer	1.550 E+9	10,764,000	1,000,000	247.1	100	1	0.3861
Sq. mile	4.014 E+9	27,880,000	2,590,000	640	259	2.590	1

C. VOLUME

UNIT	EQUIVALENT[b,c]							
	CU. INCH	LITER	U.S. GALLON	CU. FOOT	CU. YARD	CU. METER[d]	ACRE-FOOT	SEC-FOOT DAY
Cubic inch	1	0.01639	0.004329	578.7 E-6	21.43 E-6	16.39 E-6	13.29 E-9	6.698 E-1
Liter	61.02	1	0.2642	0.03531	0.001308	0.001	810.6 E-9	408.7 E-1
U.S. gallon	231.0	3.785	1	0.1337	0.004951	0.003785	3.068 E-6	1.547 E-1
Cubic foot	1728	28.32	7.481	1	0.03704	0.02832	22.96 E-6	11.57 E-1
Cubic yard	46,660	764.6	202.0	27	1	0.7646	619.8 E-6	312.5 E-1
Cubic meter[d]	61,020	1000	264.2	35.31	1.308	1	810.6 E-6	408.7 E-1
Acre-foot	75.27 E+6	1,233,000	325,900	43,560	1613	1233	1	0.5042
Second-foot-day	149.3 E+6	2,447,000	646,400	86,400	3200	2447	1.983	1

SOURCE: Tables A–G, Universities Council on Water Resources.
[a]Footnotes for all parts of table.
[b]Equivalent values are shown to four significant figures.
[c]Multiply the numerical amount of the given unit by the equivalent value shown (per single amount of given unit) to obtain the numerical amount of the equivalent unit (e.g., 5 in × 0.025 40 m/in = 0.1270 m).
[d]This is the SI expression, in base units or derived units, for the physical quantity.
[e]E-6 is a multiplication factor of 10^{-6}.

D. DISCHARGE (FLOW RATE, VOLUME/TIME)

UNIT	EQUIVALENT[b,c]				MILLION	
	GALLON/MIN	LITER/SEC	ACRE-FOOT/DAY	FOOT^3/SEC	GAL/DAY	METER^{3}SEC[d]
Gallon/minute	1	0.06309	0.004419	0.002228	0.001440	63.09 E-6
Liter/second	15.85	1	0.07005	0.03531	0.02282	0.001
Acre-foot/day	226.3	14.28	1	0.5042	0.3259	0.01428
Foot^3/second	448.8	28.32	1.983	1	0.6463	0.02832
Million gallons/day	694.4	43.81	3.069	1.547	1	0.04381
Meter^3/second[d]	15,850	1000	70.04	35.31	22.82	1

VELOCITY

UNIT	EQUIVALENT[b,c]				
	FOOT/DAY	KILOMETER/HOUR	FOOT/SEC	MILE/HOUR	METER/SEC[d]
...ot/day	1	12.70 E-6	11.57 E-6	7.891 E-6	3.528 E-6
...ometer/hour	78,740	1	0.9113	0.6214	0.2778
...ot/second	86,400	1.097	1	0.6818	0.3048
...e/hour	126,700	1.609	1.467	1	0.4470
...ter/second[d]	283,500	3.600	3.281	2.237	1

F. MASS

UNIT	EQUIVALENT[b,c]					
	POUND$_{MASS}$	KILOGRAM[d]	METRIC SLUG	SLUG	METRIC TON	LONG TON
...und$_{mass}$ (avoird.)	1	0.4536	0.04625	0.03108	453.6 E-6	446.4 E-6
...ogram[d]	2.205	1	0.1020	0.06852	0.001	984.2 E-6
...tric slug	21.62	9.807	1	0.6721	0.009807	0.009651
...g	32.17	14.59	1.490	1	0.01459	0.01436
...tric ton	2205	1000	102.0	68.52	1	0.9842
...ng ton	2240	1016	103.7	69.63	1.016	1

G. FORCE

UNIT	EQUIVALENT[b,c]			
	DYNE	NEWTON[d]	POUND$_{FORCE}$	KILOGRAM$_{FORCE}$
Dyne	1	1 E-5	2.248 E-6	1.020 E-6
Newton[d]	100,000	1	0.2248	0.1020
Pound$_{force}$	444,800	4.448	1	0.4536
Kilogram$_{force}$	980,700	9.807	2.205	1

Appendix B
Properties of Water

TEMPER-ATURE ($^\circ$F)	SPECIFIC WEIGHT, γ (LB/FT^3)	MASS DENSITY, ρ (LB-S^2/FT^4)	DYNAMIC VISCOSITY, $\mu \times 10^5$ (LB-S/FT^2)	KINEMATIC VISCOSITY, $\nu \times 10^5$ (FT^2/S)	SURFACE ENERGY,[p] $\sigma \times 10^3$ (LB/FT)	VAPOR PRESSURE, p_ν (LB/IN^2)	BULK MODULUS, $E \times 10^{-3}$ (LB/IN^2)
32	62.42	1.940	3.746	1.931	5.18	0.09	290
40	62.43	1.940	3.229	1.664	5.14	0.12	295
50	62.41	1.940	2.735	1.410	5.09	0.18	300
60	62.37	1.938	2.359	1.217	5.04	0.26	312
70	62.30	1.936	2.050	1.059	5.00	0.36	320
80	62.22	1.934	1.799	0.930	4.92	0.51	323
90	62.11	1.931	1.595	0.826	4.86	0.70	326
100	62.00	1.927	1.424	0.739	4.80	0.95	329
110	61.86	1.923	1.284	0.667	4.73	1.24	331
120	61.71	1.918	1.168	0.609	4.65	1.69	333
130	61.55	1.913	1.069	0.558	4.60	2.22	332
140	61.38	1.908	0.981	0.514	4.54	2.89	330
150	61.20	1.902	0.905	0.476	4.47	3.72	328
160	61.00	1.896	0.838	0.442	4.41	4.74	326
170	60.80	1.890	0.780	0.413	4.33	5.99	322
180	60.58	1.883	0.726	0.385	4.26	7.51	318
190	60.36	1.876	0.678	0.362	4.19	9.34	313
200	60.12	1.868	0.637	0.341	4.12	11.52	308
212	59.83	1.860	0.593	0.319	4.04	14.7	300

SOURCE: Adapted from "Hydraulic Models," *Manual of Engineering Practice No. 25,* American Society of Civil Engineers, 1942.
[a]In contact with air.

Appendix C
K Values for Pearson Type III Distribution

			RECURRENCE INTERVAL IN YEARS								
	1.0101	1.0526	1.1111	1.2500	2	5	10	25	50	100	200
SKEW COEFF., C_s					PERCENT CHANCE						
	99	95	90	80	50	20	10	4	2	1	0.5
					Positive Skew						
3.0	−0.667	−0.665	−0.660	−0.636	−0.396	0.420	1.180	2.278	3.152	4.051	4.970
2.9	−0.690	−0.688	−0.681	−0.651	−0.390	0.440	1.195	2.277	3.134	4.013	4.909
2.8	−0.714	−0.711	−0.702	−0.666	−0.384	0.460	1.210	2.275	3.114	3.973	4.847
2.7	−0.740	−0.736	−0.724	−0.681	−0.376	0.479	1.224	2.272	3.093	3.932	4.783
2.6	−0.769	−0.762	−0.747	−0.696	−0.368	0.499	1.238	2.267	3.071	3.889	4.718
2.5	−0.799	−0.790	−0.771	−0.711	−0.360	0.518	1.250	2.262	3.048	3.845	4.652
2.4	−0.832	−0.819	−0.795	−0.725	−0.351	0.537	1.262	2.256	3.023	3.800	4.584
2.3	−0.867	−0.850	−0.819	−0.739	−0.341	0.555	1.274	2.248	2.997	3.753	4.515
2.2	−0.905	−0.882	−0.844	−0.752	−0.330	0.574	1.284	2.240	2.970	3.705	4.444
2.1	−0.946	−0.914	−0.869	−0.765	−0.319	0.592	1.294	2.230	2.942	3.656	4.372
2.0	−0.990	−0.949	−0.895	−0.777	−0.307	0.609	1.302	2.219	2.912	3.605	4.398
1.9	−1.037	−0.984	−0.920	−0.788	−0.294	0.627	1.310	2.207	2.881	3.553	4.223
1.8	−1.087	−1.020	−0.945	−0.799	−0.282	0.643	1.318	2.193	2.848	3.499	4.147
1.7	−1.140	−1.056	−0.970	−0.808	−0.268	0.660	1.324	2.179	2.815	3.444	4.069
1.6	−1.197	−1.093	−0.994	−0.817	−0.254	0.675	1.329	2.163	2.780	3.388	3.990
1.5	−1.256	−1.131	−1.018	−0.825	−0.240	0.690	1.333	2.146	2.743	3.330	3.910
1.4	−1.318	−1.168	−1.041	−0.832	−0.225	0.705	1.337	2.128	2.706	3.271	3.828
1.3	−1.383	−1.206	−1.064	−0.838	−0.210	0.719	1.339	2.108	2.666	3.211	3.745
1.2	−1.449	−1.243	−1.086	−0.844	−0.195	0.732	1.340	2.087	2.626	3.149	3.661
1.1	−1.518	−1.280	−1.107	−0.848	−0.180	0.745	1.341	2.066	2.585	3.087	3.575
1.0	−1.588	−1.317	−1.128	−0.852	−0.164	0.758	1.340	2.043	2.542	3.022	3.489
.9	−1.660	−1.353	−1.147	−0.854	−0.148	0.769	1.339	2.018	2.498	2.957	3.401
.8	−1.733	−1.388	−1.166	−0.856	−0.132	0.780	1.336	1.993	2.453	2.891	3.312
.7	−1.806	−1.423	−1.183	−0.857	−0.116	0.790	1.333	1.967	2.407	2.824	3.223
.6	−1.880	−1.458	−1.200	−0.857	−0.099	0.800	1.328	1.939	2.359	2.755	3.132
.5	−1.955	−1.491	−1.216	−0.856	−0.083	0.808	1.323	1.910	2.311	2.686	3.041
.4	−2.029	−1.524	−1.231	−0.855	−0.066	0.816	1.317	1.880	2.261	2.615	2.949
.3	−2.104	−1.555	−1.245	−0.853	−0.050	0.824	1.309	1.849	2.211	2.544	2.856
.2	−2.178	−1.580	−1.258	−0.850	−0.033	0.830	1.301	1.818	2.159	2.472	2.763
.1	−2.252	−1.616	−1.270	−0.846	−0.017	0.836	1.292	1.785	2.107	2.400	2.670
.0	−2.326	−1.645	−1.282	−0.842	0	0.842	1.282	1.751	2.054	2.326	2.576

(Continued)

	RECURRENCE INTERVAL IN YEARS										
	1.0101	1.0526	1.1111	1.2500	2	5	10	25	50	100	20•
SKEW COEFF., C_s	PERCENT CHANCE										
	99	95	90	80	50	20	10	4	2	1	0.5
	Negative Skew										
−.1	−2.400	−1.673	−1.292	−0.836	0.017	0.846	1.270	1.716	2.000	2.252	2.4
−.2	−2.472	−1.700	−1.301	−0.830	0.033	0.850	1.258	1.680	1.945	2.178	2.3
−.3	−2.544	−1.726	−1.309	−0.824	0.050	0.853	1.245	1.643	1.890	2.104	2.2
−.4	−2.615	−1.750	−1.317	−0.816	0.066	0.855	1.231	1.606	1.834	2.029	2.2
−.5	−2.686	−1.774	−1.323	−0.808	0.083	0.856	1.216	1.567	1.777	1.955	2.1
−.6	−2.755	−1.797	−1.328	−0.800	0.099	0.857	1.200	1.528	1.720	1.880	2.0
−.7	−2.824	−1.819	−1.333	−0.790	0.116	0.857	1.183	1.488	1.663	1.806	1.9
−.8	−2.891	−1.839	−1.336	−0.780	0.132	0.856	1.166	1.448	1.606	1.733	1.8
−.9	−2.957	−1.858	−1.339	−0.769	0.148	0.854	1.147	1.407	1.549	1.660	1.7
−1.0	−3.022	−1.877	−1.340	−0.758	0.164	0.852	1.128	1.366	1.492	1.588	1.6
−1.1	−3.087	−1.894	−1.341	−0.745	0.180	0.848	1.107	1.324	1.435	1.518	1.5
−1.2	−3.149	−1.910	−1.340	−0.732	0.195	0.844	1.086	1.282	1.379	1.449	1.5
−1.3	−3.211	−1.925	−1.339	−0.719	0.210	0.838	1.064	1.240	1.324	1.383	1.4
−1.4	−3.271	−1.938	−1.337	−0.705	0.225	0.832	1.041	1.198	1.270	1.318	1.3
−1.5	−3.330	−1.951	−1.333	−0.690	0.240	0.825	1.018	1.157	1.217	1.256	1.2
−1.6	−3.388	−1.962	−1.329	−0.675	0.254	0.817	0.994	1.116	1.166	1.197	1.2
−1.7	−3.444	−1.972	−1.324	−0.660	0.268	0.808	0.970	1.075	1.116	1.140	1.1
−1.8	−3.499	−1.981	−1.318	−0.643	0.282	0.799	0.945	1.035	1.069	1.087	1.0
−1.9	−3.553	−1.989	−1.310	−0.627	0.294	0.788	0.920	0.996	1.023	1.037	1.04
−2.0	−3.605	−1.996	−1.302	−0.609	0.307	0.777	0.895	0.959	0.980	0.990	0.9
−2.1	−3.656	−2.001	−1.294	−0.592	0.319	0.765	0.869	0.923	0.939	0.946	0.9
−2.2	−3.705	−2.006	−1.284	−0.574	0.330	0.752	0.844	0.888	0.900	0.905	0.90
−2.3	−3.753	−2.009	−1.274	−0.555	0.341	0.739	0.819	0.855	0.864	0.867	0.8
−2.4	−3.800	−2.011	−1.262	−0.537	0.351	0.725	0.795	0.823	0.830	0.832	0.83
−2.5	−3.845	−2.012	−1.250	−0.518	0.360	0.711	0.771	0.793	0.798	0.799	0.80
−2.6	−3.889	−2.013	−1.238	−0.499	0.368	0.696	0.747	0.764	0.768	0.769	0.76
−2.7	−3.932	−2.012	−1.224	−0.479	0.376	0.681	0.724	0.738	0.740	0.740	0.74
−2.8	−3.973	−2.010	−1.210	−0.460	0.384	0.666	0.702	0.712	0.714	0.714	0.71
−2.9	−4.013	−2.007	−1.195	−0.440	0.390	0.651	0.681	0.683	0.689	0.690	0.69
−3.0	−4.051	−2.003	−1.180	−0.420	0.396	0.636	0.660	0.666	0.666	0.667	0.66

SOURCE: After *Water Resources Council, Bull. No. 15*, December 1967.

Appendix D
Survey of State Water Problems as Conducted by the General Federation of Women's Clubs

STATE	ALLOCATION METHOD	MAJOR WATER SOURCES	MAJOR WATER USERS	WATER SUPPLY AVAILABILITY	OTHER SURFACE-WATER PROBLEMS	COMMENTS
Alabama	Riparian; adjacent land water right; no specific restriction & allocation legislation; law is collection of cases; "poorly defined"	Large streams well distributed; surface water accounts for 96% usage; reservoirs	Electric power generation; thermo-electric power generation; self-supplied industrial/ commercial; public, agri-cultural	In general, state does not face a major water shortage in the future; potential problems may exist in industrialized areas; large streams & rivers well distributed	Highly variable streamflows may cause flooding or insufficient supplies; industrialized areas may have insufficient quantities during drought or for future development	State has limited water law. "However, as in the future water use conflicts may become more numerous, it may be necessary for the legislature to control water use in Alabama."
Alaska	Appropriation; state owns and appropriates the rights dependent on need & use; Water Use Act	Surface water flowing to sea nearly equal (86%) to total rest of U.S. stream discharge; much water originates in Canada; glaciers	Seafood processing; domestic use; agricultural use; placer mining largest user, but use is non-consumptive.	There is abundant water, but distribution can and does cause or relate to water shortages; non-uniform surface water distribution and seasonal streamflow	Whole range of problems: flooding, erosion, pollution, navigation, gravel extraction	Thus far, state has made best use of its groundwater sources better than surface sources because cities primarily use groundwater.
Arizona	Prior appro-priation; rights decreed by court and issued by state; com-prehensive groundwater statute	Major sources are in-state surface streams, Colorado River, and groundwater (accounting for 60% of usage)	Irrigation (89%); municipal & industrial; mineral industry	State troubled with overdrafting of groundwater; new law mandates balance supply and consumption by 2025; occasional local and short-term shortages	Problems generally related to high variability of streamflow, both seasonally and annually; erosion; sedimentation; and severe flooding	Dams and conservation reservoirs are needed to capture, store, and effectively use the surface water. "Water supply problems require further planning."
Arkansas	Riparian; ownership of surface water is determined through ownership of adjoining land	Surface-water sources from several major rivers, including Mississippi; groundwater from 2 major deposits	Electric power generation for surface water; crop irrigation (part. rice production) for groundwater	State does not face a water shortage when total resources are viewed, "but the availability of a large quantity of water does not insure an endless supply with no shortages"	Problems compounded by periods of drought	

596

California	Riparian & appropriation; riparian subject to constitutional provisions; appropriation subject to permit, license conditions, terms	75% of rainfall in north, 75% of demand in south; surface water 60% of usage, groundwater 40% of usage.	Agriculture (83.4%); urban (14.5%); fish, wildlife & recreation (2%)	With increased water conservation, reclamation, and construction of new projects, state will have sufficient water to year 2000; groundwater overdraft in some regions	State is a land of contrasts, with problems ranging from too much to too little, poor distribution, conflicting uses, poor quality, need for improved management, flooding, agricultural	Anticipated buildup of demand without state water project (defeated in 1982 referendum); planning based on project
Colorado	Appropriation; statutes and case law; rights determined through 7 Colorado Water Courts	70% of streamflow is provided by snowmelt runoff, generally in early summer months	Agriculture (95%) of surface water; municipal & industrial (5%)	Nearly all of state's streams are overappropriated; some water rights do not receive enough water to meet their needs	Not enough water to satisfy demands placed upon it; half of water produced in Colorado must go to downstream states	Situation is expected to get worse as Colorado's population grows and production of energy increases; demands met by conversion of rights & conservation
Connecticut	Riparian; statutes; interagency water resources planning board is developing long-range plan		Residential; commercial & industrial	State may be facing severe water shortages	Wide variety of problems, ranging from flooding, drinking water quality, incompatible water uses, quantity allocation	Interagency water resources board is currently developing statewide plan; need to develop data
Delaware[b]	Allocation procedure	Surfacewater sources (Brandywine River); groundwater in south	Industrial; public; agricultural	Drought biggest problem, along with inadequacy of distribution system	Quality problems, particularly along shoreline	Governor has special authority in water crisis to cut allocations
Florida	Riparian; surface water owned by state	Rainfall & groundwater major sources; most potable & much agricultural & industrial water is from groundwater	Agriculture; electric power generation; public water supply; industrial; rural uses	State will continue to have water shortages as population grows unless conservation measures are implemented and additional steps are taken to augment supply	Quantity problems in South Florida where water control systems designed to get rid of excess water quality problems	Problems caused in part because growing population is settling on water-poor coast

SURVEY OF STATE WATER PROBLEMS AS CONDUCTED BY THE GENERAL FEDERATION OF WOMEN'S CLUBS[a] *(Continued)*

STATE	ALLOCATION METHOD	MAJOR WATER SOURCES	MAJOR WATER USERS	WATER SUPPLY AVAILABILITY	OTHER SURFACE-WATER PROBLEMS	COMMENTS
Georgia	Riparian	Lakes & streams supply much of north; groundwater supplies much of south	Thermoelectric in power generation; industrial; public water supplies; irrigation	Rapid economic and population growth has caused considerable pressure on surface-water sources (particularly in north and city of Atlanta)	Municipal problems relating to inadequate water and treatment facilities	Strong state water quality laws: "Much has been done, much remains yet to do."
Hawaii	Until recently, courts have held streams are private; case currently in fed. court; groundwater statutes	Mountain stream surface waters have been developed extensively; groundwater comes from basal aquifers	Sugar plantations; municipal; hydropower; industrial uses; nearly half of use is surface	Shortages may occur in certain sensitive water resource areas by the turn of the century	Inadequate surface water as a dependable supply	Legislation to administratively regulate all water under a permit system is being considered in state legislature
Idaho	Appropriation; law governs use of surface & ground-water; permit system	Major surface-water sources and one of the nation's largest freshwater underground water sources (Snake Riv. Aqu.)	Agricultural; municipal; industrial; power generation; fish production; recreation; navigation; domestic	Sufficient water to meet needs, although shortages occur throughout state because of arid summers and the need to rely on snowmelt	Southern part of state has inadequate water supply during low-flow month; future needs require additional reservoirs	
Illinois	Riparian; state has authority to allocate water diverted from Lake Mich. & manage Kaskaskia Basin	Surface streams, reservoirs, & groundwater aquifers	Self-supplied industry (95%); public water supplies; rural; fish & wildlife; mostly use surface	Water shortages are drought-related; frequency and duration of such drought-related shortages could be increasing	"An ongoing challenge"	Increasing demands on water resources in various areas of the state

State	Water Law	Water Sources	Major Uses	Current Status	Problems	Outlook
Indiana	Riparian; relatively little statutory law	Surface water from Lake Michigan, Ohio River, & the Wabash River	Power generation; self-supplied industry; public water supply	From time to time state experiences water shortages, but overall water resource is both substantial and adequate "given proper planning and management"	Problems include variability in streamflows, flooding	Shortages generally the result of inadequate withdrawal, treatment, and/or distribution facilities or failure to anticipate & make provisions
Iowa	Riparian; statute regulates withdrawals	Major portion of use is groundwater; heavy industrial uses surface water	Thermal power generation; irrigation	Currently areas in state suffering water shortages and the problem will intensify in the near future	Quantity and quality problems	
Kansas	Appropriation; file for a water right through state agricultural board	Major rivers; major groundwater sources (Ogallala)	Agriculture	State faces water shortages in local areas now and in larger areas in the near future	Problems remain despite construction of storage reservoirs (divided planning authority)	Middle of High Plains (dependent on Ogallala Aquifer)
Kentucky	Riparian	Free-flowing surface water & groundwater; 1/3 of state population relies on groundwater	Domestic use; industrial & commercial; waterborne transportation; recreation; fish & wildlife	State currently experiencing localized water supply shortages, primarily attributable to a 2-year period of reduced precipitation and other factors	Problems not statewide, but existing localized, site specific, & basin level problems; quantity and quality	Basin level shortages are a realistic prospect in terms of both water quality and quantity within the next 10 years
Louisiana	Riparian, but "no clear definition of and distinctions for determining rights to use waters"	Groundwater aquifers; rivers; lakes; reservoirs; streams	Self-supplied industrial (electricity-generating utilities); irrigation	The region is expected to have adequate water supply through the year 2000 (last projected time)	Water quality problems from industrial and municipal point sources, as well as nonpoint sources	State has abundant water resources and boasts improvement in water quality over last 10 years
Maine	Riparian; landowners own to the thread of nontidal stream & state holds title to ponds greater than 10 acres	Large rivers; groundwater for domestic supply (57% of population rely on groundwater)	Thermoelectric power plant cooling (saltwater); self-supplied industry (freshwater)	State is water-rich; periodically droughts do cause shortages (particularly drinking water in southwest)	Active state water program	Unlikely state will face widespread water shortages before turn of century

SURVEY OF STATE WATER PROBLEMS AS CONDUCTED BY THE GENERAL FEDERATION OF WOMEN'S CLUBS* (Continued)

STATE	ALLOCATION METHOD	MAJOR WATER SOURCES	MAJOR WATER USERS	WATER SUPPLY AVAILABILITY	OTHER SURFACE-WATER PROBLEMS	COMMENTS
Maryland	Riparian; water appropriation permit system; exemptions for domestic & agricultural use; numerous statutes	Groundwater is major source on eastern shore and in southern part; free-flowing streams in Piedmont & Appal. region	Power generation (largest surface-water use); public drinking water (second)	Preliminary data indicate that state has adequate water supply to meet demands in foreseeable future; some local areas will require increased attention	No major quantity problems; localized wastewater discharge problems (particularly chlorinated discharges)	Study underway to determine possibility of shortages
Massachusetts	Riparian; legislation	Reservoirs; wells; Metropolitan District reservoir wholesales waters to 40% of population (44 localities)	Hydroelectric; thermo-electric; domestic public	No statewide shortage although a number of communities experiencing shortages; 26 communities under state emergency, 18 with volun. bans	Surface-water quality problems including acid precipitation, color turbidity, odor	Fewer communities expected to experience shortages in 1982 following higher rainfalls; but shortages predicted in 96 commun. before 1990
Michigan	Riparian; ownership of Great Lakes within the public trust domain	Owns more of Great Lakes than any other state or Canadian province; 40% of surface area of state is water	Tourism; agriculture; industry (paper, chemical, petroleum, primary metal producers); public	Water shortage is highly unlikely in foreseeable future; greater percentage of population may be served by GL due to groundwater polution	Essential that pollution control efforts are maintained to assure that the relatively unpolluted waters remain safe for human consumption	Great Lakes Governors are establishing a strategy for protecting economic and environmental interests of state
Minnesota	Riparian	Lakes; marshes; rivers; streams; surficial & buried aquifers	Surface water: hydropower (70%); self-supplied industry (20%); public water supply (9%); irrigation (7%); rural livestock (.3%)	State does not face a water shortage in the foreseeable future	Contamination in some bodies of water is a problem; quality varies across state	

State	Water law	Water sources	Major water use	Water shortage status	Problems	Future/perception
Mississippi	Riparian	Major surface stream networks; freshwater aquifers	Power generation; large pulp and paper mills	Water shortage is not anticipated	Problems relating to how state can better facilitate drainage and prevent devastating floods	Shortages short-term and caused by drought
Missouri	Riparian; no statutory law on "water rights"	Surface waters replenished from surface runoff; flows into Missouri River; precipitation varies in state	Industrial self-supplied (including industrial water & electric power production)	State is generally water-rich, but occasionally shortages occur due to short-term drought conditions	Problems include inadequate drainage, diffused surface-water flooding, water quality (point and nonpoint source)	
Montana	Appropriative; permit system; adjudications underway	Major drainage basins; water flows from state; spring melts	Irrigation (accounts for 96% of total withdrawal). Irrigation, thermo-electric, self-supplied industry primarily surface	Unique among western states because unappropriated water is still available, but development of groundwater may be necessary to supply or supplement future use	Groundwater not panacea, however, because extensive withdrawal may result in streamflow depletions; uncertainty in planning process	Perception that water may be abundant, but factors limit availability over large portion of state (hydro, instream reqts., reserved & stored rights)
Nebraska	Appropriation; surface and groundwater public	Groundwater; state overlies vast underground lake which if located on surface would inundate state to 35 ft dep.	Crop irrigation major surface water user; 85% of water consumed for agriculture	In terms of surface water immediate shortages are not anticipated; occasional periodic droughts; long-term streamflow not depleting	Surface-water problems confined to drought condition times	
Nevada	Appropriation	Major lakes (4); inflow of surface waters including Colorado River; groundwater (esp. used for drinking water)	Irrigation (accounts for 93% of consumptive requirement); industrial (3%); public (3%); other (less than 1%)	State is most arid state in the nation, and also has highest per capita growth rate; reoccurring cycle of drought predicted, competition for use	Competition among users; sediment & erosion; nonpoint pollution; point source pollution; litigation; lack of financial resources	State must plan carefully for future due to growth rate and limited supply

SURVEY OF STATE WATER PROBLEMS AS CONDUCTED BY THE GENERAL FEDERATION OF WOMEN'S CLUBS[a] *(Continued)*

STATE	ALLOCATION METHOD	MAJOR WATER SOURCES	MAJOR WATER USERS	WATER SUPPLY AVAILABILITY	OTHER SURFACE-WATER PROBLEMS	COMMENTS
New Hampshire	Riparian			State expects to face a water shortage by 1990s	More than 90% of state surface waters meet "fishable/swimmable" water goals, other problems	Problems of meeting increasing demands remedied with implementation of State Water Supply Master Plan; bond issue passed Nov. 1981
New Jersey	Riparian; permit for major diversions	Half of potable water from surface sources; south relies more on groundwater	Industry (68% of total used)	If state were to take no action it would face another drought (with less than average rainfall)	Quality problems; regulations currently being drafted to manage stormwater (to protect surface-water supplies)	
New Mexico	Appropriation	Rio Grande; San Juan River and Pecos River	Irrigated agriculture (accounts for 85–90%)	State faces shortage as supply is insufficient to meet projected requirements		When state has fully developed waters, inflow will approximately equal outflow
New York	Riparian; state permits required	Major lakes (5); major rivers (5); groundwater (upstate communities rely totally on groundwater for drinking)	Public supply (61%); agriculture (16%); industrial (17%); thermoelectric power (6%)	Shortages have occurred (1980 southeastern part of state); plans underway by state and Corps of Engineers to address problems	Water problems include pollution (organics, nonorganics, toxics, point & nonpoint, PCBs), acid rain, and oil spills	Water allocation system is under discussion in state legislature
North Carolina	Riparian; statutes	Impounded streams; wells	Electric power generating facilities; pulp & paper industry; municipalities; hydropower; growth in irrigation	Water shortages experienced by communities, industries, and agricultural interests due to lack of prudent planning and implementation of plan	Irrigation sector will continue to experience water shortage during drought periods	Periodic shortages due to lack of planning and implementation

State	Water Law	Water Sources	Major Uses	Supply Outlook	Problems	Needs/Recommendations
North Dakota	Appropriation; code sets forth procedural and substantive requirements for acquiring a right to use water	Missouri River; other sources	Irrigation (largest user); industrial; municipal	Missouri River will provide an adequate supply to meet future needs of existing rights	Flooding and drought	State needs system to distribute Missouri River water to several water-short areas in state
Ohio	Riparian	Rivers & streams (36%); Lake Erie (37%); groundwater (27%)	Thermal electric power; self-supplied industry; public supplies	State is rich in water resources, but can avoid localized water shortages only by storage and providing for treatment & distrib.	"Inadequate financial planning is a major water problem in the U.S." Problems include financial uncertainty of federal funds to solve problems Natural & manmade pollution; part has natural salt springs and salt flats emitting into streams; municipal and industrial polution	Needs long-range and modest, reliable formula for federal aid to public water systems; needs to increase water and sewer rates to reflect costs Unless water-short areas are provided with additional supplies, agricultural economy & industrial development threatened
Oklahoma	Appropriation	Reservoirs; groundwater (Ogallala, Garber-Wellington, & Roubidoux aquifers)	Agriculture (63%); municipal (17%); industrial (16%); power generation (4%)	Abundant supply but water is unevenly distributed; east boasts stream, groundwater, & rainfall; west is threatened by drought	Major water problem is that there are insuffient supplies to meet existing demands	
Oregon	Appropriation; applications submitted to water resources division	Willamette River; Snake River; Columbia River	Irrigation (largest consumptive user)	Many parts of the state face a water shortage on annual basis at present; as population grows shortages will become more widespread	Other surface-water problems	
Pennsylvania	Riparian	Morongahela River; Delaware River; Susquehana River; Ohio River; Allegheny River; Lake Erie	Power generation (69%); self-supplied industry (19%); municipal (10%); rural irrigation (2%)	State has experienced drought conditions; each of 3 major basins could easily face situation again if weather conditions are duplicated		

SURVEY OF STATE WATER PROBLEMS AS CONDUCTED BY THE GENERAL FEDERATION OF WOMEN'S CLUBS[a] *(Continued)*

STATE	ALLOCATION METHOD	MAJOR WATER SOURCES	MAJOR WATER USERS	WATER SUPPLY AVAILABILITY	OTHER SURFACE-WATER PROBLEMS	COMMENTS
Rhode Island	Riparian; restrictions to maintain streamflow and prohibit diversions which adversely affect other riparians	Surface water (37% used for water supply); Scituate Reservoir; Pawtucket Reservoir; Sneech Pond; Woonsocket Reservoir	Data are dated; water use shifting from manufacturing to service industries	Water shortages expected to occur during this decade not as widespread or serious as previously predicted; local problems	Most pressing problems caused by nonpoint source pollution and diminution of streamflow; wasteful water practices; "brush fire" situations	"Public attitudes, especially as they are shaped by water supply officials & political leaders, tend to lessen the prospects for . . . water conservation . . . . waste reduction."
South Carolina	Riparian; no special provisions	Primarily surface water, some groundwater	Thermoelectric (83.35%); self-supplied industry (6.9%); public supplies (6%); irrigation (2.2%)	A few areas of the state are currently facing groundwater problems; a growing number of surface-water conflicts are appearing	Other problems	If state continues trends of attracting water use industries and turning more toward expanded crop irrigation practices, the potential for water problems will increase
South Dakota[b]	Appropriation	Groundwater is major source; Missouri River, reservoirs, & dams	Primarily agricultural, limited industrial	State faces distribution problems (partic. in west)	Pollution from mining, erosion, along with flooding	Building distribution system in west through energy appropriation system (coal slurry development)
Tennessee	Riparian; state management under conditions of limited availability	Groundwater major source in west; groundwater & surface in east & middle; low yield of groundwater in Nashville basin	Municipalities; power generation; industry & irrigation	State has shortages; generally during summer months and limited to certain geographical areas	Problems include flooding (west and some major cities), adequacy of streamflow	

State	Water law	Water sources	Water uses	Water supply	Problems	Plans/management
Texas	Appropriation; permits	Groundwater is major source through 7 major aquifers & 17 minor aquifers; provides 70% of water used	Irrigation (largest); manufacturing; public; other	Water shortages experienced in some areas; problems expected to get worse	Variety of problems, ranging from lack of surface water to quality of water; also flooding	Plans underway to lessen the impact of impending water shortage problems
Utah	Appropriation	Surface source provide 75–80%; stems from melting in state mountain ranges; groundwater	Irrigation & livestock (51.1%); wetlands & evaporation (42.5%); public lands (2.8%); municipal (2.5%); industrial (1.1%)	State constantly faces water shortages with precipitation varying widely across state (one of dryest states)	Major problem with water distribution due to shortage in supply, lack of facilities, timing of runoffs, competing water demands, & financing	Current thrust of state plan is to develop local surface-water supplies throughout the state; need completion of Central Utah Project
Vermont[b]	Riparian	Streams, wells		Major water shortage not expected; spot shortages in summer (accompd. by contamination)	Quality more a problem than quantity	
Virginia	Riparian; little statutory law	Major rivers (9); groundwater	Steam-electric cooling (70%); industrial water (12%); public water (11%); agricultural water (6%); private (1%)	Water supply is ample for all foreseeable uses through next century, but neither supply nor demand is uniformly distributed; transient shortages	Flooding along major streams	
Washington	Appropriation; rights acquired to use specific amounts of groundwater or surface water	Considerable water enters from outside state borders; major groundwater storage	Irrigation (65%), mainly surface; industrial; municipal	State has large supply of high-quality water (more surface water generated than most states); uneven geological & seasonal distribution	Water quality problems; (65 of 179 surface-water quality segments meet "fishable/swimmable" goals)	State has river basin management programs

SURVEY OF STATE WATER PROBLEMS AS CONDUCTED BY THE GENERAL FEDERATION OF WOMEN'S CLUBS[a] *(Continued)*

STATE	ALLOCATION METHOD	MAJOR WATER SOURCES	MAJOR WATER USERS	WATER SUPPLY AVAILABILITY	OTHER SURFACE-WATER PROBLEMS	COMMENTS
West Virginia	Riparian	Large rivers; groundwater (no natural lakes)	Industrial users (part. power plants); most of large cities use rivers as public water supply	Recent water shortages have been localized & of short duration; officials currently working with the state legislature to deal with shortages	Major problems include sanitary waste problems from inadequate facilities, drainage from coal mines, lack of funding	
Wisconsin	Riparian	Lake Superior; Lake Michigan; major streams	Pulp and paper mills; cooling water for electric generating facilities; recreation, navigation; hydropower	State does not face a water shortage now, and it is unlikely there will be a shortage in the near future	Surface-water pollution problems	
Wyoming	Appropriation; use regulated by state law through state engineer	Major streams (7) account for nearly 90% of state streamflow	Irrigation farming; municipal, industrial; reservoir evaporation	State faces water shortages; during drought cycles shortages are more severe	Most pressing water problem is greatest demand for water in area of scarce water supply; geological problems which make development difficult	

[a]Data summarized in *Water Information News Service*, vol. VII, no. X, August 20, 1982 Washington, D.C.
[b]Data not provided by the state.

Index